Transatlantic Radicals and the Early American Republic

Transatlantic Radicals and the Early American Republic

Michael Durey

University Press of Kansas

© 1997 by the University Press of Kansas
All rights reserved

Published by the University Press of Kansas (Lawrence, Kansas 66049),
which was organized by the Kansas Board of Regents and is operated and
funded by Emporia State University, Fort Hays State University, Kansas State
University, Pittsburg State University, the University of Kansas, and
Wichita State University

Library of Congress Cataloging-in-Publication Data

Durey, Michael.
Transatlantic radicals and the early American Republic / Michael
Durey.
p.   cm.
Includes bibliographical references and index.
ISBN 0-7006-0823-0 (alk. paper)
1. United States—Politics and government—1789-1809.
2. Radicals—United States—History—18th century.   3. Radicals—
Great Britain—History—18th century.   4. Radicals—Ireland—
History—18th century.   5. Great Britain—Politics and
government—1760-1820.   6. Ireland—Politics and
government—1760-1820.   I. Title.
E310.D87   1997
325'.21'09410973—dc21   96-49216
                                                        CIP

British Library Cataloguing in Publication Data is available.

Printed in the United States of America

10 9 8 7 6 5 4 3 2 1

The paper used in this publication meets the minimum requirements
of the American National Standard for Permanence of Paper for
Printed Library Materials Z39.48-1984.

In Memory of

GWYN A. WILLIAMS

1925–1995

Contents

Preface

With hindsight it appears inevitable that I should have become interested in the process of emigration in the past. Nearly twenty years ago I became an emigrant myself, moving, at short notice, from England to Perth, Western Australia. Unlike the subjects of this book, I was not compelled to flee for political reasons; I was taking my young family to a new world to take up an academic post. I was, at the time, working on the history of cholera in nineteenth-century Britain, but once I had cleared the decks I returned to an era, the French revolutionary period, that had long fascinated me. Here a second unconscious influence showed itself, for in the late 1960s and early 1970s I had been a student, both at undergraduate and postgraduate levels, of Gwyn A. Williams, whose work on the Welsh emigration to the United States in the 1790s was opening up new vistas. His brilliant little book, *Artisans and Sans-Culottes* (1968), placed him firmly, with George Rudé and E. P. Thompson, among the great triumvirate of historians who were resurrecting the plebeian history of Britain in the era of the younger Pitt. At the time I studied with Gwyn, his influence on my choice of research was muted, but his love of history was inspirational. My friend and fellow student Roger Wells captured the 1790s for his thesis. I, more interested in plebeian conservatism, plumped for studying popular toryism in the 1830s, but almost by accident ended up writing on cholera (or perhaps I should follow Sir Geoffrey Elton and claim that the sources took me that way, which they did).

When I began to cast around for a new project in the early 1980s my interest in popular toryism resurfaced, and I determined to explore the career of William Cobbett in America. But again, the sources prevailed, and while working in the archives of the Historical Society of Pennsylvania I became transfixed by Cobbett's British enemies in Philadelphia, especially James Carey and James Thomson Callender. I was drawn into the world of expatriate radicals, fighting British battles on American soil. Callender, a misunderstood figure, needed a book of his own, but it soon became clear to me that the size of the radical exodus from Britain and Ireland had been underestimated, and that an extended study was required to show the full influence of transatlantic radicalism in this period. This book is the result.

I have been determined to examine the radicals not as representatives of some undifferentiated class, who followed similar paths to the New World, but as individuals, each of whom had reasons for escape and stories to tell. I have tried to weave their stories into a narrative within which certain themes are explored: political activities in Britain and Ireland; response to political defeat; motivations for expatriation; the experience of emigration; adjustment to a new society; and involvement in public life in the New World. The result is complex, because the radicals were independently minded, dogmatic, militant and pugnacious, and determined to follow their own routes. That was what made them radical, whether they lived in the deferential society of Britain, or the expanding societies of the republican United States. Highly opinionated, none was an original political thinker. Their guru, if they had one, was Thomas Paine, and it is around his ideas, and how the radicals variously interpreted them, that this study is organized. I hope to show, at least in part, the variety and vagaries of the radical exiles' experiences in an age of upheaval, and to have resurrected an exodus that has not been given the attention it deserves. (When an exile is first mentioned in the text, his name is in caps and small caps.) In some small way, I also hope to have followed in the footsteps of a man, and historian, whose own radicalism partly emerged from an understanding that the Painite vision has not yet been fully grasped. This book is dedicated to his memory.

In the course of researching this subject, I sometimes stopped to take stock, working out some of my thoughts in articles and, on one occasion, in a book. Thus, in a few passages here, where my views have remained unchanged, I have taken the liberty of plagiarizing myself, particularly when examining the career of James Thomson Callender. I am grateful to the University Press of Virginia for permission to do this.

Living thousands of miles from the archives, I could not have completed this work without the generous financial assistance of Murdoch University, the Australian Research Council in Canberra, and the Twenty-Seven Foundation of the University of London. Murdoch's Research Committee gave me grants almost annually for a number of years; a Large Grant from the Australian Research Council assisted my research on the Irish radicals; and the Twenty-Seven Foundation enabled me to visit the archives in Paris in 1990. I am also greatly indebted to the marvelously efficient and friendly staff of Murdoch University's library, whose workload obtaining interlibrary loans will have been cut in half since I completed this project.

Although when grappling with knotty parts of the manuscript I may have thought otherwise, writing history is a collaborative project. Teaching undoubtedly helps the research process, clarifying arguments, uncovering new approaches, and offering different perspectives. Three of my students in particular have been very helpful: Terry Hall, skeptical Irishman who also was my research assistant; Brian Wall, whose honors dissertation on John Stewart opened up new vistas; and Greg Brotherson, who has been inspirational in more ways than he imagines. I am grateful too for the support and assistance of other historians: my colleague Bob Reece; my e-mail correspondents Iain McCalman and Mark Philp; my research assistants Stephen Walker (Scotland), Danny Cusack (Dublin), and Trevor Parssinen (Philadelphia); Bruce Lenman and Christopher Clark, who read drafts of the manuscript; Martin Fitzpatrick and Jon Mee, who shared information with me; and the late John Dinwiddy, who gave me, as he did to so many, the benefits of his wide knowledge and understanding of this period. Jim Walvin has helped me in various ways since the time, many years ago, he first splashed red ink on my undergraduate essays at the University of York and offered me a pithy, probably Jacobin, description of William Pitt. At Murdoch, Brian De Garis has created an atmosphere conducive to the writing of history.

Any decision to uproot one's family and emigrate is a rash one; at times, I still shudder at our boldness and naivete. That it has turned out as well as it has is in no small way owing to the strength, character, and determination of my wife, Jill, who in forging an academic career for herself has created and sustained a loving, stable, and happy home life, in which Robert and Francesca have matured into young Australian citizens. Writing within this environment, it soon became clear who were the fortunate émigrés of the late eighteenth century.

Introduction

In January 1783, only days before Britain signed the preliminary articles of peace with France and Spain, which brought an end to the "Accursed American War," the cutter *Ostend,* having eluded the clutches of an English man-of-war off the capes of Virginia, brought to Baltimore the London printer, JOHN MILLER. Describing himself as one of the "most honest and boldest printers that ever lived," in the previous twelve years Miller had been hauled into the London law courts on five occasions to answer charges stemming from his patriotic activities. A Wilkite, friend of Burke and Fox, and a champion of the patriots in the American colonies, he had finally been imprisoned for a year and fined £200 for libeling the Russian ambassador to England. Released early from prison when the Rockingham Whigs came to power in 1782, Miller determined to emigrate to that new asylum of liberty, the United States.[1]

Eighteen months after Miller's arrival, MATHEW CAREY, the young but lame Roman Catholic editor and proprietor of the fiercely patriotic Dublin *Volunteer's Journal,* limped up the gangway of the *America.* Incongruously dressed in female clothing, with £25 in his pocket, Carey was escaping from the Dublin magistrates, who sought him to answer a charge of criminal libel against John Foster, speaker of the Irish House of Commons. Seven weeks later he disembarked at Philadelphia, poorer but wiser for having lost half his money to a gang of cardsharpers.[2]

Carey and Miller were pathbreakers for a host of men of advanced political principles and heterodox religious beliefs who, sometimes alone, sometimes with their wives and children, and occasionally with other men's wives, sought freedom and liberty by emigrating to the United States from Britain and Ireland in the late eighteenth century. The exact number who became refugees cannot now be ascertained, but they were only a small proportion of the nearly three hundred thousand who emigrated from Britain and Ireland between 1783 and 1819.[3] According to the Scottish political exile JAMES THOMSON CALLENDER, of the thousands of immigrants from Britain and Ireland who came to the United States in the early 1790s, "a numerous majority remove, not in search of a republic, but of bread." Most of these immigrants came from Ireland. In 1791 Mathew Carey informed JOHN CHAMBERS, a Dublin United Irish printer, that between 3,000 and 4,000 Irish immigrants had reached Philadelphia that summer alone. Following the unsuccessful Irish rebellion of 1798, this flow of immigrants temporarily swelled to a flood.[4]

This study is not concerned with mass migration, but is confined to part of a constellation of political activists who in the late eighteenth century attempted, in a variety of ways but with little success, to establish in Great Britain and Ireland a system of government that was less oligarchical, less deferential, and more popular, democratic, and equitable than the current regime of King, Lords, and Commons. Embracing a wide range of political positions—from advanced whiggery to physical force revolutionism—this group, either by self-ascription, by the attribution of its enemies, or by the determination of historians, has been collectively described in a number of ways. During the American Revolution many were happy to call themselves patriots or the Friends of Liberty, but by the mid-1790s these designations fell into disuse, or came to represent only a section of the group, particularly once patriotism was engrossed by loyalism during the war with France. Their enemies called them Jacobins and Levellers, smear words, especially the latter, from which they struggled to disentangle themselves. Modern historians, more sympathetic and aware of their heterogeneity, have variously described them, with equally varying modifiers, as reformers, radicals, revolutionaries, rebels, and even organic intellectuals.

Richard Twomey, the historian who has done much to uncover the transatlantic dimension of English-speaking radicalism of the late-eighteenth century, prefers to call them Jacobins, although not in any pejorative sense.[5] The term has the advantage of firmly fixing the group in its particular epoch, but for several reasons it is unsatisfactory. First, the activists themselves disliked being tarred with this particular brush, for Jacobinism was equated in the public mind in England with anarchists, "disorganizers," atheists, and the guillotine, and in America with these vices and foreign conspiracy.[6] Second, although Jacobinism in France went through several phases, it has usually been seen as a purely "bourgeois" phenomenon, in opposition, for example, to the sansculotte ideology of 1793–94.[7] As the radical movement in Britain and Ireland was by no means confined to the "bourgeoisie" (a term that obscures more than it explains), and as it also incorporated a "sansculotte" frame of mind, to call it Jacobin is to force it into an ideological straitjacket that is unwarranted. My personal dissatisfaction with the term was consolidated when I read the following definition of Jacobinism: "Every man who wishes the minority to trample down and rule the majority—who himself opposes, or who excites opposition to the laws—who seeks to dissolve the union under any pretext whatever—who defends the enemies of his country, right or wrong, and slanders and degrades his own government, is an enragé—a disorgan-iser—a jacobin." This could have come from the pen of Edmund Burke or of Alexander Hamilton, but actually it was written in 1814 by an Irish radical émigré, Mathew Carey, and the men to whom he was alluding were New Eng-land Federalists and separatists, who only fifteen years earlier when in govern-ment were accusing Carey and his fellow exiles of Jacobinism![8]

Although the fragment of this wider group in Britain and Ireland, the sub-ject of this study, incorporates men from all parts of the progressive political spectrum, and although the word is strictly speaking anachronistic, I have de-termined to call them radicals.[9] Radicals are, then, people who try "to change the world and to change it for the better," who seek "fundamental change by striking at the very root of contemporary assumptions and institutions."[10] To be a radical is to adopt "any position which, if fulfilled, would undermine or overturn *existing* political authority."[11] To define them thus is not to ignore the distinctions between those who sought by constitutional means to improve current practices and institutions, and those who sought, by legal or extra-legal means, to replace the status quo.[12] But it does help to avoid difficulties of nomenclature arising from two pertinent factors: that many involved in this study altered their views according to circumstances at different points in their careers; and that political positions were frequently redefined as sudden changes in the wider world warranted it. In the eyes of many, ideas and values that in Britain in 1791 would have been regarded as reformist were, by 1797-98, without significant alteration perceived as potentially revolutionary. With this in mind, to call all progressives radicals is not a serious distortion.[13]

The particular radicals in this study have been chosen because they can be confirmed as having emigrated at least partly as a consequence of their het-erodox political and/or religious beliefs, and because they can be confirmed as having subsequently spent time in the United States. These parameters re-quire the omission of known immigrants who seem to have been politically involved in America but whose activities in Britain or Ireland cannot now be ascertained. WILLIAM COBBETT, for example, in 1798 derided two "republican Britons" named Harper and Hancock, who were in a Philadelphia jail for counterfeiting.[14] As no evidence has been found to confirm their participation in political affairs before emigration, these men have not been included in this study. Similarly, an unnamed Scotsman, a participant in the Watt conspiracy of 1794, found working on the new steamboats on the Delaware river in 1809, and who "is here a very useful man, and there is no danger of his setting the Delaware on fire," has been discarded for lack of confirmatory evidence.[15] Fi-nally, those whose participation in radical activity in their home country can be proven, but whose arrival in the United States cannot be confirmed, also have been omitted. Thus of the ninety Irishmen mentioned by name in the Banishment Act of 1798, whom the government expected would emigrate to America in return for not being prosecuted for treason and rebellion, only fifteen can definitely be said to have crossed the Atlantic.[16] A number of the rest almost certainly emigrated, but they have been reluctantly discounted.

By rigidly adhering to these criteria, undoubtedly many of the rank and file British and Irish radicals who emigrated to America in this period are not included here, leaving 219 political refugees to form the subject of this book, of whom 152 were Irish (69 percent), 49 English (23 percent), and 18 Scottish (8 percent). As individuals, these men have some significance, fighting what they perceived to be intolerance and inequity in their homelands, and struggling to achieve success in their adopted country, but equally, some preliminary comments on them as a group—or rather as three clusters based on nationality—can assist in elucidating the roles they played in the drama on both sides of the Atlantic during the era of revolutions. It will be of particular value at the outset to have some idea of their collective characteristics, personal, social, and religious. It has to be said, however, that data have been hard to discover for many of the more obscure radicals. Nevertheless, sufficient information has been obtained for some general conclusions to be reached.

First, the proportions of English, Irish, and Scottish radicals who fled to the United States probably accurately reflect the relative intensity of political conflict in each of the countries in the 1790s. In Ireland, the rebellion of 1798 drew tens of thousands temporarily into the conflict; no such upheaval, capable of driving so many into exile, occurred in England or Scotland. Table 1 shows the pattern of emigration by country of origin. In England, the peak years of emigration were 1793–94, suggesting that the exiles mainly represented the victims of the first wave of loyalist and government repression that drove many Radical Dissenters overseas and culminated in the treason trials of 1794. In Scotland, some of the early radical leaders were arrested and sentenced to transportation in 1793, and accordingly had no opportunity voluntarily to leave their country. Thus the main phase of Scottish radical emigration to the United States came in 1794–95, coinciding with the exposure and aftermath of the Watt conspiracy in Edinburgh and the total victory of the government's repressive policies. In Ireland, the vast majority fled into exile after the 1798 rebellion. Many escaped in the immediate aftermath of the disaster, although a large number, mainly state prisoners, did not leave until the war between Britain and France was temporarily halted in 1802, reaching the United States as late as 1805 and 1806. Thus in each country a major response to government victories at crucial moments was an exodus of disillusioned and frightened radicals to the New World.[17]

Table 1. Dates of Emigration

	English (*n* = 49)	Scottish (*n* = 18)	Irish (*n* = 152)
pre-1791	1	0	1
1791	0	0	0
1792	2	0	1
1793	16	2	1
1794	16	9	2
1795	3	4	4
1796	2	1	5
1797	4	0	9
1798	4	1	48
1799	0	0	43
1800+	1	0	32
unknown	0	1	6

The peak years of emigration from each country need to be kept in mind when considering the age data of the radicals in Table 2. At first glance, the most obvious feature of the data seems to be the youthfulness of the Irish exiles compared with their British counterparts. Nearly 50 percent of the Irish whose dates of birth are known were born after 1770, compared with 24 percent of the English and 23.5 percent of the Scots. The 1798 rebellion, as all wars, was fought by the young. In practical terms, however, these age differences, particularly in terms of the radicals' ability to establish themselves swiftly in exile, may not be very important, for the British refugees tended to emigrate five, sometimes ten, years earlier than the Irish. In other words, they were approximately the same age as the Irish *at the time they emigrated*. A large proportion of the exiles from all three countries were in their early twenties to early thirties when they expatriated themselves, at that period in their lives when either their futures had not been fully fixed, or when they felt maximum frustration at the barriers hindering their personal advancement.

To emphasize the comparative youthfulness of the radicals is not to ignore the fact that the diaspora also included many men of mature years, whose decision to emigrate usually represented a desire to retire, both from the heat of political combat and from their accustomed, but now threatening and unpleasant, surroundings. If the young fled because of military failure, the older withdrew because their long-held political dreams had been crushed and their religious demands rejected. For many of them the United States was a place of retirement, not a place to begin anew.

Table 2. Age of Exiles

Birth Decade	England	Scotland	Ireland
pre-1739	2	0	1
1740–49	2	3	3
1750–59	6	1	16
1760–69	9	9	19
1770–79	6	4	28
1780–89	0	0	4
unknown	24	1	81

The socioeconomic composition of the three groups of exiles displays features that highlight the main radical bodies from which they derive (see Table 3). The radical movement in England in the 1790s can be divided into three main phases: an early phase (ending in 1793) dominated by middle-class reformers who had been involved in political activities since the American War of Independence; a middle phase (with some overlap in 1792–93) centered on the activities of the popular radical societies in London and the main provincial cities, which carried on with fluctuating fortunes after the repression of 1794 for three years; and a later phase in which the most desperate, including English-based Irishmen, in vain plotted revolution. Table 3 confirms the evidence from Table 1 that participants from both the first two phases of the English radical movement made up most of the emigration to America. Most of the professionals and all the merchants who expatriated themselves reflect the disillusionment of the middle-class radicals.

But this group was significantly outnumbered by other English radicals of lower social status. It is well known that the activist element of the popular radical movement in England in the 1790s included large numbers of artisans and tradesmen (small producers), as well as a roughly equal number of minor professionals (apothecaries, attorneys, clerks, teachers).[18] Together, these social groups made up that so-difficult-to-define category, the "middling sort."[19] Men "of small property, big aspiration and broad sympathy,"[20] they dominated the leadership cadres of the popular societies. They also appear to have dominated the English radical diaspora, although those who emigrated were rarely leaders of the popular societies, and certainly, those who were involved in politics during the difficult years after 1795 are infrequently found in the data.

In Scotland, the radical movement was always comparatively weak and suffered from a lack of determined leadership. The few Scottish reformers of high social status tended to be moderate in their demands and easily intimi-

Table 3. Socioeconomic Background of Exiles (percent)

Occupation	England (n = 49)	Scotland (n = 18)	Ireland (n = 152)
Gentleman	0	0	1.3
Farmer	0	0	5.9
Merchant	22.4	0	9.2
Manufacturer	2.0	0	1.3
Banker	0	0	0.8
Professional	12.2	16.6	27.6
Minor professional	26.6	27.8	11.2
Small producer	36.8	55.6	21.7
Unskilled	0	0	2.6
Unknown	0	0	18.4

dated. Such higher status radicals who were prepared to put their heads over the parapet in 1792–93 were ruthlessly picked off by the authorities, with the result that they sailed to Botany Bay rather than to Philadelphia.[21] Unsurprisingly, therefore, the exiled Scots consisted primarily of one broad social group, the middling classes. Even this group was more narrowly focused than its English and Irish counterparts, consisting mainly of aspiring young men from humble backgrounds whose radical activism developed as a result of their failure to achieve personal success in the field of literature and the arts. As will be shown later, this narrowness reflects the stunted roots and limited nature of Scottish radicalism as a whole in this period.

The socioeconomic profile of the Irish radical exiles is much more varied than the British groups', signifying the generally higher social status of the United Irish leaders, and the fact that the government, having arrested so many who were fomenting revolution, found it wiser to send them into exile rather than risk multiple trials for treason with evidence tainted by informers, its primary source. That the Irish exiles included a disproportionate number of leaders can be shown in a number of ways. First, fifty-four of the Irish exiles (38 percent) held official positions in the United Irishmen, either as members of political committees—from the baronial level to the provincial executive—or as officers in the military wing (from captain to colonel). Second, the high-status composition of the Irish diaspora can be seen in Table 4, which compares the proportional representation of selected occupations in the exile group with the occupations of those identified by Nancy Curtin as being members of the Dublin and Ulster United Irishmen in the years 1795–98.[22] Curtin's own data are skewed toward the leadership cadres, the exile data ob-

Table 4. Comparison of Occupational Groups, Ireland (percent)

Occupation	Exiles (n = 124)	United Irish (n = 1731)
Gentleman	1.6	1.4
Law	4.8	2.6
Medicine	6.5	3.6
Merchant	13.7	14.0
Presbyterian minister/teacher	23.4	6.4
Roman Catholic priest	3.2	2.6
Farmer	7.3	8.4
Clerk	3.2	3.8
Small producer	29.0	45.0
Other	7.3	12.2

viously even more so. Proportionately, nearly twice as many gentlemen and higher professionals found their way across the Atlantic. Far fewer among the lower social groups can be found to have emigrated (perhaps primarily the result of the criteria established for inclusion in this study). The exceptional difference between the data for Presbyterian ministers is partly the result of deliberate government policy, which will be discussed in more detail later, and partly the consequence of many young probationers being drafted into leadership roles in the Ulster United Irish just before the rebellion.

Not too much credence should be given to the exact percentages in Table 4, especially as the ratio of Ulster radicals to southern radicals is nearly 2:1 in the exile group, compared with 1.38:1 in Curtin's much larger sample. Nevertheless, the data offered in Table 4 are enough to show that the exiles were broadly representative of the most active cadres of radicalism in the British archipelago. As such, they reflect the vital role played by the socially marginal and the socially displaced in generating a critique of British political institutions. They bring to our attention the need to reexamine the impact of Thomas Paine's writings, by focusing on his appeal to the socially frustrated and socially aspiring as well as on his plebeian radicalism and egalitarianism. The United States was a suitable terminus for many radicals because of its positive image; they perceived it as a country where personal talents could be freely exercised, and where privilege and prescriptive status would not hinder individual advancement. One major theme of this study, however, is to demonstrate that success for even the talented frequently remained elusive; steadiness, perseverance, and good fortune remained essential prerequisites. The feckless, the improvident, and those without "bottom" were to find fame, fortune, even contentment as difficult to achieve across the Atlantic as in their homeland.

This is not to deny that for many the United States was indeed a land of opportunity. In the freer atmosphere of the New World their literary, entrepreneurial, and pedagogic talents flourished. Some grew very wealthy; many achieved a decent competence and established strong family lines. On balance, the United States gained a fund of expertise by their immigration. Institutes of higher education were graced by their learning; several fields of science and medicine received a fillip; the world of printing profited from new techniques; and the literary world, from the lowered standards of the political press to the patronage of a national literature, was transformed.

Of equal if not of more importance than the exiles' marginality and social displacement for assessing their politics was their religious stance. In his controversial but important book on ancien régime England, Jonathan Clark argues that "all forms of radicalism in early-modern England had a religious origin." In particular he emphasizes the role played in the late eighteenth-century upsurge of radicalism by "subversives" adhering to various forms of religious heterodoxy: Arianism, Socinianism, Unitarianism, and Deism. The radical impetus, he claims, "was not generally aimed against a body of doctrine defending the allocation of seats or the extent of the franchise: such doctrine there was, but it was minimal in extent and achieved even a modest prominence only at the end of the eighteenth century. The radical critique was aimed mostly against what society saw as its fundamental political ideology: Trinitarian Christianity."[23] There is considerable truth in this claim. With the possible exception of the small Scottish group under consideration, where it has been impossible to distinguish between members of the established Presbyterian church and those of the various seceding sects, the vast majority of the exiles were heterodox in belief (see Table 5).

Only a tiny minority of the Irish and only one of the English radicals gave their allegiance to the Established Church (and some of these were probably Deists or agnostics). For Ireland, of course, where established church membership reflected the privilege of a small minority, this might be expected, but the extreme heterodoxy of the great majority of the English exiles needs serious consideration. Indeed, it would not be too great an exaggeration to suggest that the English radical diaspora of the 1790s, and a significant part of the Scottish and Irish, too, was driven as much by antitrinitarianism as by secular politics. How the exiles' religious opinions developed once they inhabited a world of greater religious tolerance, and what effect they had on America's sectarian history, will be considered in this study.

In any examination of emigrant groups, as much emphasis must be given

Table 5. Emigrants' Religion (percent)

Religion	English (n = 39)	Scottish (n = 18)	Irish (n = 115)
Anti-Trinitarian	90	22	14
Presbyterian	0	61	50
Episcopal	2.5	0	8
Other Protestant	5	11	0
Roman Catholic	2.5	6	28

to whence they came as to where they were going. The radicals' translation from a society based on a limited but still powerful monarchy and an aristocratic hegemony to a republic based on the doctrines of popular sovereignty obviously had a major impact on their political ideas. They responded to America in a variety of ways. For some, life under the new U.S. Constitution represented perfection; their political activism subsided into a complacent support for Jeffersonian Republicanism or a benign disinterest. For many others, however, the realities of political warfare in America in the 1790s came as a shock. Alexander Hamilton's program of political economy and the Federalists' pro-British foreign policy seemed to signify a desire to return to the stratified, hierarchical society they had left behind in Britain. They accordingly threw themselves into party conflict, forming within the Jeffersonian party a radical phalanx dedicated to the defeat of Federalism and the promotion of a democratic, egalitarian society. Their impact on national and state politics for a time was to be profound, but after Jefferson's election success in 1800 their influence waned. How and why this happened will be major features of this study.

The political fragmentation of the radicals to a significant extent mirrored the divisions within Jeffersonian Republicanism after 1801, but it also signified the variety of positions they embraced on settling into their new lives. New surroundings can lead to new ideas and new ways of looking at things, but few of the radicals would have envisioned in Britain that so many of them would so readily have taken on the coloration of their surroundings as to accept, and even participate in promoting, the institution of slavery. But this was to be the case. Nor, in contrast, would they have guessed that so many would also fail to settle in America; many returned home when they thought the hue and cry had died down, others made their peace with the British government. Perhaps, after all, America was not the asylum of liberty they had expected?

The radical exodus to America in the late eighteenth century has not been ignored by historians, and this study is indebted to these early labors.[24] But there has been a tendency to focus on the most visible dozen to twenty radicals who made their mark on American party politics. Joyce Appleby, for instance, in her important study of republicanism in the early republic, recognized that "no fewer than twenty [British radicals] played an active role in Republican politics," but this number included men of British extraction—such as Blair McClenachan, William Findley, and even the West Indian–born Alexander Dallas—who had left the British Isles many years before the 1790s.[25] They cannot have experienced firsthand the significant impact on British radicalism of Paine's works and the French Revolution, nor have appreciated the configuration of ideas that the radicals brought with them to America. Moreover, however important the place of expatriates in the Republican party (and their role is explored in depth hereafter), the legend of America as the land of freedom for the downtrodden and dissenting cannot be fully understood in all its complexity by concentrating exclusively on the best known few. As the following chapters will testify, the radicals' experiences after emigration were too varied and problematic to allow us any longer to assume uncritically that America was a welcoming asylum for them all. For many it was Bedlam.

ONE

English Radicals

ORIGINS

The Wilkite Movement

On his return to England in 1801 from his eight-year political exile in the United States, the Painite-turned-anti–Jacobin William Cobbett wrote in the introduction to his collected American writings: "Since the Grand Rebellion [of 1642 to 1660] there has constantly been, in this kingdom, a certain portion of the leven [sic] of republicanism. Sometimes it has remained, for years together, in a dormant state; but whenever it has found materials to mix with, it has never failed to revive, to ferment, and to swell the discontents and the calamities of the country. Of late years it has been enlivened, cherished, and augmented by various means, but by nothing so much as by the success of the American rebellion."[1] For Cobbett, the American war had been the determinative event of his teenage years. He had watched the villagers of Farnham in Hampshire, previously ignorant of and uninterested in national affairs, divide into opposing political camps as the war went badly. Cobbett's father, a farmer sympathetic to the rebels but who before the war had never read a newspaper or followed political events, constantly engaged in political argument with a local loyalist gardener, a "shrewd and sensible old Scotchman." It was on a visit to the naval base at Portsmouth in 1782 that Cobbett's desire to experience this wider world in conflict was first stimulated by seeing the fleet riding at anchor. His attempt to enlist on the *Pegasus* was thwarted by its captain, George Berkley, who, presuming Cobbett to be escaping the wrath of a pregnant girl's family, persuaded him to return home to assume his responsibilities. But Cobbett's wanderlust could not be dampened; in May 1783 he secretly decamped for London, along a road that was to take him from a clerk's stool into the British army and, after many twists and turns, into the political cauldron of late eighteenth-century Philadelphia, where he swiftly rejected his early Painite opinions.[2]

Cobbett's mature insight in 1801, that the American Revolution can be viewed as one of a number of epochal events, which, since the midseventeenth century, had brought to the surface of British life a subterranean tradition of political radicalism, has since been confirmed by many historians. The roots of English radicalism in the 1790s, and thus of the English political and religious migration to the United States of that era, are to be found in the soil in which, in the early years of George III's reign, the first extraparliamentary pressure groups germinated. The Wilkite agitation and the various programs championing the American patriots, relief for dissenters, and parliamentary reform were by no means the first signs of radical opposition to the power and influence of the monarch and the Whig oligarchy in eighteenth-century Britain; nevertheless, they were singular for promoting the first organized movements to link radical ideology and popular extraparliamentary pressure in a demand for significant political and religious reforms.[3]

These reform movements of the 1760s and 1770s addressed themselves to a new and increasingly nationwide public opinion that incorporated both middle and middling classes, "men of moveable property" as John Brewer has called them.[4] Few of these primarily urban merchants, minor professionals, shopkeepers, and master artisans had a sanctioned role to play in political affairs under the constitution. Excluded from "the institutionalized political process," they were expected to accept dutifully and deferentially whatever their masters decided. The Wilkes phenomenon changed all that, insinuating the new politics of participation next to the old politics of oligarchy. Dissolute, cynical, and self-centered though Wilkes personally was, the movement that bore his name focused contemporary radicals' attention on a number of threatened liberties, including the danger to personal liberty from general warrants, the right of a constituency to elect a member of parliament of its own choice, and the right of the press to publish freely.[5]

Wilkes was a brilliant propagandist who commercialized politics by saturating the media with his opinions and examples of his outrageous political behavior. He attracted not only the raucous but still essentially "pre-political" London crowd by his public theater, but also, and more importantly in the shorter term, those commercial classes in the growing urban areas of Britain who believed most strongly that their local economic and social eminence was ignored by a political process in which only landed wealth was deemed to have value.[6]

The government was particularly alarmed by the breadth of Wilkes's support, which was garnered with the assistance of numerous London printers and publishers who kept Wilkes's name in the public eye. Probably the most useful was the publisher John Almon, but his colleague John Miller also gave Wilkes unstinting help. Miller began his career in London during the administration of George Grenville in 1763. In 1768 he became printer of the *London Evening Post,* a newspaper that he soon offered to the radical cause, assuring Wilkes that "the Paper shall be at all Time devoted to the National Service with the most persevering Constancy."[7] Miller was true to his word. In December 1769 he reprinted from the *Public Advertiser* a letter to the king from the notorious "Junius," which resulted in a charge of seditious libel. Defended by Wilkes's friend Sergeant Glynn at his trial before Lord Mansfield in July 1770, Miller was acquitted, much to the delight of the London mob.[8]

In the following year, he carried out on Wilkes's behalf a ploy that not only heaped ridicule on the pretensions of the House of Commons, but also asserted the freedom of the press. The scheme was part of a larger issue regarding the right of the press to publish parliamentary debates. Following complaints by Colonel George Onslow in March 1771, the House of Commons ordered two London printers who had published parliamentary proceedings to attend examination at the bar. The printers went into hiding, until one was "arrested" and brought before Wilkes, sitting as an alderman at the Guildhall. Wilkes, who had masterminded the whole affair, discharged the printer, informing Secretary of State Halifax that the arrest had been "in direct violation of the rights of an Englishman and of the chartered privileges of a citizen of this metropolis." Incited by Wilkes's mischievousness, the House of Commons ordered the arrest of all printers, including Miller, who had published the debates. When the parliamentary messenger arrived at Miller's house to take him into custody, however, a city constable, surreptitiously hidden, arrested him on a charge of assaulting Miller, a freeman of the city. Taken before Wilkes, the messenger, unable at first to offer bail, narrowly avoided imprisonment. Wilkes then proceeded to defy the Commons until, with an adjournment of the session, the matter was allowed to lapse, the rights of the press having been vindicated.[9]

As with many other radicals who eventually emigrated to the United States, Miller's early career can only be traced through his periodic clashes with the law. In the years after his triumph with Wilkes, he was tried three further times for his publications, on one occasion being fined £2,000, a huge sum that would have brought ruin if assistance had not been given by "gentlemen of influence." Ironically, the charge that broke him had little to do with radical politics, for he was imprisoned for copying into his newspaper a paragraph that libeled the Russian ambassador. Released early by the new Rockingham government, Miller emigrated to the United States, leaving his wife and seven children to follow him later.[10]

Dissenting Radicalism

Wilkes was nominally an Anglican but had been raised in a Dissenting household and had attended Dissenting academies, including one where the master, who thought he saw in the boy a "tincture of heretical theology," was an Arian.[11] Not the least troubling aspect of Wilkes's activities for the authorities was the possibility of his forming a union with the newly awakening Dissenting interest, which would have not only temporarily swelled the number of "Wilkites," but also more lastingly added breadth and depth to the burgeoning extraparliamentary radical movement as a whole. This conjunction, however, occurred spasmodically for only a few years before 1771; most Dissenting leaders found the Wilkites' pragmatism and their "tampering with the mob" distasteful.[12] Nevertheless, when the Wilkes phenomenon faded, radicalism in England until about 1793 came to depend, to a considerable extent both for leadership and principles, on Dissenters, particularly of the heterodox kind.[13]

The role played by Protestant Dissent in the evolution of extraparliamentary reform politics in England from the early 1770s is particularly pertinent for this study. As Table 5 in the Introduction shows, the emigration of English radicals to the United States in the 1790s consisted overwhelmingly of Dissenters, in particular Rational Dissenters, or Unitarians as most became generally known by the early 1790s. Of the thirty-seven English exiles whose religious affiliation is known, at least twenty-five were Unitarian; only one, William Cobbett, was an Anglican at the time of emigration. Moreover, most of the Unitarians went into voluntary exile in 1793–94, either accompanying or deliberately following DR. JOSEPH PRIESTLEY, the most outspoken and persecuted of their number. Their exodus not only constituted the defeat of a politico-religious movement that had been active for nearly twenty-five years, but also affirmed their sympathy for and commitment to the Birmingham scientist-preacher. It is clear, therefore, that an understanding of the English emigration requires some consideration of the part played by Dissent, by Rational Dissent, and by Priestley in particular in the development of the radical movement in the 1770s and 1780s.[14]

By the first half of the eighteenth century the Presbyterian, Baptist, and Congregational (Independent) denominations—together known as Old Dissent—were pale imitations of their Puritan ancestors. Defined by their dissent from the authority and dogma of the Established Church, their previous militancy and obduracy had sunk into a smug complacency. Although they continued to privilege the authority of the Bible over other traditional religious authorities, and retained in their ecclesiastical structures the egalitarianism of their forefathers, based on the belief that all were equal in the eyes of God, they were slowly being suffocated by a combination of official kindness and indifference.[15] True, they remained subject to the penal laws of the seventeenth century, but they saw this as a small price to pay to ensure that Popery and Jacobitism were kept at bay.[16] Not that the Corporation and Test acts bore very heavily on them as the century progressed; the Earl of Chatham, for instance, dismissed the penal laws as so many "bloodhounds held in leash."[17] The practice of occasional conformity, and, from 1727, annual Indemnity Acts, allowed the more flexibly minded Dissenters to involve themselves in the activities of their local corporation, and even to hold government offices of trust. Priestley's close friend WILLIAM RUSSELL, for example, although described in 1791 by the Treasury Solicitor as "a Rigid Dissenter and one of the most violent of that Sect in Birmingham," went through the riots of that year as a Justice of the Peace.[18] For sixty-six years during the eighteenth century Presbyterians filled the office of mayor in Nottingham. In 1777 the town was claimed to be "the most disloyal in the kingdom, owing in great measure to the whole corporation . . . being Dissenters."[19]

Nottingham, if not unique, was nonetheless unusual. Dissenter influence on a comparable scale probably existed in only a handful of boroughs. But an exhaustive analysis of the political role of Dissent in England in this period shows that where their numbers were significant, Dissenters could play a larger part in electoral politics than previously thought, possessing some influence on occasions in as many as one-quarter of the borough electorates.[20] In a few towns, therefore, by the 1770s, Dissent was "neither politically chaste nor impotent." In Yorkshire, some Dissenting leaders had even managed to attach themselves to the fringes of the Whig elite, where they began to benefit from the fruits of patronage.[21]

In return for this laxity the old denominations gave their allegiance to the Hanoverian monarchy.[22] But it came at a cost. Old Dissent had traditionally drawn much of its vitality from official persecution; in the eighteenth century, as Anglican antagonism waned, the number of Dissenters began to decline. Between 1727 and 1776 Old Dissent congregations in London and Middlesex fell from 112 to 72. The Presbyterians, Priestley's denomination, suffered most severely; their congregations throughout the country dwindled from about 637 to about 200 between 1718 and 1800, some having disintegrated, others becoming Independent congregations.[23]

Freed from the need to resist an aggressive and punitive Established Church, elements of the Dissenting clergy began to speculate on theological issues, shedding their traditional Calvinism in favor of various forms of heterodoxy. What came to be called rational religion slowly emerged, particularly among Presbyterian ministers, who began to preach Arian, Socinian, and by the 1770s, Unitarian forms of heresy.[24] Although they never agreed on a common theology—Richard Price, for instance, remained an Arian, while Priestley in the late 1760s converted to Socinianism—the Rational Dissenters united in the opinion that God's gift of reason should be applied to theology.[25]

Under the microscope of the scientific method, theology was explored as if it were just another part of natural philosophy. RALPH EDDOWES, the Chester merchant and future Unitarian lay reader in Philadelphia, epitomized their skeptical and scientific approach; he believed there to be "more than two thousand passages in the Old Testament, and more than one thousand in the New, wherein the unity and supremacy of God the Father is either directly expressed or clearly implied." Justifying his rejection of the Trinity he wrote: "in any other science than that of theology, it is impossible to conceive such theorems supported by such arguments, or, to speak more correctly, [that] such assertions, would be for a moment endured; yet in this case, however strange the fact, the spirit of inquiry seems to be laid asleep."[26] Believing they were clearing away centuries of popish and superstitious corruptions from true Christianity (which had made, claimed Priestley, "the whole system of modern Christianity less like the Christianity of the *New Testament*, than it is to the *Brachmans* of Indostan"), Rational Dissenters rejected the doctrines of the Trinity, original sin, and the atonement, as well as the less controversial Calvinist doctrines of predestination and salvation by faith alone.[27]

Although many of the theological views of the Rational Dissenters were progressive, and inspired by the scientific rationalism of the Enlightenment, they by no means rejected links with their Puritan past. The core of their philosophy remained the fundamental right of the individual to "form his own sentiments, and to pursue them by all lawful and regular methods," and its inevitable corollary, a rejection of "all civil establishments and the Church/State alliance."[28] Their defense of liberty of conscience brought them into contact with a small group of Anglican clergy, who in the 1760s also began to question, on similar intellectual grounds, the doctrines and role of the Church of England. Led by Archdeacon Blackburne and Theophilus Lindsey, a Yorkshire vicar, these liberal clergymen from the mid-1760s organized a movement seeking to modify the Thirty-Nine Articles and the subscription tests required of clergymen and university students. Unitarian in theology, from the early 1770s they merged in an unformalized way with many heterodox Dissenters to create "a galaxy of talented figures" who helped to keep radicalism alive in England until the first years of the French Revolution.[29]

The Unitarians, Dissenters, and former Anglicans were never to be a large group—their refined, rational, and reasonable preaching and writings were "too cold, too distant, too polite"[30] for the poor and middling groups—but they did attract many among the urban commercial and industrial middle classes. It is significant that a number of the Unitarian exiles of 1793–94 were themselves merchants. Ralph Eddowes was a tobacco merchant, his two sons, RALPH JR. and JOHN, china merchants; and BENJAMIN VAUGHAN was a merchant with interests in America and Jamaica, as well as being a member of Parliament for Calne for a short time. GEORGE HUMPHRIES and William Russell of Birmingham also found prosperity through commercial activities, the latter in the American trade, while THOMAS COOPER of Manchester invested heavily, and unsuccessfully, in a cotton cloth-printing business.

Joseph Priestley

This attraction of highly visible sections of the rising middle classes to heterodox Protestantism has led some historians to claim, in exaggerated fashion, that the Unitarians were "bourgeois radicals," with concerns and demands more social and political than religious, for their "constant invocation of the principle of religious laissez-faire, the withdrawal of the state from the realm of belief, became appropriated by secular arguments for economic laissez-faire." They were alienated, socially marginal men, "secular prophets, the vanguard, of a new social order. These talented and industrious Protestant Dissenters played the decisive role in transforming England into the first bourgeois civilisation." They "nearly destroyed aristocratic England and its traditional values."[31]

By the same token, Priestley has been seen as the main instigator of this purported bourgeois insurgency: "no more zealous a modernizer and liberal apologist for the middle class can be found in the ranks of British reform in these years," claims Isaac Kramnick. He "more than anyone else qualifies as the principal architect of bourgeois England."[32] Undoubtedly, Priestley had great faith in the middle classes; they were the most socially useful group in England. In his first major political work he claimed that "Persons who are born to a moderate fortune, are, indeed, generally better educated, have, consequently, more enlarged minds, and are, in all respects, more truly *independent*, than those who are born to great opulence."[33] It is their freedom from dependence on another that makes the middle classes so beneficial to society, for it enables them to display the virtue (in the political, Commonwealth sense), which, together with "right conduct," creates "those affections and actions which terminate in the public good."[34] To the end of his life Priestley believed that "there is not only most virtue, and most happiness, but even most true politeness, in the middle classes of life."[35]

But Priestley was no John the Baptist, clearing the way for the success of the bourgeoisie. Overemphasizing the political and social components of his thought, at the expense of his core religious motives, creates a distorted view of him, and of Rational Protestantism as a whole. Priestley's admiration should not be taken to reflect a revolutionary zeal to overthrow social order on behalf of a militant middle class.[36] In 1769, at the very time he first openly defended Wilkes and the American colonists, he wrote: "It is not . . . any part of the Author's intention to revive the spirit of a *party*, except, primarily, so far as the party has *religion*, that is, the interests of its members in another world, for its objects; and secondarily, so far as the interests of this particular party, in *civil matters*, is the interest of the whole society, of which they are members, having for its object the cause of liberty, and all the valuable rights of Englishmen."[37] Thus, rather than being a class apologist, Priestley saw in the middle classes many of the values that previous generations of Dissenters had embraced: personal autonomy, virtue, industry, and self-reliance. If Priestley supported the new industrialists, he did so less because of their economic function than because most—in his experience—were heterodox Dissenters whose religious views precluded them from partaking fully in local civic life. In Priestley's eyes, the middle classes were indistinguishable from the Dissenters, except that among the latter the heterodox were closer to religious truth.

Unlike their orthodox dissenting counterparts, Rational Protestants lived outside the protection of the toleration laws.[38] Non-Trinitarians were specifically excluded from the Toleration Act of 1689, exposing them to the full penalties of the penal laws still on the statute books from the sixteenth and seventeenth centuries. The 1698 Blasphemy Act also prohibited the oral and written denial of the Trinity, with graduated penalties up to a maximum of three years imprisonment in England (and in theory the death penalty in Scotland).[39] Thus the Rational Protestants had "no *legal* establishment," and although in 1769 Priestley hopefully asserted that the tolerant "spirit of the times" would continue to give them security, he nevertheless interpreted the Wilkes affair as a sign that the heterodox were potentially under threat: "The spectre of a Jesuitical court once more began to haunt" them.[40]

He was also aware that non-trinitarian heresy was unpopular. As one divine of an earlier generation had put it—he was quoted by Charles James Fox in Parliament in 1792—"The Socinians are impious blasphemers whose infamous pedigree runs back (from wretch to wretch) in a direct line to the devil himself."[41] Unitarians' denial of Christ's divinity, selective acceptance of the Bible, and rejection of the doctrine of original sin struck deeply into the heart of traditional Christianity, worrying many orthodox Dissenters as well as Anglicans.[42] They were seen as taking the penultimate step to Deism, reviving this pernicious doctrine more than a generation after it had been defeated (Priestley's Deist friend and fellow Lunar Society member Erasmus Darwin called Unitarianism "a feather-bed for falling Christians").[43]

In times of peace and stability and confined to a small group of intellectuals, unitarian views, although in theory threatening the function and status of the Established Church of England, could be tolerated. But it was a different matter in the atmosphere of unrest and uncertainty during the Wilkite agitation and the first difficulties with the American colonies. Rational Protestants were aware of this themselves, but far from shrinking from the limelight they took the initiative, justifying their actions on the duty they had to speak with "candour." By the doctrine of candour they meant "a rigorously honest examination of one's conscience, a commitment to act according to its dictates, and an obligation to act and speak with complete honesty in one's dealings with others."[44] Wrote Priestley: "Freedom of enquiry will produce its natural offspring, truth; and truth has charms that require only to be seen and known, in order to recommend itself to the acceptance of all mankind."[45] Of little community concern when confined to intellectual debating among clergymen, candour appeared more threatening when it spilled over into the political arena, as it did when Rational Protestants perceived government actions in the 1760s as evidence of a growing royal tyranny.

As Cobbett was later to say: "Presbyterians are not remarkable for a passive submission to injuries and insults, any more than they are for abstaining from a mixture of religion and politics."[46] Priestley unashamedly mixed religion with politics from the late 1760s, but this was because he believed that in a country that was a church-state, where full civil rights were possible only through membership of the Established Church, they could not be separated. Any criticism of the Church of England inevitably would be construed as a political statement. When opposition to what Priestley called "our present *politico-ecclesiastical constitution*" was combined with fears of arbitrary government and the misuse of power—as was the case with Priestley and some other Rational Protestant leaders influenced by Commonwealth ideology— events such as the Wilkes affair or the dispute with the American colonies could spark a chain reaction.[47]

Shortly before emigrating to the United States, Priestley informed the readers of the *Morning Chronicle* that "I am not, nor ever was, a member of any political society whatever."[48] To the extent that he was no political activist, and preferred his controversies to take place in print, this is true. It is also true that his natural angle of vision always highlighted the religious aspects of political situations, particularly the relation of dissent to the state, but he nonetheless entered the political stage, anonymously at first, as a Wilkite and American patriot propagandist.[49] Priestley sent Wilkes a copy of his *Essay on the First Principles of Government* (1768), which Thomas Cooper called "the first plain, popular, brief and unanswerable book on the principles of civil government," describing himself as "a member of the same community and a lover of liberty."[50] Priestley was also a member of the Club of Honest Whigs, the mainly Dissenting society at whose regular dinners pro-American discussions were as commonplace as "Welsh Rabbits and Apple-Puffs, Porter and Beer."[51] There Priestley, always a sociable man, became friends with Benjamin Franklin.[52] Indeed, he later claimed: "It is probable that no person now living was better acquainted with Dr. Franklin and his sentiments on all subjects of importance, than myself, for several years before the American war. I think I knew him as well as one man can generally know another."[53]

Priestley was thus an important member of a small group of intellectuals in London, indebted to Commonwealth and Lockean ideology, and mainly heterodox in religion, who championed political liberty in general and the rights of the American colonists in particular. But he never lost sight of the religious implications of political action; politics and religion were inextricably intertwined. "Religious liberty . . . cannot be maintained except upon the basis of civil liberty" (the right of each man "to be exempt from the controul of society"), he reminded his Dissenting readers in 1774.[54] Even political liberty, which Priestley defined as "the power which members of the state reserve to themselves, of arriving at the public offices, or, at least, of having votes in the nomination of those who fill them," was given a strong religious twist.[55] If a man, "by his birth or fortune, [is] excluded from these offices, or from a power of voting for *proper persons* to fill them," he is a "poor, abject creature," no better than a slave.[56] In these circumstances, even the Dissenters' right to vote is worthless, for their possible preference for non-Anglican representatives could not be satisfied (unless, of course, as sometimes happened—contrary to the doctrine of candour—Dissenters were prepared to conform to enter Parliament).[57]

Priestley's defense of the individual's right to free inquiry was so intense that claiming any representative qualities for his writings is fraught with danger. Nevertheless, there can be little doubt that his conviction of the intimate connection between religion and politics was shared by most of his fellow Rational Protestant intellectuals, although some were more willing than he to act on their convictions (Priestley's speech impairment probably partly explains his reluctance to participate in public life). In the 1770s they acted indiscriminately as both Commonwealth ideologues and partisans of heterodoxy, frequently—like Priestley—marrying the two at strategic moments.

Religious Subscription

A case in point is the religious dimension Rational Protestants gave to their interpretation of the disastrous relations between the British government and the American colonists that culminated in the Declaration of Independence. Richard Price, James Burgh, and other prominent heterodox supporters of the American patriots saw not only a threat to the Englishman's traditional liberties in government colonial policy, but were also quick to associate the pro-Catholic Quebec Act and the rumor of the introduction of episcopacy into the American colonies with government domestic responses to religious issues.[58] Religious issues were becoming more prominent; between 1771 and 1774 Parliament "witnessed more contentious religious debate than had appeared in the legislature at any time since the 1730s."[59] Of the business before Parliament that had religious overtones and consequences, the most important for the Rational Protestants were the attempts to revise the policy of religious subscription. In February 1772 the liberal Anglicans' Feathers Tavern petition, which sought amendments to the Thirty-Nine Articles for newly appointed or promoted clergymen, was rejected by Parliament. The failure of this and a later bill introduced in 1774 led to the secession of a small number of clergymen from the Church of England. Believing that some of the arguments used by government supporters—including Lord North, the prime minister—suggested they would not be averse to meeting some of the Dissenters' objections to subscription, in May 1772 a bill seeking to relieve Dissenting ministers and schoolmasters from some irksome provisions of the Toleration Act of 1689 was introduced into Parliament. Although it passed the Commons, it was defeated in the House of Lords. In the following year, an amended bill was also rejected, but by a smaller majority.[60]

Opposition to these reforms came from both Anglicans and orthodox Dissenters who feared that the bills were part of "an infidel and libertine design to overthrow religion."[61] Although clerical withdrawal caused minimal disruption to the Church of England, among the Dissenters the effect of these failures was more profound. Rational Dissenting leaders began to argue for the abolition of all laws that distinguished between religions. By openly questioning the validity of each denomination's own confessions they further alienated most orthodox Protestants, until by the first years of the French Revolution they were so isolated that emigration became not only an attractive but perhaps the only reasonable option open to them when the forces of order triumphed.[62]

The subscription issue occurred at the same time as relations with the American colonists deteriorated dramatically. In a sermon given in Philadelphia in 1797, Priestley claimed that many of the exiles now crowding into the city had "prayed for your success from 1776." For the crime "of wishing well to the liberty and independence of America," they "will never be forgiven by the Court of Great Britain."[63] Apart from issuing a number of political pamphlets defending the American cause before 1776,[64] however, prayers and good wishes were as much as the Unitarians had offered their colonial cousins. It is not even certain that they managed to carry most Dissenters into the pro-American camp, at least before the failure of British arms and growing trade dislocation in the late 1770s.[65] Moreover, Priestley in 1797 had seemingly forgotten that most of his Unitarian colleagues had only reluctantly accepted American independence once it was a fait accompli.[66] Benjamin Vaughan, for instance, was still hoping for a reconciliation as late as 1778, at the same time as Priestley, more realistic than most, was privately acknowledging his support for the Duke of Richmond's parliamentary motion to recognize American independence.[67]

If there were no strong feelings among English Dissenters to go beyond supporting their American co-religionists' defense of "English" liberties, the effects of the American war—or at least its catastrophes—did encourage them to seek political reform in Britain. The first thrust came from Rev. Christopher Wyvill's Yorkshire Association movement, which sought pragmatic and very moderate economical and political reforms.[68] The Association's Westminster Committee, however, was more radical, publishing in 1780 a full democratic program. From this committee emerged the Society for Constitutional Information (SCI), the major concern of which was the mass dissemination of radical literature. Many of the leading Rational Dissenters became members, including Benjamin Vaughan, who as an intimate of Lord Shelburne's Bowood Circle had at the same time an unofficial role in the Paris peace negotiations. Rather later, in 1788, Thomas Cooper and another Mancunian, the Unitarian printer MATTHEW FALKNER, joined the SCI.[69]

REPEAL MOVEMENTS

The Anti-Slave Trade Movement

Cooper and Falkner's membership of the SCI reflected an attempted renewal and widening of the reform movement in England, following its failure to achieve more than a modicum of economical reform between 1779 and 1785. From 1787 Dissenters also initiated campaigns against the slave trade and the Test and Corporation acts. In these movements, some future radical emigrants first began to make their mark. The anti-slavery movement is particularly interesting, because of the ambiguous way in which many expatriate radicals came to regard slavery when in America.[70] In England it was, with repeal of the penal laws, parliamentary reform, and, from 1793, the desire for peace, one of the four great political issues of concern to radicals in this era.[71]

The anti-slave trade movement began in England, as in America, among Quakers, but in the late 1780s, once Thomas Clarkson had begun his itinerant campaign, it was taken up and extended by other Dissenting denominations, some working within the SCI in London, others in the new manufacturing districts of the North.[72] Although Unitarians were particularly prominent—the small Anti-Slavery Society in Liverpool, for instance, was formed in 1788 by four Quakers and three Unitarians—abolitionism united all Dissenters in a common cause.[73] In Sheffield, the Unitarian JOSEPH GALES used his newspaper the *Sheffield Register* to support the local anti-slavery committee, and in Birmingham Priestley joined the abolitionist Committee of Correspondence. In January 1788 he was one of many Dissenting clergymen in the town to preach against the slave trade, the disappearance of which he foretold in apocalyptic terms.[74]

Abolitionism received its biggest boost from Manchester, where Thomas Walker and Thomas Cooper greatly extended its constituency by financing a national petitioning campaign through the media that dovetailed neatly with Clarkson's itinerancy. Their first petition in Manchester in December 1787 obtained 10,639 signatures, 20 percent of the town's total population.[75] By then both Walker and Cooper were prominent radical activists in a very conservative town, the former as a wealthy merchant, the latter as a recently arrived lawyer and partner in a cotton cloth-printing firm. Both were members of the prestigious local Literary and Philosophical Society.[76]

Cooper's connections with Manchester predated his settling there in about 1785. The son of a wealthy Londoner, he had attended University College, Oxford, from which he failed to graduate owing to his principled refusal to sign the Thirty-Nine Articles (he was both a materialist and an Unitarian). At his father's insistence, he became a lawyer, although his own preference was for medicine. In the summer of 1780, as the capital was wracked by the Gordon riots, Cooper attended a series of anatomy lectures in London, and subsequently a clinical course at Middlesex Hospital. His primary interest, however, lay with the sciences, especially chemistry, which probably explains his decision to invest his personal fortune—augmented by the dowry from his wife Alice, the daughter of a wealthy shipowner—in a Bolton cotton cloth-printing manufactory.[77]

In many ways, perhaps even more so than the nonactivist Priestley, Cooper was the archetypal radical of this era. He was prosperous, sociable, religiously heterodox, and intellectually progressive, with a supreme confidence in his own abilities. He was also narrow-minded and a zealot, committed to change and intolerant of tradition and the status quo. He would have approved of John Jebb's comment: "Show me a moderate and I will show you a rascal."[78] In one sense, his move to the booming cotton town of Manchester represented a rejection of metropolitan culture (subsequently justified when he was overlooked by the Royal Society for his radicalism) and an embracing of "the frontier," the cutting edge of socioeconomic change and progress.

Walker was undoubtedly the leader of the new men of Manchester, but Cooper was his faithful lieutenant. It was the latter's series of letters hostile to the slave trade, first published in a local newspaper in 1787, that were spread around the country before being combined in an influential pamphlet. In these, Cooper used Lockean rights theory and the populist concept of the freeborn Englishman to attack the slave trade as a form of political tyranny: "If it be our boast as Englishmen, that we (as all men ought to be) are governed by those laws only to which we have an opportunity of assenting; if we claim Freedom as our birth right, and glory that the 'very air of our country is too free for a slave to respire'; we are in honour bound to assist in exterminating the most diabolical exertion of political tyranny, which the annals of oppression can exhibit an instance of."[79] More interestingly, given the pro-slavery position Cooper was to take up in South Carolina, he specifically condemned the planters' argument that, as slaves were private property, the use of slave labor was legitimate. "No bargain is fair, where there is not a quid pro quo; a mutual equivalent. But no equivalent can possibly be received by a slave. No man has a right to purchase what he may know, if he please, that the seller has no right to sell."[80]

The Movement to Repeal the Test and Corporation Acts

The anti-slave trade agitation had the useful side-effect of acting as a unifying force for the differing strands of Dissent. As Cooper noted: "This is not the cause of Arianism or of Calvinism—it is the cause of Humanity, of Christianity."[81] At the same time, however, it polarized opinion among the manufacturing and mercantile elites in the northern towns where prosperity, to a greater or lesser extent, depended on the production of raw materials using colonial slave labor. The simultaneous renewal of agitation against the Test and Corporation acts of 1787 had a similar impact, fracturing local politics.

In the first two of the three campaigns waged against the acts between 1787 and 1790, however, the potential for social cleavage was muted by the moderation and caution of the Dissenters' organizing committee in London, which concentrated on lobbying members of Parliament rather than on a vigorous open campaign.[82] But in 1789 the more radical Dissenters in the provinces became increasingly involved; they organized regional committees with the aim of sending delegates to a national forum or convention in London. The "Committee of the Seven Congregations of the Three Denominations" in Birmingham was at the center of this movement in the Midlands. William Russell was its energetic chairman and was soon secretary and treasurer of the committee that controlled the propaganda effort in the whole region.[83]

Russell, according to his biographer, was "a broad-minded, public-spirited, if perhaps somewhat viewy man—a local personage who should have stood well with all his neighbours."[84] The conditional here is instructive; although successful in business and sufficiently prominent to be a justice of the peace in the county of Warwickshire, Russell was too intense, narrowly focused, and obstinate in his opinions to be popular. His portrait shows him to be small boned and thin, with a "Puritan" lugubriousness about his features and a downturned mouth. His aquiline nose and arched eyebrows display a touch of arrogance. Unlike the more excitable Cooper, Russell was no self-publicist; but he was a talented and indefatigable organizer, a fixer who soon after Priestley came to Birmingham made himself indispensable to the new minister.[85] Like so many of his fellow Rational Dissenters his religion gave him an innerconfidence that, combined with bulldog qualities, made him a formidable opponent.

Russell's active involvement in spreading nationwide the movement against the Test and Corporation acts coincided with the excitement and enthusiasm generated by the beginning of the revolution in France. What had previously been a pragmatic campaign now came to be waged on the grounds of natural justice and the rights of man. The carefully controlled attempt to keep a solid phalanx of Dissenting reformers together—always a hard task because of the "supineness [that] hangs about the Bulk of the Dissenters"[86]—was vitiated by this new extremism. Cooper resurrected the specter of infidelism and alienated most moderates by demanding not only the repeal of the Test and Corporation acts, but also all religious penal statutes.[87] And Priestley, still seemingly unaware that his religious disputes had political consequences,[88] widened the breach between the establishment and nonconformity in a number of published sermons. First in 1785 he compared Dissenters with sappers preparing to undermine the Established Church: they were "wisely placing, as it were, grain by grain, a train of gunpowder, to which the match would, one day, be laid to blow up that fabric which never could be again raised upon the same foundation."[89] Having thus earned the title "Gunpowder Joe," he then, in a commemoration sermon on 5 November 1789 in Birmingham, vigorously attacked Bishop Horsley.[90] He affected surprise that "the clergy here . . . now do everything they possibly can to injure me. I hear it is a measure of the clergy in general to prosecute me in the Spiritual Court, but on what ground they will proceed I cannot imagine."[91]

Local Hostilities

The two widespread movements hostile to the slave trade and the Test and Corporation acts brought some activists and future emigrants to national prominence and notoriety, but it was at the local level that the hostility against them was most pronounced, and for good local reasons. In Birmingham, for instance, which "was perhaps the greatest centre of middle-class Dissent" in Britain (with perhaps a quarter of them being Unitarians), Priestley was feared not just for his outspoken views but for the powerful local pressure group that he represented.[92] Anglican-Dissenter antagonism grew there in the years after 1785 not because the latter were knocking on the door of local authority; they were already inside, having considerable local economic power as well as holding down significant positions in both municipal and county government.[93] Rather, the fracturing of the Birmingham elites along religious lines occurred because Anglicans thought Dissenters were becoming too overbearing, too demanding at a time when their numbers, especially non-Trinitarians, were growing.[94] In disputes over religious teaching in the local multidenominational Sunday schools and over the type of religious literature that should be available in the local library, previously harmonious inter-denominational committees split asunder along religious lines.[95] On both occasions the Dissenting interest was represented most vocally by Priestley and Russell. When in 1787 the repeal of the Test and Corporation acts became an issue, smoldering Anglican-Dissenting antagonism burst into flames.

Local considerations also were influential in creating divisions in the ancient borough of Chester in the late 1780s, where the prosperous Unitarian merchant Ralph Eddowes led a campaign against the local oligarchy. He could have been bred for this role: not only had he been a pupil of Priestley at Warrington Academy, but his Dissenting "ancestry, both paternal and maternal, comprised a long succession of Old Whigs and Puritans" who were "the determined assertors of liberty, civil and religious."[96] Between 1784 and 1790 Eddowes conducted a campaign through the courts to overthrow the power of the closed Tory corporation of Chester, which was under the influence of the powerful Grosvenor family. His case rested on the provisions of the charter bestowed on the city by Henry VII, which prescribed annual elections on a freeman franchise for the aldermen and mayor.[97] His opponents rested their case on the legality of a charter issued by Charles II. After a number of trials in the King's Bench, one of the major issues was eventually brought to the House of Lords by Eddowes in February 1790. It was decided in his favor, but the judgment, having left avenues open for further litigation, was ignored by the corporation.[98]

Eddowes had originally agreed to act as relator in this campaign on behalf of a group of local Whigs who were willing to share the costs, but their subsequent reluctance to pay their debts and the loss of valuable time spent in attending the trials in London forced his decision to withdraw from the battle in 1790. He did so with understandable bitterness: "As to the part *I* have taken in the late cause, tho' a principle of honour and love of my country determined me not to abandon, after having once undertaken it, yet prudential reasons absolutely forbid me to place myself *again* in such a situation. The corporation may resemble the head of *Hydra,* or the stable of *Augeas,* but I am no *Hercules,* nor do I find myself disposed to undertake the *labour* of delivering the public from all its baneful and loathsome effects."[99]

By this time Eddowes, influenced by the French Revolution, had shed his ancient constitutionalism and his Whig admiration for the British Constitution of 1688.[100] In contrast to revolutionary France, Britain was enveloped in a "despotic atmosphere" in which thrived "the monstrous forms of monarchical, aristocratical, and ecclesiastical power, with all their engines of oppression."[101] His lurch to the left was partly a consequence of his involvement in the movement to repeal the Test and Corporation acts, but it was also a response to the increased official harassment he suffered in his business affairs.[102]

Finally, in 1793 Eddowes sold his property in Chester and moved north to Liverpool, where he became friends with a group of advanced reformers who had themselves only recently been thwarted by lack of money in a campaign similar to Eddowes's against the local corporation.[103] This group, consisting entirely of Dissenting middle-class intellectuals rather than activist radicals, remained a tiny atoll of ineffectual liberalism in an ocean of pro-slave trade and loyalist interests.[104] Increasingly, Eddowes's thoughts turned to the United States, the new constitution of which held "an irresistible attraction for the lovers and devoted adherents of liberty."[105] When his partnership in a firm of wine merchants failed, he abandoned his country and with his large family set sail across the Atlantic.

The Priestley Riots, July 1791

Eddowes's experiences in Chester and his liberal friends' ineffectiveness in Liverpool show that in towns where the corporation was a closed oligarchy and where Radical Dissenters were unable or unwilling to link their strategies

to a wider constituency, it was possible for loyalist-Anglican groups successfully to bully and overawe their rivals. In contrast, in towns where parties
were more evenly balanced and local power was vigorously contested, intimidatory tactics merely heightened conflict. In Birmingham they led to the
frightening "Priestley Riots" of July 1791.

Priestley had been forecasting an outbreak of violence against the Radical
Dissenters in Birmingham since before the failure of the third repeal campaign in March 1790. However his expectation of mischief by the mob when
the news of repeal's rejection arrived was not fulfilled.[106] Not that it probably
would have deterred him at that time. He seemed to relish the continuation of
conflict, at one time aggressively telling Lindsey "I shall now keep the ball up,
and not do it by halves," at another informing Richard Price that "I have long
since drawn the sword and thrown away the scabbard, and am very easy about
the consequences."[107]

By continuing to engage in polemical pamphleteering Priestley played into
the hands of his enemies. His main local clerical opponent, Spencer Madan,
Vicar of St. Philip's, was able to blacken all Dissenters by emphasizing Priestley's unwarranted extremism:

> The doctrine of the Trinity, we know, is a most sacred and fundamental article of
> the national creed. This the dissenters think proper to reject, and they are at *liberty*
> to reject it. But they go still further, they insult us with the charge of idolatry on
> account of this doctrine; they are at *liberty* to do *this also,* through the mildness of
> our principles. . . . It is a circumstance *well known,* that in their ordinary discourse
> and in their frequent publications, they abuse this liberty without scruple and with-
> out molestation. . . . Surely the *professed* candour of these sectaries . . . instead of
> seeking to inflame the public mind with absurd apprehensions of a dormant stat-
> ute, ought rather to approve itself by acknowledging the lenity of *such ample tol-
> eration!*[108]

Moreover, a clergyman prepared to defend the church against Priestley could
do his own prospects no harm. According to Birmingham's first historian: "To
dispute with the doctor was deemed the road to preferment. He [Priestley] had
already made two bishops; and there were several heads which wanted mi-
tres." In May 1792 Spencer Madan was to be elevated to a bishopric.[109]

Thus, although the specific cause of the Birmingham riots was the Bastille
commemorative dinner organized by William Russell, the resulting mayhem
can only be explained in terms of the longstanding conflict between High
Church toryism and radical Unitarians in the town. Priestley himself viewed
it in just this way. He rejected the view of the Whig leaders Fox and Sheridan
that the riots stemmed from Court encouragement of the High Church party

to intimidate both the opposition at Westminster and their allies, the Dissenters. "Upon the face of it," he wrote to Russell, the riots were "evidently of a purely religious nature."[110] Blame should be sheeted home to "the magistrates, and other principal high-church men at Birmingham."[111]

Russell agreed with Priestley's analysis and for the next few weeks feverishly worked to obtain affidavits from local citizens to prove that three local magistrates had not only failed to nip the riot in the bud, but had actively encouraged the rioters to attack Dissenting chapels. By the end of July he informed William Chamberlayne, a treasury lawyer sent to Birmingham: "The evidence [against the magistrates] proves so much stronger than was expected, and is withal so repeatedly and pointedly corroborated that I am persuaded it will carry conviction with it."[112] In the event, when Samuel Whitbread brought on a motion in the House of Commons against the magistrates in May 1792, it was rejected by a large majority.[113]

Birmingham Dissenters suffered serious property damage as a result of the riots. Not only were three Unitarian meeting houses and a Baptist chapel laid waste, but at least twenty-seven private homes were attacked, damaged, or destroyed.[114] Priestley lost his manuscripts and scientific instruments when his house was burnt, Russell's home at Showell Green was destroyed, and at Sparkbrook the "capital mansion" and furniture warehouse of another Unitarian, WILLIAM HUMPHRIES, were razed, although Humphries managed to shoot dead one of the rioters. Fourteen others were later found "dead drunk" on the lawn outside the house.[115]

But it could have been much worse, according to the Ulsterman JOHN CALDWELL, who retailed the following story more than fifty years later, having first heard it in a Birmingham tavern just after the riots. At the height of the riots his namesake (but no relation) JOHN CAULDWELL, a Baptist merchant, prudently and secretly moved a large consignment of fire crackers and other squibs containing gunpowder far away from the disturbances. When, however, Spencer Maden advised him to pour water over his stock before the mob arrived ("otherwise the whole neighbourhood might be blown up"), Cauldwell cannily intimated that the rioters ought to take great care if they intended to steal his stockpile of coal, for the gunpowder was hidden underneath. "This hint was sufficient," claimed Caldwell, "and the Reverend leader directed the mob to some other victim." Soon after, Cauldwell emigrated with his family and relations to America, where he became an eminent hardware merchant.[116]

Apocryphal or not, the story supports the view that the riots did not totally overawe Dissenting radicals in the Midlands. Although Priestley never returned to Birmingham, he retained his (by now rather passive) faith in the imminence of the millennium. In October 1791 he wrote to a sympathetic acquaintance: "There is indeed a glorious prospect for mankind before us. Flanders seems quite ripe for a similar revolution; and other countries, I hope, will follow in due time; and when civil tyranny is all at an end, that of the church will soon be disposed of. . . . Our court and courtiers will not like these things, and the bishops least of all."[117]

Russell and others rode out the storm in Birmingham, remaining in the region for many months, and even daring publicly to call for parliamentary reform.[118] But the dissenting triumphalism of the late 1780s had disappeared; High Church loyalism now held sway. Moreover, tensions remained high. As late as October 1793, when attempts were made to collect the county rate raised to pay for the damage caused in the Birmingham riots, troops had to be called in, and at least two people were killed in the subsequent riots.[119] In these circumstances, Dissenters ultimately had to consider carefully whether to continue struggling to remake their lives in the region or to look overseas for better opportunities.

THE INFLUENCE OF PAINE

Manchester Radicalism

In Manchester the Dissenting radicals managed to avoid disturbances on 14 July 1791 partly because their acknowledged leader, Thomas Walker, as Boroughreeve, had control of local policing, and partly because the advertisements for their commemorative dinner stressed its nonpolitical nature.[120] They were also more tightly and visibly organized, having established in the previous October, in response to a local Church and King Club, the Manchester Constitutional Society.[121] Indeed, for the loyalists the Manchester radicals were to be a tougher nut to crack than their Birmingham counterparts. Not only did they have the benefit of experience drawn from their repeal and anti-slave trade activities, but they also created a wider social base for their movement, had a more activist (if not more militant) leadership, and possessed a newspaper to attract attention and spread their views.

Perhaps the Manchester Dissenting radicals' greatest strength lay in their ability to coalesce with new strains of popular radicalism, which by 1792 began to emerge among plebeian groups in London and many provincial towns. Edmund Burke appreciated this; for him, "the Constitutional, the Revolution and the Unitarian Societies" were "objects of the greatest terror."[122] For the first time political awareness was becoming widespread in the British Isles, and secular political ideas began to jostle the older Rational Dissenting radicalism with its roots in religious conflict.[123] The Manchester Constitutional Society was one of the first societies to bridge the gap between middle-class Dissenting and more plebeian radicalism. Appropriately, given his interest in designing bridges, the keystone of this merger was Thomas Paine.[124]

Although the writings of Rational Dissenters such as Priestley and Richard Price remained influential throughout the 1790s, it was mostly Paine's writings that spoke to the radicals' needs. The publishing history of *Rights of Man* is astonishing. Part one, published in March 1791, was promoted by the renascent SCI in London and by the new provincial radical societies. The Manchester Constitutional Society asked Thomas Cooper to abridge it for popular use, and in January 1792 the Unitarian Joseph Gales of the Sheffield Constitutional Society obtained Paine's consent to print the first cheap edition.[125] The book became a bestseller, but it was eclipsed by the phenomenal success of part two, published in February 1792. As many as 200,000 copies of part two, in various forms and editions, may have been distributed in the British Isles by the end of the year.[126]

The Manchester radicals did not fail to share this enthusiasm for *Rights of Man*. Cooper told James Watt, Jr., that "It has made me still more politically mad than I ever was. . . . It is choque full, crowded with good sense and demonstrative reasoning, heightened also with a profusion of libellous matter. I regard it as the very jewel of a book. . . . Burke is done up for ever and ever by it—but Paine attacking Burke is dashing out the brains of a Butterfly with the Club of Hercules! . . . Talk of it everywhere, read it as soon as you can get it, then get it by heart and retail it."[127] The new radical *Manchester Herald*, printed by Falkner, SAMUEL BIRCH, and their young apprentice, WILLIAM YOUNG BIRCH, was filled with Painite arguments and enthusiasms written by a Constitutional Society editorial collective. It will, wrote Cooper to Horne Tooke, "*at first* be gently but always decidedly democratish, nor pestered with much presbyterian nonsense."[128] And according to JOHN WOOD, admittedly a hostile source, JAMES CHEETHAM, one of three Manchester brothers known as "the three Jacobin infidels," rushed "with the *Rights of Man* in one hand, and *Age of Reason* in another . . . from tavern to tavern and from brothel to brothel, collecting and summoning together all that wickedness had rendered contemptible, drunkenness turned idle, and indolence made destitute."[129]

Cheetham and his brothers JOHN and BEN were affiliated to the local Constitutional Society, but were also members of the Manchester Reformation Society, founded in June 1792 at the Old Boar's Head, Hyde Cross. The formation of another radical society, the Manchester Patriotic Society, had preceded it in May.[130] Whereas the Constitutional Society comprised mainly middle-class members (between fifty and one hundred merchants, manufacturers, and professional men, with a strong Unitarian element), both of these new societies were primarily plebeian in membership, with cheap subscriptions suitable for the working man, and a policy of weekly reading sessions in which Paine's works were a feature. Undoubtedly the Constitutional Society acted as both midwife and mother hen to these societies, helping to create a temporary supraclass radical alliance in the town.[131]

As Paine's ideas took hold, and revolutionary France plunged into war with Austria and Prussia, the Manchester Constitutional Society shed its narrow provincial husk to flower briefly as part of international "Jacobinism." In March 1792 Cooper and James Watt, Jr., traveled to France, taking with them a letter of introduction from Walker to Petion, mayor of Paris, which hinted at the imminent collapse of the British monarchy and aristocratic society.[132] Cooper was in his element. He later recounted that his weeks in Paris were the happiest of his life: "He laughed more than he ever did before or afterwards and in each month he lived a year."[133] Electing themselves delegates from the Manchester Society, Watt and Cooper were presented to the Paris Jacobin Club by Robespierre. Cooper delivered an address full of the currently fashionable internationalism: "The light which you have thrown upon the true principles of Politics and the natural Rights of Man, a light which in England faintly gleams amidst the darkness of civil ignorance, ought to teach us that the period is at length arrived to abolish all national prejudice, and for the freemen of every country to salute each other as brethren. Too long have the machinations of despots, always in opposition to the dictates of nature, taught the nations of the earth to regard each other as enemies."[134] With their objective of establishing a correspondence between the Manchester society and the Jacobin Club having received a warm welcome, and having marched in a huge patriotic procession in Paris—Watt carrying the British flag, the diminutive Cooper a (hopefully small) bust of Algernon Sydney—the delegates returned happily to Manchester in May 1792.[135]

Unwittingly they had raised a hornet's nest, for in their absence Edmund Burke had attacked them in Parliament for their effrontery in claiming "to represent all England" while in Paris. The notoriety they had brought to the Constitutional Society was not, however, to last long, for inexorably increasing loyalist pressure in Manchester forced the radicals on the defensive. Nationally, the cue for a loyalist reaction was given by a Royal Proclamation against seditious writings in May 1792. Writing as "Sydney" in the *Manchester Herald*, Cooper complained that "The evil spirit of criminal conjecture is let loose upon the public, by authority, to stab the reputation of the innocent; and the malignant passions of private pique and public prejudice have full play and ample gratification."[136] He may have been right. Only two days after these words were published a Church and King crowd attacked a dissenting chapel and a Unitarian meeting house in Manchester. A few trees were uprooted to use as battering rams but otherwise little damage was done.[137]

Faced with extravagant claims that they were levelers in league with Beelzebub,[138] the radicals were gradually forced into a defensive posture, responding to their opponents' accusations and jibes rather than promoting their own political program. They were even squeezed out of the public space; in September loyalist pressure on Manchester's publicans forced the societies to seek new premises in which to meet. Walker offered his home as a replacement, and thereby directed loyalist malice ever more against himself.[139]

A major crisis for the radicals emerged in the last months of 1792 when the authorities and the propertied classes in Britain began to display signs of panic.[140] France became a republic, war loomed, and the radical societies, cock-a-hoop at the military victories of the French, became increasingly militant. In Manchester, using his "Sydney" pseudonym, Cooper published a controversial antiwar leaflet, which was distributed widely, even as far as Scotland. In it, Cooper strongly intimated that war was socially and politically divisive, having no ill effects on the rich but leading to disaster for the poor:

> WAR apppears to be the present determination and the real cause of all the sudden ASSOCIATIONS and loyal declarations. . . . Will landed property become more valuable? . . . Will [war] diminish the excise, or the land tax, or the house tax, or the window tax, or the commutation tax, or any of the long, long catalogue of taxes which lies so heavily upon this devoted country? . . . The ignorance and bigotry of Church and King politics may deprive us at a stroke of every market for our manufactures which the world affords. . . . Suppose for a moment that the rich and opulent manufacturer can support this—what will the little maker, the country dealer say to such a crisis of affairs? . . . [The poor] are liable to be torn from their families by the violence of the press-gang, while the rich and luxurious repose in peace upon their beds of down.[141]

Cooper may have felt justified in stirring up passions on account of his genuine abhorrence of war and its effects. Less justifiable, however, were the attempts by Falkner and others to suborn the locally stationed Scots Greys by giving them dinners and supplying them with Paine's works gratis.[142] There is, moreover, some evidence to suggest that Cooper may have had secret dealings with republican French diplomats before he published his leaflet. The French representative in London, Chauvelin, had been ordered to stir up antiwar feeling. He reported to Lebrun, the French Foreign Minister, that he had met some very rich London and Manchester merchants in Putney on 4 December, who told him that antiwar addresses "conceived and drafted precisely in the manner that I had indicated to them" would shortly be available. A week later Cooper's leaflet was published.[143]

As the crisis deepened, and a second Royal Proclamation was issued on 1 December, a familiar response accompanied Cooper's efforts. As had happened during the repeal campaigns, more moderate reformers began to withdraw, worried not only by the threat to property, but also by Cooper's extremism. In an impressive loyalist reaction, hundreds of petitions flowed into London expressing support for the king and the constitution. One of these came from the Nonconformists of Manchester. The Unitarians, with their plebeian supporters, became increasingly isolated, tarred with the brush of French Jacobinism.[144]

On the evening of 11 December, following a crowded but well-ordered loyalist meeting in the town, a mob attacked the shop of Falkner and Birch "with stones and brick bats till the windows were almost entirely destroyed and beat in at the front of the building."[145] With the local magistrates complacently looking on, some of the rioters moved on to Walker's house. Four times they surged around it, breaking windows, before Walker, with the help of members of all three radical societies, dispersed them by firing shots over their heads.

As Walker's spirited response suggests, crowd violence was not the best way to cow the Manchester radicals; much more effective was official harassment. In the ensuing months the Loyalist Association formed at the 11 December meeting systematically set out to destroy the radicals. Their key target was the *Manchester Herald*. In January 1793 Falkner and Birch were served with four ex-officio informations relating to their newspaper's contents and six indictments relating to the sale of seditious literature. Unwilling to face the long prison terms currently being handed out to radical printers and booksellers, in March they both fled to the United States.[146] Their newspaper collapsed, resulting, said one anonymous writer, not from "an assault of an enormous battery committed upon his body about three months ago," but from "six mortal wounds" (the six indictments).[147]

The loss of their mouthpiece was a serious blow to the Manchester radicals, which became fatal when the loyalists turned their attention to those spreading radical and antiwar literature. Many members of the Reformation Society were arrested, including Thomas Dunn, a hard-drinking Irish weaver who turned informer, and thereby sealed the fate of radicalism in Manchester. He swore that three of his fellow plebeian members, McCALLUM, JOHN SMITH, and BARRETT, had "cursed the King and wished to guillotine him."[148] All three managed to escape to America before they could be arrested. Not so fortunate was James Cheetham, a young man of "robust form, large frame, and great height," who was arrested on Dunn's evidence on a charge of sedition and held in prison for three weeks before being bailed. Tried in April 1794 on this and another charge, he was acquitted.[149]

Faced with continual harassment and perjured evidence, the radical movement in Manchester collapsed. The Constitutional Society ceased meeting at the end of March. Walker prudently disappeared to London in June 1793 where he stayed for several months, knowing that on his return he too would be charged with treason. Strangely, no attempt was made to arrest Cooper. Perhaps this was because already in April he had decided to emigrate.[150] With his cloth-printing firm in financial trouble, he "resolved to quit Trade. . . . My friends wish me (I think stupidly) to follow the Law; my own wish is to live while I can, and therefore if I can muster £1000 or £2000 I will endeavour to persuade my wife to accompany me to America."[151] In August he sailed across the Atlantic with JOSEPH PRIESTLEY, JR., and two other friends on a scouting mission to find a suitable asylum for his persecuted Unitarian friends. On his return (he left New York in February 1794), he published a pamphlet extolling the virtues of the new republic, and soon after became part of the general exodus of Priestley's followers to the United States.[152]

POPULAR RADICALISM

Plebeian Radicals

All the classic accounts of English radicalism in the 1790s have rightly concentrated more on the popular societies that emerged from 1792 and the subsequent underground revolutionary movements, than on the activities of middle-class radicals earlier in the decade.[153] That an account of radical emigration to America has to reverse this emphasis is a reflection of the fact that America, as an asylum of liberty and liberal Elysium, was both more attractive and more accessible to those radicals who came out of the Dissenting political tradition.[154] This is not to ignore the point (see Introduction, Table 3) that most English radical emigrants had an artisan background; but many of these emigrated as a consequence of their connections with Dissenting radicals, as the examples from Manchester mentioned above demonstrate.

A systematic examination of the English popular societies in their open phase shows that hardly any of the most prominent members either fled or emigrated to the United States in the 1790s. Of the dozen London Corresponding Society (LCS) and SCI leaders arrested in May 1794, only one, JOHN

LOVETT, eventually made his way to America. A hairdresser, Lovett had occasionally acted as chairman of LCS meetings. But even he was not seen as particularly important by the authorities; after five months in prison, he was released by a grand jury for lack of evidence.[155] LCS leaders such as Thomas Hardy, John Thelwall, and John Baxter may possibly have contemplated emigration overseas in their darkest moments, but stoically they remained in England (although Thelwall did 'emigrate' to rural Wales).[156] They internalized their defeat, rather than escaping from it.

With slightly less certainty, the same can be said of the most prominent plotters in the underground movement in the late 1790s. Very few leaders sought America as a place of safety. Those who did included JASPER MOORE, variously described as a warehouseman and printer, who in early 1798 was acting as president of the LCS.[157] Moore can be classified as a middle-ranking radical; much more significant was the Irishman, JOHN BINNS. In late 1794, with his elder brother, BENJAMIN, Binns left Dublin for London, where he worked first in the plumbing trade, then lived off the rent from debating rooms in the Strand. He joined the LCS and was soon prominent on its executive council, being at one stage chairman of its general committee. In 1796–97 Binns traveled the provinces as an LCS delegate hoping to revive the radical movement. He visited some of the more sensitive places in Britain's war effort, such as the dockyards at Portsmouth, and was suspected of encouraging the mutiny in the fleet.[158] In March 1796 he was arrested in Birmingham for uttering seditious words in a public house. Like so many other radicals, Binns's speech at the Swan tavern was full of the politics of threat. As one onlooker claimed, Binns had called for universal suffrage and annual parliaments:

> He then told the company that their object was to obtain [their objectives] by every peaceable means in their power for it would be shocking to humanity to shed the blood of your fellow creatures, but that if they continued obstinate there should be a time when force was necessary to be used. . . . In speaking of the soldiery Binns observed that though they were buried in barracks . . . they had the same feelings as themselves . . . whether in a brown coat, a black one or a red one. That if the soldiers were called upon to act against them, like the National Guards who were called upon to fire on the people in the outset of the Revolution in France they would not dare to draw the trigger or point the bayonet against the preservers of their Freedom and their liberty.[159]

After long delays on bail, Binns was acquitted of the Birmingham charge in August 1797, probably because a sympathetic court official rigged the jury.[160] Soon after, Binns left the LCS and joined the shadowy revolutionary United Irishmen in London. Acting with his brother on liaison duties with the

United Irishmen in Dublin, he was arrested twice more, once in February 1798 on a charge of high treason, when on the point of sailing to France. At Maidstone assizes, where he shared the dock with Arthur O'Connor, O'Connor's servant JEREMIAH LEARY, John Allen, and the Catholic priest James O'Coigley, he was again acquitted, although O'Coigley was hanged. In March 1799 he was jailed under the Suspension of Habeas Corpus Act, not being released for nearly two years.[161]

The Binns brothers, perhaps reflecting their Irish background,[162] were serious revolutionaries, republicans by conviction. This made them very different from most of their English colleagues who finally ended up in America. Apart from the Unitarian exodus already mentioned, many of the English radical emigrants were small-fry who became individually entangled in the loyalist dragnets that periodically swept across the country. A good example is JOHN COOK, a Cambridge baker, who in July 1793 was tried at Quarter Sessions for seditious words. He may well have been drunk when he allegedly asserted: "I will always have a calf's head for dinner on the anniversary of the martyrdom [30 January, execution of Charles I], so long as I have money to buy one. King George's head would look well so served up in a dish; there would be cut and come again; and what a wonderful discovery there would be when you came to the brains! Damn the Monarchy; I want none; I wish to set all the churches down, and the roads mended with them and King's chapel [Cambridge] made a stable of."[163] Cook was probably lucky to escape with three months in prison, a fine of 40 shillings, and sureties for six years.

At about the same time Cook was released from prison THOMAS BRIELLAT, a pump-maker from Hackney, offered a field to the London Corresponding Society as the venue for one of its large open-air meetings. Following the meeting, at which representatives to the Edinburgh Convention were chosen and LCS committee members required police protection from loyalist hecklers, Briellat was arrested for having uttered seditious words more than ten months earlier. On the testimony of a Jewish butcher's boy, who claimed he had said that "he was a republican, and he owned it, and was certain there could be no reformation without a revolution," Briellat received a sentence of two years in Newgate and a fine of £100.[164]

Cook and Briellat are examples of small-propertied reformers and radicals whose livelihoods were seriously disrupted as a consequence of their political foolhardiness.[165] They were not leaders of radical movements; they may not even have been very active. But they are representative of the rank and file elements who became victims of loyalist rancor at a peak of reaction in the localities. Both would have found great difficulty resurrecting their businesses on release from prison. It is unlikely that their radical friends would have been able to help them. Selling and beginning again in the United States may have been for Cook and Briellat a risk not much greater than trying to convince old customers to renew their trading in neighborhoods where radicals were deliberately ostracized.

Radical Journalists

These English radicals of minor importance sought America as a haven because they tended to become victims of loyalist associations, which, following the dictates of various Royal Proclamations against seditious writings and seditious words, fixed their attention on easy targets, frequently people waxing seditious in the hop-filled atmosphere of ale houses.[166] Another prime target, potentially of much greater influence and thereby of particular concern to the government, were "the wordsmiths, the journalists who were the veritable artisans of revolution."[167] They were not just the transmitters of ideas; many also sought to be creators of a new political language to express and explain the new political world they envisioned. In France, where strenuous efforts were made to obliterate virtually every facet of the ancien régime, revolutionary words "came in torrents," invested with a "unique, magical quality," and aimed at destroying the mystique of kingship.[168] Across the channel, in a very different context, the flow was neither so fast nor so destructive. Nevertheless, an English war of the words was fought, in which a plain and democratic speech was advocated and practiced, in an attempt to find an alternative to the class-bound and hegemonic "good English" and its despised corollary, vulgar English.[169] The first campaign in the 1790s was inconclusive (it was to be fought again after 1815),[170] but in the skirmishing several of the wounded had to retreat to America.

In London especially the authorities faced a wide selection of hostile scribes; in 1793–94 the political wing of Newgate prison could have been mistaken for a press corps club.[171] The metropolis was crowded with aspiring writers and amateur philosophes, some who at times expressed radical political opinions but were easily bought off; some who attached themselves to the Foxite Whig opposition; and yet others who allied themselves with the various popular societies.[172]

Principled journalists and booksellers, therefore, need to be distinguished from the more opportunistic hacks whose pens were used in the radical cause only if the price was right, but who also at times had to seek refuge across the Atlantic. Extorting money by threatening to publish scurrilous material in newspapers or pamphlets was common practice in late eighteenth-century London; possibly three-quarters of the daily newspapers engaged in such activities at one time or another.[173] Henry Pace, for instance, who in 1802–3 was to be JAMES THOMSON CALLENDER's partner on the notorious *Richmond Recorder*, had fled to America in 1798 when an extortion attempt miscarried.[174] The Oxford-educated James Fennell, who became one of America's first tragic actors, arrived in Philadelphia in 1794 for similar reasons. He, like many genuine radicals, had gone to Paris in the first stages of the revolution, where he opened a school of declamation, an enterprise that, given the histrionics of the French revolutionaries, one might think ought to have been very successful. Unfortunately, a rival Frenchman denounced him as a spy of Pitt, and he was forced to flee. In London, close to poverty, he began an arts magazine, which he shamelessly used to extort money from the manager of the Covent Garden theatre. He obtained his money, but only on condition of going to America.[175]

Pace and Fennell have left no evidence to confirm their genuine adherence to the radical cause, but the case of JOHN MASON WILLIAMS (1761–1818) demonstrates that it is not always easy to separate the committed radical from the rogue. Exemplifying the restlessness and instability of men of minor artistic talent, the London-born Williams flirted with painting and translating before moving to Dublin in the early 1780s. There, like Mathew Carey at the same time, his satirical writings for a newspaper brought him into conflict with the authorities. Back in England to escape prosecution, for the next few years he flitted from London, to Brighton, to Bath, and again to London, establishing short-lived magazines and writing for newspapers. He left each location under a cloud. He gained minor celebrity for his verse under the nom de plume "Anthony Pasquin," and in the early 1790s wrote for two antiadministration newspapers, the *Morning Post* and the *World*. Williams was never a political activist, but used his talent for scurrilous satire to poke fun at, and undermine, British institutions. Eventually, having received a taste of his own medicine, in 1797 he unsuccessfully sued for libel. At the trial, where he was nonsuited, Lord Justice Kenyon expressed the hope "that some method will ere long be fallen upon to prevent all such unprincipled and mercenary wretches from going about unbridled in society to the great annoyance and disquietude of the public." Soon afterward, Williams emigrated to America, arriving in Boston in May 1798, where he continued his unsuccessful career as a journalist.[176]

Much less unprincipled than Williams, but of like Whiggish-cum-radical views, was another writer, poet, and political dabbler, ROBERT MERRY (1755–98). The son of a governor of the Hudson Bay Company, Merry had a privileged upbringing (Harrow and Christ Church, Cambridge) and an independent fortune, which he dissipated by the age of twenty-five. Forced by penury to live abroad, he settled in the expatriate English colony in Florence, where he pursued women and literary fame and discussed progressive political ideas with Italian intellectuals. He perceptively and at first successfully rode the wave of romanticism and feeling that rolled across Europe under the influence of Rousseau in the last years of the ancien régime.[177] Back in London, as "Della Crusca" he created the poetic movement of that name that for a few years made frothy, sensitive, and highly refined romantic verse popular. One commentator has likened him to a pale version of Lord Byron: "Merry had all of the surface traits of a Lord Byron—the spectacular love affairs, the masochistic sense of evil in his own nature, the feeling of tremendous inner power and pride in his own resources. And he had, too, many of Byron's redeeming traits—his hatred of oppression, his intense feeling about human freedom, his passionate worship of beauty."[178]

Unfortunately, he was only a mediocre poet.

Merry was also a playwright and a journalist, first for the *World,* and then, from mid-1791, for the *Morning Post.* Enthralled by the prospects of the revolution, he visited France in 1789, and in June 1791 helped to found in London a Foxite society, the Friends of the Liberty of the Press.[179] On 14 July, at the same time as Priestley, Russell, and their friends around Birmingham were hiding in fear of their lives, Merry was reciting his "Ode to Liberty" before 1,500 people at a celebratory dinner at the Crown and Anchor tavern.[180] He too was probably lucky not to be mobbed!

Merry's fatal misfortunes began in February 1792, at about the same time as he helped to write the Whig Friends of the People's reforming "Address to the People." His play, "The Magician No Conjuror," was performed for the first and only time at Covent Garden. Previously his plays had been apolitical, but in this one he ridiculed Prime Minister Pitt as The Magician.[181] The play was immediately withdrawn. Soon after, his new wife, the actress Miss Elizabeth Brunton, was dismissed from the company and was thereafter unable to find work. Twice they went to Paris; on the second occasion, in November 1792, Merry tried in vain to win a seat in the National Convention by presenting to its members a treatise on "The Nature of a Free Government."[182] This was an ill-timed offering. In 1795 Mr. and Mrs. Merry set sail for America, in the hope that both would find audiences more sympathetic to their talents.

It is hard to take Merry very seriously, although he and his wife were the victims of officious, if not official, persecution for their political views. Like

Mason Williams, Merry belonged to the demimonde that clung to the fringes of the circle comprising the opposition Foxite Whigs and the Prince of Wales.[183] Its commitment to reform had more to do with high-political maneuverings than to principle. But also in London existed a more plebeian world of journalism and publishing, which was trying to build on Paine's "intellectual vernacular prose."[184] Like so many of the metropolitan trades, printing and publishing was divided into a respectable part and a "rough" part. The latter's murky underworld of extremist, disreputable, sometimes crackpot militants has been brilliantly recreated by Iain McCalman.[185] He has shown how in convivial low alehouses and from tiny back-lane shops, from market stalls, and even from wheelbarrows, committed republicans and religious extremists sought to disseminate their ideas through the sale of their cheaply produced leaflets and pamphlets.

"CITIZEN" RICHARD LEE was one such republican bookseller who published and sold inflammatory pamphlets from "The British Tree of Liberty" in Berwick Street, Soho. His own writings were sanguinary, violent, and aimed at an English sansculotterie. A forthright republican, at times he betrayed the influence of Thomas Spence on his thinking by hinting at the need for property redistribution.[186] The titles of his leaflets and handbills were deliberately provoking: *The Reign of the English Robespierre, The Happy Reign of George the Last*, and *King Killing*. In the last, a handbill, he called for regicide:

> Shall kings alone claim an exemption from Law, an impunity of Wickedness? . . . It is a prejudice to consider the persons of Princes alone as sacred: the infliction of TERRIBLE JUSTICE BY THE PEOPLE, when the people have it in their power, is alone capable of checking the career of tyranny. If an individual believes, that an act of seasonable violence on his part will operate as a salutary example to his countrymen, and awaken them to the energy and dignity of their characters, by breaking the wand whose magic power lulled them into sloth and inaction; does he not, in committing that act of violence, perform his duty as a member of the community, whose interests are closely connected with his own? . . . Let us destroy this huge Colossus, under which the tall aspiring head of Liberty cannot pass!!![187]

Lee's admiration of the guillotine as a revolutionary instrument and his unbounded delight at the successes of French "*gingerbread bakers* and *hairdressers*" over the best European generals demonstrate the influence of the French Revolution on his thinking.[188] But in several important respects he can be seen as representing a more indigenous tradition coming out of the seventeenth-century upheavals. Lee claimed that he filched the titles for his works from pamphlets of the civil war era, which suggests that he was familiar with their contents.[189] He was also influenced by the Dissenting tradition—he is frequently called a Methodist—and by millenarianism. It was his religious views, more than his violent language or his leveling principles, that made his position in the LCS so stormy. Lee joined the society in June 1794, but within a year had twice been expelled for refusing to sell the rationalist Volney's *Ruins of Empire* and Paine's Deist *Age of Reason*. When a warrant for his arrest was issued at the end of 1795, Lee took flight to America.[190]

Lee had been allowed considerable latitude by the authorities for many months. Perhaps, like the strange JOHN "WALKING" STEWART, who also wrote, printed, and published his own unread and unreadable manifestos,[191] he was seen to be too eccentric or ineffectual. One political writer and publisher who was more respectable, and who consequently was repeatedly harassed by the authorities, was DANIEL ISAAC EATON (?1751–1814). From his shop in Bishopgate Street in the City of London he sold some of the more radical and more popular pamphlets of the time, including Paine's, for whom he was the only official publisher in England. A committed member of the LCS, and like so many of his colleagues a Deist in religious principle (he was brought up in the Roman Catholic faith), Eaton made a significant contribution to the radical movement by publishing and editing a number of intelligent and thought-provoking magazines and pamphlets. These included *Hog's Wash, or Politics for the People, Political Classics,* and the *Philanthropist;* he also printed and published John Thelwall's sophisticated journal, the *Tribune.*[192]

In comparison with other publishers who fled to America, Eaton was at the upper end of the market. This, of course, made him more of a threat to the authorities, even though his politics were decidedly nonviolent and nonrevolutionary. He did, however, publish one of Thelwall's more belligerent pieces, in which he compared George III with a tyrannical gamecock, which, when beheaded and cooked "was no better than a common tame scratch-dunghill pullet: no, nor half so good, for he was tough, and oily, and rank with the pollutions of his luxurious vices."[193] (Cannibalizing George III seems to have been a recurring image in radical polemics.)[194]

This and other paragraphs led to Eaton being indicted in December 1793 for seditious libel (he had already been acquitted twice on similar charges the previous June and July). Unable to find the exorbitant bail required, he was imprisoned in Newgate for two months, before again being acquitted. Three months later, when the government arrested the LCS and SCI leaders, his house and shop were searched by the police in his absence. He was not arrested at this time and he continued his publishing, until in July 1796 he was finally found guilty of publishing seditious works. He went into hiding. His family continued the business, but early in 1797, with new prosecutions hanging over him, he escaped to America.

BENJAMIN VAUGHAN: AN ARCHETYPE

The English radical movement in the 1790s was created from a diverse range of political traditions.[195] The English radicals themselves were a varied lot: provincials and metropolitans; Dissenters and Deists; middle class and plebeians; reformers and revolutionaries. But whatever the background and political position examined, normally at least one representative can be found who sought freedom and a breathing space by escaping to the United States (one possible exception may be the network of second-generation metropolitan Dissenting intellectuals that included William Godwin, Thomas Holcroft, and Mary Wollstonecraft, although even here John Stewart, John Binns, Merry, and Eaton probably had connections).[196]

The "ideal" English refugee was a middle-class Unitarian or Deist writer or publisher involved in extraparliamentary politics from the 1780s. He was an enthusiast for the Revolution of 1789, and an active member of a political society, who once Britain was at war in 1793 came to grief on account of his sympathies for France and extreme antiwar views. A radical reformer, he was not a man of violence, but had to flee at some point before 1795. The man who probably best fits this profile is Benjamin Vaughan.

As a young man, after being educated by Priestley at Warrington Academy, Vaughan became a member of the Club of Honest Whigs and part of the Bowood circle, the gathering of intellectuals around Lord Shelburne (later Marquess of Lansdowne). Intelligent, inquiring, and open-minded (and thus almost inevitably Unitarian and anticlerical in religion), he had little of the arrogant cocksuredness that made Priestley, Cooper, and Russell so insufferable. Briefly brought close to the center of Whig power when his mentor, Lansdowne, became Prime Minister on the death of Lord Rockingham, he was sent on an unofficial mission to smooth over difficulties at the Paris Peace conference in 1783. He had some success in this task, although his return to London at one stage as an accredited envoy of John Jay, one of the American negotiators, probably unreasonably brought him the mistrust of George III. Thereafter he saw himself as an expert on international relations, and retained the confidence of Lansdowne, who in 1792 placed him in his pocket borough of Calne.[197]

With a degree in medicine from Edinburgh, a partnership in a successful London merchant house, and heir to land (and slaves) in Jamaica and Maine, Vaughan was sufficiently independent and prosperous to indulge his interests in politics and international relations. He edited a short-lived radical journal, the *Repository*, which developed some of the utilitarian ideas of the Bowood circle. He was a member of both the London Revolution Society and the SCI, and a major figure in the Dissenters' campaigns against the Test and Corporation acts.[198]

He was, of course, delighted with the revolution of 1789, and soon was in correspondence with many of the moderate constitutionalists (Mirabeau, La Rochefoucault, Target, Lafayette).[199] In 1790 he visited France as a representative of the London Revolution Society, and in 1791 attended the opening of the new legislative assembly. In 1792 he wrote a series of articles for the *Morning Chronicle,* in which he developed his ideas on parliamentary reform and the future of Europe.

Vaughan was one of the more clear-sighted and subtle political commentators of his generation. His political vision was heavily influenced by his friend and mentor, Joseph Priestley, but sensibly was driven less by the dictates of candor. Man, he thought, "is not perfect, but a perfectible animal." In an "untutored state" humankind is slow to develop new ideas, and even slower to reject old ones. But in France it was "a happy circumstance" that the revolution has been placed in the hands of "the middle ranks of people," who by seizing liberty had appropriated the future for themselves.[200] Their success, he claimed, had strengthened France and made it potentially a formidable opponent.

One of Vaughan's primary aims in writing his articles in 1791–92 was to use the example of France to demonstrate that the governing elite ought to join with "men in middling life" to reform political institutions in Britain. Revolutionary ideas, he claimed, will inevitably spread from France: "The rights of men never can be kept a secret, nor yet the wrongs they have suffered from their rulers. The great may dream that they are of a different race from others, but they will no longer find the multitude partaking of that dream. Hence the revolution will travel into other countries, which it will enter either by sap or by storm. . . . He is no statesman, who does not see other revolutions approaching or preparing."[201] Referring to the French nation "calling their keepers to account," but cleverly directing his message closer to home, Vaughan pointed out that "No prescription . . . will be of avail against men, who possess *power,* and who think they second it with *rights.* The [French] aristocracy, consequently, never can regain their situation but by intermixing with the people, and becoming their leaders, when they can no longer be their masters."[202] How much more wise, he implied, would be the British aristocracy if they made this alliance immediately and forestalled revolution.

Vaughan's solutions were not incompatible with the political position of the Whigs, who viewed themselves as the natural leaders of the people, but they were at the extreme left of whiggery, strongly tinged with Lockeian and Jeffersonian notions. He sought better representation of the people in Parliament, and more frequent elections, aims consistent with those of the SCI. These he argued for from first principles, in particular from the natural equality of man:

> On the subject of the natural equality of man, . . . we are not to understand that there are no natural differences between men, for the fact is otherwise. Men differ essentially from each other; but men must *not judge for themselves* of this difference; since every man would judge for himself improperly. Every man then must be estimated personally by his *neighbor;* or, in other words, when a government is instituted, it must be founded upon *mutual consent.* But this consent would only be momentary, if the public established a government in which they left no place for themselves. Their consent must be resorted to perpetually; and as they are unable to deliberate in large bodies, they must possess representatives, frequently renewable, for the purpose both of guarding the constitution, and of voting upon incidental subjects. We have thus a variety of principles flowing from the leading one, that men are equal. But by equal, we mean only that they must be *viewed* as if they were equal; for though unequal in their qualifications, they are at least equal in their *rights.*[203]

It is thus understandable that he voted in the House of Commons in May 1793 in favor of parliamentary reform. He also voted against the war with France.[204] His reasons for doing so were consonant with his fears for the stability of the British polity expressed the year before, as well as with his admiration for the principles of 1789. As he had anticipated in 1792, war threatened the position of the middle classes in France and increased the power of the lower orders.[205] It had also forced the French into a policy of expansionism. But above all, he predicted, Britain's involvement in the war would greatly increase the dissemination of revolutionary ideas, at a time when "our own dominions are in a state not to make it wise for us to embark in troubles." War would soon aggravate the "causes of disquiet, visible or latent," in both Britain and Ireland, with French principles finding their way across the channel "by a sort of under-current."[206]

It may be thought that on the basis of these ideas Vaughan should not be viewed as epitomizing the English radical emigration of the 1790s. He may have been a middle-class Unitarian, he may have been involved in all the Unitarians' programs, and he may have been an active member of the SCI, but his politics seem too *moderate* adequately to represent the generality of radicals who became refugees. In reality, however, his opinions, written before France became a republic, were *for their time* representative of the majority of the political emigrants. Where he differed from most of his contemporaries was in his invulnerability to the siren calls of Thomas Paine and the surges of republican energy that pulsated from Paris after 10 August 1792. Paine, he boldly informed Evan Nepean, undersecretary at the Home Office, should have been ignored by government: "His effect in some degree was certain, and experience has proved that it was less before he was noticed, than since. . . . You and I . . . know, that Payne [*sic*] is a dangerous book for any person who does not share in the spoil, to be left alone with; and it appears, that the book is now made as much a standard book in this country, as Robinson Crusoe and the Pilgrim's Progress, and that if it has not its effect today, it will tomorrow; in short, that it is ready for the occasion."[207] Do not, he continued, make the same mistake by prosecuting Thomas Cooper.

Nor did the revolutionary excitement generated among his peers by the apparent invincibility of the new French Republic seduce him from his desire for parliamentary reform. At the height of the Great Scare of late 1792, as hyperloyalism exploded in response to the popular societies, he continued to advance his usual views: "In this country, I would seize this [time], as the most favorable moment *possible* for a limited reform; and if our court would abandon foreign affairs and consent to this limited reform, we should get easy in money matters, and the court [will] have no struggles of moment in parliament, as they all of them turn upon wars, taxes, and reforms. But in future the public opinion must always count for something."[208]

It was as well for Vaughan that he had been involved in this correspondence with the Home Office at this juncture—he was trying to obtain official help for many of the French clergy who had fled to Britain—for only a week later he learned that his foreign correspondence with public figures in France had been opened by the Post Office. This knowledge gave him some uneasiness, as he thought his comments could be open to misinterpretation. But, he informed Nepean, "I wrote during peace and under the impression of peace, in favour of the funds, and with a view to confirm sentiments of peace. I hope this will be deemed legal and loyal."[209] To prove his point, he voluntarily sent his most recent correspondence to the Home Office.

Vaughan's explanation apparently was accepted, or, at least, he seems not to have been the subject of further government interest. No doubt, especially once war broke out, he was much more circumspect in his activities. But his penchant for giving advice on political matters in writing was to be his undoing. In February 1794 Rev. William Jackson arrived in London from Hamburg. An Anglican clergyman with a checkered past (in one popular play he was caricatured as Doctor Viper), Jackson was on a secret mission for Robespierre's Committee of Public Safety, to discover the weight of support in Britain and Ireland for a French invasion. He brought with him letters from the Unitarian merchant-in-exile, John Hurford Stone, to his brother William, a London merchant, and the wily old radical, John Horne Tooke.[210]

Jackson left the task of eliciting public opinion to William Stone, who contacted a number of opposition politicians, including Vaughan. Some were naturally suspicious and refused to cooperate; others were convinced by Stone's story that he was gleaning information for a report that he hoped would prevent his brother being arrested in Paris. Vaughan naively took the bait and wrote one of his erudite state-of-the-nation papers. He made it clear that a French invasion stood no chance of success:

> The temper of England is in favour of the first French Revolution, but not of the second; however, on the whole, it shows symptoms of being adverse to the present situation of the war, not from disliking its principles, but from seeing little profit in it; at the same time that they think its main object unattainable; namely, the overthrow of the present French system. They would be more earnest for peace, had they either suffered enough, or did they think the present French government sincerely disposed to peace. There are many persons attached to the principles of the French revolution in England, if they are reckoned numerically, but they are as nothing compared to the great mass of the people, who are indisposed to them.[211]

If an invasion occurred, he concluded, "there would be but one mind through the whole nation, they must defend it."

On 8 May 1794 Vaughan, with fellow Whig members of Parliament William Smith, Thomas Maitland, and Richard Brinsley Sheridan, and Lord Lauderdale, was summoned to the home office, where they were questioned on their involvement with Jackson. Vaughan's letter had been found in Stone's house when it had been raided and Stone arrested (Jackson was arrested in Dublin). Vaughan was examined again the following day. Immediately after, he fled to France.[212]

Vaughan's response seems out of proportion to the situation in which he found himself. According to the extant evidence, he may have been indiscreet and naive, but he was not knowingly corresponding with the enemy. And he certainly was not giving succor to the French, unless his attempt to dissuade them from invading can be seen as a machiavellian way of protecting French interests. On the other hand, Vaughan had already been embarrassed once before by his foreign correspondence; perhaps he believed that he could no longer expect the government's indulgence. Certainly, a major clamp down was imminent; only four days after Vaughan's first interrogation, the authorities arrested the LCS and SCI leaders in London. To arrest a close colleague of Charles James Fox at the same time would have been a temptation hard to resist. Thus it came about that the most moderate of the Unitarians found himself escaping to France as if he were a revolutionary Painite.

CONCLUSION

In May 1793 THOMAS PAINE—now a *conventionelle* in Paris—confided to Georges Jacques Danton: "I now despair of seeing the great object of European liberty accomplished, and my despair arises not from the combined foreign powers, not from intrigues of aristocracy and priestcraft, but from the tumultuous misconduct with which the internal affairs of the present revolution are conducted. All that now can be hoped for is limited to France only."[213] His expectation that the revolution would have extended liberty "through the greatest part of Europe" had been disappointed.[214] Across the channel, Paine's disillusionment was mirrored in the decision of the Radical Dissenters to emigrate to America. This exodus was not confined to the harassed groups in Manchester and Birmingham; from smaller centers of Rational Dissent also— from Uttoxeter, from Chourbent, from Bromsgrove—whole extended families and their retainers sold off their property and booked passage across the Atlantic.[215] At the same time, an even larger emigration of Welsh Dissenters got under way.[216]

By the end of 1794 the bulk of English radical emigration to America had been completed. It had been dominated by respectable, prosperous, Dissenting family men whose confidence in the future of their country had been shattered and who looked on their destination, thousands of miles to the west, as a place to regenerate their vision of a godly and liberal society. It was almost as if the events of 1620 and the voyage of the *Mayflower* were being repeated. But, of course, these new immigrants now faced a vibrant, expanding, and increasingly sophisticated society, not a wilderness. Whether it conformed to their expectations as an asylum of liberty would ultimately determine their responses to their new home.

Scottish Radicals

SCOTLAND IN THE LATE EIGHTEENTH CENTURY

Not the least valuable feature of John Galt's novel *Annals of the Parish* (1821) is its portrayal of a rural Scottish lowland parish moving, with ever-increasing momentum, from a traditional, closed, hierarchical community in the 1760s, to one that twenty years later was modernizing its economic base, suffering from growing social instability, and opening itself to the fashions and ideas of the wider world. The turning point came in the late 1770s. As a consequence of the American War of Independence, "a wonderful interest was raised among us all to hear what was going on in the world." By the time, a decade later, that a cotton mill had been established and the township of Cayenneville built in the parish to house immigrant spinners and weavers, "the minds of men were excited to new enterprises; a new genius, as it were, had descended upon the earth, and there was an erect and out-looking spirit abroad that was not to be satisfied with the taciturn regularity of ancient affairs."[1]

Galt's Dalmailing was a microcosm of lowland Scotland in the second half of the eighteenth century. It represented one man's imaginative depiction of Scotland undergoing "the crucial transformation from an underdeveloped to a developing industrial society." Although Scottish economic expansion can be found on many fronts at this time, it was the emergence of the cotton industry in the west of Scotland, initially based on water-powered spinning mills, the vast product of which greatly boosted the handloom weaving trade, that acted as the main engine of growth.[2] This process was uneven in its impact and subject to fluctuations, but by the late 1780s traditional Scottish lowland society was about to be irrevocably undermined.

Moreover, from about 1760 Scotland began to share with the rest of Europe the unprecedented effects of a sustained growth in population. Unlike in England and Wales, where a rising birth rate seems to have been the dominant factor, population increase north of the border was determined primarily by a decline in the mortality rate, especially among infants. Infant mortality dropped from about 200 to 250 per thousand live births in midcentury, to about 170 per thousand by the 1790s. The annual rate of population growth in the last half of the century was about 0.6 percent, which, although only half the rate of England's, was nevertheless sufficient—especially when combined with rapid economic change—to lay the foundations for a fundamental alteration of Scottish society. Between 1755 and the 1790s Scotland's population increased by 250,000 to 1.5 million, one quarter of whom lived in towns with populations greater than 2,500.[3]

The Scottish Enlightenment

At the same time as the economy began to show signs of modernizing, Scottish intellectual life reached its zenith. In the fields of philosophy, sociology, history, literature, political economy, morals, and medicine, among others, the Scottish enlightenment became a major intellectual force on both sides of the Atlantic. Scottish ideas informed the makers of constitutions in the new United States; Scottish savants were feted in Europe; Edinburgh University became a favored seat of learning for young American, European, and dissenting English students alike. In the thirty years after 1750, men of striking originality, such as Adam Smith, David Hume, Joseph Black, and William Cullen, created an intellectual world in Scotland that compared favorably, if on a more compact scale, with the world of the philosophes and their salons in contemporary France. Such was their eminence that Voltaire, with a mixture of sarcasm and envy, commented: "It is an admirable result of the progress of the human spirit that it is from Scotland we receive rules of taste in all the arts—from the epic poem to gardening."[4] The literati were equally influential in their homeland; dominant in the Church of Scotland and in the universities, and with the support of the Scottish landowning ruling class, there were few obstacles to hinder their progressive approach to most fields of human knowledge.[5]

Scotland's cultural life flourished in a society that by midcentury was aristocratic, classical, urbane, and civic. Although following the Act of Union in 1707 the Scottish parliament disappeared and many of the great landed magnates sought a place under the imperial sun in London, Scotland did not, as some had feared, remain an impoverished and stagnant backwater. After a period of dislocation and uncertainty, and particularly after the final defeat of Jacobitism in 1745, the Scots began to take advantage of the economic benefits of being Britons in the new state of Great Britain.[6] The resident gentry and the newly emergent professional classes (especially in the faculty of advocates), confident in their role as a provincial elite, introduced the sociable world of clubs and debating societies to spread the Augustan ideals of civic virtue and politeness.[7]

At the hub of this new Scottish culture lay Edinburgh; it "can be regarded, like eighteenth-century Dublin, Philadelphia or Boston, as the effective centre of the political life of one of the great provinces of the English [*sic*] Crown, and the focal point of the collective life of a provincial elite."[8] The site of the Scottish law courts, theaters, academies, and the annual meeting place for the General Assembly of the Church of Scotland, it attracted a host of enlightened gentry, scholarly Presbyterian ministers, and eminent professors (both Black and Cullen were lured to Edinburgh University from Glasgow).[9]

The Scottish elites came to participate in the varied cultural life that the clubs and societies of Edinburgh offered in abundance. There they were not only educated and entertained, but also, so it was argued, they were infused with the urbane manners and morals of the cult of sociability, as had been first promoted by Addison and Steele in early eighteenth-century London. In the salons, coffeehouses, and taverns, Phillipson claims,

> men and women met each other as friends and equals and were able to enjoy the sense of ease that good conversation could bring. Addison and Steele saw coffee-house conversation as a form of social interaction that taught men tolerance, moderation and the pleasures of consensus. It also taught them to look on their own behaviour with a critical detachment which was difficult to acquire in public life. It taught them to be adaptable, thoughtful and pragmatic in their attitude to social relations and to ideas and to lead decent, pleasant lives according to the principles of propriety. To put it another way, Addison and Steele set out to show men and women who had been raised in a classical tradition that the coffee-house could play as important a part in providing them with a sense of moral identity as the *polis* had done in the case of the citizens of ancient Greece and Rome.[10]

Lads o' Parts

In two major ways, in its support of the status quo and in its manipulation of patronage, this polite culture in Edinburgh inadvertently played a significant role in determining one major feature of the radicalism that emerged so briefly in Scotland in 1792–94, its reliance on aspiring "lads o' parts"—the poor but intelligent young man who benefited from Scotland's broadly based education system and whose interest was promoted by the local clergy or gentry. For all their progressive social thinking, the Scottish literati accepted the established order, displaying their talents in a society that was profoundly conservative, if not politically moribund.[11] Owing to the absence of a local parliament, no clear locus for political development existed in Scotland. The focus of ambitious politicians was on London, not Edinburgh; the local political vacuum was filled mainly by the legal fraternity and the General Assembly of the Church of Scotland. Scottish politics revolved around personalities and their interests rather than parties; when the tenacious and overmighty Argyle interest finally collapsed in 1764, the ensuing vacuum was ultimately filled by Henry Dundas, whose power rested on his influence in London.[12] Some of the literati may have had doubts about particular aspects of this system of rule, but they never questioned its legitimacy or its fundamental principles.[13]

Thus, although the American Revolution stirred popular political interest in Scotland, no organized center of opposition existed to coordinate it. The Belfast medical student William Drennan, studying in Edinburgh, and his sister Martha McTier, for instance, noticed that the pro-Americanism prevalent among young students in the early 1780s was tempered by caution. "There is," wrote Martha, "a spark of spirit got into the young men which, tho' they dare not avow, they are cherishing in secret, and while they honour the Irish they wish much to follow their example."[14] The example was, of course, the Volunteer movement, but according to Drennan, "the rude and imperfect sketches" made at volunteering by the Scottish students collapsed because of "the immeasurable distance that takes place between the gentry and commonalty."[15]

That gap, however, was to be partially filled during the next political crisis in 1792 by lads o' parts, ironically in some measure because of the way the Scottish enlightenment reproduced itself (by patronage), but also through the effects of demographic change. Radicalism in Scotland after 1789 was to feed off the thwarted ambitions of a generation the size of which reflected the first signs of rapid and sustained population growth north of the border. This cohort came of age in the 1780s and possessed high expectations at the very moment that the Scottish enlightenment's social and cultural influence and reputation peaked. For the purposes of the argument put forward here, the absolute size of this generation, rather than the causes of its size, is its crucial feature. More educated males were reaching manhood, yet the opportunities for advancement either remained static or failed to match population growth. The result was the emergence of an undercurrent of disaffection among socially aspiring individuals, in which unfulfilled expectations and social frustrations engendered by the increasingly closed world of Scottish society and culture burst out in pursuit of an independent, egalitarian, and ascriptive social system. If Thomas Paine's *Rights of Man* was the fire that swept through Scotland in the late autumn of 1792, it was fueled by the dry timber of social and cultural alienation stacked since the 1780s.

This argument requires documentation, for it flies in the face of some respected opinion. I. R. Christie, for example, argues that opportunities as a whole in late eighteenth-century Britain generally kept pace with population growth, while Bruce Lenman, writing of Scotland in particular, claims that opportunities for the educated were generally favorable: "The frustrated and therefore alienated intellectual was unimportant in eighteenth-century Scotland."[16] T. M. Devine is even more forthright: "Economic growth at home and expansion of the British colonies in North America, the Caribbean and India in the eighteenth century, . . . released a new series of opportunities for the sons of the middle classes and the landowners." After 1793, moreover, posts in the army and navy became increasingly available.[17]

Two points may be made about Devine's comments in particular, although they also apply by implication to Christie's and Lenman's. First, in eighteenth-century Scotland competition for places occurred not just among the sons of the middle and landed classes. The talented boy from humble background also had hopes of upward social mobility. Although the "myth" of the lad o' parts may have been exaggerated,[18] it is nevertheless true that the talented were frequently picked out for advancement, even if the main purpose was to draw them into supporting the status quo.[19]

A couple of examples will help to demonstrate this process. Between 1758 and 1760 James Beattie (1735–1803) went from being an obscure school teacher to professor of moral philosophy and logic at Marischal College, Aberdeen. The fourth son of a small landowner who died prematurely, Beattie was put through college at his brother's expense. Anxious to relieve the family's financial burden, in 1753 he became the schoolmaster at Fardoun. For the next five years he quietly wrote poetry in his spare time, until he came to the attention of Francis Garden, the future Lord Gardenstone, who introduced him to James Burnet, later Lord Monboddo. In 1758 they were instrumental in his appointment to a teaching post at Aberdeen Grammar School. Two years later, again at their instigation, Beattie was raised to the chair of moral philosophy at the local university, his alma mater. All of this occurred before the publication of his famous poem "The Minstrel" and, of course, before he made his name as a major figure of the Common Sense school of Scottish philosophy.[20]

A second example of the benefits of patronage from the same era is the career of William Thomson (1746–1817), whose father was a carpenter and builder "of decent circumstances." Thomson attended parochial school and Perth Grammar School, before moving on to the University of St. Andrew's. There he attracted the attention of the chancellor, Lord Kinnoul, who introduced him to Drs. Blair and Robertson. Following graduation, Kinnoul offered Thomson the position of minister in the parish of Monivaird. Unfortunately, Thomson's taste for "field sports and jovial companionship" was not appreciated in a presbytery "remarkable for religious gloom and fanatical austerity." He decided to pursue his ungodly interest in the violin and his literary pretensions in London, being helped on his way by an annual pension of £50 from Kinnoul. Once there Blair and Robertson offered him the opportunity of completing Robert Watson's unfinished *History of Philip III*. He accomplished this "so much to the satisfaction of the public, that he soon found himself surrounded with friends, and his hands filled with employment." For the next thirty-five years he wrote voluminously on all subjects except poetry, as well as editing a newspaper.[21]

Beattie and Thomson are perfect examples of what could be achieved by the marriage of individual talent and judicious patronage. (Both, incidentally, became supporters of the status quo; Beattie became an arch-conservative and Dundas's drinking companion; Thomson was employed by the government in London in 1793 to write down the radicals.)[22] But both had received their patronage in the mideighteenth century; by the 1780s such opportunities were beginning to dry up. And this brings us to the second point about Devine's view of the sufficiency of patronage in Scotland; it fluctuated in intensity. Between about 1780 and the early 1790s the window of opportunity closed, and a generation of young hopefuls remained out in the cold.

Part of the explanation for this lies in the relative freezing of professional jobs. There were five major avenues of advancement for the ambitious Scot determined to prosper in his native land: the law, the kirk, medicine, teaching, and the world of letters. Only two of these occupations, however, were expanding in real terms by the last decades of the century. The church was chronically oversubscribed with hopeful probationers; teachers were paid a pittance, suffering from low status (the publisher, William Creech, claimed in 1784 that "even porters, pimps, and chairmen in [Edinburgh] are opulent, when compared to most country schoolmasters")[23]; and the law remained the preserve of the landed classes, who made up ninety percent of the faculty of advocates. Numbers qualifying as Writers to the Signet (attorneys) increased in the years before 1800, but the proportion of those gentry-born remained almost constant.[24] Opportunities existed in medicine, although the high reputation of the Scottish universities meant that competition was strong. To rely on one's pen for a career was extremely risky and undoubtedly required the bounties of patronage.

There were other ways of achieving success; before the American Revolution the aspiring educated Scotsman could emigrate to the colonies. Together with the thousands of Highland crofters who sought a modest competence in America before 1775 were hundreds of young men, often the sons of lairds and merchants, who became family tutors, schoolmasters, local doctors, and clerks.[25] This relief valve for the aspiring and adventurous, however, closed off during the revolutionary years and did not reopen in the immediate aftermath of 1783.[26] Thus at the very time the cohort that later joined the radical movement in 1792 came of age, the job market was temporarily cluttered with young men who in previous decades would have emigrated to the colonies.

As the example of William Thomson suggests and the complaints of both Dr. Samuel Johnson and John Wilkes testify, another possible route to success for the ambitious Scot was along the high road to London. It is not difficult to find examples of Scots who made their mark in London in the mideighteenth century. London was an attractive destination, particularly for those with literary ambitions. Opportunities of obtaining financial independence were greater there than in Scotland, for London booksellers were increasingly prepared to hazard publication on their own initiative, knowing that a rapidly growing reading public reduced the risk of failure.[27] But again, the financial assistance that Thomson received on leaving Scotland seems not to have been forthcoming a few years later. James Mill, for instance, the talented son of a cobbler, was caught on the cusp of this change in attitudes toward patronage. "Some timely patronage" enabled him to enter Edinburgh University but, coming of age in the 1790s, no further help was forthcoming and he had to move to London "to earn an arduous living in literature." Unsurprisingly, there he promoted the meritocratic ideal of intellectual powers rather than wealth or birth as prerequisites for leadership.[28]

The pressure on job opportunities made the need for patronage more, not less, necessary. Catching the eye of a potential patron became paramount. This might be accomplished in one of the many clubs and societies that the enlightenment had spawned in Scotland, where "the excitement of debate was the passion of the hour."[29] At the Pantheon, for example, a debating society open to all classes, "where the grand concerns of the nation are debated by a set of juvenile Ciceros," and which had as one of its purposes "to relieve literary merit in distress," every "liberty of speech, and freedom of debate" were allowed."[30]

Nicholas Phillipson has claimed that voluntary societies in Edinburgh created "a complex network of sympathetic relationships which extended from an aristocratic social elite through the professions to the population of young, upwardly mobile men of humbler origins which every centre of government and politics necessarily attracts."[31] Such possible class bonding presupposes the successful distribution of patronage. Particular examples of the talented being elevated in that manner, however, do not prove them to be the norm, for it is not known what proportion of social climbers failed to impress. Even Robert Burns considered emigrating to the West Indies before his first successes, and he also ensured the world knew of the lack of patronage that drove another poet, the clerk Robert Fergusson, to an early grave.[32]

The careers of the engraver John Kay and of the aspiring author William Gillan were probably more typical than either Burns's or James Mill's. Kay (1742–1830) was a barber in Edinburgh when a customer, Nisbet of Dirleton, took an interest in his sketches. Moving to Nisbet's country seat, Kay abandoned his job in favor of his art. Nisbet supported Kay's wife and eleven children in Edinburgh, promising, on his death, to leave Kay an annuity sufficient for independence. This he failed to do in 1782, leaving the artist "in somewhat awkward circumstances, having, as it were, fallen to the ground between certainty and hope." Nisbet's heir, with an annuity of £20, saved Kay from penury. In 1792 Kay was to be sympathetic to the aims of the Edinburgh Friends of the People, his engravings of Thomas Muir, Thomas Paine, and other radical leaders becoming bestsellers.[33]

William Gillan was a humble clerk in the Edinburgh Sasine office in the 1780s, with pretensions to literary merit. A member of the literary circle around Lord Gardenstone, he eventually moved to London, where he unsuccessfully sought literary fame and became involved with a group of Scots who were to agitate for parliamentary reform. He is last heard of in 1792 hoping to join the East India Company, a common source of patronage for Scotsmen. He was not very confident of success. "I have," he wrote to a friend, "met with so many disappointments already in my small progress through the world that I allow my hopes to be as little sanguine as possible."[34]

Social Closure

Gillan's despondency would make a suitable epitaph for all those aspiring young men who poured into Edinburgh at the height of its fame, only to find that the world of literature was closed to them. In the 1780s, as elite society became less flexible, avenues of advancement into the highest circles narrowed. In the societies of Edinburgh there was an undeniable polarization: aristocrats, intellectuals, and scholars separated themselves and gathered together in societies that were no longer open to those from the middling ranks of society. Landed society was increasingly giving up the Edinburgh season altogether, leaving the capital's social life in the hands of the professional classes and petty gentry, for whom the cult of patronage held little interest.[35]

The hostile attitude of the literati themselves toward aspiring young men seeking to follow them up the social ladder is reflected very nicely in an 'agony column' in the *Mirror*, a magazine published in 1779–80 by a group of major enlightenment figures including Henry Mackenzie, William Cullen, David Hume (cousin of the philosopher), and several future judges, who together formed an exclusive club called "The Tabernacle" or "The Mirror Club."[36] In

March 1780 the editor, William Creech, published a letter from "K. B.," a young man with high hopes. The son of a farmer K. B. had been encouraged by his local schoolmaster to learn Latin and Greek, with the intention of going to college. "If I studied divinity, (which was proposed), I might in time preach in the pulpit of the very parish in which my father lived; nay, I might rise to be a Professor in the University, or become *Moderator* of the *General Assembly* of the Church of Scotland." Unfortunately, his family's straitened financial position meant that he could not afford as a student to pay for all the lectures he wished to attend, nor buy the necessary books. With the help of his professors, however, K. B. was employed at £20 a year as tutor in the household of a wealthy gentleman, where he was responsible for the welfare of seven children of all ages. He was mortified to discover that he was treated worse than a servant: "When there were strangers of distinction at the house, I was not allowed to sit at table, but was placed in a corner of the room with the younger children, where my province was to attend to what they eat, and to cut their meat for them." Predictably, his young charges soon treated him with contempt; even the footman, "who wears a better coat . . . looks upon himself as a finer gentleman than me; and, as I am but little respected by those whom he considers his betters, he does not think himself bound to respect me at all." The final straw was a hint from the 40-year-old housekeeper, "thick and squabby, with a mouth a little awry, and eyes a little squint," that they might marry. What was he to do?

Although the letter is probably spurious, Creech's answer reflects the hauteur, pomposity, and fear of competition that the successful man of letters felt for those jostling him from below:

> I have of late remarked, with regret, in this country, a disposition in many, who, from their station and circumstances, ought to have been bred farmers or manufacturers, to become scholars, and men of learned professions. Let such persons and their parents be assured, that, though there may be a few singular instances to the contrary, there is no pursuit which requires a competency, in point of fortune, more than that of a man of learning. A young man who has not enough to make him easy, and to bear the expense requisite for carrying on his education, can hardly be expected to rise to any eminence. The meanness of his situation will humble and depress him, and render him unfit for any thing elegant or great. . . . Had [K. B.] followed his father's profession, he might have been both happy and useful.[37]

The message was clear; be content with your station in life.

The deliberate social closure that this response suggests was increasingly apparent by the mid-1780s, and might be compared with a similar process occurring in enlightenment Paris at the same time.[38] Moreover, the desire to pull up the social drawbridge was intensified by the French Revolution, which caused fears and doubts among the very conservative Scottish elites even in its early stages. Elite withdrawal, however, happened some time before a Scottish reform movement established itself. By the end of 1791 the popularity of open debating societies such as the Pantheon had declined. University students, always a voluble part of the audience, created their own exclusive societies, where they were free to debate more daring political topics.[39] It was not by chance that at least four prominent members of the Edinburgh Friends of the People were medical students, two of whom were to be implicated in Robert Watt's revolutionary conspiracy of 1794.[40]

ANGRY YOUNG MEN

Paisley Poets

The correlation between the processes of lowland industrial change, population increase, and social closure on the one hand, and the structure of the Scottish radical movement of 1792–94 on the other, is best displayed in the example of the so-called Paisley weaver poets. This group included ALEXANDER WILSON, JAMES KENNEDY and his brother ALEXANDER, David Brodie, Ebenezer Picken, GAVIN TURNBULL, and the musician brothers JAMES and WILLIAM MITCHELL. Their significance is usually attributed to their combining a plebeian occupation with artistic talent, but while their means of gaining a living are important, much more so for an understanding of their politics is their combined desire to escape from the tyranny of the loom and seek fame and fortune in the literary world of Edinburgh. They ought to be viewed as representatives, not of the weaving community with typically plebeian views, but of the aspiring, upwardly mobile groups whose politics were aimed at achieving a society open to talent.

Most of this Paisley group came from very humble backgrounds: Wilson's and Picken's fathers were weavers, the Mitchells' a local tavernkeeper.[41] Turnbull's parents had once been comfortably off, but were reduced to poverty during his childhood.[42] James Kennedy may have had very little formal education:

> I lay no claim to sapient lore,
> My teacher was my Mother;
> Plain Scotch I learn'd in days of yore,
> And language ken no other.[43]

Most appear to have been brought up in dissenting Presbyterian congregations, either covenanting or seceding, a factor that would have increased their sense of marginality once they entered the wider world. Exemplifying the lads o' parts mythology, their families had great plans for them. Picken, for example, was destined for the Burgher ministry; he spent five years at Glasgow University but, partly by marrying at a very young age, he failed to fulfill his early promise. Wilson's mother Mary, who was "pious after the ancient type of fervid godliness and in every way (in a good sense) a superior person," [44] hoped he would become a minister, as Wilson's poem "The Solitary Tutor" (composed in America) suggests:

> Here dwells the guardians of these younglings gay,
> A strange, recluse, and solitary wight,
> In Britain's isle, on Scottish mountains gray,
> His infant eyes first open'd to the light;
> His parents saw, with partial fond delight,
> Unfolding genius crown their fostering care,
> And talk'd with tears of that enrapturing sight,
> When clad in sable gown, with solemn air,
> The walls of God's own house should echo back his pray'r.

Unfortunately, his mother's premature death when he was ten, and his father's rapid remarriage, ended Wilson's classical education almost before it had begun.

All except Picken began their working lives as weavers, but all hoped to escape the loom as quickly as possible. The Kennedys were the most successful; by the late 1780s they had moved to Edinburgh, where James ran a small weaving manufactory and Alexander opened a haberdashery. [45] William Mitchell tried to establish himself as a music teacher. [46] Picken opened his own school in Falkirk in 1791, but it soon failed. A teaching post in Carron the following year saved him and his new wife from starvation. [47] Wilson and Brodie for a while worked side by side in a two-loom shop in Paisley. Brodie's ambition, which he achieved, was schoolteaching. Sallust and Vergil were only two of the classical writers whom he read while working; beside him, Wilson was "deep in the study of Milton, Pope and Goldsmith." [48] Their range of reading was limited only by what Picken could obtain for them from various libraries. [49] Outside working hours, they frequently met together, Wilson and the Mitchells to play the flute and violin and compose songs, Wilson, Picken, Turnbull, and James Kennedy to discuss their verse. [50]

Restless, rootless, and romantic, the Paisley poets initially were filled with that sense of limitless possibilities that is usually seen to have been a consequence of the impact on their class of the French Revolution and Paine's

Rights of Man. They were driven by "the thirst of fame, the expected applause of the world, . . . the charms of ambition," and above all by the hope of what Wilson later called "the golden rock" of independence.[51] Poetry, however, was an unsuitable medium to achieve their aims, ironically the more so after Robert Burns's success in 1786 with the Kilmarnock edition of his poems. The craze to write earthy vernacular poetry in the Burns style was not matched by a sufficiently large audience prepared to support young talent. The Paisley poets had some success, but their standards fluctuated. Turnbull had real talent as a lyric poet, but was forced into becoming a strolling actor (he was eventually very successful in America). Wilson made a small breakthrough in 1791 when he composed "Watty and Meg," a poem of sufficient quality to have been regarded as Burns's. Both James Kennedy and Wilson drew effectively on their own experiences to declare approval of the wonders and value of the new industrial machinery that was transforming their trade.[52] They also expressed great pride in their skill as weavers.

> Stern critics, carp not tho' you see
> The rules of art o'erstep'd by me;
> If you'll eclipse me as a Weaver,
> I'll own you *tolerably* clever.
>
> Gowns for an Empress and a Queen
> were wove by my direction;
> Ev'n great DUNDAS and Hopetoun JEAN
> Exclaim'd O what perfection.[53]

But as all the poets were later ruefully to admit (and as the above lines surely demonstrate), most of their verse was too crude, too local, and too immature to have wide appeal.[54] When Picken and Turnbull published small volumes of poetry in 1788, and Wilson in 1790, sales were disappointingly small.

Wilson made strenuous efforts to gain the approval of socially prominent figures for his book. William McDowell, the local MP and wealthy entrepreneur, subscribed for two copies at Wilson's personal request, but a local duchess refused his gift of a volume, and a visiting nobleman returned a copy unopened.[55] In his search for patronage, Wilson took rooms in Edinburgh, giving an oration at the Pantheon and attending "an elevated gentleman's levee" five or six times a day. Unfortunately, he was given "a distant and strange reception." Instead of lionizing Edinburgh society, Wilson took up a pack of James Kennedy's goods and tramped through the countryside, trying to sell his book to more plebeian customers.[56]

Failure led to depression and a jaundiced view of the world. To William Mitchell in November 1790 Wilson wrote: "depend little upon the encouragement of the World, which, let Merit be ever so worthy, seldom rewards it till its possessor is *no more*. And rather practice your favourite study as an Amusement, than rely on it as the means of subsistence, by which precious maxim you will be more independent."[57] To Thomas Crichton he lamented: "O that I could roll back the tide of time, and place myself in the same circumstances I was a few years ago. Then all the charms of Fame, the insinuations of ambition, the applause, renown, and admiration of the world, would in vain display their united glories to tempt me to one line of verse. . . . From repeated experience, I can here solemnly declare, that I have found poetry . . . to be productive of nameless miseries, and in reality the source of all my sorrows."[58]

On James Kennedy's advice, Wilson made one last attempt to break into Edinburgh's literary circle. In April 1791 he entered a competition at the Pantheon, where he defended, in broad Scots verse, Robert Fergusson's poetry against the claims of Allan Ramsay's. Although his contribution was a great success, he failed to win the prize. This went to Robert Cumming, a wealthy local, who paid forty of his friends to attend and vote for him. Wilson lost by seventeen votes. The symbolism seems clear; a year later Wilson, and most of the other Paisley poets, were at the forefront of agitation for radical parliamentary reform in their hometown.

James Thomson Callender

The connection between literary ambition, blasted hopes, and a subsequent involvement in the Scottish radical movement is also demonstrated in the career of JAMES THOMSON CALLENDER, who is nowadays best remembered for his political journalism in America from the mid-1790s. What little is known of his early life includes his year of birth, 1758, his father's occupation, tobacconist, and his religious upbringing, Presbyterian of the strongly Calvinist variety.[59] If a reference to himself in one of his poems as "an orphan bard" can be taken literally, his parents may have died in his youth.[60] Uncorroborated contemporary evidence suggests that he may have been a kinsman of the famous poet James Thomson.[61] He received a good classical education, but seemingly never entered university, although he attended some of William Cullen's lectures in Edinburgh.[62]

Callender first came to prominence in 1782 when he published the first of two pamphlets in which he lambasted Dr. Samuel Johnson's reputation as a lexicographer and man of letters.[63] He also subtly incorporated in his writings what at the time were regarded as advanced political views. His general attack on Johnson, who had defended government policy in his *Taxation No Tyranny* (1775), reflected Callender's sympathy for America's rebels and for the Wilkite movement in England. He was also one of those young Scottish patriots whom Drennan had noticed in Edinburgh at this time, for he applauded the example of the Irish Volunteers.[64]

Many of Callender's political ideas stemmed from the opposition Tory writings of Jonathan Swift. Such was his admiration for the early eighteenth-century Irish pamphleteer that Callender envisioned himself as potentially the Scottish Swift. At first glance this may appear incongruous, for Swift adhered to many of the same opinions as Johnson. He was a High Church Anglican, a critic—in *A Tale of a Tub*—of Calvinist theology. Politically he was a Tory, albeit with Jacobite sympathies; and he hated the Scots![65] But in Callender's eyes Swift had political and personal virtues that far outweighed these particular vices. He was, for example, virulently anti-Whig, hostile to the corrupt practices of Walpole and the Whig grandees. Above all, however, Swift had opposed the union between Scotland and England, which he claimed, in 1707, would result in a ship of state "with a double Keel," an ungovernable "crazy double-bottom'd Realm" wide open to the evils of faction.[66] He was also both a patriot and a pacifist, strongly opposed to British rule in Ireland. "His intrepid eloquence," wrote Callender of Swift in 1782, "first pointed out to his oppressed countrymen, that path to Independence, to happiness, and to glory, which their posterity, at this moment, so nobly pursue."[67]

In 1782 Callender had high hopes of a successful literary career; his *Deformities of Dr. Samuel Johnson* was sufficiently successful to go into a second edition, published in London. According to Callender, it had been received on both sides of the border with some degree of notice by "men of learning," including the influential Lord Kames.[68] Any hopes of patronage were quickly dashed, however, by Kames's death in 1782, and by the failure of Callender's second pamphlet, which was repetitive and unoriginal, swiftly sinking into a morass of minor and irrelevant detail.

Callender was compelled to seek his living as an inferior writing clerk in the Edinburgh Sasine office, where he spent the next seven years. In 1787 he passed the examination to become a messenger-at-arms, a paralegal occupation involving the executing of writs. This was a useful second string to his bow, which bestowed some social status, but any hopes of prosperity were dissipated when Callender, on behalf of his fellow clerks, unsuccessfully tried to expose the corrupt practices of his superior officers in the Sasine office.[69] In 1790 he was dismissed. His experiences in the Sasine office supplied him with firsthand knowledge of the corruption and influence within the British political system and gave particular focus to the general insights he had drawn from Swift's writings.

Ostracized by the legal profession as a troublemaker, and therefore unable to find work as a messenger-at-arms, Callender was saved from possible destitution by the patronage of Lord Gardenstone, who was attracted by some of

Callender's verse. Gardenstone (1721–93) was one of the few in the Scottish nobility to be interested in literature and to hold mildly progressive views. He was the only member of the Scottish bench to take an active part in the burgh reform movement from 1782.[70] To his country seat at Morningside, just outside Edinburgh, Gardenstone in the 1780s attracted a group of aspiring young literati: "the young and frolicsome delight in his society."[71] His eccentric behavior and the "secondary sort of company" he kept alienated him from respectable society. "He was never very choice in the selection of his convivial associates," wrote one disapproving contemporary.[72]

Callender became Gardenstone's "Fidus Achates" and his "intimate friend and adviser."[73] He edited, in 1791, *Miscellanies in Verse and Prose,* to which his mentor contributed some literary criticism. Many of the poems in this volume, however, since attributed to Gardenstone, can safely be claimed as Callender's, and others to acolytes in the Morningside group.[74] In this verse Callender rehearsed some of the political ideas that he was to publish in very different circumstances a year later. He also attacked the system of patronage, for although he was receiving some assistance, his mentor's anomalous social position meant that he remained outside the walls of the establishment.[75]

Gardenstone kept a tight purse, but he managed to put Callender in touch with the tiny elite opposition to Henry Dundas's dominance of the Scottish political system. Among these were some of the Edinburgh brewers, led by Hugh Bell, who were in conflict with the excise service over blatantly corrupt official practices. Callender was employed to bring this dispute to the public's attention. The resulting pamphlet, *An Impartial Account of the Excise,* was not merely a catalogue of specific abuses within the excise department; it was also another stealthy attempt by Callender to transpose Swift's ideas on Ireland to his own country and to propagate Scottish nationalist opinions.[76] He argued that the excise system was deliberately manipulated in Scotland to destroy industries competitive with England's. Although, in deference to the brewers, Callender mitigated his political opinions in this pamphlet, he was to use much of the information he had obtained in 1791 to buttress his radical and nationalist arguments in his major contribution to the Scottish radical movement the following year.

POLITICAL REFORM

The Influence of Paine

For young men with high opinions of their talents and a strong desire for independence, the patronage model on which most aspects of Scottish society rested in the 1780s was anathema. The need to flatter and entreat, and the sensation of perpetual constraint and confinement imposed by stifling convention could only lead to high levels of frustration. Yet, with the exception of Callender, there is little evidence that before the French Revolution the socially ambitious—whether Paisley poets or in-migrants to an expanding Grub Street in Edinburgh—had made the intellectual leap from dissatisfaction with their own circumstances to a general critique of the political system. The patronage carrot left tantalizingly dangling saw to that. But this was to change in 1792, under the inspiration and influence of Paine's *Rights of Man*, Part 2, and the victories of the new French republic. Whatever else the annus mirabilis achieved, among the lads o' parts it revived earlier enthusiasms and zeal.

This point needs to be emphasized, for the traditional interpretation of the Scottish radical movement of 1792–94 has no distinct place for them. The classic view of the Scottish Friends of the People was first provided by Henry Meikle's *Scotland and the French Revolution* (1912). Although some progress has since been made, notably in two theses,[77] the radical movement's origins and development have essentially remained fixed in a pre–World War I configuration. Gallin, for instance, following Meikle, sees the genesis of Scottish radicalism as a consequence of the onset of a major economic slump in early 1792, leading to dissatisfaction among Scottish plebeians, who—as elsewhere in the British Isles—were to make up the bulk of the radical movement's rank and file. This downturn preceded both a similar economic transformation in England by many months, and the formation of the Scottish Friends of the People. Unlike in England, therefore, radicalism in Scotland is perceived as a significant consequence of general economic dislocation.[78]

In contrast, but still following a theme developed at length by Meikle, John Brims emphasizes the primacy of the political in his analysis of the movement for change in Scotland. He points to the Pitt government's unpopular policies in 1791 and 1792, including the Corn Law and the rejection of burgh reform and of relief for dissenters, to explain why many middle-class Scots sought some measure of parliamentary reform.[79]

Gallin and Brims are not necessarily in conflict; both follow in the footsteps of Meikle, the inevitable consequence of using the same basic sources. Both are reinforcing the traditional point that Scottish radicalism consisted of two main components, an elite, mainly moderately reformist leadership, and a plebeian, more Painite, rank and file. It is a distinction both T. C. Smout and Brims have emphasized, the latter claiming that "the movement which grew up in the last months of 1792 was essentially popular in character. Paradoxically many of its leaders were gentlemen both of property and of what Lord Justice Clerk Braxfield called 'liberal education'."[80]

This dichotomy, however, erases the role of intermediary between leadership and rank and file played by the aspiring lads o' parts in radicalism's emergence and development.[81] When news of the French Revolution reached Scotland in 1789, there were only two small associations—the burgh reformers and the county reformers—representing even the slightest opposition to the political hegemony of Henry Dundas ("Harry the Ninth"), Pitt's manager of North Britain. Both organizations, which were constitutionally separate but had some overlap in membership, had arisen in the early 1780s. Although the burgh reform association was concerned primarily with local issues relating to the nature of town corporations, both it and the county reform association took spasmodic interest in parliamentary reform. The burgh reformers sought to break down the corrupt town council oligarchies that under the royal burgh franchise chose the delegates who in turn elected the fifteen MPs from urban Scotland.[82] In Edinburgh, for example, according to one contemporary Whig, the corporation was "omnipotent, corrupt, impenetrable. Nothing was beyond its grasp; no variety of opinion disturbed its unanimity, for the pleasure of Dundas was the sole rule of everyone of them. . . . Silent, powerful, submissive, mysterious, and irresponsible, they might have been sitting in Venice."[83]

In the counties, the use of taillies to create "parchment barons" had slightly extended an extremely narrow franchise. This had, however, only increased the influence of particular landowners, especially the nouveaux riches, leaving most rural dwellers, including many wealthy landlords, smaller and middling gentry, and tenant farmers, with no political influence at all. The county reform movement sought at most to extend the franchise to smaller landowners, while even the most advanced burgh reformers did not want the vote given to those below their own class. Most of the members of these associations, therefore, remained socially conservative, seeking minimal changes on behalf of the propertied.[84]

The most "extreme" burgh and county reformers were Foxite Whigs who supported the moderate and tentative demands of the London Friends of the People. When in July 1792 the burgh reformers at a meeting in Edinburgh refused to support parliamentary reform, the Scottish Foxites, including many who were already members of the London Friends of the People, formed their own organization that incorporated two other disaffected but prosperous groups, the politically excluded merchants and manufacturers of the Glasgow region and the big brewers.[85] Their objectives were distinctly moderate: "to attempt by all Constitutional means, the attainment, first, of an equal Representation of the People; and second, of a more limited duration of Parliamentary Delegation."[86]

It was the excise issue, about which Callender had acted as spokesman for the brewers in 1791, that initially seems to have drawn together the reform activity of the elitist Friends of the People and the slowly growing radical agitation among plebeians in the major urban centers. The brewers had opposed the excise because they believed it to be a way of keeping the land tax low at their expense, but in the middle of 1792 their particular grievance suddenly became a popular issue. According to Brims, "The exciseman was no longer simply the object of popular vituperation or assault: he was [now] the personification of 'Old Corruption,' the symbolic representative of a hateful political system."[87]

The first signs of this politicization predated the formation of the Associated Friends of the People, coming in the week before anti-Dundas riots broke out in Edinburgh on 4 June, the day set aside to celebrate the king's birthday. A number of handbills circulated, including one calling on tradesmen "and all others who wish well of their Country" to gather on the king's birthday to give "a general salute in the way it was given to Captain Porteous of the Town Guard"—a reference to the riots of 1736—"to Mr. Maitland, General Supervisor of the Excise who has been a Scourge to this Country for some years past, and unjust and dishonest in the Execution of his Office to the blackest degree."[88] The author of this placard remains anonymous, but whoever it was obviously had knowledge of Callender's pamphlet of the previous year, for the specific accusations of taking bribes made against Maitland came from there. The 4 June burning in effigy of Henry Dundas, and the attacks on his house and that of his nephew, the lord advocate, were in part the consequence of a convergence of elite and popular grievances.[89]

The Foxites were uneasy with this democratization of their complaints; indeed, the formation of the Friends of the People was in part an attempt to control popular agitation. But by the summer of 1792 two worrying political tendencies had appeared among the membership in the proliferating branches of the society: a "moderate" radicalism that sought to use public opinion to force Parliament to grant the franchise to all males possessing even a small amount of property; and a militant radicalism that demanded universal suffrage, even if violence had to be threatened.[90]

These programs represented the appeals of the spokesmen of an emerging and independent radical leadership to the textile workers and small property owners who in the late summer and fall of 1792 began to pour into the newly formed societies.[91] The catalyst was the second part of Paine's *Rights of Man*, the banning of which by government proclamation in May 1792 had only increased its popularity. According to the Foxite MP Norman Macleod, "the Proclamation acted like an electric shock; it set people of all ranks a-reading; and as everybody in this country can read, the people are already astonishingly informed."[92] It was some months after May before large numbers of Part 2 became available in Scotland. But as an Edinburgh journalist noted, one small northern town that had only one copy at the time of the Proclamation sold 750 as soon as they arrived.[93] Alexander Wilson in Paisley agreed about its popularity:

> The *Rights of Man* is now weel kenned,
> And red by mony a hunder;
> For Tammy Paine the buik has penned,
> And lent the court a lounder.[94]

Beginning in the large urban centers of the Forth-Clyde axis, these new radical organizations spread into smaller villages where the textile trades, fueled by rapid population growth, predominated. Eventually at least 123 radical clubs were formed in Scotland in sixty-six Scottish cities, towns, and villages (in thirty-eight of which textile trades were the main form of employment). Unsurprisingly, outside the main urban centers weavers made up the largest occupational group, probably one third of the several thousands who were to play an active part in the societies.[95]

In his multivolume *Statistical Account of Scotland*, Sir John Sinclair tried to explain why disaffection had arisen in the textile districts "in the midst of the most profound peace, and . . . of the most unparalleled prosperity." Writing of the textile printers of Campsie, he pointed to "a few half educated people" among them, "mostly lads from 17 years of age to 30," whose "vanity consisted in raising the astonishment of their more ignorant companions, by a detail of political grievances, which had never entered into the hearts of the others to conceive. . . . The young people at the different print fields are men, who have abundance of time in the evenings to cabal together."[96]

An unsympathetic commentator may have made the same comments about nearby Paisley, another textile town troubled by rapid growth, where several societies coordinated under the umbrella of the United Societies of Paisley were established. Initially, the leaders were mainly manufacturers, but on their withdrawal they were swiftly replaced by weavers, including a number of poets. William McLaren and James Paterson, friends of Alexander Wilson, were at the forefront of agitation, while the Mitchell brothers tried to organize strikes and led the successful opposition in Paisley to the customary King's birthday parade in June 1792. Wilson, whom Paterson later said was "the most expert writer of reports and resolutions" he had ever seen, "and that too in a style of elegance most astonishing to his compatriots," became secretary to the Paisley association.[97] Fueled by personal resentment, expounding a facile critique of contemporary Scottish society, with one foot in local plebeian society and the other in the world of metropolitan culture, the lads o' parts were eminently qualified to become provincial leaders and to forge links between the popular movement and the more respectable leadership in the capital.

At the same time, in Edinburgh the Friends of the People became so popular that the society had to be subdivided, with each branch supplying delegates to a central committee. By November 1792 there were between four and five hundred members in the Canongate No.1 branch, comprising mainly artisans, journeymen, and shopkeepers, but with a leadership in which attorneys, medical students, and clerks were prominent. The most active was the young lawyer Thomas Muir, the ambitious son of a successful Glasgow hop merchant. His friends included Callender[98] and Robert Forsyth, another upwardly mobile young lawyer, the son of a tailor.[99] With other enthusiasts, they met weekly in the attic of a baker called Buchanan. A mixture of militants and moderates—Muir himself was not a militant on every issue although Callender was—they discussed tactics, drank a lot, and forged links with Archibald Hamilton Rowan in Dublin and with societies in London, including the radical London Corresponding Society.[100]

Muir was not a republican in 1792, but influenced by Paine and his Irish contacts he lobbied strenuously for a national convention, at which a reform petition to Parliament would be proposed.[101] On 21 November at a meeting of Edinburgh delegates Muir obtained unanimous support for a convention to meet on 11 December. The Foxites acceded very reluctantly, but decided to attend to control events.

Between the Edinburgh delegate meeting and the first Scottish convention the political situation deteriorated dramatically. The propertied classes were frightened badly by a series of riots that stretched from Aberdeen to the border country, and included planting trees of liberty, the burning of effigies, and the destruction of property.[102] Enthusiasm for the events in France peaked, at the same time as war loomed closer. On 1 December Henry Dundas issued a proclamation against seditious writings; immediately a major loyalist reaction got under way. Almost all the burgh reformers had by then left the Friends of the People. Dundas informed Pitt that "Everybody of character, respectability and property are . . . much of one mind here in all the great principles of real Government. The contest is with the lower orders of the People, whose minds are poisoned up to the point of Liberty, Equality and an Agrarian Law."[103]

Dundas's interpretation was not strictly accurate, for some prominent Foxites attended the convention between 11 and 13 December, where with the help of moderate delegates they managed with some difficulty to control the agenda.[104] Most of the sessions were taken up with ways of responding to the upsurge of loyalism, but among the 171 delegates was a minority who were prepared to take a strong radical position. Their presence was felt on 12 December when Muir introduced an address from the Dublin Society of United Irishmen, signed by William Drennan and Archibald Hamilton Rowan. It referred to Scotland as a separate nation: the United Irish were pleased that the Scottish reformers "do not consider yourselves as merged and melted down into another Country but that in this great national question you are still Scotland—the land where Buchanan wrote, and Fletcher spoke, and Wallace fought."[105] Many at the convention were greatly concerned that these references to nationalist sentiment, combined with certain Painite opinions—"It is not the Constitution but the People which ought to be inviolable"—might be construed as a condemnation of the authority of the British Parliament. The Foxites and many of the moderate radicals believed that if the convention acknowledged the Irish address, they would lay themselves open to charges of treason or misprision of treason.[106] On three occasions the militants supported Muir's motion for a formal reply to the Irish address before they were finally defeated.

Government Reaction

Although the Convention of the Friends of the People rejected the nationalism implicit in the address of the United Irishmen,[107] reports of the debates nevertheless made their way to the lord advocate, Robert Dundas, and his uncle Henry. On 13 December the former decided, if he could obtain a copy of the United Irish address, to charge Muir with treason; a copy became available within a few days. Other inflammatory documents, preferably published in Scotland, also were required, whose authors could be prosecuted to intimidate the Friends of the People.[108] In this way Dundas unwittingly laid the foundations for Scottish radical emigration to the United States.

In addition to Muir, two likely victims were rapidly found in Edinburgh. One was the eccentric polymath and inveterate failure, JAMES "BALLOON" TYTLER (1745–1804). By turns a chemist, surgeon (on a whaler), printer, mechanic, journalist, poet, and pamphleteer, Tytler's career was a series of disasters and disappointments, even though he was intelligent, inventive and well, if unsystematically, read. Even the high point of his life, as the first Briton successfully to make and fly in a balloon, ended in farce and ridicule. As a journalist, he never rose above the level of a competent hack; as yet another aspirant who married prematurely, he was in and out of debtors' sanctuaries and prisons. Robert Burns, however, was perceptive enough to see that Tytler was by no means lacking in perseverance and ability: he was "an obscure, tippling though extraordinary body . . . a mortal, who though he drudges about Edinburgh as a common printer, with leaking shoes, a sky-lighted hat, and knee-buckles as unlike as George-by-the grace-of-God, and Solomon-the-son-of David, yet that same unknown drunken mortal is author and compiler of three fourths of Elliot's pompous Encyclopaedia Britannica."[109]

In 1791, as editor of the *Historical Register*, Tytler began his short career as a militant radical. He vehemently attacked burgh charters, monopolies, and the Scottish aristocracy, satirized Henry Dundas in verse, and, as befitted a former member of the dissenting Glasite sect in Newcastle, called for the diversion of the Church of England's income into "free schools" for the English poor.[110] In October 1791 he called on his fellow countrymen to follow the example of revolutionary France and free themselves from "a state of wretched slavery."[111]

By late 1792 Tytler was an unabashed militant extremist. In his anonymous broadside *To the People and Their Friends*, clandestinely distributed in Edinburgh in November, he targeted the elite leaders of the Friends of the People—of which he was a member—as much as the government. "Certain colonels and captains" [for example, Colonels Dalrymple and Macleod, and Lord Daer] were trying to undermine the popular movement by supporting a petition to Parliament, the "democratical part of the constitution." But they were all members of "a vile junto of aristocrats." Tytler's advice was to ignore Parliament. Petition the king directly to dissolve Parliament and allow the people to elect representatives "of good understanding and character." If the king refused: "Keep your money in your pockets [for example, refuse to pay taxes], and frame your own laws, and the minority must submit to the majority."[112]

Even without loyalist reaction intimidating the timid, Tytler's call for active resistance was beyond the pale. When he fled to Belfast after being released on bail (he was to stay there until sailing for Boston in 1795), he was both outlawed by the government and spurned by the Edinburgh Friends of the People. His own branch, Canongate No. 1, voted to support his family in January 1793, but were overruled by the Committee of Finance.[113]

The second object of Robert Dundas's scrutiny was Callender's *The Political Progress of Britain*, which had been published in parts in the *Bee*, an Edinburgh magazine, between February and June 1792, and published in revised pamphlet form in July. It was the only lengthy treatise vehemently attacking British political institutions to be published in Scotland during the era of the French Revolution. It was also the only published work to promote the virtues of Scottish nationalism and of Scottish independence from England. Although fear of arrest prevented Callender from openly avowing revolution,

The Political Progress of Britain was one of the most inflammatory, undeferential, and militant texts to be published in the 1790s. As a pungent critique of imperialism, war, and corruption only Thomas Paine's *Rights of Man* could rival it.

Callender took his stand as an historian, seeking to expose the machinations of the governing classes and to demystify their shibboleths by offering an "impartial" history of British politics since 1688. To achieve this aim he had to destroy the myth of the British Constitution, the totem behind which the propertied classes had gathered in 1792 in response to popular agitation in Britain and revolution in France. There was no need for political or social reform, the propertied claimed, because the 1688 revolution, and the subsequent Act of Settlement and Act of Union, had established a British Constitution that guaranteed everyone's liberties under the rule of law. Change, if it were to occur, should proceed piecemeal, as had always been the case.[114] Nonsense, replied Callender, the British Constitution was a phantom aimed at protecting the wealthy: "What 'our excellent constitution' may be in theory, I neither know nor care. In practice, it is altogether A CONSPIRACY OF THE RICH AGAINST THE POOR."[115]

Nor was the source of the Whig Constitution, the revolution of 1688, such a glorious event as the propertied and "the idle writers who pester us with fulsome panegyrics on *our present happy establishment*" claimed:

> What *glory* can be annexed to the affair, it is not easy to see. An infatuated old tyrant was deserted by all the world and *fled* from his dominions. His people chose a successor. This was natural enough, but it had no connection with *glory*. . . . The characters of the leaders in the revolution will not justify a violent encomium on the purity of their motives. The selection of William was reprobated very soon after, by themselves, which excludes any pretence to much political foresight. Here then is a *glorious* event, accomplished without an actual effort of courage, of integrity, or of wisdom.[116]

In the annals of modern history, he continued, real glory could be found only where the Swiss, the Scots, the Americans, and the Corsicans wrestled for national independence "against the superior forces of despotism." Switching dynasties was a mundane affair, for it was merely moving from one despotism to another. "Since the Norman conquest," Callender declared, "England has been governed, including Oliver Cromwell, by thirty-three sovereigns; and of these, two-thirds were, each of them, by a hundred different actions, deserving of the gibbet."[117]

After 1688 British monarchs and their chief ministers had presided over a mercantilist policy, "the system of war and conquest." The lust for foreign luxuries stimulated Britain's bellicosity and was at the root of the evils of Britain's political system. Denouncing the wars with Holland (one), France (five), Spain (six), the "civil wars" in Ireland and Scotland in 1688–89, two rebellions in Britain (1715 and 1745), and "the endless massacres in Asia and America," Callender computed that 30 million people had been killed, £380 million sterling wasted by the British government, and between 16,000 and 20,000 merchant ships lost, leaving a national debt of £250 million sterling. The dead, he wrote, "have been sacrificed to the balance of power, and the balance of trade, the honour of the British flag, the rights of the British crown, the omnipotence of Parliament, and the security of the Protestant succession."[118]

Imperialism brought out the worst features of the English: "At home Englishmen admire liberty. . . . Abroad they have always been harsh masters." For the sake of "tea, sugar, and tobacco, and a few other despicable luxuries," Callender continued:

> What quarter of the globe has not been convulsed by our ambition, our avarice, and our baseness? The tribes of the Pacific Ocean are polluted by the most loathsome of diseases. On the shores of Africa, we bribe whole nations by drunkenness, to robbery and murder. . . . Our brandy has brutalized or extirpated the aborigines of the western continent; and we have hired by thousands, the survivors, to the task of bloodshed. On an impartial examination, it will be found, that the guilt and infamy of this practice, exceed, by a considerable degree, that of any other species of crimes recorded in history.[119]

British belligerence had led to an enormous national debt and to a vast extension of corruption among military officers, politicians, and speculators in government securities. Government fundholders "remind us of a band of usurers, embracing every advantage over the necessities of the state; while the ministers of the crown seem like desperate gamesters, who care not by what future expence they secure another cast of the dice." In the American War of Independence, in addition to the cost of financing the army and navy, £50 million sterling was "happily for mankind, expended in jobs, and bubbles of all kinds, and in bribes to the peers, the house of commons, and their *constituents*." Expenditure on corruption was, nevertheless, preferable to expenditure on yet more mercenaries. Taxes of all kinds, including the despised excise, were extorted to pay for these wars. "After such work," wrote Callender of the wars against Louis XIV, "it is not wonderful that we are now harnessed in debts and taxes, like horses in a carriage."[120]

It is also "not wonderful" that Robert Dundas was determined to prosecute the author of this tract. Not only was it filled with bitter venom against the state of Great Britain—in that way it magnified many of Paine's points—

but it was also particularly dangerous for raising the issue of Scottish independence. Callender argued that Scotland's position within the British empire was merely that of a subservient colony, no different to that of the American colonies before 1776. To the English, he wrote, "We were for many centuries a hostile, and are still considered by them as a foreign, and in effect a conquered nation." England had conquered Scotland not by force of arms but by the trickery of the 1707 Act of Union. "It is remarkable that though the Scots are constantly talking of their constitution, and their liberties, the whole fabric is entirely founded on one of the grossest and most impudent acts of usurpation ever known. I refer to the celebrated *Union*. The whole negotiation bears on its face the stamp of iniquity." In reality, Scottish rights and liberties did not exist, for the Scots were represented in Parliament by timeservers, who were the mere satellites of the minister of the day; and are too often as forward as others, to serve his most oppressive and despotic purposes." Instead of wasting money electing forty-five Scottish MPs, he continued, "an equal number of elbow chairs, placed once for all on the ministerial benches, would be less expensive to government, and just about as manageable."[121]

What was needed, claimed Callender, was the complete breakup of Britain, with Scotland obtaining "a wise, virtuous, and *independent* government." No longer would "our southern masters" be able to destroy all Scottish manufactures that threatened English development. No longer would taxes be spent on foolish wars; instead, investment in domestic improvements would convert "the whole country, like the Swiss cantons, into gardens, cornfields, and pastures." No longer would Scotland, Ireland, and Wales be like "three plants of inferior size, whose natural growth has been stunted by the vicinity of an oak." Tinkering with the mechanism of the British Parliament was thus irrelevant; Callender's vision could be fulfilled only by snapping all connections with the warmongering, corrupt machine in London. Separate development, as the Americans had accomplished, and the Irish hoped to, was the only path to follow.[122]

The pamphlet edition of *The Political Progress of Britain* had some influence in Scotland in the last months of 1792. According to Callender, sales both in London and in Edinburgh had been lively, with five times the cover price being offered for copies in the Scottish capital. The 1,000 copies of the Edinburgh edition were quickly sold, and requests for 500 more copies in London arrived before the end of the year.[123] It therefore became important for Dundas to discover the author as soon as possible. In the days following the first Scottish convention, he and Deputy Sheriff John Pringle began questioning those involved in its printing, both in the *Bee* and as a pamphlet. After much stonewalling, one of James Anderson's journeyman printers confessed that the original manuscript letters were by Callender and that he had revised the proofs. On 1 January 1793 Pringle interviewed Callender, but did not arrest him. The next day, having received information from an agitated Gardenstone, sheriff's officers raided Callender's home, but he had already fled. Like Tytler, Callender escaped to Ireland, from where a few months later he sailed for Philadelphia.[124]

THE COLLAPSE OF SCOTTISH RADICALISM

Intimidation

Dundas and Pringle were probably unperturbed by the flight of two of their suspects; their main objective, to frighten the propertied classes into abandoning reform, seemed to have been achieved. The tone of the meetings of the Friends of the People in the first week of the new year was "now much lowered," the "most violent and most determined" having been intimidated by the vigorous measures.[125] Intense pressure was put on the propertied and professional classes in the next two years to conform to a pattern of loyalism first laid down by the authorities but taken up with relish by the Scottish elites. The harsh legal penalties meted out to Muir, Thomas Fyshe Palmer, and the other Scottish martyrs obviously had their effect; the prospect of facing Lord Justice-Clerk Braxfield across a courtroom was daunting.[126] But pressure was applied in more subtle ways too. In Edinburgh, failure to attend the official celebrations on the king's birthday was taken as a sign of disloyalty, as was a preference for the new "Jacobin" short and unpowdered hair styles. Men shedding the old fashion of "shorts, silks and buckles" in favor of trousers or gaiters were shunned as incorrigible rebels.[127] Economic harassment, which had some success, was also a powerful weapon; suspected shop-owners lost the patronage of the well-to-do.[128]

The professional classes were particularly vulnerable to forms of social intimidation. Schoolmasters and university professors found their teachings under scrutiny. The Whig rector of Edinburgh High School, Dr. Alexander Adam, was dismayed by the parental encouragement given to his pupils to give information on the curriculum of his classical history classes to the authorities.[129] Doctors thought to be not totally loyal found their patient lists mysteriously diminishing. In Glasgow, the brilliant young physician JOHN MacLEAN, who had been a member of the local Friends of the People, found his professional prospects so deflated that early in 1795 he emigrated to the United States. Within months of arrival he was professor of chemistry and natural history at Princeton University.[130] At the same time JOHN CRAIG MILLAR, lawyer son of the famous Professor Millar of Glasgow University and husband of Cullen's daughter, was so disgusted by society's ostracism that he "sought peace and freedom in the United States." A moderate reformer at the first Scottish Convention and elected to the second (though he may not have attended), and a friend of Muir, he had been counsel for Robert Watt at his treason trial in 1794. He subsequently fell foul of the widespread belief that no lawyer of liberal principles was worth employing, as the bench would not give him a fair hearing.[131]

Most of the intimidated professionals would have considered themselves Whigs or Foxites, moderate reformers rather than radicals. Their withdrawal from the reform movement left a leadership vacuum that was partially filled by the more radical, less socially exclusive, among whom were the lads o' parts. Although there was some loss of momentum and continuity as this process worked itself out, the wise strategy of promoting an antiwar policy and linking it to the economic recession prevented the movement from going into terminal decline. Indeed, the new leaders, with their close affinity with the rank and file, developed means of spreading their message that particularly suited the new circumstances. As Paola Bono's recent bibliographical study of the Scottish reform movement demonstrates, few, if any, substantial political pamphlets of a radical tenor were published in Scotland after Callender's.[132] Instead, the radicals—perhaps out of necessity—concentrated on producing more ephemeral literature, suitable to their plebeian rank and file.

Poetry remained a suitable medium to inspire the radicals. Late in 1792 Alexander Wilson wrote several poems in broad Scots that were distributed around the Paisley weaving sheds among the unemployed weavers. Strongly antiauthority but narrow in their focus, "The Hollander" and "Mab's Door" caught the resentment and sense of grievance of a local audience but sought to channel those feelings to create or sustain a wider political momentum.[133] Unfortunately, in January 1793 Wilson was arrested after attempting to extort money from the subject of another of his poems, "The Shark, or Lang Mills Detected," in which he claimed that a manufacturer, one Sharp, was underpaying his weavers by using looms slightly too long.[134] Thereafter he spent several spells in prison.

If Wilson's poems voiced the smoldering economic resentment of the weavers, giving it a class-conscious resonance, James Kennedy's poetry of this period was solidly Painite in inspiration. His long poem *Treason!!! or Not Treason!!!* was an attempt to put Paine's ideas into verse, attacking kingcraft and priestcraft, taxes and tithes, and promoting the sovereignty of the people:

> Of pow'r THE PEOPLE *are* the source,
> The fountain-head of human force;
> Spurn'd by their Subjects, WHAT ARE KINGS,
> But useless, helpless, haughty things?[135]

He continued to promote the radical cause of late 1792, still hoping the king might be persuaded to reject evil counsel:

> List to a suff'ring People's cries—
> Resign the sword of terror:
> Spurn evil *Counsellors*, *Crimps*, and *Spies*,
> Who lead you into error![136]

Defiantly, he called for revolution:

> When Faction's pow'r spreads ruin round,
> Sure then 'tis time th'alarm to sound;
> When o'er the land Oppression lies,
> Sure, Britons! then 'tis time to rise.[137]

The fruits of success would be material, claimed Kennedy:

> While you the good effects will feel
> Does not the prospect charm you?
> Say, would you love a better meal,
> A better fire to warm you?
> Less toil, a better coat to wear,
> And better drink your heart to cheer,
> Secret LIBERTY the whole to crown;
> *Reform abuses*, ALL'S YOUR OWN.[138]

Ephemeral poems, handbills, and peace petitions were the main means whereby the radicals tried to keep the movement going, but it was a hard task.[139] They still had to contend with the temporizing moderate elites, whose attention was focused as much on burgh and county reform as on the program of the Friends of the People. At the second Scottish convention in April 1793, only 117 delegates attended, fifty-three fewer than in the previous December, but now included representatives from the depressed western industrial regions around Ayr. Devoid of those dancing to the pusillanimous tune of the London Friends of the People, the convention was in the hands of more plebeian members: the inaugural chairman was a leather merchant representing Canongate No. 1, the first resolutions were proposed by a Glasgow baker, and

William Mitchell, representing Paisley, played an active role.[140] Nevertheless, the delegates divided along moderate-militant radical lines on major questions of policy. The former were ultimately victorious, ensuring the defeat of militant demands to petition the king for peace (thereby bypassing Parliament) and to draw up a comprehensive plan of parliamentary reform. The resulting petitions to Parliament for a vague political reform were easily rejected by the government in May.

The Scottish radical movement was slowly dying of inanition; active members who subsequently emigrated to America, such as the Edinburgh typefounder ARCHIBALD BINNY, the elderly goldsmith DAVID DOWNIE, and the youthful Dalkeith nailer GRANT THORBURN, would have felt the lack of direction that infused the Friends of the People by mid-1793. They would have sympathized with the statement issued by the Renfrewshire societies meeting in Paisley in July that "Those exalted statesmen," who had rejected the reform petitions, and "who look down with indifference on the ruin and distress of innumerable families, may smile in safety; NO helpless and famishing children cling around their knees, and wring their parental feelings with their weeping solicitations for bread! NO; these heartrending distresses are far removed from their sumptuous and magnificent palaces, and therefore forgotten and disregarded."[141]

But they would also have shared in the anger subsequent to Muir's trial in August, and in the renewed hopes of reform that came with the suggestion of Thomas Hardy, of the London Corresponding Society, that a British convention should be called later in the year. Their roller-coaster ride between hope and despair, however, came to a shuddering halt at this convention in December 1793, when it was broken up by the authorities after showing itself much more radical and confrontationist than its predecessors.[142] Yet another group of political martyrs was created, but this time Scottish public opinion was firmly on the side of the government. James Mitchell, the only Paisley delegate at the October convention, and who had been a vocal militant, Downie and Binny, who had both represented the Bridge Street society several times, were fortunate to escape the clutches of the law.[143]

Insurrection

As in England and Ireland, the full force of government repression in Scotland led to the defection of many but the disappearance "underground" of the most recalcitrant. A hardcore element, including a significant number of future exiles, began to plot insurrection. They did so through the Committee of Ways and Means, a subcommittee of the Committee of Union formed in Edinburgh to prepare for yet another convention. Included on this secret subcommittee of seven were Robert Watt, David Downie (as Treasurer), James Kennedy, and JOHN EDMONDS STOCK, an English Unitarian medical student. Links were forged with small militant groups in other towns, including Paisley, Stirling, and Glasgow. Regular drilling occurred in Perth and Paisley. According to Henry Dundas, at the time of Watt's arrest Paisley appeared to be "in a state of great readiness. . . . within these three weeks persons . . . have assembled themselves in a very considerable number in the nighttime, for the purpose of practising the use of arms."[144] James Mitchell was heavily involved in this, but Wilson was already in prison for writing handbills for the local society.[145]

Some historians have dismissed the Watt conspiracy as a madcap scheme; Watt's plan for simultaneous uprisings in London, Dublin, and Edinburgh seems to support that interpretation.[146] Nevertheless, evidence exists that the conspiracy was widespread and that serious attempts were made to suborn local troops.[147] Stock was responsible for writing the handbill dated Dundee, 12 April 1794, which was distributed to the Fencibles in Dalkeith and played on their dissatisfaction at being transferred illegally to Liverpool, leaving "foreign mercenaries [to] violate the chastity of your wives, your sisters, and your daughters."[148] He was also responsible for correspondence with Hardy in London, and for the distribution of such materials throughout Scotland (he was fortunate to be on mission to London when the plot was blown and thus escaped arrest).[149] James Kennedy allowed the plotters to store materials in his house, while James Mitchell and two other weavers attempted in a tavern on the Paisley-Glasgow road to suborn recruits raised for the Marquess of Huntly's regiment.[150]

The conspiracy came to light inadvertently in May 1794, when a search of Watt's house in connection with another case led to the discovery of pike heads. Watt and Downie were arrested in Edinburgh, Mitchell in Paisley. Stock was absent, Kennedy escaped into the hills around Edinburgh. With the collapse of this final phase of the radical movement, a small surge of Scottish radicals left for better climes across the Atlantic. Included among these disillusioned radicals were James Mitchell, following six months in prison without trial, James Kennedy, who had been outlawed, and Downie, whose sentence for treason was commuted to banishment.[151] For them, America was less a beacon of freedom than a refuge from the consequences of their treason.

THREE

Irish Radicals

INDEPENDENCE AND REFORM IN IRELAND:
THE FIRST STAGE, 1776–85

Ireland and America

The Gaelic poets' conviction that "England's difficulty is Ireland's opportunity" was never more apposite than during the war of American independence. Subsequent to the alliance between the American rebels and France in 1778 and the entry of Spain into the war in 1779, the distractions caused by fighting on two fronts with extended and vulnerable lines of communication led the British government to relax its hold on Ireland and to consider significant economic, social, and political reforms. Feelings of dissatisfaction among a section of Ireland's Protestant ruling class in Parliament before 1775 gained strength with the recognition that the problems of imperial policy and political representation that had led the American colonists to rebel had their analogues in the British-Irish connection.

Many of Ireland's difficulties in promoting economic advancement, and much of its residual poverty, were perceived to be the inevitable consequences of imperial regulations, which favored British manufacturers and farmers and perpetuated Ireland's colonial status. The Navigation Acts, in accordance with mercantilist theory, naturally put the welfare of the mother country before the interests of the dependent colonies. But their weight did not bear equally on Britain's overseas possessions. Although, for example, imperial policy artificially skewed American colonial economies in various ways, enterprising colonists found numerous opportunities open to them. Except in time of war, most foodstuffs and timber products could be exported freely to foreign markets; several major products were competitive only because they were protected by imperial legislation against foreign competition. In addition, much of the rigor of British mercantilism was reduced, at least until 1763, by imperial government lethargy and by the enervating effect on enforcement of the distance between center and periphery in the empire. By the 1760s, "England's colonies [in America] had developed complex and sophisticated economic patterns based upon agriculture, commerce, and limited manufacturing."[1]

In contrast, the impact of imperial policy on Ireland's economy was more debilitating and intrusive, although the extreme view—first put forward by the United Irishmen and further developed in the late nineteenth century—that imperial regulation had almost totally hamstrung Irish economic development, has now largely been abandoned.[2] Not only has the impact of Britain's economic policies been qualified in recent years, but the malign influence of middlemen and absentee landlords has also been questioned. Historians have emphasized the ability of mideighteenth-century Irish agriculture both to feed a growing population and to export grain. They have also pointed to increasing investment in agricultural improvement, to comparatively low taxation per head and to the growth of textile manufacturing, primarily linen, as evidence to qualify the exaggeratedly gloomy, though long dominant picture of imperial rule.[3]

Nevertheless, this economic revisionism has not yet succeeded in crushing the old nationalist historiography; major qualifications have been made, but not of an order to suggest that an econometric analysis of an Ireland independent of imperial economic interference would come down in favor of the colonial reality. What perhaps now can be suggested, however, is that renewed attention be given to what contemporaries perceived the reality to be as an explanation for events beginning in Ireland in the 1770s. In other words, the economic revisionism of the last twenty-five years can still be incorporated without intolerable strain into an older Whig-liberal tradition that emphasizes a growing sense of disillusionment with the imperial connection, even when it coincided with increasing prosperity.[4]

The comparison with contemporary America thus retains its vitality, for not only did British economic policy in the greatly enlarged empire after 1763 increasingly suggest to observant Irishmen that central controls were being tightened, and that similar imperial energy might eventually be expended in their own country, but new political initiatives against the American colonists also had their relevance for the Irish situation. The Declaratory Act passed after the repeal of the stamp tax was based on similar 1720 legislation that asserted the Westminster Parliament's right to legislate for Ireland. To Irish Protestant patriots the arguments of their American counterparts—that there should be no taxation without representation and that traditional 'English' liberties were being assailed—had a particular resonance at a time when the Dublin parliament's subordination to Westminster and to the Privy Councils in both London and Dublin was causing concern. Certain grievances, such as the absence of a habeas corpus act and a law limiting the term of parliament, as well as the uncertain tenure of judges and a growing desire for place and pension bills, took on additional significance in the context of the quarrel between imperial parent and colonial child. Thus, although when war broke out in 1775 the Dublin parliament voted its support for British policy, a considerable groundswell of sympathy for the Americans' plight emerged in Ireland, which was soon to find focus in the Volunteer movement.[5]

The Volunteer Movement

The Volunteers were created in 1778 ostensibly to protect Ireland from invasion. The defense of Ireland from external aggressors and its internal police requirements normally involved a military establishment of 12,000 men, but this number was swiftly reduced to 9,000, including one thousand invalids, by the needs of war. Financial constraints prevented the Irish administration from raising a militia, with the consequence that when Protestant Irish patriots, faced with the threat of French invasion, formed themselves into myriad Volunteer corps, the British government could only look on with a mixture of relief and apprehension. Patriotic enthusiasm was a double-edged sword; Ireland could now be protected from invasion, but "it was very soon seen that the formation of Irish volunteer corps meant that armed power . . . was in the hands of the politically conscious public."[6]

Initially, however, the Volunteers were more a reassurance than a threat to the status quo. They represented the embodiment of Protestant Ireland, Episcopalian and Presbyterian, "the most affluent and respectable inhabitants of the kingdom, from the knights of the shire to the most opulent freeholders in each parish." In the towns, particularly of Ulster but also in Dublin, the professional middle classes—attorneys, doctors, academics, and clergy (of both Protestant denominations)—and the better-off master artisans became involved in the Volunteer movement, impelled by a combination of patriotic sentiment, craving for excitement, and vainglorious desire to don a splendid uniform and be awarded military rank. By the fall of 1779, perhaps as many as 40,000 men wore a Volunteer uniform.[7]

At one level, the Volunteer movement was little more than an enlightening example of eighteenth-century man's commitment to the doctrine of sociability, leavened by a particularly Irish conviviality. Friends, neighbors, and colleagues joined or formed Volunteer companies together, basking in a patriotic atmosphere of clubbability. Frequent public drillings, reviews, and parades served both a military and a social psychological function (as well as attracting the interest and enthusiasm of even dour Presbyterian ladies). Like Cobbett in England, a number of Irish radical exiles were later to reminisce on the way the excitement and liberal politics associated with the American war formed an important part of their early childhood memories. John

Caldwell, for instance, a merchant's son from Ballymoney in Ulster, recalled that "in early childhood certain ideas of liberty were under various circumstances instilled on my mind, which, as I increased in years, increased with my age and strengthened my strength. Thus on the news of the battle of Bunker Hill, my nurse Ann Orr led me to the top of a mount on a midsummer eve, where the young and the aged were assembled before a blazing bonfire to celebrate what they considered the triumph of America over British despotism, when my nurse cried out—'Look Johnny, dear, look yonder at the west. There is the land of liberty and there will be your country'."[8]

Youthful Enthusiasm

Other future Irish exiles had even closer links with the patriot movement in their youth. John Binns (1772–1860) and his brother BENJAMIN (1771–1845?) were products of what on the surface appears to have been an unusual marriage, between John Binns, Sr., a Moravian whose family "were all on what was called the liberal side of politics," and Mary Pemberton, an Episcopalian whose family "were on the government side" and included a future sheriff and mayor of Dublin. Politics inadvertently encroached on the lives of the Binns brothers in 1774 when their father drowned while returning from England to canvass for the shrievedom of Dublin. The family moved into the household of a maternal uncle, but this did not protect the brothers from the strong influence of their patriotic paternal relatives, in particular their great-uncle 'Long John' Binns, a very tall, thin man known to his enemies as "the Devil's darning needle." He was a member of the Dublin Common Council and a "speaker of fearless ability on the liberal political side."[9]

The influence on the boys of the distaff side of the family was significantly reduced, however, when the widow Binns, against family advice, married a young student lawyer, George McEntegart. A Castle supporter and future mayor of Drogheda, he was to act ruthlessly in suppressing the rebellion of 1798. The marriage was a disaster for John and Ben, although their later accounts of this period of their lives differ slightly. John records both boys being beaten by McEntegart for coming home late from an outing one day, but claims that, owing to the intervention of a paternal uncle who threatened to whip their stepfather, such treatment never recurred. He also remembers the shame he felt when his Drogheda headmaster regularly informed the whole school of his stepfather's refusal to pay the quarterly fees. Benjamin, possibly because he was the elder and heir to his father's estate, appears to have borne the ill treatment. Unlike his brother he did not suppress the fact that, in 1782, they ran away from home under the care and guidance of their servant girl who witnessed our cruel usage; started for Dublin twenty miles distant; no money but what she had, only a shilling or two in her pocket. While on the road near Swords, she brought us into a little shebeen house, to get homely fare; when from the window we perceived McEntegart on his grey horse, galloping by in pursuit. We stopped there that night, and rising early reached Dublin about breakfast time, and not a little surprized our dear grandfather Jonathan Binns and family were. The girl told our sad story; he clasped us in his arms, wep'd over us, and declared we should never return; he provided for us, and was soon appointed by the Chancellor our guardian and next friend.[10]

Back under the benign influence of the Binns family, both boys were exposed to the alarums and excitement of the patriot movement in Dublin. Sixty years later Ben could still recall the pleasure he took, as a twelve-year-old, putting on a Volunteer uniform, "red faced with *green*—and I took such a fancy to that color, that I prized it ever since, and wear it still, *As the Emblem of Hope!*" Family love being so closely associated with the public face of patriotism, and ill treatment with loyalism, it was perhaps inevitable that John, and his brother, became "at an early age, a lover of republican principles."[11]

Patriotic Presbyterians

In Belfast—"the metropolis of Volunteering" where three companies were established—and in other Ulster towns, the military church parade was popular, often receiving the enthusiastic support of the local Presbyterian minister. Sinclare Kelburn, minister to the Third Presbyterian Rosemary Street chapel, Belfast, wore his Volunteer uniform while preaching, "leaning his musket against the pulpit door"; so too did Rev. Joseph Douglas, of Clough, near Ballymena, Rev. William Steel Dickson of Portaferry, and Rev. William Bruce, who looked particularly resplendent in the short blue coat with red facings, brass buttons, and white breeches of the Lisburn True Blues. Rev. Robert Black, of Dromore, County Down, commanded his local Volunteer company, and frequently preached to them using a drum as a lectern. Even some ministers of the covenanting church were involved; William Staveley, of Knockbracken, County Down, for example, became captain of the local volunteers, gaining "much notoriety in his military capacity."[12]

Most of these Presbyterian ministers, with the notable exceptions of Black and Bruce, were to become involved in United Irish agitation a decade later. Indeed, Kelburn, Staveley, and Dickson were fortunate not to be transported or banished in 1798. One not so lucky was THOMAS LEDLIE BIRCH (1754–1828), the sixth son and the youngest of nine children of the "zealous dissenter" and militia officer, John Birch, of Birch Grove, Gilford, County Down. His maternal grandfather was a prosperous linen merchant and farmer. Blessed thus with wealthy connections, Birch had attended the University of Glasgow in Scotland, where he trained for the Presbyterian ministry. He also, with other Irish students, entered the world of student politics by establishing a successful debating society, which survived their return home. Meetings were still being held in Ireland in 1775, when the political crisis reached a peak. Birch is said to have written several pro-American pamphlets while in Glasgow, but these unfortunately have never been found. Graduating in 1772 with an MA, Birch was licensed in 1775 and ordained at Saintfield, a wealthy congregation in which his relatives had influence, in May 1776. Although Birch was always to remain an orthodox member of the Presbyterian General Synod, and, moreover, had the connections to reach the highest levels of the ministry, he came to be regarded as an unstable eccentric. Birch was an enthusiast, millenarian in his theology and strongly supportive of the American patriot cause. He was soon elected chaplain to the local Volunteer corps, the Saintfield Light Infantry. In 1784 he wrote an address for the Yankee Club in Stewartstown, County Down, which was sent to George Washington, congratulating him on his success in overthrowing "slavery" in America. Washington's exertions, he wrote, had "shed their benign influence over the distressed kingdom of Ireland." Birch published both the address and Washington's reply in the *Belfast Mercury* in 1784. He was later to complain that he became "a marked object, so early as the first year of [the] American war, for bearing testimony against that unnatural business." Six times in the ensuing years he sought election as moderator of the General Synod, always unsuccessfully.[13]

The Presbyterian ministers' willingness to exchange "the rusty black . . . for the glowing scarlet, and the title of 'Reverend' for that of 'Captain' "[14] reflected the enormous impact that the Volunteer movement had on Protestant dissenters in Ulster. Although they were not so heavily burdened by official discrimination as were Roman Catholics under the penal laws, they nevertheless, at the beginning of the American War, did not possess full civil rights. Prohibited from involvement in local politics by the Test Act, the religious toleration which was extended to them by the ruling Protestant Ascendancy served only to heighten a sense of civil persecution, making a mockery of the Presbyterians' growing wealth and economic significance resulting from their role in the burgeoning linen industry. Significantly, the political crisis over the American colonies coincided with an economic recession in Ulster, which led to increased emigration across the Atlantic. Between 1769 and 1774 about

40,000 people, mostly Presbyterians, abandoned the northern province. In many cases, therefore, transatlantic family connections reinforced the Presbyterians' traditional libertarianism which was expressing itself in sympathy for the plight of the American colonists.[15]

It is thus not surprising that the Volunteer movement politicized Presbyterian Ulster, the convivial club atmosphere of the companies soon being replaced by the urgent rhetoric of the debating society. The natural leaders of the Ulster Presbyterian community stepped forward to chair meetings, organize conventions, and rally the rank and file in favor of a reform program that was to become increasingly radical with success. Understandably, the Volunteer movement has come to be seen by some historians as a northern, and particularly Presbyterian, movement.[16]

It also acted as the perfect platform for young Presbyterians of Ulster anxious to demonstrate their patriotism but also to assert their civic rights. SAMUEL NEILSON (1761–1803) was born in Ballyroney County Down, a child of the manse. Educated partly at day school and partly by his father, he "displayed in his early years an eager desire for knowledge." As an apprentice woollen draper to his brother John in Belfast, Neilson matured into a tall, well-built, and powerful young man, with a strong Presbyterian faith and an earnest manner. He was present in Belfast in the summer of 1776 when about 250 prominent inhabitants, many of whom were to be politically compromised in the 1790s, called on the king to abandon "the civil war" against the colonies. When the Volunteer movement began, he swiftly joined the elite First Belfast Battalion, whose members included many others from his congregation, the First Belfast Presbyterian. The First Battalion soon became renowned for its advanced patriotic views. His already bright prospects further enhanced by marriage to the daughter of a wealthy merchant, Neilson embarked on a very successful mercantile career, which culminated in his establishment of the wholesale Irish Linen Warehouse, the "most extensive and respectable house in that line in Belfast." Worth about £8,000 in 1792, Neilson was to sacrifice this and his other business ventures in pursuit of a radical dream of a reformed and united Ireland that had first captured his imagination in the ranks of the Volunteers.[17]

The Dublin Volunteers

Predominant as Ulstermen undoubtedly were in the Volunteer movement, much of the political activity that they enthusiastically sustained occurred in Dublin, where patriots could most influence government. Some were also attempting to unite the essentially middle-class Volunteers with the capital's

large plebeian population in one massive reform movement. The severe trade
dislocation of 1778–79, caused primarily by the war, but also by the British
policy of embargoing Irish provision exports to ensure the filling of military
contracts, was particularly useful in this regard. Patriot policy in Ireland followed the nonimportation example of their compatriots in America. In Dublin
in 1779 a trade boycott aimed at British consumer goods was successful
enough to scare the Lord Lieutenant into seeking economic concessions from
the British government. With the Castle administration temporarily losing its
grip on parliamentary affairs, tensions were heightened in November by several large demonstrations outside Parliament, in which the patriotic parliamentary opposition and "the people," in the form of the Volunteers in full
array, demonstrated their solidarity and commitment to free trade. On 4 November the Dublin Volunteer Company of Artillery drew up their two field
pieces on College Green, close to the statue of William of Orange, placarded
with threatening slogans such as "Free Trade, or this" (the legend that the
slogan was the more ominous "A Free Trade or Speedy Revolution" was explicitly denied by Benjamin Binns).[18]

The commander of artillery on this occasion was "the red-hot patriot"
JAMES NAPPER TANDY (1740–1803), a close friend of "Long John" Binns.
Born into an Episcopalian household in Dublin, Tandy received a commercial
education and worked at his father's occupation of ironmonger before becoming a land agent and rent collector. He first gained prominence in late 1775
when at the head of a group of Dublin freeholders he bypassed a protesting
High Sheriff and sent a pro-American address to the king. He belonged to a
society called the Free Citizens of Dublin, which met every quarter day for
dinner, at which they offered toasts in honor of the American cause. At one
stage he considered emigration to America to join Washington's army. A no-
ticeably ugly man, and accordingly quick to take offense, Tandy used his
assets of cunning and volubility to become a "self-appointed tribune of the
people" and a constant irritant to the authorities. He was, says one historian,
"a pushing radical politician who was to his friends the sincere promoter of
every liberal cause, and to his enemies a vulgar demogogue." He could also
irritate his colleagues. When in 1780 the Dublin Volunteer committee refused
to address a vote of thanks to the Whig politician Henry Grattan, Tandy se-
ceded and formed his own Independent Volunteer Company. Together with
"Long John" he organized the Dublin Common Council, and the mob in the
city's Liberties, for patriotic purposes. Between 1777 and 1793, whenever
street politics erupted, Tandy normally could be found at its source. His
influence among the *menu peuple* was vividly described by the Belfast reformer
William Drennan, who saw him in the Dublin streets during the 1790 election

"in all the surliness of republicanism, grinning most ghastly smiles, and as he lifts his hat from his head the many-headed monster raises a shout that reverberates through every corner of the castle."[19]

A Victory, of Sorts

The British government defused the immediate crisis by repealing all its trade laws in December 1779. For Dublin radicals like Tandy, however, this was not enough; "no illuminations, no rejoicings . . . until our constitution [is] made free" was their motto, based on their concern that without the repeal of Poyning's Law and the Declaratory Act, the British government might, at a more favorable opportunity, reintroduce the restrictive trade laws. By 1782 it appeared that their program had succeeded: the new Rockingham ministry in London reluctantly acceded to the patriots' demands for the ending of formal British control over the Irish legislature. The Dublin and Westminster parliaments were now seemingly of equal status.[20]

Much of the credit for this political success was given to the formidable extraparliamentary pressure of the Volunteers. The reviews, marches, and mock battles, although capable of being dismissed as games of toy soldiers by the cynical, had undoubtedly an intimidating aspect to them. The Volunteer movement was a classic example of the politics of threat; its orderliness, its control, its restraint, and especially its hierarchical structure—with the gentry and some aristocrats dominating the officer class, and the middle classes and better-off artisans making up the rank and file—gave it strong claims to represent the embodied nation. (When the Belfast Volunteers staged a three-day mock operation in July 1781, a visitor noted with surprise that "during three days and four nights I did not hear of an individual being drunk or disorderly, except a Lord and two blackguard sailors.") In reality, however, the influence of the movement was less powerful than was thought at the time. Free trade and legislative independence occurred primarily because of the weakness of the Castle government and the machinations of politics in Westminster. Patriot politicians cleverly took advantage of government frailties, and placed themselves in a strong position for when the Rockingham Whigs came to power at Westminster. The Castle administration, it is true, was continually aware of the shadow cast by the Volunteers; but the nation embodied was not the decisive factor in the political events of 1779 to 1782.[21]

Furthermore, the impressive unity shown by the Volunteers was conditional; cracks were already beginning to show in the Volunteer phalanx and in the Volunteer-Whig opposition axis by the end of 1782, especially once the war was effectively concluded. Opposition politicians in Dublin remained ambivalent in their attitude to the legitimacy of extraparliamentary pressure groups; the Volunteer convention at Dungannon in 1782, which had codified demands for legislative independence, had been seen as a mixed blessing and a political risk. Whig politicians like Henry Grattan no more relished the prospect of a semipermanent and independent extraparliamentary political force than did the Castle authorities. Parliamentarians of all hues were particularly outraged when radical Volunteers unsuccessfully attempted to overawe the House of Commons by appearing in the gallery in uniform and in arms in November 1783.

Moreover, while free trade and legislative independence from Britain were aims that had united the middle classes with a group of patriotic aristocrats in Ireland, the more advanced demands made by radical Volunteers—for parliamentary reform and Catholic emancipation—led to disastrous divisions, with the more moderate Whig aristocrats such as Lord Charlemont withdrawing their support. As the United Irishman Valentine Lawless was later to argue, when from 1782 some of the Volunteers, realizing that the Irish Parliament would not endure unless the legislature was "pure" as well as independent, pressed for reform, "the zeal—perhaps a little exceeding discretion—evinced by some members of that celebrated body, and the caution—perhaps much exceeding prudence—of others, created an occasion for difference of opinion between many excellent Irishmen who, up to that point, had stood shoulder to shoulder in the patriot ranks."[22]

The drive for parliamentary reform accelerated during the general election campaign of 1783. Initially spearheading the movement were the Presbyterian Volunteers of Ulster, who at conventions in Lisburn, Dungannon, and, in November, in Dublin, worked out a reform program. Their demands were influenced by prominent members of the English reform movement, whose opinions had been solicited by a committee of correspondence—another American device—established at the Lisburn convention. Much of the advice offered was relatively uncontroversial, relating to ways of avoiding "corrupt" influences in the legislature. The abolition of pocket boroughs, the proscription of placemen in Parliament, and the reallocation of parliamentary seats were by the 1780s familiar parts of the reform platform. But from the American crisis in the 1760s the issue of representation had become a major point of discussion—and disagreement—among reformers. In Ireland, with its large, but powerless, Catholic majority, this issue was particularly controversial. The advice from the English reformers on the Catholic question was cautious. The duke of Richmond, promoter of universal suffrage on the basis of natural rights, believed in Catholic enfranchisement; Richard Price, Christopher Wyville, and the Cambridge don John Jebb—all of whom favored a property qualification—concurred. But none advocated the right of Catholics to be elected to Parliament, and one, Price, privately contradicted what he had said publicly. On the crucial question of political rights for Roman Catholics, the Irish reform campaign began to founder.[23]

A Model for Hercules

One of Jebb's students at Cambridge had been ARCHIBALD HAMILTON ROWAN (1751–1835). Born in London to parents who possessed substantial estates in Killyleagh, County Down, Rowan enjoyed a life of privilege and wealth. He was educated at Westminster School and Peterhouse, Cambridge, where he was influenced by Jebb's unitarianism. Rowan was also renowned for his high spirits, nonconformity, and madcap behavior, as when on leaving an inn while on a walking tour in England he rolled himself "into the first pool he met, in order that he might be beforehand with the rain." Larger than life, he developed into what Jonah Barrington described as: "a man who might serve as a model for Hercules; his gigantic limbs conveying the idea of almost supernatural strength; his shoulders, arms, and broad chest were the very emblems of muscular energy; and his flat, rough countenance, overshadowed by enormous dark eyebrows, and deeply furrowed by strong lines of vigour and fortitude, completed one of the finest, yet most formidable figures I had ever beheld." This intimidating and slightly menacing persona—which in the event was found to be a mask—was completed by the habitual presence of a huge Newfoundland dog.

Rowan played no part in the early years of the Volunteer movement. He had visited the American colonies for three months in 1771, acting as private secretary to Gov. Lord Charles Montague in South Carolina, but had returned to England. America, in hindsight at least, seemed to stimulate a sense of political awareness; in 1794 he told the Committee of Public Safety in Paris that "I [had] regretted not being an American, but I made up my mind that if I ever could I would play the same role in Ireland." In fact, during the American War and until 1784 he remained in England, when he paid a short visit to France. He then took passage to Ireland and swiftly became involved in political affairs as a radical, pro-Catholic commander of the Killyleagh Volunteers.[24]

Rowan's company was by no means the only one in Ulster to take the unprecedented step of supporting the rights of Catholics. The first Roman Catholic to be allowed to join the Ulster Volunteers was, according to John Caldwell, Daniel Maxwell, who on a second ballot was admitted to the Ballymoney Volunteers, after the commander, Caldwell's father, had threatened to resign if he were rejected.[25] With fewer objections, on 13 May 1784 Neilson's

First Volunteer Company in Belfast opened its ranks to men of all religious persuasions, "firmly convinced that a general Union of ALL the inhabitants of Ireland is necessary to the freedom and prosperity of this kingdom as it is congenial to the Constitution." A fortnight later, marching in tandem with another Belfast Volunteer company, the First Battalion celebrated its new ecumenicalism by parading before Belfast's first Roman Catholic chapel.[26]

In Dublin, the other main branch of the reform movement also played the Catholic card. Subsequent to the failure of Henry Flood's moderate parliamentary reform bill in 1784, Tandy shed his earlier antipopery and organized intermittent meetings with younger and more radical members of the Catholic Committee, led by John Keogh, at which a new reform agenda incorporating Catholic emancipation was drawn up. Already, in 1778 and 1782, government fears of Catholic loyalty had led to amendment of the penal laws, so that Catholics now had the same rights to hold property in land as Protestants. Yet they still carried the stigma of second-class citizens. All professions except medicine continued to be barred to them, positions in both central and local government were confined to Protestants, and Catholics remained unable to vote or sit in Parliament. But by the 1780s a growing middle class of prosperous Catholics existed in many of the towns, fretting at the caution of the Catholic Committee and deeply resenting their legal marginality.[27]

Patriotic Catholic Brothers

Among this new breed of militant young Catholics were MATHEW CAREY (1760–1839) and JAMES CAREY (1762?–1801), two of five talented sons of Christopher Carey, a Dublin baker whose contracts to supply the British navy had lifted him to prosperity. Mathew, lame from a childhood accident, was serious but headstrong; James was witty but giddy. Both were committed patriots from their teenage years, James being a volunteer.[28] Mathew claimed to have read Harrington, Sidney, and Locke by the age of nineteen, as well as everything on the position of Irish Catholics that he could find in a local circulating library. The Carey family seethed with a sense of oppression. Older brother William Paulet later wrote: "Born a catholic, my slavery commenced with my existence"; he had to "drink by stealth from the fountain of learning." In 1775 Mathew was apprenticed to Thomas McDonnell, publisher of the radical, pro-American newspaper the *Hibernian Journal,* and future United Irishman. Four years later Carey was forced to flee to France, following his printing of a seditious advertisement for his pamphlet, which, by calling for the immediate repeal of all the penal laws, had antagonized the cautious Catholic Committee as much as the government. After some months at Passy, where he enhanced his skills on Benjamin Franklin's printing presses, and further time working for the prominent printer Didot le jeune, Carey slipped back to Dublin. In the fall of 1783, with his father's financial help and the assistance of his brothers and William Bingley, John Wilkes's old printer, he established the violently nationalist and uncompromisingly radical newspaper, the *Volunteer's Journal or Irish Herald*. His object was "to defend the commerce, the manufactures, and the political rights of Ireland, against the oppression and encroachments of Great Britain." The newspaper was "violent and enthusiastic. It suited the temper of the times." Republican, patriotic, and recklessly libellous, Carey was soon threatened with arrest. Less than a year after beginning the newspaper Carey was forced into exile, leaving his father and brothers to pick up the pieces. James, still involved in radical printing, did not follow him to the United States until 1792.[29]

The Failure of Reform

The radical agitation promoted by Tandy culminated in another convention in Dublin in April 1785 to which five representatives from each county and large town were invited. Rowan, armed with a reform program that included a place/pension bill, the disenfranchisement of rotten boroughs, and a secret ballot, was chosen with his father to represent County Down. The convention was a fiasco. Only about one hundred attended and when, following the withdrawal of Henry Flood after the failure of his extremely modest reform proposals, a motion was put forward supporting Catholic emancipation, it received the support of only seventeen delegates (including Rowan). With the adjournment of the convention sine die, the reform movement—the child of the Volunteers—collapsed. Shortly afterward, the Presbyterian accoucheur Dr. William Drennan visited Belfast for a final Volunteer review. He watched "the buried majesty of the people arise and cross the stage for the last time. The ghost of Volunteering was dressed in its habit as it lived and shook in vain its visionary sword."[30]

THE EARLY SOCIETY OF UNITED IRISHMEN, 1791–92

Origins

THEOBOLD WOLFE TONE was exaggerating only marginally when he claimed in his *Autobiography* that "the French Revolution changed the politics of Ireland in an instant, dividing society into Aristocrats and Democrats."[31] In retrospect, enthusiasm for the early years of the French Revolution filled the minds of old rebels; it was a golden age before the horrors of rebellion, civil war, and defeat. Charles Teeling, the Catholic Defender and United Irishman, whose brother Bartholomew was executed in 1798, remembered "a new spirit ... infused into the nation" in 1789.[32] More than sixty years after the outbreak of the revolution John Binns reflected that

> It seems scarcely possible for the people of the present century to form a correct idea of the enthusiastic rejoicings and powerful sympathy of a large portion of the human family on the outbreak of the French Revolution of 1789. In Ireland and Great Britain it was ardent and universal. All ranks and degrees, all classes and descriptions of persons, the high and the low, the rich and the poor, the learned and the ignorant, the young, the old and the middle-aged, all rejoiced and were exceedingly glad. The ministerial, the Whig and the reform parties, the pulpits and the printing presses, vied with each other in their manifestations of joy. . . . The nations of the earth, in no age of the world, had ever before exhibited such wild, enthusiastic, and general rejoicings.[33]

Popular euphoria, however, led to no immediate practical consequences. Nearly two years were to elapse before a revived radical reform movement in Ireland emerged, inspired in its rhetoric by French forms and examples but seemingly with insular aims that had been rehearsed ten years before among the Volunteers. Instead, energies were initially channelled into Whig high politics, or what THOMAS ADDIS EMMET later called "the agitation and corruption of contested elections."[34] In the County Down election of 1790 the young Robert Stewart, Lord Castlereagh, stood as the representative of the new Northern Whig Club with the support of many old Volunteers who helped him spend a reputed £60,000 to win a seat. With Samuel Neilson as his agent, Steel Dickson was an enthusiastic canvasser who over a three-month period "rode one horse, nearly to death, reduced another to half his value, and expended above £50 part of which I was obliged to borrow."[35]

Although when Acting Secretary to Ireland during the rebellion of 1798 Castlereagh was to be the nemesis of many of the more radical who had supported him in 1790, his election campaign revived more than a moderate whiggery in Belfast and Down. It was a catalyst that impelled the radicals of 1784–85 again to consider a campaign for parliamentary reform and Catholic emancipation, with the consequence that Irish politics began to gravitate toward the extremism of both ends of the spectrum.[36]

Belfast

The initial seat of this radical reform movement was Ulster, more specifically Belfast, and its founders were—contrary to Irish Nationalist hagiography—middle-class Presbyterians. The vehicle for this new reform movement was the Society of United Irishmen, created by Neilson and a group of fellow Belfast Volunteers, including JOHN RABB, soon to be printer of the *Northern Star,* and ALEXANDER LOWRY, a merchant from Rathfryland. In many respects, however, it was also the brainchild of William Drennan. Influenced by the secrecy, mystery, and mysticism of freemasonry, as early as 1784 Drennan began privately to speculate on the formation of a radical secret society:

> I would much like to see the institution of a society as secret as the Free-masons, whose object might be by every practicable means to put into execution plans for the complete liberation of the country. The secrecy would surround the proceedings of such a society with a certain awe and majesty, and the oath of admission would inspire enthusiasm into its members. Patriotism is too general and on that account weak. We want to be condensed into the fervent enthusiasm of sectaries, and a few active spirits could, I should hope, in this manner greatly multiply their power for promoting public good.[37]

In a later letter he stated that "ten or 12 conspirators for constitutional freedom would do more in a day than [an open reform club] would do in ten."[38]

Drennan's romantic daydreams came to nothing in the mid-1780s, but they resurfaced once Irish radical politics again began to stir. In May 1791 he wrote from Dublin to his brother-in-law Samuel McTier (one of Neilson's group) of his plan for a society:

> having much of the secrecy and somewhat of the ceremonial of Freemasonry. . . . A benevolent conspiracy—a plot for the people—no Whig Club—no party title— the Brotherhood its name—the Rights of Man and the Greatest Happiness of the Greatest Number its end—its general end Real Independence to Ireland, and Republicanism its particular purpose. . . . Communication with leading men in France, in England and in America, so as to cement the scattered and shifting sand of republicanism into a body . . . and when thus cemented to sink it like a caisson in the dark and troubled waters, a stable unseen power.[39]

Remarkably, given Drennan's concern for secrecy, he sent copies of the plan he drew up in June to several people, including Henry Joy at the *Belfast News-Letter* office. His proposal was soon public knowledge and was even discussed in the Four Courts in Dublin.[40] Nevertheless, he had struck a chord with Neilson and his radical colleagues, who independently of Drennan had in April formed themselves into a secret committee for the purpose of promoting a radical agenda through the Volunteer movement.[41] They organized a procession in Belfast in July 1791 to celebrate the second anniversary of the fall of the Bastille and asked both Drennan and Tone to prepare addresses for the meeting.

The parade on 14 July went well; two Volunteer companies and members of the Northern Whig Club wearing green cockades marched gaily through Belfast carrying flags commemorating the 1688 revolution and portraits of Mirabeau and Franklin. But if the secret committee had hoped to build community enthusiasm for the full radical program by this display, they were disappointed. Resolutions drawn up by Tone in favor of Catholic emancipation had to be withdrawn, because "the minds of those present were not yet fully prepared for the measure."[42]

With the intention of changing public opinion in favor of the Catholics, in October Neilson, his secret committee, and a dozen others—including Tone and Thomas Russell—met in Belfast and formally established the first society of United Irishmen.[43] A month later, the Dublin society was formed, while in some of the smaller communities in Antrim and Down the lead from Belfast was followed by the end of the year.[44]

These so-called constitutionalist and open societies were to last, with many ups and downs, until the spring of 1794. The membership differed quite markedly from society to society. In Belfast, the first society was composed primarily of Presbyterian merchants, shopkeepers, and lesser professionals. The core group centered on an elite comprising Neilson and other merchants connected together since the 1780s by marriage, business ventures, religion, and local politics, but the membership of the smaller societies that from 1792 emerged in Antrim and Down soon embraced artisans as well as Presbyterians of the second rank such as the bookseller JOHN HUGHES, whose mother ran a Belfast dram shop, and JOHN CAMPBELL WHITE, an apothecary whom Drennan's sister disparagingly described as on "the second level of physicians" in Belfast, but who "may pick up a little money and no fame among the poorer sort."[45] There was also a shadowy Jacobin Club in Belfast, which, before either merging with or being taken over by the United Irishmen, seems to have comprised only men of lower social station such as its first chairman, the chandler Rowley Osborne, and its secretary, SAMUEL KENNEDY, a compositor on the *Northern Star*.[46]

Elsewhere in Ulster United Irishmen wisely penetrated existing organizations such as masonic lodges and Volunteer companies to extend their influence, rather than attempting to establish societies of their own.[47] Particularly helpful in spreading propaganda and making, in Thomas Addis Emmet's phrase, "every man a politician," were United Irishmen who already held rank in other societies.[48] DR. JAMES REYNOLDS, for instance, who played a major role in the United Irish-inspired Dungannon Convention of February 1793 and was purportedly Tone's brother-in-law, had been president of the County Tyrone Freemasons since 1783.[49] Presbyterian ministers and licentiates (the latter usually serving as schoolmasters while awaiting a call) were particularly well placed to influence their congregations. It is probably no coincidence that in Ulster communities with "active and zealous" ministers the United Irish cause made significant inroads. In Saintfield, Thomas Ledlie Birch had a congregation of about 4,000 to inspire with his view that religion ought to be involved in politics. In Maghera, REV. JOHN GLENDY, also prominent at the Dungannon Convention, regaled his congregation with sermons proving that the French Revolution benefited from the intercession of the Almighty. So soul-stirring was he in December 1792 that thirty-seven young men in the congregation formed a new Volunteer Corps before leaving the meeting-house.[50] Both Saintfield and Maghera were to be burnt by the army during the rebellion of 1798.

Dublin

The practice of using already existing organizations, and the Presbyterian penchant for small, cohesive, and semiclandestine meetings were not followed by the United Irishmen in the South when they established their society in November 1791. The Dublin Society of United Irishmen was organized as a large-scale debating society, meeting weekly and open to all persons who were nominated by two members, acceptable to 80 percent of the membership in a secret ballot, and prepared to take a loyalty test. In December 1791 there were fifty-six names on the membership roll; by the end of 1792 there were 240. At its peak, in March 1793, the society had at least 350 members, and possibly as many as 400, although by no means all regularly attended meetings. The 150 or so consistently active members comprised nearly equal numbers of Protestants and Catholics.[51]

In social composition, the Dublin society was heavily weighted in favor of mainly Protestant professional groups—lawyers (30), barristers (26), physicians (16), teachers, students; and those involved in the cloth trade—cloth merchants (67) and textile manufacturers (31). The legally trained, as in the French Jacobin clubs at this time, were especially prominent in the day-to-day planning and running of the society. Tone, who drifted away from the United Irish society within a few months as his concern for promoting the Catholic interest took precedence, was a lawyer; so too was Thomas Addis Emmet. Indeed, a significant number of radical exiles in America whose backgrounds have led to the impression of a primarily middle-class and professional exodus, originally came to prominence as active members of the Dublin Society of United Irishmen in its early phase. Emmet has been seen in some ways as the archetypal Irish exile, the undaunted man of abilities who could shrug off disappointment and rapidly become extremely successful in his adopted country. That, at least, is how his career after emigration was used both by himself and by other Irish exiles, anxious to demonstrate that forced emigration had lost Great Britain experience and talent.[52] Yet, there was nothing to have stopped Emmet becoming as successful in his chosen profession in Ireland, if he had only been prepared to moderate his political views. Unlike Tone, for example, who was a man on the make, anxious to escape his origins as the son of a coachbuilder, or Drennan, who as an *accoucheur* always felt socially inferior, Emmet came from a family of the first professional rank. A Protestant and the son of the state physician, Emmet owned land, received a £2,000 dowry on his marriage in 1790, and earned more than £1,000 a year from his law practice.[53] The world of Dublin could have been his oyster (there was even an attempt to buy him off with a judgeship) but, cautious and wary as he was, he preferred to risk all in the pursuit of a united and independent Ireland.

Emmet brought respectability and solidity to the society, which Neilson in his different way brought to the Belfast Society of United Irishmen. Apart from its structure and the high proportion of its Catholic members, what distinguished the Dublin society from its northern counterpart was, however, the social cachet infused by the membership of several major landowners and aristocrats. Lord Edward Fitzgerald, a younger son of the Duke of Leinster, is perhaps the best known champion of the society, but the first chairman was the Hon. Simon Butler, son of Lord Mountgarret, and Hamilton Rowan was a man of large estates. So too, by fate, was HARMAN BLENNERHASSETT, who has claim to be called the most naive man in American history.[54] Born in 1764 into the Castle Conway, County Kerry branch of a family that could trace its lineage back to England in the reign of King John, Blennerhassett, as a younger son, was bred to the law. The deaths of his two elder brothers, however, brought him the family estates and the prospect of a comfortable and leisured lifestyle. Having amused himself by reading the works of the French *philosophes*, he traveled to France to view the revolution firsthand. This seemed not to alienate him, for on his return in January 1793 he joined the Dublin Society of United Irishmen. Unlike Emmet, however, who took a highly active part in the society, Blennerhassett kept more in the background, although in February 1793 he was, with six other lawyers, appointed to the Committee of Constitution and was a regular attender of meetings until the society's dissolution. According to the spy Thomas Collins, Blennerhassett was "violent" (presumably in speech, not action). But when he emigrated in 1796 he was prompted as much by his illegal marriage to his beautiful and much younger niece as by any democratic tendencies he may have picked up.[55]

Men of the first social rank naturally bulked large in the higher reaches of the society, but the majority of the membership was of lesser status, including many whom William Paulet Carey called men "from behind the counter and from the compting-house."[56] With the prospect of large printing contracts and the demand for contemporary pamphlets, booksellers and printers were prominent in the society. At least fourteen were members. Perhaps the most wealthy was the Protestant, JOHN CHAMBERS, "a dangerous fellow" according to Collins the spy, and a businessman on a large scale (when his printshop burnt down in January 1792 the damage bill came to £3,000).[57] Before becoming a foundation member of the United Irishmen, Chambers had been secretary to the Dublin Whig Club and a personal assistant to Henry Grattan. In 1793 he became master of the Printers' Guild.[58]

Many of the other printers anxious to obtain work from the new society were Catholics: William Paulet Carey, RANDAL MCALLISTER, and PATRICK BYRNE, for instance. The first two, jobbing printers working on the margin most of the time and speculating in the hazardous world of newspaper publishing, soon fell foul of the law, with McAllister falling bankrupt after being imprisoned for seditious libel, and having to emigrate in 1793. His collapse brought down Carey, who also was under indictment for his services to the United Irish society.[59] Byrne, a Grafton Street bookseller and lottery ticket agent, was both more cautious and more financially secure. A well-known liberal and member of the Catholic Committee, unhappy with the limitations placed on his career by his Catholicism, he was responsible for publishing many of the most radical pamphlets of the day, including Tone's *Argument on Behalf of the Catholics of Ireland* (1791), the first Dublin edition of Paine's *Rights of Man*, Part 2, and his own *Universal Magazine* (1789–92), a compilation of reviews, extracts, and pen portraits that supported the revolutionaries in France.[60]

The Dublin Society of United Irishmen therefore appealed in its early years to a wide constituency, from a handful in the highest reaches of society to the middling. As the only radical society in the south of Ireland in 1792, it also attracted interest from a wide geographical area. The radical zealots from Cork, John and Henry Sheares, who had returned from Paris in 1793 reputedly with a handkerchief daubed with the blood of Louis XVI, were members, linking the mother society with a smaller organization in Cork that revolved around the *Cork Gazette*, edited by the eccentric cleric, DENIS DRISCOL. At least seventeen members came from the province of Connaught, with J. J. MCDONNELL a high-profile Catholic member.[61] Closer to home, with the involvement of Napper Tandy the society had links with the Dublin mob, although in character, style, and particularly leadership, it remained essentially an upper-middle-class, professional organization.

Reform or Revolution?

At least seventy members of the Dublin Society in its formative years and a very high proportion of the Belfast society's leaders were subsequently "concerned in or sympathised with the activities of extreme radicals" in the months leading up to and including the rebellion of 1798.[62] Yet, until recently historians have been satisfied that the United Irish society, before its forced dissolution by the authorities in 1794, was an organization with purely constitutional aims, viz. a radical reform of Parliament and full civil and political rights for Catholics. To argue thus is to accept at face value the society's public pronouncements and the later protestations—in other respects frequently tendentious—of United Irish leaders as they struggled to justify their actions. Emmet, DR. WILLIAM JAMES MACNEVEN, and Arthur O'Connor, for instance, claimed that "during the whole existence of the society of United Irishmen of Dublin, we may safely aver, to the best of our knowledge and recollections, that no such object [a republic] was ever agitated by its members, either in public debate or private conversation; not until the society had lasted a considerable time, were any traces of republicanism to be met with there."[63] Valentine Lawless was even more emphatic:

> I am firmly convinced, that [before 1795] the liberal opposition which included so great a majority of the Irish people, was altogether untouched by treason. [They] were influenced by a desire to improve their own condition, to escape from bondage, by constitutional means, and by these alone. They belonged to the moral force party of that day; and that party . . . included in its ranks the vast majority of the nation; nor was a recourse to physical force or foreign aid thought of, until desperation succeeded to hope in the public mind. . . . Of my dear friend, Edward Fitzgerald, of the Emmets, and of Sampson, I can say, with not less certainty than of Grattan, Curran, Arthur O'Connor, and the late Duke of Leinster, that they were all, at the onset of their career, actuated by the most earnest love of the British constitution; and that the truly patriotic object at which they aimed, was nothing else than the extension to Ireland of those blessings and guarantees of liberty, civil and religious, the principles of which are engrained in the texture of the constitutional monarchy of England.[64]

They ought to be compared, he concluded, "with their English predecessors of 1688."

But the revolutionaries of 1688 did overthrow a legitimate monarch! Perhaps that is unfair; between 1791 and 1794 the United Irishmen openly avowed a constitutional program of parliamentary reform and Catholic emancipation, to be attained by legal and peaceful means.[65] In stable and quiet times, such a policy may have been accepted at face value, but the United Irishmen were disingenuous in arguing that in the circumstances of 1792–93, with the example of the French Revolution and the outbreak of war before them, the prospect of a major reform of political institutions did not threaten the stability of the state. Castlereagh was to put the government's point of view best in August 1798 when, examining MacNeven before the secret committee of the House of Commons, he asked whether the early United Irish societies "would have been satisfied to effect a revolution through a reform?" MacNeven acknowledged that a political revolution would have resulted from their success, but stressed that private property would have remained secure, that it would have continued to have political influence, and that such a revolution would not "much confound the order of society, or give any considerable shock to private happiness."[66]

Thus, revolutionary the early United Irishmen were, but what, conceptually, did they mean by revolution? Many historians have argued that the United Irishmen's political values owed most to the indigenous doctrines of classical republicanism and John Locke. Elliott claims that "at the outset they were republican in the manner of the classical republicanism of the English 'country' or 'real Whigs', the eighteenth-century 'Commonwealthmen' or the writers of the Enlightenment, accepting monarchy but seeking to curb the powers of central government, to preserve fundamental liberties and to secure religious toleration."[67] She also believes that Tone, despite the Irish government using one of his intercepted letters to support their contention that from the beginning the United Irishmen were aiming to overthrow the state and the monarchy, "was no revolutionary in 1791. . . . However republican his 1791 statements might appear, . . . [he] was quite prepared to work within the existing constitution to achieve radical reform, and nothing he wrote in these years suggests otherwise."[68] Moreover, Curtin argues that "A blend of classical republicanism and Lockian ideas . . . provided the United Irishmen with the vocabulary to challenge ascendancy rule—or misrule, as they would have put it—in Ireland."[69]

In this scenario, the older, more moderate tradition of republicanism in the English-speaking world is given greater weight than the novel republican ideas coming out of the United States from the 1770s and France from 1789. Classical republicanism emphasized the debilitating effects on the body politic of corruption, the antithesis of virtue, which was viewed as the essential requirement of a true commonwealth. In the eyes of the Irish radicals, corruption was indissolubly linked with Britain's system of political oligarchy, which since the days of Walpole had systematically undermined the constitution established in 1688–89. Oligarchical rule from London sustained the equally corrupt system of government in Dublin, where a small group of Anglo-Irish on both sides of Parliament (and who were just being denominated the Protestant Ascendancy at this time) kept power in their own hands, at the expense of the mass of the people, especially those of dissenting faiths. To be a republican in the Commonwealth sense thus meant striving to end corruption in the Irish system of government. This logically required an effort to destroy the influence of Britain on Irish politics, as a first step toward establishing a true Irish commonwealth.

From an Irish perspective, therefore, even classical republican doctrine could easily lead to a desire for separation from Britain, in the same way that it had influenced the American colonies in the 1760s, but it did not necessarily imply the need to reject the King of Ireland and replace the monarchy with a republic, either on American or, after September 1792, French lines.[70] Nor, of course, did it imply the need to use force to gain republican or separatist objectives, although such a possibility was not ruled out by a radical interpretation of Locke's political philosophy. The revolution that the Irish radicals wanted could, and almost certainly would have been implemented by statute, once parliamentary reform and Catholic emancipation had been achieved.

As the United Irish leaders themselves recognized, however, such a limited, legal revolution could have occurred only if they had kept control of the situation and, by implication, if the ascendancy had lost the will to govern and was persuaded, frightened, or coerced into a peaceful surrender. Remarkably, Emmet, MacNeven, and other captured leaders later tried to convince the authorities that they would have been able to keep control in such circumstances. In response to Henry Alexander's query in 1798: "How did you hope to hold the people in order and good conduct when the reins of government were loosened?," Emmet arrogantly replied:

> By other equally powerful reins. It was for this purpose that I considered the promoting of organisation to be a moral duty. Having no doubt that a revolution would, and will take place, unless prevented by removing the national grievances, I saw in the organisation [of United Irishmen] the only way of preventing its being such as would give the nation lasting causes of grief and shame. Whether there be organisation or not, the revolution will take place; but if the people be classed and arranged for the purpose, the control which heads of their own appointment will have over them, by means of the different degrees of representation, and organs of communication, will, I hope, prevent them from committing those acts of outrage and cruelty which may be expected from a justly irritated, but ignorant and uncontroled [*sic*] populace.[71]

The United Irishmen, however, by taking this stance limited what they saw as national grievances. As MacNeven had insisted in 1798, their revolution would have been purely political in character; it would not have been a social revolution. No redistribution of property, even to the dispossessed Catholics, would have occurred. As the address from the United Irishmen to the Volunteers in December 1792 made clear: "By liberty we never understood unlimited freedom, nor by Equality the levelling of property, or the destruction of subordination."[72] Neilson concurred: "A great many *fools* believe, and a great many *scoundrels* publish, that the meaning of [Liberty and Equality] is an equality of property—nothing [is] more false and absurd—the meaning of *equality*, as practised in France, is an equality of rights not of property. It means that every man shall have an equal protection from the law, and that there shall be no privileged orders—nor any class of citizens placed by law above another; in short, that there shall not be any *body* of men set up, by LAW, to plunder the BODY OF THE PEOPLE."[73] Radical parliamentary reform would lead only to the abolition of tithes and hearthmoney, lower indirect taxes, the abolition of the excise laws, and reform of the legal process, to make it cheaper. There was, however, a sting in the tail; all statute law would be made "by ourselves," and this ability was "worth 10,000" other advantages.[74]

It is possible, and in Emmet's case even probable, that most of the early United Irish leaders genuinely believed that they could peacefully persuade the government and its ascendancy supporters to surrender. If so, they were extraordinarily naive. The example of France demonstrated that achieving controlled and measured reform in a country with a disgruntled and downtrodden peasantry was difficult, if not impossible, especially if the state displayed signs of weakness. Lord Lieutenant Westmorland showed more realism when he noted that Catholics expected enfranchisement to lead not only to the abolition of tithes, but also to the nonpayment of rents and taxes.[75] Where would the purely political revolution be then? Undermining by constant criticism the constituted authorities and their landed supporters was indeed a dangerous policy, even before the United Irishmen overtly sought the aid of the lower classes for a revolution.

The Politics of Threat

But not all the United Irish leaders were so artless as to believe that the ascendancy politicians would roll over and die. Hardheaded and practical radicals realized from the very earliest stages of their campaign that intellectual persuasion was unlikely to be enough. From this group were to emerge most of those who were to be forced into exile in the years before 1798. They acted clandestinely at the same time as supporting the open propagandizing of the United Irish societies in their attempts to mobilize public opinion in favor of their reform program. Their efforts revolved around the use of the Volunteer corps as a vehicle to extort reform. How far some of the United Irishmen were prepared to take the politics of threat, which the Volunteers represented, remains a contentious point. The idea of the virtuous citizen in arms was, after all, an integral part of Commonwealth ideology. But, particularly at the height of the crisis in the last months of 1792, when France became a republic and spiraled into a frenzy of expansionism, war loomed, and the radical popular societies in England and Scotland became increasingly militant, there is some intriguing evidence that at least a few United Irishmen began to consider seriously the prospect of using the Volunteers as more than a shillelagh to wave under the ascendancy's noses. There were, for example, small cliques at work behind the scenes of the societies both in Belfast and Dublin. Drennan called them "inner Societies." Late in 1792 he wrote to his sister: "Tell Sam [McTier, her husband] not to tell anyone, even *his interior,* that we [in Dublin] are to form one of our own, *Protestant but National.*"[76] A few months later Thomas Collins confirmed the existence of "the private junto" in the Dublin society making secret plans.[77]

But what were they planning? Were they surreptitiously promoting a secret agenda that went beyond the platform of Catholic emancipation and a radical reform of Parliament, toward separation and a republic? In Dublin, at least, fear that the Catholics would be fickle allies seems to have been a major motivation for the decision to establish a secret committee. Protestant mistrust was by no means groundless. Catholics were less inspired than the Protestant professional and high-born elite by the example of the French revolution, because they had seen their religion and the priesthood coming under determined assault from the revolutionaries in Paris.[78] Moreover, British government policy, when faced with the prospect of a dangerous alliance between Catholics and Protestants (especially Presbyterians in the North), was to tempt the former away with the prospect of gradual abolition of most of the remaining penal laws.[79] There is no doubt of this policy's effectiveness; Catholics were reluctant to commit themselves fully to the radical alliance while the government carrot remained in suspension before them. This partly explains why Drennan, who never fully shed his Presbyterian bigotry, confessed to his sister that "the Catholic cause is *selfish,* compared to ours, and they will make use of *every* means for success."[80]

Thus it is likely that the secret groups within the United Irishmen resulted from the leadership's belief that the rank and file, especially the Catholics, needed to be guided, willingly or not, to an acceptance of the whole radical program, but whether this guidance was intended to move them further, remains unclear. The same uncertainty remains after examining the ways in which the Volunteers were used in the period leading up to the war with France. In March 1792 Rowan, in a speech to the Catholic members of the Dublin Corps of Independent Volunteers, who had presented him with a sword, brazenly threatened a violent revolution: "I think that repeated alterations, or if you please, REVOLUTIONS, made our Constitution *what it is,* and that further *Alteration is absolutely necessary to make it what it ought to be. . . .* Many thanks to you for the Sword . . . , I assure you that it shall never be drawn in private Quarrel, nor remain in its scabbard, when patriotism calls for manly Exertion, and IRON *only can command success.*"[81]

This sort of swaggering belligerence only increased as the year wore on. The Kircubbin Independent Volunteers' celebration of French victories in November 1792 led to the following toasts: "A revolution to every State that must be supported by the Church"; and "May that old farce, Kingcraft and Priest-craft, speedily disappear from the Theatre of the World."[82] Undoubtedly, among many Volunteers and radicals enthusiasm for the French republic had swamped whatever lingering feeling they still felt for the 1688 revolution. Neilson made this point explicitly in the *Northern Star:* "Of all Revolutions, that of France is the most glorious. That of England is not to be put in competition with it. It was neither so just in its principle, nor so glorious in its effects. Much may be said against the latter, but everything must be said in favour of the former. That of England was local; that of France, like the dew of heaven, inspires all Europe, and will extend the blessing of liberty to all mankind as citizens of the world, the creatures of one Supreme Being."[83] "THE AGE OF REASON approaches to dignify the world," he wrote apocalyptically, after seeing Rowan in the chair at a meeting of the Northern Whigs in November.[84]

This rhetoric of millenarian internationalism and intimidation should not be disparaged, especially as at the same time the number of new Volunteer corps was growing and attempts made to arm them with new weaponry. Again, at the root of this rearmament were the most radical Volunteers, particularly the newly created Independent Volunteers of Dublin, led by Rowan, Tandy, Oliver Bond, and HENRY JACKSON, men whom Emmet acknowledged held "unequivocally avowed republican principles."[85] Jackson in particular was heavily involved in weapons' procurement. One of the most neglected and underestimated of all the United Irish leaders, he was a very successful iron-founder, owner of the first steam engines in Dublin, with a large workforce most of whom were United Irishmen. He was self-confident and brash, not afraid to advertise his political opinions, as the name of his country seat,

Fort Paine, testifies. John Caldwell met him in Birmingham a few days after the Priestley riots in 1791:

> One gun manufacturer entertained us at a supper party and on discoursing on the late riots, Mr. Jackson, whom I thought was imprudent sometimes in his invectives against the town, was assured by our entertainer that all was done that could be done. "For instance," added he, "Look where they [the mob] cut off my ear that this patch is on, when I was acting as one of the sworn constables." Jackson, having learned that the gun manufacturer was a furious Church and King man, replied that it was a pity that they did not take off the other, but that that perhaps was reserved for some future time.[86]

It is unlikely, but not impossible, that Jackson was plying for guns on this particular trip to Birmingham, but with his contacts it is not surprising that when the decision was made to rearm both Dublin and Belfast in November 1792 he was deputed to obtain them. By this time, however, the authorities in Britain were sufficiently alarmed to prevent the supplies leaving Liverpool.[87]

The Bluff Called

It was Tandy, Rowan, and Jackson's new Independent Corps of Volunteers that brought the crisis to a head in Dublin, at the same time as Neilson in the *Northern Star* was publishing provocative articles on "the Advantages and Defects of Missile and Hand Weapons," and on the use of "squadrons of pikes."[88] Defiantly known as the National Guard, the new Dublin unit's uniform included sansculotte trousers, with the crown on their coat buttons replaced by a cap of liberty.[89] Determined to assemble in full array within sight of Dublin Castle, the radicals' bluff was called on 8 December when the Irish Privy Council issued a proclamation banning the Volunteers corps assembling in arms. It had the desired effect; apart from a few enragés such as Rowan, no one in Dublin was prepared to wear his uniform on the appointed day. The radical policy of coercion began to collapse.

In a vain attempt to rally the troops, a few days later Drennan read to the Dublin Society of United Irishmen an address to the Volunteers of Ireland, in which they were called on immediately to arm. However one interprets the law of the time, the "Address" was a gross seditious libel, reflecting the inflamed passions and heightened sensitivities of the radicals. At least five people in Dublin were eventually to be indicted as a consequence of its publication, the first being Hamilton Rowan, who, for distributing copies of the "Address," was arrested on 21 December, although his trial did not come on until January 1794, when he was imprisoned for two years.[90]

There followed a flurry of activity and an avalanche of legislation from the authorities in the next few months that left the policies of the more radical United Irishmen in tatters and the more moderate southerners reluctant to come out of their bunkers. The situation was, however, somewhat different in Ulster, where the old Volunteer companies continued to meet. But there, too, the most radical United Irishmen were forced to concede that a policy of republicanism and separatism, particularly if it included Catholic emancipation, could not get majority support. Martha McTier warned her brother, Drennan, in late December that the mood in Belfast was not republican, as those out of touch assumed: "In all things you know there is a time when wisdom will pause, if not stop. What a glorious thing would you a few years ago have thought it to be in daily expectation of seeing the Catholics emancipated and Parliament reformed. . . . Stop then. Reap the sweets nor risk them in chimerical fancies of a Republic. . . . Believe me, [Belfast] does not breathe that republican spirit which strangers allege, nor does it deserve the character for patriotism which many in it you know might be supposed to gain it."[91] Martha's views were confirmed at the Dungannon Convention of February 1793, where delegates from five Ulster counties met to ascertain the mood of public opinion. Although they came down in favor of Catholic emancipation and parliamentary reform, they also resolved to remain "cordially attached to the form and original principles of the British Constitution," and consequently "highly disapprove of Republican Forms of Government, as applied to this kingdom."[92]

GOVERNMENT COUNTERATTACKS AND
THE MOVE UNDERGROUND

Decline of the United Irishmen

For the older future exiles, most of whom had taken extreme radical positions from the beginning of concerted political agitation in Ireland, the failure of their efforts to persuade the more moderate reformers to accept their program made the months leading up to the outbreak of war with France in February 1793 in some respects as much a turning point as the subsequent decision two years later to go underground and prepare for an insurrection. Their disappointment and disillusionment festered; the government's counterattack seemed completely successful. The policy of using the Volunteers to threaten the government was undermined by the Gunpowder Act of February 1793 and a proclamation against assembling in arms. A few months later the Convention Act stymied the other major part of the radicals' program, by forbidding the convening of unofficial representative assemblies.[93]

Seeking to reduce the influence of radical propaganda, the government began to keep "a watchful eye . . . on the public prints," commencing prosecutions "against the publishers of sedition in all cases."[94] Warrants were issued against the owners of the *Northern Star* and other newspaper editors who were publishing United Irish material.[95] Neilson, who with dry humor mixed with wary nervousness began to see himself as "an unfortunate, persecuted northern incendiary,"[96] traveled to Dublin with his fellow proprietors, where each was bailed by one Catholic and one Protestant to demonstrate radical denominational unity, and then entertained at an ecumenical dinner.[97] A few months later Denis Driscol, defended by Emmet at the Cork Assizes, was acquitted of publishing a seditious libel in the radical *Cork Gazette*.[98]

While Driscol and others temporarily slipped out of the net, JOSEPH CUTHBERT became the first victim of the government offensive. An Antrim tailor and a Volunteer, he was pilloried and imprisoned for one year in March 1793 for trying to corrupt a soldier with an extract of Thomas Cooper's antiwar pamphlet, which had also been the cause of prosecutions in Scotland. Cuthbert was a sinister figure; for the short period he was out of prison in the 1790s he gained a reputation for violence, and may have been involved with an "assassination squad" in Ulster responsible for killing informers.[99] In August 1796 he was one of four arrested for a "murderous attack" on John Lees, a Sergeant of Invalids who was employed to obtain evidence against the Ulster radicals. The attack, during which Lees was shot at, was planned by the "Muddlers' Club" in an upper room of Peggy Barclay's Belfast pub, a favorite haunt of radicals and the site of the first preliminary meeting of Neilson and his fellow Volunteers in April 1791. Charged with conspiracy to murder, Cuthbert was acquitted (after the original complainant, a peddlar, had been conveniently drowned), but was immediately rearrested on a charge of high treason, finally becoming one of the state prisoners sent to Fort George in 1799.[100]

From early 1793 the radical leaders in Dublin also began to feel the hot breath of reaction on their necks. Dr. James Reynolds was an early victim, imprisoned in Newgate in March for refusing to give evidence on oath before a secret committee of the Irish House of Lords. Drennan reported that Reynolds was nervous and agitated before his ordeal, but "not timid." "They think they will terrify this very young man, but they are mistaken," he wrote. He was right; Reynolds defiantly nailed a print of Thomas Paine on his cell wall (it was soon stolen). He remained in prison until the parliamentary session ended five months later, by which time Simon Butler and Oliver Bond had also been incarcerated for questioning the authority of the Secret Committee.[101]

Faced with this broadside from the government, support for the United Irishmen withered, and the society in Dublin began to break up. Drennan noted in March 1793: "Every day the people are routed in their *minds*, and a Reform is now again become an idea." A few days later he pessimistically informed his brother-in-law: "The whole country seems stunned. A perfect inquisition reigns here in [Volunteer] companies, in the streets, in the shops."[102] Numbers attending the weekly meetings of the Dublin Society began to fall: It was very unusual for more than forty-five members to be present from March 1793.[103] There were a number of reasons for this, apart from the government's crackdown. The British government's policy of buying Catholic allegiance by abolishing most of the remaining penal laws had some effect in satisfying the more moderate Catholic members, even though the bad grace shown by ascendancy MPs during the debates on these measures made good propaganda for the radicals.[104] There is also some evidence that the rank and file members in Dublin were becoming increasingly disillusioned with the haughty and imperious manner in which the "inner circle" kept control of the society in their own hands. McDowell has suggested that "interminable political theorizing may have bored a good many members."[105] More likely, the very significant decline in attendance in 1793 was evidence that the commercial and industrial classes, who made up two thirds of the membership, had become disillusioned with the monopolistic stranglehold that the professionals kept on the organization.[106] As Drennan explained in June: "Our society is splitting and I suppose will soon adopt the mode of Belfast in keeping silence as I shall do."[107]

Belfast's silence was primarily the result of backsliding among those who were involved with the movement's most valuable propaganda vehicle, the *Northern Star*. From January 1793 troops had been quietly sent into Belfast, and on 9 March there was a riot, instigated by dragoons of the 17th Regiment, during which the shops of prominent radicals and Volunteers were damaged and Neilson's newspaper office threatened.[108] Although the fracas was swiftly brought under control, and the dragoons withdrawn from town, the effect on the radical movement in Belfast was more long lasting. A mild case of paranoia infected the town, with Neilson publishing a sermon by Dean Swift on "false witness," which was headed "Spies and Informers."[109] Before long, faced with no less than six indictments for seditious libel, the *Northern Star* proprietors in particular began to regret their political prominence. Some

were embarrassed by the suggestion—made even by moderate reformers—
that the outspoken nature of the newspaper had almost invited retribution
from the authorities, Martha McTier noting that "The *[Northern] Star*, it has
been said, has brought all this on us and the United Irishmen; *they* are, therefore, violently attacked."[110] By July some of Neilson's fellow investors in the
newspaper were hoping to dissolve their partnership.[111] Neilson, however, remained undaunted, although even he was forced to tone down the newspaper's
politics while the prosecutions were pending.[112]

In both Dublin and Belfast, therefore, the first year of the war with France
saw the radical movement as represented by the Society of United Irishmen
lose momentum and support. The news from France only compounded the
difficulties brought on by the Irish government's repressive policies. Enthusiasm for the French revolution waned rapidly after the Brissotins—those revolutionaries most favored by the Irish radicals—were arrested and the reign of
terror began.[113] According to Emmet, loyalist propaganda linking the guillotine with the march of democracy "alarmed the timid, revolted those whose
liberal politics were more the result of feeling than of reflection, and [they]
even cooperated with the measures of government, in compelling many of the
philosophic reformers to wait in silence a more favourable opportunity, when
what had been lost of public reason and public strength, should be again restored."[114] This left the radicals in a dilemma that they failed to solve in the
ensuing months. On the one hand, they knew that the radical Pro-French,
Painite line they favored would not garner majority support among the middle
classes; on the other, an effective strategy capable of sustaining middle-class
interest, such as their concentration on hammering out an acceptable reform
program in the second half of 1793, merely demonstrated their increasing di-
vorce from political reality.[115]

Insurrectionary Politics: The First Steps

The more militant slowly began to gravitate toward an insurrectionary policy,
which involved creating better links with the increasing number of societies
formed by plebeian radicals in 1793–94. Until recently, the importance of
these plebeian clandestine societies has gone unrecognized, mainly because so
little evidence is available on their activities.[116] But in the cities of Belfast,
Dublin, and Cork there existed a variety of clubs and societies, mainly plebeian in membership but also including a sprinkling of young and enthusiastic
students. Some began as reading clubs (with Paine as the main text), some
were "Jacobin" clubs, meeting in the back rooms of pubs. Yet others were initially journeyman industrial combinations, formed in response to the grave

downturn in the economy, especially in the cloth trades, with the onset of war. And then there were the Defenders, whose ideas spread into the cities with the new militia regiments raised amid much violence and acrimony in 1793.[117]

The purpose of the secret committee that imprisoned Reynolds had been to examine evidence on the Defenders and agrarian outrages. The Defenders was an oath-bound secret society that had emerged in County Armagh in the 1780s to protect Catholics from the depredations of Protestant groups such as the Peep-o-Day Boys.[118] By 1792–93 it had spread southward and eastward, into counties Down, Louth, Cavan, and Meath. Its aims were a mixture: the redress of local grievances; a "Jacobin" program of anticlericalism and support for revolutionary France; and an inchoate and millenarian desire for the restoration of Gaelic culture and the promotion of Catholic revanchism.[119] In Ulster, Defenderism flourished where there had been "relatively recent losses of land, a sense of lost status, unusually rapid growth of population, economic competition between [lower-class] Protestant and Catholic, [and] Protestant incursion into traditional Catholic 'territory'."[120] Where antipapist Protestant landlords were prominent, Defenderism was a likely response in the 1790s. In the cities, where plebeian sectarianism was more muted, it appeared less sectarian in character and appealed in particular to the weavers and lower-order artisans.

As a closed society with no organizational center, the Defenders confused and concerned the government of the time as much as they do historians today. It is generally agreed, however, that they were at best only crudely political, being primarily concerned with traditional issues such as the abolition of tithes and the economic protection of lower-class Catholics in the linen trade. In Emmet's view, they had only a vague "notion that 'something ought to be done for Ireland'."[121] That they might be a potential source of support and a possible means of penetrating Catholic councils was recognized by some radical United Irishmen in 1792, although it was also clear that the sectarianism pervading the local conflicts in which the Defenders were involved in the north had the capacity to alienate the more moderate reform-minded Protestants, who were increasingly disturbed by the prospect of lower-class Catholics hoarding weapons obtained from their successful arms raids. Moreover, from a United Irish perspective the conflict between Defenderism and its Protestant counterparts displayed evidence of wasted energies and resources, which might be more profitably channeled into organized political activity.[122]

It is thus not surprising, especially as the Defender movement began to move into the major towns and cities from 1792, that radical United Irishmen made some attempts to penetrate these secret societies. Initially, their objective was to arbitrate between the conflicting forces and to reduce sectarian tensions. In July 1792 Neilson, Tone, Lowry, and two prominent Dublin Catholic leaders went to Rathfryland in south Down, where there had been persistent trouble at fairs and markets between Defenders and Peep-o-Day men. At a meeting with local Catholics, gentry, and magistrates a temporary truce was hammered out. A few weeks later Tone met some Defenders in Newry and was asked to act as their defense counsel at the forthcoming assizes.[123]

The Rathfryland meeting may have been the first attempt to bring together the Defenders, radicals on the Catholic Committee, and the more advanced United Irishmen in some sort of incipient triple alliance. Certainly, radical members of the Catholic Committee, including JOHN SWEETMAN (c.1752–1826), a wealthy Dublin brewer, and William James MacNeven, a doctor trained in Vienna and Prague, raised money to pay the defense costs at Defender trials in Dundalk in August, being pilloried by the ascendancy conservatives for doing so. Neilson, contemptuous though he was of their doctrines, ensured that the Defenders' belief in the millennium was catered for in the *Northern Star*.[124]

The First Irish Exile

Napper Tandy's intervention in the affairs of the Defenders, which led him to become the first United Irish leader to be forced into exile in the United States, must be understood in this context. He was probably more intrigued by the possibilities opened up by this secret society than other United Irish leaders, because of his close links with, and understanding of, the Dublin lower classes. Whether he was acting on his own initiative cannot now be ascertained, but undoubtedly he traveled to County Louth in autumn of 1792 and, having been introduced by Rev. James O'Coigley—who was to be executed at Maidstone for treason in 1798—took the Defender oath at Castlebellingham.[125]

While there, Tandy distributed copies of a short address by "Common Sense" (probably John Keogh), which attacked the role of the ascendancy Beresford family in the county and urged local Presbyterians and Catholics to reject sectarian conflict.[126] For this Tandy was indicted, but also, unbeknown to him, preparations were made to indict him for taking the Defender oath, a capital offense, when he returned to Dundalk to take his trial in March 1793. According to Drennan, Tandy was en route to Dundalk when he was overtaken by a relative who informed him that the Dublin United Irish lawyers strongly urged him to jump bail and disappear, as they were convinced that an example would be made of him if found guilty. Tandy took this sensible advice and fled to London, where he remained for some months before sailing for America.[127]

Clandestine Societies

However much of a loose cannon Tandy may have been, in the months following his escape further links were undoubtedly made between the more extreme United Irishmen and the plebeian clubs in the major cities. The exact timing of these developments may never be known, but in Belfast plots including sending emissaries to Scotland and France in 1793 were hatched, which probably first emanated from the plebeian Jacobin club.[128] This society at some point coalesced with radical United Irishmen, so that by June 1795 its committee consisted mainly of United Irishmen from Neilson's group, although Rowley Osborne remained president.[129] By this time their test was republican, omitting reference to a comprehensive reform of Parliament.[130]

Emmet's claim that once the government closed down the Dublin Society of United Irishmen in May 1794 the leaders withdrew from politics for a year cannot be sustained, although it might be true for himself and a few of his close colleagues.[131] The reality was that in Dublin and Cork members of the moribund society became involved in a number of clandestine societies that brought them into contact both with plebeian radicals and, at one point, a French spy. The best known of these groups are the Strugglers' Club, the Athenian Society, the Philanthropic Society, and the Telegraph Society. The Strugglers, according to the government official John Pollock, consisted of "the Select Heads of the United Irishmen," including the "aristocrat" Simon Butler and the Wexford landowner, Beauchamp Bagenal Harvey of Bargay Castle (a future rebel leader).[132] It may well have been the continuation of the old "inner society" by another name, now no longer prepared to advertise its subversive activities.[133]

The Cork Connection: Driscol and Burk

The Strugglers may still have been playing at being revolutionaries; they "imitate all the forms of the Jacobin society of France," and call each other, and even waitiers, "citizen."[134] Much more purposeful were the Philanthropic, Athenian, and Telegraph societies, which were denominated "preparatory schools for the fraternity of Defenders."[135] These republican and oath-bound societies had links with the Cork society associated with the Sheares brothers,

JOHN SWINEY, and Driscol's radical *Cork Gazette*. Driscol is a fine example both of how extreme radicalism and underground plotting cannot be dissociated from marginal types unable to settle or prosper in contemporary society, and of how the United system and Defenderism came to coalesce in 1794–95. He was born in County Cork in 1762 to a Catholic family of sufficient means to give him an education on the continent. He trained for the priesthood, possibly in Spain as he later advertised his services in Philadelphia as a Spanish teacher.[136] How long he served as a Catholic priest following his return to Cork is not known. Nor is it known why, at the age of twenty-seven, his faith in Roman Catholicism apparently collapsed. For whatever reason, in July 1789 Driscol conformed to the Church of Ireland, effectively disinheriting himself from his roots and at the same time entering the new world of opportunity that membership of the established church offered. At this stage of his life he obviously believed that attachment to the norms and values of the Protestant ascendancy would best promote his career.[137]

In Cork city, Driscol was licensed as curate to the French Reformed Church. Demonstrating the holistic view that the cure of souls ought to be reinforced by the simultaneous cure of the mind, he also established a newspaper, the *Cork Gazette*, in which for a period he preached loyalism and obedience.[138] Again, however, events turned sour and in August 1791 he lost his curacy, and with it went his commitment to loyalist principles. According to his erstwhile friend, Rev. Frederick Archer, curate of St. Ann's, Shandon, by the end of 1792 the newspaper's and Driscol's political position had dramatically changed: "The French Revolution and its successes [were] panegyrised in its columns. I cautioned the editor against indulging such innovations and admonished him and remonstrated in vain, he persisting [in] promulgating these infernal theories."[139]

Driscol's advocacy of French revolutionary principles demonstrated the zealotry of a recent convert and the venom of personal disappointment. He became an early convert to Painite radicalism, which put him considerably in advance of many of the middle-class United Irish leaders in the early 1790s, and in two respects he espoused such an extreme radicalism that he became a serious menace to the authorities.[140] By openly avowing anticlerical Deism and by promoting an agrarian law, Driscol moved beyond the limits of contemporary radicalism in search of the support of the oppressed Irish peasantry of County Cork. By 1794, his appeal had become revolutionary. His anticlericalism, his attack on tithes, and his land distribution demands, when combined with his Painite Jacobinism, encouraged that union between urban radicalism and peasant Whiteboy-Defenderism that the authorities feared most and which the underground societies in the capital were beginning to represent.[141] Neilson, for instance, saw Driscol as the potential leader of Catholic peasant Defenderism in the south of Ireland.[142]

By the time Neilson began to concoct this plan, however, Driscol was languishing in Cork jail. In January 1794 he had committed the cardinal sin of promoting economic leveling in his newspaper. In a long list of "Truths" encapsulating his political testament, Driscol concluded by writing: "The earth is the common inheritance of all men. Every man has a right to a proportionate share of the country he lives in. He, who possesses a greater share of the land he lives in, than another, is a monopolist and an usurper of the rights of his fellow citizens."[143] When rumors circulated that certain printers were to be prosecuted "for telling Truths," Driscol began to retreat from his exposed position. Arguing that he had been speaking only in a "philosophical sense," he denied having claimed "that in the present overgrown state of society one should not possess by honest purchase, gift etc. more landed property than another." Honest men, thought Driscol, should be inclined to laugh at rather than prosecute for such a statement, attributing "the thought to folly rather than to malice."[144]

Driscol's transparent effort to avoid prosecution proved ineffectual. At the Cork assizes in April 1794 he was tried for seditious libel. "A rogue in ruffles," as counsellor Egan called him, Driscol—defended by the Sheares brothers and Emmet—unsurprisingly was found guilty. In his speech before being sentenced, Driscol denied ever having promoted an agrarian law; he had merely been speculating on Locke's opinions on government. "A man known to harbour such notions," he asserted, "should be pitied, as a lunatick, not prosecuted as a wicked and malicious libeller."[145] Such specious reasoning cut little ice with the judge; Driscol was sentenced to two years' imprisonment.

He continued to edit his newspaper from jail, calling for the union of all Irishmen: "Those of the North and those of the South are *brothers.*"[146] He was assisted financially by the Sheares brothers, who played an important role in the promotion of subversive societies in Dublin in 1794–95. Often in Cork or away on circuit, their main henchman in Dublin—keeping the lines of communication open between Cork and the capital—was an intimate friend of Driscol, JOHN DALY BURK (1772–1808), a young man "high and lofty in his carriage, haughty in his manners, and imperious and impulsive in his disposition."[147] Most probably Burk and Driscol had first become acquainted in 1790 when the former was appointed usher at a private school in Cork. In 1792 he entered Trinity College Dublin, as a sizar; he later boasted to Thomas Jefferson that there he had won the highest "premiums" for his prose and verse compositions.[148] The appeal of rational religion and the siren call of libertarianism ruined a promising career for Burk. Rejecting the reading prescribed by his Trinity tutors, he devoured the works of Price, Priestley, Hume, Locke, and Fontenelle, emerging from these studies a convinced Deist and political radical. At about the same time as the Dublin Society of United Irishmen was closed down, Burk was expelled from Trinity College. Although he claimed that "my love of liberty, not hatred of Religion, was the cause of my expulsion," the official reason given was his infidelism.[149]

Burk's account of the next year in Dublin gives some insight into the way in which the United Irishmen coalesced with more plebeian groups in the societies previously mentioned, suggesting that Smyth may have slightly overemphasized the role of the lower classes in the crucial period during which the Dublin societies began plotting insurrection. As we have seen, the leadership of the Strugglers club appears to have comprised the old inner circle of United Irishmen, and Burk claims that he and Dr. James Reynolds were instrumental in forming some of the other societies, which were cellular in structure and military in organization. Burk was certainly involved in early military preparations, learning the pike exercise in Dublin, according to Driscol. He was also a charismatic figure capable of harnessing political discontent, "literally leading [young men] captive at his will."[150]

The roles of Reynolds and Henry Jackson in this merging process are particularly instructive. Both were members of the United Irish inner circle. Jackson was a Dublin common councilman with good connections with the lower trades. His workforce was a cohesive group and an obvious conduit through which the United Irish could penetrate plebeian society. One of his clerks, who possibly had Defender links, was pilloried and imprisoned for three months in October 1793 for uttering seditious words in a pub, and his foundry men frequently assembled at the George on Church Street "for the purpose of rioting."[151]

With his friendships with Driscol and Burk, Reynolds, who had been chairman of the United Irish society's committee that struggled for many months in 1793 to produce a comprehensive reform program,[152] clearly bestrode both parts of the incipient insurrectionary organization in Dublin. It is thus significant that when the French spy Rev. William Jackson arrived in Dublin in April 1794, anxious to discover whether Ireland was ripe for invasion, Reynolds was one of the most willing to cooperate. The more cautious radicals feared Jackson to be a British agent provocateur; his friend and companion, John Cockayne, was Pitt's spy. Jackson met Tone, Reynolds, and Rowan, the latter at this time serving two years in prison for distributing a seditious libel (the address to the Volunteers of December 1792). After some initial reservations Rowan became enthusiastic, persuading Tone to write a report on the state of Ireland for the French (which he foolishly gave to Jackson, who sent it through the open mail to France!). Tone rejected a proposal to go to France as United Irish agent to the Committee of Public Safety, and was replaced by Reynolds.[153] But before these plans went forward, Jackson was arrested. Rowan, fatally compromised, immediately escaped from prison, fled to France, and then sailed for America. A year elapsed before Jackson was tried. After he had poisoned himself in the dock, Reynolds too fled to Philadelphia, being followed a few weeks later by Tone, who had been allowed to expatriate himself.[154] Shortly before, his underground organization having been penetrated by Lawless the spy, Burk too was on his way to the promised land.

PLOTTING REVOLUTION

Militarization

The Jackson fiasco was important for cementing in the minds of the radicals the idea that revolutionary France was seriously contemplating invading Ireland, a prospect that was to be at the center of insurrectionary planning thereafter until the disaster of Robert Emmet's rebellion of 1803. The other major objective of the radicals' strategy from early 1796, once insurrection had been determined, was to link the various forms of discontent in Ireland into one secret, highly structured, and disciplined organization, with both a political and a military wing, ready to take advantage of any French invasion: what John Fitzgibbon, earl of Clare called in 1797 a conspiracy of "a deluded peasantry aided by more intelligent treason."[155]

This revamped United Irish secret society fed off the disappointment of the failure of Earl Fitzwilliam's short period as Lord Lieutenant, when the hopes for reform and emancipation were finally and irrevocably dashed, and off the anger inspired by the spread of the Orange Order from its beginnings in Armagh in 1795.[156] Like the original Belfast societies, the basic structure of the United Irish/Defender alliance was cellular, with local societies splitting into two once thirty-six members had been reached. Above these, and deriving from them, were committees at the baronial, county, and provincial level. At the apex was a national committee.[157] The purpose of this system was to keep all plans on "a need-to-know" basis (as far as was possible in a mass organization) and to prevent penetration by informers. Compared with the large open societies in England, Neilson thought the United Irish system of cells to be watertight: "Ours are more reserved and of course more secure, we commit nothing to paper, we assemble in small numbers and without any predetermined place, and when our number exceeds 35, we split and the overplus lays the foundation of a new society. We have a very strong Test, are as cautious as possible in chusing our members nor have we yet been betrayed by anyone." Unfortunately, Neilson was expressing his confidence to William Bird, alias Smith, the government informer.[158]

Side by side with this political framework from late 1796, and mirroring its structure, was a military system, based on platoons of ten or eleven men, one a sergeant, with ten platoons commanded by a captain. Within each barony the captains elected a colonel, while each county was under the control of an adjutant general, chosen by the central leadership from a list provided by the county's colonels.[159] Probably more than half the Irish exiles to America were to hold positions in the higher echelons of either the political or the military organization in the period leading up to the rebellion.

This new organization was to be mass-based, and to achieve this objective various forms of persuasion were developed. The printed word continued to have some influence, though less than in previous years. Neilson continued, against all the odds, to publish the *Northern Star*, until his arrest in September 1796. He had survived the various indictments brought against the publication, although the printer, John Rabb, was outlawed after breaking bail and fleeing to South Carolina.[160] Neilson's policy was not only to continue promoting the old constitutional program, but also to appeal to the cruder beliefs of the lower orders. Old prophecies, millennial pronouncements were all grist to Neilson's mill. He published an account of Richard Brothers' millenarian activities in London; at least one of Neilson's Belfast colleagues, John Hughes, was a follower of Brothers, and John Binns in London was also extremely curious.[161] He also printed Thomas Ledlie Birch's eschatological sermons and even prophecies lifted from American newspapers ("presented to our readers as a support to their faith in the Millennium").[162] In 1795 the publishers of the *Northern Star* reprinted Robert Fleming's millenarian *Discourse on the Rise and Fall of the Papacy* (1701), which foretold the judgment on Catholic France as coming in 1794.[163] Neilson, of course, was both sceptical and cynical: the informer William Bird reported the arrival of a letter at the newspaper office that "contained a foolish old Prophecy which [Neilson] said he must insert to please his country readers and accordingly did."[164]

In the increasingly bitter struggle between the Defenders/United Irishmen and the loyalist Orange gangs, Neilson naturally sided with the former in his columns, reporting in detail Orange outrages, toning down Catholic revenge attacks, and relentlessly pursuing magistrates biased in favor of loyalist groups.[165] The influence of the *Northern Star* is difficult to ascertain, even though it was circulated gratis and dropped into coffeehouses and pubs over a wide area.[166] It was certainly seen as a threat by loyalists.[167] The marquess of Downshire, admittedly an alarmist, was calling for its demise by November 1796, while a Donegal loyalist prophesied: "If two or three of your inflammatory orators in the House of Commons were hanged and the [Dublin] Evening Post and Northern Star suppressed we should return to that happy state we eminently used to enjoy in this part of the kingdom."[168] Unfortunately, the solution was not that simple. The newspaper delivery men were waylaid by Orangemen and the *Star*'s offices raided by the military in September 1796 and February 1797 before the newspaper was finally suppressed three months later, yet the troubles did not fade away.[169]

By the spring of 1797, with feverish preparations for rebellion under way in Ulster, the *Northern Star* had probably served its purpose. More ephemeral print communications suitable to a lower- and middling-class readership were necessary: handbills, placards, posters, even chalkings on walls.[170] Radical songbooks were particularly popular. The Storey brothers of Belfast, John and THOMAS, printed a selection of radical songs, which, according to the will-o-the-wisp radical, William Putnam McCabe, "had done wonders among the militia who were all true fellows" (sworn to the cause).[171] When Valentine Lawless and WILLIAM SAMPSON dined in 1796 at Loughlinstown military camp with the duke of Leinster, Whig grandee and colonel of the Kildare militia, Sampson "illustrated the reckless character of his zeal by privately scattering political tracts and patriotic songs among the huts, as he walked through the camp after dinner."[172]

Watty Cox: A Conundrum

For a few months from the summer of 1797 a series of intemperate broadsheets, headed the *Union Star,* was plastered on the walls of Dublin, consisting "of names and abusive characters of persons supposed to have been informers against United Irishmen, or active opposers of their designs; and to such lists were added the most furious exhortations to the populace, to rise and take vengeance on their oppressors."[173] One who went in fear of his life as a result was William Paulet Carey, who had been finally persuaded, after receiving no help from the United Irishmen, to give evidence against Drennan in his trial for seditious libel.[174] The author of these violent diatribes was unknown. Some thought the *Union Star* was a product of loyalists, trying to blacken the name of the United Irishmen by extolling assassination as a virtuous act; others thought that Arthur O'Connor, the leader of the most militant revolutionaries in Dublin, was the promoter.[175] The more cautious revolutionaries, such as

Emmet and Sampson, were appalled; they drew up a petition in an attempt to suppress the broadsheet.[176]

McNally the informer's efforts to uncover the editor of the *Union Star* led him to two men whom he thought had knowledge of the business.[177] One was WALTER (WATTY) COX, who was brought in for questioning by Edward Cooke, under-secretary at the Castle, on 14 December. Cox (1770–1837) was the son of a Catholic blacksmith from Westmeath, a gunsmith by trade who in 1792 had commanded the 2nd Company of the Goldsmiths' Volunteers in Dublin. With a volatile private life—by 1798 he had been twice married and was openly living with his mistress in a house that was part of his second wife's dowry—and a hatred of the ascendancy spurred on by memories of the harsh treatment paid out to his father by Lord Carhampton when smashing the Defender movement in the west in 1795–96, Cox was one of the more colorful and complex characters of his generation.[178] Facing Cooke in his gloomy office in the Castle, which was festooned with captured pikes of grotesque shapes and sizes,[179] he coolly inquired if he would receive a pardon on condition of disclosing the author of the *Union Star*. When Cooke agreed, Cox confessed to being "sole author, printer and publisher." After explaining the mechanics of printing and publishing his samizdat, he proceeded to implicate the militants, O'Connor and Lord Edward Fitzgerald, in his activities, claiming the former to be "an enthusiast" and the latter "weak and not fit to command a Sergeant's Guard but very zealous."[180]

Cox's pardon was conditional on his continuing to inform on his fellow revolutionaries (as one of Fitzgerald's bodyguards he was in a good position to do so).[181] Although he concocted a reasonable cover story for his occasional visits to the Castle, he nonetheless was eyed with suspicion and carefully watched by the United men.[182] Several historians have viewed him as a double agent, working both sides off against each other in the months leading up to the rebellion. But the awkward position he found himself in was not only a reflection of circumstances, but also was evidence of his own ambivalence. From a middling-class Catholic background, he naturally despised the ascendancy; however, like many others of his class and religion, he mistrusted the Protestant United leaders, whom he felt "keep themselves behind the curtain: urge on the lower classes to their destruction; and only mean to take the lead and come forward if insurrection should be successful."[183] He was referring here to the Emmets and the Sampsons, half-hearted revolutionaries who felt that a French invasion was an essential prerequisite for a successful insurrection. Cox's own links were with the militants, but he had little faith in their plans either. In the event, being "a clever man and deep," he carefully picked

his way through the shoals of potential denouncement and ignominious informing to survive the crisis of the rebellion in one piece, a continued object
of suspicion but a spy who did not give away vital secrets nor implicate his
close compatriots.[184]

Cox's ephemeral but violent writings appealed to those full of revenge but
alienated the more timid. The former, however, were increasing in number by
1797, for there had been many acts of violence, on both sides, which called for
vengeance. In their anxiety to create a mass movement, the United Irishmen
unfortunately were not averse to playing on people's heightened emotions.
Both Neilson's *Northern Star* and Arthur O'Connor's the *Press* (published in
Dublin) found it expedient to circulate the falsehood that the test of the
Orangemen included the statement that "I swear . . . that I will *exterminate*
the Catholics."[185]

Bible-carrying Proselytizers

Reports of these outrages, however, spread more by word of mouth than by
the medium of print, and were magnified with the telling. By late 1795, as the
links between the Defenders and the United Irishmen were being forged, emissaries from the better organized regions, especially Ulster, circulated the
country swearing the unhappy, the frightened, and the disaffected into the
movement.[186] As early as May 1795 reports were received of nightly expresses
sent from Belfast to surrounding villages to administer illegal oaths.[187] One of
those implicated was the Presbyterian minister of Glenarm, Rev. Robert
Acheson. Another minister, Rev. James Porter—who was to be executed in
1798—was said to have sworn in United Irishmen while traveling the countryside giving lectures on natural philosophy.[188] Education indeed had a lot to
answer for: in a mountainous and isolated part of Londonderry a young man
from Galway, acting "as a kind of schoolmaster," paid more than one shilling
to each person he swore in. "After terrifying the ignorant people with prophecies of a general massacre in Ireland on the 29th. August next," he was eventually forced to flee.[189] From the same source (Nathaniel Alexander, possibly
an alarmist magistrate) came news more than a year later that large numbers
of men were riding the countryside "organising and neglecting their businesses," including one Dempsie, who had been waked a few weeks previously
after supposedly drowning in the River Bann, but who subsequently sent a
letter from County Donegal, where he had been administering oaths.[190] If one
anonymous Castle correspondent is to be believed, even respectable middle-
class women were involved in oath-taking. Mrs. Bond, wife of "Oliver Crom-
wel [*sic*] Bond" (and daughter of Henry Jackson), constantly carried "a prayer

Book about her, to swear women, thinking thro' their influence over the other sex to disseminate this cursed doctrine the more."[191]

The tactic of suborning the military was carried on vigorously. Joseph Cuthbert, undeterred by his punishment in 1793, was reported in July 1796 to have returned from a mission to Scotland and to have visited the militia camp at Blaris Warren, near Lisburn, with the Belfast Jacobin Daniel Shanaghan and their wives. "In high spirits," they had arrived at the camp in a hired coach and four, with coachman and footman in laced liveries. There they gave five guineas to the soldiers and inspected a "Ball Room," which was set aside for the use of sworn United men and Defenders, of whom, it was claimed, there were more than two thousand. Certainly, a few months later McNally the informer confirmed that the whole camp at Blaris was organized. Shanaghan told Bird that there would be no revolution before the harvest was in, but that if he "remained here till November, [he] should see shocking work."[192]

Perhaps the most famous case of suborning soldiers occurred in the town of Antrim in May 1796, in which one future exile was heavily involved. BILLY MCKEEVER, alias Campbell, of Upperland, County Londonderry, was present when William Orr, a popular Antrim farmer, administered the oath to two soldiers of the Fife Fencibles. The soldiers, Wheatley and Lindsay, were staying overnight at the Swan Inn in Antrim en route from Scotland to Londonderry, when they were treated so royally by a group of townsmen that they became drunk. Four of the locals, two Campbells and two Orrs, began to insinuate that soldiers were treated badly, and offered them one shilling per day if they took the United Irish oath of allegiance (the two were also offered the rank of captain and Wheatley promised part of Campbell's farm once the revolution was successfully completed). The soldiers took the oath in a back-room before William Orr, and the following day repeated the oath before a group of ten men at the other Orr's house.[193]

Orr and McKeever were both arrested, the former for the above offense, the latter for administering oaths elsewhere (he was thought to be "the most active man in the region of Londonderry").[194] Their separate trials were not held until September 1797. Orr was sentenced to death, and although furious attempts were made to gain him a reprieve, he was executed as a salutary and necessary example. He naturally became a martyr; the jurors at his trial, on the other hand, "dare not appear out after nightfall, are obliged to keep Guards on the watch all night and Lead the most Uncomfortable lifes [*sic*] Imaginable."[195] McKeever was tried for being a United Irishman at Londonderry, but was acquitted when his accuser broke down on the witness stand.[196] He remained a member of the Londonderry Provincial Committee until the rebellion broke out in Ulster, when, according to one report, although commander of the rebels at Maghera (County Londonderry), he was the first to flee on news of the approaching troops.[197] America was his goal.

During 1796 and the early months of 1797 the United Irish emissaries scoured the countryside and the towns of the North and midlands, administering oaths with virtual impunity.[198] A wave of fear—"a reign of terror" one Castle correspondent from Cookstown, County Tyrone called it—swept the region, reinforced by the intimidatory tactics of both sides.[199] Even when United Irishmen were arrested and tried, they frequently were acquitted. Jury panels were too scared to convict, and witnesses were bought off or quietly disappeared.[200]

One roving emissary who could not be brought to justice openly was the "tall, portly, hard featured, pockmarked" Quaker, JOHN SHAW. In March 1796 one Robert Carlisle of County Tyrone was stopped on his way home by two men in greatcoats. When he replied to their queries that he was not interested in party politics but supported "the Protestant interest," one waving a small sword and the other a brace of pistols forced him to take the rebel oath. A few weeks later, Carlisle recognized one of his assailants at a local fair. It was John Shaw, a well-known cloth merchant from Dree, near Dungannon (formerly of Lisburn, a Defender stronghold). Subsequent information uncovered the fact that Shaw and his colleague were paying each person they swore in, having "the command of *bushels* of money."[201]

As soon as Shaw was arrested on a charge of high treason, all the resources of the United Irishmen were brought to bear on his behalf. He was characterized in the *Northern Star* as a "persecuted Quaker," obnoxious by religious belief to the ascendancy, who had been active in "opposing the torrent of [Orange] fanaticism" in Armagh, and who had been in Tyrone trying to prevent the spread of these ideas.[202] Taken to Dublin and incarcerated in Newgate jail, he was defended by the United Irishmen's top barrister, William Sampson, who after months of effort managed to obtain his release on bail. He evidently returned to his undercover job, for in April 1797 a warrant was issued for his arrest on a charge of treasonable practices.[203]

Stalling the Rebellion

The government was hamstrung in its efforts to keep control in the disaffected areas. Many suspected persons were arrested, but finding reliable juries and credible witnesses remained difficult. Suspending habeas corpus enabled the Castle in September 1796 to order the arrest of most of the prominent United Irish leaders in Belfast, including Neilson, his clerk THOMAS KANE, Thomas Russell, Samuel Kennedy—later to become a newspaper proprietor in Maryland—and the publican JOHN YOUNG. Charged with high treason, they were all packed off to Dublin. In Lisburn Charles Teeling and his father (the Teelings were the leaders of the Defenders in Antrim)[204] met Castlereagh by chance and rode with him to the entrance of the Marquess of Hertford's property, where they bid each other adieu, only to find the young loyalist politician gently marshaling them through the gates, where troops politely put them under arrest.[205]

None of those apprehended at this time was brought to trial. Neilson, for instance, was vulnerable to the evidence of Bird the spy, but was saved from prosecution—although not from seventeen months in Kilmainham jail—by Sampson and the Whig Lord Moira, who managed to persuade a number of notorious informers, including Bird, to turn their coats.[206] Another possible witness against Neilson, one Kerr of Newtownards, who had turned informer following his arrest, was visited in his cell by Charles Teeling dressed as a clergyman. The young Defender so frightened Kerr by his warnings of the celestial punishments for perjury that the poor man retracted his confession.[207]

Government responses to these frustrations and the shrill complaints of loyalists included the implementation of the Insurrection Act in Ulster, first passed in March 1796, which gave increased powers to local magistrates in regions officially proclaimed; the establishment of a yeomanry, mainly as a local force to allow the regular army and militia to concentrate on defense against a French invasion, but increasingly penetrated by the Orange Order; and finally, in March 1797, the ordering of General Gerard Lake to disarm the North: "The Authority is full and without limitation excepting which your own discretion may suggest."[208]

Neither discretion nor sensitivity was Lake's strong point, but his rough policy of dragooning the North was very successful. Some historians may point to his crude tactics as the trigger for the subsequent rebellion in the South in May 1798, but he almost certainly prevented an explosion in Ulster in the spring and summer of 1797. He compelled the disaffected to disgorge their hidden arms, stolen in night raids, and their gunpowder supplied from Dublin and America in flax seed casks.[209] He disrupted the county organizations by arresting many of the leaders; in April 1797, twenty-five from County Tyrone, which was by no means the most organized region, were languishing in jail.[210] And he watched with equanimity as around the streets of Belfast zealous magistrates guided a masked spy, Edward Newell the painter of miniatures, to pick out men whom he had met at secret United Irish meetings.[211]

In this maelstrom of reaction and confusion Thomas Ledlie Birch was almost swept away. Always a forceful, opinionated man, he fought his battles on several fronts. A struggle with his congregation over his support for the Catholics led to a secession and the formation of a nonpoliticized Burgher congregation in Saintfield in 1796. In January of the following year Hugh McKee's farm near Saintfield was attacked at night for arms. Eleven of Birch's congregation were subsequently arrested, although they were acquitted at the next assizes (McKee's whole family was to be wiped out when the rebels were holding Saintfield in 1798).[212] Immediately after their trial Birch was arrested on two charges of high treason, probably at the instigation of Nicholas Price, the loyalist owner of much of the Saintfield estate. At the autumn assizes, where the government's control of the law was finally reasserted, the incorrigible minister was acquitted, owing to the witness being a renowned perjurer, on a charge of promising to put himself at the head of rebels if a French invasion occurred. On the other charge, of planning to assassinate Price, no true bill was found.[213] He was, nevertheless, forced to take the oath of allegiance, an action that he seemed able to square with his conscience.[214] Thereafter Birch was a marked man, claiming to be continually persecuted by Orangemen.[215] In April 1798 he was again indicted, this time for offering a £50 bribe to Joseph Harper not to prosecute a United Irishman, and for assaulting Harper's son.[216] The charges were dropped when Harper Sr. was shot dead "on the Tuesday preceding the Assize upon the road leading from Belfast to Saintfield."[217]

Birch remained defiant, but as Lake cut a swathe through the North hundreds of United Irishmen scattered, mostly making for England, Scotland, or France. Edward Newall boasted that he had been "the cause of 300 having fled from their habitations, their families, and industry, to hide in the mountains or seek for safety in some distant land."[218] Many of these were holding high positions in the militarized United Irishmen; their flight seriously reduced the effectiveness and fund of experience in the organization.[219] With the losses overseas combining with the large number of arrests, the movement in Ulster suffered a near-fatal blow in 1797.

The number who fled to America following Lake's exertions cannot now be accurately ascertained. A group of Covenanter ministers and theology students—small in number but crucial for the tiny sect—emigrated to America, mainly for political reasons, but partly because their principled refusal to take oaths at a time when oath-taking was an important symbol on both sides of the political fence put them in an intolerable position.[220] GEORGE DOBBIN (1776–1811), who later became proprietor of the Maryland newspaper, the *Baltimore American*, escaped at this time.[221] So too did ROBERT MOORE, an Antrim colonel who emigrated soon after attending a secret meeting in June 1797 of Ulster military commanders where he learned that a rising would be postponed until news arrived of a French invasion.[222] He is next heard of, with Dr. James Reynolds and WILLIAM DUANE, fomenting a riot outside St. Mary's Church in Philadelphia in February 1799.[223] Alexander Lowry, one of the founding United Irishmen and captain of the Ballyroney Volunteers in 1792, had by October 1796 become a member of the United Irishmen's first National Executive. In June 1797 he fled to France, then after the rebellion sailed to America. Subsequently he was permitted to return to Ireland. His return voyage was eventful; his ship being driven into Norway, he profitably spent his time finding a wife, but died unexpectedly a few days after returning home.[224]

An Irish Bonaparte

By the end of the year the initiative among the United Irishmen had shifted from Belfast to Dublin. It was now the capital "that became the principal exporter of sedition."[225] Within the Leinster Executive in Dublin—effectively the National Executive by late 1797—plans to coordinate a rising with French aid and in conjunction with revolutionaries in England were laid. Accredited agents from Ireland had been sent to Paris earlier, including Tone, who using a passport with the uninspiring name of James Smith had left New York on New Year's Day 1796 and arrived in Le Havre a month later.[226] In June Lord Edward Fitzgerald and Arthur O'Connor made contact with French officials on the Swiss border, and the latter may even have briefly visited Paris. A year later it was Dr. William James MacNeven's turn to slip away from Dublin, cross to England, and from Yarmouth make his way to Hamburg, where he awaited permission to enter France to offer the directory a memorial from the United Irishmen.

MacNeven (1763–1841) was one of the more level-headed leaders among the United Irishmen. Born in Galway into an old Catholic family that had lost its ancestral lands in the North in Cromwell's day, he was sent abroad to his uncle, a physician to the Empress Maria Theresa. MacNeven studied medicine in Prague and Vienna, graduating in 1783. He returned to Dublin the next year, and established a medical practice. He became very prominent in the reform movement from 1791, serving both on the Catholic Committee and in the Society of United Irishmen. By 1797 he was secretary to the underground society's national executive.[227]

MacNeven was a small, neatly made man of 5 feet 4 inches, but his personality was more impressive. One does not need to accept in full Madden the hagiographer's assessment of him as "a man of powerful intellect, singularly sagacious and far-seeing, of inflexible purpose and great solidity of judgement, . . . of first-rate power in revolutionary times," to appreciate his value to the United Irishmen.[228] His obvious abilities compelled Samuel Turner—the Ulster lawyer who arrived in Hamburg only a few days before MacNeven, and who was about to embark on his career, code name "Richardson," as William Wickham's most important spy among the United Irishmen—to subdue his anti-Catholic prejudices for a moment. He acknowledged that the emissary was "look'd upon as a Buonaparte," and that he was an "active zealous quick man, full of resource and was considered as a great genius."[229]

In terms of cementing the Franco-United Irish alliance, MacNeven's mission was not very satisfactory. He had left Ireland shortly after a major split occurred in the United Irish hierarchy, between militants who were anxious for an independent insurrection before Ulster was completely subdued by Lake's forces, and moderates who, notwithstanding the evidence of French intentions as demonstrated by General Hoche's abortive Bantry Bay invasion of December 1796, did not want to rise until a French force had landed. MacNeven's own instincts were very cautious; not only was he convinced an independent insurrection was too risky, but he was also suspicious of France's long-term intentions. Like Emmet, Sampson, and the other moderates, he had no desire to replace one foreign yoke with another, and he made this clear in Paris. Unfortunately, other emissaries representing the militant position were sent from Ulster at the same time, so the French, whose own ideas—at least, the views of the lower officials with whom the emissaries had contact in Paris—were closer to the militants', were left with the correct impression of confusion and quarreling among the Irish revolutionaries. Moreover, an unsuspecting MacNeven gave Turner the opportunity of copying a memorial he had written while awaiting a passport in Hamburg; this soon found its way to Wickham at the home office. MacNeven returned from his mission with troubling concerns about French intentions. It is perhaps not surprising that soon after he fell seriously ill.[230]

Linking with England

In addition to French aid, the other strategy central to the success of the United Irishmen's plans was the ability of revolutionaries on mainland Britain to create sufficient diversions to divide the government's forces when the insurrection broke out in Ireland. Many of the Irishmen who fled to Britain in 1797, and who settled mainly in London, Manchester, and its satellite towns, continued plotting, helping to create the United Britons, an underground organization comprising United Irish cells and militants of the LCS. Their plans were coordinated by leading United Irishmen such as John Chambers and

VALENTINE DERRY who commuted between Ireland and Britain, usually under cover of business trips.[231]

In January 1798 a delegation from the United Britons arrived in Dublin, carrying an address from the LCS and "very important verbal communications" which, Benjamin Binns later erroneously claimed in his account to Madden, "never oozed out, *nor ever shall.*"[232] The delegation included the two Binns brothers, James O'Coigley, the Armagh priest and roving revolutionary, and CAPTAIN WILLIAM BAILEY, a former East India Company officer who remained in Dublin and was involved in the insurrectionary plans of May 1798.[233] They met a number of leaders in Dublin, from networks in Cork and Ulster as well as from the capital, with Henry Jackson acting as liaison. They also conferred with "the Papists," who may have been Defenders but could also have been the Dublin Catholic militants, John Keogh and Richard McCormick. Their secret instructions, pledging support from England for an Irish insurrection, gave a fillip to those on the executive—like O'Connor, Fitzgerald, and Henry Jackson—who did not want to wait for French aid before rising.[234]

Unknown to all involved, the intelligence services in London and the Castle knew much of what was happening. A few days after returning to London Benjamin Binns was arrested by a home office messenger, who with relish said to him: "Why Mr. Binns, I have had a long journey to overtake you. I dare say I have travelled fifteen hundred miles after you. . . . I can tell where you have breakfasted, dined, supped and slept for the last twelve months."[235] Binns was imprisoned without trial in Newgate (London) until August 1799, and then transferred to Dorchester jail, where he spent much of the time in solitary confinement, until his release, a broken man, in April 1801.[236] His brother, John, in the meantime, had traveled to the south coast of England with O'Coigley and O'Connor, and was there arrested while seeking a boat to take them to France.[237]

The Leaders Undone

Neither government, in London or in Dublin, however, had sufficient evidence in the early months of 1798 to round up the other plotters. They had a good idea of what was being planned; they knew the identities of most of the leaders; but their evidence, obtained either by unreliable informers or spies who refused to be witnesses in open court, was not strong enough to justify mass arrests. What they needed was information from someone high up in the United Irish organization. This unexpectedly came to hand at the end of February 1798, when Thomas Reynolds, a colonel and member of the Leinster executive, opened communications with the Castle via a third person. The information given by Reynolds, a friend and neighbor of Lord Edward Fitzgerald, who had inveigled him into the organization, included the news that in the provinces of Ulster, Leinster, and Munster 300,000 Irishmen were now sworn to the United movement. Knowledge of this was sufficient to persuade the lord lieutenant, Camden, that the ultraloyalists had been right all along, and that a pre-emptive strike against the United Irish leadership was essential.[238] If as well as disrupting the rebels it also caused a premature explosion, so much the better.

On 12 March, using information supplied by Reynolds, town major Henry Sirr, his deputy major Swan, and a file of constables in "coloured clothes" (plain clothes) burst into Oliver Bond's house on Bridge Street and arrested fourteen members of the Leinster executive. At the same time, in other parts of the city Emmet, Sampson, Sweetman, Jackson, and MacNeven were taken up. In one sweep, not only had most of the senior United Irishmen been rendered ineffective, but a significant portion of the future Irish exiles were now in the government's clutches. Those arrested at Bond's included GEORGE CUMING, an Ulster apothecary now living in Kildare, who incongruously claimed, as an explanation for his presence, that while walking down the street he had on a whim followed Bond's clerk into the house; THOMAS TRAYNOR, a Dublin spirit merchant and ship-owner, who said he was present on business; and EDWARD HUDSON, a wealthy dentist, who did not have the presence of mind to extricate himself by claiming he was on a house call![239]

The United Irish executive had suffered a serious, if not fatal blow, but was quickly reconstituted by the Sheares brothers, Neilson, and Lord Edward Fitzgerald. The plans for an insurrection on 23 May went ahead. By this time, however, Neilson was no longer the solid, confident leader of 1792–93. His long confinement—he was released on bail only in February 1798—had broken his health and ruined his nerves: "His once powerful frame [was] shrunken and delapidated."[240] From prison in Scotland in 1801 he later confessed to his wife that "I have not enjoyed so good health since my mind was made uneasy about the *Star* prosecutions in 1793: from that period . . . I could never reckon on my liberty or my life, and was of course in a state of perpetual anxiety, which was much increased by the uneasiness of my partners. What I have been made to feel since that time has cured me perfectly of all idle apprehensions."[241] In the spring of 1798 he was also frequently drunk.[242] This was an occupational hazard at a time when conviviality and sociability often masked serious plotting. Bird the spy, when in the confidence of Neilson and his fellow radicals in Belfast, once complained that "there is one thing wherein [the radical leaders] puzzle me, which is, that they seldom say much till they are nearly drunk, and by the time I get them in this plight, I am little better myself, and tho' they were to open their hearts ever so liberally, I stand a fair chance of forgetting it by morning."[243] Not that drunkenness could not be a good cover in times of peril. In April 1798, while reconnoitering routes for the rebel armies outside Dublin, Fitzgerald and Neilson avoided arrest by a patrol when the former persuaded the officer that he was a doctor ministering to a (plainly) drunken patient.[244]

In the days before the insurrection the government dragnet covering Dublin further whittled away the new executive. The arrest of John and Henry Sheares would have tormented the quiet evenings of Patrick Byrne in Philadelphia in later years, for he was the unsuspecting author of their downfall. Byrne's bookshop was "the literary headquarters" of the radicals, where they could browse through what few radical publications remained on sale. Byrne was always on the lookout for prospective recruits. Captain John Armstrong's frequent visits to the shop over a period of two years, and his purchasing of Paine's works, suggested that he might be sympathetic to the cause. Byrne was supposed to have said to another customer: "This man wears a uniform, and he is a croppy for all that." He accordingly sounded him out, and then put him in contact with the Sheares brothers, who were looking for an officer to lead the United Irishmen among the soldiery stationed around Dublin. This was a serious misjudgment. Armstrong was a dilettante, interested in political subjects and opposed to some of the government's policies, but not to the extent of contemplating revolution. He reported the contact to Castlereagh, and then met John Sheares half a dozen times, gathering information that was to lead to the brothers' deaths. Byrne too was arrested, but never brought to trial. His wife was to die while he languished in Newgate prison.[245]

Two days before the Sheareses were arrested, the government had finally collared Lord Edward Fitzgerald, who for many weeks had evaded capture by skipping from safe house to safe house, including one belonging to JOHN CORMICK, a feather merchant and United Irish captain. Fitzgerald had been a difficult man to protect. He moved between hideouts disguised in a pigtailed wig and a countryman's greatcoat, but insisted on taking long walks through Dublin at night and on gardening during the day. Wherever he stayed, he left his boots outside his bedroom, with his name neatly written around the inside rim.[246] Dangerously wounded during the arrest, he was carried off to Newgate.

By now, although thousands of peasants around the city were preparing to rise, the rebel force in the capital had virtually disintegrated. Of the original leaders, only the tragic figure of Neilson was left. It was his idea to use the stopping of the mail coaches to signal the beginning of the insurrection, but although this was done, the few hundred putative rebels milling around Barley Fields on the evening of the 23rd had no idea what to do. Neilson went out there to meet them, then went back to the directory to get fresh instructions. According to Madden, he was caught outside Newgate trying to find a way to free John Sheares; according to Watty Cox: "On his way to the Directory, he again applied to his favourite enjoyment [in a pub], and so much did he destroy all sense of the great trust he undertook, that he deliberately staggered to the prison gate where Lord Edward lay. Immediately he was recognised and arrested by the jailer."[247]

And then there was none.

REBELLION AND DEFEAT

Escape from the South

It is a mark of the ferocity of the fighting in the South, and of the policy on prisoners of Castlereagh and the new lord lieutenant, Cornwallis, that very few of those involved in the fighting outside Ulster during the rebellion finally found their way to America. Of the nearly three thousand prisoners taken in 1798, most from the South who were not executed or eventually released on bail were sent overseas in a military capacity—either to the West Indies or Holland in the British army, or into the armies of the King of Prussia—or were transported as convicts to Botany Bay.[248]

One who escaped these fates and eventually reached America was NICHOLAS GREY, a young lawyer who became aide-de-camp to Bagenal Harvey during the Wexford uprising. "A most desperate and dangerous fellow," he so distinguished himself at the battle of New Ross that he "nearly won [it] by his own personal intrepidity."[249] Grey was arrested but released after a few weeks, for reasons that are unknown.[250] This by no means ended his revolutionary career; in 1803 he was commander of the Kildare forces that participated in Emmet's rebellion. According to William Wickham, now chief secretary to Ireland, Grey and Thomas Cloney were "the most artful desperate and incorrigible rebels in the country," part of "a handful of wandering Politicians who have neither Birth, family, character nor credit to sustain them."[251] Artful Grey certainly was. Little effort was made to capture him, for everyone thought he was dead.[252] But he was subsequently captured, spending several months in Athy prison before being transferred to Kilmainham. While there he sought from the government additional compensation for his servant's subsistence, the amount allocated being "not by any means adequate to the expence I have been at."[253] Surprisingly, he was banished, not executed; he initially settled in Hudson, New York, where he was soon "driving the quill."[254]

Another very young aide-de-camp to Harvey who escaped to America was JOHN DEVEREAUX (1778–1860), of Taghmon, County Wexford, the son of a prominent Catholic brewer and landowner. According to John Binns, Devereaux brought two thousand of his father's tenants to the rebel army, for which they fought and died at the battles of New Ross and Vinegar Hill. Two accounts of Devereaux's immediate fate exist: One claims he was hidden by a Carmelite priest until an amnesty enabled him to emigrate to America at the end of 1799; another reports his arrest and sentence to execution, which was reduced to banishment because he had spoken on behalf of loyalist prisoners during the insurrection.[255]

Disaster in Ulster

Both Grey and Devereaux were very young men, too young to have played any significant part in the years of struggle leading up to the rebellion. The same can be said of a large number of Ulster exiles, many of whom were only just embarking on adulthood when they were thrust into the spotlight in June 1798. They were the victims of the United Irishmen's escalator policy of filling vacant positions with the next in seniority. The arrests and the flight of so many experienced leaders in 1797 in Antrim and Down partly explain their promotion.[256] But also of significance was the irresolution, even cowardice, of some of the more mature leaders of Antrim and Down in the crisis of 1798. It was not just that the two core positions of adjutants general were vacant in June 1798—Steel Dickson of Down was arrested just hours before the insurrection and Robert Simms of Antrim "retired" at about the same time—but there had been an air of defeatism and languor among the leaders in east Ulster for many months previously.[257] A spell in prison had dampened the ardor of many Ulstermen. Although most had been released by early 1798, they were reluctant to take further risks. They "will not go to any public meetings from fear, but are very anxious to get the reports and hear the news."[258] According to Samuel Turner, except for Robert Simms (who had lost his nerve), the only leaders of talent had fled abroad. "He said he hardly knew who to look upon as leaders." Not that it perhaps mattered: "we had no one to obey us."[259]

With fickle and apprehensive leadership at the top, preparations for insurrection failed to occur. At a meeting of the Ulster Provincial committee in Armagh on 29 May, called to determine the province's position now that news of the insurrection in the South had been received, THOMAS BASHFORD, JR., a Belfast shopkeeper, angrily denounced the Ulster Executive for having refused to prepare for rebellion, even though delegates returning from the South had brought with them plans for a coordinated rising. "He thought they completely betrayed the People both of Leinster and Ulster, and he thought it the duty of the present Committee to denounce and vote them out of office, and to take some speedy and vigorous measures to second the efforts of the People in the Upper Provinces."[260] Meetings of colonels at the county level in the next few days showed that opinions remained divided. In Down, the colonels, including the young Presbyterian licentiate and schoolmaster JOHN MILES, REV. JAMES TOWNSEND, minister of Greyabbey, and DAVID SHAW, a merchant of Saintfield, agreed to rise, but in Antrim, only two of the twenty-three colonels assembled on 1 June were so enthusiastic.[261]

It was a recipe for disaster, which unfolded relentlessly in the next few weeks. The rebellion in east Ulster was too late, too tepid, and too unorganized. Among the young enthusiasts, disillusionment was swift. When the Down licentiate and schoolmaster Colonel WILLIAM FOX heard that Henry McCracken was advancing on Antrim at the head of a rebel army, he climbed Scrabo Hill, near Newtownards, expecting to find his regiment awaiting his orders. The hill was deserted. Looking down on the bustle in the barracks below, he realized that the element of surprise had been lost. The next day, learning that Saintfield was "up," he urged his horse toward Bangor and Donaghadee, raising the country as he went. That night he led a section of the 300-strong rebel army to attack the town of Newtownards, but his force fled when they blundered into another rebel column in the dark. By the time they had regrouped, the garrison had evacuated the town. Thereafter, his little army was reluctant to move. "I was torn by a thousand vexations," he later wrote from America, "which no person but one who may have been in my situation can understand or feel—however, after much flattery, I got them to begin to march off by companies and it was 11 o'clock [P.M.] before the rere [*sic*] marched off the hill" (into oblivion at the battle of Ballynahinch).[262]

Not the least difficult problem for the colonels to resolve was overcoming their rank and file's growing uncertainty as to why they were rebelling. The news from the south mixed accounts of rebel successes with reports of Catholic peasants massacring Protestants, hardly music to the ears of the mainly Presbyterian Ulster rebels.[263] The young officers had to urge them on, risking their lives in the process. Indeed, the brilliant young County Down tutor in mathematics and languages, ROBERT ADRAIN, was stabbed in the back by his own disaffected troops and left for dead, even before the British army had been sighted.[264]

Unlike in parts of Wexford, where Catholic priests could inspire the peasants, in Ulster there was no charismatic leadership around which the rebels
could muster. On "Pike Sunday," at Creevy Rocks overlooking Saintfield,
Thomas Ledlie Birch did his best, preaching to the "army" a frenzied, millenarian sermon from Ezekiel: "Let every man come forth, a slaying weapon in
his hand."[265] But the military leaders were uninspiring: Henry McCracken in
Antrim was widely respected, but imprisonment had reduced his prowess;
James Dickey, a Ballymena attorney, was mad and full of bloodlust; and
Henry Monro, commander in Down, was a Scottish Protestant who had never
been part of the United Irishmen's military organization. How, then, could
someone like RICHARD CALDWELL, age eighteen, and only a few months out
of Trinity College, Dublin (he had withdrawn when the student body was interrogated for signs of sedition), hope to be successful when placed "at the
head of a considerable number of undisciplined and but very partially armed
men, in fact an almost ungovernable mass, whose character may be appreciated from the very circumstance of choosing a young lad of Richard's age to
command them"?[266] The simple fact was that they could not. It was a disappointing and disillusioning set of circumstances that set them on the road to
America.

FOUR

Into Exile

MOTIVES FOR EXILE

In certain circumstances, the act of emigration may be interpreted as a political statement that challenges and repudiates the authority of the state from which one voluntarily secedes. Although they failed to see emigration in this political light, late eighteenth-century British government sources were nevertheless worried by the practice, for mercantilist theory interpreted this leakage, unless channeled into selected parts of the empire, as a loss of valuable manpower and skills that might strengthen rival states.[1] Radical enthusiasts of Enlightenment ideas, however, vigorously asserted the ideal of the right of unfettered expatriation.[2] They rejected the doctrine that a state could claim inalienable loyalty from those born within its borders in favor of the ideals of personal freedom, a qualified duty to the nation, and universal fraternity. This vision, in Anglophone countries, was most closely associated with Thomas Paine, the quintessential "citizen of the world," who was to be only one of many unfortunate revolutionaries to discover that promoting the libertarian values of universalism did not preclude imprisonment or the prospect of the guillotine in a foreign revolutionary state.[3]

Most of the radicals who went to the United States in the 1790s would have agreed in principle with Paine's internationalism,[4] but, as we shall see, their theoretical position was to come into conflict with an awareness that the emigration of radicals weakened not only the state, but also the indigenous radical movement itself. Nor was their withdrawal overseas determined by these idealized values. With varying degrees of reluctance most were impelled into exile by the authorities; expatriation signified their political defeat rather than an affirmation of free choice. In exploring their motives for emigrating—to the extent that they had a choice—the radicals can be usefully, if sometimes loosely, divided into five main types: the recalcitrant; the routed; the intimidated; the compounding; and the perfidious.

The Recalcitrant

The recalcitrant refugees were those who went into exile with the expectation of returning at some point to continue the struggle. Undoubtedly battered in confidence and pride, they nevertheless were not prepared to accept defeat, seeing expatriation as a tactical withdrawal. Although most radicals probably rationalized their predicament, convincing themselves that their exile would be shortlived, only a few fled their countries with the deliberate intention of returning to fight again. Rowan, Tandy, and Reynolds, the Dublin United Irish leaders who escaped in 1793–94, initially hoped that if William Jackson, the French spy whose activities had implicated them in treason, was exonerated at his trial, they might be able to return home.[5] Their hopes were dashed by his conviction, although Tandy did return from America to France to continue his plotting.

So too did Wolfe Tone, the best known example of a radical going to America with the express intention of swiftly recrossing the Atlantic to France. In his journal for May 1795, the month before he sailed to America, Tone recorded a ramble with some of the northern United Irish leaders, during which, at McArt's fort high in the hills around Belfast, they "took a solemn obligation, which I think I may say I have, on my part, endeavoured to fulfil, never in our efforts to desist, until we had subverted the authority of England over our country, and asserted her independence."[6] Like Rowan and Reynolds, Tone had been implicated in the Jackson affair. Although an official from London informed the ascendancy politician John Claudius Beresford that, following Rowan's escape, "Tone was the next guilty person, and ought to be hanged," an accommodation was reached whereby Tone was not prosecuted so long as he voluntarily went into exile in America.[7] Tone intended to keep his bargain but, as he told his compliant friends in Belfast, he believed his obligations would be fulfilled once he landed in America. With his conscience clear, he could return to Europe as soon as he wished.[8] This he was to do, but, like his nemesis Jackson, he was destined to die by his own hand during his trial for treason in 1798.

Tone was by no means the only Irishman in the 1790s to use France as a base for continuing the fight against English rule in Ireland. By and large, the most committed Irish revolutionaries congregated in Paris, hoping to persuade the French to invade their homeland. Although thwarted in their ambitions in 1796 and 1798, regular contact was kept with Ireland. Taking advantage of the lax intelligence services in Dublin after the Union of 1800, United Irishmen acting as French agents crossed to Ireland to build up support for a new insurrection. Among these was John Swiney, who returned to Ireland several times in 1802–3. Unfortunately, Robert Emmet's rebellion was a fiasco, and disputes within the exiled Irish community in France destroyed their unity. In the battle for political supremacy between Thomas Addis Emmet and Arthur O'Connor, Swiney sided with the former, to the extent of killing Thomas Corbet, an O'Connor supporter, in a duel. Eventually, disillusioned with Bonaparte's regime, and no longer hopeful of a successful insurrection in Ireland, Swiney and many other supporters of Emmet emigrated to the United States in 1805.[9]

Not only Irishmen were recalcitrant. Certainly the most bizarre example of a radical fleeing his country but temporarily continuing his antigovernment activities was the Scot James Tytler. According to his biographer, Tytler fled from Edinburgh in January 1793 to Belfast, "where he had no friends and no influence." During his two-year sojourn in Ulster, before sailing across the Atlantic, he published two pamphlets. One, a critique of Paine's *Age of Reason*, Fergusson speculates was written "to rehabilitate himself in the eyes of the orthodox."[10] In reality Tytler, having assumed the name Donaldson, swiftly became immersed in the radical politics of Belfast. According to the spy Bird/Smith, in 1793 "the committee of Belfast" decided to use Tytler to foment rebellion in Scotland. Having learned Gaelic, the destitute Scotsman was expected to move from town to town, dressed as a Highland piper, organizing a general insurrection. He was then to travel to Cork and finally to Paris—presumably without his bagpipes—where he was to solicit French aid for Ireland. Apparently, this tartan-clad pied piper had got as far as Donaghadee, on the Ulster coast, before the Belfast committee lost its nerve and recalled him.[11]

This story may not be so far-fetched and sanguine as it seems. Tytler's close friend in Belfast radical circles was William Putnam McCabe, the swashbuckling United Irish emissary who gained notoriety in the 1790s for his talents as an impersonator and, in a wide range of disguises, for repeatedly avoiding arrest on his missions through Ireland. McCabe's recklessness can be discerned in the plan to use Tytler in Scotland, and suggests that this harebrained plot was organized without official sanction. Certainly, the cancellation of the project caused dissension in the United Irish ranks and led to Tytler's ostracism. The radicals so neglected him that "He used to damn the Clubs altogether." By the time he emigrated to America in 1795 his political principles had changed dramatically, which helps to explain his pamphlet against Paine and a satirical attack on "the Belfast Jacobins" that he published in Boston. It also explains why, living in wretched poverty in Salem, Massachusetts, Tytler was one of the very few radical exiles to reject his past politics, favoring the Federalists rather than the Jeffersonians.[12]

The Routed

More numerous than the recalcitrant exiles were the routed, whose journey into exile normally occurred at very short notice, after defeat in battle or in response to the threat of arrest for treasonable activities that included preparations for violent upheaval. Examples of the latter are to be found scattered throughout Madden's list of United Irishmen proclaimed under the Fugitive Act of 1798. Of the fifty-one men he enumerated, at least eleven found their way to the United States.[13] The discovery of pikes and other caches of weapons was often the cause of headlong flight to escape justice. We have already seen that the discovery of "pikes, spears and other iron and steel weapons" in Robert Watt's Edinburgh house in 1794 led to the flight of some plotters, including the young Unitarian English student John Edmonds Stock, who by good fortune was on a mission to London when Watt was arrested. Alerted, he was able to sail to Philadelphia.[14] James Kennedy escaped into the heather surrounding Edinburgh, where he pined for his wife and son—patriotically named Citizen—and wrote antigovernment verse before finding a berth on an American-bound ship.[15]

Stock was up to his neck in Watt's conspiracy; Kennedy was probably only on the fringes. Both, however, given the ruthlessness of the law's application in Scotland, acted sensibly in escaping as soon as possible. In Sheffield also, the existence of pikes—the weapon of citizens ("Pikes began the revolution, pikes will finish it," wrote Brissot the Girondin)[16]—led to the rapid expatriation of two radicals, Joseph Gales and RICHARD DAVISON. When the London authorities raided Thomas Hardy's house in May 1794, they found a letter, on notepaper headed with Joseph Gales's business address, which began: "Fellow Citizens: The Barefaced aristocracy of the present administration has made it necessary that we must be prepared to act on the defensive against any attack they may command their newly armed minions to make upon us. A plan has been hit upon, and, if encouraged sufficiently, will, no doubt, have the effect of furnishing a quantity of pikes to the Patriots, great enough to make them formidable."[17]

Gales's denial of all knowledge of this letter was possibly genuine, but his implied ignorance of pike-making in Sheffield was not. According to one witness at Horne Tooke's trial, the fiery Sheffield radical Henry Redhead Yorke had told him in April 1794 that Gales would buy a dozen pike staffs, the metal heads for which would be obtained by Gales's journeyman, Richard Davison. The witness, a turner named Widdison, made the pike handles as requested. However, he claimed that Gales wanted the weapons "for his own defence. I believe they were never intended for any other purpose [than self-defense]; I remember, in particular, that Gales's house had been attacked once or more, by a great number of people, when some particular news was come to town; they swore vengeance against him, on account of his paper, and several of his friends were then obliged to defend his house—several were solicited to come on that account. And that was what I understood they wanted those arms for."[18] Whatever Gales's role was in this episode by which he was fatally compromised and forced into exile, he held no grudge against Davison, the only other possible author of the letter found at Hardy's. When they met again in Philadelphia Gales reemployed him, later helping him to establish his own newspaper in Warrenton, North Carolina.[19]

Stock, Kennedy, Gales, and Davison were lucky; they had some intimation of government intentions that enabled them to flee before arrest. Gales even had time, before departing, to write a final editorial for his newspaper, in which he justified his actions and asserted his reformist, rather than revolutionary intentions.[20] Less fortunate were those who fought in the Irish rebellion of 1798; vanquished in battle, they had little option but to flee precipitately, frequently only a few frenzied paces in front of their vengeful pursuers. Some followed what seems to have been a particular Irish tradition of dressing in women's clothes to escape detection. Not only did Mathew Carey thwart his hunters in that manner in 1784, but so too did John Burk eleven years later. So grateful was he to a Miss Daly for the loan of her petticoats, which enabled him to pass unrecognized through lines of troops who had surrounded him in a Dublin bookshop, that he subsequently also appropriated her name.[21] Legend has it that REV. JOHN GLENDY, minister at Maghera, a United Irish colonel in 1798 and later chaplain to the U.S. Senate, escaped to America in women's clothes.[22] Others, however, were less successful in hiding their masculinity. Female attire helped William Sampson escape in 1798 with his servant-cum-chaperon from Ireland to Whitehaven in Cumberland, but he was arrested soon after; his shaving had aroused suspicions![23] George Birch, nephew of Rev. Thomas Ledlie Birch and a participant with his brother at the battle of Saintfield, was arrested in bed wearing a nightdress, with his distraught mother claiming him to be her nonexistent daughter.[24]

Some of those who retained their breeches also failed to avoid their pursuers, were imprisoned, but thereafter managed to escape. The Belfast printer Thomas Storey, whose brother John was executed after the battle of Ballynahinch, was captured and taken to Belfast, but he managed to break out of prison before trial.[25] Thomas Kane had similar experiences. Formerly a clerk in the office of the *Northern Star*, he had acted as aide-de-camp to General Monro at the battle of Ballynahinch. After two days on the run, he was betrayed on a farm near Ednavady and taken to Belfast. There he managed to jump from a third-story window of the provost prison, successfully eluded the guard, and eventually reached America.[26]

Many hundreds of rebels spent weeks as fugitives, desperately seeking help to escape. ARTHUR KENNEDY, a young man who fought at the battle of Antrim, successfully eluded capture by hiding for three weeks in his uncle's coal hole in Belfast.[27] Others made their circuitous way to ports and tried to board American-bound vessels without detection. When John Caldwell made his first abortive attempt to emigrate in October 1798, the vessel, the American-owned barque *Pallas*, was forced into Larne by bad weather. This caused great consternation among the passengers, for many of them were proclaimed fugitives who had only broken cover once the ship had sailed. Theirs was a fraught passage to safety; although they were never betrayed, they also had to go back into hiding several weeks later, when storms forced the ship into Cork harbor for major repairs.[28]

Others were less fortunate. JAMES HUNTER, a farmer from Glenarm, County Antrim, managed to escape through his burning house when on the point of being hanged as a rebel. With another fugitive he made his way to Ballygally Bay, where the local Presbyterian ministers were trying to arrange a boat to take them to Scotland when they were arrested.[29] John Cormick, the feather merchant, in whose house Lord Edward Fitzgerald concealed himself for some weeks, hid in Dublin for a week before successfully escaping to London. Dressed as a sailor, he stayed there a fortnight until, fearing that he had been recognized, he fled to Guernsey under the name of Coppinger, where he was discovered and arrested.[30]

Betrayal by those among whom the fugitives were hiding was by no means uncommon in the immediate aftermath of the rebellion. It must have tasted particularly bitter to rebels who had risked their lives for a united Ireland. Cormick was recognized and apprehended by an Irish soldier in Guernsey. Richard Caldwell, only eighteen when he left the family home at Harmony Hill in the spring of 1798 to become a general at the battle of Ballymena, escaped with two or three others to Scotland. Known to have been a rebel, he was nevertheless assisted with his plans to escape to America. Unfortunately, he became complacent, attending a dance where he was betrayed by a local clergyman, sent back to Coleraine, and sentenced to death by a court martial, a punishment later reduced to exile in America by Lord Cornwallis.[31]

According to his brother, Richard Caldwell's sentence was commuted only after the rest of his family—against whom not enough evidence of treason existed to expect guilty verdicts at trial—agreed to expatriate themselves. A less official and far more unsavory form of blackmail was used on PAUL DOUGLAS, a Parkgate, County Antrim, farmer. Douglas was an old hearts of steel man, who in the past had not shunned the use of blackmail and intimidation himself when defending neighboring farmers from dispossession. After the battle of Ballynahinch he had escaped, killing two dragoons in the process. According to local report, a Major Siddons proposed to Mrs. Douglas that if she slept with him, he would gain permission for her husband to return to the family farm. The suggestion was accepted, Douglas was allowed home, but both husband and wife immediately sold up and emigrated to America.[32]

The Intimidated

The routed were men who either contemplated or actually took up arms in the 1790s; hanging or life terms served in Botany Bay or the army for treason were their only alternatives to expatriation. The intimidated emigrated to America because of their inability to withstand the social, economic, and political pressures placed on them by community and state disapproval of their "sedition" and Francophilia, or because imprisonment had worn down their resilience. In Scotland, as we have seen, several members of the professions succumbed to public ostracism in 1794–95, but in England, Wales, and Ireland the individually rejected were outnumbered by groups who collectively decided at about the same time to cut their losses and emigrate. In Wales, whole congregations of dissenters, some inspired by the myth of a Jacobin Madoc, took a well-worn path to America.[33] In England, of course, the Radical Dissenting diaspora represented a communal answer to loyalist intimidation. The key to this decision was Joseph Priestley, who for many months after the riots in Birmingham was reluctant to contemplate emigration. William Russell, his *fidus Achates*, had determined to leave by mid-1792, but Priestley only began to contemplate the inevitable in April 1793.[34] In June, preparatory to leaving, he sent one of his three sons, with Cooper, to America to scout for a suitable settlement. His reasons for emigration he explained to a correspondent in Savannah, Georgia:

> I cannot give you an idea of the violence with which every friend to liberty is prosecuted in this country. Little of the liberty of the press on political subjects is now left, and the country goes heartily with the court into all their measures, so that nothing but general calamity, which I fear is approaching, will open their eyes. The source of all this evil is want of knowledge in the lower, and some, not of the lower, orders of the people. The French are wisely providing against this evil by a system of public instruction. Here, even Sunday-schools begin to be reprobated, as making the common people too knowing.[35]

Priestley's hopes of educating the people into right principles had been shattered. His own situation, although not hazardous, had become "unpleasant, so that I thought my removal would be of more service to the cause of truth than my longer stay in England."[36] With that decision made, he found himself at the head of a large band of followers, determined to follow his example.

In Ireland the troubles also led another small group of religious dissenters, the Covenanters, to emigrate. Presbyterianism in the eighteenth century was notorious for its tendency to fissure, evidence perhaps of its roots in the reformed theology of the sixteenth century, which stressed both the primacy of the individual conscience and the ideal of the covenant. Divisions within Irish Presbyterianism in the eighteenth century, however, in large part were generated from outside, most particularly from Scotland, for the Irish church remained "in practice an autonomous branch of the Church of Scotland," with many of its ministers being Scottish by birth and most being trained at Glasgow University.[37] The presence of Burgher, Anti-Burgher, and Covenanting connections in Ulster, for instance, was the consequence of developments within Scottish Presbyterianism. The Burghers and Anti-Burghers, at first united as the Seceding Church, emerged in 1737 following theological disagreements in the Church of Scotland over the emphasis to be given to the Calvinist doctrine of justification by faith alone and the continued significance of the 1638 National Covenant and 1643 Solemn League and Covenant. When further disputes arose over the rights of congregations or patrons to choose their ministers, the seceders broke away, only themselves to split into two separate sects over the legitimacy of taking the "burgess" oath in Scotland. Ministers from both the ensuing connections soon began to settle in Ulster; the first Burgher synod was formed in Ireland in 1779, the first Anti-Burgher synod in 1788.[38]

Underlying the apparently abstruse nature of these disputes lurked an important issue: Would Presbyterianism remain faithful to its original principles, or would it evolve, via Arianism and Socinianism, into an Arminian and liberal unitarianism, influenced by the Enlightenment? The seceders withdrew because they believed that the Church of Scotland, with the growing influence of the "enlightened" Arian faction (the moderates), was rejecting its past and shedding its Calvinism. There were some Presbyterians, however, known variously as Covenanters, Cameronians, Mountain Men, or Reformed Presbyterians, who had preempted the seceders and had refused to join the Church of Scotland when it was formally anointed as the established church in 1689. A small and persecuted sect, especially during the "Killing Times" in the 1680s, the Covenanters remained strictly faithful to the principles of their Calvinist forebears, who had refused to accept the church settlement imposed on Scotland after the restoration of Charles II. For them, even more so than for the seceders, the National Covenant and the Solemn League and Covenant remained living documents. As the latter called for the destruction of popery and prelacy, the Covenanters were both anti-Catholic and hostile to established episcopal churches. More importantly, they refused to give allegiance to a monarch who was not covenanted and a polity that did not explicitly recog-

nize that all worldly authority derived ultimately from God. They thus refused to make oaths of allegiance, a position that in troubled times left them
open to accusations of disloyalty. In Ireland, after one false start, a Reformed
Presbytery, serving about seven scattered congregations but focused on
County Antrim and County Londonderry, was first permanently organized in
1792.[39]

In Covenanter theology all politics was profane, unless one was striving to
establish a covenanted state. But in times of excitement it was difficult to remain aloof. Rev. William Staveley's active membership of the Volunteers in
1792, as captain of the Drumbracken Company and secretary at a meeting
that resolved on the citizen's right to bear arms, was not an isolated example
of political involvement supposedly in contravention of Covenanting ideas.[40]
Covenanting theology was at root republican ("republicans by religion and
descent," Thomas Addis Emmet called its adherents),[41] antiauthoritarian, and
heavily impregnated with the doctrines of millenarianism. Although unable
to join uncovenanted oath-bound societies such as the United Irishmen or the
Defenders, the Covenanters were not prevented from preaching the rights of
man as well as the rights of God. By so doing, they brought themselves to the
attention of a government determined to silence all threats to the status quo.

REV. JAMES McKINNEY (1759–1802), pastor of the small congregation of
Dervock in County Antrim, was the first to suffer. In 1792, on behalf of the
Reformed Presbytery, he published a sermon entitled "Causes of Fasting," in
which in apocalyptic terms he proclaimed that "the signs of the times call
upon all who have any interest to employ it with God that he would hasten the
downfall of Popery, Prelacy, Judaism, together with Mahometan delusion."
He proceeded to regret that those striving "for the abolition of tyranny and
oppression from the whole earth, and especially from the lands of our nativity,
that have long groaned under the unrelenting jaws of cruel despots," had
failed to realize "that God's covenant interest in his Son and his Church is the
surest pledge the world has for overturning oppression and the introduction
of universal liberty."[42]

As this suggests, Covenanting politico-theology was ambiguous in its
seemingly uncompromising stance; if the government could take no comfort
from it, the radicals too did not avoid criticism. On balance, however, the
United Irishmen had greater cause for optimism. Knowing that the Covenanters had influence among the poor farmers and weavers, it was potentially
profitable to gain their allegiance, although they could not work on McKinney,
who in 1793 fled to America under two indictments for publishing sedition.[43]
As we have seen, the Belfast United Irishmen played the millenarian card for
all it was worth.

From 1796, as the revolutionary United Irishmen sought links with the disaffected in the countryside of the North, the Covenanters' passions were stirred up by three itinerant field preachers, William Staveley, WILLIAM GIBSON (1753–1838), and Joseph Orr. Gibson drew thousands to hear his fiery six-hour sermons. A graduate of the universities of Glasgow and Edinburgh, he had become pastor of the Kellswater, County Antrim, congregation in 1787, beginning his itinerant campaign in April 1796.[44] His flamboyant oratory appealed strongly to the emotions and prejudices of his audience, but also showed the ambiguity of antediluvian Covenanting theology as a revolutionary doctrine in an era when the United Irishmen were trying to neutralize sectarian tensions. According to Samuel McSkimin, the Ulster antiquarian, Gibson, "on entering upon his mission . . . at times so forgot himself as to relapse for a moment into his holy hatred of popery, by introducing the antiquated dogmas of his sect, in allusions to the men of sin, and even [to] an old jade dressed in scarlet, dyed with the blood of the saints, said to reside near Babylon. These untimely slips of his reverence were overlooked by his hearers with a truly Christian forbearance, for which kindness he was afterwards sure to make amends by pointing out the immediate destruction of the British monarchy."[45]

Gibson's favorite text was the eighteenth chapter of Revelations (foretelling the fall of Babylon); Staveley's sermons too were strongly millennial, representing the contemporary period as the sixth vial, during which time the Battle of Armageddon was to occur, with the Jews and Gentiles flocking into the Christian church. But even the Reformed Presbytery became alarmed when he published his sermon, *An Appeal to Light,* in which, although it was meant to be a critique of Paine's *Age of Reason,* he wrote: "Was my arm long enough, I would stretch it over to the Gallic shore and take you by the hand as a friend of the liberties of men and a pointed opposer of despots."[46] In October 1796 the Presbytery issued a disclaimer, declaring that "We hold in the highest abhorrence and detestation, all tumultuous and disorderly meetings; and we utterly disclaim all connection with such, whether publicly or privately held, where anything is said or done that is prejudicial to the peace, the safety, or property of any individual or society."[47]

But it came too late. According to Emmet, thanks to the persuasive skills of the United Irishmen: "Men who had previously been separated by sectarial abhorrence, were now joined together in cordial, and almost incredible amity."[48] This was probably an exaggeration, but the field preachers continued their work until they were forcibly stopped during the pacification of Ulster in 1797. Staveley was imprisoned for a month in June (he and Orr were also arrested during the rebellion a year later),[49] and Gibson went into hiding. Linking up with four Covenanter theology students, JOHN BLACK, SAMUEL BROWN WYLIE, Thomas McAdam, and JOHN REILLY, who were also under suspicion for their activities, Gibson sought relief by sailing to America.[50] A considerable part of the next generation of Covenanting leaders went with him.

The Compounding

One feature common to all the radicals in the 1790s was their belief in progress. Many of those who continued to view the world through theological spectacles defined progress within a millenarian framework. This perhaps best explains why prominent members of two such theologically different sects, the Unitarians and Covenanters—the former Arminian and rational, the latter strictly Calvinist and Bible fundamentalist, but both millenarian—exiled themselves. Persistent intimidation undermined their faith in the future; perhaps they could renew their expectations in the New World? For the Compounders, the desire to emigrate was less easily accomplished, for they comprised many of the Irish who were imprisoned in 1798 and who desperately had to bargain for their lives. To understand why so many rebel prisoners were exiled to America, it is necessary to examine in some detail British and Irish government policy toward their opponents in the months before and after the rebellion of 1798.

By October 1798 the Irish government had several thousand rebel prisoners on their hands, partly the result of a very successful intelligence operation before the rebellion broke out, and partly as a consequence of the compassionate and practical policy of the new lord lieutenant, Cornwallis. The arrests of the Leinster directory and others in March 1798, and the subsequent roundup of United Irish leaders in Ulster in June, had left the government with nearly 150 important prisoners in custody, most of whom could only be convicted of treason and rebellion if various spies and informers were prepared to give evidence in open court. Moreover, when Cornwallis first arrived in Dublin to replace Camden he had been sickened by the apparently revenge-driven slaughter being carried out by ill-disciplined units of the yeomanry. It was essential, he informed the duke of Portland, to "soften the ferocity of our troops."[51] He immediately ordered a general pardon for all rank and file rebels who surrendered their weapons and took the oath of allegiance.[52] He intended to exempt "only those who have been guilty of cool and deliberate murder, and to leave the leaders liable to banishment for such terms as the safety of the state may require, to be extended in some cases to banishment for life."[53] By the end of July thousands of rebels had taken advantage of the pardon, while "most of the leaders have either been seized and executed, or have availed themselves of the Clemency of Government and surrendered on condition of Banishment."[54]

At the same time, orders had been given to bring courts-martial more under the control of the higher military in the field.[55] Cornwallis extended this by insisting that he review all court-martial verdicts before their implementation. Not only did he reduce the numbers condemned to death between July and December 1798 by one third (from 380 to 258), but he also more than trebled, from eighteen to fifty-six, the number to suffer banishment rather than transportation or general service (service in the "condemned regiments" in the West Indies).[56]

Cornwallis's policy of leniency was, however, more favorable to the Ulster rebels than to those from the rest of the country. For example, all but three of the thirty-eight rebels who had their sentences reduced to banishment overseas came from the northern province. A high proportion of these were Presbyterian ministers or licentiates. One can only speculate why this should have been the case. Certainly, the authorities were reluctant to punish to the limit rebel clergymen of all denominations, and there were more Presbyterians in prison than Catholics. Some Catholic rebel priests who had led the insurrection in the South had been summarily executed, and three Presbyterian clergymen and licentiates suffered the same fate in Ulster, but from July 1798 Cornwallis was just as willing to reduce the sentences of Catholic clergy whose cases he reviewed as he was those of their Presbyterian counterparts. For example, three Dominican priests, Fathers JAMES BUSHE, BARTHOLOMEW MACMAHON, and MICHAEL MULHALL, from the Denmark Street seminary in Dublin, were permitted to expatriate themselves, although their activities in the United Irishmen had been known for more than a year.[57]

On the evidence available, perhaps four reasons can be given for the seemingly preferential treatment afforded to Ulster rebels in general, and Presbyterian clergymen in particular. First is the more widespread nature and extreme ferocity of the rebellion in the South. More lives were lost, more property destroyed in the South; consequently, larger numbers of prisoners were charged with the most heinous crimes. Second, as we have seen, in Ulster the leaders of the various rebel "armies" tended to be very young men, many licentiates or schoolteachers, who were drafted into senior military roles only at the last minute, when their elders either had been arrested or had withdrawn. The Presbyterian licentiates WILLIAM ADAIR, a commander at the battle of Saintfield, William Fox, an officer at Newtownards, James Townsend, second in command at the battle of Ballynahinch, and John Miles, a Down colonel, were all in their twenties, as were JAMES SCOTT, commander of the Bangor rebels, and schoolmaster JOHN ALEXANDER, another rebel commander.[58] In theory, as rebel military officers and members of United Irish county and baronial committees, they were all liable to the death penalty. But, virtually forced into positions of authority both by their youthful enthusiasm and by the pusillanimity of many of their elders, the authorities regarded them as suitable subjects for mercy, although too dangerous to be allowed to remain in the country.

The third reason for the disparity of treatment between Ulster and the South lies in the consideration the Castle authorities gave to the recommendations on behalf of individual rebels from family, friends, and influential members of the local community. Pleas on behalf of rebels from the South were by no means ignored; a wealthy Catholic brewer from Carlow named McDonnell, who had helped the United Irishmen financially, was saved by the intercession of local poor Protestants, and John Joseph McDonnel, a prominent Catholic appointed general in County Mayo by Humbert, commander of the French invasion force, had his sentence remitted to banishment at the instigation of future Prime Minister George Canning, even though Denis Browne—a Mayo MP and brother of Lord Altamont—and the provincial gentry vigorously sought his execution.[59] But, as these two examples suggest, successful pleas were likely to be heard on behalf of Catholics only if the appeal came from Protestants. The Catholic gentry themselves were tainted with rebellion; their voices were rarely acknowledged by the government in 1798.

In addition, the influence of Chief Secretary Castlereagh, himself reared as a Presbyterian, may perhaps be seen working behind the scenes on behalf of his fellow Ulstermen. He knew many of the Presbyterian ministers, and was personally able to value the weight of influence that each prisoner could bring to his cause. He certainly gave his full support to Cornwallis's moderate policy. There was, however, a limit to Castlereagh's sympathy: Rebel ministers who had deliberately fooled the authorities with pious but false attempts to show loyalty before the rebellion were given short shrift. Rev. William Sinclair, for example, assisted Castlereagh and his father in administering the oath of allegiance to 300 of the latter's tenants in November 1796. A dinner was then given to the tenants in Newtownards market house. "We had a jolly dinner," Castlereagh reported. "Cleland quite drunk, Sinclair considerably so, my father not a little, others lying heads and points, the whole very happy, and God Save the King and Rule Britannia declared permanent."[60] In July 1798 Sinclair was found guilty of treason and rebellion. Sentenced to banishment overseas, he attempted in vain to persuade Castlereagh to allow him to remain in Ireland by producing a certificate signed by many of rank and distinction in his neighborhood, including Rev. Henry Montgomery, the

Episcopal clergyman of Rosemount, and the lieutenant-colonel of the York Fencibles.[61] Biting the hand that (literally) feeds you was not a sensible way to gain government sympathy.

One key, then, to the number of Ulster rebels, and particularly of Presbyterian clergymen, who were exiled to America was their access to influence. Richard Caldwell received the "powerful interest and incessant exertion" of lords Belmore and Enniskillen, "the good and humane" Henry Alexander, MP for Londonderry, and Joseph Wilson, the American consul.[62] The millenarian minister of Saintfield, Thomas Ledlie Birch, was saved by his brother Dr. George Birch, a loyalist in the yeomanry in 1798 and a friend of Castlereagh and Lord Londonderry. In April 1798 Birch had been elected chaplain of the United Irish forces in County Down. On 9 June he was present at the battle of Saintfield. The following day, "Pike Sunday," he preached to the rebels at Creevy Rocks, exhorting them: "We have grasped the pike and musket and fight for the right against might: to drive the bloodhounds of King George the German king beyond the seas. This is Ireland, we are Irish and we shall be free."[63] Much to the chagrin of the troops, "who were very near going out and hanging him themselves," Birch was acquitted owing to insufficiently strong evidence when he faced a court-martial a week later. The waters were muddied by witnesses swearing the defendant had been elsewhere during the rebellion and by the prosecution's failure to present evidence of the Pike Sunday sermon. Dr. George Birch's pleas had been heard. A deal was reached during the trial, for just as the verdict was about to be pronounced, Thomas Ledlie informed the court that, although he was innocent, he was prepared to exile himself to America.[64]

The Caldwells and Birch were from prominent Presbyterian families, and could expect to be able to appeal to people of influence in the local community, but such good fortune also appeared further down the social scale. WILLIAM GREER, of Wellbrook, County Tyrone, for instance, was arrested in June 1798 for breaking curfew by attending an illegal meeting, and for uttering seditious words, viz. "Down with the Orange and up with the Green and to Hell with any one who Dare Say against the Roman Catholics Getting what they Want." In the atmosphere of the time, such (probably drunken) statements in Ulster would usually have led courts-martial to sentence the offender to Botany Bay or the condemned regiments in the West Indies, and Greer's position became particularly vulnerable when evidence was given that in 1796 he had been administering illegal oaths. At this point his "wealthy and respectable relations" intervened, and with the support of other prominent county gentlemen bail was obtained, on condition Greer transported himself to America for seven years.[65]

The fourth possible reason for government policy favoring Ulster rebels was the uncertainty of evidence against many of them, with a sympathetic Cornwallis being prepared to give them the benefit of the doubt. He and Castlereagh had to be careful, however, for ascendancy politicians and Orangemen were fiercely hostile to the policy of leniency.[66] This probably partly explains why three Presbyterian clergymen were executed (Rev. James Porter of Greyabbey, and licentiates Robert Gowdie of Bangor, and Archibald Warwick of Kircubbin). Their deaths could be used to show ascendancy militants that suitable government vengeance was being applied in the North as well as in the South.

In the meantime, other Ulstermen were benefiting from the government's scrupulousness. The licentiate CHARLES WALLACE, found guilty of treasonable practices, which included leading armed men through the countryside on the outbreak of the rebellion in Maghera, had his sentence remitted from 800 lashes and transportation for life, although not before he was stripped for punishment opposite his chapel in Tobermore.[67] DAVID BAILIE WARDEN was a young probationer minister (of the New Light persuasion), who had been closely watched by the authorities since his return from Glasgow University in 1797. Suspected of writing for the United Irishmen, and notorious for inflammatory sermons, he was commissioned colonel in the rebel forces and was aide-de-camp to Monro at Antrim. Evidence of his involvement in the uprising was not conclusive, but hearing that his neighbors in Killinchy were prepared to give him up to prevent the village being burned, he surrendered to the authorities. Sentenced to life transportation for treason and seditious practices at Downpatrick in July 1798, he was eventually allowed to sail for America.[68] Even long-term United Irish officers such as REV. ROBERT STEELE of Dungiven and REV. JAMES SIMPSON could escape from a court-martial verdict of execution or life transportation.[69]

Not all rebels benefited only from government lenity; the absence of evidence to ensure conviction was sometimes more than fortuitous. When the Ulsterman John Caldwell was arrested in Dublin in May 1798, he was allowed to breakfast with the sheriff's men before being taken into custody. At the table, he felt confident that his luggage contained no incriminating evidence, but he was disconcerted to discover a list of names—purportedly of participants in a United Irish lottery—in his pocket. Fortunately, the lady of the house distracted the guards sufficiently to allow him to throw the paper on the fire undetected. Or so he thought. Later he was asked by Major Swan, Deputy Town-Major of Dublin, not to mention the paper in interrogation, as he would be disciplined for failing to search the prisoner.[70]

At least Caldwell had a fire nearby to dispose of the evidence. When

Town-Major Sirr and his minions burst into Oliver Bond's house in May 1798 to arrest the Leinster directory, Thomas Traynor was forced to put an incriminating document in his mouth. Pretending to faint, he took a glass of water from a solicitous Sirr and swallowed![71]

Although successful in bringing the rebellion to an end and the army to heel, Cornwallis's policy of leniency did not resolve all the government's difficulties. Indeed, in one respect it compounded them. The prisons and hastily commandeered buildings were now nearly full to bursting. What was to be done with these prisoners? Some had been languishing in cells for many months, untried; some, ordinary felons as well as prisoners under the Insurrection Act, had been awaiting transportation to Botany Bay since 1797; others had surrendered on condition of banishment; and yet others had been captured, tried by court-martial, and were awaiting sentence review.

The Irish government eventually came up with a two-pronged strategy that sought to deal both with the sentenced and the untried prisoners by shuffling them all off overseas, either by agreement or by compulsion.[72] Those already tried by court-martial and who could not persuade Cornwallis to lighten their sentences were packed off to a holding camp in New Geneva, near Waterford. Most had been sentenced to Botany Bay or general service. As it happened, transportation was not a viable option in 1798; no suitable transport ships could be found for the long trip to Australia until early the next year. Moreover, Cornwallis felt that Botany Bay was too harsh a punishment for many of the rebels, "who have not been sufficiently criminal to justify their being sent."[73] For most of the prisoners held in New Geneva, therefore, service in either the regiments in the West Indies, or in the army of the King of Prussia, was to be their fate.

Those whose sentences had been remitted to banishment Cornwallis could also force overseas. But there still remained several hundred, including the prime movers of the rebellion, who had been in custody before the insurrection or who had since been arrested but against whom there was not enough evidence to bring to trial without the testimony of turncoats and informers.[74] Thomas Reynolds had been used to convict some of the United Irish Leinster executive, and one or two other prominent leaders in the South (MacNeven and Neilson, for instance) were vulnerable, but it was believed that juries would be reluctant to convict a large number on the basis of one man's testimony alone. In the North, the evidence of Nicholas Magin (or Magean) could have brought "home guilt to every Leader of consequence in Ulster, most of whom are in custody," but he refused to give testimony in open court.[75] So too did John Hughes, another reluctant informer on whose evidence the authorities were reliant.[76]

Ironically, the solution to the government's problem came from the state prisoners themselves. Following the capital conviction of William Michael Byrne and Oliver Bond in July, but before their executions, feelers were put out to the government through intermediaries on behalf of the state prisoners. According to MacNeven, "persons not at all implicated in the insurrection" took the lead, acting initially without the prisoners' knowledge.[77] This is not strictly true, for the process was instigated by Neilson, then in solitary confinement in Newgate, in consultation with his solicitor, one Crawford. In the middle of July they considered the possibility of entering into some arrangement with the government. Neilson requested Crawford to contact Lord Charlemont, the elderly former commander of the Volunteers of 1779–84. Charlemont pleaded infirmity and passed the problem on to Francis Dobbs, a Whig MP and kinsman of Sampson, one of the most prominent state prisoners.[78]

The first the government heard of the maneuvers was on the morning of 23 July, when Dobbs sought an opinion from Castlereagh. The Irish Secretary was predictably cautious in his response, saying that nothing could be decided until the verdict in Bond's trial (then under way) was known.[79] But the following day Neilson was permitted to visit Bond and Byrne in their cell, where he also found William Archer, a sheriff of Dublin, and Henry Alexander, MP for Londonderry, member of the secret committee, and kinsman of Bond. At Alexander's instigation, Neilson drew up a proposal seeking a stay of execution for Byrne and Bond, which Dobbs then undertook to take around the three prisons (Kilmainham, Bridewell, and Newgate) to obtain the assent of the state prisoners.[80]

That evening (24 July) Dobbs and Archer brought to Castlereagh a document signed by sixty-four of the state prisoners, which set out their proposals for saving their necks and bringing the rebellion to a close. They agreed to acknowledge in general terms their treason in return for life banishment for themselves, the remittance of the sentences of Byrne and Bond, and an end to the prosecution of Neilson.[81] This proposition had distinct political advantages for the more farsighted ministers such as Cornwallis and Castlereagh. Not only did it offer a possible way of ridding the country of a great number of state prisoners, but it also gave the opportunity of manufacturing a massive propaganda coup, justifying the defensive actions of the government during the past few years. It would prove beyond doubt that a conspiracy involving the United Irishmen and the French had existed, as the government had repeatedly asserted. To convince the public of this (and to confound the opposition Foxite Whigs) was "a matter of much more consequence than the lives of twenty such men as Oliver Bond," Cornwallis informed Portland.[82]

The problem was, however, that the Protestant ascendancy in Ireland was still baying for blood; to allow prominent rebel leaders to escape justice would only compound the intense irritation felt by loyalists at Cornwallis's conciliatory policies. This attitude became apparent at a meeting held on 25 July by the lord lieutenant with most of his senior law officers (Clare, who was to prove sympathetic to the prisoners, was absent in the country). Cornwallis reluctantly rejected the offer. The execution of Byrne went ahead as planned that day.[83]

One of the factors influencing Cornwallis's decision was the omission from the document of the signatures of a number of significant rebel leaders, including Arthur and Roger O'Connor's, and William Sampson's. Arthur O'Connor's confession of treason was particularly sought, for he had greatly embarrassed the British government by being acquitted of that offense at Maidstone only a few months earlier (aided by the Whig opposition, who had attended in large numbers to give him a character reference).[84] Unbeknown to the government, however, these rebel leaders had deliberately declined to sign the document. Certainly in Sampson's case, and probably in the O'Connors' too, they were confident that the government had no evidence with which to convict them, and were accordingly dismissive of Dobbs's blandishments.[85]

The execution of Byrne therefore came as a shock, jolting them out of their selfish complacency. Next in line for the scaffold was Oliver Bond, to be followed, so it was thought at the time, by Neilson, against whom Cornwallis believed there to be sufficient evidence to convict capitally.[86] Unsurprisingly, it was Bond who acted as catalyst for the next step, entreating his kinsman Henry Alexander to visit him on the morning of 26 July (the day of his execution). "In the plenitude of French conceit" Bond made it plain that he was prepared to die if necessary, but wished government to know that "An opportunity might be lost not regainable if He was executed and that he conceived nothing could more lead to the tranquillity of the State than the communications and exertions of him and his associates. That his mind was reconciled to death and that he would not sollicit [*sic*] Life except as a man acting with a class of men anxious to save him. He added that He and they could give the only information capable of saving this Country from an aggravated Civil War. He proposed Banishment for some, Emigration for all."[87] Although Alexander passed on this message to the Castle, he did so with some repugnance. Bond should certainly die, he suggested, if the state prisoners failed to offer enough information. Unwilling further to besmirch his reputation, he happily thereafter left negotiations to Cooke and Dobbs.[88]

During the rest of that day Dobbs must have feverishly circulated the Dublin prisons, not only working on the recalcitrant prisoners, but also persuading the majority to modify their previous requirements. By the evening he and Alexander were able to inform Castlereagh that a revised set of propositions was being drawn up, acceptable to all the prisoners, which, in return for Bond's life and an end to the trials, reiterated their willingness to confess their guilt and acknowledged their acceptance of banishment to any part of the world once the war ended. With the powerful support of Clare, Cornwallis was able to use these propositions as the basis for negotiation. In the meantime, Bond's sentence was respited for a week.[89]

On Sunday, 29 July MacNeven, Arthur O'Connor, and Emmet, representing all the state prisoners, met Castlereagh, Clare, and Cooke in the latter's gothic rooms in the Castle, where they thrashed out a scheme acceptable to both sides. The rebels agreed to give full information on their previous activities, both within Ireland and with all "foreign states," without implicating anyone by name. In return, the government confirmed that only those rebels guilty of murder or conspiracy to murder would thereafter be tried, and that at some future point the prisoners would be banished.[90]

On 4 August the state prisoners presented a memoir to Cornwallis, in which they gave details of their treason.[91] Naturally, they did not explain themselves in those terms; rather, they sought to justify their actions by blaming the government for rejecting their reform and emancipation program. Cornwallis conceded that the memoir "admitted fairly enough the most material parts of their guilt, [but] was written (on the pretence of its being an apology for their conduct) in the style of a controversial pamphlet, and was in some parts rather inflammatory." This made it impossible to publish the memoir under government auspices. Not that Cornwallis was particularly concerned by the memoir's tone; it gave him an opportunity, on 6 August, of rejecting it with mock indignation. As he had anticipated, this led to the state prisoners' representatives agreeing with alacrity to give oral evidence before the secret committee of the Irish House of Lords, which Cornwallis had particularly desired, for he would now be able to keep under wraps the information he had received from covert sources.[92]

Even allowing for their special pleading, both in the memoir and before the secret committee, MacNeven, O'Connor, and Emmet fulfilled their side of the bargain. Understandably, other rebels and radicals not in their predicament were unhappy with this open confession by the Leinster leaders. Rumors began to spread that they had bribed government officials to save their lives, and even that they had secretly disclosed the names of their compatriots.[93] Many state prisoners probably began to realize that they had been outmaneuvered in the bargaining.

With both the Irish and British governments exulting in their propaganda victory, attention turned to the future fate of the state prisoners. But what in July may have been viewed as an easily solved administrative problem, became in the next few months a political nightmare. To begin with, exclusive of the eighty-one state prisoners who signed the declaration in Dublin, there may have been as many as 300 more who were subject to banishment.[94] Those who had been tried and sentenced, either to banishment in the first instance or after review, could be ordered out of the country with little compunction. But there still remained a large number in Dublin and at least thirty-six in Belfast who had not yet been tried. Under the terms of the agreement with the Dublin state prisoners, the Belfast prisoners could no longer come before the courts. Nor, however, could they be freed, even on security. Too many of them, like Robert Simms and ROBERT HUNTER, had been too prominent in United Irish circles for loyalist public opinion to tolerate their immediate return to society.

The Irish government was as anxious to rid themselves of this incubus as the prisoners themselves wanted to get out of prison. They were an enormous drain on the public purse, Castlereagh (with pardonable exaggeration) complaining that "the expence of this regiment of traitors exceeds five-fold that of the best regiment in the King's service."[95] In a bid to force the Belfast prisoners voluntarily to accept banishment, on 23 August General Nugent offered them the same terms as had been accepted in Dublin.[96] But only nine of thirty-six were prepared to acknowledge their guilt.[97] One was subsequently freed on bail; another, the County Antrim shopkeeper JOHN DICKEY, had already been tried (he was sent to the West Indies but escaped to America). The rest called the government's bluff.

In the authorities' opinion, loyalist prejudice against the prisoners was in most cases unwarranted; only about twenty, fifteen in Dublin and five in Belfast, were "the active and intelligent heads of the party." The remainder were "inferior, insignificant persons, very little formidable from their talents."[98] Nevertheless, Ireland would be better off if all were exiled. But where were they, especially the twenty incorrigibles, to be sent? What had been agreed in the July negotiations? In answering the last question, it needs to be remembered that there were several phases of negotiation; that intermediaries were involved whose private comments to both government and prisoners are not always known; and that the prisoners were scattered about in three prisons, receiving different information from different people at different times. Further complicating the issue is that Emmet, MacNeven, Sampson, and Neilson subsequently published accounts of this episode, giving a disingenuous spin to their interpretation of the negotiations to claim that the government, and the American ambassador, Rufus King, had acted in bad faith by not allowing them to migrate to the United States in the fall of 1798. Working in tandem, they insisted, King and the government had conspired to ensure that the United Irish leaders were kept in captivity in Scotland until 1802. In reality, however, neither the British and Irish governments nor King acted dishonorably over the fate of the rebel leaders, although in one respect at least the prisoners probably did not have the information to appreciate that at the time.

There exist a number of accounts, some from prisoners, some from government quarters, of what was agreed during the negotiations, which were spread over six days. Sampson was one prisoner who was kept in solitary confinement for most of the time; he did not have direct contact with the negotiators. His understanding was that the state prisoners could emigrate to any country "as should be agreed upon" that was not at war with Britain. In his case, the country settled on was Portugal, to which he was permitted to go in October 1798 on account of ill health and the recommendation of his county MP.[99] Neilson, too, incarcerated in Newgate, had little or no contact with "the Kilmainham Directory," as Emmet, MacNeven, and O'Connor came derisively to be called.[100] He understood the agreement of 29 July 1798 to be "that [the state prisoners] are ready to emigrate to such country as shall be agreed upon between them and Government, and give security not to return to this country without the permission of Government, and not to pass into any enemy's country."[101] Nor did MacNeven, in his account published in New York in 1807, deny the main points made by Sampson and Neilson, although he claimed that the United States was the place of banishment accepted by both parties at the 29 July negotiations.[102] Emmet also, in his attack on Rufus King in New York in 1807, made it plain that the state prisoners had expected to be allowed to go to America.[103]

If we are to believe the published accounts of the major state prisoners, therefore, they wished to go to America and they believed they could leave as soon as their examinations had been completed. This, of course, was what did *not* happen, at least to the twenty leaders sent to Fort George in 1799, and this later gave the state prisoners the opportunity of abusing both the Irish and British governments and Rufus King. Emmet even accused King of being instrumental in the death of his brother, Robert, who in 1803 was executed following his abortive twenty-minute insurrection in Dublin. If the state prisoners had been permitted to emigrate to America in 1798, he claimed, Robert would have accompanied him and thus would not have instigated his forlorn hope.[104]

It is true that on 13 September 1798 King informed Portland that the state prisoners would be unwelcome in America: "I certainly do not think that they will be a desirable acquisition to any Nation, but in none would they be likely to prove more mischievous than in mine, where from the sameness of language and similarity of Laws and Institutions they have greater opportunity of propagating their principles than in any other country."[105] But far from this announcement pleasing the government, allowing them to keep the prisoners in custody—as the rebel leaders asserted—it threw them into temporary confusion. Although they realized that, like Tone and Tandy, the leaders would easily be able to return to Europe across the Atlantic, ministers had, until King's intervention, been prepared to send the prisoners to America. Ironically, however, contrary to what was later suggested, when the prisoners were asked in August where they wanted to go, both MacNeven and Emmet said they wished to be sent to Germany, the former because he had relatives there, the latter—my destination "decidedly is not America"—because of the yellow fever epidemic then raging and the hardships that his six children would suffer on the journey.[106] That part of the Irishmen's publications during the New York election campaign of 1807 that aimed at discrediting King by claiming he thwarted their wishes was thus not true, and can only be interpreted as political propaganda.

At first glance, the leaders' complaints that the timing of their leaving the country broke the agreement of July seems to have more validity. Cornwallis's official dispatch to Portland immediately after King's decision in September certainly implies that at the 29 July meeting the possibility of the state prisoners being banished before the war's end was discussed. However the same dispatch also claimed that Dobbs, when he met Castlereagh three days previously, had said that the prisoners were prepared "to leave the time of their liberation so long as the war lasted to the discretion of Government," and that the three rebel representatives subsequently agreed to this proviso.[107] Whether this agreement was indeed made cannot now be ascertained, nor is it known if Dobbs ever told the leaders what he had promised on their behalf, but undoubtedly the government's statement that they reserved the right to determine when the rebels could leave the country was buttressed in part by Dobbs's commitment.

Moreover, the rebel leaders' protests ignored the fact that by early 1799 most of the state prisoners had been ordered out of the country, many of them migrating to America. So anxious was the government to rid itself of all but a handful of the prisoners that in December they gave them one month to expel themselves; failure to do so would lead to trial (an empty promise). They even threatened to make the prisoners pay their own mess bills![108]

The key leaders also ignored the fact that once America was no longer seen as a viable refuge for the prisoners, the Irish government made plans to send them to Hamburg, in conformity with their wishes. Unfortunately, the ghastly visage of Napper Tandy arose to thwart them. In September 1798, bearing the French rank of general of brigade, and commanding a force of eighty seamen, marines, and cannoneers, Tandy had landed on the northwest coast of Ireland from the *Anacreon.* He remained only long enough to discover that Humbert's invasion had been a failure and that the Irish were unwilling to flock to his colors. He returned to Norway and from Oslo made his way overland to Hamburg, where on 23 November he and three other Irishmen were arrested in their beds by the local police, at the behest of Sir James Crauford, the British ambassador.[109]

Tandy's arrest and the call for his extradition to face a charge of high treason in Ireland caused a major diplomatic incident that lasted for months. Its most immediate impact was to shatter the government's plans to ship all the state prisoners in a group to Hamburg.[110] It was still hoped that, as happened with America, lesser lights among the prisoners might be allowed to travel to the Hanseatic port individually; but for the leaders, virtually no options were now left. The British government finally decided to take up a suggestion first made by Cornwallis in September, that the leading state prisoners be held in captivity in Fort George, Scotland, until the end of the war.[111]

In Dublin Castle, ministers favored the scheme as the only one that would keep the prisoners, "this most inconvenient and dangerous possession," secure during the war, and prevent them from continuing to stir up trouble in Ireland.[112] Castlereagh admitted that the authorities had been unable to prevent the prisoners from communicating with their supporters outside, even when they had been kept in solitary confinement.[113] This gave credence to information received in March 1799 that the "Kilmainham Directory" had been the source of a plot for an insurrection in London as soon as the French landed, which included plans for training an assassination squad for the purpose of killing either the king or Pitt.[114]

On 19 March 1799, after twenty-four hours notice, fifteen state prisoners were embarked on a ship bound for Scotland. Arthur O'Connor, ever the showman, "was dressed in Green, and talked of Robespierrian cruelty etc."[115] En route, the ship berthed briefly in Belfast to pick up another five prisoners. The Dublin prisoners were to remain incarcerated in Fort George for more than three years; the more fortunate men from Belfast were freed on bail and allowed to return to Ireland in December 1801.[116] Of the fourteen southern prisoners sent to Hamburg in June 1802 (Roger O'Connor was allowed to return to Ireland because of ill health), eleven—after continuing their plotting in Napoleon's France—eventually emigrated to the United States. It had been a long and tortuous route.

The Perfidious

In 1843 Benjamin Binns quoted Plutarch for the benefit of R. R. Madden, the United Irishmen's hagiographer: "To deceive a friend is impious, but to outwit an enemy is not only just and glorious, but profitable and sweet."[117] He was remembering with satisfaction his ability to thwart the aims of a committee of the English Privy Council when interrogated by them following his arrest in 1798. But he was also recalling unfaithful friends and comrades, in particular John Hughes (a "lying traitor" and a "scared traitor"), who in the extremity of fear for his life had in 1797–98 sold his soul to the government. Such perfidy was by no means uncommon at the time. Perhaps ironically, for a number who failed to keep the faith, America became a place of refuge. Most were Irish. Although English and Scottish turncoats and informers existed in significant numbers in the 1790s—the Scot Robert Watt and the Londoner William Bird were only two to oscillate in unfathomable ways between loyalism and radicalism, acting as political weathercocks—the greater certainty of violent revenge in Irish politics and the more desperate circumstances in which captured United Irishmen found themselves during the government onslaught of 1797–98 made flight and a new identity almost a necessity. The sheer size of the United Irish movement also ensured that the weak, the greedy, and the timid were involved in numbers.

We have already seen that at the time "the battalion of testimony"—the band of spies and informers who resided in Dublin Castle—was systematically denouncing suspects to the authorities, Watty Cox had embarked on a career of enforced informing. John Hughes found himself in a similar predicament. Born into an extended family of respectable Ulster Presbyterian farmers, Hughes's early years were disrupted by a quarrel of unknown cause between his parents. His father James was ostracized by the family, and his mother, a Carson, left her husband and settled in Belfast, where she opened a dram shop. According to Madden, John Hughes was apprenticed to the editor of the *Belfast Newsletter*, before becoming a prosperous stationer and bookseller.[118] It is possible, however, that he may also have run away to sea during the American War of Independence, anxious to avoid the unhappiness of family life.[119] In 1793 Hughes joined the Belfast United Irishmen; in 1796 Robert Orr swore him into the underground organization. Forming his own cell in Belfast, he acted as its secretary, swearing in new members (a capital offense). He also became a colonel in the military wing of the County Down organization. On several occasions he acted for the Belfast United Irishmen in Dublin, where he met most of the leading figures on the executive. Until his arrest in Newry in October 1797, Hughes was a trusted and committed member of the United Irishmen.[120]

Faced with the threat of a trial for treason and the collapse of his business, Hughes's nerve quickly broke. For the next six months he acted under the orders of Major Sirr in Dublin, incriminating among others Samuel Neilson (his kinsman) and Henry Grattan, the latter, he claimed in his evidence before the House of Lords, having been sworn into the United Irishmen by the former.[121] To his credit, however, although he could have condemned many of the Belfast leaders, Hughes refused to give evidence in open court. Intense pressure from John Pollock, the government official leading the Ulster investigations, was ultimately to no avail, greatly adding to the administration's difficulties.[122]

Spying and informing were unsavory activities, and so were many of the participants, as William Sampson exhibited to the world when he persuaded Edward Newell and William Bird to recant early in 1798. But Hughes and others like him should not, perhaps, be tarred with that brush. Madden admitted that in later life many former rebels had come to understand Hughes's predicament, and acknowledged that he had been truthful and free of "personal rancour."[123] Many informers were trapped by circumstances and personal fear into betraying their fellow conspirators. Unlike William Michael Byrne, who rejected with scorn the promise of his life if he informed on Lord Edward Fitzgerald,[124] the perfidious lacked the moral and mental courage to accept their fate philosophically. They also probably did not possess the imagination necessary to dream of themselves romantically covered in glory as future martyrs. To suggest thus is not to condone what they did; rather, it helps to explain their actions at a time when "turning the spit"—the cant phrase for informing—was rife and no one could be certain that his neighbor was not preparing to denounce him to the authorities. If even prominent figures such as Neilson and John Binns could be accused of peaching to the government, who could one trust?[125] It might be prudent when in a tight corner to denounce before being denounced.

But there were limits to what one could impart without losing self-respect. GEORGE WARNOCK, a Belfast soap boiler, saved himself by telling John Pollock where the two six-pounder brass cannons of the Belfast Blue Volunteer Company had first been hidden in 1794 (they were subsequently buried in Warnock's cow house). But he refused "to disclose the names of the persons who were concerned with him in concealing the Cannon, because the party were bound by the Obligation of an Oath to each other, to keep the Transaction secret." Nor would he tell who swore him into the United Irishmen in

1796.[126] Warnock was nevertheless permitted to emigrate. He doubtless would have considered that he had offered the minimum consistent with his future safety, and that his betrayal, if that is what it was, was no worse than the Dublin Compounders'.

If a combination of scrupulousness and realism can be seen in Warncok's confession, the tactics of Francis Henry Gordon are less justifiable. Son of the agent for the ultraloyalist Price family's estate; a relative of Rev. Arthur McMahon, the United Irish leader who had fled to France in 1797; and a member of Thomas Ledlie Birch's Presbyterian congregation in Saintfield, Gordon had fought at the battle of Saintfield and had commanded the rebel artillery at Ballynahinch. Faced with execution when captured, he saved his life by turning crown witness, not only against ANDREW BRYSON, JR., who was sent to the condemned regiments in the West Indies before escaping to America, but also against his own minister, Birch. Perhaps providentially, he was accidentally drowned in Lake Ontario a few years after being permitted to emigrate to the United States.[127]

Similarly, John Cormick, the Dublin feather merchant, probably went beyond tolerable bounds with his confession. He was sworn into the United Irishmen in early 1797, but for a year had remained "passive." His troubles began when in April 1798 the surgeon William Lawless brought to his house the fugitive Lord Edward Fitzgerald, who remained for a month. Cormick was drawn into the conspiracy by attending the meetings that took place in his home. After troops raided the house he fled, first to London, then to Guernsey, where he was arrested. Cormick was "obviously terrified" when he gave his confession to Gen. Sir Hugh Dalrymple.[128] Uncertain whether he would be pardoned, he not only betrayed individuals in his statement, but also "offered, if his pardon should be granted, to correspond with [Edward Lewins, the United Irish representative in Paris], who he was certain would write confidentially to him."[129] En route to Ireland a week later, he escaped from Fabiani, the king's messenger. William Wickham, brilliantly organizing the government's intelligence system in London, expressed little concern at this turn of events. He doubted whether Cormick would have given evidence in court against Neilson (who with Hughes had visited Fitzgerald at Cormick's house); he also realized that Cormick's "reputation has gone for ever with his own party."[130] As it happened, Cormick was soon recaptured and became one of the state prisoners sent to Fort George. MacNeven recalled meeting him "in France, shortly after their release from Fort George, but he seemed rather inclined to shun his former associates than to renew their acquaintance."[131] When he emigrated to America he settled, with his brother JOSEPH, in Georgia, far from the main concentrations of Irish radical émigrés.

MacNeven noted that Cormick's "principles were much changed" in France, but it is likely that the young merchant had only flirted with revolution until he came under the charismatic gaze of Fitzgerald. His year-long passivity suggests that he was one of many who probably had not thought through the implications of joining a secret organization led by ruthless and implacable "hard men." He almost certainly did not willingly offer his residence as a safe house. Faced with his own personal crisis in July 1798, alone in a foreign country, his spirit collapsed and he demeaned himself before the contemptuous eyes of General Dalrymple.

Cormick's sense of guilt went with him to America, but he did at least remain an honest man. This is more than can be said of some radicals who emigrated to the United States. The consequences of debt and financial disaster frequently played a significant role in turning some radicals into rogues. In this respect they were little different from the professional informer and spy, for this covert world was filled with desperate debtors and bankrupts. Some were just plain crooks. When General Lake dragooned Ulster in 1797 DUNN, the treasurer of the Belfast United Irishmen, fled to America, taking with him £1000 of the society's money.[132] CHARLES SMITH, a Catholic grocer of Mary's Abbey, Dublin, who had been a United Irishman since 1792, was sworn into the underground organization only after he had gone bankrupt. In 1800, soon after his illicit still had been seized, he suddenly fled to America. Shortly after, he was accused of forgery. This did not prevent Emmet and his wife dining with him in New York a few years later.[133]

Undoubtedly the most picaresque of the perfidious radicals was the young Scotsman, JOHN WOOD (1775–1822). Wood was one of those characters who embraced the mantle of radicalism when it suited him (for example, when he first arrived in New York), but whose commitment to the doctrines of progress and change must remain questionable. Like Callender, Wilson, and other Scottish radicals, he was a young man on the make. Born in Edinburgh to the wife of a gentleman's servant, Wood displayed precocious talents as a classicist, mathematician, and artist.[134] What schooling he had cannot now be confirmed, but he probably received some patronage, perhaps from his father's employer, for in his late teens he had "resided for some time past in Switzerland improving himself in landscape [drawing]."[135] In 1794 he established himself in Edinburgh as a teacher of drawing, advertising both public classes and private lessons.

In 1797 the trustees of the board of manufactures and arts in Edinburgh advertised for a master of their drawing academy, who needed to be "a man of great inventive genius and knowledge of the fine arts qualified to direct and improve the taste of the public and to influence artisans and manufacturers of all descriptions in the principles of Drawing and Design."[136] Applicants had to present a range of exhibits displaying their talents, including a portfolio of their drawings, which were sent to London, where the president of the Royal Academy, ignorant of the applicants' names, adjudicated on their merits. Nine portfolios were examined; two, denominated by the letters B and C, possessed "most distinguished excellence," but C had "extraordinary merit, and [was] much preferable to the others."[137] Before the trustees in Edinburgh made their final decision, but after the London rankings had been reported, the committee received a flurry of letters objecting to some exhibits put forward by Wood as part of his candidature. Robert Cummins, a carver and gilder, and Edward Mitchell, an engraver, claimed that two chalk drawings presented by Wood in addition to his portfolio had been executed "almost wholly" by the latter. In consequence, one of the candidates, Alexander Nasmith, submitted that Wood's works sent to London probably were not his: "It is notorious that Mr. Wood is incapable of doing *figures* in any way passable." Wood, he argued, should be made to redraw his submissions under the eyes of the committee. In response, Wood presented a paper signed by four gentlemen who confirmed that they had seen Wood at work on his compositions at various times.[138]

The committee established to examine these accusations met on the day that the trustees voted for a new master. Wood was exonerated on the charge relating to his portfolio, but the committee found suspicious circumstances surrounding his chalk drawings. The trustees then proceeded to discuss their main business, the position of drawing master. The envelopes containing the names of the applicants and their respective cover letters had already been opened a few days previously, so it was known that C referred to John Graham, a London painter of historical scenes, and B to Wood. The former's referees were strong, including the chairman of the Society of Polite Arts at the Adelphi in London and the painters George Romney and J. F. Rigaud. Wood's were more local, but included professors Dugald Stewart and John Playfair of Edinburgh University, and the Scottish solicitor general. On the casting vote of the chairman, Lord Balgomy, Wood was elected, for a probation term of three years at a salary of £120 per annum.[139]

It was a victory for parochialism and, perhaps, for the last remnants of Whiggery in the Scottish capital. Both Stewart (professor of moral philosophy) and Playfair (professor of mathematics) were part of what has been called a "small, isolated, and sometimes suspected Whig caucus" in Edinburgh, surrounded by a sea of Dundas toryism and loyalism.[140] Both were deemed by loyalists to be sympathetic to "Jacobinism," and too encouraging of students giving blasphemous and radical speeches in the student societies, although they were too securely placed to be ousted from their university positions. Wood's election was a sign that they still had some influence in Edinburgh society (a few years earlier, one potential student of the academy was refused entry for having been a member of the Friends of the People).[141]

The hostile rumblings that continued for six months after Wood's victory coincided with the publication by John Robison—professor of natural philosophy at Edinburgh, and political enemy of Playfair and Stewart—of his infamous anti-Jacobin and anti-infidel book, *Proofs of a Conspiracy against All Religions and Governments of Europe* (1797), which emphasized the role of freemasons, *Illuminati*, and other secret societies in the spread of revolution and contempt for revealed religion. Priestley was one of Robison's main targets.[142] It was no accident that when Wood came to write his history of Switzerland, published in 1799, he explicitly rejected the ultraconservative Robison's analysis of the influence of secret societies on the revolution in that country; instead, he partly blamed "Dissensions between the Catholic and Protestant cantons, occasioned by the arts and intrigues of the clergy."[143] His book was in one sense a repayment to those who had supported him a few years earlier.

Wood was genuinely anticlerical; this was to be partly the cause of his downfall, for in the last years of the century in Scotland heterodox religious ideas were firmly associated with the underground revolutionary group, the United Scotsmen.[144] In 1799, with two Presbyterian clergymen and a small group of young Whig enthusiasts who met regularly at the home of Robert Anderson, a successful man of letters, he was involved in the establishment of a very short-lived magazine, the *Edinburgh Clerical Review*. Its aim was to publish weekly reports, with commentary, on the sermons given at all the established churches in Edinburgh. News of this project broke before the first number was printed, with the result that the Presbytery of Edinburgh intervened and forced the clergymen involved to recant. Wood was one of those ordered to appear before the Presbytery for examination. Although the editors denied any subversive intentions, the magazine had been intended to lampoon the clergy and to criticize the loyalist politics that lurked in their sermons. The Presbytery's preemptive strike was successful; only two innocuous numbers of the magazine appeared.[145]

The embarrassment of this fiasco was not enough to force Wood abroad, but it played its part, for while the Presbytery was relentlessly pursuing its lines of enquiry the trustees of the board of manufacturers received a memorial from Peter E. Sime, a drawing master, who confessed that the five drawings in Wood's portfolio that went to London in 1797 had been "composed and executed wholly" by him, locked up in Wood's house. He had come forward because Wood had subsequently failed to pay him for the commissions. The deputy sheriff of Edinburgh's enquiries confirmed Sime's story. A letter from Wood was read to the meeting, in which he claimed illness prevented him from attending, and that "he understands he has been accused of Atheism and Sedition and of getting his office by improper means; but that though his enemies believe it, his friends will not; And that God and his conscience acquit him of those charges." The Board understandably dismissed him immediately.[146]

When Wood reached New York later in the year, he sensibly took on the mantle of a persecuted martyr forced overseas for his political and religious opinions. It was a guise that attracted much sympathy at the time in certain quarters. And there was some truth in it, even though used to hide his corrupt past. It would obviously be wrong to suggest that Wood, or John Hughes, or the thief Dunn were typical of the radical diaspora; they manifestly were not. But they remain counterweights to the idealized view that all the radicals were saints, unjustly persecuted by an authoritarian government for their politics. The efflux of radicals to the United States was more complex than that.

THE CHOICE OF AMERICA

John Wood emigrated to hide his shame, shed his past, and begin anew. Most other radical exiles had no personal disgrace to expunge, but they were influenced to greater or lesser extent by Wood's other motivations. But why did they choose the United States as the preferred place of exile? To some extent, their choice was made for them. Those formally banished from Ireland, for instance, were forced to go to a neutral country outside the British empire; this somewhat reduced their options. For the rest, especially for those with wives and children to consider, the European war also diminished the range of choices. The Low Countries, for instance, the resort of exiles since the sixteenth century, was a cockpit of war and under the thrall of France. Given the circumstances of the time, therefore, the English-speaking United States remained perhaps the only sensible and prudent place in which to settle.

Nevertheless, most exiles did not perceive America as a refuge of last resort; rather, they saw it as having decided advantages, promising a prosperous future. Many already had close connections with the new republic, either through trade links or with friends and family already settled there. As a tobacco merchant, Ralph Eddowes had obvious commercial connections in America; William Russell had both family and long-standing business links.[147] William Sampson's uncle was a rich landowner in Sampson, North Carolina.[148]

The Caldwells of Ballymoney could boast two ancestors who, emigrating after surviving the siege of Londonderry in 1688–89, had helped to found Londonderry, New Hampshire, and other relatives who fought for America in the Revolutionary War.[149] Benjamin Vaughan, himself half-American (his mother was a Boston Hallowell), not only had a prosperous merchant brother in Philadelphia, but another holding considerable lands in the Kennebec region of Maine.[150] As for the less affluent, more middling-class exiles, especially the Irish, many must have had relatives or neighbors who had been among the thousands to emigrate to the United States in the years prior to, and immediately after, the war of independence.[151]

Images of America

Important though personal connections were for some exiles, for most their perceptions of the land in which they were to settle were determined partly by the general accounts of the new world that were circulating in the 1790s, and partly by the image of freedom and liberty that America possessed within current radical ideology. With tongue in cheek Daniel Boorstin once commented that modern America inevitably became the center of advertising through the process of natural selection. Its inhabitants were descended from a long line of immigrants originally seduced by advertising to leave their homelands for a brave new world![152] Certainly, in the early 1790s the radicals themselves contributed significantly to the cultivation of America's image as a land of potential plenty and of religious and political liberty. But the message they presented was curiously ambiguous: On the one hand they seemingly encouraged emigration to America; on the other, they promoted the new republic's political system as exemplary, worthy of emulation and thus a beacon in the battle to bring radical change to Britain's polity.

This ambiguity was, perhaps, at times unwitting. Extolling the virtues of America for a mass audience, as well as using the new republic as a benchmark against which to contrast hierarchical and corrupt Britain, inevitably involved emphasizing the material benefits available there. The letters from Irish immigrants in America that Neilson's *Northern Star* published in numbers between 1792 and 1794 highlighted the superior lifestyles that were possible across the Atlantic. One typical letter from Pennsylvania set out a veritable feast for oppressed Irishmen: "The lowest here (unlike those of poor Ireland) are well fed, well dressed, and happy. . . . they stand erect and crouch not before any man."[153] Another claimed that "in not many years hence, [America] will form probably the greatest, the freest, and the happiest Empire in the world."[154] In his *Cork Gazette*, Denis Driscol wrote glowingly of "Happy—thrice happy

America—instead of taxing for hateful war, you are paying off the debt of your independency, cultivating the fruits of industry, and building cities as asylums, for persecuted Europeans."[155]

The radicals' encouragement of emigration to America was, at least until the defeat of their political aims, inadvertent. Rather than endorsing emigration, they were trying to make the link between material prosperity and a system based on representative government and popular sovereignty, holding out the prospect of private happiness and contentment as the consequence of a successful bid to reform Britain's political system along lines similar to America's. In 1793 Joseph Gerrald—who had lived in America for much of the previous decade—wrote of the new republic as a "happy land of freedom and an equality of rights. . . . The poor are not broken down by taxes to support the luxury of an insolvent nobility. No lordly peer tramples down the corn of the husbandman, and no proud prelate wrings from him the tythe of his industry." With the political point came the bait: "Plenty is the lot of all, superfluity of none."[156]

The most important booster of America and American institutions among the radicals was, of course, Thomas Paine. In *Rights of Man*, Part 2, he idealized America's system of government, which enabled it to overcome all obstacles:

> If there is a country in the world, where concord, according to common calculation, would be least expected, it is America. Made up, as it is, of people from different nations, accustomed to different forms and habits of government, speaking different languages, and more different in their modes of worship, it would appear that the union of such a people was impracticable; but by the simple operation of constructing government on the principles of society and the rights of man, every difficulty retires, and all the parts are brought into cordial unison. There the poor are not oppressed, the rich are not privileged. Industry is not mortified by the splendid extravagance of a court rioting at its expense. Their taxes are few, because their government is just; and as there is nothing to render them wretched, there is nothing to engender riots and tumults.

Like a new laundry soap attacking stubborn stains, "Representation ingrafted upon democracy" apparently dissolved all society's problems.[157]

Mark Philp has shown that Paine and other radicals following his example deliberately inserted American republicanism into the torrid debate in England, which followed the publication of Edmund Burke's *Reflections on the French Revolution* in 1790, as a counter to loyalist emphasis on the violence and instability of the French Revolution.[158] In England, America was used in this manner for only a brief period (1792–93), but it was a tactic that Irish revolutionaries were also prepared to use later in the decade, justifying their activities by claiming American, and therefore moderate precedents, rather than French. John Daly Burk talked of the United Irishmen walking "in the footsteps of the Americans in '74."[159] MacNeven asserted that the Irish immigrants "had proved on their native soil their adherence to the principles of the American declaration of independence. . . . The principles of the American constitution were their principles."[160] DANIEL McCURTIN indignantly reminded his fellow immigrant Mathew Carey in 1798, when they were sheltering from the storm of Federalist triumphalism, that "Never had this country [America] more sincere friends. Ireland considered its emancipation irreparably connected with American independence."[161] And when Emmet stated before the secret committee of the House of Lords that "My wish was to overturn the establishment of the church," and was asked: "And have it as in France?," he replied, "As it is in America, my lord."[162]

Some of these Irish protestations can be taken with a grain of salt, although most emigrants—especially those attracted by America's reputation for religious freedom—were sincere.[163] John Thelwall, probably the most erudite of the LCS political thinkers, noted that more advanced radicals were impressed by France, the moderate by America.[164] There was, as we have seen, some truth in the distinction, at least in the early years, but even some of the most radical saw America's material advantages once defeat stared them in the face and the specter of first Robespierre, and then Napoleon, loomed large. Thomas Cooper, for example, in 1792 had criticized both the American Constitution and the French constitution of the previous year for being insufficiently democratic,[165] but by the time he had returned from his visit to America two years later his enthusiasm for France had dissipated. France was not "a more eligible country than the United States." The French revolutionaries' "ferocious injustice . . . compleat and absolute despotism . . . perfect annihilation of the liberty of the press, [and] the liberty of speech; their detestable want of private honour . . . [and] their unnecessary execution of females" put them beyond the pale. "They are," he admitted, "a wonderful people; but in my opinion rather to be admired at a distance, than fit for a peaceable man to reside among."[166] In contrast, in America "The government is the government *of* the people, and *for* the people," with no tithes or game laws, no excessively rich people, very few beggars, no military parading the streets, and with robberies "very rare." For the potential immigrant with a family, "France is not, and America in my opinion is, the country to be chosen."[167]

America, therefore, in the eyes of many radicals turned from being a useful tactical ploy in a political argument, to an asylum for the defeated. For others, this shift in emphasis raised concerns as to the viability of the radical movement at home, when so many of its principal leaders came to believe their own propaganda and emigrated. As the Liverpool radical William Roscoe put it in 1793: "The leaders have apostacised and the disciples perish."[168] In the Norwich radical magazine the *Cabinet,* editor Charles Marsh wrote "that departure to America was a gross violation of the duty to stay and check the precipitate degeneracy of the age."[169] Felix Vaughan, the natural son of John Horne Tooke, pleaded with Cooper not to emigrate: "If *good men* would not leave us, what might we not attempt for the good people of England! As to the bad, it signifies little what becomes of them. In sober sadness cast in your mind whether you cannot bear with us for a few years more and help us to stem the torrent of folly."[170] The absence of a viable alternative place to settle possibly might have persuaded the emigrants to think twice, but America, as beacon of freedom, asylum of liberty, and prospective elysium, had taken too strong a hold on their imaginations.

TO THE FAR SIDE

The Voyage

The logistics of removing family and estate from the British Isles to the United States in the late eighteenth century were complex even for prosperous emigrants who enjoyed the luxury of drawing up their plans at a leisurely pace. For the radicals—suffering from the pressures of social antagonism, economic hardship and outlawry—the disruption of family life, loss of property, and prospects of an uncertain future compounded the problems of expatriation. Nevertheless, several managed to take considerable sums of money with them. According to the London *Oracle,* Vaughan sailed to America from Europe with £100,000.[171] This was almost certainly an exaggeration, but Harman Blennerhassett received $100,000 for his property in Ireland, Ralph Eddowes took £26,000 onto the *Hope* when it left Liverpool, and his fellow Dissenting refugees sailing with him took similar amounts.[172] Others, of course, suffered financial penalties by being forced to sell their property too rapidly. In November 1798, while in prison, the brewer John Sweetman auctioned his paintings, including a Vermeer, a Rubens, a Holbein, and a Caracci. He claimed to have received only two-thirds value for his property. Henry Jackson obtained only half the value of his ironfoundry and other industrial concerns when he sold them.[173] William Russell was compensated with £1,600 for the damage to his property during the Priestley riots, £1,000 less than he had demanded.[174] Not everyone, however, suffered from a buyer's market. When the respected Catholic United Irishman McDonald sold up in Carlow, the locals ensured he got a fair price for his property because of his help for poor Protestants during the rebellion. He sailed to New York with £3,000 in his pocket.[175]

The voyage across the Atlantic in the late eighteenth century, given an un-interrupted passage, a seaworthy vessel, and tail winds at the right season of the year, could take about six weeks. For some radicals the trip came as a blessed relief from their sufferings. On board the *Swift*, which left Belfast in May 1794, there were a number of radical refugees, including the Scot Alex-ander Wilson and the Irishman Dr. James Reynolds. A few days out, when they felt safe, Reynolds "treated all passengers and crew with rum-grog, which was drunk to the confusion of despots, and the prosperity of liberty all over the world." The highlight of the party was the hanging of George III in effigy.[176]

Although Elizabeth Brunton, Anthony Merry's wife, could not have known it at the time, by traveling to America with a company of actors she was ac-companied by her three husbands. Following the sudden death of Merry from apoplexy in 1798, she was to marry her manager, Thomas Wignall. Widowed again, she married the company's comedian, William Warren.[177] With a come-dian on board, as well as Merry, who was a noted punster, the cabin passengers must have been kept amused.

Most of the radicals who left accounts of their journeys traveled as cabin passengers, and thus were insulated from the worst rigors of long-distance sea travel. John Daly Burk had the leisure to write his blank verse play, "The Battle of Bunker Hill," which was a success when performed at the newly opened (and Republican) Haymarket Theatre in Boston soon after he ar-rived.[178] Priestley, however, was rather offended by the levity and secularism of his companions: "Our society in the cabin was agreeable enough, tho' the majority were aristocratically inclined; but all in the steerage were zealous re-publicans, and persons of good character, and several of good property. In the steerage, also, there was more religion than in the cabin, but they were univer-sally Calvinists, though the majority very moderate."[179]

A dose of fatalistic Calvinism was probably appropriate for travel in steer-age. JAMES ORR, the County Antrim weaver-poet and United Irishman, was one of very few among the poorer radicals to mention the journey across the Atlantic.[180] His account, in verse, accords well with the doom-and-gloom sce-nario, which habitually is associated with emigration by the poor:

How hideous the hold is!—Here, children are screaming—
There, dames faint through thirst, with their babes on their knee!
Here, down every hatch the big breakers are streaming,
And there with a crash, half the fixtures break free!
Some court, some contend, some sit dull stories telling;
The mate's mad and drunk, and the tars tasked and yelling;
What sickness and sorrow pervade my rude dwelling;—
A huge floating lazar-house, far, far at sea![181]

Although some pastimes were similar, there is a striking dissimilarity between Orr's lament and other radicals' travel accounts (although the wealthy Ralph Eddowes wrote of the *Hope:* "Such a bum-boat as ours surely never went to sea!").[182] Another Ulsterman, David Bailie Warden, had been incarcerated in a prison ship in Carrickfergus Bay for many months before he sailed to America. He had lost his appetite, had "a dry cough, with short breathing," and found himself "extremely wasted." The sea air had an immediate effect. "I walked much on the deck, and escaped the sea sickness, except a slight vomiting, which was a real use. In a few days I found myself in perfect health, and felt not a moment's indisposition during the voyage." Sea travel brought out the romantic streak in Warden's nature: "The beauties of the rising and setting sun; the grandeur of the ship ploughing the waves; the water as if sparkling with fire after evening; the sight of birds many hundred miles from land, and the fishes sporting in the water, will afford much entertainment to a mind so fond of admiring nature." He enjoyed plenty of amusements to while away the time. His fellow cabin passengers were "pleasing and interesting." Reading, conversation, songs from the ladies, and dancing on the quarterdeck "when the vessel had little motion" were some of the things that occupied him. At other times he played "a rubber of whist or a bit of backgammon." "I speak with sincerity," he wrote to an unknown friend in Ireland, "when I assure you that I was grieved that our passage was no longer than six weeks."[183]

Strangely, however, another account of the same voyage gives a less idyllic impression of the journey. Warden sailed on the *Peggy,* chartered by John Caldwell, whose passenger list including six other Presbyterian ministers or licentiates: James Simpson, William Sinclair, Charles Wallace, John Miles, William Adair, and John McNeill (or McNeish). These were part of a group of exiles who had hoped to be dropped off in France to continue the struggle. Caldwell's refusal to reroute the ship caused discontent, which was only reduced "by exhibiting a few iron shackles and hand irons together with the pistols on the top of the companion [way], accompanied by a few pithy but deter-

mined remarks."[184] Nor was the companionship so pleasing as Warden intimated. Rev. James Simpson had been so "disorderly" before they left port that
the captain agreed to take him only because his wife and children were desperate. On the voyage, he was sent to Coventry for repeated disputations on
arcane religious matters, which he continued against Sinclair in New York
City.[185]

There were, of course, far greater dangers involved in crossing the Atlantic than being ranted at by a zealous Presbyterian clergyman. Storms frequently caused serious damage to the ships. William Sampson's ship taking
him to Portugal was hit by one and forced into a port in Wales for several
weeks. So obnoxious did he make himself to the local gentry that they officially sought his removal.[186] John Caldwell's first attempt to emigrate in October 1798 was thwarted in this way also; his ship, the barque *Pallas,* was twice
forced into Irish harbors, the second time after being dismasted. After spending weeks in Cork, Caldwell was allowed to return to Belfast and restart his
transatlantic journey. His shipmates DR. JACKSON and ANDREW BRYSON, SR.,
were given similar privileges, as was the Newtownards rebel leader, WILLIAM
HERON, whose court-martial sentence of life transportation had been reduced
to banishment. General Nugent had given Heron a travel pass to Liverpool to
embark for America, but he was caught hiding near his home a few months
later by a yeomanry unit.[187]

The Atlantic was a major cockpit of war, and the exiles faced danger from
privateers and, depending on which flag they were sailing under, from the
navies of either Britain or France. In 1795 Theobald Wolfe Tone sailed in an
American ship that was hove to by three British frigates, asserting their right
to inspect neutral shipping. Fifty men were pressed, including all but one of
the crew. Tone was certain he would have been taken if his name had become
known. Telling the story in a letter to Thomas Russell after safely reaching
terra firma, he could see the potential irony of his "nearly having the honour
myself to serve the King." Fortunately for the now almost unmanned ship, the
weather was mild and only a week of the journey remained.[188]

At about the same time as Tone was writing his letter, the Sheffield radical
Joseph Gales and his wife were setting off from Altona in Denmark for the
voyage across the Atlantic. This was their second attempt, the first having
foundered on account of bad weather and a rebellious crew a year earlier. Just
off the American coast their ship was captured by the notorious privateers,
Hutchins and Bethel. If the story can be believed, Winifred Gales—upper-
class born and bred—turned her considerable wit and charm on the privateers
and personally persuaded them to forego their prize.[189]

Caldwell's second attempt to reach America was also interrupted by a privateer, *Bordelieu,* sailing with a French letter of marque, and with orders to send ships sailing under the American flag into Bordeaux. The captain of the *Peggy* and Caldwell, as supercargo, were ordered onto the French ship. Caldwell was taken to the captain's cabin, where he was "struck with horror on viewing the immense number of guns, pistols, hatchets, pikes, and other instruments of death and destruction with which the cabin was decorated." The captain, one Derrygrand, was equally horrific. The side of his face he presented to Caldwell was disfigured with St. Anthony's fire and the scars of several severe sword cuts. He had "the very hideous outline of a bloody pirate." On turning his cheek, however, he displayed "a countenance replete with humanity and kindness." In broken French Caldwell tried to persuade Derrygrand to allow them—poor persecuted people seeking an asylum in America—to proceed; in equally broken English Derrygrand regretted that it was impossible. With a flash of inspiration Caldwell gave a Masonic sign; he immediately became Derrygrand's "tres bon frere." After some heated discussion with the officers, one of whom was an Irishman, the privateers decided to let the ship go. "The French nation was never so happy as when protecting those, who were persecuted by the British," Derrygrand elegantly summed up the discussion. After supplying the travelers with good French bread and exchanging a number of French National cockades for some green Erin Go Bragh ribbons, Derrygrand sailed away (to be captured shortly after by the British). For the rest of the *Peggy's* voyage to America, Derrygrand's health was drunk daily by all except the captain.[190]

Not all the exiles had such fortunate escapes as the Galeses and Caldwell's bevy of Presbyterian clergymen.[191] JOHN and SAMUEL NEILSON of Ballycarry, County Antrim, were on board a ship that was carried off by the French as a prize. They were the sons of a poor widowed schoolmistress and had been arrested in June 1798 when guns were found in their house. Their younger brother William, aged fifteen, had been executed after the battle of Antrim. The brothers were never tried, but John agreed to banishment for seven years, Samuel for life. They sailed from Belfast in May 1799. The French did not possess their ship for long, for it was retaken and sailed for the West Indies. Samuel died on the voyage; John, fearing recruitment into the army, managed to escape and made his way to America, where he was later to achieve some celebrity as an architect and builder.[192]

An Interrupted Journey

One of the most prolonged and distressful journeys to America fell to William Russell, his family, and his fellow Unitarian exile, REV. HUDDY, who suffered a trip that lasted for more than a year and badly dented their enthusiasm for republicanism. Four days out from Falmouth in August 1794, with most of the passengers still badly seasick, their vessel, the American-owned *Mary,* was stopped by a French frigate. Russell's party, unfortunately without American passports, was taken on board the *Proserpine.* There they stayed for the next few weeks while the French captured, burned, or sank thirty vessels, much to the enthusiasm and pleasure of Russell's daughters, Mary and Martha. But the increasing number of prisoners taken aboard led to cramped conditions below deck. Thus they were pleased when the *Proserpine* avoided a large British fleet—"our enemies and countrymen"—and tied up in Brest harbor on the last day of August.[193]

Naively, the Russells expected immediate release; instead, they were taken on board the prison ship, *La Ville d'Orient,* with one hundred others. Conditions were deplorable, with Russell's son Thomas soon falling sick with fever, but they improved when they were transferred to another vessel at the end of September. There they were permitted to cook for themselves, and thus avoided the detestable French food, varieties of garlic-flavored sauce covering suspicious-looking vegetables. Another removal soon after, however, and news that they would be detained until the war's end, greatly lowered their spirits.

They also had the misfortune to be given berths in a cabin in which thirty people slept, two of them captured steerage passengers. To save their feelings, the "ladies and gentlemen" decided to divide the group into two messes, one for themselves, and one for the children, the servants, and the steerage passengers. The republican Russells were shocked when, having determined that their mess should always eat first while the other went on deck, the two steerage passengers "both objected, saying they had as much right to the cabin as any of us, they were as good as we, all being prisoners alike. In short their behaviour was very impertinent and disagreeable, and they proved sad plagues to us the remaining time of our imprisonment, particularly Mrs. Bevan, who was really a virago."[194] The arrival of a large group of captured English sailors caused further problems. According to Martha Russell:

> They were a most desperate set of fellows—a complete contrast to the French sailors—fine, tall, lusty men, well clothed, and clean to a degree. They obliged us all, very soon after they came on board, to take off our cockades. My father and we were the last who did it, not being willing to submit to English tyranny in France. At last we were obliged to take them out, hardly daring to go on deck with them for fear of their insults. My father continued obstinate till they threatened to throw him overboard if he did not take it off. . . . These fellows threatened to get off with

the ship, and, had they been on board after the fleet sailed, I have no doubt but that they would. The French certainly were a little in awe of them.[195]

And Martha, despite her republicanism, was certainly a little in love with them.

The Russells' shipboard imprisonment ended on 30 December 1794 when they set out for Paris, leaving their servants and retinue still incarcerated. They were to stay there for six months, making the acquaintance of such radical luminaries as Archibald Hamilton Rowan, whose privations following his escape to France nearly rivaled theirs, but who now appeared to have taken consolation in the arms of a mistress; Mary Wollstonecraft, who, wrote Mary Russell drily, "had much information, and was fond of communicating it"; and John Hurford Stone, the Unitarian radical whose brother had been acquitted of treason, and who had as his mistress the radical feminist Helen Maria Williams.[196] The Russells' republican principles probably received a fatal blow when they visited the National Convention:

> The confusion, noise, low language, the nervous attempts to overpower one another by the loudness of voice in place of the strength of argument, the stamping, raving, and uncouth attitudes, menacing each other with clenched fists, some jerking their arms suddenly as if throwing stones at their adversaries, others while speaking moving their whole bodies like a pendulum of a clock—in fact such a variety of uncouth gestures and vulgar-looking people I should have thought could be found but among a set of old-clothesmen. . . . This day the President broke two bells trying to keep silence . . . but this was [not] an uncommonly tumultuous meeting. . . . In short, the whole scene excited in my breast a degree of disappointment, disgust, and astonishment scarcely to be imagined.[197]

They also, on one occasion, passed a tumbrel carrying a man to the guillotine: "We were not only hurt by seeing the poor man that was to be soon launched into eternity, but also by meeting such throngs of people going with the greatest gaiety to witness the execution."[198]

By mid-year, having watched from the sidelines two Parisian *journées,* the Russells were anxious to depart France. They left from Le Havre on the American ship, *Nancy,* in July, and, having survived several storms, arrived off the American coast near Sandy Hook on 19 August, more than one year after leaving Falmouth. Martha was, like so many of the other exiles after their varied adventures, understandably overjoyed: "Never did I see such a beautiful land before: it had a thousand charms not to be described: it was the land to which my eyes had been directed for more than a year; it was the land of virtue, of peace, and of plenty. In short it was America."[199]

Land of Opportunity?

FIRST IMPRESSIONS

Culture Shock

With the exceptions of John Miller and Mathew Carey, who arrived earlier, and Benjamin Binns, who arrived later, the radical exiles reached the United States during a fifteen-year period, from 1792 to 1807. They encountered a society that was undergoing rapid social and economic change; a new federal system of government that had yet to be properly bedded down; a continued uncertainty about the new nation's place in a world at war; and, closer to home, an ambiguous attitude toward the thousands of immigrants brought to the country by international revolutionary forces and the prospects of economic rewards, which at times in this period was to erupt into outbursts of nativism.[1] To help them cope with these uncertainties, the radical exiles arrived laden down with cultural and political baggage, of which some parts were to be useful, but other parts needed to be jettisoned if they were to settle comfortably in their new home.

Of course, the exiles were immigrants as well as radicals, and thus had to cope with most of the practical difficulties inevitably faced by all who seek to settle in a foreign land. Similarly, they also had to negotiate a transitional or adjustment period, the length of which varied with each individual and was determined by a number of factors, including the personal psychology and abilities of each immigrant, the availability of support networks to ease the transition, and current responses to emigration among the native inhabitants. Few immigrants could genuinely emulate John Daly Burk's claim to have made a swift transition from Irishman to American: "I too am a citizen of those States—from the moment the stranger puts his foot on the soil of *America,* his fetters are rent to pieces, and the scales of servitude which he had contracted under *European* tyrannies fall off, [and] he becomes a FREEMAN; and tho' civil regulations may refuse him the immediate exercise of his rights, he is *virtually* a citizen."[2] More realistically, the transition from Englishman, or Irishman, or Scotsman to American was a long and uncomfortable process, as Burk himself was later to discover, and many were never to make it.[3]

One of the main pitfalls facing an immigrant is the natural tendency to compare the past with the present, contrasting what is in one's haversack with what is on offer. In 1794 the French Girondin exile Brillat-Savarin had wise advice on that score for those contemplating emigration to the United States: "I spoke like them, I dressed like them, I was careful not to give the impression of being cleverer than they were, I found everything they did good; thereby repaying their hospitality by a consideration which I believe necessary and which I counsel to all those people who find themselves in a similar position."[4] Embellishing these insights at a later date, John Caldwell advised that immigrants ought not make "invidious and almost always ill-founded comparisons between the country they left and that which opened its arms for their hospitable reception." Nor should they "too often" sigh "after the flesh pots of Egypt, or rather . . . after the misery, famine and tyranny of the ill-starred country they left, if they should not at once succeed equal to their foolish hopes and expectations."[5]

Another radical who quickly worked out that keeping one's counsel and being nonjudgmental was a key to acceptance and success in a foreign country was the Belfast doctor, John Campbell White, who settled in Baltimore. Within a few years of arrival he had become an enthusiastic booster of the country, adopting local ways and manners, "and admits he never felt real comfort and happiness to the degree he now enjoys, in the land he left." Understandably, "He is held in high estimation, and what is extraordinary, by the very violent people of both [political] parties."[6] White was also aware that the upheavals of emigration could only subside following a long process of settling in. To Robert Simms he confided: "You must know that a settlement in a new country is attended with many inconveniences, and that a considerable time must elapse before a new settler will find himself at his ease. He must serve a kind of noviciate, or apprenticeship, in acquiring a knowledge of the trade of the country, of its inhabitants, and more particularly, such part of them as he does any business with."[7] Probably the greatest problem facing new arrivals, he thought, was the absence of a kinship network, which in the old country acted as a security blanket for most functional families. Settling the eldest children in suitable positions so that disaster would not result if the main breadwinner died prematurely was one strategy White highly recommended.[8]

Again and again radical exiles, after their own period of adjustment, were to hammer home the injunction that an immigrant's successful "apprenticeship" required perseverance, unremitting toil, and eternal optimism. Mathew Carey wrote of gradually advancing in the world only "by care, indefatigable industry, the most rigid punctuality, and frugality," good advice, he ruefully admitted in his autobiography, that he failed to follow himself.[9] John Chambers, who became a prosperous stationer in New York, warned that "nothing but misery and disappointment" awaited Irish immigrants who failed to display "unquestioned evidence of industry and firmness of mind."[10] The Scot Alexander Wilson—whose introduction to America was disillusioning ("We made free to go into a good many farm-houses on the road [from Wilmington to Philadelphia], but saw none of that kindness and hospitality so often told of them")—took a metaphor from nature to explain the acclimatization process. "Assure all my friends this is a good country," he informed a friend in Paisley; "The transplanting a tree or flower checks its growth for a little, but let them persevere, and they will finally prosper, be independent, and wealthy, and happy, if they will."[11]

Today these virtues promoted by the exiles would probably be called Victorian values, but in the late 1790s, more than most immigrants, the radicals emphasized these necessary attainments because they had imbibed Paine's views that republican government offered the best prospects of a society open to the talented, and that the ideal form of republican government was America's.[12] They had migrated with the expectation of using the wasted or underused talents that had been denied to them by the highly structured social world of Britain. In a New York sermon in 1794 REV. THOMAS DUNN, who had emigrated after being persecuted by his neighbors for his religious heterodoxy, both quoted Paine's *Common Sense* almost verbatim on the value of republicanism and placed his mentor's fate in England in a long historical context of talents being ignored: "From the murder of righteous Abel, down to Dr. Priestley, the first philosopher of the present age, superior integrity and superior talents have always been persecuted by narrow-minded, malignant, and wicked men."[13] Two years earlier Thomas Cooper, replying to Edmund Burke, the great defender of prescription and hereditary claims, had written that "strength, and wisdom, and talents, and good dispositions, superior capacity of body or mind—superior industry or activity, do, and ought to create proportionate distinctions, and to bring with them their own reward."[14] Now free from the British constitution, which aimed "above all to cramp the inventive genius and the enterprising spirit of Englishmen,"[15] the radicals hoped to spread their wings and fly like birds in the New World.

For many radical exiles, however, these high expectations were not swiftly fulfilled. They experienced severe culture shock in the first months after their arrival. John Binns, who had devoured every travel book he could find before emigrating, discovered that the reality did not conform to the naive images they had planted in his imagination: "I expected that among the people, even in the large towns, I should occasionally meet one of our red brethren with his squaw leaning lovingly on his arm. I expected to find the white men so plain and quakerly in their dress that I had the lace ripped from my neckerchiefs, and the ruffles from my shirts."[16] This was Binns laughing at himself in old age, but even Benjamin Vaughan, half-American and with extended family firmly settled in Maine, was out of touch. Believing that republican America mirrored his ideal image of patriarchal simplicity, from Switzerland—whence he had fled after his hostile welcome in France—he ordered his plate sold and advised his family to dress in the plainest manner before embarking for the New World.[17]

More seriously, it does appear that the radicals genuinely believed they were entering a society in which republican and democratic institutions had fundamentally altered not only the human condition, but also human nature. In a real sense, many had come to believe their own propaganda. Inevitably, there was early disappointment. Some of the criticism that ensued was unreasonable. Tone, for instance, informed Thomas Russell that America "is beautiful, but it is like a beautiful scene in a theatre; the effect at a proper distance is admirable, but it will not bear a minute inspection."[18] At the time of writing, Tone had been in the country for precisely two days!

With greater percipience—given that others also complained about the same problem—Tone whined that Americans "do fleece us émigrés at a most unmerciful rate."[19] But such treatment was not meted out only to radicals; it truly denoted egalitarianism in practice. A respectable English lawyer, Charles William Janson, visiting a city market in 1793 with other new arrivals, soon found "that we had paid at least a halfpenny per pound more than the market price." Wryly, he conceded that in other countries "the perversion of the scriptural expression 'I was a stranger and you took me in,' is perhaps still more strikingly exemplified."[20] Henrietta Liston, wife of the British minister in Philadelphia, suffered equally. "Of *Us*," she wrote, "all advantages are taken, Foreign-Ministers are esteemed lawful Game, and there is less real principle in this Country than I expected to find, particularly in the lower orders of the People." Yet, she continued, leaving the house unlocked at night probably would go unpunished: "*cheating not stealing* seems to be the error in America."[21]

Those arriving at the height of the nativist upsurge in 1798–1801 (including a large number of Irish rebels, involuntary exiles unprepared for migration) were the most likely to feel early disappointment with their new country. Caldwell noted that his family was hospitably received by his countrymen already settled in New York, but rather grudgingly stated that "from the natives we met a cordial reception."[22] In Philadelphia Thomas Ledlie Birch felt decidedly unwelcome, possibly because his reluctance to emigrate had left him psychologically unprepared for life in new surroundings: "When God in his providence restores us back to our country, we hope he will dispose us to act to others as becomes freemen, we will not meet you on our shore in hostile array, armed with an Alien Bill and a naturalization law, extended from two to fourteen years."[23] Birch was eventually to live in America for thirty years, but it took him nearly one-third of that time to come to terms with his predicament.[24]

Homesickness was another natural emotion that struck nearly all the exiles at one time or another, usually when things were not going well. Those who had been forced to leave their families in the British Isles were particularly prone to this complaint. John Binns claimed to feel the pangs even "after an absence of more than half a century" from his friends and relatives.[25] After two years in America the usually extrovert Hamilton Rowan had been reduced to misery. According to one of his American friends, writing to Mrs Rowan: "Your husband's every feeling—all his happiness seems centred in you and your children; he thinks of nothing else; he scarce thinks of any thing but of schemes for being restored to you; it is the theme of all his conversations with me. He leads a recluse life, and mixes little in society."[26] Any small event or recollection could trigger homesickness. In April 1799 David Bailie Warden was writing home to Ireland, concerned with explaining the state elections then taking place in New York. He mused: "Some unhappy destiny seems, at present, to torment the nations of the earth." This turned his mind to Ireland. "I must," he wails, "lay down my pen. My imagination pictures Ireland, and every gleam of joy departs."[27]

Scots suffered the pangs as much as the Irish. A Scotsman in Baltimore in 1803 noted how most of the Highlanders—thrown off their homelands by the clearances and now reluctantly trekking to the backcountry—would rather have returned home: "They expected riches and liberty, but found nothing but a struggle to keep themselves alive."[28] The outlawed James Thomson Callender, dispirited by his lack of success, and forced to take refuge in Virginia from the outrage his political writings had caused in Philadelphia in 1798, confided to his mentor, Thomas Jefferson, that he hoped to return to Scotland in a few years, once "matters clear up on the other side of the Atlantick."[29]

Thoughts of home usually only became oppressive when expectations remained unfulfilled and prospects appeared bleak. Binns, after all, remained in America for the rest of his long life; Warden had only days before been waxing lyrical about the beauties of an American spring; and Callender, once more involved in political warfare in 1799, must have startled Jefferson by writing that if he could save some money, he would "come up the James River . . . and try to find fifty acres of clear land, and a hearty Virginian female, that knows how to fatten pigs, and boil hommany, and hold her tongue."[30] Alexander Wilson's roller-coaster feelings about his homeland probably best reflect the experiences of most exiles who eventually determined to remain in America. His first unfavorable opinions on his new country soon gave way to contentment once he realized that he could "live ten times better than in Scotland and still save." However, forced to spend longer as a schoolmaster than he wished, his optimism waned. A disappointing romance further depressed him. To his friend Charles Orr he wrote: "I have lost all relish for this country and if Heaven spares me I shall soon see the shores of old Caledonia. . . . Let us contrive a plan to leave this country and try old Scotia once more in company." Wilson never remigrated; soldiering on, he eventually found satisfaction and a degree of fame in his new country. He always thought of Scotland and his absent relatives with affection, and at least once suggested his desire to visit them. But he would not have considered remaining in Scotland: "Like a true bird of passage, I would again wing my way across the western waste of waters, to the peaceful and happy regions of America."[31]

Radical exiles may have faced the same practical difficulties as other immigrants, but when all is said and done, a great many were very different from the masses. Often better educated, generally more prosperous, and trained for professional occupations, they had higher expectations and were thus inevitably more prone to disappointment. There is an irony in the complaints of some radicals at the difficulty they found obtaining reliable servants. "The badness of servants," Emmet claimed, was "the most crying grievance of America."[32] The English radicals agreed. Henrietta Liston, who received social calls from many of those who had voluntarily emigrated, including Priestley and Russell, was forced to listen politely to their complaints about America, although she felt it improper that she should hear their "confessions." The climate (naturally!), virulent diseases, and the exorbitant cost of living were high on their list of woes, but the complaint most frequently voiced was the servant problem. Priestley confided to her that "the *Servants* alone are sufficient to render a native of Britain miserable in this Country." Mrs. Liston was convinced only shame and poverty kept the radicals in America, and mischievously suggested that the British government should send all the country's "Democrates" to America. "The cure," she believed, "would be as effectual as Botany Bay."[33]

The task of finding and keeping servants in America was difficult, of course, because in this rapidly democratizing society there was no longer a tradition of deference, at least in the cities north of the Mason-Dixon line, and because the wide open spaces of the western lands were a continual attraction for the lower classes.[34] Priestley soon came to appreciate that the traditional master-servant relationship of Britain hardly existed across the Atlantic. The poor preferred independence to well-paid service: "If there was more subordination," he believed, "it would be better for them all."[35] Yet this combination of democratic pretensions and economic opportunity was precisely what had been at the root of America's reputation among radicals in Britain; for some of those who encountered it firsthand, however, it was, at least initially, hard to endure.

First Steps

The servant problem was a symptom of a wider crisis among the exiles, which involved a natural sense of disorientation, a loss of status, and a realization that many were either ill-equipped or unqualified for the types of occupations that were readily available. Those from a middle-class urban background who had visions of establishing new communities in the semicleared wilderness of the backcountry were particularly ill-suited. If the tough Baptists of the Welsh valleys found it too difficult to preserve their Beula in western Pennsylvania,[36] it is not surprising that the followers of Priestley and Cooper who tried to create a community for gentlefolk in Northumberland were totally out of their depth. Joseph Priestley, Jr., came to acknowledge that it was as well for them that their project was abandoned, for: "The generality of Englishmen come to this country with such erroneous ideas, and, unless previously accustomed to a life of labour, are so ill qualified to commence cultivation in a wilderness, that the projectors would most probably have been subject to still more unfounded abuse than they have been, for their well meant endeavours to promote the interests of their countrymen."[37]

More sensible were those who had the time and money to sit back and consider the options available, rather than rashly striking out on a new occupation (as did the city-dwelling engineer Henry Jackson, who precipitately bought a farm in the middle of nowhere and consequently suffered mind-numbing boredom).[38] William Russell took his family on a long circular journey incorporating New York, Philadelphia, Northumberland—where he visited Priestley and sensibly declined to join the colony—and Boston, before they finally settled in Middletown, Connecticut.[39] John Chambers, a year before he embarked on a business in partnership with his son in New York, took a grand winter tour to the South, visiting Campbell White, Jackson, and the Irish poet, Robert Moore. He satisfied his longstanding curiosity by attending many sittings of Congress in Washington, and seeing (if not meeting) Thomas Jefferson, "the great character who presides over the destinies of this happy country."[40] William Sampson, seeking to repair his shattered health, soon after arrival traveled up the Hudson to Ballston Springs where, in his efforts to become a registered New York lawyer, he happily became "acquainted and in many cases intimately, with what may be safely called the first company of America." He would, he anticipated, eventually "profit by them."[41]

The majority of the radical exiles, however, had neither the time nor the money leisurely to contemplate their future. Finding work was their first priority and many were forced to take whatever was available. Some who had previous experience in the higher branches of the print and publishing trades nevertheless had to start at the bottom. Joseph Gales was first employed in 1795 as a compositor for Claypole and Dunlap on their Philadelphia newspaper, the *American Daily Advertiser*. His talent was soon recognized; promoted to bookkeeper, he also replaced an inefficient stenographer and reported congressional debates, quickly making a deserved reputation for accuracy and impartiality.[42] James Thomson Callender followed a similar path, although no one ever accused him of being impartial. Armed with letters of recommendation from friends he had met while hiding in Dublin, he was initially employed part-time by Mathew Carey as editor of the Old World sections of a new edition of Guthrie's *Geography*. At the same time, until the yellow fever epidemic of 1793 totally disrupted the publishing trade, he acted as Dunlap's assistant on the *Advertiser*. Thereafter, he became congressional reporter for Andrew Brown's *Federal* (later *Philadelphia*) *Gazette*, a job he used to attack the pretensions of (mainly Federalist) politicians.[43]

Both Gales and Callender were, in their very different ways, to have a significant impact on American journalism. William Duane, another exile who had to start at the bottom and work his way up, was to be even more influential. Born near Lake Champlain in 1760 to Irish Catholic parents, Duane was taken by his widowed mother to Ireland when he was about eleven.[44] His teenage years were spent amid his landed relations who were, despite their religion, reasonably prosperous. He was a difficult young man; by the age of nineteen, and while still serving an apprenticeship in the printing trade, he had not only rejected the teachings of his church, but had also married a probably pregnant Protestant girl. Duane moved to London, where for several years he worked for John Almon as a parliamentary reporter on the Foxite *General Advertiser*. In 1786, leaving his wife and family behind, he sailed to Bengal, where he produced several newspapers, including the Calcutta *World*, which unusually included much European news. It became a forum for those opposed to the policies of the East India Company. Duane's opposition to the established powers, and his moderate pro-French Revolution stance brought him spells in a Calcutta prison. Eventually he was expelled, arriving back in England in July 1795. For the next few months he was involved both in antigovernment journalism, as editor of the *Telegraph*, and in the last major open push of the LCS to gain a mass base for their policies.[45]

The following year Duane and his family arrived in New York, virtually destitute. His equally radical friend and traveling companion Thomas Lloyd, a Welsh-born American veteran of the war of independence who had spent several years in Newgate for seditious libel, helped to pay the fares of Duane's family.[46] For several months Duane worked on contract for a publisher before he traveled with Lloyd to Philadelphia, where they traipsed around the printing shops seeking employment. At Richard Folwell's establishment Duane's rather slapstick interview included an invitation to sing. He "bellowed forth tremendously," but Folwell, unimpressed by Duane's long beard and wild hair, refused to employ him. With tongue in cheek (he was to be no friend to Republicans), Folwell later admitted he might have decided otherwise if he had known the hirsute Irishman would become a colonel and "look so pretty about the head" after cropping.[47] Duane's prospects were not harmed by this rejection; he and Lloyd were soon working for the *Merchant's Daily Advertiser.*

Exiles with practical skills, a determination to succeed, and a realistic approach to what was possible stood the best chance of falling most rapidly on their feet. Those with clerical skills found adjustment more difficult.[48] Alexander Wilson noted in 1801 that "New York swarms with newly imported Irishmen of all descriptions, clerks, schoolmasters, etc."[49] It is a debatable point whether young men who in the recent past had been wielding weapons and holding military rank would have desired to revert to the mundane task of "driving the quill" in a bank or counting house, but in the event, with such positions being rarely available in the American cities, few were given the opportunity. Schoolteaching, however, remained the stopgap for the educated young exile with few other skills.[50] It was common in Ulster for Presbyterian licentiates to teach while awaiting a call from a congregation. So many were obliged to continue this practice across the Atlantic that Cobbett contemptuously claimed in late 1798 that "one half of the country-schools in Pennsylvania are in the hands of these 'poor ignorant creatures.' " He was referring in particular to the group of Covenanting Presbyterian students, including Wylie, Black, and McAdam, who initially kept body and soul together by establishing a school in Lower Dublin township in Philadelphia, traveling as far as Lancaster in search of pupils.[51] Wylie and Black were to go on to greater things at the University of Pennsylvania, as too was Bailie Warden, who began teaching at a seminary at Kinderhook, New York, before graduating to principal tutor at Kingston Academy.[52]

The most graphic account of the drudgery of teaching came from Alexander Wilson, who struggled to escape its clutches. In July 1801 he was earning the miserable sum of $160 a year as a teacher in "a settlement of canting, preaching, praying and snivelling ignorant Presbyterians." His lot was not a happy one: "The scholars have been accustomed to great liberties by their former teacher. They used to piss and put stones in his pocket etc. etc. I was told that the people did not like to have their children punished, but I began with such a system of terror as soon established my authority most effectually. I succeed in teaching them to read, and I care for none of their objections." To while away the time he composed self-pitying verse:

> There lonely and sad in his country box sitting,
> The windows unglazed, and the floor all beshitten;
> A wretched exile murmers ABC grieving,
> In sounds slow and solemn from Morning to Even.

When Wilson moved to a new position at Gray's Ferry in 1802 he unhappily recorded: "I shall recommence that painful profession once more with the same gloomy resignation that a prisoner re-enters his Dungeon or a Malefactor mounts the Scaffold; Fate urges him, necessity me."[53]

Wilson had thwarted ambitions that turned his mind against the practice of teaching the young. Others, grateful for the succor it gave, viewed teaching as an honorable profession. BERNARD MCKENNA, a young County Tyrone Catholic who fled Ireland during the harrying of the North in 1797, on arrival in America—"a land of peace and plenty, and . . . garden spot of the world"—walked from Newcastle, Delaware, to Long Island, New York, where he was swiftly offered the position of schoolmaster in "a very respectable neighbourhood." He soon recognized his unfitness for the job, but doggedly set out to improve his education. Having obtained books on English grammar, bookkeeping, navigation, and geography: "I began my studies and gave myself up entirely to a recluse life appropriating every hour (when absent from the school) to the business. In the summer season I frequently retired to the woods: here I spent my time in solitude and in close retirement, as long as the temperance of the weather prevailed; in the winter I shut myself up in the schoolhouse where I have spent whole nights: still continuing myself disengaged from everything that I thought might retard my progress in the attainment of those desirable accomplishments, for about the space of two years." McKenna's reward for perseverance was his appointment at "a superior school" fifteen miles away, where he earned $300 a year, "and found in everything but clothes, with every accommodation suitable to any gentleman, a horse, or horse and chair, any time at my command."[54]

Wilson and McKenna did not possess formal qualifications to help them settle comfortably into their new lives. One might expect that experienced men in the liberal professions would have found the transition easier. Charles Janson, for example, thought that the medically qualified ought to have been welcomed in America. "Gentlemen of that profession have opportunities of pushing themselves forward which lawyers cannot adopt. A medical man, with tolerable address, may plant himself in any town in the United States, without undergoing the probation required from the lawyer."[55] Campbell White's success in Baltimore appears to confirm this, but it is significant that he did not play down the initial difficulties involved, and he had the advantage of settling among a city élite which shared his Presbyterianism.[56] The early fate of GEORGE CUMING, a prisoner in Fort George for three years, further qualifies Janson's optimism. He arrived in New York in late 1802 with, according to John Caldwell, "an eminent surgical character, strongly recommended, and with good certificates from Edinburgh." He "could not fail of succeeding."[57] But if Cuming did not fail, neither did he prosper. So dissatisfied was he with his New York practice that in 1805 he agreed to move to Natchez, in the Mississippi Territory, at the behest of a wealthy friend who promised him "a competency."[58] In the event, another outbreak of yellow fever in New York prevented him from realizing his assets, and with Emmet and Chambers now settling in the city, Cuming decided to remain.[59]

Local Aid

Undoubtedly, the exiles who fared best in their early years benefited from local assistance, either from influential American contacts or from their fellow radicals. Mathew Carey had only been in Philadelphia a few days when he was summoned by the Marquis de Lafayette, who had read of the young exile's Dublin escapades in the press. When he learned that Carey intended to edit a newspaper, not only did the French hero offer to recommend him to his Philadelphia friends Robert Morris and Thomas Fitzsimons, but he also subsequently sent Carey an unsolicited $400.[60]

Similarly, Thomas Addis Emmet's reputation appears to have preceded him. When he first arrived in New York in November 1804 he had intentions of visiting Harman Blennerhassett on his island paradise on the Ohio river, before settling down as a farmer. He had deliberately left his law library in Ireland. But as he later admitted: "My principles and my sufferings were my first passport and introduction here and they procured me the effective friendship of the leading characters of this state [New York] and in the union at large."[61] At a dinner at John Caldwell's, where he met many of the city's Republican élite, he was firmly advised to consider taking up law. As an alien, however, he was unqualified. Almost at once he traveled to Washington, where Jefferson and others told him that his lack of citizenship should not be a disqualification. One lawyer even obtained his admission to the bar at Alexandria, Virginia. Disliking the idea of living in a slave society, however, Emmet returned to New York where, with the assistance of the Republican party leaders Governor George Clinton, New York mayor De Witt Clinton, and future governor Daniel D. Tomkins, the Supreme Court permitted him to practice law despite his alien status. With the bar denuded of talent by the death in a duel of Alexander Hamilton, and the subsequent withdrawal from the state of his killer Aaron Burr, Emmet was swiftly on the road to success.[62] In August 1806 William Sampson was given the same privilege to practice, but thereafter this loophole was blocked.[63]

Only a small fraction of the exiles possessed a sufficiently high reputation to be courted on arrival by influential Americans. The majority, seeking assistance in the first instance, came to rely on either immigrant aid societies or the friendship of other, longer-settled radicals.[64] Immigrant aid societies existed in most of the large ports, some for the benefit of immigrants in general, others for particular nationalities.[65] In Philadelphia there were the long-established St. Andrew's Society for indigent Scots and the Society of St. George for the English; in 1792 the Hibernian Society was created for the Irish. There was also the general Philadelphia Society for the Information and Assistance of Persons Emigrating from Foreign Countries, on several committees of which William Young Birch sat in 1796 (he was to be a prominent member of the Society of St. George by the 1820s).[66] Members of the Hibernian Society, who were mainly Jeffersonian Republicans from the middling groups in society with a sprinkling of the wealthy, visited all ships coming from Ireland to check on the treatment of immigrants and help the newly arrived find their feet. Mathew Carey played a prominent role from its inception, and devised a program for the society that included attending to the education of newcomers, as well as helping them integrate and become "Americans."[67]

In New York, too, longer established aid societies, such as the conservative Friendly Sons of St. Patrick, were paralleled by Republican-dominated societies such as the Hibernian Provident Society by the early years of the new century, with exiles such as George Cuming, Emmet, and MacNeven taking a prominent part in their activities.[68] Among the English exiles, John Caudwell was secretary of the Albion Benevolent Society.[69] MacNeven, John Chambers, Sampson, and Emmet also were involved in establishing in 1816 the New York Association for the Relief of Emigrant Irishmen. This society promoted the idea that Irish migrants should move into the country away from the snares of metropolitan life as soon as they arrived. The problem of Irish reluctance to leave the relative security of friends in the seaboard cities had been noticed by

John Caldwell as early as 1802. Scottish and German farmers or agricultural laborers were always prepared to seek work in the countryside, where their talents were best suited. "I wish I could say," he informed Simms,

> the same for our countrymen. The labourer, the farmer, the weaver, on coming here, all incline to live in *large towns*. This may arise from the *known* character of the Irish. We are, to use a trite saying, so warmhearted, we wish to live together and to be in the way of hearing often from our friends. But this disposition is often attended with ruin to individuals, and dishonour to our national character. I have often seen the man, who, with his family might have made a figure a hundred miles from town, and there been respectable as a citizen and a man, lose his little property in the dram shop he kept, lose his time by attending to political controversy, and matters that *as an alien did not concern him*, or at all events, which his interference could not better, and lose the respectability of himself and of his family.[70]

One scheme to help disperse the Irish came from the Wexford rebel Nicholas Gray, who in Ireland had been a lawyer but by 1816 was a landowner in Mississippi Territory, from where he offered to provide land, rent-free for three years, to Irishmen willing to move so far from the eastern seaboard.[71] Whether anyone took up his offer is not known, but it would not have reduced the number of Irishmen in New York significantly. The bolder solution that the Association put forward, which would have dispersed the migrants but also appealed to Irish sociability, was for Congress to grant a large tract of land in Illinois on easy terms, specifically for Irish immigrants. In 1818, on a mission that took two months, John Chambers carried a memorial to Washington seeking federal assistance, but the idea was defeated in the House of Representatives by twelve votes. Although the society persisted, the scheme was never put into practice.[72]

Mutual Aid

How many radical exiles sought assistance from these aid societies is not known. Probably only the most indigent turned to them, as Callender was forced to in the spring of 1798 when he was provided with food for his family by his friend Thomas Leiper of the St. Andrew's Society. One of his dying wife's last meals included the leftovers from a wedding banquet.[73] More common was the unstructured assistance that the exiles gave to each other. Much of this was low-level, but nonetheless helpful for men striving to make their way while adjusting to new circumstances. Dr. James Reynolds and other United Irish exiles, for instance, helped collect material for John Daly Burk's pamphlet on the Irish rebellion, while Denis Driscol was later to promote Burk's history of Virginia by printing extracts in his Augusta newspaper.[74] James Cheetham was the only New York editor prepared to accept advertisements for Driscol's Deist *The Temple of Reason;* Duane helped Driscol when he moved the magazine to Philadelphia.[75] In 1798 William Young Birch presented a number of books to the Welsh radical Morgan John Rhees's library in Beula.[76] Rhees's settlement was advertised in Joseph Gales's Philadelphia newspaper, as were the publications of Richard Lee. In North Carolina, Gales reprinted Lee's editorials from the *American Universal Magazine,* and printed an account of Thomas Cooper's trial for seditious libel in 1799 from his own notes.[77]

Connections already forged in Britain and Ireland were strengthened in America. DAVID BRUCE, on arrival in Philadelphia, where he worked for Thomas Dobson on the *Philadelphia Gazette,* deliberately sought out fellow members of Scotland's Friends of the People, including Archibald Binny and JAMES RONALDSON.[78] Thomas Cooper saved Thomas Lloyd from penury in 1801 by hiring him as his secretary when he was appointed commissioner to settle Connecticut's land claims in the Wyoming Valley. Joseph Gales not only continued to employ Richard Davison, his old journeyman in Sheffield, when he started the *Raleigh Register,* but he later helped him establish his own newspaper, the Warrenton *Messenger.*[79] When David Bailie Warden returned to America in 1810 to seek confirmation of his position as American consul-general in Paris, his case was supported by Sampson, MacNeven, Emmet, and Duane. In Paris, Warden acted as an unofficial cultural agent, regularly sending back books and the latest scientific, social, and literary information to his correspondents, including Jefferson, Chambers, and Duane.[80]

In Philadelphia some of the exiles formed "The Club," a society that met regularly on Mondays for companionship and conviviality until 1820. This was in some ways an unusual gathering, for it transcended nationality, Englishmen like Cooper and William Young Birch mixing with Irishmen like Edward Hudson and John Binns.[81] More commonly, nonpolitical connections tended to remain intranational. Elaborate transatlantic and interstate networks of correspondence and communication ensured that personal news—marriages, births, and new jobs—was widely spread, with certain individuals, such as Robert Simms in Belfast, Andrew Bryson's sister in Newtownards, and Bailie Warden in Paris, acting as sorting officers, receiving and passing on information.[82] Tight-knit Irish communities evolved in Baltimore, Philadelphia, and New York, and were strengthened by intermarriage. One of Emmet's sons married MacNeven's stepdaughter (the widower MacNeven married "an amiable pretty little widow" in 1810); Tone's son William married Sampson's daughter Catherine; Richard Caldwell, who in 1812 was to die of fever as a captain in the U.S. army fighting for his new country, married John Chambers's daughter; and one of Edward Hudson's three wives was the daughter of Patrick Byrne.[83]

The Bonding of Religion

Undoubtedly, religion played a key role in assisting the exiles to acclimatize in America. For those belonging to the major denominations, membership of settled congregations swiftly helped them assimilate into the community. Of all the exiles' expectations of their new home, their religious hopes were to be the most nearly fulfilled. Nevertheless, for the more heterodox there were shocks in store, and for all the exiles the instability, enthusiasm, and variety of religious practices in America came as an unexpected surprise. This was partly because the radicals were not fully aware of the main tumultuous impulses, harnessed in the Second Great Awakening, that drove American religious movements in the years following the war of independence. English Rational Dissenters, for example, had forged strong links with men of a similar religious outlook in New England before and during the war. Their correspondence tended to leave the impression that the liberal Arianism of Jonathan Mayhew, or the anti-enthusiastic beliefs of Charles Chauncy were commonplace in America.[84] Knowledge of Benjamin Franklin's and Thomas Jefferson's Deism reinforced the impression both that rational religion was the norm, and that complete religious liberty existed in America. The latter view seemed to be confirmed first by Jefferson's Virginia Statute for Establishing Religious Freedom of 1786, which gave equal protection to the profession of all religions, Christian or otherwise, and then by the famous "no establishment" clause of the First Amendment to the Federal constitution in 1790, which forbade the national government to legislate on religious matters, leaving the beliefs of each individual to his or her conscience. It is thus not surprising that when Thomas Cooper published his *Information Concerning America* in 1794—it was written in the form of letters to an English Rational Dissenter—he failed to mention religion at all. He assumed it would not be an issue in America for the exiles.

In reality it was, for a number of reasons. First, Cooper, like many other radicals, had failed to grasp the complexities of the new federal system of government, and in particular the fact that the state constitutions also included articles on religion, some of which were not so liberal, nor so indifferent as

Virginia's and the national government's. Although all state constitutions confirmed the right of individual religious liberty, in a few there were significant limitations. Maryland, New Hampshire, and South Carolina, for example, offered toleration only to Christian religions; in New Jersey, full civil rights were protected only for Protestants. Moreover, many states required a religious test for men holding public office; even democratic Pennsylvania required members of the legislature to take an oath acknowledging the divine origin of the Bible.[85] New York did not abolish its religious test for office, offensive to Roman Catholics, until February 1806.[86]

Protean Presbyterians

Compared with British law, of course, American state religious policies were remarkably generous. Nevertheless, the law by no means conformed to popular attitudes, which often were less tolerant. Some of the exiles were to face this reality on several occasions, but particularly during the height of nativist and high Federalist fears between 1797 and 1801. The careers of the young Presbyterian licentiates suffered perhaps the greatest dislocation from the suspicion of foreigners shown by certain denominations, for they became victims of a set of regulations issued by the American Presbyterian General Assembly in 1798, whereby only ordained clergymen from overseas with satisfactory credentials were to be admitted to the church, following a year's probation. Any hopes the probationers may have had of being ordained in America were dashed by the refusal of the Ulster Presbyteries to give them certificates of probation. John Miles, James Hull, and Warden were all denied certificates by the Bangor Presbytery, leading the last to fulminate in a pamphlet against the hypocrisy of a Presbytery which had previously circulated "Republican Morality" turning itself into "an Ecclesiastical Court Martial."[87] It is significant that, with the exception of Warden, it has been impossible to discover the ultimate fates of the ten non-Covenanting Presbyterian licentiates who emigrated. All must have moved into different careers.

Even some ordained and certified Presbyterian ministers discovered that the path to acceptance was not easy. They were shaken to discover that as American Christianity became democratized, it took on an increasingly evangelical and enthusiastic character. The connection between rational religion and political liberty, which so many radical exiles took for granted, was sundered in America by a powerful movement that married an unsophisticated Bible Christianity with doctrines of personal freedom, individualism, and an egalitarian spirit.[88] In this situation, the radicals adhering to Enlightenment religious values found themselves regarded as outsiders in a society that they had anticipated would be freely welcoming.

Thomas Ledlie Birch suffered from this rising evangelical fervor. He preached in Philadelphia for three months shortly after his arrival, but when he moved to Washington, western Pennsylvania in 1800, he (and Robert Steele) found themselves in difficulties. Querulous and quarrelsome, Birch stirred up a hornet's nest among local Presbyterians. The local newspaper called him "a dog to eat children's bread," a "renegado, fugitive from justice," and a "traitor to his country." In 1802 he was acquitted on a charge of adultery, but in the following year he was rejected by the General Assembly of the Presbyterian Church in Philadelphia, and subsequently by the Ohio Presbytery. Birch claimed that all his misfortunes stemmed from his Jeffersonian and democratic republican politics, although it is likely that his distaste for the frontier's individual conversion-type evangelicalism and his preference for academic millenarian prophesying were also influential.[89]

That was certainly the case with Rev. Robert Steele, whose call to the Pittsburgh congregation in 1799 brought together in an unfortunate alliance his suavity of manners and the backcountry's greater earthiness. Tall, well-spoken, with all the social graces, Steele lived (or, perhaps, tried to live) in the style of a gentleman, never being seen without satin breeches, silk stockings, kneebuckles, and pumps. At a time when the Second Great Awakening was reviving enthusiastic preaching and the necessity of repentance, Steele was easy-going, cool, and indulgent toward backsliders in his congregation. He was an active pastor; he opened a Sunday school, at which he personally attended Bible classes, and in 1802 replaced the old log chapel with a more solid brick edifice. For a large part of his congregation, however, who thought education "unessential" and the revivalist message vital, Steele was unsatisfactory. In June 1802 they withdrew, forming the Second Presbyterian Church in Pittsburgh. Until his death in 1810, from pneumonia contracted when fighting a fire on a wintery night, Steele's congregation remained small, growing only slowly over the years. He was thus considered a failure.[90]

Steele had found his position even though he had not brought his certificates with him from Ulster. His example suggests that most ordained ministers were able eventually to find a congregation. The Burgher exiles REV. JAMES HARPER and REV. THOMAS SMITH, likely by their theology to be sympathetic to the direction of American religious practices, each secured a congregation within a year or two of arrival.[91] The New Light William Sinclair, even though he had been disannexed by the Presbytery of Antrim in 1798 when found guilty of treason, ministered to a congregation in Baltimore.[92]

John Glendy, too, was to find Baltimore a haven, but his change of fortune arrived when he visited several towns in Virginia on a preaching tour. There he caught the eye of Thomas Jefferson, who was later to inform Governor McKean of Pennsylvania that Glendy was "without exception the best preacher I ever heard."[93] His reward was the chaplaincy of the federal House of Representatives in 1805, and a similar role for the Senate in 1816.[94]

The Unity of Unitarians

The diversity of Presbyterian theology in America helped exiled ministers of various arcane beliefs eventually to find a congregation that suited them (and vice versa). For them, the process of acclimatizing to their new world could begin relatively swiftly. But it was another matter for the more heterodox exiles such as Unitarians and Deists. They found that the profound transformations that American religion was undergoing placed them on the margins, the object of scorn and hatred. In Philadelphia in June 1796 fourteen men formed themselves into the Society of Unitarian Christians, which was the first church in the United States openly to bear the scare-name unitarian. Uninfluenced by the liberal Christianity that was to become unitarianism in New England, this new sect consisted almost entirely of English-born immigrants. By the end of the year, when the membership stood at twenty-one, the radical exiles William Young Birch, Samuel Birch, Ralph Eddowes, Joseph Gales, and William Russell were members. Other exiles, Mathew Falkner, John Eddowes, and Ralph Eddowes, Jr., joined within a few months. Their inspiration remained Joseph Priestley, who in 1796 and 1797 made the long and uncomfortable trip from Northumberland to preach a series of lectures in the capital.[95] Priestley was the obvious person to be their pastor, but his wife, who had never recovered fully from the Birmingham riots of 1791, persuaded him to remain in the isolation and safety of the backcountry, even though the settlement of English gentlemen that Cooper and Joseph Priestley, Jr., had originally envisioned in Northumberland had collapsed. Nor would the radical exile REV. HENRY TOULMIN, son of Priestley's old friend Joshua, accept an offer to go to Philadelphia: "He was comfortable in his situation at Lexington, and could not remove except upon a certainty of improving it."[96] The result was that until the stiffbacked and autocratic REV. WILLIAM CHRISTIE, who had formed the first unitarian congregation in Scotland in 1782 and who went into exile at the same time as Priestley, became their first ordained minister in 1806, the Philadelphia group was compelled to remain a lay society.[97]

The Philadelphia Unitarians were quietist and uninterested in gaining converts. They were content to support each other through the medium of their church. They met weekly in a small room at the University of Pennsylvania to listen to their regularly elected lay readers. Gales was frequently chosen, until his removal to North Carolina in 1799. He was later, in 1824, to explain to a skeptical Roman Catholic bishop, when justifying the practice of distributing Bibles without insisting on subsequent religious instruction, how simple and uncomplicated Unitarian theology and practice was:

> We have always believed that the Scriptures contained many things hard to understand, yet there is sufficient in them, which is plain and intelligent to the meanest capacity, to produce the best effects on the life and character; and sufficient even without a guide to teach men their duty to God and to their fellow-men. Nor do we conceive the diversity of opinion among men on the subject of religion as an evil to be lamented. All that is necessary to produce happiness under such circumstances is that men should think charitably of each other, and agree to differ, believing that every one who professes himself to be guided by the principles of the Gospel, is sincere in his profession and will hereafter be approved by his Maker.[98]

With such principles, the Philadelphia Unitarians ought to have been able to worship peacefully, confirming their belief that the American Republic championed religious liberty and toleration. Instead, however, establishing themselves just at the time that political warfare began to move toward a crescendo in the city, they found themselves tarred with the brush of pro-French radicalism, even though most seem to have shed their political pasts with emigration. Partly this was the inevitable consequence of their close connection with Priestley who, notwithstanding his determination to keep clear of all political entanglements, found himself the focus of bitter attacks in the Federalist press. Partly, also, their unpopularity stemmed from their supposed theological beliefs, which were commonly perceived to be no better than "deistical, infidel, Christ-denying."[99] The Episcopalians alleged Unitarianism to be a step on the road to atheism; the Presbyterians contended that it was heresy and blasphemy; and the Baptists asserted that the Unitarians were the confederates of Satan. In January 1798 the room at the university allocated to them was withdrawn, and they became a peripatetic society. Men of sympathy and understanding, like President John Adams, distanced themselves from the sect.[100] Even at late as 1813, long after the political frenzy of the Adams years had dissipated, Ralph Eddowes complained that the building of a Unitarian chapel in Philadelphia was "viewed with a kind of religious horror; and not a few have been the harsh epithets and uncharitable expressions to which it has given occasion."[101]

The Unitarian society scarcely survived until the turn of the century. The yellow fever epidemics took their toll on the congregation, which never numbered more than forty-two.[102] For seven years after 1800 it was virtually moribund. The society's historian tentatively suggests that this might be explained by the congregation—which included a large number of merchants—turning their attention to making a living during this period.[103] Furthermore, by 1800 the social (rather than the religious) function of the society had served its purpose for the newly arrived immigrants, helping them to adjust to their new environment. Unable owing to their religious beliefs to assimilate easily, they drew common strength from mutual support. When the congregation was reactivated in 1807, three years after Priestley's death, only Ralph Eddowes remained of the original exile membership, although in later years William Y. Birch and other members of the Eddowes family returned to what continued to remain thereafter a tiny fold.

Conscience-salving Covenanters

Another group of exiles who used their common religious beliefs as a means of survival and acclimatization in America were the Reformed Presbyterians or Covenanters. As with the Unitarians, no formal Reformed organization existed in America at the time William Gibson, Samuel Brown Wylie, John Black, John Reilly, and Thomas McAdam arrived, local congregations having arisen only with the occasional arrival of individual immigrant ministers. In 1797 James McKinney, one of only three ordained Reformed ministers in America (Gibson made a fourth, but one soon died), was in Chester County, South Carolina, so the Covenanters in Philadelphia had to fend for themselves until McKinney arrived the following year. This was easy enough for Wylie and Black; they had been friends since their school days and attended Glasgow University together in 1792. Although they were to separate once they had landed on their feet and Gibson and McKinney had established a Reformed Presbytery—Wylie was to remain in Philadelphia, Black became the first Covenanting minister west of the Allegheny Mountains—they were to marry sisters in Pittsburgh in 1802 and keep in close contact for the rest of their lives. In 1832, when Wylie created the New School Covenanters by splitting the church over the issue of acknowledging the legitimacy of the federal government, Black, with his ordained son and Wylie's nephew, was to take his side.[104]

The Covenanters survived by pulling together and adhering to a common set of religious principles. Their commitment to the seventeenth-century Solemn League and Covenant, even in America, gave them the strength to endure throughout the nineteenth century. They remained an eccentric church, "marked by very distinctive peculiarities."[105] They were undoubtedly republican in politics, but refused to acknowledge the legitimacy of any uncovenanted government, including the federal government: "The [American] Constitution is radically and wilfully defective in that it does not recognise the existence of God, the supremacy of Christ the King of Nations, and the word of God as the supreme law."[106] As God was not mentioned in the oath, Covenanters would never swear allegiance to the United States, and thus neither voted nor held public office (church members who accepted jury service or voted had to confess their sin or face excommunication).[107] However, in other respects they accepted the authority of the state; they paid their taxes and were prepared to bear arms in its defense.

Extremely strict in its modes of discipline—although committed to the universal and immediate abolition of slavery, members were not allowed to join anti-slavery societies that were in any way "political"—but unaffected by the culture of revivalism, the Covenanting church remained small, catering mainly for poor Ulster migrants and their descendants. At first, Wylie ministered in Philadelphia to a congregation of about twenty in a schoolhouse, but as numbers grew they built a modest meeting house in a neighborhood between Cedar and Lombard Streets in 1800 that soon became "each day more repulsive by the bad quality of the occupants." Forced to abandon their church in 1817 (it was taken over by an African-American Presbyterian congregation), they moved to a fine brick church on 11th and Marble Streets.[108]

In 1809 Wylie informed Bailie Warden that he had a small but thriving and healthy congregation, which soon promised to give him a reasonable income.[109] He kept body and soul together by teaching classical languages at the University of Pennsylvania (Black did the same at Dickinson College, Carlisle). A year later Wylie became foundation professor of theology at the new Presbyterian seminary in Philadelphia; in 1828 he was appointed professor of Greek and Latin (two of fourteen languages in which he was competent) at the university, a position he held until 1845.[110]

Undeniably, Wylie and Black and their fellow Covenanting exiles made a successful transition to America. They did so partly by adhering strictly to their covenants, which acted as a protective capsule, insulating them from what they saw as the sins of the secular world. In one sense, their rejection in 1832 of their previously held belief that the federal government gave "legality to gross heresy, blasphemy, [and] idolatry under the notion of liberty of conscience,"[111] and their admission that America was now a Christian country, reflected not only the decline of enlightenment infidelism and the reascendancy of traditional Bible Christianity since the late 1790s, but also the early Covenanters' absorption into and acceptance of American life.

Disappointed Deists

Neither the Unitarians nor the Covenanters were evangelizing societies, hell-bent on converting the nation. In this they can be distinguished from the Deists, who for a number of years after 1796 did make attempts to spread their controversial message of rational religion. Politically engaged, as militant Jeffersonian Republicans, they found acceptance in their new country hard to achieve. But unlike the Unitarians and the Covenanters, at least they found a pre-existing religious organization to which they could attach themselves, for in 1795 the blind peripatetic preacher, Elihu Palmer, had founded the deist Society of Theophilanthropists in New York.[112]

Palmer's Deism was part of an ultraradical ideology that sought a democratic republican society in which not only aristocratic power, but also superstitious religious creeds had been ousted. His attack on the "double despotism" of political oppression and religious bigotry naturally appealed to exiled radicals who, like Palmer himself, had been inspired by Thomas Paine's *Age of Reason* as well as *Rights of Man*. A number of exiles joined the New York Society of Theophilanthropists in late 1801, when it was revived and put on a firmer footing with a new constitution. According to one hostile source: "The imported scum of the Edinburgh Convention, and the refuse of the banished rebels of Ireland, joined also their hearts and hands with the Infidels of New-York, in planning this society."[113] Certainly, the three Cheetham brothers from Manchester, James Mitchell from Scotland, and John Binns and Denis Driscol from Ireland were members, with Benjamin Cheetham offering a large room in his house for meetings.[114] They helped to make up a membership that probably never rose above 100, consisting mainly of artisans and professionals.[115]

Denis Driscol was for two years to be Palmer's right-hand man, first in New York and then in Philadelphia. He had arrived in America in 1799, after finally giving up his subversive activities in Ireland. Released from prison in 1796, he had continued publishing his *Cork Gazette*, which for a time gained a national circulation. But faced with another spell in prison in 1797 he capitulated, informing the government that he would close his newspaper if the prosecution against him was dropped and he was permitted to leave the country. How he survived for the next eighteen months is not known, although it is possible that he took up Samuel Neilson's plan and traveled through the south of Ireland helping to forge the Defender/United Irish coalition. According to two contemporary sources, a wandering hermit called Driscol, found with two Catholic prayer books in his possession, was half-hanged three times and flogged four times in the barrack room at New Ross in 1798, on suspicion of having administered illegal oaths. Denis Driscol may have been this victim, but the ubiquity of his surname in the region precludes a positive identification. Certainly, by the spring of 1799, when Driscol was in Dublin, he lived in dire poverty. Claiming that "want of means in this country compels me to seek bread in America," he successfully obtained a passport from the authorities. He left for America "as a freeman, and voluntarily."[116]

On arrival in New York Driscol threw himself enthusiastically into the Theist Society's activities. Given his editorial experience, his credentials as a promoter of deist principles in Ireland, and his urgent need of subsistence, Driscol was the obvious choice as editor of the new magazine the Deists decided to establish. The first number of the *Temple of Reason* appeared on 8 November 1800; thereafter it was published weekly in New York until 8 February 1801, when Driscol transferred it to Philadelphia, where it lasted for another two years. Driscol's editorial policy aimed at achieving two objectives: defending President Jefferson against accusations of atheism, which had circulated during the dirty presidential campaign of 1800 and were continuing to be used to undermine his presidency; and destroying Christianity's social position by shattering its intellectual pretensions. Driscol was convinced of Jefferson's commitment to Deism, although he admitted that firm evidence was lacking. The president was, however, too strong-minded to be "superstitious" and too "philosophical" to be an atheist. Rejecting accusations that he openly defended Jefferson in the expectation of patronage, Driscol claimed—with little evidence except the general decline of debate on Jefferson's beliefs—to have succeeded in defeating the president's detractors.[117]

Unfortunately for Driscol and his fellow Deists, most Americans preferred to remain mired in irrationalism or, like many in the public eye, to keep their heterodox opinions to themselves. They were swimming against the tide. Palmer had tapped into a small reservoir of infidelism in the mid-1790s, at a time when Paine's *Age of Reason* was going through seventeen American editions, but by the time the exiles appeared on the stage a few years later the various forms of Enlightenment free thought were about to be swept away by the whirlwind of the second Great Awakening.[118] Only a tiny number ever came to hear of the *Temple of Reason* and its doctrine of rational religion. With little advertising revenue and falling subscriptions, Driscol came under serious financial pressure. In January 1802, after agreeing to stay on in a caretaker role for a few months, he announced that "a society of citizens" had taken over the financial management of the magazine. He was replaced as editor of

The Temple of Reason by another radical exile, JOHN LITHGOW, who was equally unsuccessful. In February 1803 the publication closed down.[119]

Deism as an organized religion had collapsed by the time Thomas Paine—its most notorious promoter—returned to America in October 1802, where he suffered grievously for his heterodoxy. Undoubtedly, many exiles still adhered to Deism's tenets, but increasingly they did so in silence, or covered their views by attending church. To do otherwise could be a risk: when the Scottish exile Grant Thorburn, a Baptist minister in New York, publicly shook Paine's hand in 1803, he was dismissed from his pulpit.[120] Some United Irish leaders whose religious beliefs in the 1790s had been openly anticlerical and, more quietly, dismissive of organized religion in any form, in America regularly attended public worship.[121] Even the militant Driscol gradually moderated his proselytizing; as owner of the Georgia *Augusta Chronicle* from 1804 he defended his Deist principles only in response to occasional attacks from rival editors.[122] The trajectory of the religious odyssey of De Witt Clinton, the New York Republican leader, perhaps best sums up the victory of orthodox Christianity over Deism and other forms of infidelism. Heavily involved, if behind the scenes, with the New York Theophilanthropists in the first years of the century, he lived to become vice president of the American Bible Society and a pillar of the Presbyterian Church.[123] As that process unfolded, many of the hopes of freethinking exiles that America was a land of religious freedom slowly disappeared.

Summation

The acclimatization period for the exiles depended for its duration and intensity on a number of factors, some the product of the migration process itself, some the consequence of the character of American society and the disposition of its citizens, and some the result of the willingness of groups of exiles to work together for the common good. Undoubtedly, adjustment was most awkward and uncomfortable during the years 1797 to 1801 when the largest numbers of exiles arrived, for the radicals were used as stooges in partisan American politics and became the victims of heightened nativist and anti-rationalist sentiment.[124] Ironically, much of the heat of political contention in these years was exacerbated by established exiles who had arrived a few years earlier becoming embroiled in the propaganda wars leading up to Jefferson's victory in 1800. The exiles of 1797–1801 were also the least prepared, both psychologically and socially, for the traumas of expatriation, frequently having to flee without adequate preparation, or being forced out of their country immediately following months of imprisonment. On the other hand, assistance to fellow exiles increased in consequence of a growing awareness of the problems being faced by the new arrivals. Circumstances were better for those arriving after 1802; not only did they encounter nativist sentiment on a diminished scale, but many had had time to plan their departures with care, or, like the Fort George prisoners, had been able to mature their plans on the continent preparatory to sailing the Atlantic. All the exiles were thus compelled to endure a period of "seasoning," but the process as it unfolded over time remained distinctive and uneven.

FORTUNE

Finding Elysium

The Augustan poet and satirist Charles Churchill was making a statement with wider resonance when he wrote of an actor:

> Where he falls short, 'tis Nature's fault alone;
> Where he succeeds, the merit's all his own.[125]

Among the exiles there probably were many who at various times thought along such lines, but equally, there must have been others who recognized the benefits they had gained by emigration. By single-mindedly using their talents to take advantage of the many opportunities to which they became exposed in what was still an unsophisticated but extrovert and open society, some of them became spectacularly successful. Success, of course, means different things to different people: wealth, fame (national or local), the achievement of personal goals, or merely gaining the respect of one's friends, relations, and community. The recognition—election to the Columbian Society of Artists, the American Philosophical Society, and the Philadelphia Academy of Natural Sciences—that Alexander Wilson achieved for his original researches on American ornithology, did not bring him the sort of huge wealth that Edward Hudson accumulated as a highly successful dentist, but both had reasons for harboring feelings of satisfaction with their decision to abandon the Old World and embrace the New, and can be viewed as successful. However, they used the opportunities afforded by America in different ways. Hudson kept to a path along which he had begun to travel in Ireland. He had already gained prominence in Dublin as a dental practitioner; in Philadelphia he developed the technique of root-filling teeth with gold foil to become acclaimed as a pioneer in his field.[126] Wilson, on the other hand, had to shed much of his past, including his hunger for fame as a poet, before discovering, with the support of a neighbor, the naturalist William Bartram, an avenue that both brought to life previously unrecognized talents and opened up new vistas and opportunities.[127]

Of those exiles who appear to have been successful in America, few followed Wilson's risky approach by branching out into a totally new occupation or calling. John Cook, the seditious Cambridge baker, took a degree in medicine in America, and later visited England as a chaplain in the U.S. Navy.[128] Grant Thorburn, a nailer in Scotland and New York, became (eventually) a successful seed merchant after a nail-making machine made his former skills redundant.[129] Either James Kennedy or his brother Alexander, previously small manufacturers in Edinburgh, owned in 1830 a Washington theological bookstore.[130] And the LCS hairdresser John Lovett retained his skills with his scissors, but also successfully diversified into the grocery and tavern businesses.[131]

Undoubtedly the most successful exile who had to dig deep within himself for new talents was the Catholic Irishman, JOHN CORISH DEVEREUX. With his brothers Luke, Thomas, and NICHOLAS, he came to dominate the economy of Utica, New York, by the 1830s. The Devereuxs' father, a prosperous landowner from Enniscorthy, County Wexford, had died in prison during the rebellion of 1798. One brother, James, had been killed at the battle of Vinegar Hill, another had escaped to the East Indies. John arrived in America at the age of twenty-four with no money and no relevant experience, except his skills in dancing, which he energetically displayed throughout New England until he had saved enough money to enter trade in upstate Utica, a region still suffering from frontier conditions. In a series of partnerships with his brothers, Devereux's mercantile concerns soon had a turnover of $100,000 a year, helped after 1821 by relocation close to the newly opened Erie Canal. He became president of the Utica branch of the Bank of the United States, and with Nicholas formed the Utica Savings Bank. Several times elected mayor of the town, he died in 1848 one of the most wealthy and prominent businessmen in a region that had now entered, thanks in no small part to the Devereux brothers, the mainstream American economy.[132]

The Devereux brothers were decidedly unusual. Most of the successful exiles cautiously and sensibly took advantage of their previous experience, skills, and knowledge to advance their fortunes. They took their known talents further, rather than discovering new ones. Like Hudson, a few became extremely wealthy. Thomas Addis Emmet, as a premier advocate in New York, was earning $15,000 a year at the height of his career.[133] William Young Birch, an apprentice in his uncle's bookshop in Manchester, left $250,000 in his will to the Pennsylvania Institute for the Blind, the product of his successful bookselling and publishing company.[134] John Chambers, whose fortune had suffered severely during his years of imprisonment after 1798, amassed another as a stationer in partnership with his son in New York. In 1820 he retired, to live another sixteen years in comfort doing good works.[135]

The accumulation of large fortunes was, however, relatively rare among the exiles. Although evidence is sparse, it is likely that for most who could be deemed successful a much more modest competence, capable of ensuring personal respectability and independence, was the norm. John Neilson of County Antrim, exiled under the Banishment Act, had been apprenticed to an architect and builder in Belfast. In Virginia he followed the same line with some success, at one point working for James Madison, whose wife Dolly treated him very kindly.[136] Further north, in Albany, New York, PATRICK MATHEWS, a Dublin Catholic who fled after taking up arms in 1798, made a comfortable living as a merchant, although he lost his new wife to yellow fever soon after their arrival. By 1811 he was president of the charitable Albany Sons of St. Patrick, and an ensign in the local militia.[137] JOHN CHAMBERS of County Armagh, who was swept up onto a Belfast prison tender only days before the Ulster rebellion broke out, within a few years of arriving in America was contentedly reporting having rented a farm in New Jersey, and owning a good horse and other valuable livestock.[138] As he had begun as a poor laborer in Ireland, becoming a tenant farmer in his adopted country he considered social advancement, and a major step toward becoming a free and independent citizen.[139]

Creating and Disseminating Knowledge

As these few examples, and others mentioned earlier suggest, exiles who could claim success in America were involved in virtually every occupation imaginable: entrepreneurial (including land speculation), agricultural, and professional. But in one respect at least, a very significant number of radical refugees focused their considerable energies and abilities on one general area, the creation and dissemination of knowledge, cultural, political, pedagogical, and scientific. They did this in a number of ways, some becoming involved in both generating and making accessible new knowledge (as authors, translators, newspaper editors, and teachers), others joining the trades and occupations on which the production of knowledge for an ever-widening literate public depended (typefounding, printing, publishing, and bookselling). By their involvement in the production and marketing of knowledge the exiles made their greatest contribution to the development of American society in the early republic.

Like so many other industries in what was still an underdeveloped economy, printing and publishing in America was subject to recurrent and frustrating bottlenecks, a consequence either of the reliance on European-manufactured products or of the inability of Americans to make efficient use of their own resources, both human and natural. Paper, for example, was frequently in short supply; it was not unusual for newspaper editors to advertise for the public to provide old rags for paper production, and on rare occasions to be forced into using colored paper.[140] Worn-down fonts of type frequently had to be used, for at a time when the number of printing shops was increasing, finding adequate replacements was difficult. Attempts to solve the problem by establishing typefoundries in America before the 1790s had been defeated by cheaper British competitors.[141] Three Scottish exiles, David Bruce, Archibald Binny, and James Ronaldson did much to change that situation. Sons of a tanner, Bruce and his brother George had emigrated from Edinburgh to Philadelphia in the mid-1790s, moving first to Albany and then to New York following the yellow fever epidemic of 1798. After three years as printer and publisher of the *New York Daily Advertiser,* Bruce went into book printing in 1806. Six years later he returned from a trip to Britain, bringing with him the secret of stereotyping (industrial espionage of this kind was common at the time). Bruce, however, had trouble establishing the process, because of the unavailability of suitable type. Not only did he cast his own type to solve his problem, but he also improved the stereotyping process while doing so. Thereafter, for the next ten years he successfully built up his typefoundry in New York.[142]

In Philadelphia, Archibald Binny and James Ronaldson formed one of the most successful partnerships among the exiles. Binny arrived in America in 1795 with typefounding equipment valued at $880.80; Ronaldson had the finance capital, which he was prepared to invest in Binny's many skills. For two years they struggled to make their operation successful, undercutting the price of the popular European types, working long into the night, and devising new, labor-saving production techniques (which were patented). Within a decade they were employing more than thirty men and boys in a thriving and lucrative business. They succeeded by the use of astute business methods—Mathew Carey, for example, owed them almost $4,000 on long-term credit in 1804—and by producing type of a quality and beauty equal to the very best Europe could offer. When William Duane was preparing for publication *Diversions of Purley,* John Horne Tooke's work on linguistics, Saxon and Gothic types were specially cast by Binny, for the first time in America. Binny and Ronaldson were also far-seeing. With war on the horizon in 1809 Ronaldson, knowing that typefounding relied on supplies of antimony available only from Europe, sailed to France and Germany with a supportive letter from Thomas Jefferson to obtain supplies sufficient to tide them over if hostilities broke out. The partnership continued to be highly successful; when Binny sold his share of the business to Ronaldson and retired with his very large family to his plantation in Maryland in 1815, he received $62,000.[143]

The fonts were needed, among other things, to produce the ever-increasing number of newspapers that proliferated in the years spanning the turn of the century. One estimate has 450 newspapers and seventy-five magazines founded in the United States between 1783 and 1800.[144] Large numbers were established in the next decade too, extending newspaper production across ever larger areas of the states.[145] Between the end of the American War of Independence and 1818 twenty-three British and Irish radicals edited and produced no fewer than fifty-seven newspapers and magazines, mostly in the politically sensitive middle states but at one time or another covering all the eastern seaboard, from Georgia to Massachusetts, and as far west as St. Louis.[146] Some of these titles were ephemeral; James Carey, for instance, published nine newspapers in five different locations between 1792 and 1800. But others became firmly established: Duane edited the *Aurora* from 1798 to 1829, Gales the *Raleigh Register* from 1799 to 1833, Cheetham the *American Citizen* from 1801 to 1810, JOSEPH CHARLESS the *Missouri Gazette* from 1808 to 1820, and John Binns the *Democratic Press* from 1807 to 1829.

The political impact of these newspapers will be examined in following chapters; here it is sufficient to mention that newspapers were probably the best way to get a message across in late eighteenth-century America. William Cobbett switched from publishing pamphlets to producing the daily *Porcupine's Gazette* in Philadelphia in 1797 because "the thousands who read [in America] read nothing else." John Ward Fenno, editor of the Federalist *Gazette of the United States*, claimed in the 1790s that "more than nine-tenths of the scanty literature of America is made up of newspaper reading." On this issue Callender agreed with his former Philadelphia rivals: "It is certain that the citizens of America derive their information almost exclusively from newspapers."[147]

Hamstrung by the limitations of the contemporary printing press, the newspaper industry did not make many significant changes in this period, but what were made the radical exiles often either originated or helped to institutionalize. Benjamin Franklin Bache is usually credited with first using the editorial in American newspapers (in his *Aurora*),[148] but Mathew Carey began using the technique in the 1780s, and other exiled editors such as Cobbett, Gales, and Duane made the practice permanent. Gales, for example, had introduced the editorial column in his *Sheffield Register* as early as 1787. Duane, James

Carey, Cheetham, Gales, and Cobbett all risked producing daily newspapers, still at that time unusual (there were about twenty-four dailies in 1800).[149] The Carey brothers and their great rival Cobbett were innovative in their attempts to attract customers. Mathew, from August 1785, was the first editor in America to report the debates of the Pennsylvania Assembly; he also appealed to merchants and shipowners with his *Complete Counting House Companion,* a free weekly supplement to his Philadelphia *Evening Herald.* James unsuccessfully tried to turn his *Charleston Daily Evening Gazette* into a hybrid newspaper-cum-magazine by occasionally publishing essays suitable as "Companions to the Tea-Table"; and Cobbett printed weekly German and country editions of his *Porcupine's Gazette,* from which irrelevant city advertisements had been omitted.[150] All were aware of the need to cater for consumer demand.

One of the most innovative of the exiled journalists was James Thomson Callender, who in 1800 came up with a crafty plan of synchronized syndication to promote the efficient and national distribution of Republican political information throughout the country, and to bypass the problems caused by the competitive dog-eat-dog instinct among newspaper editors. He suggested that if a particularly important article was written in, say, Philadelphia, numerous copies of it should be sent to one or two sympathetic editors in every state before publication. They in turn would distribute further copies to other Republican editors in the state, and on a specified day the article would be simultaneously printed in all the newspapers. "By their receiving, and publishing all these articles at the same time," wrote Callender later, "the jealousy of competition would have been destroyed; while the federal editors were to struggle after them, at the distance of several days, and very often of several weeks. The effect of such an arrangement must have been infinitely superior to the present disorderly crowd of republican newspapers. . . . What is the line of battle firing in platoons, or the ship that pops by single guns, compared with the impression of a general attack, or a series of full broadsides? The result is very much the same in printing, as in fighting."[151] Unfortunately, this particular idea was never taken up.

Editing a newspaper might occasionally bring some fame, certainly frequently caused notoriety, but rarely made anyone wealthy. To cover costs, editors had also to be printers, publishers, and even patent medicine vendors. Altogether, at least thirty-two exiles were involved in printing and publishing at some point, and at least another five were solely booksellers. Callender was hardly exaggerating when he noted a preponderance of expatriate booksellers by the mid-1790s: "Take away all the Scots and Irish booksellers from Philadelphia, and [a reader] could hardly supply his library. With three or four exceptions the whole trade centres among foreigners. The case is much the same in New York and Baltimore."[152] (He could also have drawn attention to the English booksellers in Philadelphia, including Cobbett, Lee, and Eaton.) To some extent, as we have seen, this was one consequence of the printers and publishers having been a target of the British government's counter-radical policies in the 1790s.

Undoubtedly the most successful of these publishers, and the most innovative, was Mathew Carey. Perhaps partly owing to his being an immigrant, Carey's ambition was never confined by state boundaries, nor was he a victim of a cultural cringe toward Europe. From the time he joined in a partnership to produce the *Columbian Magazine* in 1786 he aimed to achieve a national circulation for his publications, which extolled the virtues and potentialities of the new republic. His magazine the *American Museum* (1787–92) deliberately sought a national audience, mixing reprints of major political writings from newspapers—especially debates surrounding the acceptance of the new Federal Constitution—with original poems and essays by American writers on political economy and American culture. "No publisher," it has been said, "did more to encourage American writers in the Federal period," and "no other publishing firm, even in proportion to its size, published so many works of native production between 1787 and 1824."[153]

Much of Carey's ultimate success can be attributed to his unwearying efforts to establish a national network of outlets for his productions. He had realized from the outset that access to a growing but widely dispersed market would be a key to success. At first, he was prepared to submit himself to the hardships of traveling long distances over poor roads to establish useful connections and collect his subscriptions. In the summer of 1789 he rode more than 1,300 miles on horseback.[154] His uncomfortable experiences must have encouraged his later enthusiasm for internal improvements. Subsequently he came to rely on a network of promotion agents, the most successful of whom was the indefatigable American nationalist, Parson Mason L. Weems, many of whose own writings Carey published. At the same time he devised various schemes to promote the book trade: a cooperative in Philadelphia (1794–96), that encouraged joint publishing ventures; and an annual booksellers' fair in New York (1802–6).[155] Altogether, between 1785 and 1821 Carey published more than a thousand titles.[156]

The exiles were involved not only in the dissemination of knowledge through the medium of print; as teachers of the sciences, the classics, and medicine they left their mark on the next generation at many of the emerging universities. At least eight of the radical refugees were to hold professorships at or presidencies of American institutes of higher learning. Thomas Cooper held chairs at the universities of Pennsylvania and South Carolina, becoming president of the latter as well as one of the most prominent pedagogues in the antebellum South.[157] Henry Toulmin, a Unitarian minister in Lancashire when he emigrated in 1793, having "praised the French Revolution too warmly," was appointed president of Kentucky's Transylvania College in 1794, before becoming the state's secretary and later a prominent judge in Mississippi Territory.[158] John Maclean was appointed to the chair of chemistry and natural history at Princeton within months of arrival in America, and the United Irishman Daniel McCurtin taught at Washington College in Maryland.[159] Another United Irishman, Robert Adrain, who was wounded by his own troops before the battle of Saintfield in 1798, taught at a number of American academies before, in 1810, becoming professor of mathematics and natural philosophy at Queen's College, New Brunswick. In 1813, regarded as the best mathematician in the country, he transferred to a similar chair at Columbia College, New York. He ended his career as professor and vice provost at the University of Pennsylvania.[160] Other successful Irish academics were the two Covenanting ministers, Samuel B. Wylie and John Black, the former holding a chair in classics at the University of Pennsylvania, the latter at what became the University of Pittsburgh.[161] Last, but by no means least, William James MacNeven became professor of midwifery at the New York College of Physicians and Surgeons in 1808, exchanged this chair for that of chemistry in 1811, and in 1816 added materia medica to chemistry. His chemistry laboratory was said to be the first in New York. Between 1826 and 1830 he lectured at the new Duane Street Medical School. MacNeven published several scientific works, the best known being his *Exposition of the Atomic Theory of Chemystry* (1819), and co-edited the *New York Medical and Philosophical Journal and Review.*[162]

MISFORTUNE

Heirs to Disappointment

The weight of evidence appears to support Thomas Ledlie Birch's opinion that the British and Irish exiles made up "the most respectable" group to emigrate to America "since the settlement of the New England colonies."[163] That they were also successful immigrants seems to be confirmed both by contemporary accounts and by the conclusions of more recent historians.[164] Yet it is noticeable that much of this contemporary praise converged on the successful examples of a few men in New York: MacNeven, Sampson, and particularly Thomas Addis Emmet, whose exceptional career was promoted as a model by those anxious to demonstrate that the exiles had made a successful transition to a republican society. A wider focus, however, strongly suggests that failure was as common as triumph among the exiles.

Many, for instance, were never given the opportunity of fulfilling their potential in America; premature death was to be their fate. At least ten died within two or three years of arrival. The ubiquitous fever took its inevitable toll of the unseasoned. The young Tyrone United Irishman, THOMAS BELL, settled as a merchant in Amelia County, Virginia, in 1798. Early in 1800 he married a young local lady, who unfortunately died within months. In mourning, Bell took a business trip to the North. He had only been back a few weeks when he too died of fever, aged twenty-one.[165] Father MacMahon, the Dublin Dominican priest, died of yellow fever in Philadelphia in 1800, as too, in Poughkeepsie, did Samuel Neilson only months after his arrival. Never having fully recovered from his illness in 1798, Neilson had secretly (and illegally) travelled to Ireland after being freed from Fort George. He then sailed to America, where he had plans to establish a newspaper devoted to Irish interests. His sudden death in August 1803 left his young son, who had followed him to America, unprovided for.[166]

Both John Craig Millar and Robert Merry were victims of America's harsh climate. Millar and his wife, the daughter of the famous Scottish doctor, William Cullen, had been well received in Philadelphia on arrival in 1795. A few months later, however, pursuing his speculative interests in a Scottish land company in the Pennsylvania backcountry, he collapsed and died of heatstroke.[167] Merry too died of apoplexy, in Baltimore in 1798. He had never really settled, relying for subsistence on his wife's acting ability. According to Cobbett, Merry "was never noticed in America; he pined away in obscurity" because the people had, "thank Heaven, no taste for the Della Cruscan poetry or politics."[168] He had not, however, lost his appetite for quips and jests. When asked by John Bernard, a visiting English actor, why he had settled in America (he had always claimed an aversion to living there), he supposedly replied: "Nonsense, John, you know that I always liked to be in A-merry-key." "Poor fellow," wrote Bernard, "here was the ruling passion strong in exile: he had given up home, friends, fame, poetry, pleasure, politics—everything but punning."[169]

Neilson, Millar, Bell and the rest had only begun to sort out their new lives when they were cruelly cut short. Other exiles, at least sixteen, also died within a dozen years of arrival. A few, like Priestley, McKinney the Covenanter, and Rev. James Harper, were already elderly when they chose America as a place of retirement. But the rest were still relatively young when they died. Most had failed to strike deep roots in the community, remaining either restless and dissatisfied, or sunk in torpor and despair. James "Balloon" Tytler, for instance, disillusioned with radicalism, settled with his third (probably bigamous) wife in a small cottage on a peninsula outside Salem, Massachusetts. There he barely kept himself from starvation by unoriginal and verbose hack writing, mostly scientific and medical, and an unsuccessful venture into salt production. William Bentley, a local Unitarian minister, noted in his diary after a massive storm had destroyed Tytler's salt pans in 1798: "His pans have not produced salt for his porridge and his medicines have not relieved him from extreme indigence." Tytler became increasingly reclusive; with his long white hair and high bald forehead he gained a reputation as the local eccentric philosopher. Prone to drink, when he could get it, Tytler drowned late one January night in 1804 while staggering through the darkness and rain to borrow a candle from a neighbor.[170]

A drunken death by drowning was not common among the exiles, but another Scotsman whose life ended in this manner, only six months before Tytler's, was James Thomson Callender. Unlike his countryman, Callender had lived an exciting, dangerous, but ultimately futile life in Philadelphia as one of the Republican party's most notorious propagandists. In July 1798, having just lost his wife and under threat from the Sedition Act, he had fled to Virginia, leaving his four young boys in the hands of a friend. He continued his political activism in Richmond, until in 1801 he was sentenced to nine months in prison for sedition. On his release, being—in his view—abandoned by the now successful Republicans, Callender began a campaign of vilification against his former mentor, Thomas Jefferson. When his sensational revelations dried up without the president's reputation having received a fatal blow, Callender found himself unemployed, penniless, and ostracized. Always a heavy drinker, in July 1803 he was found dead floating in the shallows of the James River. The coroner's verdict was accidental drowning while drunk, but many thought Callender had committed suicide in a fit of remorse.[171]

In Philadelphia Callender had been part of a small nucleus of exiles who, as radical penmen, had kept the columns of Bache's *Aurora* filled with political squibs and comments between 1795 and 1798. Except for Duane, all were dead before the end of Jefferson's second term of office. Dr. James Reynolds, whose career as a doctor had been threatened by his outspoken radicalism, died in 1808. According to Mathew Carey, he had been consistently disappointed: "Unlike Midas . . . every thing in which the Doctor was concerned, eventuated unprosperously." On one occasion Carey had told Reynolds, in "half jest, half earnest—that if I were a leading federalist, I would give him 500 dollars a year to take an active part in the affairs of the Democrats; for so surely as he did, so surely would they be utterly blasted."[172]

Reynolds's fellow Irish penman, James Carey, died in 1801. In many ways Carey epitomized a significant element of the radical diaspora from Britain and Ireland. He was young, high-spirited, footloose, and improvident, but firmly committed to Jeffersonian Republicanism and determined to add his mite to the battle with Federalism. A continual cause of frustration and affectionate amusement to his older brother Mathew, James appeared unable to concentrate his undoubted talents on an objective for any length of time. Between 1792 and 1795 he failed on no fewer than six occasions to establish newspapers, one in Richmond; one in Wilmington, North Carolina; one in Savannah; and three in Charleston. His brother was prompted to ask: "Are you not too prone to change, and too easily discouraged?"[173] Unheeding, James embarked on a series of loan requests that brought Mathew close to bankruptcy on several occasions in the next few years. James himself only escaped debtors' prison in New York in 1794 by boarding a boat for Charleston, leaving what few goods he had behind him.[174] Always a sucker for the stage (and for actresses), at one point during his last unsuccessful sojourn in Charleston he deserted his newspaper business to play the part of Melidor in Voltaire's tragedy "Zara, or the Generous Frenchman" at the Church Street Theatre.[175]

In 1796 James Carey finally settled in Philadelphia, where he established a printery that relied for much of its work on Mathew's publishing company. He could not, however, refrain from newspaper ventures. Three more newspapers collapsed under his editorial guidance between 1797 and 1800. In August 1800 he finally saw the inside of Philadelphia's debtors' prison, where he waited for his brother to bail him out. "Should I be disappointed in my expectations," he wrote, "send me at least a few dollars, as I have not a single cent in my possession."[176] When a few months later he died, following bouts of gout and a bilious complaint, James left only $424.79 after his goods were sold and his debts paid. It was not much to show for nearly ten years in America.[177]

Carey's wayward career in America displays a sense of rootlessness, St. Vitus's dance spasms that reflect more than youthful caprice. It also exhibits elements of loss: of direction; of sense of place; and of ultimate purpose. Yet Carey, it will be remembered, had not been compelled by the threat of outlawry to emigrate; it was ultimately his voluntary choice. He also had two brothers and a sister living in Philadelphia to whom he could turn for emotional and financial support. His comment to Mathew, that they were "heirs to disappointment,"[178] is testimony to a dual anguish, partly relating to their Catholic Irish roots, from which they were sundered, and partly to their status as unwilling exiles, evidence of defeat. It also reflects a cast of mind that is suffused with a mixture of pride, shame, and frustration; it explains much of the restlessness that so many radicals felt in America. It can, for instance, be seen dominating the activities of John Daly Burk, and was probably a direct contributor to his untimely death. Burk's upbeat introduction to America did not survive his move from Boston to New York early in 1797, his editorship of Boston's first daily newspaper, the *Polar Star,* having ended in failure. His growing reputation in New York as a playwright was discountenanced in July 1798 when, as editor of the Jeffersonian newspaper, the *Time-Piece,* he and his partner Dr. James Smith fell foul of the Alien and Sedition Acts. Following his arrest for seditious writings against President Adams, Burk was bailed on the surety of several leading Republicans, including Aaron Burr, who had befriended him. The *Time-Piece* staggered on for another month, but collapsed after quarrels between the editors. With the connivance of Burr the charges against Burk were dropped, on condition that he left the country. But although under surveillance, Burk managed to slip quietly away to Amelia County, Virginia, where for a while he lived under an assumed name.[179]

Burk now faced a predicament common to many radical exiles at this juncture. He was, in modern parlance, multiskilled; he was intelligent, young, and in good health. He was also safe from prosecution (Amelia County was strongly Republican, its electorate voting unanimously for Jefferson in the election of 1800).[180] But he appeared unable to keep out of trouble, or, as he rationalized it: "I was destined to be the sport of fortune." No sooner was he appointed principal of the newly established Jefferson College in Amelia County than he was, possibly falsely, accused of adultery. The irate cuckold, as might be expected in aristocratic Virginia, tried to kill him, and the Irishman was forced to resign his position in disgrace.[181]

Although Burk at one point contemplated returning to Ireland, he remained in Virginia, moving to Petersburg, where his seesaw career for a while unexpectedly improved. Mysteriously, he was accepted as an accredited lawyer, possibly through the same sort of influence that later served Emmet and Sampson so well further north. He certainly began to move in élite circles, where his charm and clubbability were welcomed. He also remarried—like Tytler, bigamously?—his new wife being a widow who had time to give him a son to go with two from her previous marriage before dying prematurely. Despite this setback, Burk continued his writings and was well advanced on his massive history of Virginia when in April 1808, while dining in a tavern, he patriotically and loudly insulted the French nation (they were "a pack of rascals") in earshot of a Frenchman, Felix Coquebert. Disdainfully refusing to apologize, Burk was shot through the heart in a duel the next day, the hotheaded part of his character having finally and fatally prevailed.[182]

The premature deaths of James Carey, Callender, and Burk have their tragic aspects; *Fortuna,* to which all three appealed in times of despair, seemed to reject them at crucial times. But until the denouement, their careers reflected a doggedness and persistence that allowed them to bounce back from moments of adversity. Other exiles, however, failed to demonstrate the same flexibility and commitment. They appeared totally unable to cope with their new surroundings and the demands put on them by their expatriation. Before his death in Philadelphia in 1806 JEREMIAH LEARY, who, as the body servant of Arthur O'Connor had been acquitted of treason at Maidstone Assizes in 1798, led a disreputable life, which John Binns refused to divulge in his autobiography.[183] In New York, some former United Irishmen remained a considerable burden on those who had settled quickly. Nine years after John Shaw, the Quaker clothier and United Irishman, had been accused of administering illegal oaths in Ulster, he remained mired in debt in New York City, unable to feed his large family. John Caldwell gave another unfortunate Ulsterman, ROBERT SWAN, an opportunity of painting his house. Being a "broken-down old man," he made a poor fist of it, and remained in "abject poverty." The New York Irish thought of raising a subscription for his passage back to Ireland, where it was hoped his family might take care of him (a curious case of the traditional roles of Ireland and the United States being reversed).[184]

Naturally, not all the abject failures in America were Irishmen. Cobbett took great pleasure in divulging the fates of unsuccessful English exiles, including the LCS Methodist printer, "Citizen" Richard Lee, who in 1798 was "comfortably lodged in New-York jail," presumably for debt.[185] The Paisley brothers James and William Mitchell's experiences probably best reflect the consequences of despair taking ineradicable root in the soul. Restless in Scotland, they found America equally unsettling. For two years they mooched around Philadelphia; when they finally moved on, to New York, Alexander Wilson for one was glad to see their backs.[186] Both tried to make use of their musical talents in New York. James opened a music school, but whatever strength of character he may once have had soon deserted him. Addicted to alcohol and gambling, he even took his young pupils to the gaming house. Having ruined his reputation and his business, in 1801 he was jailed for debt, an unpleasant welcome to greet his elderly father when he crossed the Atlantic to visit his sons that year. James was last heard of as a dancing master in Halifax, Nova Scotia.[187]

William Mitchell too tasted the dregs of life in New York. He seemingly "had lost all ambition. He was unkempt, swore constantly, was abandoned to wretched companions, and lost to every good purpose in the world."[188] For some time he worked as a "hocus-pocus" man, playing his flute in the streets to gain an audience for his partner. Later he took up his old career of weaving, before eventually, a last resort, he joined the army. With a large draft of un-seasoned troops he was sent to New Orleans, to become part of General James Wilkinson's army protecting the newly acquired western lands. Owing to Wilkinson's notorious greed and corruption, the troops were camped on a swampy, pestilential site outside the city, where sickness soon was rife. In Oc-tober 1809, on a disastrous trip up the Mississippi to Natchez to escape the fever, Mitchell was one of ten in his boat to die of dysentery. The mortality among the troops became a scandal (the force was reduced by half by disease and desertions), although Wilkinson, as usual, escaped censure at the follow-ing inquiry.[189] As far as is known, of all the exiles' burial places, Mitchell's is the farthest from the British Isles. His was a wasted death, but, so too, was much of his life.

REPATRIATION

Transients

It is clear that the traditional view of the radical exiles successfully transplant-ing themselves to the New World needs modification. From the evidence available, at least as many failed to make the transformation as succeeded. Moreover, of the 106 exiles whose ultimate fate is known, no less than thirty (28.3 percent) returned to the British Isles, rejecting the advantages of living in a republican society. Rates of return among emigrants have always been high; the repatriation rate of the exiles seems to be about the same as British and Irish rates from colonial times until the 1920s.[190] It would appear, there-fore, that in this respect the conduct of those making up the radical exodus was not dissimilar to emigrant behavior in general. This can partly be ex-plained by the common forces—homesickness, lack of capital, inflexible atti-tudes, and the like—acting on all immigrants. Yet the radical exiles, it might be thought, ought to have possessed more staying power than the average emigrant, for their vision of America transcended economic aspirations to embrace an ideological commitment to republican and democratic institu-tions, which the United States exemplified. Moreover, whereas normal emi-grants probably left their homelands carrying with them only generalized dis-contents with their lot in life, the radicals had suffered almost a personal rejection that sent them on their way across the Atlantic, committed anglo-phobes. They were hardly likely to look back nostalgically or affectionately on their former homelands.

The examples of Tone, Tandy, and Swiney, who left America's shores after a short sojourn to renew the battle against British imperialism in Europe seem to suggest that repatriation was less a sign of rejection of republican society than a commitment to its dissemination elsewhere, but such motives for return were held by remarkably few exiles. The only other example of a rebel who returned to Ireland and became politically active again was the Ulsterman JAMES FINLAY, who had trained for the Presbyterian ministry without proceeding to ordination, fought in the rebellion, and had been banished in 1798. A few years after settling in New York he returned (illegally) to his home in Cotton, County Down, where his neighbors and the local magistrates turned a blind eye to his presence. In 1803 he became involved in Robert Emmet's rebellion, was remanded in prison for two years, but was never brought to trial. Sensibly, he spent the rest of his life peacefully on his farm, dying in 1811.[191]

Much more common than a relish for retribution among both exiled leaders and rank and file, was the desire to return home and live as quietly as possible, eschewing politics altogether. DR. THOMAS WILSON, an Ulster United Irish leader, returned in 1802, and seemingly had no difficulty practicing his profession in Magherafelt, County Derry.[192] Even some rebels known as "Fifty-Pounders," who had been named in the 1798 Fugitive Act and whose failure to surrender had led to their outlawry, successfully slipped back to Ireland a few years after the rebellion. WILLIAM CURRY and WILLIAM McCLELLAND both returned to their haunts in Island Magee without being prosecuted. McClelland subsequently became a lieutenant in the local yeomanry, as well as continuing his secret trade as a successful smuggler.[193] A victory of sorts may be discerned here. More tragic was the case of MATTHEW SCOTT, a Catholic merchant from Carrick-on-Suir, who fled to America after imprisonment and a severe flogging from the notorious magistrate, Sir Thomas Fitzgerald. He never recovered from the experience, returning from America a few years later only to lose his sanity and commit suicide.[194]

No doubt a significant number of the smaller fry who were in danger from the authorities only during the height of the disturbances in 1798–99 surreptitiously returned home at a later date, where they quietly and successfully picked up the threads of their lives. The same can be said of some of the English printers and publishers who had voluntarily emigrated; once the hue and cry died down, they felt safe to recross the Atlantic.[195] Cobbett, the Manchester Unitarian Matthew Falkner, Daniel Isaac Eaton, and the Norwich radical RICHARD DINMORE all returned to England after 1800 (Cobbett, of course, traveling in very different political colors). All had reached a hiatus in their careers in America, as Dinmore's experiences demonstrate. An apothecary by trade and the son of a saddler who for a time was president of the Norwich

Patriotic Society, Dinmore was a victim of the loyalist upsurge of 1792–93, being "marked out as an object of persecution" and ostracized for his reformist views.[196] He emigrated in 1797, soon after publishing a work defending the English reformers from the taint of French Jacobinism.[197] In America he bestowed on himself the title "Doctor," but mixed medicine with the quintessentially Jacobin stimulant, printing and publishing.[198] Indeed, Dinmore displayed considerable entrepreneurial talents in Washington, running a circulating library, selling tobacco and patent medicines, as well as being employed as editor of the Washington Printing and Bookselling Company, of which he was one of a dozen directors. He might have made himself a tidy fortune, if he had kept clear of publishing newspapers and magazines. His first publication, the *National Magazine,* which covered politics, the sciences, and general literature, lasted only eight very boring numbers before succumbing to lack of support in January 1802. A few months later, in partnership with James Lyon, an enthusiastic Republican editor who had gone bankrupt in the previous year, Dinmore took over another magazine, the *American Literary Advertiser,* which he removed to Alexandria, where it lasted until March 1804.[199] At the same time he and Lyon began a triweekly newspaper, the *Alexandria Expositor,* which after some months when it was in danger of "fainting and drooping under the terrors and effects of poverty," managed to last for a respectable five years.[200] In 1807, having shed his partner, he moved back to Washington and for two years edited the *Washington Expositor,* but this collapsed after fifty-four editions. His writings were strongly anglophobic and greatly irritated the English Tory traveler, Charles Janson, who was particularly piqued by Dinmore's ability to get many of his pieces published in a London monthly magazine.[201]

In 1809 Dinmore migrated back to England, where he died two years later. His decision to leave was predicated on more than economic failure, for he always had more than one string to his bow. Perhaps the success of his publications in London, which included an account of a trip he made between Washington and Kentucky, suggested that his prospects as a writer were better back home. Certainly he had no personal ties to keep him in America, for not only had his wife died soon after childbirth in 1804, but eleven of her twelve children, most presumably from a previous marriage, had predeceased her.[202]

Begging Pardon

Unlike most other English exiles, Dinmore was not prevented by outlawry or threat of arrest from returning home. For most of the Irish, however, implicated in the rebellion and subject to the Banishment or Fugitive Acts, it was a different matter. Yet it was not only the small-fry who wished to return. Perhaps the most surprising feature of the repatriation data is the number of prominent United Irishmen who put out feelers to obtain permission to return to Ireland. Rowan, Henry Jackson, John Sweetman, Patrick Byrne, John Chambers, John Devereaux, Alexander Lowry, and William Sinclair were all given the opportunity of returning home. Significantly, the United Irish leaders whose careers in America have been most lauded—Emmet, MacNeven, and Sampson—were not part of this push to acknowledge defeat and show remorse, although in 1806 Sampson was prepared to await the results of the efforts of his wife and family to persuade the British government to allow his return before pursuing "with vigor and determination our future career."[203] Emmet was the most unequivocally opposed to return, but then he had little to return to. He wrote to a friend in Dublin who had asked him if he had contemplated remigration: "I am too proud, when vanquished, to assist by my presence in gracing the triumph of the victor, and with what feelings should I tread on Irish ground? as if I were walking over graves, and those graves of my nearest relations and dearest friends. There is not now in Ireland an individual that bears the name of Emmet."[204]

Emmet was, however, in a minority in his intransigence. Attempts to open a dialogue with the British government on behalf of individual exiles occurred almost as soon as the exodus began. In Hamilton Rowan's case, it preceded his escape to France, starting while he was still under threat of imprisonment in January 1794. His wife, who had no sympathy at all with Rowan's politics, was the instigator of the attempted reconciliation with the authorities. According to William Drennan, Mrs. Rowan's activities caused immense marital discord:

> The disputes between [Rowan] and his wife are most outrageously violent, often on the brink of separation, yet she still gains something and has an insurmountable obstinacy that will, or I am much mistaken, cause the ground to be again opened for negotiation, which Government would wish and triumph in. [James] Reynolds still stays at his house and, I believe, is necessary as a domestic relief. He is a good staunch man and Mrs. Rowan will find it easier to work on the ferocity of her husband, than on his mild firmness. I am on the best footing with all, and as good with Mrs. Rowan as the case will admit of, for no doubt she wishes us often to the devil.[205]

Indeed she did, especially once she was separated from her husband by three thousand miles of ocean. She wanted her husband back, whatever political capitulation was necessary. Her strategy was twofold: to open up lines of communication with government; and to harry her husband into eschewing all forms of political activity in America. Letter after letter from his wife slowly increased the pressure. First she blamed his political friends for his predicament: "All your faults originated from your connecting yourself with wicked and artful men, who cared not for you nor anybody else."[206] When she heard that Tone was en route to Philadelphia, she warned Rowan "to avoid all connection with him; and it is well to say at once what is the fact—*his friends cannot be mine;* his wicked principles and artful manners have destroyed us." (Later, Mrs. Rowan softened a little, when she realized that her husband could hardly avoid the other Irish exiles without raising suspicions: "There is no reason for absolutely shunning even Tone.")[207] Her next ploy was to advise Rowan not to meddle with politics, American or expatriate Irish. Finally, she played on his own doubts about his political capabilities: "You do not use your own understanding sufficiently, from some error in your education or temper, but catch your opinions and ideas from those immediately about you. I am doubtful whether nature ever did intend you for a public character."[208]

It is unlikely that Rowan required much persuading from his shrewd and faithful wife. His unfortunate experiences in France—where he was imprisoned for a while as a suspected spy and suffered a serious illness—and his dislike of "the climate, manners and the exorbitant rate of everything" in America, helped him make up his mind, although the torrent of advice from Ireland left him "much agitated."[209] By March 1798 Drennan was reporting a rumor of the government's willingness, because of Rowan's good behavior, to allow him back to Ireland, with full possession of his estates, once the war was over.[210] In August, while the rebellion was still being mopped up, Mrs. Rowen asked Cornwallis for access to her husband's rents. Again, the prospect of Rowan's pardon at the end of the war was hinted at.[211] Nearly a year was to pass, however, before Rowan formally asked the Irish government if he might return to Europe, not to Ireland but to Denmark. Cornwallis, who accepted that Rowan had "expressed great Contrition for his former Conduct" and had refused to conspire in America, pointed out that the king had no power to order his subjects to reside in any specific country, but neither would he lift Rowan's outlawry.[212] Mrs. Rowan's tactics, however, were close to success; once the war temporarily ceased, Rowan was allowed back to London, and in 1806 was permitted to reside on his Irish estates.[213]

Rowan's final pardon came from an administration that was headed by Charles James Fox. It was this so-called Ministry of All the Talents that relaxed the hardline against the exiles taken by previous administrations. Fox, and his rump Whig opposition in the 1790s, had had close connections with many of the United Irish leaders, links that had caused great embarrassment when the state prisoners had confessed to their revolutionary intentions in 1798. Nevertheless, by 1806, with the war now being fought against Napoleon's imperial rather than revolutionary France, and with Ireland again firmly under control, it was thought that suitably contrite rebel leaders could safely be allowed to repatriate themselves. Accordingly, extinct volcanoes like John Sweetman and Henry Jackson returned to Europe (the latter, however, owing to family pressures, subsequently remigrated).[214]

But the window of opportunity afforded by Fox's position in government remained open only a short time, for Fox died in September 1806 and the ministry did not long survive him, collapsing over the intractable issue of Catholic relief. Its replacement, headed by the elderly Portland, brought back to power many of the Irish radicals' greatest enemies, including their bête noire, Lord Castlereagh. Thus a number of former United Irish leaders, who might have taken the opportunity of returning to Europe, subsequently decided not to do so.[215] Possibly, they were right to be suspicious, for younger rebel leaders such as John Devereaux of Taghmon found that hopes raised by the Foxite ministry were dashed by Portland's. He had been given permission to visit Ireland for twelve months, but arriving in London after the change of government his request to travel to his estates in Wexford was denied. In this case, however, the government's caution was probably merited, for they had intercepted a letter from Arthur O'Connor in France, which included an invitation to Devereaux to join the French army at "a flattering rank." Devereaux subsequently took an Irish Legion to fight (disastrously) for South American independence, became a trusted friend of Simon Bolivar, who, claimed John Binns, gave Devereaux a gold mine as reward for his services, and was appointed to a number of Colombian diplomatic posts overseas. He lived to a ripe old age, dying in Mayfair, London, in 1860.[216]

Family Dilemmas

Henry Jackson's dilemma when given the chance of returning to Ireland was that one of his daughters wished to live there, the other in Baltimore. This is a reminder that family pressures were a major factor for many exiles when considering where permanently to settle, and probably explains a significant part of the remigration that occurred. Many of the exiles who were fortunate enough to be accompanied by their relatives found that their nearest and dearest—unfortunate victims of politics with which they may have disagreed—

had great difficulty acclimatizing to their new surroundings. This was often the case for older radicals whose children were young adults, their characters and attitudes already formed before emigration. It can be seen with at least one of Priestley's sons (William, whom it was rumored tried to murder his father with poisoned flour), and one of Cooper's (who fought a Federalist editor in a Philadelphia street in 1800 and who lost his commission in the navy for habitual drunkenness).[217] But the clearest example relates to the widower William Russell, whose children became disillusioned with America and influenced their father to return to Europe. Although Martha and Mary Russell had been infatuated with republicanism while in France, a closer acquaintance with the more prosaic version in small-town America soon brought out an inherent snobbery and aristocratic hauteur in their characters. Settled in Middletown, Connecticut, they distanced themselves from their neighbors, complaining of their narrow minds and limited horizons, which made them unsuitable society for "the feeling and enlarged mind of an European." Their brother Thomas was an unreconstructed prig, openly hostile to republican manners and customs. In contact with local business practices through his father's commercial activities, Thomas was scornful of the social status that money brought in a democratic society: "Here a man may break his word with impunity, and may without disgrace flagrantly violate those established customs, the infringement of which would in England irretrievably ruin his character. He may have been two or three times a bankrupt and be known to have defrauded his creditors, and if he thereby reacquires considerable wealth, he will nevertheless be received in the first company. . . . In short, as wealth is the darling object of their attention, so a person with that needs no other letter of recommendation."[218] Soon after Martha married an English businessman, the three children returned to Britain, and William Russell removed to Brittany until the end of the Napoleonic Wars. Before his exile, Russell had tried to give his children all the opportunities open to the second generation of a successful and upwardly mobile family. Perhaps he succeeded too well; creating young gentry, he made them unfit for American society.

Other exiles, either because they departed so hastily or because of poverty, had been compelled to leave their families behind, and fretted over their situation. Sampson, for example, after his solitary wanderings through Wales, Spain, and France, naturally wanted his wife to join him in America as soon as he had established a suitable sanctuary. But she was reluctant to emigrate, using her widowed mother as an excuse to put off the evil day. Whatever Sampson wrote—that America was a surprisingly sophisticated society, or that he was surrounded by beautiful ladies at balls—he failed to influence her, until, nearly four years after he had landed in America, he boldly informed her:

> I have now to conclude with this final sentiment, that I wish you by no means to come to this country if you feel no other motive but a sense of duty, for as this duty may be understood to be in great measure towards me I have often said that I release you from every claim that can belong to me and would much rather deprive myself of ever seeing you than be the means of punishing you by such suffering as you seem to apprehend. I should much rather request you to consult your case with your mother and friends. . . . I must request of you that you come to a determination at once for the state of suspense is a cruel and painful one.[219]

It was a risk, but this persuasive letter had the desired result; Mrs. Sampson was soon on her way to New York.

Although in the cases of Russell and Sampson the family maneuverings are possible to follow, in most others it is difficult to be certain of the role played by wives, parents, and children in the lives of the radicals, both in the British Isles and in America, for by and large the exiles were extremely reticent about their personal lives. Cobbett was an exception, always prepared to extol the virtues of his family life (some of his boasting has subsequently been found to be a mixture of fiction and flummery).[220] Most, however, either kept their counsel or paraded pious platitudes about their marriages and families. Mathew Carey and John Binns both paid tribute to their wives as helpmeets in their autobiographies, the former acknowledging that Bridget Carey took an active part in his business affairs when he was struggling to make headway.[221] Undoubtedly, especially among the artisan and small business categories of exile, wives seem to have participated in their husband's public and business affairs. The formidable Winifred Gales, for example, was obviously a tower of strength for her husband (and not just when putting pirates in their place!). When Joseph Gales was away from Sheffield on a business trip and a visitor warned her of an official raid on the shop, Winifred hid all the dangerous books and pamphlets before the authorities arrived.[222] Not only did Henry Jackson's daughter (and wife of Oliver Bond) help organize the female branch of the United Irish society in Dublin, but on Christmas Day 1796 she brought writing paper, pens, newspapers and letters to the incarcerated state prisoners, hidden, classically, under the crust of a large pie.[223] It is not surprising that with such strongwilled daughters, Jackson havered between settling in Ireland or Baltimore. It is also not surprising that when a radical's wife gave practical and sympathetic assistance, and shared his political opinions, the family not only usually stayed in America but also made a success of it.

IN RETROSPECT

Between Devereaux's gold mine and Hudson's dental fortune on the one hand, and the fates of the Mitchells and John Craig Millar on the other, lies a chasm, loosely filled by the silent majority of the exiles, whose lives in America remain shrouded in darkness. Hints and glimpses are occasionally seen: the one-time assassin Joseph Cuthbert working hard at his tailoring trade in New York City, eschewing all politics; Richard Davison watching his printshop burn down in Warrenton, North Carolina; and Andrew Bryson, Jr., riding through the New York snowdrifts—a welcome change from the heat and mosquitoes of Martinique?—in a vain attempt to gather in his firm's debts and find new orders for the books.[224] How long they lived in America, and whether they remigrated, cannot now be ascertained. It would be an assumption, but probably not an unwarrantable one, to state that most of the exiles eventually lived out their lives as quiet and inoffensive American citizens, working at their trades or on their farms, marrying, having large families, and occasionally dreaming of what might have been if their political activities in the British Isles had been successful. Perhaps the fates of the three Cheetham brothers can be taken as typical: in New York City John kept to the family trade of hatter; Ben went into partnership in a livery stable; only James branched out, into the quintessential "Jacobin" occupation of political journalism.[225]

Memories seem not to have softened with the passage of time but, especially for the Irish, news years later of continued unrest in the homeland stirred the feelings of defeat and despair rather than the enthusiasm of the early 1790s. Musing over Irish agrarian outrages in 1822, John Chambers wrote to Robert Simms, now an old man in Belfast:

> Looking at these things with a cooler mind and more matured judgement than when I lived in the country, I can find no grounds for hope of any change for the better, as . . . they proceed from causes beyond the probability of reform or alteration. I mean the constant absence of the great landholders, and the difference of religion between the Governors and the Governed, which contains in itself a principle of perpetual repulsion, strengthened by various contributing and aggravating causes. It is a heavy denunciation, but it is the conviction of my humble judgement, that our poor country is doomed to long, if not perpetual distraction and unhappiness and poverty.[226]

Samuel Brown Wylie, too, in retrospect contemplated the mistakes made by the United Irish movement in the 1790s, although he continued to console himself that it had been "a blow stricken . . . for the rights of man."[227] John

Caldwell, however, mourned, and warned against, a youth misspent pursuing a will o' the wisp:

> Politics however virtuous may be the intention of the patriot, however advantageous to the general weal would be the accomplishment of the hopes and efforts of the youthful aspirant, yet must be admitted to be a dangerous study, profession or pursuit for a young man of ardent temperament and for a young man in mercantile life, particularly so, when a degree of secrecy is necessarily attendant on the pursuit. The midnight meetings, the exposure to all classes of kindred politicians and amongst them too often the wicked, the reckless, unworthy, and often unprincipled base informer and spy, who under the cloak of patriotism and solemn oaths, wheedle themselves into the confidence of virtuous but unwary associates to lead them to destruction. How many young men I have known to be led astray by designing, corrupt demagogues, and not infrequently by well intentioned individuals, who ever forgetful of their duties to their families and to their callings would waste away the hours listening to idle harangues and declamations for the "public good" at the expense of their health, their fortunes, and all the comforts of domestic life. I do not make these observations to paralyze the efforts of aspiring and virtuous ambition, but to guard the young and inexperienced against splitting on the rock on which so many in my young days were wrecked.[228]

America may have been a haven, but it could not keep away the ghosts.

SIX

Defending the Republic, 1793–1801

JEFFERSONIAN REPUBLICANS

Out of the Frying Pan

However temporarily dispirited many radical emigrants were by the reality of exile, and however difficult it was to establish themselves in their new country, their transition to the New World at least offered them the opportunity to shed a heavy burden of political concerns and worries. In republican America, no longer would they have to struggle with the inequities of the Church-State establishment. No longer would they need to decide between reform and revolutionary strategies; to attack the glorious consequences of the 1688 revolution and the mythical and supposedly perfect British Constitution; to assail the pretensions of monarchy and an hereditary aristocracy; to condemn the war; or to seek to undermine the foundations of Old Corruption and its perennial servant, the oligarchic financial system rooted in an ever-expanding national debt. The strain of opposing the myriad tentacles of the British state would now dissipate. Many of the most heavily used parts of their philosophical arsenal could be decommissioned, unnecessary in the republican society to which they were bound.

Or so they thought. In reality, the exiles soon came to realize that the battles they had fought (and lost) in Britain had to be fought again in America. The war was by no means over; its campaigns had merely been transferred to fresh fields.

One cause of this inevitable renewal of hostilities was the influence in the new federal government then settled in Philadelphia of a William Pitt doppelgänger, Alexander Hamilton.[1] When George Washington became the first president of the United States, he chose for his two premier secretaries in the tiny cabinet one strong promoter of the fledgling constitution, Alexander Hamilton, and one skeptical but tolerant critic, Thomas Jefferson.[2] Both were stout republicans and both had been committed patriots during the Revolutionary War, but in the aftermath, while Jefferson was distanced from domestic events as ambassador to France, Hamilton had become convinced of the need for a strong and consolidated government with the powers necessary to harness and restrain what he and other Nationalists saw as the runaway democratic tendencies being shown by many state legislatures and their unruly constituents. Democracy needed to be reined in, which the new federal constitution, drawn up at the Philadelphia convention in the summer of 1787, sought to achieve. With the help of Jefferson's fellow Virginian and friend James Madison, and John Jay, Hamilton played a key role in selling the constitution to the public. His reward, from his mentor Washington, was a seat in the cabinet, with responsibility for national finances.

The United States in the years after 1787 was a land filled with visions of the future, emanations from that which Thomas Paine called "the wilderness of imagination."[3] Paine's statement in *Common Sense* that "We have it in our power to begin the world over again" had struck a chord in the minds of Americans.[4] Some were bold in their dreams, envisioning a large agricultural empire stretching from the Atlantic to the Pacific, filled with small, independent yeomen farmers supplying the world with its food. Others, usually either western settlers or with a frontier mentality, considered the virtues of a separate empire beyond the Appalachians, free of the sectional influences of the older, more commercialized states. Yet others, equally rapacious, looked with covetous eyes on the silver mines of the tottering Spanish empire to the south. Hamilton, too, had his grand design, but it focused less on the endless landscape to the west than on the example presented by the sophisticated and wealthy economies of western Europe, especially that of old enemy Britain. The United States would become a great empire encompassing the whole of North America, Hamilton dreamed, but it would also be a great world power, based not only on its function as a world granary, but as the supreme commercial and industrial power on the globe. The United States would compete with Great Britain at her own game and beat her.[5]

Ironically, to achieve that end, Hamilton had initially both to copy many of Britain's economic and financial institutions and to lean on her goodwill, interest, and above all, investment. In 1790 and 1791 he put forward, in a series of controversial reports to Congress, his plans for setting the finances, and the future, of the federal government on a sound footing. These included funding the national debt at par, assuming state debts resulting from the war of independence, creating a national bank and a mint, raising an excise tax on distilled liquors to supplement the federal government's main source of income, import duties, and encouraging domestic manufacturing by the introduction of selected tariffs. Hamilton's financial policy "contained within it a vision of an America with a strong national government protecting and stimulating commerce and industry and fostering close ties between the government and men of affairs and influence."[6]

Unfortunately, many of the men of affairs and influence looked askance at this apparently monarchical-oligarchical policy dressed in republican clothing. Far from drawing America's élites into supporting the federal government ever more closely, it fractured the pro-constitution élite combination of 1787–88. Men with a different conception of America's republican future, like Jefferson and Hamilton's erstwhile colleague Madison, were aghast. Not only did his plans favor a small group of monied men and speculators, but they were also certain to open sectional fissures, by seeming to favor northern interests over southern and western in a variety of ways. The Virginian version of America's future, as a simple commercial-agrarian republic based on a society of autonomous independent farmers, seemed at risk from the outset: "with Hamilton's plan there were now two utopias where previously there had been one."[7]

Opposition to Hamilton's program was at first tentative and diffuse, without a clear focal point around which to coalesce. This core of opposition was only to emerge as the decade wore on, centering on Thomas Jefferson and his more activist lieutenant, James Madison. Jefferson's commercial-agrarianism attracted both western farmers and the southern plantocracy, but in addition the Republicans, as the formal opposition came to be called, appealed to other groups disillusioned with Federalist policies. In particular, the Jeffersonian Republicans began to make headway in the seaport cities, among both the mercantile classes and the artisans. The great weakness of Federalism was its too narrow social base, a consequence of the conservatives' fear of democracy and disdain for the common man, who lacked virtue. Influenced by classical notions of virtue, Hamilton was convinced that the republican experiment would succeed only if a governing class was created that acted on behalf of the national interest, subordinating its own and local interests. This policy required the wooing of the holders of traditional aristocratic proprietary wealth, "who are in every society the only firm supporters of government."[8] In pursuing this objective, Hamilton ignored the interests of many other social groups, including the commercial farmers, urban tradesmen and mechanics, upwardly mobile professional men, and the growing number of nouveau riche merchants and manufacturers. Although many of these had supported the federal constitution in 1788, by the mid-1790s they were coalescing with old Anti-Federalists and drifting into the Republican opposition, creating a coalition of different interests and ideas, but united by a common antipathy to the thrust of government foreign and domestic policies.[9]

Hamilton's program was only one factor in the forging of the Republican coalition. Another, equally if not more influential, was the French Revolution. However excited many Americans were at the thought of the French following their example by ridding themselves of their king and establishing a republic, supporters of Hamilton's policies were aware that the country's future depended on retaining cordial ties with Great Britain, at least in the medium term.[10] At certain times during the 1790s this was difficult to accomplish, as Britain's war policy on the high seas acted against America's mercantile interests. For the Republicans, however, ideological rather than economic factors determined their stance. They applauded the French Revolution, for it represented an attempt to implement New World political doctrines in an Old World setting.[11] Popular opinion in America regarding the French Revolution fluctuated, sometimes dramatically, throughout the decade, but the Republicans' position remained fixed. On two basic issues, hostility toward the pro-British, "monarchical" policies of the Federalists, and sympathy for the French republicans in a war against despotism, the Republicans defined themselves.

Such were the growing divisions in American political society—Jefferson, for instance, later claimed that "two very distinct parties had formed"[12] by the time the Second Congress met—that even the few exiles who had arrived as early as 1793 could be forgiven for having thought that their ships had silently turned around one night and secretly returned to Britain, so familiar to them were the political arguments and divisions agitating the American public. Given the circumstances, it is not surprising that the radical exiles almost unanimously favored Jefferson's opposition party. There were, of course, a few exceptions. In New England, Rev. William Wells, John Mason Williams, James Tytler, John Humphries, and Benjamin Vaughan gave muted allegiance to Federalism, the last, however, remaining in correspondence with Jefferson through their mutual interest in the American Philosophical Society and agricultural improvement.[13] Callender and James Cheetham, as we shall see, became anti-Republicans, if not Federalists, while Cobbett soon after his arrival in America became a leading propagandist for Pitt's Britain and, incidentally, Federalism.[14] A great many others supported the Jeffersonian Republicans, but deliberately eschewed the "low, vindictive and degrading squabbles" associated with partisan politics.[15] A few, Cooper, Priestley, and Sampson, for example, hoped to remain free of political entanglements, but were eventually dragged in.[16]

Probably as many as ten percent of the radical exiles did much more than give their electoral support to the Republicans in the two decades following the introduction of the new federal system of government. In America, they represented the most militant elements of the emigration and threw themselves into the battle against Federalism, most as editors, pamphleteers, and propagandists promoting their conception of republicanism.[17] As we have seen, theirs was a politics strongly influenced by Painite ideas, and while their radicalism and the rambunctious manner in which they promoted it did not always appeal to all sections of the Republican party, it nevertheless neatly conformed both to the political needs of the party's leader, Thomas Jefferson, and to the radical strain in his political philosophy.

Jefferson, Paine, and Painites

All commentators agree that Jefferson was a many-sided, intellectually subtle figure, whose philosophy can be interpreted in a number of ways. He has been categorized, pari passu, as an enlightened patrician, a liberal pluralist, a libertarian with a "darker side," and a radical democrat. His protean character stems partly from his long public life, in which he played many different roles and confronted a variety of important, and sometimes unique political issues; partly from his unwillingness to say or write anything controversial for public consumption, while expressing forthright, partisan, and even at times bloodthirsty views in private correspondence;[18] and partly from the various symbolic uses to which his name has been put since his death.[19] Although conscious of the need to avoid what has been called the "fallacy of misplaced coherence"[20]—a tendency to fashion either groups' or individuals' political views into too logical systems of belief—it is nevertheless possible to suggest that in his radical persona and as the rather secluded, but not isolated leader of the opposition in the 1790s, Jefferson can plausibly be denominated a "Painite," in the same way that Paine may legitimately be called a "Jeffersonian." In the 1790s the exiled activists, most of whom were partisans and ideologues rather than political philosophers, certainly would have recognized and acknowledged the parallel. As their role in the political struggles increased, both Jefferson and Paine came to represent in the radicals' minds the Spirit of '76—a rallying cry encompassing the doctrines of *Common Sense* and the Declaration of Independence—which helped to take Jefferson to the presidency in 1800.[21]

During the battle with Federalism, there were few fundamental political principles on which Paine and Jefferson (and the exiles) disagreed. Indeed, in 1791 Jefferson told John Adams that an attack on Paine's principles was synonymous with an attack on "the principles of the citizens of the United States."[22] Both Paine and Jefferson were children of the Enlightenment, internationalist in orientation and transfixed by the possibilities inherent in the new natural philosophy. Both believed in social progress and in the ultimate perfectibility of humankind. Jefferson has been called "a virtual Pollyanna about everything," forever optimistic that science and reason would eventually solve every problem.[23] The exiles too held similar sanguine views of the future, based on similar premises. Priestley, Cooper reminded Americans, had advanced "the doctrines of the perfectibility of the species, or at least its continually increasing tendency to improvement, and to happiness," long before Franklin, Richard Price, Condorcet, and Godwin had followed in his footsteps.[24] Unlike Condorcet and Godwin, however, the exiles' optimism was more pragmatic than utopian, premised, said John Daly Burk, on the ability of Newtonian science and the reforming spirit to ensure that Americans will come to "enjoy the plenty and the spirit of the golden age."[25] How fortunate it was, declaimed Richard Dinmore, that "To *man* is given a peculiar prerogative; a power of progressive improvement."[26]

Neither Jefferson nor Paine and his acolytes eschewed revolution as a means of progress. It would perhaps be an exaggeration to suggest they believed in permanent revolution, but they certainly aspired to regular political upheavals. In *Rights of Man* Paine argued in favor of generational self-determination. "Every age and generation must be free to act for itself, *in all cases*, as the ages and generation which preceded it," he wrote. "The vanity and presumption of governing beyond the grave, is the most ridiculous and insolent of all tyrannies. . . . I am contending for the rights of the *living*, and against their being willed away, and controlled and contracted for, by the manuscript assumed authority of the dead."[27] Jefferson, too, rejected the dead hand of the past, and the threat of the present dominating the future. Even his own generation's contributions to the practice of government, the state and federal constitutions, ought to be seen as provisional.[28] He first expressed his belief "that the earth belongs in usufruct to the living" and that "the dead have neither powers nor rights over it" in a letter to Madison in 1789, but in one of his last letters before his death in 1826—to the English radical Major John Cartwright—he both plagiarized himself and paraphrased Paine: "Can one generation bind another, and all others, in succession forever? I think not. The Creator has made the earth for the living, not the dead."[29] At the very least, this cast of mind lent itself to accepting the necessity of continuous change and systemic reform, as the radicals were to urge even after Jefferson's accession to the presidency.

Both Paine and Jefferson held tenaciously to their fundamental principles, altering their positions only under the force of circumstances. Both resolutely adhered to a radical version of natural rights from the mid-1770s until their deaths, although many other patriotic leaders, fearful of the implications of a doctrine that brought the state of nature "into imaginable history," had veered away once independence reduced the value of natural law arguments.[30] Both, as a logical outcome of their natural rights' views, believed in minimalist government. With Paine's (and Locke's) famous distinction between government and society—that "Society is produced by our wants and government by our wickedness; the former promotes our happiness *positively* by uniting our affections, the latter *negatively* by restraining our vices"[31]—Jefferson (and the exiles)[32] fully concurred. Indeed, one historian has claimed that "Paine's conventional liberal division between society and government was the premise of Jefferson's political thinking—his faith in the natural ordering of society, his belief in the common moral sense of ordinary people, his idea of minimal government."[33]

Enough has been shown here of the many features common to the ideologies of Paine and Jefferson to explain why the Painite radicals' adherence to the Republican party was inevitable. Their loyalty to Jefferson, however— and it was a loyalty as much to the man as to the Jeffersonian coalition—was conditioned by more than the intricacies of political philosophy. Although there was never a close friendship between Paine and Jefferson, they were seen as compatriots and allies, a view Paine at least was happy to promote.[34] Moreover, in May 1791 Jefferson had written favorably of Paine in a private letter enclosed with a copy of *Rights of Man*, Part 1, which at Madison's behest he was passing on to the brother of a printer who intended to publish an American edition. He had commented: "I am extremely pleased to find it will be reprinted here, and that something is at length to be publickly said against the political heresies which have sprung up among us. I have no doubt our citizens will rally a second time round the standard of Common Sense." To Jefferson's embarrassment, the printer published his comments in a preface to the work, which soon found their way into the newspapers too. Jefferson thus, in the public mind, became associated with Paine's most radical ideas.[35]

Furthermore, however reluctant he was to involve himself in the rough and tumble of politics, Jefferson appealed to the radicals because he was the only obvious figurehead for the Republican opposition, capable of holding together, by his reputation alone, various groups without intolerable strain. His fame among the radicals, resting primarily on his authorship of the Declaration of Independence, was a major contributing factor, for it was that document, far more than the federal constitution, that they believed summed up the philosophical essence of American republicanism. Important too, for the exiles, was his known anglophobia, which they naturally shared. Suspicion of British intentions and a lingering dislike of the former mother country among Americans in general was understandable so soon after fighting a long war for independence, but Jefferson's anglophobia was particularly acute because of its personal nature, stemming from the embarrassment he felt when as governor of Virginia a mere 900 British troops under Benedict Arnold had forced him and his council to retreat from Richmond, seemingly in panic. Being snubbed by George III when he had attended the court in 1785—an intelligible response, considering what Jefferson had written of the king in the Declaration of Independence—had only soured him further. He responded in a classic manner by transposing his own feelings onto his opponent: "In spite of treaties," he wrote to John Langdon later that year, "England is still our enemy. Her hatred is deeprooted and cordial, and nothing is wanting with her but the power to wipe us and the land we live on out of existence."[36] It was a position from which he was scarcely to deviate throughout the rest of his long political career, much to the comfort of the radical exiles.[37]

The political careers of the activist Republican exiles, both before and after Jefferson's presidential victory in 1800, are best understood within this framework of what they perceived to be a militant Painite-Jeffersonian radicalism, premised on the doctrines of participatory democracy. Determined to involve themselves in the partisan battles of their new homeland, they saw their role as creating the conditions to undermine the power of Federalism and to clear the way for the victory of a radical Jefferson.

PARTISANS AND PROPAGANDISTS

A Free Press

The impact of the radical exiles on American politics in the 1790s far outweighed their small numbers because of the strategically important positions they held within the media communications of the opposition. As one historian has written: "Foreigners seemed to get one sniff of printers' ink and become loyal Jeffersonians."[38] Throughout the decade Republican newspapers were consistently outgunned by the much larger number supporting the government, the most prominent of which enjoyed the financial advantages of government printing and advertising patronage. Before the Alien and Sedition Acts stirred the Republicans to feverish activity from the summer of 1798, fewer than ten percent of newspapers throughout the country consistently supported the opposition, and by 1801 there were still twice as many Federalist as Republican newspapers.[39] In this situation, the influx of even a relatively small number of combative Republican journalists made a significant difference.

Leaving aside for the moment consideration of the exiled writers' influence on the outcome of Federalist-Republican conflict, it was generally thought at the time that access to knowledge, widely dispersed among the sovereign people, was a fundamental requirement for the success of the republican experiment, with a free press playing a vital role in sustaining republican institutions.[40] Jefferson, who personally was to find press freedom a double-edged sword, informed Washington in 1792 that "No government ought to be without censors; and where the press is free, no one ever will be. . . . Nature has given to man no other means of sifting out the truth, either in religion, law, or politics."[41] In old age, having survived the years of slander, he continued to assert the Enlightenment view that a free press was "the best instrument for enlightening the mind of man, and improving him as a rational, moral, and social being."[42] Denis Driscol summed up exile opinion when he wrote: "Information is like the dew of heaven, to the tree of liberty. It is with this, that its leaves must be continually moistened. Knowledge prevented, is death to the liberty of mind. . . . The press, being the only weapon, which reason, in the cause of liberty, should use, never let it rust or be used against you."[43]

The martial language often used in this era when discussing the role of the press—press warfare, newspapers as weapons, and the like—reflected both the growing partisanship in American political life and the belief that a fundamental conflict over principles and the future of the United States was in progress. Yet Americans still remained uncertain about the use of the media in political debate. That the press should remain unfettered and free to publish was a sine qua non; even Hamilton, in the *Federalist*, acknowledged that in a state founded on the doctrine of popular sovereignty only public opinion could ultimately decide the amount of liberty and latitude the press could achieve.[44] At the same time, however, American understanding continued to fluctuate between the concepts of a "free" and an "open" press, the former being defined as a press that was at liberty to defend the community as a whole against the inevitable usurpations of government, the latter as a press consisting of newspapers that even-handedly published every viewpoint, the value of which could then be determined by public opinion. In the period leading up to independence the free press idea dominated patriot thinking; it was a perfect rationale for those claiming to protect the community against a power-hungry British government.[45] After 1783, however, the open press doctrine revived, best exemplified by Mathew Carey's magazine *American Museum*, which opened its pages to various points of view concerning the federal constitution and America's future political economy.[46] The ubiquitous prerevolutionary newspaper masthead, "Open to all Parties, but Influenced by None," continued to be used into the 1790s, even for a few months by James Carey in his *Wilmington Chronicle*.[47]

The open press doctrine could not survive long in an age of aggressive partisanship,[48] but doubts remained: Could a newspaper legitimately broadcast a sustained opposition to a legally constituted government elected by the community? As James Thomson Callender acutely pointed out: "A representative government is, from its very nature, liable to embarrassment from *conflicting opinions*."[49] From the various possible solutions to this conundrum, a militant phalanx of Republicans in Philadelphia in mid-1795 chose a policy of attempting to overwhelm the Federalist political agenda by saturating the public with its own, radical interpretation of political events. Via this overtly partisan process, that in effect imitated the role of British radical newspapers such as the *Northern Star, Cork Gazette, Manchester Herald,* and *Sheffield Register,* a number of exiles stormed onto the American political stage.

This is not to deny that bursts of partisan newspaper warfare had preceded the advent of the exiles. In response to Hamilton's early use of John Fenno's *Gazette of the United States* to support his political agenda, Jefferson and Madison, with the promise of government patronage and a job as a translator, had persuaded Philip Freneau in July 1791 to establish the *National Gazette* in the capital. The ensuing warfare, which peaked in 1793 with Freneau's defense of Edmund Genet, the reckless and arrogant French ambassador, gave a taste of what was to come, but the prospect of a sustained promotion of Jeffersonian views in the media failed to survive the demise of Freneau's newspaper in October 1793. The ostensible cause of its failure was the disastrous impact on circulation of the yellow fever epidemic, but Freneau had already been losing readers owing to his obstinate refusal to abandon Genet's cause, even after the ambassador had lost the confidence of Jefferson and had destroyed his popularity by insolently refusing to abide by the consequences of America's policy of neutrality.[50]

Thereafter, the main prop for the dwindling Republican position in the capital was Benjamin Franklin Bache's *General Advertiser* (renamed *Aurora* in 1794). Bache, the favored grandson of Benjamin Franklin, had spent much of his youth from 1777 to 1785 in Geneva and France, where he trained as a printer. In 1790, using his grandfather's presses, he established his newspaper in Philadelphia, espousing the millennial cause of universal liberty in general and the French revolutionaries in particular. Bache's reputation as an unprincipled enragé and fifth columnist for revolutionary France stems primarily from his activities in the last few years of his short life, when he was allied with some of the most radical Painite exiles. In the preceding years, however, although he consistently championed the French republic, his overall political position was equivocal, the result in part of his commitment to the doctrines of an open press. Supportive of a nationalist fiscal policy, he did not criticize Hamilton's policies in a partisan manner. Nor, in the congressional elections of 1792, which were fought in Pennsylvania on proto-party lines, did he recoil from an impartial editorial policy. His biographer has even described him as "timid (and sometimes almost sycophantic)" in his public approach to Federalist luminaries such as Washington and John Adams.[51]

Emigré Journalists

Bache's decision to adopt a strong partisan stance emerged only in the early months of 1794, and coincided with his initial contact with James Thomson Callender, the first of the militant exiles to arrive in Philadelphia. Callender had sailed from Dublin, where he had gone into hiding following his outlawry in Edinburgh, arriving in America in May 1793. He brought with him letters of introduction from sympathetic United Irishmen, which persuaded Mathew Carey to employ him as a "scissors-and-paste" author, first part-time and then at $12 a week. A second job, a few month's work on the *American Daily Advertiser*, was followed in December 1793 by an offer from Andrew Brown to report on congressional debates for his newspaper, the Republican *Philadelphia Gazette*.[52] As Bache recorded the debates for his own newspaper, it probably would have been at the desk reserved for shorthand writers in Congress that he first became acquainted with Callender.[53]

There were few nuances in Callender's approach to journalism; he perceived the world as having but two colors, black and white, and but two moral positions, good and evil.[54] It took him no more than a few weeks to decide that the Republicans were good, and the Federalists evil. His reports of debates, which either from inexperience, laziness, or mischievousness sometimes appeared in garbled form in the *Gazette*, soon had the House in uproar. He gained the enmity of several powerful Federalists by the unscrupulous practice of adding to his reports personal comments in parentheses, and by the judicious use of italics, both subtle ways of influencing the reader without straying too far from the spoken text. Although prominent Federalists suffered most acutely from these techniques, more moderate Republicans such as William Branch Giles and Madison were also occasionally targeted.

How Bache, who took his role as congressional reporter very seriously, responded to Callender's antics is not known, but from the beginning of 1794 he began to accept for publication in his newspaper regular paragraphs and squibs from the Scotsman, which he published under the heading "From a

Correspondent" (anonymity had to be preserved, because Callender was still working for Brown). Between January 1794 and June 1798, when Callender fled Philadelphia, exactly 300 paragraphs were published under that heading in the *General Advertiser/Aurora*.[55] Although it is impossible to prove, it appears that many, if not most, of these political comments and sarcastic squibs came from Callender's virulent pen. Bache himself was no paragraphist, capable of participating in the cut and thrust of daily journalistic jousting, but Callender, with his caustic wit, large fund of invective, and hatred of the powerful, was perfectly suited.[56] From the moment of their association, the *Aurora*'s subject matter became more partisan and more scurrilous. The rather schizophrenic policy the newspaper displayed on such issues as the excise tax in 1794 reflected a combination of Bache's own indecision and ignorance of economics, and the increasing influence on him of the militant Callender, an expert on the evils of excise from his Edinburgh days.[57]

With Bache's printery and bookshop as a rallying point, there began to emerge in Philadelphia a group of radical activists who in the next few years were to engage Federalism in open and bitter warfare in conjunction with the local Republican party. Philadelphia Republicans had begun to organize themselves in 1791, in opposition to the ruling Junto of longstanding and wealthy merchant-gentry families who, following the upheavals of the Revolutionary War, had regained control of Pennsylvania in 1786. With the aid of many nouveau riche merchants and compliant small businessmen, they had successfully supported the new federal constitution and, in 1790, replaced the old democratic state constitution of 1776 with a more conservative form of government. Once firmly in control, however, the old élite ignored the legitimate aspirations of the nouveaux riches, who were seeking a share of political power commensurate with their economic status. The result was that by 1791 a disaffected part of the Philadelphia gentry began to organize itself into an opposition. Led by the British-born secretary of the Commonwealth, Alexander J. Dallas, and the diminutive, ex-tory merchant, John Swanwick, they sought to use national issues to widen political participation at the state level. In 1792 their tactic of appealing to disaffected newcomers, ethnic groups, and the numerous city small producers had its first minor success, with Swanwick winning one of Philadelphia's assembly seats on a ticket "to support the Rights of Man."[58]

Involvement in the numerous state and federal elections in Philadelphia was slight, with usually no more than 20 percent to 25 percent of those eligible casting a vote. Republican tactics sought to achieve much greater voter participation, especially among the middling classes.[59] The creation of the Democratic Society of Pennsylvania in 1793 was one attempt to widen Philadelphia's active political constituency. Republican leaders such as Dallas, Swanwick, the rich snuff manufacturer Thomas Leiper, Dr. Michael Leib, and the "burly, gouty old gentleman" Blair McClenachan were prominent in its activities.[60] When the society collapsed under the weight of presidential disapproval and tactics over policy toward the whiskey rebels, the Republicans turned to less contentious forms of proselytizing, with Bache's newspaper taking on a major role.[61]

As outsiders, the radical exiles conformed to the social profile of the Philadelphia Republican organization. Although the leadership was mainly the moderately wealthy and from the mercantile class, most were foreign-born (Dallas, Leiper, Swanwick, and McClenachan were British or Irish-born, Leib was German). By 1794 they had been joined by another arriviste, Mathew Carey. From the moment he became involved in American politics as a newspaper editor in 1785, Carey had promoted economic nationalist policies and the drive for a new, more powerful federal government. In state affairs he initially leaned toward the Constitutionalists, who wished to retain the 1776 constitution, joining, with Dallas, the Newly Adopted Sons of the United States, a society with links to the Philadelphia radicals. But by 1787 Carey had united with the Federalist Junto (confusingly called Republicans at the state level), and remained supportive of them and Hamiltonian economics at the national level, until his anglophobia came to the surface during the conflicts over foreign policy and the French Revolution in 1793. The publication in 1794 of his pamphlet, *A Short Account of Algiers,* that denounced British imperial policies and took a Madisonian line on possible American responses, marked Carey's entry into the Republican party. He brought with him his presses, his links with the immigrant Irish, and his skills as a political propagandist, all of which were to be of considerable value to the nascent opposition.[62]

The Jacobin Scandal-Club

The Republican party in Philadelphia before 1796 had little formal organization or structure, except on an ad hoc basis at election times, and on major issues tended to divide into moderate and radical factions.[63] At the leadership level, political discussions probably took place at business meetings or social gatherings. Such tactics as were decided on were spread via small networks of friends and colleagues.[64] By 1795 two men, John Beckley and Tench Coxe, played central roles in holding these networks together, sustaining lines of communication from the national and local leadership to the rank and file. As clerk to the federal House of Representatives, Beckley was ideally placed to act as the Republicans' "political manager," for little occurring in Congress escaped his attention, and having responsibility for the newspaper reporters in the chamber, he had easy access to Bache, Callender, and later Duane and Gales. Beckley was an incorrigible intriguer, gossip, and rumormonger, although Jefferson thought him at times too credulous.[65] A regular correspondent of Jefferson's, he "had extremely strong and dedicated Republican convictions, verging on fanaticism at times. He was very bold in his political approach, much too bold in the opinion of some more conservative Republicans."[66]

Beckley had been acquainted with Tench Coxe for several years before, in 1795, they became firm political allies. Coxe was a turncoat, Hamilton's assistant secretary at the treasury from 1790 to 1794. There he had produced much of the data on which Hamilton based his famous reports, and was also, according to Senator William Maclay of Pennsylvania, one of the treasurer's early propagandists. He also secretly assisted Jefferson when he was secretary of state, and continued a correspondence after Jefferson had retired to Monticello. A neutral, if not a tory, in the war of independence, a dandy, and an amusing dinner companion, Coxe was from an old West Jersey family, but in Philadelphia was regarded as an arriviste. His doubts about Federalist policies and his growing anglophobia in 1794 were accentuated when, following Hamilton's decision to resign from government, Coxe failed to obtain his anticipated promotion to the top treasury position. Thereafter, he moved ever more inexorably into the Republican orbit, although he continued to hold a government post as commissioner of the revenue. Little wonder that Abigail Adams, when First Lady, called him "A Man of no sincerity of views [or] of conduct, a Changling as the Wind blow, and a Jacobin in Heart."[67]

The Beckley-Coxe combination was the axis around which the Republican party and the militant exiles revolved. They picked up information and political tidbits, schemed, and, in the former's case especially, tried to organize the troops.[68] With their close connections to both the Philadelphia and the national leadership, they liaised between the hierarchy and the propagandists who congregated around Bache's printshop. Most of these penmen were radical exiles: Callender, James Carey, Duane, Reynolds, Lloyd (an honorary exile, although he first emigrated to America before the revolution), and, more marginally, Gales, Lee, Eaton, and Tandy. With the exceptions of Callender, Tandy, and Reynolds, all were involved in establishing their own printing shops, and publishing or editing newspapers and magazines. Just how close their connections were cannot now be ascertained with certainty, but Tandy in a letter to Ireland said Reynolds belonged to an anti-Washington "political club" in Philadelphia, and Mathew Carey in his autobiography recalled an "association" in 1796 led by Leib, Reynolds, Beckley, Duane, and Bache.[69]

In some ways, these exiled radical journalists were a godsend for the Republicans. They had considerable experience of acting against an entrenched government and a clear understanding of the mechanisms of Old Corruption, which enabled them swiftly to confirm the Republicans' conviction that Federalist policies were putative Pittite policies.[70] They also were proficient in the art of popular politics and were experienced in the use of political propaganda. Moreover, they had no qualms about creating political conflict; to them, party divisions were natural, not something to be avoided, as many Americans, entrapped by Commonwealth ideology, still thought.[71] They also realized that to be polite and reasonable in print was to play into the hands of the élite. A democratic society was an earthy, boisterous, and brash society, where social pretensions were pricked, pomposity ridiculed, and the legitimacy of even the most exalted questioned. As good Painites, fearful of aristocracy's revival under Federalism, the exiles sought to push Americans toward acknowledging and accepting the more democratic implications of their revolution.

The radical exiles, too, were not inhibited by contemporary American imperatives that sometimes narrowed political options and hindered prospects of change. They were not diverted, for instance, by sectional interests (at least in their early years) and could take a detached, ironically more national view of events than their American counterparts. They also did not carry the burden of uncertainty caused by a (usually reluctant) admission among Republicans that many of the government's supporters were themselves good republicans who had played patriotic roles in the war of independence. For the exiles, Hamilton, John Adams, and Washington were not former colleagues; they were aristocratic wolves in republican sheep's clothing.

The advent of this clique of highly opinionated, militant journalists in Philadelphia in 1795–96 was not, however, without its problems for the Republicans. By no means all of them, especially among the members of Congress, where first Madison and then William Branch Giles were moderate House leaders, were amenable to an extreme, "democratic" form of politics. They were reluctant to embrace the aggressive and very public tactics that the exiles and their main Philadelphia allies—Leib, Bache, and Beckley—favored. Moreover, the Whiskey rebellion had alarmed local leaders such as Dallas and Swanwick, who thereafter retreated from the dangers of popular democracy toward a Madisonian moderation.[72] The result was that although the militants fought on behalf of the Republicans, they were never fully under party control and frequently slipped the leash.

Recognizing this last point is crucial for understanding the manner in which, in 1795, American politics degenerated into unrestrained partisan warfare. The key issues were the reception of Jay's treaty in America, and the president's role in its acceptance. With war a possibility owing to Britain's maritime policy of ignoring America's neutral status, Washington had sent Chief Justice John Jay to England in May 1794 to negotiate a treaty aimed at resolving all the major points of contention that had lingered since 1783. The treaty was provisionally signed in November 1794, but its articles remained secret throughout the first half of 1795 while the Senate examined them behind closed doors. During this unpopular news blackout political tensions were kept at high pitch by a Republican press convinced of Jay's failure to defend America's interests.[73] The cauldron boiled over when on 29 June 1795 Bache, having received a leaked copy of the treaty, published a rough synopsis.[74] He then rode through the northern states distributing copies of the treaty and organizing demonstrations, causing a surge of anger to sweep the country.[75] In New York, Hamilton was stoned by an irate crowd. In Philadelphia in July, at the second of three protest meetings called by the Republicans against the treaty, Blair McClenachan jumped up on the platform and shouted: "What a damned treaty! I make a motion that every good citizen in this assembly kick this damn treaty to hell." While a mob marched to the homes of the French and British ambassadors, burning a copy of the treaty outside the latter, one interested onlooker, Hamilton Rowan, "who has taken refuge amongst us, from the despotism of his native country," received an ovation. The new secretary of the treasury, Oliver Wolcott, Jr., who observed the meeting, sourly noted that the Republicans' supporters seemed to be composed of the "ignorant, violent, disaffected and alien."[76]

Destroying an Icon

Agitation at this high level of intensity could not be sustained, and slowly hostility to the Jay treaty subsided. But as soon as Washington signed the treaty into law, the Republican journalists in Philadelphia, independently of the leadership, took the crucial decision to turn their guns on him personally. They did so because they recognized that the Federalists were using his immense prestige as successful military commander and father of his country for their own partisan purposes. Washington was a living legend, whose lengthy shadow blanketed national politics, deflecting the light of reason and republicanism.[77] Public criticism of the president had occurred since 1790, but it had been muted, spasmodic, and indirect. The restraint caused by Washington's cult status was abandoned by the radical exiles; in August 1795 Callender broke the taboo by declaring war on the president. Claiming that by signing the treaty Washington had ignored public opinion and descended to the level of a partisan political leader, Callender informed the president that "he must expect to be no longer viewed as a saint; as he had spoken daggers to [the people's] feelings, he must no longer expect a blind devotion to his will. His conduct has impaired their obligations to him, and instead of being viewed as the father of his country, we behold him as a master. The new character he has disclosed ought to awaken us to our situation, and teach us to shake off the fetters that his name has hitherto imposed upon the minds of freemen."[78] In harsh, sarcastic tones Callender pilloried Washington for his aristocratic hauteur and self-imposed segregation from the people. "Ye swinish creatures," he wrote, alluding to Edmund Burke's famous slur, "dare not approach the presidential sanctuary with your gruntings. Is he to be pestered with your impertinent opinions, and to have his delicate nerves unstrung, by your advice? Is he not your *sovereign*, is he not *paramount* to you and your *constitution*, is he not *infallible, immaculate, omniscient?* . . . Ye hardened and presumptuous wretches, ye deserve not so good a monarch, for thus profaning his hallowed name."[79]

This high-risk strategy of iconoclasm, of playing the man to destroy the Federalist insinuation "that the President is the constitution, and the constitution is the President,"[80] was regarded with apprehension and distaste by leading Republicans. Neither Jefferson nor Madison commented directly on the personal abuse aimed at Washington, but the former thought the president should remain sacrosanct until his retirement, and both were disappointed with the ineffectual nature of the newspaper campaign against the Jay treaty.[81] They were concerned that by attacking Washington, the symbol of national unity, the radical penmen unwittingly risked casting the Republicans as un-American, unpatriotic, and unheeding of the new nation's fragile cohesion.

Once, however, a foreigner claimed the emperor had no clothes, the floodgates opened. The attacks continued throughout 1796, as the Republicans sought to destroy the treaty with Britain in the House of Representatives; to prevent Washington seeking the presidency for a third time; and to ensure Jefferson's presidential election. Dallas, Bache, and Beckley were three of the Americans involved in the attempted destruction of Washington's reputation, but the most virulent abuse continued to pour from the poisonous pens of the exiles.[82] Bache published Paine's letter to Washington, in which the former prisoner of Robespierre, recuperating in Paris, accused the president of deliberately refusing to help in his release from the Luxembourg prison, and of surrendering America's interests to Britain. Washington, Paine claimed, was "treacherous in private friendship . . . and a hypocrite in public life. The world," he continued, "will be puzzled to decide whether you are an apostate or an imposter; whether you have abandoned good principles, or whether you ever had any."[83]

At the same time William Duane burst into print against Washington. Duane emphasized the disappointment felt by "the stranger who flies from the bondage and oppression of Europe," when he realizes that "the affections of America" for Washington are misplaced. As the president's comments on the democratic societies had demonstrated, his "principles go as far, and [his] sympathy of sentiment falls nothing short of Mr. Pitt." His supporters are "the constant and no less ardent eulogists of privileged orders, the advocates of an Established Church, and the eulogists of a British form of government. British maxims in morals as well as politics are with them the standard of perfection." By ignoring the voice of the American people over the Jay treaty, Washington's reputation sank from the elevated rank of a Solon or a Lycurgus to "the insignificance of a *Venetian Doge* or a *Dutch Stadtholder!*" American politics "became discoloured with the jaundiced hue of despotism and cabinet cunning."[84]

The campaign against Washington lasted nineteen months, from August 1795 until March 1797. Strangely, the most strident attacks came after he had officially announced his intention to retire in September 1796. Duane's effort had been in part a response to the president's farewell address, and what has been called "one of the most famous diatribes ever written against Washington" was published in the *Aurora* in December.[85] Again, it was Callender's pen dripping the vitriol:

> If ever a nation was debauched by a man, the American nation has been debauched by WASHINGTON. If ever a nation has suffered from the improper influence of one man, the American nation has been deceived by WASHINGTON. Let his conduct then be an example to future ages. Let it serve to be a warning that no man may be an idol, and that a people may confide in themselves rather than in an individual. Let the history of the federal government instruct mankind, that the marque of patriotism may be worn to conceal the foulest designs against the liberties of the people.[86]

The campaign came to a close only with the inauguration of John Adams. The coup de grâce came from yet another radical exile, Dr. James Reynolds, who wrote that "Every heart, in unison, with the freedom and happiness of the people ought to beat high with exaltation, that the name of WASHINGTON from this day ceases to give a currency to political iniquity, and to legalized corruption." March 4, he continued, "ought to be a jubilee in the United States."[87]

The malicious glee expressed here at first glance seems out of proportion, for it was not Jefferson, but John Adams, who was being inaugurated in Philadelphia, even though the Republican ticket for the electoral college had carried Pennsylvania (and thus seemed to vindicate militant tactics).[88] But as the relentless campaign even after Washington's decision to retire shows, the exiles' eyes were less on one particular election campaign than on the more fundamental issue of destroying Federalism as a political force. Adams was no Jefferson, it is true; but on the other hand, nor was he a Washington (as even Hamilton, who tried to swing the election to his preferred candidate, Thomas Pinckney, realized).[89] In March 1797 the Republicans did not see Adams as a Federalist stooge. Rather, he was assumed to be malleable, capable of being influenced by Republican arguments, especially as his links with the Hamiltonian Federalists were so fragile. In expectation of better relations with the executive, Bache's dogs had been called off once the election result was known. Jefferson, who feared the prospect of Hamilton becoming president in the future, viewed Adams, suitably influenced "to administer the government on its true principles," as a bulwark against the former treasurer's ambitions.[90] Their leader's views were soon known. According to Callender, Bache informed his clique of writers: "Let us give [Adams] a fair trial and then, if he actually does wrong, our censures will fall with greater weight."[91]

In contrast to Adams, or rather, to this naive Republican version of Adams, Washington remained a much greater threat. Closely allied to the even more dangerous Hamilton, in the view of the exiles Washington not only represented the pro-British faction in America, but he was also a leader in the insidious plot to turn the country into a monarchy on the British model. If the plot ever succeeded, Washington would return to take his anointed position. Such a possibility now seems a fantasy, the product of paranoid minds. But this was not the case. Although few Americans doubted Washington's commitment to republicanism, even at the end of his presidency, the radical exiles possessed a different set of experiences, understandings, and insights. They had watched the Pitt government at work; they had suffered at its hands, as victims of its machinations. Fearful of having jumped from the frying pan of one King George into the fire of another, they could see more clearly than most Americans how closely Federalist policy corresponded with Pitt's. As the symbol of aristocratic Federalism, Washington had to be destroyed at all costs, even if Jefferson's candidacy was threatened by a reaction to their efforts. Ironically, therefore, in one sense their sustained and unique campaign against Washington was not aimed at him personally, for the exiles were seeking to destroy the icon that the man had become.

INTERNECINE STRIFE

The Making of Peter Porcupine

The overwhelming prominence that the exiled journalists gave to the British plot they saw simmering in the minds of Federalists was justified, in their eyes, by a parallel campaign that they were fighting in Philadelphia, ironically against an Englishman who had emigrated in 1792 as an acknowledged Painite. William Cobbett's significant intervention in the murky world of Philadelphia journalism in 1795 had the effect of reinforcing the radicals' conviction that the influence of the British government was insidiously poisoning American politics and subverting the republic.

Cobbett claimed in his autobiography published in 1796 and in subsequent writings that he had arrived in America in October 1792 a republican and a Painite.[92] As he had fled to France in March 1792 with the threat of arrest for his political activities hanging over his head, Cobbett undoubtedly fits the category of radical exile. Yet during his eight years in America he was to gain a formidable reputation as Peter Porcupine, the ultra-tory scourge of radicals, democrats, and Republicans. His first foray into American politics in 1794 was a literary assault on Joseph Priestley and those who had given him a very public welcome on his arrival in New York.[93] In the following year Cobbett published another four pamphlets, in which he articulated his hatred of revolutionary France, his contempt for American democrats and British exiles, and his strident English patriotism.[94] Thus at some point in the two years following his flight to France he had turned his political ideas upside down.[95]

Cobbett's own explanation for this somersault rested on his youth and political immaturity, and the growth of his patriotism when confronted in America with "the atrocious slander that was continually vomitted forth against Great Britain."[96] His biographers have tended to add the effects of his experiences in revolutionary France in 1792, his contacts as a teacher of English with obnoxious Frenchmen in Wilmington and Philadelphia, and his general disappointment with republican society in America.[97] All these factors undoubtedly played their part in his rejection of radical principles, but the origins of his disillusionment can be found in the manner in which he was treated by his fellow reformers during the few months he spent in England from November 1791. He had returned to Britain from a seven-year tour of duty with the Fifty-Fourth Regiment of Foot in Nova Scotia and New Brunswick with the rank of Regimental Sergeant Major and an angry determination to prosecute those officers whom he believed had been systematically pillaging the regiment's accounts.[98] While waiting for the court-martial that was established at his insistence, he came into contact with a group of reformers in London, who gave him advice and support and with whom he collaborated in the production of a pamphlet critical of the administration of the army and the treatment of the troops.[99] These reformers remain shadowy, but probably included members of the Society for Constitutional Information and several Foxites with connections to the Prince of Wales. They had their own reasons for attacking Pitt's administration and happily made use of Cobbett's inside knowledge of army corruption.[100]

Among those assisting Cobbett in preparing his case for the court-martial of his former officers was Captain George Lane, of the 54th, whom Cobbett had first met when he enlisted at Chatham in 1784, but who did not accompany the regiment overseas. Lane regularly visited Cobbett at his London lodgings in early 1792, probably partly in connection with the writing of *The Soldier's Friend,* and partly to keep him up to date with the regimental preparations for the court-martial. It was Lane who fuelled Cobbett's (unfounded) fears that the court-martial would be a whitewash, and that soldiers would give evidence questioning Cobbett's loyalty. What Cobbett did not discover until after he fled to France was that Lane himself had been accused of the same "corrupt" practices as the officers due to come before the court-martial. Lane, in an unsuccessful effort to curry favor with the authorities (he was forced to sell his commission), encouraged Cobbett to leave the country and subsequently condemned him to the authorities. When Cobbett discovered Lane's treachery, his opinion of the reformers in London must have been severely shaken. Thus when Priestley turned up in New York as a radical hero, and was so warmly greeted, Cobbett saw red. Soon after, Peter Porcupine was born.

Cobbett showed himself to be a prolific writer. While in America he published at least seventeen pamphlets, nine issues of a monthly magazine dedicated to congressional politics, and, between March 1797 and August 1799, a daily newspaper filled with his political comments and observations, which for a time was very influential. His selections from his American writings, published in 1801, filled twelve volumes. Almost all this output sought to achieve one objective: to convince Americans that their economic interests, their political happiness, and their future prosperity depended on their recognition that Britain, not revolutionary France, was their country's natural friend and ally.[101] From January 1795, when he defended the Jay Treaty in *A Bone to Gnaw for the Democrats*, until his final desperate attacks on John Adams in *Porcupine's Gazette*, for not declaring war on France, he openly defended British interests, which were, he claimed, also America's interests.[102]

Cobbett was never a Federalist, nor their propagandist; he remained an English ultra-tory patriot who happened to be fighting his battles against his country's enemies on the wrong side of the Atlantic. But inevitably, he became associated in the public mind with the more extreme, pro-British Federalists such as congressmen Fisher Ames and Robert Goodloe Harper (Cobbett often helped the latter with his speeches).[103] For the Republican penmen, of course, the temptation to tar the Federalists with the brush of Cobbett's toryism was too great to resist. But at the same time, Cobbett's relentless defense of Britain and his persistent attacks on everything French meant that to a significant extent the propaganda war in Philadelphia was as much a continuation of the ideological battles of Britain, from which the exiles had escaped, as a struggle over America's future. The radical exiles thus fought in the 1790s on two fronts: as Republicans against Federalists; and as British radicals against British toryism. America became part of an extended battlefield.

Literary Wars

This goes far to explain why in the 1790s American bookstores were filled with radical publications concerned with the ideological conflicts within Britain and between Britain and France. Radical exiles were to the fore in ordering books from overseas for sale in America, printing American editions of significant pamphlets, and republishing their own efforts.[104] Pro-French sympathizers in America obviously wanted to refute Federalist heresies as comprehensively as possible, and thus encouraged the reprinting of publications from Europe, but the radical exiles also needed to defend their position against Cobbett's condemnation of the British popular movement in particular, a "trick" that Cobbett was not slow to notice.[105] In their defense of British radicalism, Paine remained a bestselling antidote to Cobbett. Although the exiles had no monopoly on Paine's works, they reproduced his writings in a number of ways. Mathew Carey republished both parts of *Rights of Man* in 1796, and brother James printed a two-volume edition of Paine's works in 1797, which could be bought with or without *The Age of Reason* and with or without Bishop Richard Watson's reply to Paine's deist pamphlets.[106] Some of the exiles' own

British publications came out in American editions: Callender's *Political Progress of Britain,* Lee's *King Killing,* Eaton's *The Philanthropist* and *Politics for the People,* and Burk's *Trial of John Burk* are examples. They also supplemented their British writings with new volumes on their past activities. Callender wrote a second part of *The Political Progress,* and there were three accounts of the United Irishmen published by exiles (by Birch, Burk, and McNeven). In addition, exiled newspaper editors filled their columns with news from Britain and Ireland, putting the home radical movement in a favorable light.[107]

Engaging Cobbett in literary combat was an unenviable experience. He was as competent as any of the radical penmen at dropping bucketsful of slander, sarcasm, and satire on his enemies, but had the additional advantage of possessing real literary wit, which even at this distance in time, if the context is appreciated, sometimes retains its capacity to amuse. ("I have endeavoured to make America laugh instead of weep," Cobbett wrote of his essays).[108] His caricatures of his enemies were frequently sharp and unerringly directed at their weak points. The outlawed Callender he happily skewered as "*Newgate* CALLENDER." He consoled his female readers with the opinion that the effeminate bachelor Swanwick, known for his fondness for speaking at young ladies' academies, will "do you no violence" even when he presses his attentions on you. Paine, Cobbett claimed, wrote *Age of Reason* to save "his ugly uncombed head from the guillotine. . . . The Second Part of the Age of Reason he wrote for a living, and the First Part he wrote for his life."[109]

In the literary war fought out in Philadelphia between 1795 and 1799, when the combatants "lived antagonistically,"[110] the battles fought by the British radical and tory exiles with raillery and billingsgate were a dishonorable draw, but in terms of an effective demolition of one's opponent's case and arguments, Cobbett usually won, if not by a knock-out, certainly handsomely on points. Callender, Cobbett's second radical exile victim after Priestley, tried to counterattack, but was outbludgeoned.[111] Bache, whom Abigail Adams thought was afraid of Cobbett, refused to respond when hostile articles in *Porcupine's Gazette* appeared.[112] The enthusiastic James Carey was a more persistent opponent, bravely willing to meet Cobbett " 'hand to hand and foot to foot' on any ground."[113] Although always teetering on the edge of financial disaster, he had the capacity to meet Cobbett's "dunghill wit" on even terms. His satire, "The Death and Dissection of Peter Porcupine," rivaled the crude humor of Cobbett at his best. It was published twice in the *Daily Advertiser* and as a broadsheet, belying Cobbett's claim that the newspaper had come "into the world with death written on its front."[114]

Carey's claim to have "completely unhinged" Cobbett was premature.[115]

When the *Daily Advertiser* collapsed during the yellow fever epidemic in September 1797, Cobbett had survived the daily pinpricks that Carey had bestowed.[116] In much more threatening circumstances in January 1798, Carey tried again, establishing *Carey's United States Recorder*. Not only was Republicanism in full retreat as the demands for war with France grew apace, but Cobbett was busily stirring the nativist pot. He teased the Careys with his knowledge of their brother's political disgrace in Dublin in 1794.[117] James responded by publishing an anonymous report claiming that Cobbett, when living in Wilmington, had beaten a young black girl as well as his own wife.[118] He also accused Cobbett of seeking a civil war in America and "the total *annihilation* of the democratic-republicans."[119] Cobbett's reply was yet more abuse, and the repeated claim that Mathew Carey was the secret financial backer of, and real influence behind, the "O'Careys'" newspaper. His attacks forced the reluctant Mathew Carey into public debate, which lasted into 1799, months after James Carey's second attempt at producing a newspaper in Philadelphia had collapsed.[120]

Mathew Carey was a more formidable opponent than his brother. When he published "A Plum Pudding for Peter Porcupine," Cobbett sent him some venison and jelly between two plates. Carey sent it back, in the hands of "a stout Irish porter," with orders to drop the plates in the middle of Cobbett's shop.[121] He followed up with a long Hudibrastic poem, "The Porcupiniad," which powerfully satirized Cobbett's abusive style of writing. The fact remains, however, that Cobbett remained impervious to the literary assaults of his radical exile opponents. What brought him down in 1799 was the determination of two Republican heavyweights, Dr. Benjamin Rush and the newly elected state governor Thomas McKean, to convict him of criminal libel. Rush was the plaintiff, indignantly protecting his professional reputation, McKean the recently retired chief justice, who kept his old position vacant until Justice Edward Shippen, the favorite for elevation, had successfully presided over Cobbett's demise.[122] A huge fine of $5,000 compelled Porcupine to return to England.

PENMEN IN RETEAT

The ruining of Cobbett was but one consequence of the great turn around in Pennsylvania politics, for by the time his case came to trial, in December 1799, the Republicans had control of the state executive and the lower house of the legislature. But the personal cost of victory had been high for those—Hamilton called them "the Jacobin Scandal-Club"—who had carried the Republican banner in Philadelphia from middecade.[123] The uneasy rapprochement that Jefferson had called for in the early weeks of 1797 did not survive President Adams's first public statement on foreign affairs in May, in which he fruitlessly called for defensive preparations against the threats from the French Directory, who were angered by the Jay Treaty.[124] The swift end to the honeymoon was a relief to both sides. Adams had predicted it a month earlier; his wife reported that the Republican press's praise "for a few weeks mortified him, much more, than all their impudent abuse does."[125] The *Aurora*'s big guns began firing the day after Adams's speech.

A few days earlier the first of the Philadelphia Republican propagandists had fallen victim to Federalist intrigue. John Beckley was dismissed from his office as clerk of the House of Representatives on a vote that followed party lines. "A man's private opinions, it appears, are to be the test of his fitness for office," Bache rather disingenuously declared.[126] Unprepared for this calamity, Beckley was forced to advertise his hastily established law practice in the newspapers.[127] Understandably, the desire for revenge filled his mind.

The means were close at hand. The victim was to be Alexander Hamilton, the would-be president. In April 1797 Callender wrote that Hamilton "still flatters himself, that he will one day become President, and if he can render those who have the public opinion in their favour, obnoxious, part of his plan will be effected."[128] But if Hamilton did have that ambition, he also knew that a sword of Damocles was hanging over his head. In December 1792 he had extricated himself from a possible charge of official corruption by confessing to three congressmen, including James Monroe, that he had been blackmailed by the speculator husband of Maria Reynolds, with whom he had had an affair in New York. The congressmen accepted his explanation and the matter remained confidential, although news of it soon reached Jefferson at Monticello. Copies of the documents and letters in the case, however, remained in the hands of John Beckley, a potential timebomb waiting to be primed.[129]

Tactically, the Republican cause would have been best served by keeping the matter secret until the most propitious moment—either when Hamilton moved on the presidency or when he took up another official position (as second in command of the army in 1798, for instance)—but Beckley's need for revenge, and a more general Republican desire to counter Federalist attacks on James Monroe for his performance as ambassador to France, persuaded the Philadelphia radical clique to set their bomb off in June 1797.[130] As with the verbal assault on Washington, a radical exile was used as the frontman. Again, Callender was prepared to take the odium and brickbats for destroying the reputation of one of the Federalists' main leaders. With much journalistic acumen, he initially gave the information to the public in small installments in pamphlet form, before, in late July, he published the whole sorry story in *The History of the United States for 1796.*

Hamilton's public humiliation represented the zenith of the Philadelphia Jacobin Scandal-Club's political efforts. Thereafter their fortunes began to plummet. Their association with the cause of an increasingly unpopular France became a deadweight that they found almost impossible to shake off. The refusal of the French Directory to receive the new ambassador, Charles Cotesworth Pinckney, and their policy of seizing neutral American ships carrying British goods or touching British ports, greatly diminished Americans' sympathy for their sister republic. If the United States were forced into choosing sides in the war, the national interest and economic exigencies would impel the country into the arms of Britain. Adams's policy of sending a negotiating team to France—following the precedent set down in 1794 during the crisis with Britain—was a difficult one to criticize effectively, with the result that Republican propaganda became increasingly shrill and querulous.[131] Adams himself remained a prime target; otherwise, the Republicans could do little more than weakly defend the French by blaming Britain for first ignoring America's neutral rights. Raising the standard of patriotism, the Federalist press found their opponents an easy target.[132]

At the same time, the Federalists began to seek vengeance for their leader's discomfiture. Within a year of the publication of the *History of 1796,* the Republican group in Philadelphia had been broken up, even before the Alien and Sedition Acts had come into force. The first to feel the Federalists' wrath was Tench Coxe, who, like Beckley, was particularly vulnerable because he held a government position. Insidious attempts to discharge him, which had begun soon after Adams's accession to the presidency, culminated in his dismissal for improper conduct in December 1797.[133]

As a speculator with financial difficulties, Coxe faced a bleak future, for 1797 was a year of major economic stagnation and many bankruptcies, the result, the Republicans predictably charged, of the impact of the Jay Treaty.[134] Businessmen's need for loans to tide them over the slump put (usually Federalist) bank directors in a position to aggravate their political opponents' financial woes.[135] Mathew Carey's publishing business wobbled uncertainly several times in 1797–98. He had underwritten the costs incurred when James Carey bought out his newspaper partner in July 1797 and only narrowly escaped bankruptcy when James failed to meet his commitments. In September, one of his notes was protested. Early in 1798 financial disaster again loomed when for a whole month the Bank of the United States refused to discount his bills.[136]

Carey survived the crisis; John Swanwick did not. Prevented by the war from realizing his assets in Europe; facing usurious rates of interest from the local banks; and failing to recoup the debts owed to him by "the splendid bankrupts" (and Federalists) Robert Morris and John Nicholson, in September 1797 his mercantile firm collapsed. Forsaken by most of his erstwhile colleagues, pilloried by Cobbett, he died of yellow fever the following July, "a victim," claimed James Carey, "of political persecution . . . [and] a martyr in the cause of liberty."[137]

The Republican editors and their writers also found themselves in serious difficulties. Since March Duane had been conducting, with the assistance of Lloyd, the Bradford family's *Merchant Daily Advertiser,* which was not in the arch-Republican stable.[138] In July, not having been regularly paid, he resigned, but a dispute over salary arrears led to a public scuffle, which resulted in Duane being bound over to keep the peace.[139] Fortunately for Duane, the tragic death of Andrew Brown of the *Philadelphia Gazette* in a fire at his premises offered him an opportunity of acting as Andrew Brown, Jr.'s, assistant, but this position too lasted only a few months. In the spring of 1798 he was forced back into journeyman printing.[140] By this time both Richard Lee and Thomas Lloyd, who had remained with the Bradfords when Duane resigned, were in jail for debt, the former in New York, the latter in Philadelphia.[141] Callender too was in abject poverty, compelled to seek poor relief and handouts from sympathetic Republican colleagues.[142] In mid-1798 Cobbett claimed to have seen Daniel Isaac Eaton living "in a log-hut over Schuylkill, where he cohabited with an Indian squaw. The proprietor of the hut, finding what gentry he had for tenants, turned them out bag and baggage. I happened to be going out on a shooting party, when the miscreant and his yellow hided frow were coming into Camp-town, traipsing thro' the dirt."[143]

Even Bache and the *Aurora* were in deep trouble by the spring of 1798. Unlike Cobbett, who financed his newspaper from the profits of his other printing ventures, Bache fell deeply into debt. His total losses from the *Aurora* between 1790 and 1798 came to $14,700.[144] Cobbett happily revealed in November 1797 that Bache had been unable to pay a five-dollar fine in the mayor's court, and in the following April claimed he could not pay his paper maker.[145] Such was Bache's distressed situation by June that his wife's brother suggested that Bache legally transfer property into her name and that she and the children should come to live in St. Croix.[146]

Bache's bankruptcy loomed even though the Republican leaders made valiant attempts to keep him solvent. Jefferson warned Madison in April 1798 that the Federalists were aiming to destroy "the Whig press." Referring particularly to Bache's and Carey's newspapers, he wrote: "We should really exert ourselves to preserve them, for if these papers fail, republicanism will be entirely brow-beaten."[147] With much difficulty funds were raised to pay Callender to act as Bache's assistant, and efforts were made to increase subscriptions, enabling an amused John Fenno to accuse Jefferson of traveling to Virginia to solicit for customers for the *Aurora*.[148]

NATIVIST ONSLAUGHT

The financial crisis and the unpopularity of the French cause were not the only reasons for the distressed and disillusioned state of the Republican penmen by the spring of 1798. Added to their woes was a vicious and public campaign of nativist bile that was promoted, ironically, by Cobbett. Antiforeigner sentiment was not new, being expressed in the alien debates in Congress as early as 1794, and was soon augmented by claims that French-supported spies and emissaries, of whom Bache was preeminent, were working with "the disaffected and disappointed" to undermine the federal government.[149] But from the time of Adams's inaugural, a more sustained campaign of nativism began, which was to taper off only in the aftermath of Jefferson's presidential victory. The credit for occasioning this unappetizing period of American hostility toward newcomers can be given primarily to the radical exiles, for it was not only the greater influx of immigrants that agitated the more xenophobic conservatives, but also the fact that they so swiftly became both politically conscious and politically active, a tribute to the organizing abilities of the exiles.[150] As early as April 1797 Pennsylvania Governor Thomas Mifflin's veto of a bill that would have tightened up voting procedures in state elections caused one correspondent to Fenno's newspaper to ask: "Why should aliens be permitted to interfere in our politics? No doubt this is agreeable to certain friends of disorder and confusion, because the greatest number of those aliens who are so eager to have a hand in our affairs come here discontented with the government they have left, and with an abhorrence of all settled governments: these men's votes will suit a certain party; for that reason are they courted, and *societies* instituted, *patronized* by those who will never get along by mere American aid."[151]

Among the "Gallo American Harpies," "imported felons," and "covenanted foes of Britain" who had the gall to involve themselves in American politics, the Irish became major targets for the nativists.[152] Attacks on their loyalty were a primary means whereby the loud demands for alien and sedition laws were justified. Cobbett began his witch-hunt in a relatively mild mood: "We want no more of your ESCAPING folks," he wrote in response to a letter regarding Irish immigration in the *Daily Advertiser;* "We have too many of them already. We keep no gallows here; and consequently are at a total loss how to dispose of them."[153] But when the disclosure of the XYZ dispatches created a huge wave of francophobia and war hysteria in the spring of 1798, his attitude hardened. In May Cobbett reported the existence of a United Irish conspiracy that aimed to assist the French by subverting the American government. He began his exposé by recounting the efforts of the French to organize an effective force in the United States to promote their interests. The Democratic societies had failed, because the native-born, although initially credulous, were ultimately loyal to their country's interests. Thwarted, the French had turned to the recent immigrants from Ireland and Britain, who had arrived expecting to wallow in anarchy and plunder. Finding the government too strongly entrenched, the immigrants formed a league with indigenous French interests and established another secret society, the United Irishmen.[154]

Cobbett's evidence comprised printed material sent anonymously to him on two occasions in January and February. It included the constitution of a society of United Irishmen, dated August 1797, which had most of the provisions and secrecy requirements of the United Irish societies of 1793–98 in Ireland, including a test (a commitment to seek "Liberty and Equality for *all* mankind"), a secret oath, an hierarchical committee system, and the splitting of groups when members reached a certain number. Membership was open to all—not, apparently, just Irishmen—"who have suffered in the cause of freedom" and were zealous for the Rights of Man.

Cobbett's interest had been raised by the name of the man who had signed most of the documents: Dr. James Reynolds, one of Bache's penmen. Confirming Mathew Carey's opinion that he was a prize blunderer,[155] Reynolds had recently been in the public eye, and was currently under threat of legal action, for falsely accusing Secretary of State Timothy Pickering of extorting illegal fees from people seeking passports to travel overseas.[156] Cobbett's revelations of Reynolds's covert activities had an immediate impact; the local hospital authorities dismissed the Irishman from his honorary position as physician to the dispensary, and confirmed their decision even though five other doctors resigned in sympathy. Cobbett remained unrepentant: "A man's politics at this time are *everything*," he wrote. "I would sooner have my wounds dressed by a dog than by a democrat."[157]

Cobbett claimed that United Irish societies existed in New York and Baltimore, that one was about to be formed in Chambersburg, Pennsylvania, and that there were 1,500 members in Philadelphia and its surrounding region. Their objective was to assist in an insurrection when the French invaded. They would coordinate their activities with the 30,000 Frenchmen currently living in America, and with Republican planters in the South, who would free their slaves to help spread the rebellion. Already, he hinted darkly, membership of the United Irishmen included "free negroes."[158]

Most of this was black propaganda, aimed at frightening Americans into accepting draconian laws hostile to aliens and seditious Republicans, but the United Irish society did exist, and it is worth considering its purpose and importance. Unfortunately, no society records are extant, but it appears to have been formed around June 1797, when Mathew Carey attended a meeting and declined to become a member.[159] The fall yellow fever epidemic disrupted its organization, but it was active again by December, and was still publicly advertising its meetings two years later, when Daniel Clark, a shoemaker, was its secretary.[160] It is impossible to say how large its membership was, but it was in the interests of Cobbett, the Fennos, and subsequent Irish nationalist historians to exaggerate their numbers for political reasons.[161] John Ward Fenno claimed there were 40,000 involved, but this was a gross exaggeration, and probably represented his view of all those in America who opposed the government.[162] Having asked his readers for names of members, he was given a paltry seventeen. One was John Daly Burk, who before fleeing to Virginia had resided in New York; another was Matthew "Spitting" Lyon, the Irish-born congressman from Vermont, who was soon to fall foul of the sedition law. Of the others, ten were radical exiles: Callender, Lloyd, Duane, the Careys, Reynolds, and the four Covenanting licentiates Wylie, Black, McAdam, and Reilly.[163] Five of the seventeen publicly denied membership almost immediately: the Careys, Wylie, Black, and Samuel Parks, a tavernkeeper.[164]

Given the paucity of evidence, the conclusion must be that the Society of United Irishmen in America was made up of a few tiny groups in Philadelphia, New York (while Burk was there), and perhaps Baltimore. Most likely, they were nothing like the Dublin society in its open phase, nor were they the beginnings of a Defender-like national organization. Rather, they probably mimicked the small clubs in Dublin in 1794–95 such as the Strugglers and the Telegraph, in which both Reynolds and Burk had been heavily involved.[165] They were not secretly planning revolution in America, on behalf of the French or anyone else; but they would have been a society, incorporating lower and middling-class Irish immigrants, working legitimately on behalf of the Republicans.[166] They would also have been doing what little they could for the cause of freedom in their homeland. It is possible that they had some involvement in raising money, which a spy on the executive of the United Irish reported being received from America in August 1797.[167]

THE TIDE TURNS

To be denounced in 1798–99 as a United Irishman in America was to be exposed to the possibility of becoming a victim of the Alien and Sedition Acts. These laws were passed in June and July 1798 and were part of a package of measures that the extreme Federalists drove through Congress in response to the quasiwar with France. With these, the Federalists sought to muzzle, if not destroy, all domestic opposition to the government. One of the acts related only to enemy aliens in time of war, but the radical exiles were vulnerable to the deporting provisions of the Alien Friends Act (if they were not naturalized), and to the imprisonment provisions of the Sedition Act if they falsely, scandalously, and maliciously criticized either the government, its officers, or the constitution, with the intention of bringing them into contempt or disrepute.[168] The Sedition Act is perhaps the best memorial to the radical exiles, for it was primarily their constant goading from 1795 that persuaded the Federalists to pass what turned out to be an act of folly. As both Cobbett and Fenno Jr. repeatedly emphasized, 90 percent of those "who have constantly employed the press in annoying the government, and in encouraging and justifying the hostility of France" were "malcontents from Great Britain and Ireland."[169] Ironically, however, the legislation's main target, the radical clique around the *Aurora,* had broken up before the acts came into force. On the day before Adams signed the sedition bill into law, with the positions of most of the other radicals increasingly untenable, the newly bereaved Callender fled Philadelphia for Republican-dominated Virginia.[170] When a few months later Bache died of yellow fever, it appeared that the propaganda arm of the Republicans had been totally destroyed.

Republican Revival

But in their moment of triumph the Federalist ultras overstretched. By so artlessly seeking to silence dissent, by embarking on a huge military buildup, and by raising direct taxes to pay for the army and navy, they opened avenues for

criticism that enabled the Republican party, with the radical exiles again acting as *tirailleurs*, to claw back popular support.[171] The crisis brought both
Priestley and Cooper back into public life. Alexander Wilson, after several
years avoiding politics, reemerged in 1799, riding around the countryside
making Jeffersonian speeches, and writing political poems, including "The
Aristocrats' War Whoop," in which the Federalists were caricatured as enemies of their country, determined to surrender America to Britain.[172] Duane
took over Bache's *Aurora* and, in 1800, his widow. Callender, after a period of
recuperation, was by 1800 "firing through five port holes, at once," writing for
the Richmond, Virginia, publications the *Examiner*, the *Friend of the People*,
and the *National Magazine*, as well as James Lyon's Petersburg *Republican* and
Staunton *Scourge of the Aristocracy*.[173] In 1799 Senator Nathaniel Macon persuaded Joseph Gales to establish a Republican newspaper in Raleigh, North
Carolina. The *Raleigh Register*, a clone of the *Sheffield Register*, was an immediate success and quickly broke the Federalist monopoly of news and opinion
in the state.[174] In New York, where yellow fever and the sedition act had left
the Republican media in disarray, the recently arrived James Cheetham began
editing the *Republican Watchtower*. The great disruption of 1798, therefore,
was only temporary. The renewed impact of the radical exiles was such that
one plaintive Federalist claimed that "three foreign emissaries, . . . under the
Chief Juggler" (Jefferson) had between them divided the country into "three
Grand Departments" for the purpose of disseminating Jacobin principles.
Callender ran the southern department, Duane the eastern, and Cooper the
western.[175]

The years 1799–1801 were *anni mirabiles* for the radical journalists, when
their effectiveness reached new heights. This was partly because they had such
inviting targets to attack. Not only was there the ultra-Federalist war program
to aim at, but once Adams decided in February 1799 to send another delegation to France in a final (and this time successful) attempt to avoid full-scale
war, the Federalist party split asunder, allowing the Republican propagandists
great opportunities to pick at the wound.[176] Defending a policy was never the
radicals' strength. They were at their best, even after Jefferson's presidential
victory, as an *opposition* press, criticizing those with power rather than erect-
ing defensive ramparts.

They also began to show greater maturity, more frequently being prepared to argue their case rather than simply abusing their opponents. Partly
this may have been the consequence of the decline of Peter Porcupine, but
also of help were new men stepping into the breach. Cooper, for instance, in
his letters to the electors of Northumberland during the state gubernatorial

campaign of 1799, showed a restraint and wisdom that helped to convince readers that the Republicans were not rabble-rousing anarchists, as their opponents had been asserting for so long:

> It is well known that the Republican party are attached to a representative Constitution; to a Constitution of equal rights; free from all hereditary honours and executive privileges; where the officers of Government are responsible for their conduct, and liable to be recalled at stated periods into the mass of the people, by whom, and for whose benefit, they were chosen. This party is averse to war, to unnecessary and exorbitant taxes, to Standing Armies and permanent Navies. They are careful of people's lives, and frugal of the people's money. They are friendly to the right of investigating with perfect freedom, public characters, and public measures; and they wish that every nation upon earth may enjoy a constitution founded upon the same basis with our own.[177]

This neatly encapsulates what the Republicans, including the exiles, had been saying for years, but now its tone was more reasonable and less frenetic.

Duane too seems to have made a commendable effort to keep himself in check. When he became involved in the so-called "St. Mary's riot" in February 1799, he not only failed to mention it in the *Aurora*—possibly because of the embarrassment it might cause—but he did not report the favorable trial outcome either. Duane, Dr. James Reynolds, and two others, a clerk and a journeyman printer, had gone to St. Mary's Catholic church on Fourth Street during Sunday mass to seek signatures to an anti–Alien and Sedition Act petition. While Reynolds was putting his case from atop a tombstone, he was attacked by members of the congregation, and pulled a gun to make his escape. The four were arrested and taken before the mayor, who charged them with making an affray, and Reynolds with attempted murder. While bail was being taken, Chief Justice McKean stormed in, accused the Federalist mayor of playing politics, and loudly proclaimed that the prisoners ought to be freed without charge. Potentially, this was a disaster for the Republicans, as McKean was their candidate for governor, and Cobbett did not fail to fill several of his columns with his attacks on "the Democratic Judge." When the trial was heard on February 21, Reynolds was defended by Dallas, and McKean was absent from the bench. All those charged were found not guilty, but rather than take up the challenge offered by Cobbett and Fenno, Duane and the other Republican editors kept silent, and the issue died away.[178] A new sense of party responsibility was being shown by the press.

This is not to say that the old personal attacks and overcharged abuse disappeared, especially to the south where Callender used his regular columns in

the Richmond *Examiner* to vent his spleen. He continued his campaign against
the Adams government, concentrating on its supposed maladministration and
malfeasance.[179] Callender was particularly dangerous because of the plausibil-
ity and the slipperiness of his criticisms. He had the unerring ability to focus
on particular issues and to twist them into shapes that conformed to his predetermined conclusions. Even seemingly minor issues, such as the number of
outfits funded when John Quincy Adams rapidly moved from one European
ambassadorial post to another or Abigail Adams's refurbishment of the president's residence, were used to pile up evidence of Adams's alleged misappro-
priation of funds. This tactic was very effective, because the Federalists had
no simple counter to use. They were caught between denying every claim
Callender made, with no certainty of being believed, or ignoring them altogether, thereby leaving the field to him. Either way, the Federalist press was
permanently on the defensive, as Callender gleefully harassed them from all
sides. As a purely destructive force, but with an assured instinct for knowing
what his democratic constituency wanted to read, no one could compete with
Callender in America in 1800.[180]

"Sticks and Stones Will Hurt My Bones . . ."

The Federalist response to this revivified and increasingly confident Republican press was the bludgeon and the sedition act. The threat of violence had
been an occupational hazard for writers and printers on both sides of the political fence since 1797. In April Bache had been assaulted in the Philadelphia
shipyard by the son of the designer of the navy frigate then being built, who
objected to accusations of bribery published in the *Aurora*. At the same time,
Cobbett was threatened by a group of Republicans who resented his comments on Governor Mifflin.[181] Soon after the exposé of Hamilton, an "assassin" twice entered Callender's house, alarming his family. He was also threatened just before fleeing Philadelphia a year later.[182] In the crisis months of
spring 1798 bands of youths, some wearing the black cockades of Federalism,
and others the Republican tricolor, roamed the streets of Philadelphia, harass-
ing passers-by and "serenading" outside the establishments of Cobbett,
Bache, and James Carey.[183] Later in the year Bache and Fenno Jr. fought in the
street, and the latter was bludgeoned by two assailants outside his house
(Fenno headlined the news, "United Irishmen").[184]

   As this last case suggests, being a Federalist editor was as dangerous as
being a known Republican, especially when the Irish were involved, for they
were not prepared to tolerate intimidatory tactics. In January 1799 JOHN
RICHARD MCMAHON, a United Irish refugee, was fined $20 for assault and

bound over for twelve months for challenging Andrew Brown, editor of the *Philadelphia Gazette,* to a duel, after he had written offensively about the United Irishmen. That same month, Dr. James Reynolds called out Fenno. When the challenge was refused, he pasted up a notice in a coffeehouse calling the editor a liar, a scoundrel, and a coward.[185] Reynolds certainly appears to have been at the center of much of the violence and counter-intimidation that existed at this time. He was the one with the gun in St. Mary's churchyard, and in 1800 he led a group of United Irishmen who attacked the new editor of the *Gazette of the United States* after he had abused Thomas Cooper in his columns.[186]

With the increasingly confident Republican printers refusing to be cowed into silence, threats and violence became counterproductive. Gales took a rival editor to court in Raleigh after an assault and won £100 in damages; James Lyon ignored threats to his printshop in Staunton; and even the normally timid Callender threw defiance at the Federalist Richmond Associators, who attempted to railroad him out of town.[187] It was, however, Duane's sufferings in defense of his political beliefs that most discredited the activities of the frustrated ultra-Federalists. The vicious beating he received from some officers of a mainly Federalist volunteer militia company after he had refused to name his source for a critical account in the *Aurora* of their activities in Northampton during the Fries rebellion not only inspirited the Republican party, but also shifted public opinion in Philadelphia decisively away from Federalism.[188]

Duane achieved a sort of martyrdom for his bravery, and the lifelong friendship of Thomas Leiper, whose name he protected, but he was by no means the only radical exile to achieve this status in the period leading up to the presidential election of 1800, for the Federalists' use of the law to silence their political opponents gave others an opportunity to demonstrate their commitment to Jefferson and Republicanism. The exercise by the Federalists of the common law of seditious libel, the sedition act, and their prerogative powers in the federal Senate to imprison Duane, Cooper, Callender, and other opposition journalists is well known and has been thoroughly discussed elsewhere.[189] What needs to be emphasized here is that the exiled journalists deliberately encouraged their political foes to indict them, knowing that their trials would make the courtrooms ideal theaters for their dramatic performances as victims of Federalist despotism.[190] The public martyrdom of the editors combined neatly with the constitutional arguments concurrently being argued in the Virginia and Kentucky Resolutions to convince public opinion of the extremism of their opponents, who, unable to win the intellectual argument, were forced into jailing their antagonists.[191] As John Daly Burk, one of the first radical exiles to be threatened with arrest for seditious libel, wrote of the Alien and Sedition Acts: "The Aristocrats could not for their soul fight the battles of liberty better."[192]

". . . But Words Will Never Hurt Me"

Two years after Jefferson's first presidential victory Denis Driscol wrote that the campaign of 1800 "was a contest between democracy and aristocracy— THE SOVEREIGN PEOPLE were to be *unkinged,* and the few upstart (self-stiled, *well-born*) intended to seize on the reins of government and rule the NATION with the high hand of usurpation and insolence."[193] If John Adams, Fisher Ames, and many other disappointed Federalists can be believed, Jefferson's success was primarily the consequence of the émigré journalists' concerted campaigns against the government. In 1801 a devastated Adams complained, "Is there no pride in American bosoms? Can their hearts endure that Callender, Duane, Cooper, and Lyon should be the most influential men in the country, all foreigners and degraded characters?" Ames was equally distraught: "The newspapers are an overmatch for any Government. They will first overawe and then usurp it. This has been done; and the Jacobins owe their triumph to the unceasing use of this engine."[194] William Coleman, Hamilton's protégé on the *New York Evening Post,* concurred with this analysis. Jefferson had lost in 1796 because "*Modern* patriotism had not yet numbered its proselytes; a little accession of strength was still wanting, and powerful auxiliaries were found in those restless and discontented spirits, who, spurning the restraints of Government in the old world, had traversed the ocean in search of freedom in the new; of that freedom that would give full indulgence to their profligate and licentious dispositions."[195] With the exiles working for the Republicans in numbers, democracy's victory over aristocracy in 1800 was assured.

Many modern historians do not agree with this bald assessment. Mindful of the contemporary conceit that governments tend to lose elections rather than oppositions win them, some accentuate the divisions within Federalism and the antediluvian character of Federalist philosophy to explain Adams's defeat.[196] Others focus on the superior organization of the Republicans, with Beckley playing a key role.[197] Only Joyce Appleby has taken the views of the defeated Federalists seriously enough.[198] She has recognized that the Republican victory came with words, "those *printed* words that had for so long been owned and exchanged by the world's élites." With words "ordinary men, political parvenus, outsiders, interlopers, [and] mere voters without office" engaged in political debate. "With words they formed a democratic network, with words they created loyalties among strangers, with words—often anonymous words—they defied their social superiors, with words they repelled intimidation."[199] Callender, for one, understood this very well, as early as 1795. For all his visceral hatreds and rabid insults, he was a very astute political animal. Free speech, he wrote, "is the right of discussing and expressing an opinion on public men or measures—of influencing by arguments—by words, as many of our fellow-citizens, whether rulers or ruled, over to our opinions. This is the right of every citizen in his individual or in an aggregate capacity."[200] It was a right that he and his fellow émigrés pushed to the limit.

However organized the Republican party had become by 1800, and however clearly Jefferson and the other leaders enunciated the doctrine of "the Spirit of '76" in philosophical treatises such as the Virginia and Kentucky Resolutions, these ideas had to be diffused to the people. America, it is true, was still in many ways an oral culture, but with politics, the written word stimulated political discourse and disseminated it over a wide enough area for public opinion to be both created and molded. No medium performed this role so well as the newspaper, and in the late 1790s the most influential and widely copied newspaper writers and editors in America were the radical exiles.

In their writings they produced just what was needed in a democratic society, a vulgarized politics. Modern-day teachers who are advised to remember the limited attention span of their students will acknowledge Callender's dismissive scorn for the New York *Argus,* which during the debates on the Jay Treaty filled six columns a day with the arguments of Hamilton, writing as "Camillus." Jefferson and Madison might have worried that he was not being answered satisfactorily, but Callender, Burk, Duane, and Cobbett knew that only the most educated, politically aware, and committed reader would be open to complex and weighty arguments of this sort. If one wanted to influence the ordinary person, now part of the new "political nation," different tactics were needed. With the *Argus,* "instead of miscellaneous articles of intelligence, instead of that variety, vivacity, and brevity, that *curiosa felicitas* of selection that constitutes the very essence and soul of a newspaper, the eye is condemned to wander in dejection from adverts to Camillus, and from Camillus to adverts."[201] A democratic constituency would only be roused by excitement, anger, blood, and commitment. That is what the radical exiles brought to the Republican party in the 1790s with their writings, and that is why the war within a war—the struggle with Cobbett—was so important. If the Republican leadership wanted to reform the ordered, élitist, and aristocratic ancien régime of the Federalists, the radical émigrés sought to demolish it, with the people wielding the sledgehammers.

SEVEN

Reforming the Republic

REPUBLICAN FACTIONALISM

Jefferson's inauguration on 4 March 1801 was one of the most satisfying moments in the lives of the radical exiles. To savor Jefferson's victory, proclaimed John Daly Burk in a 4 March oration, was "to taste the sweetness and fragrance of *Elysium*."[1] In Philadelphia, Republicans celebrated in customary style by dining in public, rounding off the evening with convivial bumpers, speeches, and myriad toasts. But at this pinnacle of victory there were already incipient signs of disunity and disharmony. According to one grumpy onlooker, the Republicans met at two separate venues not because of the large numbers wishing to celebrate, but because already they were dividing into two factions, the respectable "Democrats" and the unrespectable, alien "Jacobins," who "breathed naught but the foul breath of *sedition* and *insurrection*." The latter dined at a tavern in Chestnut Street, where Thomas Cooper presided, and James Reynolds was vice president for the evening. One of the toasts was "A speedy revision to *our* constitution, and a reform to the senatorial branch of *our* legislature." There was much talk of the need for a general dismissal of all federal office holders.[2] So much, therefore, for Jefferson's speech earlier that morning, in which he stated that "We are all republicans: we are all federalists."[3]

The Federalist observer was engaging in wishful thinking in March 1801, but he was nevertheless correct in surmising that the potential for division existed within the Republican party, especially in the middle Atlantic states. Jefferson had been borne to power on the back of a powerful coalition, that united around a hostility to Federalism but that had less cohesion when promoting a positive program of policies, both at state and national levels. All Republicans supported Jefferson, of course, but which Jefferson? The "radical" Jefferson of the Kentucky Resolutions, of the "spirit of '76," and of the "Revolution of 1800" was the inspiration of most of the exiles, with his Declaration of Independence their guiding light.[4] But more moderate, senior Republicans—for example, Madison and Albert Gallatin, who formed "a virtual triumvirate" with Jefferson, and Thomas McKean—saw much of the Republican theory of 1798 to 1800 as mere rhetoric, necessary to win an election but not to be taken as the fundamental basis for action by the new Republican administration in Washington.[5] "In power Republican leaders sought to dampen partisanship, end polemics, and make the practitioners of these arts political pariahs."[6] In Pennsylvania, the Dallas-McKean faction, which dominated the state executive from 1799, "were not democrats in the usual sense," nor were the dominant Republican factions in New York, the Clintonians and the Livingstons, both groups adhering to the traditional idea of prominent families controlling government. Although the Pennsylvania Republicans had used the radicals—Duane, Leib, and the *Aurora* penmen—in their march to victory, they were "at heart conservatives who had a real aversion to popular politics, and believed that the talented, wealthy, and virtuous should govern."[7] They naturally championed Jefferson's inauguration speech, which reflected a strategy of conciliation aimed at wooing moderate Federalists away from their high-flying leaders.[8] The radicals, however, although accepting the broad outlines of Jefferson's policies, also sought revenge, reform, and a place at the table.[9]

At the moment of victory, therefore, the vision of participatory democracy that had sustained the activist émigrés during the 1790s was threatened by powerful, "aristocratic" elements within the Republican party. Republican divisions after 1800, which Jefferson somberly perceived to be inevitable once Federalism had been beaten into the ground,[10] were to a considerable extent created by factionalism based on personalities and the scramble for offices, but it would be a mistake to ignore the role also played by ideological differences. Since the mid-1790s there had existed a moderate-radical fissure within Republicanism, but it had remained, for the most part, concealed by the imperative of destroying Federalism. With the successful election of 1800 having overthrown the ancien régime, it was perhaps to be expected that factional differences would arise, as each group sought to influence the outcome of their collective endeavors.[11] The more the Federalist party shrank after 1800, the more the Republican party became riven, at times dividing into various forms of third-party "Quiddism," as Tench Coxe first termed the process.[12]

Divisions Among the Exiles

As also might be expected, given the variety of political positions that the exiles as a whole had embraced on both sides of the Atlantic, they too were not immune from the effects of factionalism themselves, and frequently did much to encourage it. For many, Jefferson's victory represented the successful culmination of their long political struggle on both sides of the Atlantic. They had every confidence not only in the new president, but also in his lieutenants, and were convinced that Federalism had been struck a mortal blow. Early in 1804 the dying Priestley asked Pennsylvania Republican leader George Logan to "Tell Mr. Jefferson that I think myself happy to have lived under his excellent administration. . . . It is, I am confident, the best on the face of the earth, and yet I hope to rise to something more excellent still."[13] The exiles contented with Jefferson's rule by no means anticipated "the end of history," but they did expect a reduction in political ardor, their acceptance as republican citizens, and the opportunity to pursue their private interests and develop their talents in a free, open, orderly, and genuinely republican society. Moderates such as Mathew Carey, Joseph Gales, and Archibald Binny—all in the process of becoming very successful in their chosen fields—thus plumped for social and political stability and, putting their trust in Jefferson, resiled from a radical Painite philosophy that in the Federalist years had been the political ground defended most strongly by the exiles. They certainly backed away from the prospect of continual popular involvement in all aspects of political affairs, favoring the more limited doctrine of representative government, leaving power in the capable hands of an elected "natural aristocracy."[14] When factionalism raised its head within the Republican party, they stayed true to Jefferson and his anointed successor, Madison, and in state politics clung to a moderate, middle-of-the-road republicanism.[15]

In contrast other exiles, belligerently truer to democratic republicanism, saw the battles of the 1790s as uncompleted. During the years of Jefferson's presidency the militant exiles continued to promote the democratic doctrines that they associated with the "Spirit of '76." In policy terms these included strict construction of the federal constitution, an emphasis on states' rights, a free press, limited government, a foreign policy seeking peace with all countries, and no standing army or deepwater navy.[16] In effect, they accepted the program set out by Jefferson in his inaugural speech of 1801, but went further, rejecting the possibility of a *rapprochement* with their Federalist enemies (seeing this policy as part of a plot foisted on Jefferson by his untrustworthy advisors), and seeking further constitutional reform. They aimed at a system that allowed, indeed encouraged the perpetual involvement of the people in political action. The Declaration of Independence continued to best represent their core values. It contained "the essence of representative government"; its bedrock was the sovereignty of a continually active people. The Declaration encapsulated "the immutable principles which exist in the nature of human society," based on "*virtue*, . . . liberty, truth, candor, sincerity, integrity, honor, and probity," all values essential to the success of democratic government.[17] It was the task of the radicals, particularly through their newspapers, to ensure that even Republican politicians and statesmen conformed to the principles and values of participatory democracy.

Among the militants the deepseated suspicion of power, and its ability to unhinge even the most virtuous, which was a continuing legacy of Commonwealth and Anti-Federalist ideology, retained its influence after 1800. Duane, critical of members of Jefferson's cabinet, wrote that "power always blinds those who possess it." It "should always be conferred with a sparing hand, guarded with a watchful eye."[18] Alexander Wilson, in a 4 March oration, told his audience that it was their duty "to be vigilant and watchful of the prowling enemy of your peace, your prosperity, religion, and happiness."[19] Binns wrote of the "unremitted watchfulness" required "to guard the Liberty of the Press and the Freedom of Speech."[20] Most Republicans were reassured by Jefferson's election; he was incorruptible. But Thomas Cooper could not dismiss his residual fears of executive power. Nor could he refrain from warning the president that "We have to learn even in this mildest of Governments, how easy it is to govern too much and how prone the best of rulers are, from the best of principles, to overact their part." You, he hastily added, should be excepted from these strictures. Nevertheless, a kernel of doubt remained. "Almost," he continued, "am I persuaded that your principles are too habitual, and your character too fixed, for your practice to be warped, or your conduct to waver. *Almost*, for looking at the Bonapartes of present and former times, who of us can say he can completely trust himself, under every vicissitude of popular favour and popular ingratitude?"[21]

Convinced of their political rectitude, the radical exiles also remained assured that they were promoting the genuine ideals of Jefferson. From the relative peace of Augusta, Georgia, Driscol claimed: "We are convinced that Thomas Jefferson will, to the end of his life, remain—a Jacobin—a Democrat; in a word, a decided friend to the liberties of his country, and the freedom of mankind."[22] The ever-suspicious Duane explained Jefferson's reticence on radical reform by pointing to the shady characters surrounding him in government. "We believe most sincerely," he wrote, "that Mr. Jefferson's purposes have been the purest, and his views the wisest that could be contrived for the national policy; but we believe also, that he has been marred in the prosecution of many of the purposes nearest his heart, for the good and glory of his country; and that the concealed designs of persons near him have produced the evils . . . that now exist."[23]

Others, of course, especially those Republicans who were the targets of the radicals' arrows, disagreed with this analysis. The result was continual infighting within the Republican party. As champions of the people, the militants remained unamenable to party discipline when authority was in the hands of those who saw themselves as superior guardians of the public interest. One consequence was that in the cut and thrust of factional warfare, they frequently found themselves at odds with the leadership cadres, and often on the losing side. This was, however, by no means altogether their own fault. As will be shown, they often were treated shabbily by their own supposed allies, who although perhaps fearing their sharp pens, nevertheless never fully accepted these foreigners into the Republican camp.

VIRTUE IS ITS OWN REWARD

An early manifestation of the Republican tendency to neglect the radical exiles was the patronage and removals policy of the new federal government. What to do with the Federalist-appointed officials who dominated the bureaucracy of the central government, especially in the states, remained a divisive problem for Jefferson throughout his first period of office, for he had to balance the legitimate demands of his supporters with the desire to soothe the fears of moderate Federalists, whose detachment from High Federalism his conciliatory policy sought. The dispensing of patronage was of particular interest to some of the politically active exiles, who naturally hoped that their sacrifices on behalf of Republicanism would be rewarded with access to the loaves and fishes. On this issue some showed their first signs of disillusionment.

On arrival in office Jefferson privately made it clear that he did not intend to make a clean sweep of all federal appointments. Apart from federal attorneys and marshals (in a branch of government totally dominated by Federalists), all officials appointed by John Adams after he knew of his electoral defeat, and Federalists who had used their offices for partisan purposes, no person holding a government post was to be removed solely because of his politics. "Malconduct," Jefferson informed William Findley of Pennsylvania, "is a just ground of removal: mere difference of political opinion is not."[24] In practice, however, unable to withstand pressure from needy state politicians, Jefferson ultimately was maneuvered into accepting a partisan policy that removed far more incumbents than he personally thought politic.[25] But even though the number of openings increased, the exiles' begging bowls remained virtually empty.

The Radicals and Patronage

The radical exiles were at the forefront of those who loudly called for a clean sweep of Federalists from office. In Richmond, Virginia, Callender proclaimed that Jefferson would "degrade his own character to a level" with his opponents if he did not follow Governor McKean's policy in Pennsylvania and kick out all the Federalists.[26] In New York James Cheetham argued that "It is rational to suppose that those who removed John Adams from office, because of his manifold transgressions of the constitution, and his pointed hostility to liberty . . . would naturally expect the removal of lesser culprits in office. If this should not be the case, for what, in the name of God, have we been contending? Merely for the removal of John Adams, that Mr. Jefferson might occupy the place which he shamefully left?"[27] Privately, Cheetham and his partner David Denniston informed the president that "The people of this City and State look to the new administration with full Confidence for a thorough Change in the different offices," and warned that "Republican exertions will certainly be relaxed in this quarter if unhappily the people ever be convinced that all their efforts to Change the Chief Magistrate, have produced no consequent effects in renovating the Subordinate Stations of our government."[28] In Philadelphia, Denis Driscol initially believed that "Hitherto everything has gone on right: the augean stable of aristocracy continues to be purged; royalist agents continue to be removed, and men devoted to liberty and their country—to succeed them." But a year later, now settled in Baltimore, Driscol expressed bitter anger at the pusillanimity of the removals policy. There should be, he inveighed, no compromise with the enemies of American freedom. Jefferson had shown himself "a better philosopher than he is a General" by failing to destroy his enemies.

> It has never been the wish nor the desire of the democracy of the United States to *temporise* with their declared enemies, much less to continue them in office, while their best friends remain idle spectators and unrewarded expectants. Those who fought the battles of America want bread, while those who leagued with the enemy, are still in office. Nay, those who would turn out again, if occasion required, in defence of Liberty, are shamefully neglected by the executive, and grossly abused by the hirelings of St. James', while those on the other hand, who would *range* themselves with the enemy, and *conduct* them *once more*, to lay waste, are caressed and rewarded, enjoying the wages due to freemen, through the mistaken lenity of the President, or by the shameful policy of influential individuals, who take certain tories under their wings.[29]

Neither Cheetham nor Driscol sought federal patronage and therefore could argue their case for removals on purely selfless political grounds.[30] Both had arrived in America too late to be heavily involved in the struggle against the Federalists and had no strong case for preferment. But it was a different matter for Duane, Callender, Burk, and Cooper, all of whom had made considerable sacrifices in the Republican cause. If patronage was to be spread among the faithful, they surely had powerful claims to receive some reward. Effectively, however, they were all disowned by the republican government. In June 1801 Burk explained in considerable detail to Jefferson the story of his sufferings since arriving in America. Forced to live under a false name, incapable of earning a living consistent with his abilities, but assured by friends that his "political compositions and exertions" had been "of some use to the cause of liberty," Burk asked for a government position paying "a small stipend," possibly as a secretary in a government department, where he could continue his writing. The president politely refused his request.[31]

The most notorious case of a radical exile being refused patronage was Callender's. He was released from prison in March 1801, having served the full term of his imprisonment under the Sedition Act. He was in debt to Thomas Leiper; he still had to pay part of his fine, as Republican subscribers reneged on their promise to pay his prison costs; and he was unable to afford to bring his young, motherless family to Virginia. Unlike other victims of Federalist oppression, he had no financial assets to fall back on. Understandably, he thought his previous exertions deserved some reward. He did not expect much, just the postmastership of Richmond.[32] This was not in Jefferson's gift, but in the postmaster general's, Gideon Granger. The president, however, could have exerted his influence, if he had so wished. Indeed, when Augustine Davis was dismissed as Richmond postmaster in December 1801, Jefferson asked James Monroe for the name of a suitable replacement.[33] By this time Callender was persona non grata among Republicans, although his infamous publications on Jefferson's supposed relationship with his slave, Sally Hemings, still remained in the future.

Callender, and the other exiled penmen of the 1790s, were victims of their own notoriety. In the course of his career as propagandist, Callender had given hard knocks not only to the Federalists, but also to now important moderate Republican chiefs. Quite rightly, he had a reputation for extreme militancy and scurrility, and was not popular in many circles within his own party. He also was no gentleman, a fact he recognized himself. "I am not, to be sure," he wrote to Madison, "very expert in making a bow, or at supporting the sycophancy of conversation. I speak as well as write what I think; for God, when he made me, made that a part of my constitution." But remember, he continued, "that it is not by beaux, and dancing masters, [or] by editors, who would look extremely well in a muslin gown and petticoats, that the battles of freedom are to be fought and won."[34] Jefferson's ideal candidate for the Richmond postmastership, incidentally, was a gentleman "of respectable standing in society."

Lack of social skills and a gentlemanly manner were not, however, the only reasons why the radical exiles were denied preferment. After all, James Lyon, Callender's equally radical, destitute, and unsophisticated colleague in Virginia, received a position carrying a salary of $500 a year from Albert Gallatin, the new secretary to the treasury.[35] What prevented the exiles from receiving federal patronage was the Republican policy of conciliating moderate Federalists. Quite simply, the radical penmen of 1797 to 1800 were too hot to handle. By their belligerence, their democratic ideology, and their willingness to be the advance guard of Republicanism, they had acted as lightning conductors, attracting all the fireballs thrown by the opposition (as well as throwing their own, of course). Jefferson was prepared to sacrifice them in his quest for a union of "honest men."[36]

Gallatin and Madison were even less sympathetic to the radicals than Jefferson.[37] In the throes of political triumph they, together with the newly reappointed House clerk John Beckley, seemed to forget the needs of William Duane. Duane may have exaggerated his role in the victory of 1800, but he was undoubtedly the premier Republican newspaper editor of these years. With Gallatin dominating federal patronage in Pennsylvania, none of the militants could expect anything locally. Duane, therefore, decided to open a printshop in the new capital, where he naturally anticipated significant Republican support. Unbeknown to him, however, Jefferson had already persuaded Samuel Harrison Smith to establish a newspaper in Washington, which would become the official voice of the party and would be supported by lucrative printing contracts. Smith, previously editor in Philadelphia of the *New World* (1796–97) and the *Universal Gazette* (1797–1800), was "a rare specimen: a native . . . , a gentleman, and a scholar." He was also young, moderate, and flexible in his republicanism, and untainted by the vulgarity of the press campaigns of the years of opposition.[38]

When Duane sought to establish his printery and newspaper in Washington, he found himself, very politely, marginalized. Gallatin persuaded him of the importance of the *Aurora* remaining in Philadelphia; Jefferson listened passively to his claims that patronage in Washington would help his business thrive. But when the new Congress met in December 1801, Duane failed to receive the contract for publishing the House journals. Beckley made the decision, but it is unlikely he did so without the acquiescence of cabinet members. Smith scooped virtually all the printing patronage available. After protests, Duane was given a contract to supply the Treasury with paper, but even this lasted only a year or two.[39]

Several layers of irony are uncovered when the issue of patronage in a Republican society is examined from the perspective of the radical exiles. First is the sight of the most voluble opponents of the British system of patronage—"Old Corruption" or "The Thing" in the radical Cobbett's terminology—baying for the Ins to be turned out so that the Outs could suckle on the teats of government. The radicals may have argued that the circumstances were totally different, and that true talent could only be rewarded by a general spill. Nevertheless, both Pitt and Jefferson (and state leaders such as McKean and the Clintons) manipulated spoils systems that at root sought the same ends, the attachment to government of the influential and the powerful, and the rewarding of the faithful and loyal.

The second irony is that the most militant exiles were almost as far away from the magic circle in Jeffersonian America as they had been in Britain. It is significant that exiles who succeeded in obtaining patronage were either moderate in their politics, and thus toed the dominant party line, or could call on the good offices of influential men. The moderate Republican Joseph Gales, protégé of Nathaniel Macon, now speaker of the House of Representatives, made a comfortable fortune from being state printer in North Carolina, a position he held from 1800 until after the election to the presidency of Andrew Jackson.[40] Mathew Carey, who except in his dealings with Cobbett had remained a shadowy figure behind his more ebullient brother James during the "phrenzy of 98," and who by 1802 was to be involved in the Rising Sun movement in Philadelphia that was to lead to the union with moderate Federalists in a Quid movement, fared well in Pennsylvania. He beat Duane to the contracts for printing new editions of the laws of Pennsylvania and of the United States, and he made a small fortune from his directorship of the Bank of Pennsylvania, a position bestowed on him by the state senate.[41] Thomas Cooper, admittedly a militant in 1800 but soon to be a champion of Governor McKean, benefited from his close links with Jefferson's friend Priestley. In March 1801 the new president wrote to McKean praising Cooper's qualities. The governor promised Cooper the position of president judge in what was to become, in 1804, the third district of the Pennsylvania circuit. "This will be sufficient for me," Cooper informed Jefferson. "So far as I am concerned I want nothing more," although in the following year he obtained a midshipman's position in the navy for his wayward son. In the meantime he was appointed commissioner of the Luzerne land claims.[42]

The third irony, as Jefferson soon realized, was that the distribution of patronage was a double-edged sword. Demand always outstripped supply. For every one happy Republican there were three or four crabbily discontented. Equitably balancing sectional and factional interests was a major task, and in one respect at least the efforts of the Republican managers were a failure. By slighting the militants, especially of Philadelphia where McKean ruthlessly blocked out Duane's Democrats, they enhanced prospects of permanent divisions within the party and helped to create a situation that they had wished to avoid. With Duane the acknowledged leader of the immigrant Irish in Philadelphia,[43] it was not he alone of the exiles who was thus banished from the Republican party's inner sanctum.

NATIVISM REVIVED

The militant exiles—Duane, Binns, Driscol, Paine (after 1803), Cheetham, Cooper (until 1803), and Callender—were zealots, intolerant of all who failed to meet their exacting republican standards. During Jefferson's administrations they used their control of influential newspapers to broadcast their democratic political views, promote constitutional reform, and crucify all those with whom they disagreed. They believed the press to be the most vital weapon in the defense of republicanism. According to Duane: "The *press* is the *engine* which every *tyrant* fears. Put out the press, and there is an end to democracy. You'll have first a conflagration of civil war—and then the calm of despotism."[44] There is no cause to question their sincerity, although like all other political activists, in the whirlpool of factionalism they found themselves at times with strange bedfellows or taking up contradictory political positions. Inevitably, their arrogance made them many enemies among the Republicans. But they were also marginalized because of their politics and, as the patronage issue has already suggested, because of their alien status.

The exiles had survived the nativist upsurge during Adams's administration without fatal damage and thereafter were immune to the worst taunts that the Federalists could hurl at them. Binns, for example, could ignore the nativist rantings of the Federalist editor of the *Sunbury Gazette*, who complained when Binns was elected adjutant of the local militia regiment that foreigners should be excluded from the officer corps.[45] But they were less immune to the sly and insidious innuendoes made by prominent Republicans, who used their foreignness to undermine their political influence. In the last months of 1803 Andrew Ellicott, a prominent mathematician and secretary of the Pennsylvania Land Office, was criticized by Duane in the *Aurora* for his surreptitious attempts to create a third party in the state, dedicated to defending the increasingly unpopular governor, Thomas McKean.[46] Ellicott privately complained to Jefferson, obviously hoping that the president would publicly refute Duane's hints that he was doing the federal cabinet's bidding. His protest included an outburst against the influence of foreign editors. "It appears," he wrote, "that the United States are to take their tone from three foreign printers, Messrs. Duane, Cheetham, and Binns. . . . What may eventually be the consequence of this influence of foreigners (if not foreign influence), time alone must determine: and whatever other native born citizens may think, and feel on this subject, it appears to me, that the conduct of these men is calculated to depress the American character, and carries with it an evidence, that we have decreased in vigour of mind, and independence of sentiment, since we were lopped off from the original stock."[47]

Ellicott's sentiments mirrored the Federalists', and he was soon to join many of them in the Quid party, but they also mirrored the feelings of many moderate Republicans who believed that while the foreign-born were welcome to settle in America, they ought not to be involved in politics (except, of course, to vote for the legitimate Republican ticket).[48] Part of the problem was that democratic politics seemed to be inextricably linked with the foreign-born, for activists like Duane and Cheetham had achieved considerable success in marshaling immigrants into solid voting blocs. A crucial element in this development was the pressure brought to bear on Congress, with exiles in the vanguard, to reduce the fourteen-year period of residence necessary before admission to citizenship, a provision of the Naturalization Act of 1798.[49] An initial attempt to influence Congress in 1803 was unsuccessful. In Baltimore, Driscol strongly supported a memorial that sought a reduction of the period of residence to two years. Alluding to the United Irish leaders, he pointed out that many of the recent arrivals from overseas were respectable men of property anxious to demonstrate loyalty to their adopted country by taking out citizenship. He extolled the virtues of an open immigration policy, which would lead to an influx of agricultural and manufacturing skills, and, eventually, to a white labor force large enough to permit the abolition of slavery. Driscol was annoyed when Congress rejected the memorial for its "indecorous language," but it had included a personal attack on John Adams and contained none of the deferential periods still expected by the people's representatives.[50] A better organized and more circumspect campaign in the following year was successful, with the period of residence being reduced to five years, and with special exemptions being given to those immigrants who in the late 1790s had been too scared by the Alien and Sedition Acts to announce their intention to become citizens. In Philadelphia, Leib and Duane reaped the political rewards of this campaign, and in New York the followers of De Witt

Clinton were the beneficiaries, with Cheetham gaining the reputation of being the intimate friend of the "newly imported *wild* Irishmen."[51]

Duane and the Philadelphia Irish

The role played by Duane and his radical partner Michael Leib in altering the naturalization laws helped them to consolidate a very successful democratic constituency in Philadelphia city and county, centered on the immigrant Irish and German middling and lower classes. Their domination of Pennsylvania politics until 1809 was also sustained by their ability—through the politicization of the militia, the control of various democratic clubs and societies (especially the Tammany Society), and the efforts of a committee to help immigrants acquire citizenship—to bring out large numbers of newcomers on election days.[52] A phalanx of foreign-born plebeians regularly voting as a unit in elections was an innovation in American politics, but it conformed to Duane's democratic vision of popular participation in government. But for those who still shrank from the full implications of living in a society based on the will of the majority, it smacked more of manipulation than of democracy. Even Mathew Carey was disapproving. He hoped that Irish immigrants would quickly melt into their communities, becoming indistinguishable Americans rather than remaining targets for nativist resentment.[53]

The successful mobilization of the immigrants inevitably brought a backlash in both New York and Pennsylvania. Most exiles were canny enough to realize that if they wanted to influence American politics, they should either stay in the wings, acting through American-born "frontmen" (as Binns was to do when Simon Snyder was governor of Pennsylvania), or limit themselves to printing and publishing. Standing for elective office was asking for trouble. Duane, however, was so confident of his power in Pennsylvania that in 1807 he sought the nomination for a seat in the House of Representatives, to replace his retiring friend, Joseph Clay. His apprehensive supporters reminded him that as he had not been a citizen for seven years, he was ineligible.[54] As a consolation, he was selected to stand for the state Senate in that year's elections. The result was a humiliating disaster. A torrent of nativist abuse, led by Richard Folwell's *Spirit of the Press* and George Hembold's new magazine, the *Tickler,* the latter established on principles "purely American—excluding all foreign partialities or prejudices," overwhelmed Duane.[55] In the debacle, the Democrats lost control of the city for the first time since Jefferson's election in 1801. Duane's Quid opponent gained 56 percent of the vote. Duane won a majority in only four of the fourteen wards.[56] So devastated was he that he never commented on the result, although a week later he published an article by "Mentor," who attributed the loss statewide to Republican divisions.[57] There is much truth in that, but Duane's particularly miserable performance—he received less support than the rest of the Democratic ticket—can be attributed to his unpopularity as a "foreign" interloper with ideas above his station.

Cheetham and the New York Irish

In contrast to the activities of Duane and Leib in Philadelphia, in New York no Republican faction thought of the immigrants as more than a captive vote, unlikely because of their anglophobia ever to support the Federalists. In the early years of the century, with no prominent leaders themselves, the immigrant Irish accepted their status as voting fodder, but once some of the United Irish leaders settled in the city, attempts were made to obtain official recognition of their political weight. When in 1807 the Republican General Committee refused to nominate Thomas Addis Emmet for the state assembly, 200 irate Irishmen wrecked the headquarters of the Tammany Society.[58] Their exasperation, however, was aimed not only at the Republicans' refusal to acknowledge their political importance; some old political scores were also paid off. Emmet's involvement in New York's politics in 1807 was primarily owing to his determination to defeat Rufus King's candidacy for the assembly, as a payback for his treatment of the United Irish leaders in 1798.[59] Running on an "American ticket," King was defeated.

In the serpentine twistings and turnings of New York Republican politics, Emmet, MacNeven, and lesser former United Irishmen such as George Cuming normally kept the Irish vote firmly attached to the Clintonians, one of three Republican factions in New York (the others being the Burrites and the Livingstons). Cheetham was generally seen to be the immigrants' unofficial spokesman, as his *American Citizen* was the Clintonians' mouthpiece. He had joined the *Citizen* in May 1801 as partner to David Deniston, a kinsman of the Clintons, after refusing an offer from Aaron Burr to edit a new newspaper dedicated to the vice president's interests.[60] Having been closely connected to Burr during the tense maneuverings in Congress in 1801 following the famous tied vote in the presidential electoral college, Cheetham earned his spurs in New York Republican politics by accusing Burr of seeking Federalist support in his efforts to become president.[61] Thereafter he was associated in the public mind with De Witt Clinton, but from 1805 Cheetham found himself on a roller-coaster ride, as Clinton lost his influence over his supposed puppet, Governor Lewis, and the alliance with the Livingston faction broke down.

Cheetham happily promoted Clinton's attempts to forge an interstate alliance with the Duane-Leib Democrats of Pennsylvania, but the first signs of cracks in the Cheetham-Clinton connection came when the latter, desperately thrashing around for greater support in New York, secretly made plans for a political understanding with the Burrites.[62] Although Cheetham had been instrumental in destroying Burr's political hopes in New York, he loyally followed in Clinton's footsteps, and in February 1806 published a long, approving account of the negotiations.[63] Immediately, large sections of the Republican party raised a storm. A general meeting of Republican citizens met to denounce the plans. Clinton backed off, leaving Cheetham high and dry, and with his reputation for republican consistency in tatters.[64]

There is no doubt that for a number of years Cheetham had less freedom of political movement than Duane in Philadelphia. His newspaper had begun as a vehicle for Clintonian interests, and he was dependent on state printing contracts, worth $3,000 a year, which he obtained from his Clintonian connections.[65] Like Duane, his strength lay with his influence on the Irish constituency, but this began to ebb following the arrival of the United Irish leaders from France in 1805. Pursuing De Witt Clinton's political somersaults was a dispiriting experience, and by 1808 Cheetham was showing dangerous signs of political independence. Like the other militant exiles, he had always been suspicious of James Madison, whom he felt was not a true Republican.[66] When Madison was selected as the next presidential candidate by an "unofficial" Republican congressional caucus in January 1808, Cheetham came out in open opposition, promoting instead the elderly vice president, George Clinton. Caucuses, he later bitterly wrote, are political cabals. A caucus is "an assemblage of intriguers, privately convened to plot their own elevation, upon the ruin, not unfrequently, of better men."[67]

At the same time, Cheetham began a newspaper campaign hostile to Jefferson's policy of enforcing an embargo in response to the unfriendly commercial policies of Britain and France. Needless to say, the embargo was widely unpopular, both among merchants in New York and settlers on the border with Canada, but the majority of New York Republicans supported the president's stand.[68] Cheetham, who believed that Jefferson's policy was a surreptitious attempt to aid Napoleon in his struggle against Britain—the embargo was "that complicated act of national folly and atrocious suicide"— found himself publicly denounced at two Republican ward meetings, after he wrote that his opposition to Republican policy was "a great, sacred and imperious duty; one which is infinitely superior to the party disputes of party men." That quintessential party man, De Witt Clinton, once again cast him adrift. Having initially chaired an antiembargo meeting in New York

City, Clinton blithely switched sides when he arrived in Albany as a state senator.[69]

To protect his political career, De Witt Clinton needed to ally himself with the Madisonian Republicans in New York, a collection of Burrites and Livingstons who went by the name of Martlingites, and who by the beginning of 1809 were dominant in the party. The anti-Madisonian Cheetham was expendable. In late February 1809 a group of Martlingites, accusing him of being "a base libeller, a political assassin, an enemy to the government of our country, a secret foe to the republican cause, [and] an insidious factionist," drove Cheetham out of the Tammany Society.[70] A month later, with De Witt Clinton in the chair, the state senate confirmed the assembly's decision to dismiss four of the five state printers, including Cheetham. Cheetham published an account of the debate under the heading "And you too, Brutus?"[71]

Faced with this hostile union of Republican factions, Cheetham turned to the Irish. In the weeks leading up to the April state assembly elections in New York City, he undertook a sustained campaign to dissuade the immigrants from voting. Claiming that the *American Citizen* was the only New York newspaper to have consistently championed the Irish, Cheetham cleverly appealed to their sense of grievance at not being represented on Republican committees, including the powerful nominating committee that was choosing candidates for the election.[72] Two weeks before the election, 500 members of the Adopted Republican Citizens of New York met at Lyon's Hotel and resolved to boycott elections until their importance was duly recognized by the Republican party. "We are denominated foreigners and treated as slaves," they complained.[73]

The issue divided the immigrant community, for the "natural" leaders of the Irish, including Emmet, MacNeven, and David Bryson (the last the son and brother of two radical exiles, the Andrew Brysons, Sr. and Jr.), retained their links with Clinton, whereas DR. STEPHEN DEMPSEY had been secretary at the Adopted Citizens' meeting. The United Irish chiefs responded to the threat by calling a meeting of the Hibernian Provident Society, at which they denied that they were being maltreated as foreigners.[74]

Cheetham's attempt to defeat the Republican "Throat Cutters" failed, but he did succeed in considerably reducing their majority in the city assembly seats. About 600 voters stayed at home on election day.[75] Undoubtedly, Cheetham had touched a chord of resentment and disenchantment among a significant number of immigrants. Nativism was an issue in the large American cities where immigrants congregated, and it was not confined to conservative Federalists alone. As Cheetham wrote: "Is a man an alien? Does he meddle with politics? If so, he is told, and with few exceptions he is universally told that, being an alien, he has no right to speak, much less to write, on our political concerns. Native opposition to alien meddling extends much further. Emigrants, settled with their families and fortunes for ever, and naturalized by all the forms of law, are always considered, and by *all* parties treated, as *foreigners. . . .* Against foreigners by birth and citizens by adoption, universal prejudice has formed an universal conspiracy."[76] Republicans, however, to some extent learned their lesson from this episode. In 1812 De Witt Clinton made Emmet state attorney general, and other Irish radical exiles also received the benefits of Republican patronage.[77]

Cheetham's purging from the Republican party had a devastating effect on him. At first, he tried to make light of the humiliation. When a Federalist newspaper, ironically called the *Spirit of '76*, published a satire on his expulsion from the Tammany Society, in which he was tied at the stake in the wigwam and forced to endure a range of tortures, including "having to eat his own words every morning for breakfast, and forced to listen to a 'long talk' by Sagamore John," Cheetham responded by claiming that he was "still alive and hearty, smoking my segar and drinking my glass of wine as usual."[78] In reality, however, his life was fast going to ruin. He was still a young man, probably no more than forty, tall and robust. A man of great personal courage—he was a duelist—and with a warm temperament, he was always ready to help the needy, on one occasion "expending his best energies to extinguish the flames of the humble residence of a common citizen." But his whole life was bound up in his politics; he "promulgated with little circumspection the strongest doctrines in behalf of the widest democracy."[79] With his proscription, he lost his raison d'être and his faith in democracy. The publication of his scurrilous *Life of Thomas Paine* in October 1809 needs to be seen in the context of his blind desire for revenge. When he died only fourteen months later, his disordered mind took him back to his roots. "With herculean strength he now raised himself from his pillow; with eyes of meteoric fierceness, he grasped his bed covering, and in most vehement but rapid articulation, exclaimed to his sons, 'Boys, study Bolingbroke for style, and Locke for sentiment.' He spoke no more."[80]

REFORM

Constitutional Reform

Their alien background was of some significance in explaining the militant exiles' difficulties integrating themselves into the ascendant Republican party, but of greater influence on their exclusion was their continued efforts on behalf of political and constitutional reform. An important factor in Cheetham's slide from Republican grace had been his public disapproval of the congressional caucus that selected Madison as the Republicans' presidential candidate in January 1808. Opposition to this procedure, which was first used in 1804 to readopt Jefferson for his second term, tended to emphasize its oligarchical character and its unconstitutional nature. The caucus violated the separation of powers by giving one branch of government an undue influence over the affairs of another, at the expense of the rights of the people.[81] By resorting to strict construction principles, Cheetham was following the practice common among the radical exiles when Federalists had dominated government. So far as the exiles were concerned, the "Spirit of '76/'98," or "Old Republicanism," was not narrowly confined to a "conservative" definition of states' rights (although this is how subsequently it has come to be seen when associated with John Taylor and John Randolph).[82] It also embraced a skeptical and nondeferential approach to the federal constitution, and was reflected in demands for constitutional reform. Although the radical exiles did not put forward a unified program to amend the constitution in the 1790s, they had shared common opinions on the weaknesses in the form of government instituted after 1787. They were suspicious of the potential power of the president; they queried the role, purpose, and in some cases the necessity of the senate; and they thought the judiciary too independent of the people. In their comments, the exiles made it clear that their concerns were premised on their belief in the need for republican institutions to be responsive to the people at all times, capable of expressing the will of the majority. In effect, they took their stand on Anti-Federalist principles.[83]

The militant exiles' reforming impulses did not diminish with the defeat of John Adams. Indeed, their activities during Jefferson's presidency can best be interpreted as the logical continuation of their political philosophy when in opposition. They continued in "opposition" because the Republican leadership, in their view at least, had sold the pass. The full implications of the "Revolution of 1800" still needed to be worked out, requiring reforms at federal, state, and municipal levels to ensure that the exiles' democratic ideals came to fruition.[84] Even with Jefferson sitting comfortably on the presidential throne, they retained concerns about executive power, primarily because their moderate opponents were so influential in the cabinet. Duane, whose longevity as an important political figure in Pennsylvania was owing in considerable part to his crafty ability never to criticize Jefferson directly, nevertheless was obliquely censorious of the federal executive.[85] When he wanted to condemn his factional opponents in Washington, his approach was to attack Jefferson's "Quiddish" lieutenants, Granger and Gallatin, for acting unconstitutionally by slyly appropriating the president's powers. In August 1806 Duane began to question the constitutionality of the cabinet. Taking a strict constructionist approach, he claimed that the constitution put executive power solely in the hands of the president. The president had the right to seek written submissions from government officers, but nowhere in the constitution was a cabinet mentioned. It was a constitutional "fiction" that had developed during Washington's administration, and had appropriated the Senate's function of advising the president.[86] Gallatin, "the evil genius . . . in the cabinet," and Granger had, according to Duane, used their cabinet positions to breach the constitution by performing "executive acts" without Jefferson's knowledge. Gallatin had hired and fired government officials illegally; Granger had both helped Burr in his plot to supplant Jefferson as president in 1801, and had used his executive position to put pressure on congressmen to alter their stance on a bill opposed by his friends in the New York Chamber of Commerce. These men, Duane charged, were "the most *fatal friends* or the *worst enemies* of the chief magistrate."[87]

Duane's attacks on Jefferson's lieutenants were fueled by the assertions and arguments of the maverick Old Republican John Randolph in Congress, but his strategy had its roots in Pennsylvania's factional politics and was aimed at discrediting his enemies in the eyes of Jefferson.[88] In this he failed, for the president never lost his faith in either Gallatin or Granger, but by the same token, Jefferson also never disavowed Duane and his radical wing of the party. Indeed, during his second administration he gave more patronage to the Pennsylvania Democrats than Gallatin for one thought appropriate. In part this was a consequence of his trying to keep a balance between factions, but it was also the result of his awareness that the ideology espoused by Duane, stripped of its factional connotations and petty caviling, was genuinely republican in spirit. Jefferson retained a soft spot for Duane, informing Madison that he believed him to be "honest, and well-intentioned, but over zealous."[89] It may not be too farfetched to see Duane as Jefferson's democratic conscience; he appealed to the radical part of Jefferson's nature, that part which the exigencies of office had shrivelled since the heady and irresponsible days of 1798. Nevertheless, Jefferson's presidential actions never betrayed the influence of his whimsical radicalism, and Duane and the other militants had to proceed without official approval.[90]

Radical Reform in Pennsylvania

The militant exiles in Pennsylvania, including William Young Birch and Dr. James Reynolds,[91] and with Duane and, increasingly, John Binns in the vanguard, were part of a democratic movement that between 1801 and 1809 carried out a policy of seeking a return to the values and principles of the old "Painite" and democratic Pennsylvania constitution of 1776, that had been overturned in 1790. Their points of attack were aimed at the executive, in the considerable shape of Governor McKean, and at the judiciary, seen as the least democratic part of the government system.

The intraparty warfare during McKean's administrations has often been seen as little more than two avaricious groups of politicians seeking to lay their hands on the perquisites of power and office.[92] The democrats' widespread attack on the state judicial system, for instance, has been viewed as a malicious attempt to threaten the career paths of many of McKean's moderate supporters, who were lawyers, and as a pragmatic assault on a weak part of the governor's defenses.[93] In reality, however, although there is some truth in these allegations, there was a continuous ideological conflict being fought out over the law. The democrats' targets were lawyers, the common law, and the power and position of the judiciary. In the British radical tradition out of which the exiles had emerged, lawyers had always been despised, seen, like clergymen, as self-interested defenders of the aristocratic social and political order.[94] "Next to priests," thought Driscol, "lawyers are the greatest scourge that society can be cursed with." "The present age," wrote Duane, "is as much in danger from lawyers as the last three have been the victims of priests." Lawyers are "the *only remaining ancient imposture.*"[95]

Lawyers were a canker, claimed Duane and the militants, because of their capacity to thwart the democratic aims of simplifying the process of the law and simplifying the law code. Clergymen used the Bible to mystify the people; lawyers used the common law.[96] In the years following the revolution in America the position of the common law came into question. Increasingly it was seen to be not the collected wisdom of the past, but law determined by the whim of judges, "lawyer's law" as Paine called it in 1805.[97] The principle of popular sovereignty moved Americans toward accepting only codified laws, which were seen to represent the collective will of the people. In the 1780s Jefferson thought that the common-law powers of judges should be curtailed. By the 1790s, most Jeffersonian Republicans opposed the inclusion of the common law in American jurisprudence. But in the following decade, there was a change in tack; most moderate Republicans came to defend the common law and the independence of the judges as bulwarks against unrestrained democracy.[98] In this process of a growing defense of the common law, the militants stood out for the primacy of written, statute, and democratic law.

The position of the radicals, both American and exile, on the common law was premised partly on their anglophobia. Common law was English law, the unwanted detritus of an earlier régime. It consisted of "antiquated precedents" inapplicable to American conditions.[99] It was "the mixed progeny of feudal tyranny and monarchical idolatry."[100] Many of the exiles had suffered under its vagaries, on both sides of the Atlantic, and thus felt a personal animus to its influence. Duane, for instance, claimed to have been the victim of "near sixty malicious suits" in a few years.[101] But the militant exiles made their case against the common law mainly on principled grounds. Paine appealed to Americans' patriotism: "Our courts require to be domesticated, for as they are at present conducted, they are a dishonor to the national sovereignty. Every case in America ought to be determined on its own merits, according to American laws, and all references to foreign adjudications prohibited."[102] Duane and Cheetham appealed to Americans' fear of despotic government. For Cheetham, the common law was "arbitrary. . . . It has no limits. . . . It imparts a perfect idea of full and complete tyranny. . . . It is not recognised by our constitution."[103] According to Duane, the common law was "a pretended law which was neither proposed, digested nor written, nor deliberated upon, either by the constituting power of the state, nor by the legislature, [and] which remains still *unwritten.*"[104]

Rallying under "the monstrous mass of iniquity sanctioned by the common law" were the judges and their Federalist cohorts, "the enemies of representative democracy, driven from the executive and legislative branches."[105] In all but the most extreme divine right political theory the independence of the judiciary had been a cornerstone of Anglo-American conceptions of liberty and freedom for generations, but in the circumstances of republican America after 1801 the Democrats queried its usefulness. The judiciary remained dominated by Federalists, and they and their moderate Republican allies used the common law to hinder progress and thwart the will of the majority. Duane claimed that the idea of an independent judiciary, as customarily accepted, might be necessary in Britain, to keep the monarch at arm's length. But in a republic based on popular sovereignty it was "the reverse of wisdom," for "it stands in open contradiction to the principles of representative government."[106] The law should not be independent of the people, whose civil liberties depended on their right to alter or influence all parts of government. Appointment of judges during good behavior "is one of the greatest absurdities in a democracy that can possibly be imagined." Justices of the Peace should be elected for three years, county court judges for five, and Supreme Court judges for a maximum of seven.[107]

Abolishing the common law would not only diminish the need for lawyers and reduce the power of judges, it would also help to simplify the law. "When the laws of any country extend beyond what can be contained in the memory of a man," wrote Driscol, "they are too voluminous."[108] Laws should be simple enough both for the average citizen to understand and to apply himself in resolving disputes. Practicing what they preached, the Pennsylvania militants tried on several occasions to pass legislation that would allow laymen to plead their own cases before locally chosen arbitrators, but were rebuffed by the gubernatorial veto.[109]

Although eventually successful in 1805, when following his reelection McKean allowed a tamer version of the arbitration bill to become law, the agitation lost to the militant exiles one of their erstwhile supporters. Thomas Cooper, a trained lawyer, and from 1804 a judge, publicly opposed the measure, generously being allowed to promote his views by John Binns in his *Republican Argus*, even though Binns disagreed with him. Claiming that his sufferings in 1800 had earned him the right to give his opinions to republicans, Cooper argued that the arbitration bill was motivated by animosity toward lawyers and the law, being "a blow expressly and avowedly aimed at the aristocracy of Talents."[110] Its proponents were men who appear "to proceed too much in the manner of the French revolutionists; ridiculing all moderate and gradual reform, denouncing all those to whom experience has taught caution, and who are desirous of setting some bounds to political innovation."[111] It was founded on ignorance of human nature, for it would be mainly "the idle, the ignorant, the conceited and the meddling that would press to be arbitrators." The result would be confusion and the extension of local disputes; dissatisfaction would lead to yet more court cases (and the undesirable augmentation of the wealth of lawyers).[112]

Although Cooper claimed that "the leading features of my political creed, and of my conduct, are to the best of my knowledge, unchanged," the militants charged him with apostasy and a loss of confidence in democracy.[113] They were right to do so, for he was about to undergo the most conservative period of his undulating career. In 1807 he informed Jefferson that "The longer I live, the more cautious I am of pulling down without clearly seeing how I can build up. I cannot go with the democrats throughout. They introduce too strong habits of insubordination. . . . This is too strong a dose for me."[114] But as the ideological split widened in the Pennsylvania Republican party, Cooper did not line up with the opposition to the Democrats. Rather, he remained aloof as Duane and his militants made a comprehensive push to obtain a convention to achieve changes to the Pennsylvania constitution.

The drive for constitutional reform, of a constitution that had no built-in mechanism for change, was the centerpiece of the democratic movement in Pennsylvania in the first decade of the nineteenth century. It was promoted by Duane and Leib's Democrats in Philadelphia (the Friends of the People), and by the country Democrats led by Simon Snyder, Nathaniel B. Boileau, and their propagandist, John Binns. Opposing the reform push were the Federalists and the Quids (the Society of Independent Republicans), who were propping up McKean on the gubernatorial chair. In addition to the day-to-day arguments for reform in the press—by 1807 there were two major radical newspapers in Philadelphia, Binns having established the *Democratic Press,* supposedly as an aid to Duane's *Aurora*—significant contributions to the intellectual debate on reform came from Paine and Duane. The quest for a constitutional convention in Pennsylvania was probably the last occasion that a concerted political effort by the radical exiles can be found.

Paine's Last Insertion

Paine had returned to America in late 1802, to a storm of abuse from Federalists anxious to blacken Jefferson's name by associating him with this atheist and maligner of the sacred Washington. He was elderly, sick, and increasingly querulous. To their credit Jefferson, Gallatin, and Henry Dearborn had Paine as a dinner guest in Washington, but all hoped that he would willingly go into retirement. At first, Paine had other ideas, replying to his detractors in a series of letters published in Smith's *National Intelligencer,* which were notable mainly for the egotism they displayed. More discreetly, he offered advice to Jefferson, including the suggestion that Napoleon might be prepared to sell Louisiana, an idea that the president had already considered. He then settled down into semiretirement, his occasional writings mainly concerned with religious matters and the evils of Federalism.[115]

Paine remained, however, interested in constitutional issues, especially relating to the states, and in August 1805 he wrote his last political pamphlet, on the democrats' proposal to call a convention in Pennsylvania. It was vintage Paine, plain, straightforward, and seemingly full of common sense, reiterating simple democratic principles. In it, Paine defended the integrity of the state's defunct 1776 constitution, contrasting it favorably with its 1790 replacement. Recognized as the most democratic frame of government in an era of state constitution making, the 1776 constitution had been the product of radicals heavily influenced by Paine's *Common Sense,* although Paine himself was absent from Philadelphia with the militia when the convention met.[116] Nearly thirty years later, having participated in another revolution in another hemisphere, Paine's views had changed hardly a jot. The 1776 constitution had, he claimed, "many good points," and could be criticized only for being "subject, in practise, to too much precipitancy" in the unicameral legislature. The solution was annually to elect a single legislature, divided by lot to sit in two chambers, where bills would be debated sequentially, so that one chamber could always review the arguments of the other. The final outcome would be decided on the basis of the combined votes of the chambers. Such a procedure, he thought, would prevent precipitate and flawed legislation, but at the same time preserve the egalitarian and democratic nature of the system of government, obviating the need for an "upper house" on the aristocratic style of the British House of Lords.[117]

With this revision, Paine's preferred constitution of 1805 was the same as that of 1776. In contrast, the existing constitution was not "conformable to the Declaration of Independence and the Declaration of Rights." It was a departure from the principles of representative government. With the veto, it gave the governor "a dangerous power" that was "discretionary and arbitrary." It also gave him too much power over patronage. The New York constitution, although flawed, had the better system, a council of appointment with membership consisting of the governor and state senators elected by the legislature. Moreover, the four-year tenure of Pennsylvania's senators was too long; it allowed them to ignore the principle of accountability. Franklin's maxim, "Where annual election ends, tyranny begins," should be heeded. Similarly, judges too should be accountable to the people. There is no reason why those who executed the laws should not be subject to popular approval, in the same way as those who make the laws.[118]

Duane the Reformer

Paine's pamphlet was published by Duane. An engraving of the Irishman's profile made in 1802 shows him to be firm, pugnacious, and steely eyed, with a retroussé nose that continually cocks a snook at the world. Of Duane's many weaknesses, none was so politically damaging as his fierce loyalty to his friends. He protected Leiper at the expense of a severe beating in 1799, and he never betrayed the unpopular Leib, even though it ultimately cost him his political influence. Nor did his friendship for Paine falter, which is more than could be said of most of the radicals, British and American. Indeed, Duane paid Paine the ultimate compliment of plagiarizing his opinions, for in *Experience the Test of Government*, the other important political pamphlet produced during the agitation for a constitutional convention (in 1807), Duane put forward a reform plan that essentially mirrored Paine's and was founded on the same political values.

Duane began his case for a convention by arguing that constitutional revision was a sign of political health, not of democracy's fickleness. The best time for change was "when virtue and wisdom are in office; there is scarcely any other time." And much needed to be done. Those who had written the constitution of 1790, argued Duane, were "either very ignorant, or very adverse to the principles of free and equal government." Like the Founding Fathers of the federal system, they "had nothing more constantly in view, than the British system of king, lords, commons, and the court of king's bench as their model." Reviling "the ignorance of the *swinish multitude*," and dreading "the wisdom, virtue, and vigilance of the people," they had instituted a system of checks and balances, and vested "exorbitant power" in the organs of government that were most distant from popular influence. But institutional checks and balances do not stop government officials appropriating power: "Experience proves that there is *no check*—there *can be none*, but the *people*." Liberty and freedom can only be protected by diluting the powers of the executive (the governor would be assisted on matters such as patronage by a small annually elected council); by replacing the Senate with an annually elected legislature divided along the lines suggested by Paine; and by making all judicial positions elective, with periods of office subject to a maximum time limit. Every ten years a convention rather than a legislature would be elected, to consider further amendments to the constitution.[119]

The movement for constitutional change along democratic lines in Pennsylvania was by no means an initiative stemming only from the exiles, but they contributed a considerable part of the political guidance, and were heavily involved in mobilizing support. Their efforts achieved a modicum of success. They enlarged the scope of the arbitration system and widened the powers of justices of the peace, at the expense of county court judges. In March 1810 an act was passed that prohibited the reading of British precedents, created after 4 July 1776, in Pennsylvanian courts. But their attempts to democratize the judiciary failed, as did their demand for a constitutional convention.[120] McKean served out his maximum three terms as governor, withstanding all attempts by Duane, Binns, and Leib to have him impeached.[121] Even worse, the country democrats and the urban democrats split once Simon Snyder became governor. For many years Duane and Binns were inveterate enemies, with the former losing his statewide influence and the latter becoming a powerful adviser to Snyder behind the scenes. At one particularly rambunctious ward meeting in 1810 Binns called Duane a paltroon; Duane responded by drawing a dagger and hurling two lighted candlesticks at his rival.[122] Amid the recriminations, the impetus for reform was lost and the last, lingering political influence of the exiles withered away. By 1812, of the most prominent activist émigrés, Callender, Burk, Cheetham, Driscol, Reynolds, James Carey, and Paine were dead. Only Binns, Duane, Cooper, and Mathew

Carey were left, and although individually they continued to play a part in America's future, they no longer acted in concert.

SOCIAL REFORM: SLAVERY

The movement for constitutional reform in Pennsylvania represented the authentic voice of Painite radicalism that runs like a golden thread through the history of the exiles, both before and after their emigration. Apart from the act of emigration itself, the authority of Paine is the one factor that gives some sort of unity to the exiles. Regardless of whether the émigrés openly acknowledged a debt to Paine, they all were influenced by his abiding concern for equal rights and personal autonomy. Oppression in various forms impelled them to America; Paine best portrayed the vision of egalitarian opportunity that gave them hope.

It would be futile, however, to expect the exiles to have responded to opportunities and circumstances in similar ways, or permanently to have retained their youthful idealism. The fates of three young Dubliners, all of whom were bold young men of promise when they emigrated, make the point. The reckless Mathew Carey became in Philadelphia a respectable pillar of the community, moderate in his politics and commercially successful. The revolutionary John Binns confirmed his radicalism in Philadelphia, and surprisingly gained real influence in state politics, but much to his bemusement found himself a Whig and supporter of John Quincy Adams in the 1820s.[123] The headstrong John Burk, however, died as rashly as he had lived. Who could have foreseen these outcomes?

Looked at another way, the exiles' wide range of backgrounds and formative experiences, and the "fragmented ideology of reform" in Britain, almost inevitably ensured considerable diversity in sentiments and political postures among the emigrants in America, even though the exact configurations that occurred could not, in many cases, have been anticipated. It is thus explicable, for instance, that exiles could be found promoting various forms of political economy, from Cooper's and Priestley's commercial laissez-faire of 1798 to Carey's and John Lithgow's mercantilism.[124] On the issue of the utility of banks—undoubtedly one of the most divisive questions of the era—exiles also adopted a range of positions, frequently at odds with each other.[125] Such heterogeneity is understandable, when the social and political contexts are understood. Far less explicable, however, are the attitudes of many of the exiles toward slavery, attitudes that help to establish both the limits of Paine's influence and the sinuous and insidious impact of American society on their pre-emigration philosophies.

From his earliest writings in the *Pennsylvania Journal* before the war of independence, Paine had called for the freeing of all slaves. Using the Bible, ancient history, and natural rights' theory to support his arguments, he echoed Dr. Samuel Johnson by asking how Americans could complain that they were about to be enslaved, when they held hundreds of thousands of humans in bondage themselves?[126] He never reneged from this position.[127] As good Painites, the radicals too were hostile to slavery and in their homeland had expounded abolitionist and emancipationist rhetoric, which neatly dovetailed with their political egalitarianism.[128] Yet in America the common front against this evil broke down. Of the thirty-two émigrés whose views in America have been discovered, only thirteen were adamantly opposed to slavery, no fewer than eleven owned slaves, and the views of the remaining eight were ambiguous or altered over time.[129]

Adapting to Slavery

There are three possible general explanations for this surprising diversity, one environmental, one party political, and one religious. The environmentalist explanation emphasizes the acculturation of the exiles to the regions in which they settled.[130] Not only did they become increasingly American, but as time passed they also inevitably identified themselves with particular states or sections. This helps to explain why not one of those exiles who settled in slave states can be said to have been unequivocally hostile to the institution of slavery. In 1796 slave labor built the wealthy Harman Blennerhassett's two-story "mansion," in the "style of a Persian pavilion," on his hideaway island in the middle of the Ohio river.[131] Three, possibly five, former United Irishmen owned slaves in Georgia, as did John Hughes in South Carolina and Priestley's son William in Louisiana.[132] Archibald Binny, on selling his business in Philadelphia to James Ronaldson, retired to a 5,000-acre plantation in Maryland, where he employed fifty slaves weaving, milling sulphur and grist, and raising crops.[133]

The trajectory of Joseph Gales's career highlights both the environmentalist argument and some of its problems. He had led the anti-slave trade movement in Sheffield in the early 1790s and in Philadelphia had published articles condemning the trade in his *Independent Gazeteer*. In Raleigh, North Carolina, however, where he was mayor for nineteen years, Gales owned slaves, although he claimed to be an abolitionist.[134] In 1806, when the twenty-year moratorium on anti-slave trade legislation imposed by the Philadelphia

Federal Convention was coming to a close, he supported the banning of the trade. But a decade later, when a group of Quakers asked him to publish an anti-slavery address, he refused. His reasons were typically pragmatic. Their request was "on a subject which the people of the state will not hear discussed with temper at present, it might also produce consequences of a direful kind by getting into the hands of Slaves, for many of them can read. I wish with you that an end could be put to Slavery but it will be of no use to attack the people's prejudices directly in the face, it must be brought about by slow, but gradual means."[135] These means included establishing a colony in Africa for free blacks, a solution that appealed to both antislavery and proslavery advocates.[136] When the American Colonization Society got under way in 1816, Gales became a member. During the 1830s he was for six years both a regional secretary and treasurer, but resigned under a cloud shortly before the society became moribund.[137]

Membership of the American Colonization Society did not make Gales unequivocally an abolitionist. Part of its appeal to its varied constituencies—including slave-owners, traditional Federalists, and Northern Protestant clergymen—was the prospect of creating an orderly white man's country by expunging the impurity and contamination that blacks, especially free blacks were thought to represent.[138] What his involvement does show is his continued commitment to Enlightenment lines of thought on the slave question. In effect, he took a Jeffersonian position on the question of the black population, wringing his hands on the issue but failing to find a viable solution.[139]

Jeffersonians and Slavery

He was by no means alone; slavery was a continually embarrassing issue for the exiles who involved themselves in the political arena in America. The problem was, of course, the southern Republican leaders' ownership of slaves, which made them a prime target for northern Federalist jibes. Callender weakly tried to turn the tables in 1795 by asking how Federalists could reconcile their anti-slavery with support for Washington. "If to hold men in slavery be criminal," he wrote, "he who has the greatest number of slaves increases his criminality with their numbers, and if this is admitted, there are few who could vie with the President in this species of human outrage."[140] Responding to Cobbett's taunts, James Carey put forward the disingenuous argument suggested by Jefferson in his draft of the Declaration of Independence. Slavery was the fault of the English and "eastern sharpers" who sold slaves to the southerners. "The Virginians," Carey extolled, "are generous, they are humane, they are honest; they are brave, they fought for the liberties of their country, they have defended them and they will defend them; they are not monarchy men, they deserve your hatred Peter, and that of your masters. They will be happy to see negro slavery abolished, when time, nature, and the real good of their country will permit it."[141]

With Binns, Duane, and Driscol, Carey acknowledged slavery to be an evil. During the Nullification Crisis in 1832 Binns, taking up the Colonisation Society's program, in vain proposed at a Philadelphia town meeting that the federal government, having paid off the national debt, should use the surplus to compensate owners for slaves, who would be freed and sent back to Africa. Twenty years later, however, he confessed never to have been "a zealous, active abolitionist."[142] Nor was Duane, who like Gales opposed the slave trade. Echoing an ancient justification for slavery, he argued that slavery in the southern states, by buttressing a highly civilized society, enabled more white men of ability and talent to be produced than in Pennsylvania.[143]

Driscol was far more outspoken in his opposition to slavery, but he too after a number of years tempered his position. In Ireland he had hotly asserted that the French Republic could not boast of liberty and equality until the "persecuted sons of Africa" in the French West Indies had been "restored to the Rights of Man."[144] In slave-holding Maryland he prophesied that "The period of deliverance . . . is fast approaching, when the disgraceful *stigma* will be wiped away, by the government of this country, and the example set to all nations that American freemen revolt at the idea of governing slaves. . . . We must not boast too loudly of 'Hail Columbia, happy land,' for where slavery is practised, there real happiness cannot be."[145] Nevertheless, Driscol made considerable concessions to the American practice of slave-holding. The treatment of slaves in the European-held West Indian islands was far more reprehensible than America's, "where, after all, slavery is freedom, comparatively speaking."[146] Moreover, after he moved to Georgia and took over the *Augusta Chronicle,* he continued to espouse Republican principles but remained forever mute on the question of slavery.[147] Whether he owned slaves in Augusta has not been ascertained.

The exiles in their political pursuits were forced into an uncomfortable position by their Enlightenment commitment to universal rights coming into conflict with the reality of Republican slavery. They put forward no original justifications either for or against slavery, but reiterated increasingly jejune Jeffersonian rationalizations. Neither were they averse to using racist arguments, an inevitable development, perhaps, in response to the heightened awareness of slavery's anomalous position in a republican society.[148] Duane confided to Jefferson that he thought slavery to be "congenial" to the temperament of Africans.[149] Even in death the black was inferior. The noted philanthropist James Ronaldson in 1827 laid out a new cemetery in Philadelphia, in which double lots were allocated to "friendless Scots" and single lots to poor "deceased human beings other than people of colour."[150] Callender came into close contact with slaves in a Richmond jail soon after the Gabriel Prosser rebellion of 1800. He was both disgusted and frightened by them. "To a negro mere imprisonment is almost nothing," he wrote. "You might as well put a horse in jail. Provided his belly is tolerably crammed, he cares very little about it. . . . The idea of death does not make an impression upon the mind of a black man, which it does upon a white one. He is too stupid for acute reflection; and a sense of shame is out of the question."[151]

By the time Callender wrote these comments he was a rogue Republican, highly embittered and close to drinking himself to death. No such excuses can be made for Thomas Cooper, one of the best known antislavery advocates in Britain.[152] As a freeborn Englishman he claimed that slavery was "the most diabolical exertion of political tyranny"; as a South Carolinian he wrote: "I do not say the blacks are a distinct species; but I have not the slightest doubt of their being an inferior variety of the human species; and not capable of the same improvement as the whites."[153] Cooper was a utilitarian; he found no difficulty in opposing slavery in the 1830s because it was uneconomic, yet continued to publicize his philosophical defense of the peculiar institution (a materialist arguing from the Bible was perhaps a little hypocritical, however).[154]

Gales and Cooper were both closely associated with the English doctrines of rational religion, both friends of Priestley, who retained his principled antislavery stance in America, and both citizens of southern states (Cooper settled in South Carolina in 1820). Priestley's other close friend and Unitarian confidant, William Russell, established himself in Connecticut, but on a visit to Virginia in 1797 he too was seduced by the advantages of slavery. He found a "capital black cook, a man cook (the female cooks are not valued here)," available for $500. He contemplated buying a set of black servants to fill his household, but once he heard that slavery was gradually being abolished by law in Connecticut, he backed out of the negotiations. Nevertheless, Mary Russell admitted that although her father was upset by the harsh treatment meted out to slaves in the South, he never condemned the institution.[155]

Enlightenment Rationalism and Slavery

The pro-slavery or equivocal positions taken by believers in rational forms of religion—Gales, Cooper, Russell, and Driscol, for instance—raise the question of a third influence on exile opinions toward slavery; that of Enlightenment rationalism, especially that stream of thought that led to utilitarianism.[156]

The answer cannot be straightforward; both Paine and Priestley's hostility be-
lie the explanation that rational modes of thought on their own could be manipulated into acceptance of slavery. Moreover, David Bailie Warden, who as
a licentiate in Ireland was committed to rational New Light Presbyterian doctrines, not only gave much practical assistance to Abbé Grégoire in the preparation of his influential anti-slavery book (published in 1808), but also trans-
lated it into English.[157] But Warden lived in Paris; he, like Paine and Priestley,
was not subject to the influences inevitably imposed by immersion in a slave
society. It is possible that some radicals of a rationalist utilitarian bent, be-
witched by the benefits that slavery appeared to bring to Southern civilization,
could have come to acknowledge its ultimate usefulness.[158] If so, it appears that
proximity to slavery needed to be united with utilitarian modes of thought for
antislavery sentiments to be eroded. Political commitment to the slave-holding
Jefferson would only have added to the possibility of abstract moral views
held in Britain being discarded when faced with the realities of America.

Abolitionism Defended

What can be said with confidence is that most of the exiles who openly condemned slavery were more influenced by Calvinist or evangelical strains
of Protestant theology than by rational religion. The radical Welsh Baptist
Morgan John Rhees was a fervent abolitionist, boldly traveling throughout the
states from Georgia to Maine to "administer abolition pills." At Mount Vernon
he cheekily composed a prayer to Washington to free his slaves. Rhees and the
Methodist Richard Lee were both committee members of the Philadelphia Society for the Abolition of Slavery in the 1790s, with the latter publishing the
former's writings in his *American Universal Magazine*.[159] Lee had no time for
republican slave-holders: "Of all the slave-holders under heaven those of the
United States appear to me the most reprehensible; for man never is so truly
odious as when he inflicts on others that which he himself abominates."[160]

The equally unvarnished antislavery sentiments of another Methodist
gave Jefferson a few sleepless nights. THOMAS BRANAGAN was from Dublin
and for a time had been a sailor on a slaver and overseer of a plantation in
Antigua.[161] Living as a lay preacher in poor circumstances in Philadelphia in
1805, he sent Jefferson a "preliminary Essay on Slavery" that was the introduction to a "Tragical Poem" on slavery. He sought the president's assistance
in its publication. Innocently he wrote: "Of all the publications which may be
productive of public utility, there is none more deserving of general attention;
none more intrinsically momentous to the citizens of America, than the subject matter of my Tragical Poem. To every nation, savage or civilised, it must

be deemed important, but to the Body Politic whose very existence exclusively depends upon the purity of political principles, it must be doubly important." As Jefferson confided to George Logan, when asking him to visit Branagan, the request left him in a dilemma. Branagan's cause was "holy," and Jefferson was prepared to act on the slave issue "with decisive effect" if ever the occasion arose, but openly to support the abolition of slavery would "by lessening the confidence and goodwill of a description of friends composing a large body, only lessen my powers of doing them good in the other great relations in which I stand to the publick." Jefferson was doubtless relieved to hear from Logan that Branagan, "a modest inoffensive poor man," had been perfectly satisfied with a personal explanation of the president's *real politick*.[162]

Among all the radical exile groups, the most consistent and principled opposition to slavery came from the incorrigible and punctilious Covenanting Presbyterians. Uninfluenced by the Enlightenment, refusing to acknowledge the legitimacy of the Federal government, strong in their Calvinist faith, in 1800 their new Presbytery unanimously agreed that "no slaveholder should be allowed the communion of the church." James McKinney and Samuel Brown Wylie traveled to South Carolina, to inform the Covenanting congregations of the decision. In one day, at Rocky Creek, Covenanters voluntarily freed slaves to the value of 3,000 guineas. Thereafter, the Covenanting exiles consistently preached abolitionism; their successors were to be prominent in establishing underground railways running into Canada for escaped slaves.[163] Without their active hostility to slavery, the conduct of the exiles would have been embarrassing indeed.

Conclusion

Hostility to slavery and the slave trade had helped to unite all sections of the radical movement in Britain and Ireland in the 1790s. It brought together Painites, Unitarians, United Irishmen, Enlightenment rationalists, and Presbyterians with a seventeenth-century theology as well as those of the New Light who had rejected Calvinism. No such unanimity can be found in their reactions to slavery after their emigration. As an abstract issue, anti-slavery had bonded the exiles; as a practical problem in America, it divided them. There were particular reasons for this, as we have seen, but the slavery question can also be viewed more broadly as representative of many other centrifugal forces in American society that acted on the exiles to undermine the relative harmony of thought and belief that once had been their strength and the cause of their emigration.

Gordon S. Wood has brilliantly analyzed how in the postrevolutionary war period the United States underwent a profound transformation. "By every measure there was a sudden bursting forth, an explosion—not only of geographical movement but of entrepreneurial energy, of religious passion, and of pecuniary desires. Perhaps no country in the Western world has ever undergone such massive changes in such a short period of time."[1] The ideological driving forces were the doctrines of democracy and equality, the products of the revolutionary generation and the cornerstones of the radical exiles' philosophy. The speed, intensity, and anarchy of these developments had not been foreseen, even by those of the founding generation who had most willingly first embraced change and republicanism. "In many respects," writes Wood, "this new democratic society was the very opposite of the one the revolutionary leaders had envisaged."[2]

If Jefferson, Madison, and Hamilton underestimated the forces that had been unleashed, it is hardly surprising that the radical exiles too were frequently dumbfounded by what they experienced in the United States. They had perceived the United States to be both asylum and elysium, and many were disconcerted by the reality. For the majority, blending into the background became a priority. America gave them anonymity, a blessing after their tribulations across the Atlantic. For a significant number, repatriation was the response to disappointment or homesickness. They came; they saw; they concurred that America was uncongenial.

Perhaps 20 percent of the exiles took neither of these options, but set out to play a role in their new homeland, in business, in politics, and in intellectual life. For a few years, those who rode the tiger made a mark on American politics, and some individuals retained an influence in their chosen fields for much longer. If one were not aware that he or she was part of a much larger diaspora, one might suggest that the radical exiles comprised one of the most significant intellectual migrations to the United States between the arrival of the Puritan ministers in the seventeenth century and the Jewish exodus from Germany in the 1930s. But knowledge of the larger body of ordinary exiles who blended into the background forbids such a conclusion, although it nevertheless remains true that, considering their numbers, the weight of influence the most prominent exiles exerted is impressive.

The exiles did not bring with them political ideas that were uniquely original. They were part of a transatlantic community of radicalism that had existed since the first years of colonial intransigence in the 1760s. Undoubtedly, these patterns of interaction were disrupted by the ferment of ideas created by the French Revolution, but if British and Irish radicals sometimes danced to melodies with a distinctly French tone, the background harmonies were normally Anglo-American.[3]

Between Britain and America in this era there existed a genuine reciprocity of radical ideas based on a common ideological inheritance and common political languages. Allowing for individual interpretations and emphases, as examined in detail above, there were two broad radical traditions in the Anglo-American world. The first, which appealed most strongly to both societies' middle groups—lawyers, merchants, heterodox intellectuals and clergymen—was the Commonwealth tradition encompassing the writings of John Locke, Algernon Sydney, Trenchard and Gordon, and their successors. The other, which matured more swiftly in America than in Britain in the years from 1766 to 1780, was the small producer tradition. Appealing to the middling classes—artisans, mechanics, shopkeepers, and journeymen—this stream of radicalism had its roots in the sectarianism of the Quakers and the Leveller movement of the midseventeenth century.[4]

In the years of the American Revolution these traditions had enough in common for their adherents to act in concert in support of political reform and the protection of "English" liberties. American patriots received the ideas of the Commonwealthmen from Britain, where they were circulating among a new, if small, generation of radicals who looked with suspicion and apprehension on the activities of the king and his ministers, whom they thought were attempting to establish a new despotism. Fueled by the Commonwealth belief that only a virtuous, self-denying, and independent citizenry could prevent the misuse of state power, British radicals feared that political corruption had undermined the constitutional gains achieved by the Glorious Revolution.

The Commonwealth emphasis on self-denial and independence conformed neatly with the small producer ideology of community, independence, and competency, in which the ideal society was envisaged as a community of small producers mindful of the common good, whose labor and skill gave them independence and an income sufficient to support a family and save for their old age. Both ideologies were corporatist, both frowned on excessive luxury and wealth, and both extolled the virtues of independence as a bulwark against corruption.

In the context of an increasingly acrimonious conflict with Britain, political debate in America focused on such potentially revolutionary issues as the right of representation, the locus of sovereignty and, ultimately, independence. At the same time, the language of radical politics began to mutate, as old words took on new meanings. Republicanism and democracy, for example, shed their negative images in 1776; the radical version of Locke's natural rights theory, promoted in Paine's *Common Sense* and the Declaration of Independence, was accentuated. Popular sovereignty, previously a doctrine used to combat the absolutist pretensions of the monarch, was combined with democratic ideals and the concept of actual (rather than virtual) representation to create a powerful political weapon. In a temporary alliance with small producer radicalism, it was capable of uniting middle-class merchants, the planter squirearchy, small farmers, and urban small producers in a patriotic coalition against imperial authority, which remained stable long enough to achieve and consolidate independence.

In Britain and Ireland, where radicals had expressed solidarity with the American patriots, and had given help where possible, the war of independence offered both opportunities and difficulties. With the British government distracted by the logistics of long-distance warfare and threatened by invasion, Irish patriots embodied in the Volunteers won legislative independence, although the more radical failed to achieve catholic emancipation and parliamentary reform. In Britain, the war forced radicals painfully to reexamine their adherence to both patriotism and libertarianism. Most only reluctantly accepted the fact of American independence, although they willingly imbibed American arguments on representation in an ultimately vain attempt to achieve parliamentary reform. To British radicals after 1783, although only a very small number emigrated, the new United States became an asylum, a beacon of liberty and a land of freedom and opportunity, a reputation that it was to lose only for brief periods in the next fifty years.

Such perceptions, however, were increasingly based on outdated or superficial assumptions. Ambiguity surrounded the British radicals' attitude to republicanism, which to many remained of more theoretical than practical relevance. The retreat from majoritarianism in the United States, reflected in the defeat of the small producer democratic movement by 1780 and in the federal system established by the new Constitution of 1787, was not fully comprehended. Nor were the conservative implications of the two most important philosophical innovations in the debates at the Philadelphia Convention, James Wilson's defense of a divided popular sovereignty and James Madison's argument in favor of a large republic to negate conflicting economic or sectional interests. With most of their New England informants proponents of the new federalism and its implicit elitism, British radicals remained unaware of the growing distance between their image of America and its reality.

Radical exiles seeking asylum were the first to confront this variance between image and reality. Arriving in the United States from the early 1790s, their expectations of a democratic, egalitarian, and republican society were swiftly confounded when they analyzed Federalist policies. Some jumped wholeheartedly into the political fray, their newspapers and pamphlets becoming the main conduits by which Jeffersonian Republican policies reached a mass audience. In Philadelphia, New York, and Richmond, Virginia, among other places, British and Irish journalists worked assiduously between 1796 and 1800 with Republican apparatchiks to undermine the dominant Federalist party, both locally and nationally, and to ensure that the thousands of new immigrants gave their allegiance to Jefferson. Confronted by the Alien and Sedition laws of 1798, many British and Irish radical exiles suffered harassment and in some cases imprisonment for their political activities. Jefferson's victory in 1800 owed a great deal to their efforts.

Although many exiles believed that America's political problems would be solved merely by the defeat of Federalism, a number of militants recognized that the Federal Constitution was itself a source of corruption, for it had distanced the people too far from the locus of power by its system of checks and balances and indirect elections. Aiming its message primarily at urban mechanics, small masters, and shopkeepers, exiled radical activists promoted participatory democracy, an intermediate position between direct democracy, which was believed to be unworkable in a large republic, and representative democracy, which the radicals believed in its current form had reduced the influence of the people and allowed a "natural" aristocracy to engross power.

Influenced by their experiences in the popular societies in Britain, swayed also by the Anti-Federalist arguments of 1788, the exiles attempted to revive the "Spirit of '76." Committed to a democratic republicanism in which everyone was actively involved in politics, they added to the radical wing of the Jeffersonian coalition, suggesting the need for constitutional revision, questioning the utility of the Senate, the mode of appointment to and tenure of the judiciary, and the powers of the president.

Before 1800 the radicals had the ambiguous support of Jefferson, but thereafter they were increasingly marginalized. Useful while the Federalists were powerful opponents, they were a nuisance when Republican policy aimed at conciliating the moderate Federalists. The factionalism that broke out in the state Republican parties in Jefferson's first term was less the result of fighting for the spoils of office than the consequence of the militant Republicans' ostracism by power brokers anxious to distance the party from the radicals' participatory form of democratic politics. By the War of 1812 the militant exiles had been defeated. Excluded from the Republican party's councils, they were reduced to a rump.

Another generation of radicals, still believing the United States to be both asylum and elysium, were to exile themselves to America in the years after 1815, bringing with them communitarian socialist ideas as well as further installments of Painite radicalism, but they were not to have the influence of their predecessors. Fewer in number than in the 1790s, they nevertheless were among the leaders of the workingmen's political movement and involved in the resurgence of communitarianism in America, introducing a secular millenarian strain to coexist with the indigenous religious millennial communities.[5] But this generation did not attach itself to one of the major political parties and thus always remained of minor importance. Nor did the radicals' experiences in Britain have much to offer an indigenous radicalism, which from the 1830s increasingly coalesced around the issue of slavery.

William Duane has been shown to have forged a political link between the two generations of exiles, and John Lithgow's Deist and utopian writings resurfaced in the 1830s, but most of the exiles by then were either dead or living in obscurity.[6] They lived out their lives pursuing personal dreams, some reaching the end of the rainbow, others failing in the attempt. The last two survivors died in 1860, John Binns in Philadelphia, John Devereaux in Mayfair, London. None thus lived to see the union split asunder, on an issue over which they too had been divided. By their divisions, the British and Irish reaffirmed the roots of their radicalism and acknowledged their transformation into American citizens.

APPENDIX:
Radical Emigré Serial Publications

Editor	Title and Place	Dates
J. Binns	*Republican Argus* (Northumberland, Pa.)	1802–7
	Democratic Press (Philadelphia)	1807–29
D. Bruce	*Daily Advertiser* (New York)	1803–6
J. D. Burk	*Daily Advertiser* (Boston)	1796
	Polar Star (Boston)	1796–97
	Time-Piece (New York)	1798
J. T. Callender	*Aurora* (Philadelphia)	1797–98
	Examiner (Richmond)	1800–1802
	Recorder (Richmond)	1802–3
J. Carey	*Virginia Gazette* (Richmond)	1792
	Star (Charleston)	1793
	Georgia Journal (Savannah)	1793–94
	Wilmington Chronicle (N.C.)	1795
	Daily Evening Gazette (Charleston)	1795
	Telegraph (Charleston)	1795
	Daily Advertiser (Philadelphia)	1797–98
	Carey's United States Recorder (Philadelphia)	1798
	Constitutional Diary (Philadelphia)	1799–1800
M. Carey	*Pennsylvania Evening Herald* (Philadelphia)	1785–88
	Complete Counting House Companion (Philadelphia)	1785–88
	American Museum (Philadelphia)	1787–92
J. Charless	*St. Louis Missouri Gazette*	1808–20
J. Cheetham	*Republican Watchtower* (New York)	1800–1801
	American Citizen (New York)	1801–10
T. Cooper	*Sunbury and Northumberland Gazette* (Pa.)	1797
W. Cox	*Exile* (New York)	1817–18
R. Davison	*Messenger* (Warrington, N.C.)	1802–9
R. Dinmore	*National Magazine* (Washington, D.C.)	1801–2

	American Literary Advertiser (Alexandria, Va.)	1802–4
	Alexandria Expositor (Va.)	1802–7
	Washington Expositor (D.C.)	1807–9
G. Dobbin	*American* (Baltimore)	1810–11
	Baltimore Price Current	1805–1810
	National Museum (Baltimore)	1813
D. Driscol	*Temple of Reason* (New York & Philadelphia)	1800–1802
	American Patriot (Baltimore)	1802–3
	Augusta Chronicle (Ga.)	1804–10
W. Duane	*Merchant's Daily Advertiser* (Philadelphia)	1797
	Philadelphia Gazette	1797–98
	Aurora General Advertiser (Philadelphia)	1798–1829
	Apollo (Washington, D.C.)	1802
J. Gales	*Independent Gazeteer* (Philadelphia)	1796–97
	Raleigh Register (N.C.)	1799–1833
B. Irvine	*Morning Chronicle* (New York)	1804– ?
	Whig (Baltimore)	1807–13
S. Kennedy	*American Patriot* (Baltimore)	1803
R. Lee	*American Universal Magazine* (Philadelphia)	1796–97
J. Lithgow	*Temple of Reason* (Philadelphia)	1802–3
J. Miller	*South-Carolina Gazette* (Charleston)	1783–85
	Back Country Gazette (Pendleton, N.C.)	1795
	Miller's Weekly Messenger	1807
J. M. Williams	*Columbian Gazette* (New York)	1799
	Democrat (Boston)	1804
J. Wood	*Virginia Gazette* (Richmond)	1802–4
	Western World of Kentucky (Frankfort)	1806
	Atlantic World (Washington, D.C.)	1807
	Petersburg Daily Courier (Va.)	1814

Abbreviations in Notes

Am. Cit.	[New York] *American Citizen*
Aug. Chron.	[Georgia] *Augusta Chronicle*
BL	British Library
BWJ	*Berrow's Worcester Journal*
Castlereagh Corr.	Charles Vane, Marquess of Londonderry, ed., *Memoirs and Correspondence of Viscount Castlereagh*
Cornwallis Corr.	Charles Ross, ed., *Correspondence of Charles, First Marquis Cornwallis*, 2nd ed.
Cork Gaz.	*Cork Gazette*
CUSR	*Carey's United States Recorder*
DAB	*Dictionary of American Biography*
DEP	*Dublin Evening Post*
DNB	*Dictionary of National Biography*
Drennan Letters	D. A. Chart, ed., *The Drennan Letters*
Exam.	[Richmond] *Examiner*
Gaz. U.S.	*Gazette of the United States*
HSP	Historical Society of Pennsylvania
IHS	*Irish Historical Studies*
Jeff. Papers	Thomas Jefferson Papers, Library of Congress (microfilm edition)
KCRO	Kent County Record Office
NAM	National Army Museum, London
NLS	National Library of Scotland
N. Star	[Belfast] *Northern Star*
PMHB	*Pennsylvania Magazine of History and Biography*
Porc's Gaz.	[Philadelphia] *Porcupine's Gazette*
PRO	Public Record Office (London)
PRONI	Public Record Office of Northern Ireland
Ral. Reg.	[N.C.] *Raleigh Register*
Reb. Pap.	Rebellion Papers, National Archives, Dublin
Rec.	[Richmond, Va.] *Recorder*
Rep. Argus	[Northumberland, Pa.] *Republican Argus*
RSCIHC (1798)	*Report from the Secret Committee of the [Irish] House of Commons*

RSCIHL (1793)	*Report from the Secret Committee of the [Irish] House of Lords*
RSCIHL (1798)	*Report from the Secret Committee of the [Irish] House of Lords*
Rutt, ed., *Works*	John T. Rutt, ed., *The Theological and Miscellaneous Works of Joseph Priestley*
Sampson Letters	Letters of William Sampson, Library of Congress
TCD	Trinity College Dublin
Warden Papers	David Bailie Warden Papers, Maryland Historical Society
WMQ	*William and Mary Quarterly*

Notes

INTRODUCTION

1. Delbert H. Gilpatrick, "The English Background of John Miller," *The Furman Bulletin* 20 (1938): 14–20; *Pennsylvania Packet*, Jan. 14, 1783.

2. "The Autobiography of Mathew Carey," *New England Magazine* (July 1833): 412.

3. Between 1790 and 1799, 15,000 Britons and 61,000 Irish people immigrated. For the breakdown of figures, see Hans-Jurgen Grabbe, "European Immigration to the United States in the Early National Period, 1783–1820," *Proceedings of the American Philosophical Society* 133 (1989): 194, Table 2.

4. James Thomson Callender, *A Short History of the Nature and Consequences of the Excise Laws* (Philadelphia, 1795), 45; Edward C. Carter, "A 'Wild Irishman' Under Every Federalist's Bed: Naturalisation in Philadelphia, 1789–1806," *PMHB* 94 (1970): 332–33; [Baltimore] *American Patriot*, Feb. 17, 1803.

5. Richard J. Twomey, "Jacobins and Jeffersonians: Anglo-American Radicalism in the United States, 1790–1820" (Ph.D. diss., Northern Illinois University, 1974), now published unchanged (New York, 1989).

6. For America, see, e.g., Alan V. Briceland, "The Philadelphia *Aurora*, the New England Illuminati, and the Election of 1800," *PMHB* 100 (1976): 23.

7. See, e.g., Albert Soboul, *The Parisian Sans-Culottes and the French Revolution, 1793–4* (Oxford, 1964), 1–17.

8. Mathew Carey, *The Olive Branch: or, Faults on Both Sides, Federal and Democratic*, 10th ed. (Philadelphia, 1818; reprinted Freeport, New York, 1969), 312. The first edition was published in 1814.

9. This is a change of mind on my part, caused by a growing awareness of the sheer size, as well as variety, of the political and religious emigration in the 1790s. See Michael Durey, "Transatlantic Patriotism: Political Exiles and America in the Age of Revolution," in Clive Emsley and James Walvin, eds., *Artisans, Peasants and Proletarians: Essays Presented to Gwyn A. Williams* (London, 1985), 7–31.

10. J. Ann Hone, *For the Cause of Truth: Radicalism in London, 1796–1821* (Oxford, 1982), 1; Richard L. Greaves and Robert Zaller, eds., *Biographical Dictionary of British Radicals in the Seventeenth Century* (Brighton, 1982), vol. 1, viii. See also Alfred F. Young, "Introduction," in Young, ed., *Beyond the American Revolution. Explorations in the History of American Radicalism* (DeKalb, 1993), 9–10.

11. John Brewer, *Party Ideology and Popular Poli···s at the Accession of George III* (Cambridge, 1976), 19.

12. Richard L. Greaves, *Deliver Us from Evil: The Radical Underground in Britain, 1660–1663* (Oxford, 1986), 5.

13. For recent attempts to understand the heterogeneity and variety of English radicalism in this era, see Mark Philp, "The fragmented ideology of reform," in Philp, ed., *The French Revolution and British Popular Politics* (Cambridge, 1991), 50–77; Jon Mee, *Dangerous Enthusiasm: William Blake and the Culture of Radicalism in the 1790s* (Oxford, 1992).

14. According to Cobbett, Harper turned to counterfeiting after his offer of a "killing machine" was rejected by the British government at the outbreak of war with France in 1793. William Cobbett, *Porcupine's Works; containing various writings and selections; exhibiting a faithful picture of the United States of America* (London, 1801), vol. 8, 70.

15. A. Hook, *Scotland and America: A Study of Cultural Relations* (Glasgow, 1975), 240.

16. The list of names, representing only those imprisoned in Dublin during the rebellion, can be found in PRO HO100/88/99–105. What happened to most of them is uncertain; another six may have gone to America; one was transported to Botany Bay; and some others may have gone to France.

17. The data in Table 1 suggest that the government's victory over the revolutionary parties in England in 1798–99 did not result in the expatriation of radicals. There were some, but as they were Irish they have been placed in that column.

18. Mary Thale, ed., *Selections from the Papers of the London Corresponding Society, 1792–1799* (Cambridge, 1983), xix; H. T. Dickinson, *British Radicalism and the French Revolution, 1789–1815* (Oxford, 1985), 10–11; Ian R. Christie, *Stress and Stability in Late Eighteenth-Century Britain: Reflections on the British Avoidance of Revolution* (Oxford, 1984), 49.

19. For a recent definition of the middling sort as members of "independent trading households," see Shani D'Cruze, "The Middling Sort in Eighteenth-Century Colchester: Independence, Social Relations and the Community Broker," in Jonathan Barry and Christopher Brooks, eds., *The Middling Sort of People: Culture, Society and Politics in England, 1550–1800* (London, 1994), 181–82.

20. Gwyn A. Williams, *Artisans and Sans-Culottes: Popular Movements in France and Britain during the French Revolution* (London, 1968), 18.

21. Christina Bewley, *Muir of Huntershill* (Oxford, 1981).

22. Nancy J. Curtin, *The United Irishmen: Popular Politics in Ulster and Dublin, 1791–1798* (Oxford, 1994), 127.

23. J. C. D. Clark, *English Society, 1688–1832* (Cambridge, 1985), 277–78.

24. See, in particular, Richard Twomey, *Jacobins and Jeffersonians: Anglo-American Radicalism in the United States, 1790–1820* (New York, 1989); Twomey, "Jacobins and Jeffersonians: Anglo-American Radical Ideology, 1790–1810," in Margaret Jacob and James Jacob, eds., *The Origins of Anglo-American Radicalism* (London, 1984), 284–99;

Arthur Sheps, "Ideological Immigrants in Revolutionary America," in Paul Fritz and David Williams, eds., *City and Society in the Eighteenth Century* (Toronto, 1973), 231–46; Kim Tousley Phillips, "William Duane, Revolutionary Editor" (Ph.D. diss., University of California, Berkeley, 1968); Edward C. Carter, "The Political Activities of Mathew Carey, Nationalist, 1760–1814" (Ph.D. diss., Bryn Mawr College, 1962).

25. Joyce Appleby, *Capitalism and a New Social Order: The Republican Vision of the 1790s* (New York, 1984), 60–61.

CHAPTER ONE. ENGLISH RADICALS

1. William Cobbett, *Porcupine's Works; containing various writings and selections; exhibiting a faithful picture of the United States of America* (London, 1801), vol. 1, 15.

2. "Peter Porcupine" [William Cobbett], *The Life and Adventures of Peter Porcupine,* 2nd ed. (Philadelphia, 1796), 13-19.

3. Caroline Robbins, *The Eighteenth-Century Commonwealthman* (New York, 1968), 271–319; J. G. A. Pocock, "Radical Criticism of the Whig Order in the Age between Revolutions," in Margaret Jacob and James Jacob, eds., *The Origins of Anglo-American Radicalism* (London: Allen and Unwin, 1984), 33–57; Linda Colley, "Eighteenth-Century English Radicalism before Wilkes," *Transactions of the Royal Historical Society,* 5th. Ser., 31 (1981): 1–19; H. T. Dickinson, "The Precursors of Political Radicalism in Augustan Britain," in Clyve Jones, ed., *Britain in the First Age of Party, 1680–1750* (London, 1987), 63–84.

4. John Brewer, "English Radicalism in the Age of George III," in J. G. A. Pocock, ed., *Three British Revolutions: 1641, 1688, 1776* (Princeton, 1980), 323–67.

5. John Brewer, *Party Ideology and Popular Politics at the Accession of George III* (Cambridge, 1981), 3, 21; Edward Royle and James Walvin, *English Radicals and Reformers, 1760–1848* (Lexington, 1982), 17–19; Albert Goodwin, *The Friends of Liberty: The English Democratic Movement in the Age of the French Revolution* (London, 1979), 45.

6. Brewer, *Party Ideology,* 274; Paul Langford, *Public Life and the Propertied Englishman, 1689–1798* (Oxford, 1991), 468; J. H. Plumb, "Merchant, Gentry and Intellectual: British Opinion and the American Revolution," in Charles W. Toth, ed., *Liberté, Égalité, Fraternité: The American Revolution and the European Response* (Troy, N.Y., 1989), 66.

7. [Philadelphia] *Pennsylvania Packet,* Jan. 14, 16, 1783; John Sainsbury, *Disaffected Patriots: London Supporters of Revolutionary America, 1769–1782* (Kingston, Ontario, 1987), 30. Almon had a financial interest in the London *Evening Post.*

8. D. H. Gilpatrick, "The English Background of John Miller," *The Furman Bulletin,* 20 (1938): 15.

9. Gilpatrick, "Miller," 16; Audrey Williamson, *Wilkes 'A Friend to Liberty'* (London, 1974), 163–64; Ian R. Christie, *Wilkes, Wyvill and Reform: The Parliamentary Reform Movement in British Politics, 1760–1785* (London, 1962), 47.

10. Gilpatrick, "Miller," 17–19.

11. J. C. D. Clark, *English Society, 1688–1832* (Cambridge, 1985), 309; Williamson, *Wilkes*, 17. Arians held that Christ, though divine, was created by and subordinate to God the Father.

12. Brewer, "English Radicalism," 342–43; James E. Bradley, *Religion, Revolution and English Radicalism: Non-conformity in Eighteenth-Century Politics and Society* (Cambridge, 1990), 58; Colin Bonwick, *English Radicals and the American Revolution* (Chapel Hill, N.C., 1977), 117.

13. Mark Philp, *Godwin's Political Justice* (London, 1986), 39; Bernard Semmel, *The Methodist Revolution* (London, 1974), 70.

14. Not all emigrant unitarians went to the United States. John Hurford Stone and Thomas Christie, for example, went to Paris, while Priestley's friend William Russell also finally settled in France.

15. Bradley, *Religion*, 4; H. T. Dickinson, *Liberty and Property: Political Ideology in Eighteenth-Century Britain* (New York, 1977), 240; E. P. Thompson, *The Making of the English Working Class* (London, 1968), 33.

16. Clark, *English Society*, 317; Bradley, *Religion*, xi.

17. Goodwin, *Friends of Liberty*, 77.

18. William Chamberlayne to Joseph White, Aug. 3, 1791, PRO HO42/19.

19. Michael R. Watts, *The Dissenters from the Reformation to the French Revolution* (Oxford, 1978), 482–83.

20. Bradley, *Religion*, 17, 38, 98–99, 113, passim.

21. John Seed, "Gentlemen Dissenters: The Social and Political Meanings of Rational Dissent in the 1770s and 1780s," *Historical Journal* 28 (1985): 308–9.

22. Joseph Priestley, *A View of the Principles and Conduct of the Protestant Dissenters*, in Rutt, ed., *Works*, vol. 22, 354.

23. Bradley, *Religion*, 92; Seed, "Gentlemen Dissenters," 302–3. For Priestley's own explanation for this decline, see *A Free Address to Protestant Dissenters, as Such* (1769), in Rutt, ed., *Works*, vol. 22, 289–93.

24. Clark, *English Society*, 318. Socinians rejected the divinity of Christ and the Trinity.

25. Watt, *Dissenters*, 474; Joseph Priestley, *The Memoirs of Dr. Joseph Priestley* (Northumberland, Pa., 1806), vol. 1, 57; Mark Philp, "Rational Religion and Political Radicalism in the 1790s," *Enlightenment and Dissent* 4 (1985): 36–37.

26. Ralph Eddowes, *The Unity of God, and the Worship That Is Due to HIM Alone* (Philadelphia, 1813), 14–15.

27. Priestley, *Free Address*, in Rutt, ed., *Works*, vol. 22, 256. See pp. 247–48 for Priestley's own list of corruptions.

28. Russell E. Richey, "The Origins of British Radicalism: The Changing Rationale for Dissent," *Eighteenth-Century Studies* 7 (1973–74): 189; Philp, "Rational Religion," 36–37.

29. Robbins, *Commonwealthman*, 324–35; Clark, *English Society*, 320.

30. Thompson, *Making of the English Working Class,* 31.

31. Isaac Kramnick, *Republicanism and Bourgeois Radicalism: Political Ideology in Late Eighteenth-Century England and America* (Ithaca and London, 1990), 22–23, 54, 43, 44. In the original version of this chapter, published as "Religion and Radicalism: English Political Thought in the Age of Revolution," *Political Theory* 5 (1977): 505–34, the adverb "nearly" was omitted. James J. Hoecker, *Joseph Priestly and the Idea of Progress* (New York, 1987), and Ursula Henriques, *Religious Toleration in England, 1787–1833* (London, 1961), also support variants of the "bourgeois radical" thesis.

32. Kramnick, *Republicanism,* 180, 45.

33. Joseph Priestley, *Essay on the First Principles of Government,* in Rutt, ed., *Works,* vol. 22, 14.

34. Ibid., 13. For analyses of Commonwealth ideology, see Bonwick, *English Radicals,* 13–26; Lance Banning, *The Jeffersonian Persuasion: Evolution of a Party Ideology* (Ithaca, N.Y., 1978), 21–69; Robbins, *Commonwealthman.*

35. Priestley, *Memoirs,* in Rutt, ed., *Works,* vol. 1, Part 1, 205.

36. Martin Fitzpatrick, "Heretical Religion and Radical Political Ideas in Late Eighteenth-Century England," in Eckhart Hellmuth, ed., *The Transformation of Political Culture* (Oxford, 1990), 363.

37. Priestley, *Free Address,* 249.

38. Lord Chief Justice Mansfield's decision in the sheriff's case in 1767, that "it was now no crime for a man who is within the description of the Toleration Act that he is a Dissenter," seemed to give protection to the orthodox. Richard B. Barlow, *Citizenship and Conscience* (Philadelphia, 1962), 160.

39. G. M. Ditchfield, "Anti-Trinitarianism and Toleration in Late Eighteenth-Century British Politics: The Unitarian Petition of 1792," *Journal of Ecclesiastical History* 42 (1991): 40–41.

40. Joseph Priestley, *A View of the Principles and Conduct of the Protestant Dissenters, with respect to the Civil and Ecclesiastical Constitution of England* (1769), in Rutt, ed., *Works,* vol. 22, 352; Seed, "Gentleman Dissenters," 316.

41. Rev. Robert Smith, quoted in Clark, *English Society,* 320.

42. Robert Hole, "English sermons and tracts as media of debate on the French Revolution, 1789–99," in Mark Philp, ed., *The French Revolution and British Popular Politics* (Cambridge, 1991), 34–35; Clark, *English Society,* 281.

43. Raymond V. Holt, *The Unitarian Contribution to Social Progress in England* (London, 1938), 67. Priestley was aware of the rise of Deism, but saw his brand of Unitarianism as an antidote. He blamed the Church of England for the growing popularity of Deist ideas. *Principles of Protestant Dissenters,* in Rutt, ed., *Works,* vol. 22, 348.

44. Philp, "Rational Religion," 37.

45. Priestley, *Free Address,* 257. See also similar statements by Cooper, quoted in Dumas Malone, *The Public Life of Thomas Cooper, 1783–1839* (New Haven, 1926; reprinted 1979), 18, and Thomas Paine, *Rights of Man,* Part 2, in Philip S. Foner, ed., *The Complete Writings of Thomas Paine* (New York, 1945), vol. 1, 354.

46. Cobbett, *Porcupine's Works*, vol. 9, 209.

47. Priestley, *Free Address*, 256.

48. *Morning Chronicle*, March 7, 1793, quoted in R. B. Rose, "The Priestley Riots of 1791," *Past and Present*, vol. 18 (1960), 86n.

49. Margaret E. Leslie, "The Social and Political Thought of Joseph Priestley" (Ph.D. diss., Cambridge University, 1966), 7; Priestley, *Memoirs*, vol. 1, 60–61; Holt, *Unitarian Contribution*, 90.

50. Cooper in Appendix to *The Memoirs of Dr. Joseph Priestley* (1806 ed.), vol. 2, 354–55; Fitzpatrick, "Heretical Religion," 364n; Clark, *English Society*, 333.

51. James Boswell, quoted in Goodwin, *Friends of Liberty*, 54.

52. Verner W. Crane, "The Club of Honest Whigs: Friends of Science and Liberty," *WMQ* 3rd Ser., 23 (1966): 210–33. Another exile of 1794, Benjamin Vaughan, was also a member, as was the Whig Bishop, Jonathan Shipley, a kinsman of the Shipleys of Uttoxeter who emigrated at the same time. Fifteen of the approximately twenty-five members were Rational Protestants.

53. Priestley, *Memoirs*, vol. 2, 448.

54. Joseph Priestley, "An Address to Protestant Dissenters of All Denominations," in Rutt, ed., *Works*, vol. 22, 483; Priestley, *First Principles*, 11.

55. Priestley, *First Principles*, 11.

56. Priestley, *First Principles*, 12, 37 (my italics).

57. For as many as thirteen possible Unitarians in Parliament between 1790 and 1820, including Benjamin Vaughan, see R. G. Thorne, ed., *The History of Parliament: The House of Commons, 1790–1820* (London, 1986), vol. 1, 295.

58. For Blackburne's fears of an American episcopate, which would augment the Crown's powers at the expense of the public's, see Sainsbury, *Disaffected Patriots*, 10–11.

59. G. M. Ditchfield, "The Subscription Issue in British Parliamentary Politics, 1772–79," *Parliamentary History* 7 (1988): 47. I am indebted to this article for much of what follows on the politics of subscription.

60. Barlow, *Citizenship*, 168–71. A more restricted bill became law in 1779, despite the absence of outside pressure.

61. Rev. W. Cole to Father Charles Bedinfield, June 7, 1771, in Rutt, *Works*, vol. 1, 140–41n; Barlow, *Citizenship*, 183–85.

62. John Money, *Experience and Identity: Birmingham and the West Midlands, 1760–1800* (Manchester, 1977), 189–90; Clark, *English Society*, 336.

63. Joseph Priestley, *The Case of Poor Emigrants Recommended* (Philadelphia, 1797), 23.

64. Bonwick, *English Radicals*, 44–52.

65. Historians arguing that the Dissenters' support of America has been exaggerated include Sainsbury, *Disaffected Patriots*, 80; Christie, *Stress and Stability*, 46; Seed, "Gentleman Dissenters," 324. Bradley, *Religion*, 6, 13, argues that the majority of Dissenters "were clearly pro-American in orientation," but his evidence is localized.

66. Bonwick, *English Radicals*, 99–101.

67. Bonwick, "Dissenters," 105; Priestley to Rev. Rotherham, April 1778, in Rutt, ed., *Works,* vol. 1, 313–14.

68. The classic account of Wyvill is Christie, *Wilkes, Wyvill and Reform.*

69. Fitzpatrick, "Heretical Religion," 353; Thorne, ed., *History of Parliament,* vol. 5, 442; Goodwin, *Friends of Liberty,* 103; James Walvin, "English Democratic Societies and Popular Radicalism, 1791–1800" (D.Phil. diss., University of York, 1970), 748.

70. See below, 282–88.

71. J. E. Cookson, *The Friends of Peace: Anti-War Liberalism in England, 1793–1815* (Cambridge, 1982), 1.

72. Seymour Drescher, *Capitalism and Antislavery: British Mobilisation in Comparative Perspective* (New York, 1987), 209n, 67, 71.

73. Ian Sellers, "William Roscoe, The Roscoe Circle and Radical Politics in Liverpool, 1787–1807," *Transactions of the Liverpool and Cheshire Historical Society* 120 (1968): 49; Money, *Experience and Identity,* 217; Watts, *Dissenters,* 479.

74. Goodwin, *Friends of Liberty,* 161; Priestley to Newcome Cappe, Jan. 23, 1788, in Rutt, ed., *Works,* vol. 2, 7; Jack Fruchtman, Jr., "Politics and the Apocalypse: The Republic and the Millennium in Late Eighteenth-Century English Political Thought," *Studies in Eighteenth Century Culture* 20 (1981): 158.

75. James Walvin, "The Rise of British Popular Sentiment for Abolition, 1787–1832," in Christine Bolt and Seymour Drescher, eds., *Anti-Slavery, Religion and Reform: Essays in Memory of Roger Anstey* (Folkstone, 1980), 151; Drescher, *Capitalism,* 70.

76. For Walker, see Frida Knight, *The Strange Case of Thomas Walker* (London, 1957).

77. Malone, *Cooper,* 4–6; Patricia K. Hill, "Thomas Cooper," in Joseph O. Baylen and Norbert J. Gossman, eds., *Biographical Dictionary of Modern British Radicals* (Hassocks, 1979), 95.

78. Holt, *Unitarian Contribution,* 87.

79. Thomas Cooper, *Letters on the Slave Trade: First Published in Wheeler's Manchester Chronicle* (Manchester, 1787), 4.

80. Ibid., 31.

81. Ibid., 27.

82. Goodwin, *Friends of Liberty,* 90–91; Henriques, *Religious Toleration,* 59. Benjamin Vaughan was a member of the London committee and Russell, who had been in regular contact with London Dissenters since 1784, was an associate member. Thomas W. Davis, ed., *Committees for Repeal of the Test and Corporation Acts: Minutes, 1786–90 and 1827–8* (London, 1978), 3; Money, *Experience and Identity,* 220; Lindsey to Russell, Jan. 30, 1784, PRO HO42/19.

83. Priestley to Theophilus Lindsey, Oct. 21, 1789, in Rutt, *Works,* vol. 1, ii, 37.

84. Samuel H. Jeyes, *The Russells of Birmingham in the French Revolution and in America, 1791–1814* (London, 1911), 8–9.

85. Priestley, *Memoirs,* vol. 1, 94.

86. Samuel Haywood to William Russell, Oct. 27, 1789, PRO HO42/19.

87. Goodwin, *Friends of Liberty*, 90; G. M. Ditchfield, "The Campaign in Lancashire and Cheshire for the Repeal of the Test and Corporation Acts, 1787-1790," *Transactions of the Historical Society of Lancashire and Cheshire* 126 (1977): 118-19.

88. The repeal agitation of 1787-90 "was altogether without any concurrence of mine." Priestley, *Memoirs*, vol. 1, 116-18.

89. Joseph Priestley, "The Importance and Extent of Free Inquiry in Matters of Religion," quoted in Clark, *English Society*, 341. Money, *Experience and Identity*, 219, points out in mitigation that Priestley continued: "until things are ripe for such a revolution, it would be absurd to expect it, and in vain to attempt it."

90. For a moderate Dissenter's uneasiness with Priestley's reckless extremism, see Heywood to Russell, Nov. 25, 1789, PRO HO42/19.

91. Priestley to Lindsey, March 29, 1790, in Rutt, *Works*, vol. 1, ii, 61.

92. Thompson, *Making of the English Working Class*, 79; Rose, "Priestley Riots," 71.

93. Rose, "Priestley Riots," 70; Money, *Experience and Identity*, 220; Seed, "Gentleman Dissenters," 306.

94. Only a month before the Priestley riots the Unitarians in Birmingham were considering opening a new chapel for the overflow of new members. At the same time the anti-trinitarian Swedenborgians opened "an elegant chapel here." Priestley to Rev. John Bretland, June 26, 1791, in Rutt, ed., *Works*, vol. 1, ii, 112-13.

95. Money, *Experience and Identity*, 220, 127-28.

96. Ralph Eddowes, *Sermons Delivered Before the First Society of Unitarian Christians in the City of Philadelphia* (Philadelphia, 1817), v-vii.

97. Eddowes's counsel was Serjeant Adair, a Wilkite lawyer who supported the American patriot cause and the demands of the Dissenters. Clark, *English Society*, 312.

98. Ralph Eddowes, *State of Facts Relating to the Franchises of the City of Chester, and all other Corporations in the Kingdom* (Chester, 1788), 1-2; Eddowes, *The Whole Proceedings, in Several Informations . . . against Mr. Thomas Amery . . . and Mr. John Monk . . . on the Relation of Ralph Eddowes* (Chester, 1791); D. H. Weinglass, "Ralph Eddowes," in Baylen and Gossman, eds., *Biographical Dictionary*, 145-47.

99. Eddowes, *Whole Proceedings*, Appendix 43.

100. For Eddowes's historical account of the origins of annual elections based on the idea of the ancient constitution, see *Whole Proceedings*, i-ii.

101. Eddowes to William Roscoe, quoted in Weinglass, "Eddowes," 148.

102. For loyalist activities in Chester, see Richard Mytton to John Moore, Feb. 2, 1793, BL Add.MSS. 16925.

103. Sellers, "William Roscoe," 51.

104. T. Hartley to John Moore, Dec. 1, 1792, BL Add.MSS. 16920.

105. Quoted in Weinglass, "Eddowes," 147.

106. Priestley to Lindsey, Jan. 27, Feb. 26, 1790, in Rutt, *Works*, vol. 1, ii, 52, 54. For a suggestion that Church and King disturbances were planned in March 1790, see J. L. Lotichius to Pitt, July 17, 1791, PRO HO42/19.

107. Priestley to Lindsey, March 11, 1790, Priestley to Richard Price, Jan. 27, 1791, in Rutt, *Works*, vol. 1, ii, 56, 99.

108. Quoted in Ditchfield, "Anti-Trinitarianism," 45.

109. Hutton, quoted in Rutt, *Works*, vol. 1, ii, 188n.

110. Priestley to Russell, July 29, 1791, in Rutt, *Works*, vol. 1, ii, 125.

111. Priestley, *Memoirs*, vol. 1, 202.

112. Russell to Chamberlayne, July 31, 1791, PRO HO42/19.

113. Rutt, *Works*, vol. 1, ii, 185. Seventeen rioters were eventually tried, four were found guilty, and three were hanged.

114. On the morning before the riots, the Unitarian chapels had been chalked with: "This barn to lett." Earl of Aylesford to Home Office, July 14, 1791, PRO HO42/19.

115. Goodwin, *Friends of Liberty*, 181–82; Jeyes, *Russells*, 33; Rose, "Priestley," 74; "Intelligence from Birmingham received in London, Sunday July 17, 1791," PRO HO42/19.

116. John Caldwell, "Particulars of [the] History of a North County [*sic*] Irish Family," PRONI T3541/5/3, 79.

117. Priestley to Adam Walker, Oct. 21, 1791, in Rutt, *Works*, vol. 1, ii, 38.

118. Money, *Experience and Identity*, 233.

119. *BWJ*, Oct. 24, 31, 1793.

120. Walvin, "English Democratic Societies," 617.

121. Malone, *Cooper*, 27.

122. Quoted in Ditchfield, "Anti-Trinitarianism," 59.

123. For the key role Rational Dissent played in "providing a social substratum for radicalism," see Philp, "Rational Religion," 36–41.

124. For a further analysis of the radical emigrants' indebtedness to Paine's ideas, see below, 67–68, 225–28.

125. Goodwin, *Friends of Liberty*, 177.

126. Royle and Walvin, *English Radicals*, 54.

127. Quoted in Knight, *Walker*, 63–64.

128. See, for example, *Manchester Herald*, April 28, 1792; Knight, *Walker*, 71. By presbyterian Cooper meant moderate.

129. John Wood, *A Full Exposition of the Clintonian Faction and the Society of the Columbian Illuminati* (Newark, N.J., [1802]), 11.

130. Walvin, "English Democratic Societies," 626.

131. Goodwin, *Friends of Liberty*, 147; Walvin, "English Democratic Societies," 626–27.

132. Goodwin, *Friends of Liberty*, 201–2.

133. Malone, *Cooper*, 34.

134. Thomas Cooper, *A Reply to Mr. Burke's Invective against Mr. Cooper, and Mr. Watt* (Manchester, 1792), Appendix, 86.

135. Goodwin, *Friends of Liberty*, 202–3.

136. *Manchester Herald*, June 2, 1792.

137. Pauline Handforth, "Manchester Radical Politics, 1789–1794," *Transactions of the Lancashire and Cheshire Antiquarian Society* 66 (1956): 98; Ditchfield, "Lancashire and Cheshire," 131.

138. On sale in Manchester was a handkerchief with a motif of Paine, Marat, Robespierre, and Brissot shaking hands with the devil, and the words: "Father Beelzy, I'll lye and sware with you or any of your dark subjects."

139. Walvin, "English Democratic Societies," 628–29.

140. Clive Emsley, "The London 'Insurrection' of December 1792: Fact, Fiction, or Fantasy?" *Journal of British Studies* 17 (1978): 66–86.

141. Quoted in Knight, *Walker*, 92.

142. Col. H. De Lancey to Nepean, Nov. 30, 1792, PRO HO42/22; Digby Hamilton to Home Office, Dec. 14, 1792, PRO HO42/23; Edward Roberts to J. Moore, Dec. 13, 1792, BL Add.MSS. 16922.

143. Goodwin, *Friends of Liberty*, 268–69.

144. Handforth, "Manchester Radical Politics," 99–101.

145. Walker, quoted in Knight, *Walker*, 94.

146. Ray Boston, "The Impact of 'Foreign Liars' on the American Press (1790–1800)," *Journalism Quarterly* 50 (1973): 724; Handforth, "Manchester Radical Politics," 101.

147. Goodwin, *Friends of Liberty*, 271–72; Knight, *Walker*, 119.

148. Knight, *Walker*, 126.

149. John W. Francis, *Old New York: or, Reminiscences of the Past Sixty Years* (New York, 1865), 335; T. B. Howell and T. J. Howell, eds., *A Complete Collection of State Trials* (London, 1817), vol. 23, 1067–68.

150. See below, 47, for Benjamin Vaughan's advice to the Home Office about prosecuting Cooper.

151. Quoted in Knight, *Walker*, 146.

152. Thomas Cooper, *Some Information Respecting America* (Dublin, 1794).

153. Thompson, *Making of the English Working Class;* Gwyn A. Williams, *Artisans and Sans-Culottes*, 2nd ed. (London, 1989); Goodwin, *Friends of Liberty;* Hone, *For the Cause of Truth;* Roger Wells, *Insurrection: The British Experience* (Gloucester, 1983); Iain McCalman, *Radical Underworld: Prophets, Revolutionaries and Pornographers in London, 1795–1840* (Cambridge, 1988).

154. For more detail on motivations for emigration, see below, 163–67.

155. Alan Wharam, *The Treason Trials, 1794* (Leicester, 1992), 133; Thale, ed., *London Corresponding Society*, 241.

156. Penelope Corfield, "John Thelwall in Wales: New Documentary Evidence," *Bulletin of the Institute of Historical Research* 59 (1986): 231–39; E. P. Thompson, "Hunting the Jacobin Fox," *Past and Present* 142 (1994): 111–23.

157. Thale, ed., *London Corresponding Society*, passim; Interrogation of Benjamin Binns, March 1798, ISPO Reb. Pap. 620/36/22.

158. [John Binns], *Recollections of the Life of John Binns: Twenty-Nine Years in Europe and Fifty-Three in the United States* (Philadelphia, 1854), 66.

159. Joseph Guest's affidavit, PRO TS11/541/1755.

160. Daniel Parker Coke to White [Treasury Solicitor], Aug. 17, 1797, PRO TS11/541/1755; *The Trial of John Binns, deputy of the London Corresponding Society, for Sedition* (Birmingham, 1797).

161. Binns, *Recollections*, 82; McCalman, *Radical Underworld*, 10.

162. For the early lives of the Binns brothers, see 83–84.

163. *The Times*, July 26, 1793. As his comments on the churches suggest, it is possible Cook was a Unitarian, certainly a republican Puritan of the old school. See Priestley to Lindsey, Aug. 5, 1793, in Rutt, *Works*, vol. 1, ii, 206.

164. *BWJ*, Oct. 31, 1793; BL Add.MSS. 27809, fo. 269; BL Add.MSS. 27812, fos. 76–78; Howell and Howell, eds., *State Trials*, vol. 22, 922.

165. For other examples, see *BWJ*, April 11, Aug. 1, 1793. For John Pearce, an LCS delegate and tallow chandler who emigrated to America in about August 1793, see PRO TS11/956/3501.

166. Most of the 200 trials in the 1790s for treason, seditious words, or seditious libel resulted from local loyalist or individual JPs prosecutions. Clive Emsley, "Revolution, War and the Nation State: The British and French Experiences 1789–1801," in Philp, ed., *French Revolution and British Popular Politics*, 114.

167. Williams, *Artisans*, 2nd ed., xvi.

168. Lynn Hunt, *Politics, Culture, and Class in the French Revolution* (London, 1984), 20–21.

169. Williams, *Artisans*, 2nd ed., xviii–xix.

170. Olivia Smith, *The Politics of Language, 1791–1819* (Oxford, 1986), 77. See also Gregory Brotherson, "The Social and Political Thought of John Horne Tooke" (M.Phil. diss., Murdoch University, 1993), chaps. 12 and 19.

171. At one point James Ridgway, Henry Symonds, Daniel Holt, and Daniel Isaac Eaton, all printers and publishers, were in Newgate simultaneously. They shared space with Rev. William Winterbotham, who was also busily writing. Michael Durey, "William Winterbotham's Trumpet of Sedition: Religious Dissent and Political Radicalism in the 1790s," *Journal of Religious History* 19 (1995): 141–57.

172. Lucyle Werkmeister, *A Newspaper History of England, 1792–1793* (Lincoln, Nebr., 1967); Donald Read, *Press and People, 1790–1850: Opinion in Three English Cities* (London, 1961).

173. Werkmeister, *Newspaper History*, 21.

174. *Exam.*, Sept. 18, 1802.

175. John Bernard, *Retrospections of America, 1797–1811*, ed. Mrs. B. Bernard (New York, 1887), 73–76.

176. Williams's own justification can be found in [Philadelphia] *Aurora*, July 3, 4, 1799. *DNB*, vol. 22, 422–23; *Porcupine's Works*, vol. 10, 75; Werkmeister, *Newspaper History*, 89. After Williams's death in poverty from typhus in Brooklyn in 1818, the Irish poet Thomas Moore wrote that a friend had said that "Anthony Pasquin (who was a very dirty fellow) died of a cold caught from washing his face."

177. Simon Schama, *Citizens* (London, 1989).

178. James L. Clifford, "Robert Merry—A Pre-Byronic Hero," *Bulletin of John Rylands Library* 27 (1942): 74.

179. Werkmeister, *Newspaper History*, 39.

180. Goodwin, *Friends of Liberty*, 179.

181. Merry also produced a number of mock advertisements and playbills that satirized Pitt. I am grateful to Jon Mee for this information.

182. Clifford, "Merry," 94; Werkmeister, *Newspaper History*, 92–95.

183. For the troubles that befell William Cobbett when he became entangled in this same circle at about this time, see Michael Durey, "William Cobbett, Military Corruption and London Radicalism in the Early 1790s," *Proceedings of the American Philosophical Society* 131 (1987): 348–66.

184. Smith, *Politics of Language*, 35.

185. McCalman, *Radical Underworld*.

186. Thompson, *Making of the English Working Class*, 155; Williams, *Artisans*, 98; P. Mary Ashraf, *The Life and Times of Thomas Spence* (Newcastle-upon-Tyne, 1983), 55–56.

187. "Citizen" Richard Lee, *King Killing* (London, 1794).

188. Twomey, *Jacobins and Jeffersonians*, 96.

189. For the importance of London print culture in the continuity of seventeenth-century sectarian radicalism and radical criticism in the following century, see J. G. A. Pocock, "Radical Criticism," 34. See also Christopher Hill, *The Experience of Defeat: Milton and Some Contemporaries* (London, 1984), 42.

190. William Hamilton Reid, *The Rise and Dissolution of the Infidel Societies in This Metropolis* (1800; reprinted London, 1971), 6; Information from Jon Mee.

191. Bertrand H. Bronson, *Facets of the Enlightenment: Studies in English Literature and Its Contexts* (Berkeley, Calif., 1968), 266–97; David Masson, ed., *The Collected Writings of Thomas De Quincey* (London, 1897), vol. 3, 93–120; Brian Wall, "The Social and Political Thought of John 'Walking' Stewart" (B. A. Hons. diss., Murdoch University, 1994).

192. Daniel L. McCue, Jr., "Daniel Isaac Eaton and 'Politics for the People' " (Ph.D. diss., Columbia University, 1974).

193. Ibid., 58–59.

194. For the image of the French sans-culottes as "The People, Eater of Kings," see Hunt, *Politics, Culture, and Class*, 108.

195. Mark Philp, "The Fragmented Ideology of Reform," in Philp, ed., *French Revolution and British Popular Politics*, 51–54.

196. This is not to suggest that Godwin's *ideas* failed to be taken to the United States; they were. Binns was a member of the London Philomethean Society (a debating club) with Godwin and Holcroft. They were, he claimed, "among the most diffuse and tiresome of speakers." Binns, *Recollections*, 45. Mary Wollstonecraft's brother was in Philadelphia in the mid-1790s, where for a time he was in partnership with the Irish exile Hamilton Rowan.

197. George S. Rowell, "Benjamin Vaughan—Patriot, Scholar, Diplomat," *Magazine of History* 22 (1916): 45–47; Crane, "Honest Whigs," 220–21.

198. John H. Sheppard, *Reminiscences of the Vaughan Family* (Boston, 1865), 8–9; Goodwin, *Friends of Liberty*, 103.

199. Benjamin Vaughan to Home Office, Dec. 7, 1792, PRO HO42/23.

200. [Benjamin Vaughan], *Two Papers by the Calm Observer, not printed in the Collection of his Letters Extracted from the Morning Chronicle* (n.p., 1795), 28–30.

201. Ibid., 18.

202. Ibid., 19.

203. Ibid., 28.

204. Thorne, ed., *History of Parliament*, vol. 5, 443.

205. Vaughan, *Two Papers*, 1–2.

206. Ibid., 11.

207. Vaughan to [Nepean], Nov. 30, 1792, PRO HO42/22.

208. Vaughan to Nepean, Nov. 30, 1792.

209. Vaughan to [Nepean], Dec. 7, 1792, PRO HO42/23.

210. Frank MacDermott, "The Jackson Episode in 1794," *Studies* (Ireland) (1938), 77–81.

211. *Proceedings on the Trial of William Stone, Merchant, for High Treason*, in Howell and Howell, eds., *State Trials*, 25, 1173, 1182–86.

212. Rowell, "Vaughan," 51–52; Thorne, ed., *History of Parliament*, vol. 5, 443.

213. Paine to Danton, May 6, 1793, in Moncure Daniel Conway, ed., *The Writings of Thomas Paine* (New York, 1967), vol. 3, 135.

214. Paine to Thomas Jefferson, April 20, 1793, in Conway, ed., *Writings of Paine*, vol. 3, 133.

215. For the Shipley family of Uttoxeter, [Philadelphia] *Aurora*, Oct. 30, 1794. For Henry Toulmin, *DAB*, vol. 9, 601–2. For James Redman and family, Richard Bache to Benjamin Franklin Bache, Feb. 7, 1793, Bache Papers, Castle Collection, American Philosophical Society. For William Wells, Mrs. W. Byng Kenrick, ed., *Chronicles of a Non-Conformist Family: The Kenricks of Wynne Hall, Exeter and Birmingham* (Birmingham, 1932), 84.

216. Gwyn A. Williams, *The Search for Beulah Land* (London, 1980).

CHAPTER TWO. SCOTTISH RADICALS

1. John Galt, *Annals of the Parish* (Oxford, 1986), 88, 128.

2. W. Hamish Fraser, *Conflict and Class. Scottish Workers, 1700–1838* (Edinburgh, 1988), 11–14.

3. R. A. Houston, "The Demographic Regime," in T. M. Devine and Rosalind Mitchison, eds., *People and Society in Scotland, Volume 1, 1760–1830* (Edinburgh, 1988),

12–14; Richard G. Gallin, "Scottish Radicalism, 1792–1794" (Ph.D. diss., Columbia University, 1979), 19.

4. Quoted in Christina Bewley, *Muir of Huntershill* (Oxford, 1981), 2. The English, too, were reluctant to recognize the Scots' achievements. Davis D. McElroy, *Scotland's Age of Improvement: A Survey of Eighteenth-Century Literary Clubs and Societies* (Pullman, 1969), 71.

5. The literature on the Scottish Enlightenment is increasingly large, but see in particular Anand C. Chitnis, *The Scottish Enlightenment: A Social History* (London, 1976); Alexander Murdoch and Richard B. Sher, "Literary and Learned Culture," in Devine and Mitchison, eds., *People and Society*, 127–42.

6. The most recent analysis of this process is Linda Colley, *Britons: Forging the Nation, 1707–1837* (New Haven, 1992), 117–32. See also Angus Calder, *Revolutionary Empire: The Rise of the English-Speaking Empires from the Fifteenth Century to the 1780s* (New York, 1981), 532–39, 676–82.

7. N. T. Phillipson, "Lawyers, Landowners, and the Civic Leadership of Post-Union Scotland," *Juridical Review* 21 (1976): 97–120; N. T. Phillipson, "The Scottish Enlightenment," in Roy Porter and Mikulas Teich, eds., *The Enlightenment in National Context* (Cambridge, 1981), 19–40.

8. Phillipson, "Lawyers, Landowners," 99.

9. Chitnis, *Scottish Enlightenment*, 5; Phillipson, "Scottish Enlightenment," 19; N. T. Phillipson, "Towards a Definition of the Scottish Enlightenment," in Paul Fritz and David Williams, eds., *City and Society in the Eighteenth Century* (Toronto, 1973), 125–26.

10. Phillipson, "Scottish Enlightenment," 26–27.

11. T. M. Devine, "The Failure of Radical Reform in Scotland in the Late Eighteenth Century: The Social and Economic Context," in T. M. Devine, ed., *Conflict and Stability in Scottish Society 1700–1850* (Edinburgh, 1990), 56.

12. Michael Fry, *The Dundas Despotism* (Edinburgh, 1992), chap. 2.

13. Although Adam Smith and David Hume thought that the American colonies might be given independence without harm to the mother country, most of the Scottish literati favored the suppression of the rebels by force. Bruce Lenman, *Integration, Enlightenment and Industrialisation: Scotland, 1746–1832* (London, 1981), 60–61.

14. Mrs. McTier to Samuel McTier, Oct. 2, [1782], in *The Drennan Letters*, 9.

15. Drennan to Samuel McTier, Sept. 1782, in *The Drennan Letters*, 9.

16. Ian R. Christie, *Stress and Stability in Late Eighteenth-Century Britain: Reflections on the British Avoidance of Revolution* (Oxford, 1984), 93; Lenman, *Integration, Enlightenment and Industrialisation*, 90.

17. Devine, "Failure of Radical Reform," 59.

18. R. A. Houston, *Scottish Literacy and Scottish Identity: Illiteracy and Society in Scotland and Northern England, 1600–1800* (Cambridge, 1985); Murdoch and Sher, "Literary and Learned Culture," 128.

19. Robert Anderson, "In Search of the 'Lad of Parts': the Mythical History of Scottish Education," *History Workshop Journal* 19 (1985): 83–85.

20. *DNB*, vol. 2, 22–23; R. S. Walker, *James Beattie's London Diary, 1773* (Aberdeen, 1946), 13–14; M. Forbes, *Beattie and His Friends* (London, 1904), 10; Robert Chambers, *A Biographical Dictionary of Eminent Scotsmen* (Edinburgh, 1835), vol. 1, 109–10.

21. *The Annual Biography and Obituary for the Year 1818* (London, n.d.), vol. 2, 83–99; *Gentleman's Magazine* 87 (1817): 647–48; Chambers, *Biographical Dictionary*, vol. 7, 378–79.

22. Fry, *Dundas Despotism*, 20; Phillipson, "Scottish Enlightenment," 37; George Dempster to William Pultney, Dec. 1792, PRO HO102/6.

23. William Creech, "A letter respecting the situation of the schoolmasters of Scotland," in Creech, *Fugitive Pieces* (Edinburgh, 1815), 210.

24. Lenman, *Integration*, 35–36; Bewley, *Muir*, 9; T. C. Smout, *A History of the Scottish People, 1560–1830* (London, 1985), 351–52.

25. W. R. Brock and C. H. Brock, *Scotus Americanus* (Edinburgh, 1981), 2–18.

26. C. Duncan Rice, "Scottish Enlightenment, American Revolution and Atlantic Reform," in O. D. Edwards and G. Shepperson, eds., *Scotland, Europe and the American Revolution* (Edinburgh, 1976), 78; Smout, *Scottish People*, 246.

27. Gerald Newman, *The Rise of English Nationalism* (New York, 1987), 92–93. The number of printing presses in Scotland increased markedly in the second half of the century; twenty-nine existed in Edinburgh in 1779, and others were scattered throughout the provincial towns. But most publishers preferred to publish classical texts or English books not protected by copyright. See NLS, *Four Hundred and Fifty Years of Scottish Printing* (Edinburgh, 1958), 10–11; S. H. Steinberg, *Five Hundred Years of Printing*, 2nd ed. (London, 1959), 146.

28. W. E. S. Thomas, *The Philosophic Radicals* (Oxford, 1979), 17.

29. Phillipson, "Scottish Enlightenment," 26–27; John A. Fairley, "The Pantheon: An Old Edinburgh Debating Society," *The Book of the Old Edinburgh Club*, vol. 1 (1908), 47.

30. Fairley, "The Pantheon," 50, 70, 72.

31. Nicholas Phillipson, "Adam Smith as Civic Moralist," in Istvan Holt and Michael Ignatieff, eds., *Wealth and Virtue* (Cambridge, 1983), 199.

32. John D. Brims, "The Scottish Democratic Movement in the Age of the French Revolution" (Ph.D. diss., Edinburgh University, 1983), 98.

33. Chambers, *Biographical Dictionary*, vol. 3, 280–82.

34. William Gillan to J. T. Callender, May 14, 1792, PRO HO102/7.

35. McElroy, *Scotland's Age of Improvement*, 87; Phillipson, "Definition of the Scottish Enlightenment," 137–38.

36. W. J. Couper, *The Edinburgh Periodical Press* (Stirling, 1908), vol. 2, 152–55.

37. *The Mirror*, No. 88 (March 1780), 349–52.

38. Robert Darnton, *The Literary Underground of the Old Regime* (Cambridge, Mass., 1982).

39. Fairley, "Pantheon," 65; Chitnis, *The Scottish Enlightenment*, 61–62.

40. *Edinburgh Evening Courant*, Sept. 6, 1794.

41. Robert Cantwell, *Alexander Wilson: Naturalist and Pioneer* (Philadelphia, 1961),

16, 60; Robert Brown, *Paisley Poets, with Brief Memoirs of Them, and Selections from Their Poetry* (n.p., 1889), vol. 1, 62.

42. [Thomas Crichton], *Biographical Sketches of the Late Alexander Wilson, Communicated in a Series of Letters to a Young Friend* (Paisley, 1819), 35.

43. James Kennedy, *Treason!!! or Not Treason!!! alias The Weavers Budget* (London, 1795?), 23.

44. Cantwell, *Wilson*, 16.

45. James Kennedy's name first appears in the Edinburgh directories in 1790.

46. Alexander Wilson to William Mitchell, Nov. 21, 1790, in Clark Hunter, ed., *The Life and Letters of Alexander Wilson* (Philadelphia, 1983), 140.

47. Wilson to David Brodie, Nov. 23, 1792, in Hunter, ed., *Wilson*, 145.

48. Cantwell, *Wilson*, 43.

49. Ibid., 31.

50. Alexander Wilson to William Mitchell, Nov. 21, 1790, Wilson to David Brodie, April 28, 1788, in Hunter, ed., *Wilson*, 141, 119–20.

51. Wilson to Thomas Crichton, Sept. 20, 1790, Wilson to David Wilson, June 6, 1811, in Hunter, ed., *Wilson*, 136, 386.

52. Cantwell, *Wilson*, 49–51; Kennedy, *Treason*, 24.

53. Kennedy, *Treason*, 24. Hopetoun Jean was Lady Jane Hope, elder sister of the Earl of Hopetoun, whom Dundas married as his second wife in 1792. Fry, *Dundas Despotism*, 157.

54. Brown, *Paisley Poets*, 67; Wilson to Thomas Crichton, Oct. 28, 1811, in Hunter, ed., *Wilson*, 392.

55. Crichton, *Wilson*, 22; Cantwell, *Wilson*, 58.

56. Wilson to Crichton, Nov. 2, 1790, in Hunter, ed., *Wilson*, 139.

57. Wilson to William Mitchell, Nov. 21, 1790, in Hunter, ed., *Wilson*, 141.

58. Wilson to Crichton, Nov. 2, 1790, in Hunter, ed., *Wilson*, 137–38.

59. [Richmond, Va.] *Recorder*, Jan. 12, 1803; *Exam.*, Nov. 21, 1800. A full account of Callender's life can be found in Michael Durey, *"With the Hammer of Truth": James Thomson Callender and America's Early National Heroes* (Charlottesville, Va., 1990).

60. [J. T. Callender], "The Present State of Parnassus," in Callender, ed., *Miscellanies in Prose and Verse*, 2nd ed. (Edinburgh, 1792), 327.

61. Robert Anderson, *Life of Samuel Johnson LLD*, 3rd ed. (Edinburgh, 1815), 231.

62. Callender to Thomas Jefferson, May 28, 1796, in W. C. Ford, ed., "Thomas Jefferson and James Thomson Callender," *New England Historical and Genealogical Register* 51–52 (1896–97): 325–26.

63. [J. T. Callender], *Deformities of Dr. Samuel Johnson* (Edinburgh, 1782); [J. T. Callender], *A Critical Review of the Works of Dr. Samuel Johnson* (Edinburgh, 1783).

64. Callender, *Deformities*, 12, 27, v.

65. Bernard Tucker, *Jonathan Swift* (Dublin, 1983); R. J. Cook, *Jonathan Swift as Tory Pamphleteer* (Seattle, 1967).

66. Jonathan Swift, "Verses on the Union," in C. J. Horne, ed., *Swift on His Age* (London, 1953), 127.

67. Callender, *Deformities*, 12.

68. Callender, *Critical Review*, iii.

69. Michael Durey, "The Radical Critique of 'Old Corruption' and the Beginnings of Public Service Reform in Late Eighteenth-Century Scotland: The Edinburgh Sasine Office as a Case Study," *Scottish Tradition* 16 (1991): 33–55.

70. J. Ramsay, *Scotland and Scotsmen in the Eighteenth Century* (Edinburgh, 1888), vol. 1, 379; *Scots Magazine* 51 (1789): 411.

71. Ramsay, *Scotland and Scotsmen*, 370.

72. John Kay, *Original Portraits* (Edinburgh, 1879), vol. 1, 24; William Forbes to George Chalmers, May 21, 1794, Edinburgh University Special Collections Department, Ms. La.11.451/2.

73. John Pringle to Henry Dundas, Jan. 7, 1793, PRO HO102/5; Robert Dundas to Henry Dundas, Jan. 13, 1793, PRO HO102/7.

74. Durey, *Callender*, 23–25.

75. Callender, ed., "On the Diversities of Life," *Miscellanies in Prose and Verse*, 36. Callender's verse made no great mark on the contemporary literary world, but a generation later, when Gardenstone was thought to be the author, it was regarded with some respect, one critic suggesting it to be the best Scottish satire of the previous fifty years. [Society of Ancient Scots], *Lives of the Scottish Poets* (London, 1822), vol. 3, 90. I find this opinion hard to fathom.

76. [J. T. Callender], *An Impartial Account of the Conduct of the Excise towards the Breweries of Scotland* (Edinburgh, 1791).

77. Gallin, "Scottish Radicalism, 1792–94"; Brims, "Scottish Democratic Movement."

78. Gallin, "Scottish Radicalism," 89, 94.

79. Brims, "Scottish Democratic Movement," 126.

80. Smout, *Scottish People*, 415; Brims, "Scottish Democratic Movement," 199–200.

81. Brims, whose thesis is by a considerable margin the best work on the Scottish radical movement, misses the significance of the lads o' parts when he includes in the lower classes making up the popular societies clerks, students, schoolmasters, dissenting clergy, apothecaries, and writers. Brims, "Scottish Democratic Movement," 126.

82. Brims, "Scottish Democratic Movement," 45–47; Gallin, "Scottish Radicalism," 82–89; Richard B. Sher, "Moderates, Managers, and Popular Politics in Mid-Eighteenth Century Edinburgh: the 'Drysdale Bustle' of the 1760s," in John Dwyer et al., eds., *New Perspectives in the Politics and Culture of Early Modern Scotland* (Edinburgh, 1982), 180; Ronald M. Sunter, *Patronage and Politics in Scotland, 1707–1832* (Edinburgh, 1986), chaps. 10–12.

83. Henry Cockburn, *Memorials of His Time* (1856; reprinted Edinburgh, 1971), 81.

84. *Scots Magazine* 51 (1789), 412; Gallin, "Scottish Radicalism," 90–94; Brims, "Scottish Democratic Movement," 52; John Dwyer and Alexander Murdoch, "Para-

digms and Politics: Manners, Morals and the Rise of Henry Dundas, 1770–1784," in Dwyer et al., eds., *New Perspectives*, 235–37.

85. Gallin, "Scottish Radicalism," 31–32, 63, 80–81.

86. Quoted in Brims, "Scottish Democratic Movement," 173.

87. Brims, "Scottish Democratic Movement," 148.

88. Gallin, "Scottish Radicalism," 103; Brims, "Scottish Democratic Movement," 147.

89. Callender, *Impartial Account*, 51; Henry W. Meikle, *Scotland and the French Revolution*, 2nd ed. (London, 1969), 81. Fry, *Dundas Despotism*, 167–68, argues that the June 4 riots were common in Edinburgh and that the 1792 riot had no political overtones. He also points to some aggravating features. Although Henry Dundas was not in Scotland when the rioters appeared before his house, two nephews "foolishly provoked the rioters by rushing out and attacking them with a golf-club and Lady Armiston's crutch. Forced to retreat, they presented their backsides for kissing before disappearing indoors."

90. Gallin, "Scottish Radicalism," 4–5.

91. A Friend to the Constitution to John Moore, Nov. 26, 1792, BL Add.MSS. 16919; James Mathison to Home Office, Nov. 16, 1792, PRO HO42/23; Meikle, *Scotland and the French Revolution*, 92.

92. Quoted in John Brims, "From Reformers to 'Jacobins': The Scottish Association of the Friends of the People," in Devine, ed., *Conflict and Stability*, 33. Macleod was writing in November 1792.

93. Meikle, *Scotland and the French Revolution*, 81.

94. "Address to the Synod of G[lasgo]w and A[y]r," in *Poetical Works of Alexander Wilson* (Belfast, 1845), 203. A "lounder" was a heavy blow. I am grateful to Iain Brash for this information.

95. Gallin, "Scottish Radicalism," 14, 20–21, 27, 43–44.

96. Sir John Sinclair, *The Statistical Account of Scotland* (Edinburgh, 1796), vol. 15, 380–81.

97. Cantwell, *Wilson*, 48, 69, 71.

98. Thomas Muir to John Millar, Jr., July 1796, NLS, MS 3825, letter 1, p. 3.

99. Brims, "Scottish Democratic Movement," 96.

100. William Gillan to Callender, May 14, 1792, PRO HO102/7; George Dempster to William Pulteney, Dec. 1792, PRO HO102/6; Bewley, *Muir*, 42.

101. Brims, "Scottish Democratic Movement," 97, 297.

102. Meikle, *Scotland and the French Revolution*, 96–98.

103. Brims, "Reformers to 'Jacobins'," 39–40.

104. Gallin, "Scottish Radicalism," 143.

105. Callender had written a short biography of Buchanan. Callender, ed., *Miscellanies in Prose and Verse*, 247–86.

106. *The Parliamentary History of England, from the Earliest Period to 1803* (London, 1816–18), vol. 24, 615–17; Meikle, *Scotland and the French Revolution*, 245–47; Brims, "Scottish Democratic Movement," 315.

107. For considerations of the depth of nationalist sentiment in Scotland at this time, see Durey, *Callender,* 42–43; John D. Brims, "The Scottish 'Jacobins', Scottish Nationalism and the British Union," in Roger A. Mason, ed., *Scotland and England 1286–1815* (Edinburgh, 1987), 247–65.

108. Thomas Cooper's radical antiwar pamphlet, published under the pseudonym "Sydney," was widely circulating in Scotland in December 1792. Robert Dundas obviously could not get at the author, but he was determined to prosecute the Scottish publisher if he could be found. Robert Dundas to Evan Nepean, Jan. 3, 1793, PRO HO102/7.

109. Sir James Fergusson, *Balloon Tytler* (London, 1972), 13, 18, 26, 97.

110. Brims, "Scottish Democratic Movement," 233, 160, 230.

111. Fergusson, *Tytler,* 116.

112. [James Tytler], *To the People and Their Friends* (Edinburgh, 1792); reprinted in Gallin, "Scottish Radicalism," 259–62.

113. Gallin, "Scottish Radicalism," 151.

114. For examples of these sorts of arguments see Harry T. Dickinson, *Liberty and Property: Political Ideology in Eighteenth-Century Britain* (New York, 1977), chap. 8; Gayle T. Pendleton, "English Conservative Propaganda during the French Revolution, 1789–1802" (Ph.D. diss., Emory University, 1976).

115. [J. T. Callender], "The Political Progress of Britain," in *The Bee,* Feb. 29, 1792, 307.

116. [Callender], "Political Progress," June 20, 1792, 241.

117. James Thomson Callender, *The Political Progress of Britain,* Part 1, 2nd ed. (Philadelphia, 1794), 77, 30.

118. James Thomson Callender, *The Political Progress of Britain,* Part 2 (Philadelphia, 1795), 5; Callender, *Political Progress,* Part 1, 5–7. For a similar critique of mercantilism and the wastage of wars, although without the radical nationalist conclusions, see John Knox, *A View of the British Empire, More Especially Scotland* (London, 1784). Callender may have read Knox's work, but it is more likely that he obtained information from it through Dr. James Anderson's work on Scotland, which he did use extensively. Anderson, editor of *The Bee,* used Knox's writings without attribution. See A. J. Youngson, *After the Forty-Five: The Economic Impact on the Scottish Highlands* (Edinburgh, 1973), 87–89.

119. Callender, *Political Progress,* Part 1, 74, 16–17, 78.

120. [Callender], "Political Progress," *The Bee,* Feb. 22, 1792, 271, March 14, 1792, 45, May 9, 1792, June 20, 21, 1792, 241; Callender, *Political Progress,* Part 1, 11–12.

121. [Callender], "Political Progress," *The Bee,* 4 Feb. 22, 1792, 265–66; Callender, *Political Progress,* Part 1, 58.

122. Callender, *Political Progress,* Part 1, 62, 43–45; [Callender], "Political Progress," *The Bee,* Feb. 22, 1792, 267.

123. Callender, *Political Progress,* Part 1, 3; T. B. Howell and T. J. Howell, eds., *A Complete Collection of State Trials* (London, 1817), vol. 23, 82.

124. Examinations of James Robertson and Walter Berry, Dec. 29, 1792, PRO

HO102/6; Howell and Howell, eds., *State Trials*, vol. 23, 79–115; Examination of J. T. Callender, Jan. 1, 1793, PRO HO102/6; Examination of Lord Gardenstone, Jan. 2, 1793, Robert Dundas to Evan Nepean, Jan. 3, 1793, William Scot to Robert Dundas, Jan. 3, 1793, PRO HO102/7.

125. J. Pringle to Henry Dundas, Jan. 7, 1793, PRO HO102/5.

126. The latest account of the Scottish trials is Alan Wharam, *The Treason Trials, 1794* (Leicester, 1992), 47–67.

127. Cockburn, *Memorials*, 68–69.

128. Brims, "Scottish Democratic Movement," 378–80; Meikle, *Scotland and the French Revolution*, 123.

129. Cockburn, *Memorials*, 8. Loyalist parents may have had some justification; in 1795 John Thelwall was avoiding the law in England by giving political lectures masked as classical history.

130. Cantwell, *Wilson*, 160; Andrew Hook, *Scotland and America: A Study of Cultural Relations, 1750–1835* (Glasgow, 1975), 241.

131. Gallin, "Scottish Radicalism," 132; *DNB*, vol. 13 (sub. John Millar), 402; *Autobiography of Mrs. [Archibald] Fletcher with Letters and Other Family Memorials* (Edinburgh, 1875), 65–66, 71; Brims, "Reformers to 'Jacobins'," 42; Brims, "Scottish Democratic Movement," 394. Unfair treatment was particularly the case in civil trials, where there was no jury.

132. Paola Bono, *Radicals and Reformers in Late Eighteenth-Century Scotland* (Frankfurt am Main, 1989).

133. A. B. Grosart, ed., *The Poems and Literary Prose of Alexander Wilson, the American Ornithologist* (Paisley, 1876), vol. 1, 62–69.

134. Wilson's actions have never been satisfactorily explained. It has been claimed that he did it to get money for the unemployed weavers. It has also been suggested that he was covering up for the real extortionists, the Mitchell brothers. Cantwell, *Wilson*, 78; Brown, *Paisley Poets*, vol. 1, 46–47.

135. Kennedy, *Treason*, 20. Kennedy's poems were not published until 1795, but it is likely that some of them circulated in manuscript earlier than that.

136. Ibid., 20.

137. Ibid., 27.

138. Ibid., 27.

139. Bain Whyte to John Moore, Feb. 26, 1793, BL Add.MSS. 16925, for claims that the radicals were still quietly persisting.

140. Gallin, "Scottish Radicalism," 163; Meikle, *Scotland and the French Revolution*, 125.

141. Gallin, "Scottish Radicalism," 177.

142. Brims, "Reformers," 46–47.

143. Gallin, "Scottish Radicalism," 208, 256.

144. Ibid., 222.

145. Brims, "Scottish Democratic Movement," 514.

146. Meikle, *Scotland and the French Revolution*, 152, claims that "the proposed in-

surrection is to be regarded as the work of Robert Watt." Fry, *Dundas Despotism*, 172, calls Watt "potty and disreputable" and his plot "implausible." Gallin and Brims take Watt more seriously.

147. [An English Barrister], *The Trials at Large of Robert Watt and David Downie, for High Treason . . . at Edinburgh, 1794* (London, 1794), 9–10.

148. [An English Barrister], *Trials of Robert Watt*, 16; Gallin, "Scottish Radicalism," 220–21.

149. [An English Barrister], *Trials of Robert Watt*, 25.

150. *Edinburgh Evening Courant*, Sept. 4, 1794; Brims, "Scottish Democratic Movement," 555.

151. [Philadelphia] *Aurora*, June 1, 1796.

CHAPTER THREE. IRISH RADICALS

1. Angus Calder, *Revolutionary Empire: The Rise of the English-Speaking Empires from the Fifteenth Century to the 1780s* (New York, 1981), 633–35; Oliver M. Dickerson, "Were the Navigation Acts Oppressive?," in John C. Wahlke, ed., *The Causes of the American Revolution*, 3rd ed. (Lexington, Mass., 1973), 26–48; Lawrence H. Leder, *America—1603–1789: Prelude to a Nation*, 2nd ed. (Minneapolis, 1978), 124–25.

2. Thomas Addis Emmet, "Part of an Essay Towards the History of Ireland," in William J. MacNeven, ed., *Pieces of Irish History* (New York, 1807), 1–2.

3. The classic interpretation is W. E. H. Lecky, *A History of Ireland in the Eighteenth Century*, 5 vols. (London, 1892). The revisionist position is associated particularly with the writings of K. H. Connell and L. M. Cullen. See also Francis Godwin James, *Ireland in the Empire, 1688–1770* (Cambridge, 1973), 190–217.

4. Commercialization of the Irish economy, together with population increase, resulted in inevitable dislocation in sectors of the economy and increasing pauperization. Growing prosperity was not evenly distributed. See, e.g., Kerby A. Miller, *Emigrants and Exiles: Ireland and the Irish Exodus to North America* (New York, 1985), 31–33.

5. Owen Dudley Edwards, "The Impact of the American Revolution on Ireland," in R. R. Palmer, ed., *The Impact of the American Revolution Abroad* (Washington, D.C., 1976), 132; R. B. McDowell, "Colonial Nationalism and the Winning of Parliamentary Independence," in T. W. Moody and W. E. Vaughan, eds., *A New History of Ireland* (Oxford, 1986), vol. 4, 196–216. The Townshend Viceroyalty from 1767, which ended the undertaking system in the Irish Parliament and established a "Castle party," was also important in resurrecting constitutional issues. See Gerard O'Brien, *Anglo-Irish Politics in the Age of Grattan and Pitt* (Blackrock, 1987), 25–27.

6. McDowell, "Colonial Nationalism," 215–19.

7. R. B. McDowell, *Ireland in the Age of Imperialism and Revolution* (Oxford, 1979), 257–58; McDowell, "Colonial Nationalism," 222–23; James Kelly, "A Secret Return of the Volunteers of Ireland in 1784," *IHS* 26 (1989): 269.

8. John Caldwell, "Particulars of [the] History of a North County [sic] Irish Family," 4 (the pagination is from the typed version of the manuscript held at PRONI).

9. R. B. McDowell, *Irish Public Opinion, 1750–1800* (London, 1944), 103; [John Binns], *Recollections of the Life of John Binns: Twenty-Nine Years in Europe and Fifty-Three in the United States* (Philadelphia, 1854), 14–16.

10. Binns, *Recollections,* 24–25.

11. Benjamin Binns to R. R. Madden, Jan. 30, 1843, TCD, Madden Papers, 873/451.

12. *Drennan Letters,* 7; Mary McNeill, *The Life and Times of Mary Ann McCracken, 1770–1866* (Belfast, 1988), 31; A. T. Q. Stewart, "The Transformation of Presbyterian Radicalism in the North of Ireland, 1792–1815" (M. A. diss., Queen's University, Belfast, 1956), 4; James Seaton Reid and W. D. Killen, *History of the Presbyterian Church in Ireland,* 2nd ed. (London, 1853), vol. 3, 397–98; Patrick Rogers, *The Irish Volunteers and Catholic Emancipation (1778–1793): A Neglected Phase of Ireland's History* (London, 1934), 45–46; W. Desmond Bailie et al., eds., *A History of Congregations in the Presbyterian Church in Ireland 1610–1982* (Belfast, 1982), 315.

13. *Irish Presbyterian Fasti,* no. 209; Aiken McClelland, "Thomas Ledlie Birch, United Irishman," *Proceedings of the Belfast Natural History and Philosophical Society* 7 (1963), 24–27; McDowell, *Public Opinion,* 49; Thomas Witherow, *Historical and Literary Memorials of Presbyterianism in Ireland (1731–1800),* 2nd Ser. (London, 1880), 285–86; [Thomas Ledlie Birch], *A Letter from an Irish Emigrant to His Friend in the United States, Giving an Account of the Rise and Progress of the Commotions in Ireland* (Philadelphia, 1799), 22.

14. William Steel Dickson, *Scripture Politics* (1812; reprinted Belfast, 1991), ed. Brendan Clifford, 16.

15. Reid and Killen, *Presbyterian Church,* vol. 3, 405; David Dickson, *New Foundations: Ireland 1660–1800* (Dublin, 1987), 143–44; R. F. Foster, *Modern Ireland, 1690–1972* (London, 1988), 214; A. T. Q. Stewart, *The Narrow Ground: Aspects of Ulster, 1609–1969* (London, 1977), 105.

16. John Wallace Nelson, "The Belfast Presbyterians, 1670–1830: An Analysis of Their Political and Social Interests" (Ph.D. diss., Queen's University, Belfast, 1985), 177–78; Marianne Elliott, *Watchmen in Sion: The Protestant Idea of Liberty* (Derry, 1985), 19.

17. McDowell, *Ireland in the Age of Imperialism,* 242; R. R. Madden, *The United Irishmen: Their Lives and Times* (Dublin, 1858), vol. 4, 2.

18. Dickson, *New Foundations,* 147–51; Binns to Madden, Jan. 30, 1843, TCD, Madden Papers, 873/451.

19. Rupert J. Coughlin, *Napper Tandy* (Dublin, 1976); Albert J. Hamilton, "James Napper Tandy," in Baylen and Gossman, eds., *Biographical Dictionary,* vol. 1, 466–67; McDowell, *Irish Public Opinion,* 43–44, 64–65; James Smyth, "Dublin's Political Underground in the 1790s," in Gerard O'Brien, ed., *Parliament, Politics and People: Essays in Eighteenth-Century Irish History* (Blackrock, 1989), 132; Binns, *Recollections,* 24–25; *Drennan Letters,* 51.

20. Dickson, *New Foundations,* 151–55; Foster, *Modern Ireland,* 246–47.

21. Reid and Killen, *Presbyterian Church,* vol. 3, 376; Charles Dickson, *Revolt in the*

North: Antrim and Down in 1798 (Dublin, 1960), 76; McDowell, "Colonial National-ism," 230.

22. R. B. McDowell, "Parliamentary Independence, 1782–9," in Moody and Vaughan, eds., *New History of Ireland*, vol. 4, 274; Foster, *Modern Ireland*, 250; O'Brien, *Anglo-Irish Politics*, 56–57; Stewart, *Narrow Ground*, 106.

23. McDowell, *Ireland in the Age of Imperialism*, 301–2; Thomas Bartlett, *The Fall and Rise of the Irish Nation: The Catholic Question 1690–1830* (Dublin, 1992), 105.

24. Madden, *United Irishmen*, vol. 2, 174–75; [Valentine Lawless, Lord Cloncurry], *Personal Recollections of the Life and Times, with extracts from the correspondence of Valentine Lord Cloncurry*, 2nd ed. (Dublin, 1850), 136; Archibald Hamilton Rowan, *The Autobiography of Archibald Hamilton Rowan*, ed. William H. Drummond (Dublin, 1840; reprinted Shannon, 1972), 100, 147; Joseph J. St. Mark, "The Red Shamrock: United Irishmen and Revolution, 1795–1803" (Ph.D. diss., Georgetown University, 1974), 31.

25. Caldwell, "North County Family," 63. Caldwell may not be strictly accurate; some Catholics were allowed into Armagh Volunteer units as early as 1779. Bartlett, *The Fall and Rise of the Irish Nation*, 99.

26. *N. Star*, Jan. 11, 1792; A. T. Q. Stewart, " 'A Stable Unseen Power': Dr. William Drennan and the Origins of the United Irishmen," in John Bossy and Peter Jupp, eds., *Essays Presented to Michael Roberts* (Belfast, 1976), 86.

27. Maureen Wall, *Catholic Ireland in the Eighteenth Century: Collected Essays of Maureen Wall*, ed. Gerard O'Brien (Dublin, 1989).

28. [Philadelphia] *Carey's Daily Advertiser*, July 6, 1797.

29. "The Autobiography of Mathew Carey," *New England Magazine* (July 1833): 405–12; Edward C. Carter, "The Political Activities of Mathew Carey, Nationalist, 1760–1814" (Ph.D. diss., Bryn Mawr College, 1962); Earl L. Bradsher, *Mathew Carey, Editor, Author and Publisher: A Study in American Literary Development* (1912; New York, 1966); [Dublin] *The Rights of Irishmen, or, National Evening Star*, Feb. 18, 1792; Thomas Carey to Mathew Carey, July 17, 1792, Lea and Febiger Collection, HSP.

30. Rowan, *Autobiography of Rowan*, 122–23; McDowell, "Parliamentary Independ-ence," 274–75; Drennan to Mrs. McTier, c. August 1785, in Drennan Letters, 34–35.

31. Quoted in A. T. Q. Stewart, *A Deeper Silence: The Hidden Origins of the United Irishmen* (London, 1993), 143.

32. Charles Hamilton Teeling, *Sequel to the History of the Irish Rebellion of 1798: A Personal Narrative* (Glasgow, n.d. [1828?]), 186.

33. Binns, *Recollections*, 52–53.

34. Emmet, "Part of an Essay," 1.

35. Dickson, *Scripture Politics*, 20.

36. T. A. Emmet, A. O'Connor, and W. J. MacNeven, "Memoir," in MacNeven, ed., *Pieces of Irish History*, 29.

37. Drennan to Dr. William Bruce, Feb. 7, 1784, PRONI D.553/20, quoted in Stewart, "Stable Unseen Power," 84.

38. Drennan to Bruce, undated [1785?], quoted in Stewart, "Stable Unseen Power," 84–85.

39. Quoted in Stewart, *Deeper Silence*, 156–57.

40. *RSCIHC* (1798), 86–92; Drennan to McTier, July 11, 1791, in *Drennan Letters*, 58. Lord Lieutenant Westmorland called Drennan's plan "a very dangerous paper." Quoted in Bartlett, *Fall and Rise*, 126.

41. Stewart, "Stable Unseen Power," 82–83.

42. Emmet, "Part of an Essay," 16.

43. Drennan to McTier [c. Nov. 1791], in *Drennan Letters*, 62–63.

44. Samuel McSkimin, *Annals of Ulster*, new ed. (Belfast, 1906), 5.

45. Marianne Elliott, *Wolfe Tone: Prophet of Irish Independence* (New Haven, 1989), 135; V. G. Kiernan, "The Emergence of a Nation," in C. H. E. Philpin, ed., *Nationalism and Popular Protest in Ireland* (Cambridge, 1987), 20; Madden, *United Irishmen*, vol. 1, 463; Mrs. McTier to Drennan, [c. Feb. 1788], in *Drennan Letters*, 46. For one example of United Irishmen making up the bulk of directorships (of the Belfast General Insurance Company), see *N. Star*, No. 5, Jan. 14, 1792.

46. McSkimin, *Annals of Ulster*, 14. This may have been the club that sponsored the planned trip of James Tytler to Scotland and France in 1793. See below, 136.

47. Nancy J. Curtin, *The United Irishmen: Popular Politics in Ulster and Dublin 1791–1798* (Oxford, 1994), 92; *N. Star*, No. 102, Dec. 22, 1792.

48. Emmet, "Part of an Essay," 74.

49. Richard Twomey, *Jacobins and Jeffersonians: Anglo-American Radicalism in the United States, 1790–1820* (New York, 1989), 216.

50. *N. Star*, No. 4, Jan. 11–14, 1792, No. 99, Dec. 12, 1792, No. 100, Dec. 15, 1792.

51. R. B. McDowell, "The Personnel of the Dublin Society of United Irishmen," *IHS* 2 (1940–41): 13–14.

52. See, for example, John Chambers to R. Simms, May 9, 1806, PRONI D1759/3B/6/36; T. A. Emmet to Harman Blennerhassett, in William H. Stafford, ed., *The Blennerhassett Papers* (Cincinnati, 1864), 528–29.

53. Thomas P. Robinson, "The Life of Thomas Addis Emmet" (Ph.D. diss., New York University, 1955), 28.

54. Blennerhassett was duped by Aaron Burr in 1805–6.

55. R. B. McDowell, "Proceedings of the Dublin Society of United Irishmen," *Analecta Hibernica* 17 (1949): 62, 140; Raymond E. Fitch, ed., *Breaking with Burr: Harman Blennerhassett's Journal, 1807* (Athens, Ohio, 1988), xi.

56. William Paulet Carey, *An Appeal to the People of Ireland* (Dublin 1794), 4–5.

57. *N. Star*, No. 3, Jan. 7–11, 1792.

58. McDowell, "Proceedings," 140; Seamus O'Casaide, "John Chambers: Printer and United Irishman," *The Irish Book Lover*, July 1940; Thomas Pakenham, *The Year of Liberty* (London, 1972), 45.

59. Michael Durey, "The Dublin Society of United Irishmen and the Politics of the Carey-Drennan Dispute, 1792–1794," *Historical Journal* 37 (1994): 89–111.

60. McDowell, *Ireland in the Age of Imperialism*, 387; Curtin, *United Irishmen*, 179; Elliott, *Tone*, 62; *N. Star*, No. 6, Jan. 18, 1792.

61. Michael Durey, "Irish Deism and Jefferson's Republic: Denis Driscol in Ireland and America, 1793–1810," *Éire-Ireland: A Journal of Irish Studies* 25 (1990): 56–76; Jim

Smyth, *The Men of No Property: Irish Radicals and Popular Politics in the Late Eighteenth Century* (London, 1992), 60.

62. McDowell, "Personnel," 18, for the Dublin figure. There are no reliable figures for the Ulster United Irishmen, but certainly nearly all the leaders of the period 1791 to 1794 were implicated in the rebellion of 1798.

63. Emmet, "Memoir," 207–8. For Neilson's similar views, see *RSCIHL* (1798), 48. See also, for Sampson, [William Sampson], *Memoirs of William Sampson*, 2nd ed. (Leesburg, Va., 1817), 46–47.

64. Lawless, *Personal Recollections*, 17–18.

65. See, for example, *N. Star*, No. 1, Jan. 4, 1792, No. 23, March 17, 1792, No. 72, Sept. 5, 1792, No. 95, Nov. 28, 1792, No. 98, Dec. 8, 1792.

66. MacNeven, *Pieces of Irish History*, 246–47.

67. Marianne Elliott, *Partners in Revolution: The United Irishmen and France* (New Haven, 1982), xiii.

68. Elliott, *Tone*, 106.

69. Curtin, *United Irishmen*, 17.

70. Thomas Bartlett, "The Burden of the Present: Theobald Wolfe Tone, Republican and Separatist," in David Dickson, Daire Keogh, Kevin Whelan, eds., *The United Irishmen: Republicanism, Radicalism and Rebellion* (Dublin, 1993), 1–15.

71. MacNeven, *Pieces of Irish History*, 269.

72. Quoted in John [Daly] Burk, *History of the Late War in Ireland, with an account of the United Irish Association* (Philadelphia, 1799), 37.

73. *N. Star*, No. 95, Nov. 28, 1792.

74. *N. Star*, No. 97, Dec. 5, 1792.

75. Thomas Bartlett, "An End to Moral Economy: The Irish Militia Disturbances of 1793," *Past and Present*, no. 99 (1983): 61.

76. Drennan to Mrs. McTier, Nov. 25, 1792, in *Drennan Letters*, 97–98.

77. McDowell, "Proceedings," 82.

78. Drennan to McTier, Jan. 21, 1794, in *Drennan Letters*, 182.

79. Emmet, "Part of an Essay," 46–47; Lawless, *Personal Recollections*, 2–28.

80. Drennan to Mrs. McTier, Nov. 25, 1792, in *Drennan Letters*, 98.

81. *N. Star*, No. 24, March 21, 1792.

82. *N. Star*, No. 89, Nov. 7, 1792.

83. *N. Star*, No. 28, April 4, 1792. See also the Address of the Dublin Society of United Irishmen, signed by Tandy in Jan. 1792, *N. Star*, No. 3, Jan. 7, 1792.

84. *N. Star*, No. 89, Nov. 7, 1792.

85. Emmet, "Part of an Essay," 41.

86. Caldwell, "North County Family," 80.

87. T. Collins to Giffard, Nov. 29, 1792, in McDowell, "Proceedings," 42; *N. Star*, No. 97, Dec. 5, 1792.

88. *N. Star*, No. 99, Dec. 12, 1792, No. 100, Dec. 15, 1792.

89. William Paulet Carey, *Appeal*, 51, claimed later that he was instrumental in persuading the unit to forego this "mischievous" button. It was hoped that between 6,000

and 10,000 would join the National Guard; in the event, only about 200 did so. Curtin, *United Irishmen*, 52.

90. William Paulet Carey and Randal McAllister were two of the three Dublin printers indicted for their role in publishing the "Address." See Durey, "Carey-Drennan Dispute," 105.

91. Mrs. McTier to Drennan, Dec. 25, 1792, in *Drennan Letters*, 113.

92. *N. Star*, 2, No. 15, Feb. 20, 1793. For Neilson's view that the proceedings were "not entirely up to my ideas," see [Neilson to Drennan], Feb. 17, 1793, in Drennan Letters, 136.

93. Emmet, "Part of an Essay," 46–47; [Drennan to McTier], Feb. 25, 1793, in *Drennan Letters*, 82; McDowell, "The Age of the United Irishmen: Reform and Reaction, 1789–94," in Moody and Vaughan, eds., *New History of Ireland*, vol. 4, 331.

94. Westmorland to Dundas, Nov. 17, 1792, PRO HO100/38.

95. Carey, *Appeal*, 16.

96. Neilson to Richard McCormick, [early 1793?], in Madden, *United Irishmen*, vol. 4, 98.

97. Emmet, "Part of an Essay," 42; Drennan to McTier, Jan. 28, 1793, in *Drennan Letters*, 122.

98. Madden, *United Irishmen*, vol. 3, 41.

99. He was released in March 1794. See N. Star, No. 235, March 31, 1794.

100. *N. Star*, 2, No. 28, April 6, 1793; [Baltimore] *American Patriot*, Oct. 16, 1802; McSkimin, *Annals of Ulster*, 24, 101; Cooke to Nugent, Aug. 6, 1796, Nugent Papers, NAM; J. Lees to Edward Cooke, Aug. 27, 1796, Reb. Pap. 620/24/163; Andrew MacNeven to Cooke, May 23, 1797, Reb. Pap. 620/30/167; Caldwell, "North County Family," 86; Madden, *United Irishmen*, vol. 1, 536–37.

101. Drennan to McTier, March 26, 1793, in *Drennan Letters*, 144–45; Madden, *United Irishmen*, vol. 2, 83; Emmet, "Part of an Essay," 59; *N. Star*, 2, No. 26, March 30, 1793.

102. Drennan to McTier, March 6, 9, 1793, in *Drennan Letters*, 140–41.

103. McDowell, "Proceedings," passim.

104. Elliott, *Watchmen in Sion*, 25.

105. McDowell, *Ireland in the Age of Imperialism*, 388.

106. For a more detailed examination of this, see Durey, "Carey-Drennan Dispute," 89–111.

107. Drennan to Mrs. McTier, June 18, 1793, in *Drennan Letters*, 164.

108. *N. Star*, 2, No. 21, March 13, 1793; Samuel McTier to Drennan, April 22, 1793, in *Drennan Letters*, 151; Stewart, *Deeper Silence*, 185.

109. *N. Star*, 2, No. 23, March 20, 1793.

110. Mrs. McTier to Drennan, April 1, 1793, in *Drennan Letters*, 148.

111. Drennan to Mrs. McTier, July 1, 1793, in *Drennan Letters*, 165.

112. *N. Star*, 2, No. 66, Aug. 17, 1793.

113. See, for example, *N. Star*, No. 78, Sept. 26, 1792.

114. Emmet, "Part of an Essay," 78–79.

115. Elliott, *Partners*, 47.

116. But see Smyth, *Men of No Property*, chap. 6; Nancy Curtin, "The Transformation of the Society of United Irishmen into a Mass-based Revolutionary Organisation, 1794–6," *IHS* 24 (1985): 463–92; Durey, "Denis Driscol," 60–64.

117. Bartlett, "Moral Economy," 41–64.

118. Thomas Bartlett, "Defenders and Defenderism in 1795," *IHS* 24 (1984–85): 374.

119. Tom Garvin, "Defenders, Ribbonmen and Others: Underground Political Networks in Pre-Famine Ireland," in Philpin, ed., *Nationalism and Popular Protest in Ireland*, 229–32.

120. Marianne Elliott, "The Defenders in Ulster," in Dickson et al., eds., *United Irishmen*, 225.

121. Emmet, "Part of an Essay," 56.

122. Emmet, "Memoir," 212–13.

123. Smyth, *Men of No Property*, 68–69.

124. John Sweetman, *A Refutation of the Charges Attempted to Be Made Against the Secretary of the Sub-Committee of the Catholics of Ireland* (Dublin, 1793); *RSCIHL* (1793), ii–iii; Madden, *United Irishmen*, vol. 4, 94; *DNB*, vol. 19, 197–98; Daire Keogh, *"The French Disease": The Catholic Church and Radicalism in Ireland, 1790–1800* (Dublin, 1993), 71, 101.

125. Emmet, "Part of an Essay," 57; Elliott, *Partners*, 44; Smyth, *Men of No Property*, 70; Coughlan, *Tandy*, 97–98.

126. A copy of the address can be found in McDowell, "Proceedings," 32–34. Patrick Byrne printed thousands of copies of this tract.

127. Drennan to McTier, March 6, 1793, in *Drennan Letters*, 141; Coughlan, *Tandy*, 98–99. Tandy arrived in America, via Hamburgh, in September 1795. [Philadelphia] *Aurora*, Sept. 10, 1795.

128. See below, 136, for Tytler's role in this.

129. See the enclosure in Roger O'Connor's letter of June 7, 1795, intercepted by the Belfast Post Office. KCRO U840 0147/4/2. Curtin, *United Irishmen*, 360, suggests that the union in Belfast may have occurred as early as December 1792.

130. Enclosure in A. M. [Andrew MacNeven?] to "John Patrickson," April 5, 1795, KCRO U840/0144/3/2.

131. Emmet, "Memoir," 215; William J. MacNeven, "An Account of the Treaty," in MacNeven, *Pieces of Irish History*, 195; *N. Star*, No. 250, May 22, 1794; Drennan to McTier, May 3, 1794, in *Drennan Letters*, 198.

132. Pollock to Thomas Pelham, April 16, 1795, KCRO U840 0143/7.

133. "J. W." [Leonard McNally] to [Cooke?], April 22, 1795, KCRO U840 0143/11.

134. Curtin, *United Irishmen*, 109.

135. Quoted in Smyth, *Men of No Property*, 147.

136. [Georgia] *Aug. Chron.*, March 15, 1811; [Philadelphia] *Temple of Reason*, passim.

137. *DEP*, Aug. 6, 1789.

138. F. Archer to Judge Robert Day, Dec. 23, 1802, Reb. Pap. 620/61/80; Brian Inglis, *Freedom of the Press in Ireland* (London, 1954), 88.

139. Archer to Day, Dec. 23, 1802; John T. Collins, "A Memorable Cork Trial of 1794," *Cork Evening Echo*, Dec. 10, 1962.

140. For a more detailed discussion of Driscol's political philosophy, see Durey, "Denis Driscol," from which much of this section is taken.

141. For Cork Whiteboyism, see Maurice Bric, "Priests, Parsons and Politics: The Rightboy Protest in County Cork, 1785–1788," in Philpin, ed., *Nationalism and Popular Protest in Ireland*, 163–90.

142. Information of Bird/Smith, No. 29, Reb. Pap. 620/27/1.

143. *Cork Gaz.*, Jan. 15, 1794.

144. *Cork Gaz.*, March 19, 22, 26, 1794.

145. *Cork Gaz.*, April 26, 1794; *N. Star*, No. 243, April 28, 1794.

146. *Cork Gaz.*, May 31, 1794.

147. *Aug. Chron.*, Nov. 11, 1809; Charles Campbell, ed., *Some Materials to Serve for a Brief Memoir of John Daly Burk* (Albany, N.Y., 1868), 43.

148. Joseph I. Shulim, "John Daly Burk, Irish Revolutionist and American Patriot," *Transactions of the American Philosophical Society*, New Ser. 54 (1964), 6.

149. John Burk, *The Trial of John Burk, of Trinity College, for Heresy and Blasphemy* (Dublin, 1794); reprinted, in installments, in [Boston] *Polar Star*, Oct. 15–26, 1796.

150. Burk, *History of Ireland*, 44; *Aug. Chron.*, Nov. 11, 1809; Campbell, ed., *Some Materials*, 43.

151. *DEP*, Oct. 22, 1793; "J. W.'"s Report, April 22, 1795, KCRO U840 0143/11.

152. [Philadelphia] *Aurora*, Sept. 10, 1794.

153. Emmet, "Part of an Essay," 86–87.

154. Frank MacDermott, "The Jackson Episode in 1794," *Studies* (Ireland) (1938), 81–86; Elliott, *Partners*, 62–68.

155. R. B. McDowell, "The Age of the United Irishmen: Revolution and the Union, 1794–1800," in Moody and Vaughan, eds., *New History of Ireland*, vol. 4, 351.

156. Emmet, "Memoir," 211; Charles Hamilton Teeling, *History of the Irish Rebellion of 1798: A Personal Narrative* (Glasgow, 1828), 5, 9–10.

157. *RSCIHL* (1798), 7–8; Curtin, *United Irishmen*, 102–3.

158. Bird/Smith Information, No. 29, Reb. Pap. 620/27/1.

159. Thomas Graham, " 'An Union of Power'? The United Irish Organisation: 1795–1798," in Dickson et al., eds., *United Irishmen*, 246–47.

160. *N. Star*, Nos. 252, 253, May 29, June 2, 1794, No. 491, Sept. 12, 1796; Downshire to Castle, Nov. 25, 1796, Reb. Pap. 620/26/77; McSkimin, *Annals of Ulster*, 27; Jean Stephenson, "Records Furnished to the D. A. R. Library; . . . U.S. District Court, Charleston, SC, 1792–1800," *National Genealogical Society Quarterly* 30 (1942): 127.

161. Binns, *Recollections*, 47–51; Michael Durey, "John Hughes, Reluctant *Agent Provocateur* and Millenarian: A Note and New Documents," *Eighteenth-Century Ireland* 7 (1992): 141–46.

162. *N. Star*, 2, No. 33, April 24, 1793, Nos. 360, 398, June 11, Oct. 22, 1795.

163. Peter Brooke, "Controversies in Ulster Presbyterianism, 1790–1836" (Ph.D. diss., Cambridge University, 1980), 27.

164. Bird/Smith Information, No. 29, 1796, Reb. Pap. 620/27/1.

165. *N. Star*, Jan. to March 1796, No. 477, July 25, 1796.

166. Lees to Cooke, Aug. 27, 1796, Reb. Pap. 620/24/163.

167. See, for example, Dillon to Cooke, Feb. 14, 1798, quoted in Patrick Hogan, "Civil Unrest in the Province of Connaught 1793–1798: The Role of the Landed Gentry in Maintaining Order" (M.Ed. diss., University College, Galway, 1976), 79.

168. Downshire to [Cooke], Nov. 25, 1796, Reb. Pap. 620/26/77; J. Rea to Sackville Hamilton, March 27, 1797, Reb. Pap. 620/29/116. Driscol's *Cork Gaz.* attracted similar responses. Heron to Cooke, Jan. 2, 1797, Reb. Pap. 620/28/16.

169. *N. Star*, No. 488, Sept. 2, 1796; Mrs. McTier to Drennan, May 19, 1797, in Drennan Letters, 256.

170. The best discussion of print culture in general is Curtin, *United Irishmen*, chaps. 7 and 8.

171. Bird/Smith Information, No. 29, 1796, Reb. Pap. 620/27/1.

172. Lawless, *Personal Recollections*, 141.

173. *RSCHC* (1798), 253.

174. Carey to Hardwicke, March 30, 1801, Reb. Pap. 620/49/94; Durey, "Carey-Drennan Dispute," 105–10.

175. "J. W." to Cooke, Dec. 15, 1797, Reb. Pap. 620/10/121/85.

176. Sampson, *Memoirs*, 87.

177. "J. W." to Cooke, Dec. 12, 1797, Reb. Pap. 620/10/121/84.

178. [Walter Cox], *Irish Magazine, or Monthly Asylum for Neglected Biography* (Oct. 1810): 471–72; W. J. Fitzpatrick, *The Sham Squire, and Informers of 1798*, 3rd ed. (Dublin, 1895), 259–60; Madden, *United Irishmen*, vol. 2, 270–73; Seamus O'Casaide, "Watty Cox and His Publications," *The Irish Book Lover* (1933), 18–25.

179. Sampson, *Memoirs*, 24.

180. Cooke to Pelham, Dec. 14, 1797, Pelham Papers, BL Add.MSS. 33105, fos. 262–63.

181. Fitzpatrick, *Sham Squire*, 144.

182. "J. W." to Cooke, Jan. 1, 1798 [misdated 1797], Reb. Pap. 620/10/121/41.

183. Cooke to Pelham, Dec. 14, 1797. For a similar suspicion of United Irish leaders by a middling-class Catholic, see Durey, "Carey-Drennan Dispute," 99–103.

184. Cooke to Pelham, Dec. 14, 1797; Cooke to Wickham, March 10, 1798, Reb. Pap. 620/3/32/28; *Irish Magazine* (Oct. 1810), 472.

185. *N. Star*, No. 471, July 4, 1796; *Press* (Dublin), Oct. 17, 1797.

186. For a long list of the different tactics used by United Irish emissaries, see KCRO U840/0152/1.

187. Edmond A. McNaughton to Arthur Wolfe, May 9, 1795, KCRO U840 0146/8.

188. Robert M. Young, *Ulster in '98: Episodes and Anecdotes*, 3rd ed. (Belfast, 1893), 59.

189. Nathaniel Alexander to Henry Alexander, June 3, 1795, KCRO U840 0147/1. It is likely that this emissary was a Defender rather than a United Irishman.

190. Nathaniel Alexander to Henry Alexander, Nov. 15, 1796, Reb. Pap. 620/26/85.

191. "Left Hand" to Pelham, May 27, 1797, Reb. Pap. 620/30/211.

192. "J. H. Smith" to Cooke, July 23, 1796, PRO HO100/62, fo. 142; Cooke to General Nugent, July 25, 1796, NAM, Nugent Papers, 6807/174, fos. 147–48; "J. W." to Cooke, Oct. 5, 1796, Reb. Pap. 620/10/121/38. For other examples of soldiers being seduced, see Reb. Pap. 620/26/133 (re. the 24th. Regiment); *RSCIHC* (1798), 14.

193. Colonel James Durham to Clotworthy Soden, May 29, 1796, Reb. Pap. 620/23/129.

194. *DEP*, Sept. 26, 1797.

195. Lucius Barber to Cooke, Oct. 10, 1797, Reb. Pap. 620/32/160.

196. Madden, *United Irishmen*, vol. 1, 489.

197. Black Book of Northern Ireland, PRONI D272/1; Young, *Ulster in '98*, 7.

198. For one Armagh emissary, who traveled the South each month on behalf of the Defenders, and who claimed to have sworn in most of the Limerick militia and the Irish Brigade, see "J. W." to Cooke, Oct. 6, 1796, Reb. Pap. 620/36/227.

199. ? to Cooke, Nov. 27, 1796, Reb. Pap. 620/26/83.

200. *RSCIHC* (1798), 6, 14–15, 63.

201. Deposition of Robert Carlisle, April 2, 1796, Reb. Pap. 620/23/65; ? to Thomas Knox, June 11, 1796, Reb. Pap. 620/23/165.

202. *N. Star*, Nos. 452, 453, 468, April 28, May 2, June 24, 1796.

203. *N. Star*, No. 466, June 17, 1796; Reb. Pap. 620/29/255; McDowell, *Ireland in the Age of Imperialism*, 541.

204. Elliott, "Defenders in Ulster," 224.

205. Teeling, *History of the Irish Rebellion*, 12. For the Belfast arrests, see Mrs. McTier to Drennan, Sept. 16, 1796, in *Drennan Letters*, 240.

206. Sampson, *Memoirs*, 77–78, 367–69; Bird to Camden, Feb. 3, 1798, KCRO U840 0197/2; Edward Newell to Camden, Feb. 21, 1798, KCRO U840 0197/3; McSkimin, *Annals of Ulster*, 62.

207. Madden, *United Irishmen*, vol. 1, 483–84.

208. McDowell, *Age of Imperialism*, 353; *RSCIHC* (1798), 6–7; Camden to Downshire, Nov. 12, 1796, KCRO 0160/12; Thomas Pelham to Lake, March 3, 1797, Nugent Papers, 6807/174, fos. 222–29.

209. Durham to Soden, May 29, 1796, Reb. Pap. 620/23/129; Andrew MacNeven to Pelham, Feb. 24, 1796, Reb. Pap. 620/23/36.

210. *RSCIHC* (1798), 58.

211. Curtin, *United Irishmen*, 113.

212. Birch, *Letter from an Irish Emigrant*, 38–40; McClelland, "Birch," 29.

213. Birch, *Letter from an Irish Emigrant*, 41–46.

214. For the view of a radical that Ulstermen took the oath of allegiance in 1797 only "to protect their property from being destroyed by the military," see Lord Vis-

count Bulkley to Henry Dundas, April 30, 1798, in Londonderry, ed., *Castlereagh Corr.*, vol. 2, 207–8.

215. Birch, *Letter from an Irish Emigrant*, 21.

216. McSkimin, *Annals of Ulster*, 66.

217. Downshire MSS, quoted in McClelland, "Birch," 30.

218. Quoted in Dickson, *Antrim and Down*, 114.

219. *RSCIHC* (1798), 23.

220. For more on these emigrants, see 140–44.

221. [New York] *Shamrock*, Dec. 7, 1811.

222. McSkimin, *Annals of Ulster*, 57.

223. [Philadelphia] *Porcupine's Gazette*, Feb. 12, 1799.

224. Elliott, *Partners*, 108, 133; McSkimin, *Annals of Ulster*, 59.

225. "J. W." to Cooke, Oct. 2 [1797], Reb. Pap. 620/10/121/79; Smyth, "Dublin's Political Underground," 144.

226. Elliott, *Tone*, 278–79.

227. "Memoir of William James MacNeven," in Madden, *United Irishmen*, ed. James J. O'Neill (Dublin, n.d.), 2–6.

228. Madden, *United Irishmen*, vol. 2, 240–41.

229. Downshire to Camden, April 4, 1798, KCRO U840 addn. 0196/2.

230. Emmet, "Memoir," 226–27; Elliott, *Partners*, 150–53; "J. W." to Cooke, Nov. 4, 1797, Reb. Pap. 620/10/121/82.

231. "J. W." to Cooke, June 21, Aug. 11, Sept. 11, 1797, Reb. Pap. 620/10/121/68, 73, 75; McDowell, "Personnel," 26.

232. Benjamin Binns to Madden, Jan. 30, 1843, Madden Papers, 873/451; *RSCIHC* (1798), 148–51.

233. *DEP*, Sept. 15, 1798; Elliott, *Partners*, 178, 200. Bailey at one time was thought to have betrayed the Leinster Executive. "J. W." to Cooke, March 14, 1798, Reb. Pap. 620/10/121/96.

234. Roger Wells, *Insurrection: The British Experience 1795–1803* (Gloucester, 1983), 123.

235. Quoted in Marianne Elliott, "Irish Republicanism in England: The First Phase, 1797–9," in Thomas Bartlett and D. W. Hayton, eds., *Penal Era and Golden Age: Essays in Irish History, 1690–1800* (Belfast, 1979), 213–14.

236. Binns to Madden, Jan. 30, 1843, Madden Papers, 873/451.

237. See above, 38.

238. Curtin, *United Irishmen*, 257.

239. Madden, *United Irishmen*, vol. 1, 411; McDowell, "Personnel," 51.

240. Madden, *United Irishmen*, vol. 4, 52; Drennan to Mrs. McTier, Feb. 8, 1798, in *Drennan Letters*, 266–67.

241. Madden, *United Irishmen*, vol. 4, 122.

242. Pakenham, *Year of Liberty*, 69.

243. "J. H. Smith" to Cooke, July 26, 1796, PRO HO100/62, fos. 144–45.

244. Pakenham, *Year of Liberty*, 106.

245. Madden, *United Irishmen*, vol. 1, 438, vol. 4, 251; W. J. Fitzpatrick, *Secret Service under Pitt* (London, 1892), 310; McDowell, *Age of Imperialism*, 602.

246. Stella Tillyard, *Aristocrats: Caroline, Emily, Louisa and Sarah Lennox, 1740–1832* (London, 1994), 382.

247. Madden, *United Irishmen*, vol. 4, 58; *Irish Magazine* (July 1808), 324. Pakenham further embellishes Cox's account.

248. See Michael Durey, "The Fate of Irish Rebel Prisoners, 1797–1804," Paper presented at the Australasian Modern British History Association Conference in Melbourne, February 1995.

249. William Wickham to Pole Carew, Sept. 4, 1803, PRO HO100/113, fo. 24.

250. *DEP*, July 24, 1798; Thomas Cloney, *A Personal Narrative of . . . 1798* (Dublin, 1832), 155.

251. Wickham to Pole Carew, Sept. 27, 1803, PRO HO100/113, fo. 229.

252. Wickham to Pole Carew, Sept. 4, 1803. There was a reward of £300 for his capture.

253. Nicholas Gray to Alexander Marsden, May 7, 1804, Reb. Pap. 620/13/174/23.

254. Madden, *United Irishmen*, vol. 3, 183.

255. Binns, *Recollections*, 317; Letter from E. T. D. Lambert, in [Wexford] *The People*, July 4, 1980. There is no record of his court-martial in the (incomplete) documentation in the Rebellion Papers for 1798.

256. *RSCIHC* (1798), 144–45.

257. For the role of adjutants general in the United system, see *RSCIHC* (1798), 152–53.

258. *RSCIHC* (1798), 147.

259. Downshire to Camden, April 4, 1798, KCRO U840 addn. 0196/2.

260. Black Book, PRONI D272/1; *DEP*, Sept. 17, 1798; Nicholas Magin's Report, PRO HO100/77, fos. 44–46.

261. Magin's Report, fos. 44–46; *RSCIHC* (1798), 161.

262. Narrative of William Fox, Reb. Pap. 620/4/61.

263. Cooke to Wickham, June 2, 1798, PRO HO100/77, 22; Althea Hayter, ed., *The Backbone: Diaries of a Military Family in the Napoleonic Wars* (Durham, 1993), 39; Curtin, *United Irishmen*, 261–62.

264. Thomas D'Arcy McGee, *A History of the Irish Settlers in North America* (Boston, 1851), 83.

265. At his court-martial, Birch denied being present at Creevy Rocks.

266. Caldwell, "North County Family," 70, 107.

CHAPTER FOUR. INTO EXILE

1. For examples of concern at emigration from Britain at this time, see Malcolm Campbell to Collector, Campbeltown, Aug. 12, 1792, PRO HO105/2 (who claimed

that "Poverty and Oppression of Landlords and encouraging Letters from their Freinds" [*sic*] were the reasons for 400 Scotsmen emigrating to North Carolina); Herbert Heaton, "The Industrial Immigrant in the United States, 1783–1812," *Proceedings of the American Philosophical Society* 95 (1951): 519–23 (for the loss of skills overseas); Rowland Tappan Berthoff, *British Immigrants in Industrial America, 1790–1850* (Cambridge, Mass., 1953); Doren Ben-Atar, "Alexander Hamilton's Alternative: Technology Piracy and the Report on Manufactures," *WMQ* 3rd Ser., 52 (1995): 389–414. Spokesmen for the emigrants frequently saw immigration contributing significantly to the strength of the United States. Edward Gillespy, editor of the New York *Shamrock*, for instance, reiterated this point whenever he dealt with emigration from Ireland.

2. Thomas Jefferson, for example, believed the right to migrate was more fundamental than the right to property. John M. Murrin, "Fundamental Values, the Founding Fathers, and the Constitution," in H. Belz, R. Hoffman, P. J. Albert, eds., *To Form a More Perfect Union: The Critical Ideas of the Constitution* (Charlottesville, Va., 1992), 21.

3. Eric Foner, *Tom Paine and Revolutionary America* (New York, 1976), xix; J. C. D. Clark, *The Language of Liberty, 1660–1832* (Cambridge, 1994), 20; Ian Dyck, "Local Attachments, National Identities and World Citizenship in the Thought of Thomas Paine," *History Workshop Journal* 35 (1993): 117–35. For the fate of European "citizens of the world," Paine's political colleagues in France, see Gary Kates, *The Cercle Social, the Girondins, and the French Revolution* (Princeton, 1985). Cobbett, in his anti-Jacobin phase (1798), predictably was contemptuous of internationalism: "I hate the citizens of the world, and their indiscriminating benevolence. 'I love my dog—you love yours.' That's my motto." William Cobbett, *Porcupine's Works; containing various writings and selections; exhibiting a faithful picture of the United States of America* (London, 1801), vol. 8, 31.

4. See, for example, the Irishman Rowan's comment to the Scottish reformer Norman Macleod in July 1793: "The votarys [*sic*] of liberty are of no country, or rather of every country, and . . . the destruction or establishment of the rights of mankind in one Nation conduces a similar consequence in its neighbouring state." Quoted in John D. Brims, "The Scottish Democratic Movement in the Age of the French Revolution" (Ph.D. diss., Edinburgh University, 1983), 428. See also Samuel Neilson's comment that "the happiness of the human race is with us a SUPERIOR OBJECT" to the welfare of Ireland alone. *N. Star*, No. 43, May 26–30, 1792.

5. Archibald Hamilton Rowan, *The Autobiography of Archibald Hamilton Rowan*, ed. William H. Drummond (Dublin, 1840; reprinted Shannon, 1972), 282–83; Marianne Elliott, *Wolfe Tone: Prophet of Irish Independence* (New Haven, 1989), 250.

6. Quoted in R. R. Madden, *United Irishmen: Their Lives and Times (Dublin, 1858)*, 2nd ser., vol. 1, 101.

7. W. J. Fitzpatrick, *Secret Service Under Pitt* (London, 1892), 170.

8. Frank MacDermott, *Tone and His Times* (1939, Dublin, 1980), 272–73. The more recent Elliott, *Tone*, 260, suggests that Tone's French plans were less fixed when he left Ireland than his journal entry intimates. The government in Dublin received

information, probably from intercepted correspondence, that Tone's real destination was France. Rowland O'Connor to Sackville Hamilton, June 7, 1795, KCRO, U840 0147/4/1.

9. The definitive account of the Irish in France is Marianne Elliott, *Partners in Revolution: The United Irishmen and France* (New Haven, 1982). For Swiney, see 318, 337; PRONI D1759/3B/6. He had links with French émigrés in America. He was married to the sister of the wife of the brother of General Moreau, Bonaparte's unsuccessful rival who was living across the Atlantic. Swiney had returned to France by 1810. William MacNeven to Warden, March 12, 1810, Warden Papers.

10. James Fergusson, *Balloon Tytler* (London, 1972), 134–35.

11. Smith/Bird Information, No. 29, 1796, Reb. Pap. 620/27/1.

12. Smith/Bird Information, No. 29. For McCabe's colorful career, which included sojourns in Scotland and France, see R. R. Madden, *Down and Antrim in '98* (Dublin, n.d.).

13. Madden, *United Irishmen*, 2nd ser., vol. 2, 521. The eleven were: William Adair, Thomas Gunning Bashford, Andrew Bryson, Jr., William McKeever, John Cormick, Valentine Derry, James Hull, John Nevin, Napper Tandy, Wolfe Tone, and James Townsend. Nine of these were from Ulster.

14. *Edinburgh Evening Courant*, Sept. 6, 1794; *Scots Magazine* 61 (October 1794): 652; "An English Barrister," *The Trials at Large of Robert Watt and David Downie, for High Treason . . . at Edinburgh . . . 1794* (London, 1794), 25.

15. "An English Barrister," *Trials of Robert Watt*, 4, 27; *Edinburgh Evening Courant*, May 29, Sept. 4, 1794; *Times*, Sept. 9, 10, 11, 12, 15, 18, 19, 20, 1794.

16. David V. Erdman, *Commerce des Lumières: John Oswald and the British in Paris, 1790–1793* (Columbia, Mo., 1986), 176.

17. Quoted in Willis G. Briggs, "Joseph Gales, Editor of Raleigh's First Newspaper," *North Carolina Booklet* 7 (1907): 111.

18. T. B. Howell and T. J. Howell, eds., *A Complete Collection of State Trials* (London, 1817), vol. 25, 236–38.

19. Richard Twomey, *Jacobins and Jeffersonians: Anglo-American Radicalism in the United States, 1790–1820* (New York, 1989), 68. Gales later claimed he emigrated because he preferred freedom to despotism and republicanism to monarchy. *Raleigh Register*, Dec. 10, 1804.

20. Briggs, "Gales," 111.

21. Charles Campbell, ed., *Some Materials to Serve for a Brief Memoir of John Daly Burk* (Albany, N.Y., 1868), 11.

22. W. Desmond Bailie et al., eds., *A History of Congregations in the Presbyterian Church in Ireland 1610–1982* (Belfast, 1982), 620. The story is unlikely to be completely true; he was given permission by the authorities to expatriate himself. Perhaps he was arrested in disguise.

23. [William Sampson], *Memoirs of William Sampson*, 2nd ed. (Leesburg, Va., 1817), 19–21; Thomas Pakenham, *The Year of Liberty* (London, 1972), 268.

24. John Caldwell, "Particulars of [the] History of a North County [*sic*] Irish Fam-

ily," 87. See also, Edward Cooke to William Wickham, June 5, 1798, PRO HO100/77, fos. 50–51. One Englishman, Richard Lee, escaped in women's clothes. I am grateful to Jon Mee for this information.

25. Charles Dickson, *Revolt in the North: Antrim and Down in 1798* (Dublin, 1960), 135. It was later suggested that Thomas was more deeply implicated in the rising than John, and that the authorities had executed the wrong brother. This is unlikely. John's name appears far more frequently than Thomas's in the sources.

26. Dickson, *Antrim and Down*, 154–55; John [Daly] Burk, *History of the Late War in Ireland, with an account of the United Irish Association* (Philadelphia, 1799), 135.

27. Robert M. Young, *Ulster in '98: Episodes and Anecdotes*, 3rd ed. (Belfast, 1893), 43. Kennedy, age 25, died only a few years after reaching New York. There a monument was raised "To the handsome Young Irishman."

28. Caldwell, "North County Family," 119.

29. Young, *Ulster in '98*, 20, 40; Madden, *Down and Antrim in '98*, 132.

30. General Dalrymple to William Wickham, July 17, 1798, in *Castlereagh Corr.*, vol. 1, 238–40.

31. Caldwell, "North County Family," 87, 109–10; Reb. Pap. 620/3/51/5.

32. This version of the events comes from James Burns, known as "old Croppy." Its accuracy cannot be verified. See Young, *Ulster in '98*, 41.

33. Gwyn A. Williams, *Madoc: The Making of a Myth* (London, 1980). See also John Hammond Moore, "Theophilus Harris's Thoughts on Emigrating to America in 1793," *WMQ* 3rd Ser., 36 (1979): 602–14; H. M. Davis, " 'Very Different Springs of Uneasiness': Emigration from Wales to the United States of America during the 1790s," *Welsh Historical Review* 15 (1990–91): 368–98. Davis emphasizes the variety of reasons among the Welsh for emigration.

34. Priestley to Russell, June 12, 1792, in Samuel H. Jeyes, *The Russells of Birmingham in the French Revolution and in America 1791–1814* (London, 1911), 48; Priestley to Russell, April 30, 1793, in Rutt, ed., *Works*, vol. 1, ii, 199.

35. Priestley to J. Gough, Aug. 25, 1793, in Rutt, ed., *Works*, vol. 1, ii, 208.

36. Priestley, *The Memoirs of Dr. Joseph Priestley* (1806 ed.), vol. 1, 125.

37. John Wallace Nelson, "The Belfast Presbyterians, 1670–1830: An Analysis of Their Political and Social Interests" (Ph.D. diss., Queen's University, Belfast, 1985), 37. This is not to suggest that the general assembly of the Church of Scotland had any formal authority over the general synod of Ulster. The former was an established church, subject, after 1707, to the authority of Parliament. The latter was an autonomous assembly, although its ministers received the *regium donum*.

38. Peter Brooke, "Controversies in Ulster Presbyterianism, 1790–1836" (Ph.D. diss., Cambridge University, 1980), ix–x; David Stevenson, *The Covenanters: The National Covenant and Scotland* (Edinburgh, 1988), 73.

39. Thomas Hamilton, *History of the Irish Presbyterian Church* (Edinburgh, 1887), 131–32; Ian B. Cowan, *The Scottish Covenanters, 1660–1688* (London, 1976); W. Melancthon Glasgow, *History of the Reformed Presbyterian Church in America* (Baltimore, 1888), 45–46; Brooke, "Controversies," x–xi, 9; Stevenson, *Covenanters*, passim.

40. *N. Star*, No. 102, Dec. 22, 1792.

41. Emmet, "Part of an Essay," in William J. MacNeven, ed., *Pieces of Irish History* (New York, 1807), 119.

42. Quoted in Brooke, "Controversies," 26–27.

43. Glasgow, *Reformed Presbyterian Church*, 600–601; Thomas Witherow, *Historical and Literary Memorials of Presbyterianism in Ireland (1731–1880)*, 2nd Ser. (London, 1880), 336.

44. Glasgow, *Reformed Presbyterian Church*, 521–22.

45. Samuel McSkimin, *Annals of Ulster*, new ed. (Belfast, 1906), 35.

46. Quoted in Brooke, "Controversies," 32.

47. *N. Star*, Oct. 3, 1796.

48. Emmet, "Part of an Essay," 118.

49. McSkimin, *Annals of Ulster*, 102; James Seaton Reid and W. D. Killen, *History of the Presbyterian Church in Ireland*, 2nd ed. (London, 1853), vol. 3, 424; Caldwell, "North County Family," 117.

50. Gilbert McMaster, *The Upright Man in Life and at Death* (Philadelphia, 1852), 44. That the four students were members of the United Irishmen is strongly implied by Wylie in [Philadelphia] *Gazette of the United States*, Dec. 26, 1798.

51. Cornwallis to Portland, June 28, 1798, in Ross, ed., *Cornwallis Corr.*, vol. 2, 356.

52. *Castlereagh Corr.*, vol. 1, 149–50.

53. Cornwallis to Portland, July 8, 1798, in Ross, ed., *Cornwallis Corr.*, 359–60.

54. William Elliot to Pelham, July 29, 1798, BL Add.MSS. 33106, fo. 27.

55. Castlereagh to Sir James Steuart, June 25, 1798, in Ross, ed., *Cornwallis Corr.*, vol. 2, 355.

56. Michael Durey, "The Fate of Irish Rebel Prisoners, 1797–1804," Paper presented at the Australasian Modern British History Association Conference in Melbourne, February 1995.

57. "J. W." to Cooke, May 22, 27, 1797, May 24, 1798, Reb. Pap. 620/10/121/58, 60, 104; Daire Keogh, *"The French Disease": The Catholic Church and Radicalism in Ireland, 1790–1800* (Dublin, 1993), 173; Fitzpatrick, *Secret Service Under Pitt*, 188.

58. Young, *Ulster in '98*, 15, 66; Dickson, *Antrim and Down*, 160, 242; McCance Collection, PRONI 272/35A; Fox, "Narrative of the Proceedings of the Rebel Army in Down," Reb. Pap. 620/4/41; Madden, *Down and Antrim in '98*, 129–30.

59. Roger J. McHugh, ed., *The Autobiography of William Farrell of Carlow* (Dublin, n.d.), 118, 213–17; Castlereagh to William Wickham, Feb. 6, 1799, PRO HO100/88, fos. 88–90.

60. Wendy Hinde, *Castlereagh* (London, 1981), 47–48.

61. Sinclair to Cornwallis, Aug. 22, 1798, Reb. Pap. 620/4/29/26; Reb. Pap. 620/3/28/17. Montgomery was not a clever choice. He was an inactive magistrate "who is no friend to Government, or its measures, and whom I strongly suspect." Col. Q. Atherton to Gen. Nugent, June 20, 1798, quoted in W. J. Fitzpatrick, *The Sham Squire, and Informers of 1798* (Dublin, 1895), 348.

62. Caldwell, "North County Family," 113–14.

63. Aiken McClelland, "Thomas Ledlie Birch, United Irishman," *Proceedings of the Belfast Natural History and Philosophical Society* 7 (1963): 30–31.

64. *Irish Presbyterian Fasti,* no. 209; Dickson, *Antrim and Down,* 143–44. Dr. Birch in addition managed to save his son, also called George, who was allowed to go to the East Indies, where he became a lieutenant in the Bengal infantry.

65. Reb. Pap. 620/3/23/1.

66. Robert Craufurd to William Wickham, July 25, 1798, Hampshire County Record Office, Wickham Papers, 38M49/2/14/5; Henry Alexander to Pelham, July 26, 1798, BL Add.MSS. 33106, fos. 21–24.

67. Reb. Pap. 620/3/28/6; Reb. Pap. 620/3/19/7.

68. Graduation Certificate, Warden Papers, MS871; Francis C. Haber, *David Bailie Warden, A Bibliographical Sketch of America's Cultural Ambassador in France, 1804–45* (Washington, D.C., 1954), 2; David Bailie Warden, *A Farewell Address to the Junto of the Presbytery of Bangor* (Glasgow, 1798); reprinted in W. T. Latimer, "David Bailie Warden, Patriot 1798," *Ulster Journal of Archeology* 23 (1907): 34; Reb. Pap. 620/3/28/18.

69. Reb. Pap. 620/3/28/7; Dickson, *Antrim and Down,* 145.

70. Caldwell, "North County Family," 98. Caldwell's claim that his position as treasurer of the Ulster United Irishmen involved no more than organizing a lottery can be taken with a grain of salt.

71. Madden Papers, TCD S.3.19–33/166 (statement of Mrs. Murray).

72. Castlereagh to Wickham, Aug. 12, 1798, in *Castlereagh Corr.,* vol. 1, 261.

73. Cornwallis to Portland, Oct. 29, 1798, in Ross, ed., *Cornwallis Corr.,* vol. 2, 428.

74. Castlereagh to Wickham, Oct. 29, 1798, in Ross, ed., *Cornwallis Corr.,* vol. 2, 426.

75. Castlereagh to Wickham, June 22, 1798, PRO HO100/77, fos. 180–81; John Pollock to E. Cooke, Aug. 26, 1798, Reb. Pap. 620/39/213.

76. John Pollock to Castlereagh, Aug. 26, 1798, Reb. Pap. 620/4/29/30.

77. W. J. MacNeven, "An Account of the Treaty between the United Irishmen and the Anglo Irish Government in 1798," in MacNeven, ed., *Pieces of Irish History,* 172.

78. Neilson's Account of the Negotiation, in Madden, *United Irishmen,* 2nd Ser., vol. 1, 153–54.

79. Madden, *United Irishmen,* 2nd Ser., vol. 1, 149, 155.

80. Neilson's Account, 155–56.

81. *Castlereagh Corr.,* vol. 1, 347; Cornwallis to Portland, July 26, 1798, in *Cornwallis Corr.,* vol. 2, 372.

82. *Cornwallis Corr.,* vol. 2, 374.

83. Byrne, as a former member of the Mount Kennedy yeomanry cavalry, and thus a turncoat, was in one of the categories of offenders that few people thought ought to be shown clemency, irrespective of the negotiations. Howell and Howell, eds., *State Trials,* vol. 27, 455–522, for Byrne's trial.

84. For Clare's view of the effect of O'Connor's subsequent acknowledgment of treason on the reputation of the Foxites, see Clare to Camden, Aug. 13, 1798, KCRO U840 0183/12.

85. Sampson, *Memoirs*, 37.

86. *Cornwallis Corr.*, vol. 2, 373. John Hughes could have condemned Neilson with his evidence. Cooke, who knew Hughes better, was sceptical.

87. Henry Alexander to Pelham, July 26, 1798, Pelham Papers, BL Add.MSS. 33106, fos. 21–24.

88. Alexander to Pelham, Aug. 4, 1798, Pelham Papers, BL Add.MSS. 33106, fos. 39–40.

89. Francis Dobbs to Castlereagh, July 28, 1798, Reb. Pap. 620/4/29/15; Cooke to Wickham, July 28, 1798, in *Cornwallis Corr.*, vol. 2, 378.

90. MacNeven, "Account of the Treaty," in *Pieces of Irish History*, 182. This applied only to those already in prison or who had been involved in the rebellion of June and July. It did not apply to those who joined the French invasion of August 1798. But even in the courts-martial after August, Cornwallis was prepared to confirm death sentences only for those who were leaders or who were "Guilty of deliberate Murder and Robbery." [Castle] to Nugent, Sept. 27, 1798, PRO HO100/86, fol. 69.

91. Copies of this document can be found in *Castlereagh Corr.*, vol. 1, 353–72, and MacNeven, ed., *Pieces of Irish History*, 207–30.

92. Cornwallis to Portland, Aug. 7, 1798, in *Cornwallis Corr.*, vol. 2, 382–83; Clare to Camden, Aug. 13, 1798, KCRO U840 0183/12.

93. Henry Alexander to Pelham, Aug. 4, 1798, Pelham Papers, BL Add.MSS. 33106, fol. 40; Elliott, *Partners in Revolution*, 209.

94. Castlereagh to Wickham, Oct. 29, 1798, in *Cornwallis Corr.*, vol. 2, 426.

95. Castlereagh to Wickham, Oct.29, 1798, in *Castlereagh Corr.*, vol. 1, 414.

96. [Dublin] Freeman's Journal, Aug. 30, 1798.

97. The names of those offered the deal, and their responses, can be found in Reb. Pap. 620/39/203.

98. Cornwallis to Portland, Oct. 29, 1798, Castlereagh to Wickham, Oct. 29, 1798, in *Cornwallis Corr.*, vol. 2, 428, 426.

99. Sampson, *Memoirs*, 50, 52.

100. Portland to Cornwallis, Nov. 12, 1798, in *Cornwallis Corr.*, vol. 2, 438.

101. Neilson's account, in Madden, *United Irishmen*, 158. Thomas Russell's views were the same. See Russell to Dobbs, Sept. 14, 1798, Reb. Pap. 620/16/3.

102. MacNeven, "Account of the Treaty," in *Pieces of Irish History*, 183.

103. Emmet to Rufus King [April 8, 1807], in Charles R. King, ed., *The Life and Correspondence of Rufus King*, vol. 5 (New York, 1898), 21–22.

104. King, ed., *King Correspondence*, vol. 5, 19.

105. King to Portland, Sept. 13, 1798, in King, ed., *King Correspondence*, vol. 2, 639–40.

106. Castlereagh made this point that the leaders did not wish to go to America (*Castlereagh Corr.*, vol. 1, 414), but it is confirmed by MacNeven to Cornwallis, Oct. 11,

1798, Reb. Pap. 620/15/5/34; Emmet to Cornwallis, Oct. 11, 1798, Reb. Pap. 620/15/2/13.

107. Cornwallis to Portland, Sept. 14, 1798, in *Castlereagh Corr.*, vol. 1, 348–49.

108. Lord Londonderry to Castlereagh, Dec. 10, 1798, in *Castlereagh Corr.*, vol. 2, 40; *DEP*, Dec. 8, 1798; Hugh Wilson to Thomas Russell, Dec. 5, 1798, Reb. Pap. 620/16/3; Neilson's account, reprinted in [Baltimore] *American Patriot*, Feb. 2, 1803; Madden, *United Irishmen*, vol. 4, 75.

109. Rupert J. Coughlin, *Napper Tandy* (Dublin, 1976), 124–54.

110. Castlereagh to Wickham, Jan. 2, 1799, Wickham to Castlereagh, Jan. 10, 1799, PRO HO100/85, 7, 31–32.

111. Cornwallis to Portland, Sept. 13, 1798, in *Cornwallis Corr.*, vol. 2, 405.

112. Castlereagh to Wickham, Jan. 2, 1799, PRO HO100/85, 7.

113. Castlereagh to Wickham, April 1, 1799, PRO HO100/86, 240.

114. Wickham to Cooke, March 23, 1799, Wickham to Castlereagh, March 26, 1799, PRO HO100/86, 179, 198–99.

115. Alexander Marsden to Wickham, March 19, 1799, PRO HO100/86, 189.

116. PRO PRO30/9/156, 133; Russell to Miss Russell, Dec. 20, 1801, Sirr Papers, TCD MS868/2, 291.

117. Benjamin Binns to Madden, Jan. 30, 1843, Madden Papers, TCD 873/451.

118. Madden, *United Irishmen*, 2nd Ser., vol. 1, 463, 451.

119. John Hughes to Thomas Jefferson, March 5, 1802, Jeff. Papers; Michael Durey, "John Hughes, Reluctant *Agent Provocateur* and Millenarian: A Note and New Documents," *Eighteenth-Century Ireland* 7 (1991): 146.

120. *RSCIHL* (1798), 23–29; Black Book of Northern Ireland, PRONI D272/1; Fitzpatrick, *Secret Service Under Pitt*, 94.

121. Madden, *United Irishmen*, Ser. 1, 451; *RSCIHL* (1798), 32.

122. John Pollock to Cooke, Aug. 26, 1798, Reb. Pap. 620/39/213. According to John Caldwell, "North County Family," 99, Hughes never mentioned the role of William Tennant in the United Irishmen because he was bribed to remain silent.

123. Madden, *United Irishmen*, Ser. 1, 455.

124. MacNeven, "Account of the Treaty," in *Pieces of Irish History*, 177–78.

125. Fitzgerald, *Secret Service Under Pitt*, 117, 122; Madden, *United Irishmen*, 2nd Ser., vol. 4, 56–57; Pakenham, *Year of Liberty*, 55.

126. Examination of George Warnock, Reb. Pap. 620/39/203. John Caldwell also was examined by Pollock at the same time. He confessed that Samuel Neilson had sworn him into the United Irishmen, but later retracted his statement and signed Nugent's Proclamation. Reb. Pap. 620/39/203. Understandably, he failed to mention this in his family biography.

127. PRONI 272/42; McClelland, "Birch," 32. Strangely, another Ulsterman who gave evidence to the government in 1798, the Ballymoney woollendraper James Huey, also accidentally drowned in America. PRONI 272/26; Caldwell, "North County Family," 136.

128. Dalrymple to Wickham, July 17, 1798, in *Castlereagh Corr.*, vol. 1, 238.

129. *RSCIHC* (1798), cclxxxvi.

130. Wickham to Castlereagh, July 23, 1798, in *Castlereagh Corr.*, vol. 1, 228–29.

131. Madden, *United Irishmen*, vol. 4, 258–59.

132. Report of "J. W.," May 24, [1797], Reb. Pap. 620/10/121/59.

133. R. B. McDowell, "The Personnel of the Dublin Society of United Irishmen," *Irish Historical Studies* 2 (1940–41): 47; Report of "J. W.," No. 197, 1805, Reb. Pap. 620/14/188/3.

134. Edinburgh City Parish Register, Dec. 27, 1775; [Petersburg, Va.] *Daily Courier,* Dec. 1, 1870. I am grateful to Stephen Walker for his assistance in uncovering Wood's career in Scotland.

135. *Edinburgh Evening Courant,* Jan. 11, 1794.

136. "The Edinburgh School of Design," *Book of the Old Edinburgh Club* 27 (1949): 74.

137. Minutes of the Trustees of the Board of Manufacturers in Scotland, Scottish Record Office, West Register House, NG 1/1/29, vol. 29, May 24, June 21, 1797, 272, 307.

138. Minutes of the Trustees, June 28, 1797, 310–11.

139. Minutes of the Trustees, July 5, 1797, 320–21. An appeal by Graham was dismissed in December.

140. J. B. Morrell, "Professors Robison and Playfair, and the *Theophobia Gallica:* Natural Philosophy, Religion, and Politics in Edinburgh, 1789–1815," *Notes and Records of the Royal Society* 26 (1971): 45.

141. Anand C. Chitnis, *The Scottish Enlightenment and Early Victorian English Society* (London, 1986), 61; "Edinburgh School of Design," 73.

142. Morrell, "Robison and Playfair," 47.

143. John Wood, *A General View of the History of Switzerland, with a particular account of the origin and accomplishment of the late Swiss revolution* (Edinburgh, 1799), 300–301. Wood's book was reviewed favorably in the *Scots Magazine* 62 (February 1800): 108–9.

144. Brims, "Scottish Democratic Movement," 567.

145. Records of the Presbytery of Edinburgh, SRO CH2/121/20a, vol. 17, 44–58; John Reith, *Life of Dr. John Leyden, Poet and Linguist* (Galashiels, 1908), vi–vii; *Edinburgh Clerical Review* 2 (Nov. 17, 1799): 4.

146. Minutes of the Trustees, vol. 30, Feb. 5, March 5, 1800, 128–29, 139–40.

147. Elizabeth M. Geffen, *Philadelphia Unitarianism 1796–1861* (Philadelphia, 1961), 37; Jeyes, *Russells of Birmingham,* 48.

148. Sampson, *Memoirs,* 238.

149. Caldwell, "North County Family," 4. John Caldwell also had strong trading links with America in the 1790s.

150. *DAB,* vol. 10, 233–35.

151. For "the sort of emigrating madness" affecting the tradesmen of Dublin at the war's end, see [Dublin] *Freeman's Journal,* February 18–20, 1783. I am grateful to Bob Reece for this reference.

152. Daniel J. Boorstin, *Hidden History: Exploring Our Secret Past* (New York, 1989), 127.

153. *N. Star*, No. 273, Aug. 14, 1794. See also *N. Star*, vol. 2, No. 23, March 20, 1793.

154. *N. Star*, No. 6, Jan. 18–21, 1792.

155. *Cork Gaz.*, Jan. 11, 1794.

156. Joseph Gerrald, *A Convention the Only Means of Saving Us from Ruin*, quoted in Arthur Sheps, "The Edinburgh Reform Convention of 1793 and the American Revolution," *Scottish Tradition* 5 (1975): 31.

157. Thomas Paine, *Rights of Man*, Part 2, in Philip S. Foner, ed., *The Complete Writings of Thomas Paine* (New York, 1945), vol. 1, 360, 371.

158. Mark Philp, "The Role of America in the 'Debate on France' 1791–5: Thomas Paine's Insertion," *Utilitas* 5 (1993): 221–37.

159. Burk, *History of the Late War*, iii.

160. MacNeven, ed., *Pieces of Irish History*, iv.

161. Daniel McCurtin to Mathew Carey, June 13, 1798, Lea and Febiger Collection, HSP.

162. Thomas Addis Emmet, "Substance of Thomas Addis Emmet's Examination," in MacNeven, ed., *Pieces of Irish History*, 265. This part of the interrogation is not recorded in *RSCIHL* (1798).

163. For Dissenters' preference for America, see above, 49.

164. Colin Bonwick, *English Radicals and the American Revolution* (Chapel Hill, 1977), 234.

165. Thomas Cooper, *A Reply to Mr. Burke's Invective against Mr. Cooper* (Manchester, 1792), 29.

166. Thomas Cooper, *Some Information Respecting America* (Dublin, 1794), 75–76.

167. Ibid., 53, 77.

168. Ian Sellers, "William Roscoe: The Roscoe Circle and Radical Politics in Liverpool, 1787–1807," *Transactions of the Lancashire and Cheshire Historical Society* 120 (1968): 53.

169. C. B. Jewson, *The Jacobin City: A Portrait of Norwich in Its Reaction to the French Revolution 1788–1802* (Glasgow, 1975), 59.

170. Frida Knight, *The Strange Case of Thomas Walker: Ten Years in the Life of a Manchester Radical* (London, 1957), 176.

171. R. G. Thorne, *The History of Parliament* (London, 1986), vol. 5, 443.

172. William H. Stafford, ed., *The Blennerhassett Papers* (Cincinnati, 1864), 26; [Philadelphia] *Aurora*, 30 October 1794.

173. Elliott, *Tone*, 162; Madden, *United Irishmen*, vol. 4, 92, 167.

174. *N. Star*, No. 25, March 24–28, 1792. Thomas Ledlie Birch sold his farm to his brother James for £500 in 1798. Eight months later James sold it for £1,111. McClelland, "Birch," 27.

175. McHugh, ed., *Carlow*, 216.

176. Cobbett, *Porcupine's Works*, vol. 8, 70; Clark Hunter, ed., *The Life and Letters of Alexander Wilson* (Philadelphia, 1983), 149.

177. James L. Clifford, "Robert Merry—A Pre-Byronic Hero," *Bulletin of the John Rylands Library* 27 (1942): 95.

178. Joseph I. Shulim, "John Daly Burk, Irish Revolutionist and American Patriot," *Transactions of the American Philosophical Society*, New Ser. 54 (1964): 11; [Philadelphia] *Daily Advertiser*, March 2, 1797.

179. Priestley to Lindsey, June 6, 1794, in Rutt, ed., *Works*, vol. 1, ii, 244.

180. Bernard McKenna's account of his journey in 1797 is perfunctory. See McKenna to Rev. Henry Conwell, Sept. 15, 1811, NLI, MS. 2300.

181. Coleborne, "Image of Exile," 1.

182. D. H. Weinglass, "Ralph Eddowes," in *Biographical Dictionary*, ed. Baylen and Gossman, 147.

183. Warden to [Anon, Sept. 1799?], Kinderhook Letterbook, Warden Papers.

184. Caldwell, "North County Family," 130.

185. Caldwell, "North County Family," 128. Simpson and Sinclair were both from Newtownards; the dispute, over the level of Sinclair's Calvinism, may have been long-running.

186. Cooke to Wickham, Jan. 11, 1799, PRO HO100/85, 51. Sampson, *Memoirs*, 167, denied "improper conduct and language in Wales."

187. Caldwell, "North County Family," 119–20; Londonderry to Castlereagh, n.d., Nugent to Alexander Marsden, March 27, 1799, Reb. Pap. 620/8/85/13.

188. Tone to Thomas Russell, Aug. 7, 1795, Russell Correspondence, Sirr Papers, MS868/1, 2.

189. Briggs, "Gales," 114.

190. Caldwell, "North County Family," 128–29.

191. Bernard McKenna's ship also was stopped after a two-hour chase by a French vessel, which let them go without damage.

192. Madden, *United Irishmen*, vol. 1, 336–38.

193. This and the following paragraphs are indebted to the long account of the Russells' journey, based on the diaries of Martha and Mary Russell, in Jeyes, *Russells of Birmingham*.

194. Ibid., 87.

195. Ibid., 93–94.

196. Claire Tomalin, *The Life and Death of Mary Wollstonecraft* (London, 1974), 127.

197. Jeyes, *Russells of Birmingham*, 125–26.

198. Ibid., 135.

199. Ibid., 164–65.

CHAPTER FIVE. LAND OF OPPORTUNITY?

1. Two good recent studies of America in the 1790s are Stanley Elkins and Eric McKitrick, *The Age of Federalism: The Early American Republic, 1788–1800* (New York, 1993), and James Roger Sharp, *American Politics in the Early Republic: The New Nation*

in Crisis (New Haven, 1993). The best older source is John C. Miller, *The Federalist Era 1789–1801* (New York, 1963).

2. [Boston] *Polar Star*, Oct. 6, 1796.

3. For Burk's account of his troubles a few years after he emigrated, see Burk to Jefferson, June 1801, Jeff. Papers.

4. Giles MacDonagh, *Brillat-Savarin: The Judge and His Stomach* (London, 1992), 117.

5. John Caldwell, "Particulars of History of North County Irish Family," 158.

6. John Caldwell to Robert Simms, Oct. 18, 1802, PRONI D1759/3B/6/51.

7. White to Robert Simms, Nov. 16, 1804, PRONI D1759/3B/6/55.

8. White's son was sent to New York to become a lawyer, assisted by the Irish immigrants there. William Sampson to Mrs. Sampson, July 18, 1806, Sampson Letters.

9. Mathew Carey, "The Autobiography of Mathew Carey," *New England Magazine*, 1833–34, Letter 5, 93.

10. John Chambers to Simms, June 6, 1818, PRONI D1759/3B/6/44.

11. Wilson to parents, July 25, 1794, Wilson to anon, 1796?, in Clark Hunter, ed., *The Life and Letters of Alexander Wilson* (Philadelphia, 1983), 150, 152.

12. See above, 165–66.

13. Thomas Dunn, *A Discourse, Delivered in the New Dutch Church, Nassau Street* (New York, 1794), 4, 13–14.

14. Thomas Cooper, *A Reply to Mr. Burke's Invective against Mr. Cooper, and Mr. Watt, in the House of Commons, on 30th. April, 1792* (Manchester, 1792), 22.

15. Timothy Telltruth [John Lithgow], *The Collected Wisdom of Ages, the Most Stupendous Fabric of Human Invention, the English Constitution* (Philadelphia, 1799), v.

16. [John Binns], *Recollections of the Life of John Binns: Twenty-Nine Years in Europe and Fifty-Three in the United States* (Philadelphia, 1854), 73.

17. George S. Rowell, "Benjamin Vaughan—Patriot, Scholar, Diplomat," *Magazine of History* 22, no. 3 (1916): 56.

18. Tone to Russell, Aug. 7, 1795, Sirr Papers, MS 868/1, 2.

19. For Rowan's complaint at "the exorbitant rate of everything," see Archibald Hamilton Rowan, *The Autobiography of Archibald Hamilton Rowan*, ed. William H. Drummond (Dublin, 1840), 282.

20. Charles W. Janson, *The Stranger in America, 1793–1806* (London, 1807), 20.

21. Bradford Perkins, "A Diplomat's Wife in Philadelphia: Letters of Henrietta Liston, 1796–1800," *WMQ* 3rd Ser., 11 (1954): 602.

22. Caldwell, "North County Family," 130.

23. [Thomas Ledlie Birch], *A Letter from an Irish Emigrant to His Friend in the United States, Giving an Account of the Rise and Progress of the Commotions in Ireland* (Philadelphia, 1799), 55.

24. For evidence of a better welcome for exiles arriving both before and after the hostile years 1797–1801, see Sarah Bache to William Bache, June 4, 1795, Bache Papers; Sampson to Mrs. Sampson, July 18, 1806, Sampson Letters.

25. Binns, *Recollections*, 338.

26. Rowan, *Autobiography*, 306.

27. Warden, Kinderhook Letterbook, April 28, 1799. For Watty Cox's homesickness, see *Exile*, Jan. 4, 1817.

28. W. R. Brock and C. H. Brock, *Scotus Americanus* (Edinburgh, 1982), 162.

29. Callender to Jefferson, Sept. 22, 1798, in Worthington C. Ford, ed., "Thomas Jefferson and James Thomson Callender," *New England Historical and Geneological Register* 51 (1896): 328.

30. Warden, Kinderhook Letterbook, April 20, 1799; Callender to Jefferson, Sept. 26, 1799, in Ford, ed., "Jefferson and Callender," 448.

31. Wilson to ?, 1795?, Wilson to Orr, July 12, 1801, Wilson to Alexander Wilson, Sr., June 15, 1809, in Hunter, ed., *Wilson*, 152, 182–83, 224.

32. Emmet to Simms, June 1, 1805, PRONI D1759/3B/6/27.

33. Perkins, "Liston," 602. Robert Liston affectionately acknowledged in 1800 that his wife "had the gift of the gab." Esmond Wright, "Robert Liston, Second British Minister to the United States," *History Today* 11 (1961): 119.

34. For a nonradical emigrant's views on these "evils of a republican form of government," see Janson, *Stranger in America*, 200, 304.

35. Priestley to Lindsey, July 12, 1795, quoted in Margaret Evelyn Leslie, "The Social and Political Thought of Joseph Priestley," (Ph.D. diss., Cambridge University, 1966), 229.

36. Gwyn A. Williams, "Morgan John Rhees and His Beula," *Welsh History Review* 3 (1967): 441–72.

37. Joseph Priestley, *Memoirs of Dr. Joseph Priestley*, vol. 1 (Northumberland, Pa., 1806), 166–67.

38. Caldwell to Simms, Oct. 18, 1802, PRONI D1759/3B/6/51.

39. S. H. Jeyes, *The Russells of Birmingham in the French Revolution and in America 1791–1814* (London, 1911), chaps. 13 and 14.

40. Chambers to Simms, May 9, 1806, PRONI D1759/3B/6/36.

41. Sampson Letters, Aug. 17, 1806.

42. Willis G. Briggs, "Joseph Gales, Editor of Raleigh's First Newspaper," *North Carolina Booklet* 7 (1907): 114–15.

43. Michael Durey, *"With the Hammer of Truth": James Thomson Callender and America's Early National Heroes* (Charlottesville, Va., 1990), 52–55.

44. In law, Duane was thus an alien when he returned to America in 1796, having been born in the empire and not residing in America when independence was proclaimed.

45. Kim T. Phillips, "William Duane, Revolutionary Editor" (Ph.D. diss., University of California, Berkeley, 1968), 4–34.

46. For Lloyd, see Richard J. Twomey, *Jacobins and Jeffersonians: Anglo-American Radicalism in the United States, 1790–1820* (New York, 1989), 44–46; Marion Tinling, "Thomas Lloyd's Reports of the First Federal Congress," *WMQ* 3rd Ser., 18 (1961): 519–45.

47. Phillips, "Duane," 49, 231.

48. Thomas P. Robinson, "The Life of Thomas Addis Emmet," (Ph.D. diss., New York University, 1955), 282.

49. Wilson to Charles Orr, July 12, 1801, in Hunter, ed., *Wilson*, 181. See also *Temple of Reason*, June 17, 1801.

50. John W. Francis, *Old New York: or, Reminiscences of the Past Sixty Years* (New York, 1865), 339, claimed that New York communities had difficulty finding teachers in the first years of the century.

51. William Cobbett, *Porcupine's Works*, vol. 10 (London, 1803), 64–65.

52. Francis C. Haber, *David Bailie Warden: A Bibliographical Sketch of America's Cultural Ambassador in France, 1804–45* (Washington, D.C., 1954), 3; Articles of Agreement, Oct. 8, 1802, in Warden, Kinderhook Letter Book.

53. Wilson to Orr, July 12, 23, Aug. 7, 1801, Feb. 14, 1802, in Hunter, ed., *Wilson*, 182–84, 187, 191.

54. Bernard McKenna to Rev. Henry Conwell, Sept. 15, 1811, NLI MS. 2300.

55. Janson, *Stranger in America*, 419. Thomas Cooper, *Some Information Respecting America* (London, 1794), 63, thought that American-born doctors were preferred to immigrants, but that the profession was open.

56. For this Presbyterian nouveau riche elite in Baltimore, see William Bruce Wheeler, "Urban Politics in Nature's Republic: The Development of Political Parties in the Seaport Cities in the Federalist Era" (Ph.D. diss., University of Virginia, 1967), 34–35.

57. Caldwell to Robert Simms, Oct. 18, 1802, PRONI D1759/3B/6/49.

58. George Cuming to Simms, Aug. 30, 1805, PRONI D1759/3B/6/31.

59. Cuming to Simms, May 10, 1806, PRONI D1759/3B/6/32.

60. Carey, "Autobiography," Letter 2, 490; Edward C. Carter, "The Political Activities of Mathew Carey, Nationalist, 1760–1814" (Ph.D. diss., Bryn Mawr College, 1962), 52.

61. Emmet to Peter Burrows, Nov. 19, 1806, quoted in Robinson, "Emmet," 225.

62. Caldwell, "North County Family," 158–59; Robinson, "Emmet," 227–30; John Chambers to Simms, May 9, 1806, D1759/3B/6/36; *Aurora*, July 26, 1806.

63. Sampson to Mrs. Sampson, Aug. 17, Oct. 15, 1806, Sampson Letters.

64. According to Rev. Thomas Dunn in 1794, and Priestley in 1797, most of the immigrants required only information and advice from the aid societies, not financial assistance. Dunn, *Discourse*, 25; Joseph Priestley, *The Case of the Poor Emigrants Recommended* (Philadelphia, 1797), 18–19. This had probably changed ten years later.

65. Wheeler, "Urban Politics," 12; Erna Risch, "Immigrant Aid Societies before 1820," *PMHB* 60 (1936): 15–16.

66. Elizabeth M. Geffen, *Philadelphia Unitarianism 1796–1861* (Philadelphia, 1961), 291–92.

67. Carey, "Autobiography," Letter 6, 96–97; J. Thomas Scharf and Thompson Westcott, *History of Philadelphia, 1609–1884* (Philadelphia, 1884), vol. 2, 1465–67; Carter, "Mathew Carey," 120, 194–95.

68. *Am. Pat.*, Jan. 15, 1803; Robinson, "Emmet," 297–98; Sampson, *Memoirs*, 392–93.

69. *Am. Cit.*, Dec. 31, 1807.

70. Caldwell to Simms, Oct. 18, 1802, PRONI D1759/3B/6/49–50.

71. Robinson, "Emmet," 289.

72. R. R. Madden, *The United Irishmen: Their Lives and Times*, vol. 3 (Dublin, 1858), 232; Chambers to Simms, June 6, 1818, PRONI D1759/3B/6/43.

73. Durey, *Callender*, 106.

74. Richard J. Twomey, "Jacobins and Jeffersonians: Anglo-American Radical Ideology, 1790–1810," in Jacob and Jacob, eds., *Origins of Anglo-American Radicalism*, 72; *Aug. Chron.*, Dec. 7, 1805.

75. *Temple of Reason*, March 13, 1802; Twomey, *Jacobins and Jeffersonians*, 73–74.

76. Gwyn A. Williams, "Morgan John Rhees and His Beula," 462.

77. Twomey, *Jacobins and Jeffersonians*, 67–68.

78. Rollo G. Silver, *Typefounding in America, 1787–1825* (Charlottesville, Va., 1965), 73.

79. Twomey, *Jacobins and Jeffersonians*, 71, 68.

80. John Chambers to Simms, May 24, 1811, PRONI D1759/3B/6/40–41; Haber, *Warden*, 14, 27–28.

81. Binns, *Recollections*, 294.

82. See, generally, the Simms and Bryson Papers in PRONI, and the Warden Papers.

83. Madden, *United Irishmen*, vol. 3, 182; Sampson to Mrs. Sampson, April 29, 1810, Sampson Letters; Caldwell, "North County Family," 5, 145.

84. Colin Bonwick, *English Radicals and the American Revolution* (Chapel Hill, 1977), 33, 198.

85. The religious sections of the state constitutions can be found most conveniently in Edwin S. Gaustad, *Neither King Nor Prelate: Religion and the New Nation 1776–1826* (Grand Rapids, Mich., 1993), 159–74.

86. *Am. Cit.*, Feb. 12, 1806.

87. David Bailie Warden, *A Farewell Address to the Junto of the Presbytery of Bangor, which met in Belfast, on the Sixth of November 1798* (Glasgow, 1798).

88. Jon Butler, *Awash in a Sea of Faith: Christianizing the American People* (Cambridge, Mass., 1990); Nathan O. Hatch, *The Democratization of American Christianity* (New Haven, 1989). For a reasoned attempt to moderate the more extreme claims of evangelicalism's influence, see Jon Butler, "Coercion, Miracle, Reason: Rethinking the American Religious Experience in the Revolutionary Age," in Ronald Hoffman and Peter J. Albert, eds., *Religion in a Revolutionary Age* (Charlottesville, 1994), 1–30.

89. Thomas Ledlie Birch, *Seemingly Experimental Religion, Instructors Unexperienced—Converters Unconverted—Revivals Killing Religion* (Washington, Pa., 1806); David W. Miller, "Presbyterianism and 'Modernisation' in Ulster," *Past and Present* 80 (1978): 67–68. Steele became minister of the First Pittsburg congregation in 1802, remaining there until his death in 1810. Birch was eventually received by the Baltimore

Presbytery, but bought a farm in western Pennsylvania, where he died in 1828. Aiken McClelland, "Thomas Ledlie Birch, United Irishman," *Proceedings of the Belfast Natural History and Philosophical Society* 7 (1963): 33–35; *Irish Presbyterian Fasti*, 3002.

90. William Wilson McKinney, *Early Pittsburgh Presbyterianism* (Pittsburgh, 1938), 105–26; David A. McKnight, *Historical Sketch of the Sabbath-Schools Connected with the 1st. Presbyterian Congregation of Pittsburgh from 1800 to 1867* (Pittsburgh, 1867), 10–12.

91. David Stewart, *The Seceders in Ireland, with Annals of Their Congregations* (Belfast, 1950), 271, 331–32, 341.

92. Minutes and Records of the Presbytery of Antrim, Oct. 10, 1798, PRONI T1053/1; Sinclair to Warden, April 18, 1808, Warden Papers.

93. Thomas Jefferson to Gov. Thomas McKean, March 3, 1805, Jeff. Papers.

94. Glendy to Jefferson, Dec. 5, 1801, Jeff. Papers; *Am. Cit.*, Dec. 14, 1805.

95. Ralph Eddowes, *Sermons Delivered Before the First Society of Unitarian Christians* (Chester, 1788), vii.

96. Geffen, *Philadelphia Unitarianism*, 33; Henry F. May, *The Enlightenment in America* (New York, 1976), 227; *DAB*, vol. 9, 601–2.

97. L. Baker-Short, *Pioneers of Scottish Unitarianism* (Narberth, Pa., 1965), 44–47; Geffen, *Philadelphia Unitarianism*, 69.

98. Quoted in Briggs, "Gales," 127–28.

99. Eddowes, *Sermons*, x.

100. Standish Meacham, "Priestley in America," *History Today* 12 (1962): 570.

101. Ralph Eddowes, *The Unity of God* (Philadephia, 1813), 6.

102. Priestley, *Memoirs*, vol. 2, 768 (comments of William Christie).

103. Geffen, *Philadelphia Unitarianism*, 67.

104. W. Melancthon Glasgow, *History of the Reformed Presbyterian Church in America* (Baltimore, 1888), 438–41, 470–71, 740–43; [Anon.], *A Narrative of Recent Occurrences within the Bounds of the Eastern Subordinate Synod of the Reformed Presbyterian Church* (New York, 1834), 37.

105. Scharf and Westcott, *Philadelphia*, vol. 2, 1277.

106. Glasgow, *Reformed Presbyterian Church*, 53, 67–69.

107. Samuel B. Wylie, *Two Sons of Oil* (Philadelphia, 1803); Wylie, *The Obligation of Covenants* (Philadelphia, 1804).

108. Scharf and Westcott, *Philadelphia*, vol. 2, 1277.

109. Wylie to Warden, Nov. 15, 1809, Warden Papers.

110. Cobbett, *Porcupine's Works*, vol. 10, 66; John Neil McLeod, *Preparation for Death the Business of Life: A discourse on the death of the Rev. Samuel Brown Wylie* (New York, 1852), 23; *DAB*, vol. 10, 581.

111. Samuel B. Wylie, *Sentiments of the Rev. Samuel B. Wylie, A. M. in 1803* (Philadelphia, 1832).

112. For Palmer, see Roderick S. French, "Elihu Palmer, Radical Deist, Radical Republican: A Reconsideration of American Free Thought," *Studies in Eighteenth-Century Culture* 8 (1979): 87–108; Kerry S. Walters, *The American Deists: Voices of Reason and Dissent in the Early Republic* (Lawrence, Kans., 1992).

113. John Wood, *A Full Exposition of the Clintonian Faction, and the Society of Columbian Illuminati* (Newark, 1802), 28.

114. Michael Durey, "Irish Deism and Jefferson's Republic: Denis Driscol in Ireland and America, 1793–1810," *Éire-Ireland: A Journal of Irish Studies* 25 (1990): 67; *Temple of Reason*, Oct. 2, 1802.

115. Howard B. Rock, *Artisans of the New Republic: The Tradesmen of New York in the Age of Jefferson* (New York, 1979), 316.

116. Durey, "Denis Driscol," 65.

117. *Temple of Reason*, May 13, 1801, Jan. 6, 1802.

118. Eric Foner, *Tom Paine and Revolutionary America* (New York, 1976), 256–57; James Turner, *Without God, Without Creed: The Origins of Unbelief in America* (Baltimore, 1985), 52–53.

119. For Lithgow's career in America, see Michael Durey, "John Lithgow's Lithconia: The Making and Meaning of America's First 'Utopian Socialist' Tract," *WMQ* 3rd Ser., 46 (1992): 675–94.

120. Jerry W. Knudson, "The Rage Around Tom Paine: Newspaper Reaction to His Homecoming in 1802," *New York Historical Society Quarterly* 53 (1969): 60.

121. For John Caldwell, see Caldwell to Simms, Oct. 18, 1802, PRONI D1759/3B/6/51. John Binns, who in the 1790s belonged to an infidel club in London and was fascinated by the deist views of John "Walking" Stewart, rejoined the Moravians in Philadelphia in 1812. William Hamilton Reid, *The Rise and Dissolution of the Infidel Societies in this Metropolis* (London, 1800), 13; Binns, *Recollections*, 325.

122. *Aug. Chron.*, April 21, 1804, May 18, 1805.

123. G. Adolf Koch, *Republican Religion: The American Religion and the Cult of Reason* (New York, 1933), 104.

124. See below, 248–51.

125. *The Rosciad* (1761).

126. *DAB*, vol. 10, 337.

127. Wilson wrote in 1804: "While others are hoarding up their bags of money, without the power of enjoying it, I am collecting, without injuring my conscience, or wounding my peace of mind, those beautiful specimens of Nature's work that are for ever pleasing." Wilson to William Bartram, March 31, 1804, in Hunter, ed., *Wilson*, 210.

128. Rutt, ed., *Works*, vol. 1, ii, 206.

129. *DAB*, vol. 9, 490–91.

130. Andrew Hook, *Scotland and America: A Study of Cultural Relations, 1750–1835* (Glasgow, 1975), 240.

131. Mary Thale, ed., *Selections from the Papers of the London Corresponding Society, 1792–1799* (Cambridge, 1983), 241.

132. Bagg, 137–42.

133. Madden, *United Irishmen*, vol. 3, 145.

134. Scharf and Westcott, *Philadelphia*, vol. 2, 1405.

135. Carter, "Mathew Carey," 19; Seamus O'Casaide, "John Chambers: Printer and

United Irishman," *Irish Book Lover*, July 1940), 234. For Thomas Traynor, a ship-builder in Dublin who successfully followed the same occupation on the Hudson River, see Madden, *United Irishmen*, vol. 3, 182–83.

136. Madden, *United Irishmen*, vol. 1, 338.

137. [New York] *Shamrock*, Sept. 14, 1811.

138. [Dublin] *Freeman's Journal*, June 9, 1798; Kerby A. Miller, *Emigrants and Exiles: Ireland and the Irish Exodus to North America* (New York, 1985), 190.

139. See also, for Andrew O'Cuinn, another successful and contented Irish refugee, *Irish Magazine*, Sept. 1809, 406–8.

140. James Tagg, *Benjamin Franklin Bache and the Philadelphia Aurora* (Philadelphia, 1991), 93; *Ral. Reg.*, Feb. 11, 1808; James Carey to Mathew Carey, Sept. 6, 1792, Mathew Carey to James Carey, Nov. 21, Dec. 11, 1792, Lea and Febiger Collection, HSP.

141. Seven typefoundries had collapsed in America before the successes of the Scottish exiles. Silver, *Typefounding in America*, 25.

142. *DAB*, vol. 3, 181.

143. Silver, *Typefounding in America*, 19–25; *Aurora*, July 10, 1806; I. Finch, *Travels in the United States of America and Canada* (London, 1833), 218. For Ronaldson's career as an entrepreneur, see M. Tait, "James Ronaldson, Baker, Typefounder, Philanthropist, and His Connexions in and around Edinburgh," *Book of the Old Edinburgh Club* 28 (1953): 44–50.

144. Walter Francis Brown, Jr., "John Adams and the American Press, 1797–1801: The First Full Scale Confrontation between the Executive and the Media" (Ph.D. diss., University of Notre Dame, 1974), 72.

145. Jerry Wayne Knudson, "The Jefferson Years: Response by the Press, 1801–1809" (Ph.D. diss., University of Virginia, 1962), 4, implies that more than 200 new newspapers were founded in the decade after 1800.

146. See Appendix.

147. Paul M. Spurlin, *The French Enlightenment in America* (Athens, Ga., 1984), 64–65; *Rec.*, Dec. 1, 1802.

148. Tagg, *Bache*, 95.

149. James Carey was the earliest innovator, in partnership with the Quaker Samuel Pleasants. Their daily *Virginia Gazette and Richmond Daily Advertiser* reverted to a triweekly after only two months in December 1792. Clarence S. Brigham, *History and Bibliography of American Newspapers, 1690–1820* (Worcester, Mass., 1947), vol. 2, 1149.

150. Carter, "Mathew Carey," 56; Brigham, *American Newspapers*, vol. 2, 897; *Charleston Daily Evening Gazette*, Jan. 10, 1795.

151. *Rec.*, Dec. 3, 1802.

152. *Rec.*, Dec. 3, 1802.

153. James N. Green, *Mathew Carey: Publisher and Patriot* (Philadelphia, 1985), 20; Earl L. Bradsher, *Mathew Carey: Editor, Author and Publisher* (1912, New York, 1966), 54.

154. Bradsher, *Carey*, 17.

155. [Washington] *National Magazine, or, Cabinet of the United States*, No. 8, Jan. 1802, 62–64; Janson, *Stranger in America*, 426; Francis, *Old New York*, 353–54. *Am. Pat.*, Dec. 11, 1802, for Carey being elected president at the New York literary fair, having previously been its secretary.

156. Green, *Carey*, 22.

157. Dumas Malone, *The Public Life of Thomas Cooper, 1783–1839* (New Haven, 1926), 230, 251–53.

158. Janson, *Stranger in America*, 291; *Monthly Repository* 14 (1819): 81–83; 19 (1824): 179–81.

159. Hook, *Scotland and America*, 241; Carter, "Mathew Carey," 244. For Valentine Derry, who in temporary exile in France had been professor of languages at Lafleche College and who opened an academy at Bloomingdale on settling in America, see *Shamrock*, April 20, 1811.

160. Thomas D'Arcy McGee, *A History of the Irish Settlers in North America* (Boston, 1851), 83–85.

161. Scharf and Westcott, *Philadelphia*, vol. 3, 1943.

162. Deasmumhan O'Raghallaigh, "William James MacNeven," *Studies: An Irish Quarterly Review* 30 (1941): 253; *DAB*, vol. 6, 153–54; *DNB*, vol. 12, 696–97.

163. Quoted in Twomey, *Jacobins and Jeffersonians*, 50.

164. Chambers to Simms, May 9, 1806, PRONI D1759/3B/6/36; Sampson to Mrs. Sampson, July 8, 1806, July 18, 1806, Sampson Letters; Emmet to Blennerhassett, Sept. 15, 1809, in William H. Stafford, ed., *The Blennerhassett Papers* (Cincinnati, 1864), 528–29; Theodorus Bailey to Warden, Nov. 28, 1809, Warden Papers; *Shamrock*, April 6, 1811; Twomey, *Jacobins and Jeffersonians*, 83; Miller, *Emigrants and Exiles*, 103.

165. PRONI D272/1; *Exam.*, Oct. 14, 1800.

166. Madden, *United Irishmen*, vol. 4, 139, 154. Other exiles who probably died of yellow fever were Arthur Kennedy, Joseph Cormick, and William Mitchell. For Kennedy, see Robert M. Young, *Ulster in '98: Episodes and Anecdotes* (Belfast, 1893), 43; for Cormick, *Aug. Chron.*, Aug. 23, 1806; and for Mitchell, see below, 210–11. Neilson's son died of yellow fever in Jamaica in 1817, aged 23.

167. Glasgow University Matriculation Records, Entry 3403; Madden, *United Irishmen*, vol. 2, 205. Mrs. Millar swiftly returned to Scotland, where she befriended the infamous Fanny Wright. Celia Morris, *Fanny Wright: Rebel in America* (Urbana and Chicago, 1992), 14.

168. Cobbett, *Porcupine's Works*, vol. 9, 258n.

169. John Bernard, *Retrospections of America, 1797–1811* (New York, 1887), 49.

170. James Fergusson, *Balloon Tytler* (London, 1972), 136–46 (quotation at 139).

171. Durey, *Callender*, chaps. 5–7. See below for Callender's political activities in more detail.

172. Carey, "Autobiography," Letter 5, 105–6.

173. Mathew Carey to James Carey, Dec. 19, 1792, Lea and Febiger Collection, HSP.

174. James Carey to Mathew Carey, Nov. 20, 28, 1794, Lea and Febiger Collection, HSP.

175. *Charleston Daily Evening Gazette*, Jan. 10, 1795.

176. James Carey to Mathew Carey, Aug. 16, 1800, Lea and Febiger Collection, HSP (misfiled in the correspondence for 1796).

177. *Aurora*, Feb. 6, 1801; Letters of Administration, No. 18, K64, 1801, Philadelphia City Hall Archives.

178. James Carey to Mathew Carey, Sept. 22, 1792, Lea and Febiger Collection, HSP.

179. James Morton Smith, *Freedom's Fetters: The Alien and Sedition Laws and American Civil Liberties* (Ithaca, N.Y., 1966), 206–20; Joseph I. Shulim, "John Daly Burk, Irish Revolutionist and American Patriot," *Transactions of the American Philosophical Society*, New Ser. 54 (1964): 25–36.

180. *Exam.*, Oct. 14, 1800.

181. Burk to Jefferson, June 1801, Jeff. Papers.

182. Shulim, "Burk," 39–51. Ironically, Skelton Jones, who contracted to finish Burk's *History of Virginia*, was also killed in a duel. Virginius Dabney, *Richmond: The Story of a City* (New York, 1976), 66–67.

183. Binns, *Recollections*, 79–80.

184. Caldwell to Simms, May 15, 1806, PRONI D1759/3B/6/53.

185. *Porcupine's Gazette*, Aug. 29, 1797; Cobbett, *Porcupine's Works*, vol. 9, 258n.

186. Robert Cantwell, *Alexander Wilson: Naturalist and Pioneer* (Philadelphia, 1961), 89.

187. Wilson to Orr, July 12, 23, Sept. 14, 1801, in Hunter, ed., *Wilson*, 181, 183, 188; Robert Brown, *Paisley Poets*, vol. 1 (N.p., 1889), 45.

188. Cantwell, *Wilson*, 106.

189. Wilson to Orr, July 12, 23, 1801, Wilson to James Gibb, March 4, 1811, in Hunter, ed., *Wilson*, 181, 183, 385–86; David Leon Chandler, *The Jefferson Conspiracies: A President's Role in the Assassination of Meriwether Lewis* (New York, 1994), 269–74.

190. Wilbur S. Shepperson, *Emigration and Disenchantment: Portraits of Englishmen Repatriated from the United States* (Norman, Okla., 1965), 3–6. Twenty percent of emigrants to Australia have returned to their countries of origin since 1945. [London] *Weekly Telegraph*, no. 204, June 14–20, 1995, 14.

191. Reb. Pap. 620/3/28/13; *Shamrock*, Nov. 30, 1811.

192. PRONI D272/14; Dr. S. M. Stephenson to Warden, 25 April 25, [1802?], Warden Papers.

193. Young, *Ulster in '98*, 41.

194. *Irish Magazine*, June 1812, 288. See also *Irish Magazine*, Sept. 1809, 432, for the return and death of the sickly Richard McCormick.

195. E. P. Thompson, *The Making of the English Working Class* (London, 1968), 197, erroneously suggests that only one English printer repatriated himself.

196. Richard Dinmore, *A Brief Account of the Moral and Political Acts of the Kings*

and Queens of England, from William the Conqueror to the Revolution in the Year 1688
(London, 1793), i.

197. Richard Dinmore, Jr., *An Exposition of the Principles of the English Jacobins*,
2nd ed. (Norwich, 1797).

198. For Dinmore's use of the medical title, see James Lyons to Jefferson, June 21,
1801, Jeff. Papers.

199. Brigham, *American Newspapers*, vol. 1, 98.

200. Matthew Lyon to Jefferson, Dec. 17, 1803, Jeff. Papers.

201. Janson, *Stranger in America*, 421–23.

202. *Rep. Argus*, March 2, 1804.

203. Sampson to Mrs. Sampson, Oct. 15, 1806, Sampson Letters.

204. Quoted in Henry Martyn Field, *The Irish Confederates, and the Rebellion of 1798*
(New York, 1851), 340.

205. Drennan to Samuel McTier, Jan. 17, 1794, *Drennan Letters*, 180.

206. Rowan, *Autobiography*, 285.

207. Madden, *United Irishmen*, vol. 2, 204–5.

208. Rowan, *Autobiography*, 288–89.

209. Corr. Pol. Ang. 588, fos. 195, 262–64, 268–69, Archives des Affaires
Étrangères, Paris; Rowan, *Autobiography*, 282; Report of "J. W.," Oct. 24, 1796, Reb.
Pap. 620/10/121/40.

210. Drennan to Martha McTier, c. March 1798, *Drennan Letters*, 270–71.

211. Cornwallis to Portland, Aug. 2, 1798, in Ross, ed., *Cornwallis Corr.*, vol. 2, 382.

212. Cornwallis to Portland, July 21, Aug. 29, 1799, PRO HO100/89, 111, 158–60.

213. Madden, *United Irishmen*, vol. 2, 208.

214. Chambers to Simms, June 17, 1807, PRONI D1759/3B/6/37; Madden, *United
Irishmen*, vol. 3, 159, vol. 4, 94; [Valentin Lawless], *Personal Recollections of the Life and
Times* (Dublin, 1850), 139; *Shamrock*, Oct. 12, 1811.

215. Chambers to Simms, June 17, 1807, PRONI D1759/3B/6/37. Chambers,
Byrne, and Sinclair were among those who changed their minds.

216. John Devereaux to Harman Blennerhassett, Oct. 12, 1807, Sept. 7, 1808, Mrs.
Blennerhassett to Blennerhassett, Jan. 3, 1824, in Stafford, ed., *Blennerhassett Papers*,
292–93, 523–25, 611; W. J. Fitzpatrick, *Secret Service under Pitt* (London, 1892), 207–8;
Binns, *Recollections*, 317–18; [Wexford] *The People*, July 4, 1980 (letter from E. T. D.
Lambert).

217. Caroline Robbins, "Honest Heretic: Joseph Priestley in America, 1794–1804,"
Proceedings of the American Philosophical Society 106 (1962): 66; James J. Hoecker, *Joseph
Priestly and the Idea of Progress* (New York, 1987), 242–43; Jefferson to Thomas Coo-
per, Nov. 29, 1802, April 9, 1803, Cooper to Jefferson, July 16, 1804, Jeff. Papers;
Malone, *Cooper*, 133–34.

218. Quoted in Jeyes, *Russells of Birmingham*, 267, 204–5.

219. Sampson to Mrs. Sampson, Jan. 25, [1807], April 1810?, Sampson Letters.

220. George Spater, "The Quest for William Cobbett: A Revisionist View of an

English Radical," *Times Higher Education Supplement,* Sept. 18, 1981, 12–13; George Spater, *William Cobbett: The Poor Man's Friend* (Cambridge, 1982), vol. 2, 518–22.

221. Carter, "Mathew Carey," 100–101; Binns, *Recollections,* 179.

222. Briggs, "Gales," 107–8.

223. Charles Hamilton Teeling, *History of the Irish Rebellion of 1798: A Personal Narrative* (Glasgow, 1828), 28–29.

224. Caldwell to Simms, Oct. 18, 1802, PRONI D1759/3B/6/52; Brigham, *American Newspapers,* vol. 2, 777; Andrew Bryson, Jr., to Miss Bryson, May 28, 1801, PRONI T1375/5.

225. *Am. Cit.,* March 6, May 9, 1806.

226. Chambers to Simms, Feb. 12, 1822, PRONI D1759/3B/6/46.

227. John Neil McLeod, *Preparation for Death the Business of Life: A discourse on the death of the Rev. Samuel Brown Wylie* (New York, 1852), 17.

228. Caldwell, "North County Family," 71.

CHAPTER SIX. DEFENDING THE REPUBLIC, 1793–1801

1. Jefferson called Hamilton "the servile copyist of Mr. Pitt." Jefferson to James Monroe, May 26, 1795, in Paul Leicester Ford, ed., *The Works of Thomas Jefferson* (New York, 1904), vol. 8, 176.

2. Glenn A. Phelps, *George Washington and American Constitutionalism* (Lawrence, Kans., 1993), 183.

3. Thomas Paine, "Letter to George Washington," in Moncure D. Conway, ed., *The Writings of Thomas Paine* (New York, 1967), vol. 3, 216.

4. Thomas Paine, *Common Sense,* in Philip S. Foner, ed., *The Complete Writings of Thomas Paine* (New York, 1945), vol. 1, 45.

5. Lance Banning, *The Jeffersonian Persuasion: Evolution of a Party Ideology* (New York, 1978), 129.

6. James Roger Sharp, *American Politics in the Early Republic: The New Nation in Crisis* (New Haven, 1993), 40.

7. Stanley Elkins and Eric McKitrick, *The Age of Federalism: The Early American Republic, 1788–1800* (New York, 1993), 93.

8. Gordon S. Wood, *The Radicalism of the American Revolution* (New York, 1993), 263.

9. John Ashworth, "The Jeffersonians: Classical Republicans or Liberal Capitalists?," *Journal of American Studies* 18 (1984): 425–35; Joyce Appleby, *Capitalism and a New Social Order: The Republican Vision of the 1790s* (New York, 1984), 48; William Bruce Wheeler, "Urban Politics in Nature's Republic: The Development of Political Parties in the Seaport Cities in the Federalist Era" (Ph.D. diss., University of Virginia, 1967), 55–57; Wood, *Radicalism,* 263–64. For the Anti-Federalists, see Gordon S. Wood, "Interests and Disinterestedness in the Making of the Constitution," in Rich-

ard Beeman et al., eds., *Beyond Confederation: Origins of the Constitution and American National Identity* (Chapel Hill, N.C., 1987), 69–109.

10. For analyses of American enthusiasm for the French Revolution, see Beatrice F. Hyslop, "American Press Reports of the French Revolution, 1789–1794," *New-York Historical Society Quarterly* 42 (1958): 329–48; Anne Catherine Hebert, "The Pennsylvania French in the 1790's: The Story of Their Survival" (Ph.D. diss., University of Texas at Austin, 1981), 103–4; Ruth Bloch, *Visionary Republic: Millennial Themes in American Thought, 1756–1800* (Cambridge, 1988), chap. 7; David Brion Davis, *Revolutions: Reflections on American Equality and Foreign Liberations* (Cambridge, Mass., 1990), chap. 2; David L. Waldstreicher, "The Making of American Nationalism: Celebrations and Political Culture, 1776–1820" (Ph.D. diss., Yale University, 1994), 115–17.

11. Appleby, *Capitalism*, 80. For Jefferson's championing of these ideals until his death, see Gordon S. Wood, "The Trials and Tribulations of Thomas Jefferson," in Peter S. Onuf, ed., *Jeffersonian Legacies* (Charlottesville, 1993), 409. "A True Republican" neatly put this ideological case in [Charleston] *City Gazette*, May 1798; reprinted in *CUSR*, June 7, 1798.

12. Jefferson's "Notes on Prof. Ebeling's Letter [of July 30, 1795]," in Ford, ed., *Works of Jefferson*, vol. 8, 208. He was referring to parties in Congress, not in the wider community.

13. Henry F. May, *The Enlightenment in America* (New York, 1976), 227; William Cobbett, *Porcupine's Works* (London, 1803), vol. 10, 75, vol. 11, 6; S. H. Jeyes, *The Russells of Birmingham in the French Revolution and in America 1791–1814* (London, 1911), 207; George S. Rowell, "Benjamin Vaughan—Patriot, Scholar, Diplomat," *Magazine of History* 22, no. 3 (1916): 53.

14. For Cobbett, see below, 240–42.

15. For example, Henry Jackson, Hamilton Rowan, Edward Hudson, and Joseph Cuthbert. *Shamrock*, July 17, 1817; David N. Doyle, *Ireland, Irishmen and Revolutionary America 1760–1820* (Dublin, 1981), 216; Hudson to Henry Jackson, Jan. 20, 1803, copy in Jeff. Papers (quotation); John Caldwell to Robert Simms, Oct. 18, 1802, PRONI D1759/3B/6/52.

16. Dumas Malone, *The Public Life of Thomas Cooper, 1783–1839* (New Haven, 1926), 82; Margaret Evelyn Leslie, "The Social and Political Thought of Joseph Priestley" (Ph.D. diss., Cambridge University, 1966), 18; Sampson to Mrs. Sampson, Feb. 6, 1807, Sampson Letters.

17. The major activists in the period up to 1801 include: James Thomson Callender, Mathew Carey, James Carey, John Daly Burk, Denis Driscol, James Cheetham, Joseph Priestley, Thomas Cooper, Richard Lee, Joseph Gales, Dr. James Reynolds, and William Duane.

18. See, for example, Jefferson to Tench Coxe, May 1, 1794, Jeff. Papers.

19. For a recent analysis of the ways in which Jefferson has been characterized, see Peter S. Onuf, "The Scholar's Jefferson," *WMQ* 3rd Ser., 50 (1993): 671–99.

20. Daniel T. Rodgers, *Contested Truths: Keywords in American Politics Since Independence* (New York, 1987), 10.

21. For a radical reading of the Declaration of Independence, "which traced its intellectual ancestry more to Paine than to Locke," see Staughton Lynd, *Intellectual Origins of American Radicalism* (London, 1969), 4–7. For an exile's view, see James Cheetham, *A Dissertation Concerning Political Equality, and the Corporation of New York* (New York, 1800), v.

22. Quoted in Daniel Sisson, *The Revolution of 1800* (New York, 1974), 148. See also the connections made between Jefferson and Paine in Anthony Gronowicz, "Political 'Radicalism' in New York City's Revolutionary and Constitutional Eras," in Paul A. Gilje and William Pencak, eds., *New York in the Age of the Constitution 1775–1800* (Cranbury, N.J., 1992), 98–99.

23. Wood, "Trials and Tribulations," 413. For Priestley's influence on Jefferson's optimistic expectations of science, and commitment to modernity, see Isaac Kramnick, "Eighteenth-Century Science and Radical Social Theory: The Case of Joseph Priestley's Scientific Liberalism," *Journal of British Studies* 25 (1986): 2n.

24. Joseph Priestley, *Memoirs of Dr. Joseph Priestley* (Northumberland, Pa., 1806), vol. 2, 344.

25. John Daly Burk, *An Oration, Delivered on the 4 of March 1803, at the Court House in Petersburg* (Petersburg, 1803), 16.

26. Richard Dinmore, *A Long Talk Before the Tammany Society of Alexandria, District of Columbia* (Alexandria, 1804), 4. See also John Binns's comments on progress in *Rep. Argus*, April 15, 1803.

27. Paine, *Rights of Man*, Part 1, in Foner, ed., *Complete Writings*, vol. 1, 251–52.

28. Hannah Arendt, *On Revolution* (Harmondsworth, 1973), 233.

29. Quoted in Richard K. Matthews, *The Radical Politics of Thomas Jefferson: A Revisionist View* (Lawrence, Kans., 1984), 20, 134n. See also Sisson, *American Revolution of 1800*, 109–14.

30. Rodgers, *Contested Truths*, 56–57, 67; David S. Lovejoy, "Two American Revolutions, 1689 and 1776," in J. G. A. Pocock, ed., *Three British Revolutions: 1641, 1688, 1776* (Princeton, 1980), 257–59.

31. Paine, *Common Sense*, 4.

32. See, for example, Thomas Dunn, *A Discourse, Delivered in the New Dutch Church, Nassau Street* (New York, 1794), 13–14.

33. Wood, "Trials and Tribulations," 406.

34. For their "friendship" in Paris in 1788, see David Freeman Hawke, *Paine* (New York, 1974), 184–85. See also Alf J. Mapp, Jr., *Thomas Jefferson: A Strange Case of Mistaken Identity* (New York, 1987), 297: "Though their association was by no means close, the diplomatic Jefferson and the contentious Paine were soon to be linked in the American imagination." Jeffersonian partisans still, apparently, feel the need to distance their hero from the disreputable Paine.

35. Dumas Malone, *Jefferson and the Rights of Man* (Boston, 1951), 357.

36. Jefferson to John Langdon, Sept. 11, 1785, quoted in Sisson, *American Revolution of 1800*, 130. For Madison's anglophobia, see Elkins and McKitrick, *Age of Federalism*, 83, 269.

37. Jefferson's private correspondence is littered with anti-British outbursts. One particularly malignant comment was his hope, if General Pichegru invaded Britain in 1795, "to leave my clover for awhile, to go and hail the dawn of liberty and republicanism" in London. Jefferson to William Branch Giles, April 27, 1795, in Ford, ed., *Works of Jefferson*, vol. 8, 172.

38. Walter Francis Brown, Jr., "John Adams and the American Press, 1797–1801: The First Full Scale Confrontation between the Executive and the Media" (Ph.D. diss., University of Notre Dame, 1974), 45.

39. Benjamin Franklin Bache to James Monroe, Sept. 7, 1797, quoted in Manning J. Dauer, *The Adams Federalists* (Baltimore, 1968), 99; James Tagg, *Benjamin Franklin Bache and the Philadelphia Aurora* (Philadelphia, 1991), 593n; John C. Miller, *Crisis in Freedom: The Alien and Sedition Laws* (Boston, 1951), 220; Frank Luther Mott, *American Journalism: A History of Newspapers in the United States Through 250 Years, 1690 to 1940* (New York, 1941), 122. Donald H. Stewart, *The Opposition Press of the Federalist Period* (Albany, N.Y., 1969), 867–93, rates the political position of most newspapers of the time. He tends to discount the partisan nature of many nominally Federalist newspapers, although his method fails to allow for changes of allegiance among editors.

40. William David Sloan, "The Party Press: The Newspaper Role in National Politics, 1789–1816" (Ph.D. diss., University of Texas at Austin, 1981), 56–67; Jefferson to Madison, Feb. 15, 1794, Jeff. Papers.

41. Quoted in James R. Wiggins, "Jefferson and the Press," in *Thomas Jefferson: The Man, His World, His Influence* (London, 1973), 142.

42. Quoted in Jeffery A. Smith, *Printers and Press Freedom: The Ideology of Early American Journalism* (New York, 1988), 41.

43. *Temple of Reason*, April 10, 1802. For the similar views of James Carey, see [Philadelphia] *Daily Advertiser*, April 27, June 26, 1797, and for Joseph Gales, *Ral. Reg.*, Oct. 22, 1799.

44. Smith, *Printers and Press Freedom*, 69.

45. The free and open press distinction is argued in Robert W. T. Martin, "From the 'Free and Open' Press to the 'Press of Freedom': Republicanism and Early American Press Liberty," *History of Political Thought* 15 (1994): 505–34.

46. Personally, Carey was in favor of the constitution.

47. *Wilmington Chronicle: and North-Carolina Weekly Advertiser*, July 3, 1795 and passim. Significantly, James Carey dropped the masthead in Sept. 1795, soon after a concerted Republican press campaign began in Philadelphia. He never lost his sense of humor; in the Philadelphia *Daily Advertiser*, when constrained by a partner who wished to be impartial, he entitled one regular column: "From Both Sides of the Gutter."

48. In his very first newspaper edition Cobbett wrote: "To profess impartiality here, would be as absurd as to profess it in a war between Virtue and Vice, Good and Evil, Happiness and Misery." *Porc's Gaz.*, March 4, 1797.

49. [James Thomson Callender], *The Prospect Before Us* (Richmond 1800), vol. 2, 73.

50. Editorial Note, "Jefferson, Freneau, and the Founding of the *National Gazette*,"

in Julian P. Boyd, ed., *The Papers of Thomas Jefferson* (Princeton, 1950), vol. 20, 718–53; Jacob Axelrad, *Philip Freneau: Champion of Democracy* (Austin, Texas, 1967), 206–8, 259–61; Martin S. Pernick, "Politics, Parties, and Pestilence: Epidemic Yellow Fever and the Rise of the First Party System," *WMQ* 3rd Ser., 29 (1972): 580.

51. Tagg, *Bache and the Aurora*, 160–61.

52. A fuller account of Callender's career at this point can be found in Michael Durey, *"With the Hammer of Truth": James Thomson Callender and America's Early National Heroes* (Charlottesville, Va., 1990), chap. 4.

53. Tagg, *Bache and the Aurora*, 100.

54. Jefferson's comments on the second part of Callender's *Political Progress of Britain* are instructive here: "The Political Progress is a work of value & of a singular complexion. The eye of the author seems to be a natural achromatic, which divests every object of the glare of colour. The preceding work under the same title had the same merit. One is disgusted indeed with the ulcerated state which it presents of the human mind: but to cure an ulcer we must go to its bottom: & no writer has ever done this more radically than this one. The reflections into which he leads one are not flattering to our species." Jefferson to Madison, Jan. 1, 1797, in Ford, ed., *Works of Jefferson*, vol. 8, 263–64.

55. Sixty-one were published in 1794, 60 in 1795, 74 in 1796, 62 in 1797, and 43 in the first six months of 1798.

56. Tagg, *Bache and the Aurora*, 106–7. A very large number of these squibs were later incorporated into Callender's pamphlets published in America, or came originally from his Scottish writings. Contemporaries were aware of Callender's role. One correspondent to a Federalist newspaper called the *Aurora* "the Calendar of infamy." *Gaz. U.S.*, March 14, 1797. There can be no doubt Callender was a major contributor to the *Aurora;* the only real issue is whether other anonymous writers also contributed.

57. [James Thomson Callender], *A Short History of the Nature and Consequences of Excise Laws* (Philadelphia, 1795). For Callender's writings on the excise in Edinburgh, see Durey, *Callender*, 27–28.

58. Richard G. Miller, *Philadelphia—The Federalist City: A Study of Urban Politics 1789–1801* (Port Washington, N.Y., 1976), 20–51; Roland M. Baumann, "Philadelphia's Manufacturers and the Excise Taxes of 1794: The Forging of the Jeffersonian Coalition," *PMHB* 106 (1982): 3–39. For Dallas, see Raymond Walters, Jr., *Alexander James Dallas: Lawyer-Politician-Financier* (Philadelphia, 1943), 4, 34–35. For Swanwick, see Roland M. Baumann, "John Swanwick: Spokesman for 'Merchant-Republicanism' in Philadelphia, 1790–1798," *PMHB* 97 (1973): 131–82.

59. See, e.g., Callender's views on the importance of popular participation in elections, *Aurora*, Oct. 18, 1794.

60. Philip S. Foner, *The Democratic-Republican Societies, 1790–1800* (Westport, 1976), 439–41; John F. Watson, *Annals of Philadelphia* (Philadelphia, 1830), 168.

61. Eugene Perry Link, *Democratic-Republican Societies* (New York, 1973), 147–48. The newspapers' role was not limited to rebutting the arguments of political opponents; they were also crucial for publicizing, and expounding the meanings of, the

regular public celebrations by which the political parties popularized their positions. See Waldstreicher, "American Nationalism," chap. 3, for an excellent analysis of political celebrations in the 1790s.

62. Edward C. Carter, "The Political Activities of Mathew Carey, Nationalist" (Ph.D. diss., Bryn Mawr College, 1962), 60–61, 74–75, 84–85, 131, 210–11.

63. Roland M. Baumann, "The Democratic-Republicans of Philadelphia: The Origins, 1776–1797" (Ph.D. diss., Pennsylvania State University, 1970), 494, 524–25, 541; Noble E. Cunningham, Jr., *The Jeffersonian Republicans: The Formation of Party Organisation, 1789–1801* (Chapel Hill, N.C., 1957), 110–14.

64. In the early years of the decade Dallas, Bache, and others sometimes met Jefferson at George Logan's property, Stenton. Frederick B. Tolles, *George Logan of Philadelphia* (New York, 1953), 123.

65. Edmund Berkeley and Dorothy Smith Berkeley, *John Beckley: Zealous Partisan in a Nation Divided* (Philadelphia, 1973); Jacob E. Cooke, *Tench Coxe and the Early Republic* (Chapel Hill, N.C., 1978), 283; Sisson, *American Revolution of 1800,* 155–56.

66. Berkeley and Berkeley, *Beckley,* 284.

67. Cooke, *Coxe,* 283, 261–80; Berkeley and Berkeley, *Beckley,* 67; Stewart Mitchell, ed., *New Letters of Abigail Adams, 1788–1801* (New York, 1973), 127.

68. Cunningham, *Jeffersonian Republicans,* 101–6.

69. "J. W." to Cooke, July 26, 1796, PRO HO100/62, 150; Mathew Carey, "The Autobiography of Mathew Carey," *New England Magazine,* 1833–34, Letter 8, 105. See also Archibald Hamilton Rowan, *The Autobiography of Archibald Hamilton Rowan* (Dublin, 1840), 283.

70. There is extensive evidence for this, but see, e.g, Thomas Cooper in *Aurora,* July 12, 1799.

71. Elkins and McKitrick, *Age of Federalism,* 263–64; Joseph J. Ellis, *Passionate Sage: The Character and Legacy of John Adams* (New York, 1993), 30. Both Jefferson and Madison were reluctant to form a "political party" in the 1790s. They hoped that once Federalism had been eradicated from government, party divisions would disappear. Wood, *Radicalism,* 298; Sisson, *American Revolution of 1800,* 63. For an American exception, Robert Goodloe Harper, a Federalist whose belief in the benefit of parties "made him almost unique in Federalist circles and probably in advance of the thinking of most Republicans, see Joseph W. Cox, *Champion of Southern Federalism: Robert Goodloe Harper of South Carolina* (Port Washington, N.Y., 1972), 87. For exile views on party, see Carter, "Mathew Carey," 85–86; *Ral. Reg.,* Nov. 26, 1799; *CUSR,* Feb. 22, 27, 1798. For Campbell White's belief that the "extreme virulence" of "our political animosities" was evidence of "our government being preeminently free," see White to Simms, Nov. 16, 1804, PRONI D1759/3B/6/55.

72. Link, *Democratic-Republican Societies,* 202.

73. *Aurora,* March 4, June 16, 1795.

74. *Aurora,* June 29, 1795.

75. Brown, "Adams and the Press," 28. Beckley's contribution was secretly to send an anti-treaty petition throughout the states. Edmund S. Morgan, *Inventing the People: The Rise of Popular Sovereignty in England and America* (New York, 1988), 230.

76. Miller, *Philadelphia*, 72; *Aurora*, July 27, 1795; J. Wendell Knox, *Conspiracy in American Politics, 1787–1815* (New York, 1972), 69. Rowan also attended the third meeting in August. *Gaz. U.S.*, Aug. 27, 1795. Baumann, "Democratic-Republicans," 520–21, claims that Rowan was present to seek financial aid for the United Irishmen.

77. Simon P. Newman, "Principles or Men? George Washington and the Political Culture of National Leadership, 1776–1801," *Journal of the Early Republic* 12 (1992): 477–98; Waldstreicher, "American Nationalism," 107–15.

78. *Aurora*, Aug. 22, 1795.

79. Ibid., Aug. 29, 1795.

80. Ibid., Sept. 16, 1795.

81. Tagg, *Bache and the Aurora*, 300n, 254.

82. Beckley used the pseudonym "A Calm Observer," the same nom de plume used by Benjamin Vaughan in Britain.

83. Paine, "Letter to Washington," 252; Jack Fruchtman, Jr., *Thomas Paine: Apostle of Freedom* (New York, 1994), 351–52.

84. "Jasper Dwight" [William Duane], *A Letter to George Washington, President of the United States* (Philadelphia, 1796), 6, 19, 13, 11.

85. Tagg, *Bache and the Aurora*, 526.

86. *Aurora*, Dec. 23, 1796.

87. *Aurora*, March 6, 1797. In my book on Callender I attributed this paragraph to him, but according to Tagg, *Bache and the Aurora*, 285, citing J. Thomas Scharf and Thompson Westcott, *History of Philadelphia* (Philadelphia, 1884), one of Bache's journeymen claimed it was written by Reynolds, with Leib's assistance, while Bache was absent. Leib certainly worked on the newspaper when Bache had been absent previously, and Mathew Carey later claimed Reynolds helped with the campaign against Washington. M[argaret] H. Bache to B. F. Bache, July 2, 1795, Bache Papers, Castle Collection, 8L/137, American Philosophical Society; Carey, "Autobiography," Letter 8, 105.

88. Miller, *Philadelphia*, 88.

89. Sharp, *American Politics*, 147–49.

90. Dauer, *Adams Federalists*, 112, 116; Jefferson to Archibald Stuart, Jan. 4, 1797, in Ford, ed., *Works of Jefferson*, vol. 8, 266–67.

91. James Thomson Callender, *Sketches of the History of America* (Philadelphia, 1798), 232–33.

92. Cobbett, *Peter Porcupine*, 32; *Cobbett's Weekly Political Register*, Oct. 5, 1805.

93. [William Cobbett], *Observations on the Emigration of Dr. Priestley, and on the Several Addresses Delivered to Him on His Arrival at New York* (Philadelphia, 1794).

94. [William Cobbett], *A Bone to Gnaw for the Democrats: or, Observations on a Pamphlet, entitled The Political Progress of Britain*, 3rd ed. (Philadelphia, 1795); [Cobbett], *A Kick for a Bite* (Philadelphia, 1795); "Peter Porcupine," *A Bone to Gnaw for the Democrats*, Part 2 (Philadelphia, 1795); "Peter Porcupine," *A Little Plain English, Addressed to the People of the United States* (Philadelphia, 1795).

95. "A Friend to Political Equality" [James Carey?], in *A Pill for Porcupine: Being a Specific for an Obstinate Itching which That Hireling Has Long Contracted for Lying and*

Calumny (Philadelphia, 1796), 79, wrote that several gentlemen who lodged in the same house when Cobbett first arrived in Philadelphia claimed "he was then so warm a republican, and an admirer of Paine's writings; that his *Rights of Man* were seldom out of his hands."

96. *Cobbett's Weekly Political Register*, Oct. 5, 1805; "Peter Porcupine" [Cobbett], *The Democratic Judge: or the Equal Liberty of the Press* (Philadelphia, 1798), 7.

97. Daniel Green, *Great Cobbett: The Noblest Agitator* (Oxford, 1985), 108; George Spater, *William Cobbett: The Poor Man's Friend* (Cambridge, 1982), vol. 1, 47–49; David A. Wilson, *Paine and Cobbett: The Transatlantic Connection* (Kingston and Montreal, 1988), 114–15.

98. Cobbett to Sir George Yonge, 14 Jan. 1792, PRO WO1/1051.

99. [Anon.], *The Soldier's Friend; or, Considerations on the Late Pretended Augmentation of the Subsistence of the Private Soldiers* (London, 1792).

100. The evidence for this interpretation is discussed more fully in Michael Durey, "William Cobbett, Military Corruption and London Radicalism in the Early 1790s," *Proceedings of the American Philosophical Society* 131 (1987): 348–66.

101. "Peter Porcupine" [William Cobbett], *Political Censor, or Monthly Review of the Most Interesting Political Occurrences Relative to the United States of America* (Philadelphia, 1796), Introduction; *Porc's Gaz.*, March 23, 1798.

102. See, e.g., *Porc's Gaz.*, March 16, 1797: "To unite the American Eagle with the British Lion against an ambitious and determined enemy . . . is a purpose no American need to be ashamed of, the alliance would be productive of equal honour and advantage to both."

103. Spater, *Cobbett*, vol. 1, 104.

104. For many examples, see Durey, "Thomas Paine's Apostles," 684–85; Carter, "Mathew Carey," 189–90; *Aurora*, Nov. 4, 1797. For Driscol's justification for informing Americans of "the bloody deeds of [English] tyrants," see *Am. Pat.*, Sept. 4, 1802.

105. Cobbett, *Porc's Gaz.*, Feb. 9, 1798.

106. Charles Evans, *American Bibliography* (Worcester, Mass., 1925–1955), vols. 9–13, nos. 31174, 32633; *CUSR*, Jan. 23, 1798. For the popularity of *The Age of Reason* in New York, see John W. Francis, *Old New York: or, Reminiscences of the Past Sixty Years* (New York, 1865), 133.

107. [Charleston] *Daily Evening Gazette*, passim; *Aurora*, Nov. 4, 6, 7, 1797, July 9, 10, 11, 12, 16, 17, 25, Aug. 10, 1799; *CUSR*, Feb. 27, May 17, 19, 31, Aug. 16, 1798; *Am. Pat.*, Sept. 4, 1802.

108. Cobbett, *Political Censor*, Sept. 1796, 54. Even his exiled enemies acknowledged his wit. See *Am. Pat.*, Dec. 11, 1802.

109. "Peter Porcupine" [William Cobbett], *A Bone to Gnaw for the Democrats*, Part 2 (Philadelphia, 1795), 4; Cobbett, *Political Censor*, May 1796, 189, 200, 203. Cobbett was not alone in satirizing Swanwick's sexual prowess. See "Geoffrey Touchstone," *He Wou'd Be a Poet; or, "Nature Will Be Nature Still": An Heroic Poem* (Philadelphia, 1796), 26. A more sympathetic, and female, view of Swanwick can be found in Baumann, "Democratic-Republicans," 535–36.

110. The phrase is used to describe the newspaper war between James Cheetham and the Federalist Edward Coleman in New York. Francis, *Old New York*, 336.

111. *Aurora*, July 28, Aug. 8, 12, 1796, Feb. 25, April 19, 1797; Cobbett, *Bone to Gnaw*, Part 1, 4–5, 27; Cobbett, *Political Censor*, March 1796, 26–27; *Porc's Gaz.*, Sept. 9, 1797; Durey, *Callender*, 91.

112. Mitchell, *Abigail Adams*, 143–44; *Aurora*, March 7, 1797.

113. [Philadelphia] *Carey's Daily Advertiser*, Aug. 26, 1797.

114. *Daily Advertiser*, May 5, 1797; *Porc's Gaz.*, May 4, 1797.

115. *Daily Advertiser*, May 8, 1797.

116. Cobbett reported the demise of the *Advertiser* with a black-lined column, headed "Melancholy," a tasteless triumphalism at a time so many people were dying of yellow fever. *Porc's Gaz.*, Sept. 14, 1797.

117. *Porc's Gaz.*, Jan. 24, 1798. William Paulet Carey gave evidence for the prosecution at Dr. William Drennan's trial. See Michael Durey, "The Dublin Society of United Irishmen and the Politics of the Carey-Drennan Dispute, 1792–1794," *Historical Journal* 37 (1994): 89–111.

118. *CUSR*, Feb. 23, 1798.

119. Ibid., Feb. 27, 1798.

120. The last number of the *CUSR* was Aug. 30, 1798.

121. Carey, "Autobiography," Letter 7.

122. Spater, *Cobbett*, vol. 1, 95–105; Green, *Great Cobbett*, 170–73. Shippen's summing up, in which he told the jury that "damages should be exemplary, but not so great as to ruin the offender," can be found in James Carey's *The Constitutional Diary and Philadelphia Evening Advertiser*, Dec. 17, 1799.

123. Alexander Hamilton, *Observations on Certain Documents Contained in No. V & VI of "The History of the United States for 1796,"* in Harold C. Syrett and Jacob E. Cooke, eds., *The Papers of Alexander Hamilton* (New York, 1974), vol. 19, 243.

124. Elkins and McKitrick, *Age of Federalism*, 539–49. Compare Callender's comments favorable to Adams in *Aurora*, March 14, 20, 1797, with his statements that the president was "a poor old man" and "in his dotage" in *Aurora*, May 23, 1797.

125. Dauer, *Adams Federalists*, 128; Mitchell, ed., *Abigail Adams*, 94.

126. *Aurora*, May 16, 1797. The vote was 41 to 40. *Gaz. U.S.*, May 15, 1797.

127. Berkeley and Berkeley, *Beckley*, 159.

128. *Aurora*, April 15, 1797.

129. The fullest accounts of this episode are Syrett and Cooke, eds., *Papers of Hamilton*, vol. 19, 121–44; Boyd, ed., *Papers of Jefferson*, vol. 18, 613–88. My own views can be found in Durey, *Callender*, 97–102.

130. Duane later claimed that it was the Hamiltonians' "arbitrary and scandalous persecution of an individual" (Monroe?) that provoked publication of the Reynolds affair. *Aurora*, quoted in *Exam.*, Oct. 16, 1802.

131. *Aurora*, June 6, July 24, 1797, for some examples. For the "cavilling" of Bache's "nefarious faction," see "Correspondent," *Gaz. U.S.*, July 17, 1798.

132. Tagg, *Bache and the Aurora*, 321–30.

133. Cooke, *Coxe*, 293–308. Abigail Adams admitted that Coxe, who had attacked Adams in print during the election campaign of 1796, was dismissed "for opposing the Government in its opperations [*sic*]." Mitchell, ed., *Abigail Adams*, 127.

134. Dauer, *Adams Federalists*, 136; *Aurora*, Jan. 31, March 28, 1797.

135. See the French observer Moreau de St. Mery's comments on the power of the banks, quoted in Wheeler, "Urban Politics in Nature's Republic," 49.

136. Mathew Carey to James Carey, May 16, 1797, James Carey to Mathew Carey, Sept. 23, 1797, Lea and Febiger Collection, HSP; Carter, "Mathew Carey," 254–55.

137. Baumann, "Swanwick," 178–80; Cobbett, *Porcupine's Works*, 8, 19–20; *CUSR*, Feb. 10, Aug. 2, 9, 1798; [James Thomson Callender], *The Prospect Before Us* (Richmond, 1800), vol. 1, 57–58.

138. Stewart, *Opposition Press*, 886, says it "apparently tried to be impartial." But while Duane was editor, Cobbett attacked it for anti-British bias. *Porc's Gaz.*, April 21, 1797.

139. *Daily Advertiser*, July 24, 1797.

140. Kim T. Phillips, "William Duane, Philadelphia's Democratic Republicans, and the Origins of Modern Politics," *Pennsylvania Magazine of History and Politics* 101 (1977): 352–53; *Rec.*, Aug. 25, 1802.

141. Cobbett, *Porcupine's Works*, vol. 9, 258n; *Porc's Gaz.*, Feb. 17, May 2, 1798.

142. Durey, *Callender*, 105–6; Callender to James Carey, Feb. 22, 1799, Edward Carey Gardiner Collection, HSP. The wives of both Duane and Callender were very sick; both were dead by July 1798.

143. Cobbett, *Porcupine's Works*, vol. 9, 258n.

144. Mott, *American Journalism*, 128.

145. Tagg, *Bache and the Aurora*, 106.

146. Francis Markoe to Margaret Bache, Aug. 4, 1798, Bache Papers, Castle Collection.

147. Jefferson to Madison, April 26, 1798, Jeff. Papers.

148. *Gaz. U.S.*, March 8, April 4, June 4, 1798, Aug. 11, 31, 1802. The paragraph accusing Jefferson was headed: "Help! OH! HELP!"

149. Vernon Stauffer, *New England and the Bavarian Illuminati* (New York, 1918), 93; John Howe, Jr., "Republican Thought and the Political Violence of the 1790s," *American Quarterly* 19 (1967): 150; Knox, *Conspiracy in American Politics*, 57–58, 91; Cobbett, *Porcupine's Works*, vol. 2, 208–9; Cobbett, *Political Censor*, May 1796, 196, 225; *Gaz. U.S.*, April 18, 1797; *Porc's Gaz.*, March 15, 1797.

150. Baumann, "Democratic-Republicans," 554, says that "the urban Irish went strongly Republican in 1796."

151. *Gaz. U.S.*, April 21, July 17, 1797.

152. Ibid., July 14, 19, Aug. 5, 1797.

153. *Porc's Gaz.*, April 14, 1797.

154. Ibid., May 8, 1798.

155. See above, 207.

156. *Gaz. U.S.*, Jan. 26, 1798; Cobbett, *Porcupine's Works*, vol. 9, 257n.

157. *Aurora*, June 9, 1798; Callender, *Prospect Before Us*, vol. 1, 37; *Porc's Gaz.*, June 7, 1798.

158. *Porc's Gaz.*, May 10, 15, 1798.

159. *Gaz. U.S.*, Dec. 20, 1798.

160. *CUSR*, Aug. 16, 1798; [Philadelphia] *Constitutional Diary*, Dec. 19, 1799.

161. Thomas D'Arcy McGhee, *A History of the Irish Settlers in North America, from the Earliest Period to the Census of 1850* (Boston, 1851), 87, claims that in 1797 the United Irishmen in Philadelphia "were a very formidable body." Maurice J. Bric, "The Irish and the Evolution of the 'New Politics' in America," in P. J. Drudy, ed., *The Irish in America: Emigration, Assimilation and Impact* (Cambridge, 1985), 143–67, is much more circumspect.

162. *Gaz. U.S.*, Dec. 18, 1798.

163. Cobbett, *Porcupine's Works*, vol. 10, 58–59; *Gaz. U.S.*, Dec. 18, 1798.

164. *Gaz. U.S.*, Dec. 20, 22, 26, 1798.

165. See above, 112–13.

166. For an answer to the charge of seeking to overthrow the state, see "A Friend to Liberty," *CUSR*, May 31, 1798.

167. *RSCIHC* (1798), civ.

168. The Alien and Sedition acts are comprehensively examined in James Morton Smith, *Freedom's Fetters: The Alien and Sedition Laws and American Civil Liberties* (Ithaca, N.Y., 1956); Miller, *Crisis in Freedom;* Leonard W. Levy, *Emergence of a Free Press* (Oxford, 1985).

169. Cobbett, *Porcupine's Works*, vol. 10, 75; *Gaz. U.S.*, Sept. 3, 1800.

170. *Gaz. U.S.*, July 13, 1798.

171. Elkins and McKitrick, *Age of Federalism*, 581–618.

172. Robert Cantwell, *Alexander Wilson: Naturalist and Pioneer* (Philadelphia, 1961), 102.

173. Callender to Jefferson, March 14, 1800, Jeff. Papers.

174. Willis G. Briggs, "Joseph Gales, Editor of Raleigh's First Newspaper," *North Carolina Booklet* 7 (1907): 117–18.

175. *Exam.*, April 11, 1800; Callender, *Prospect Before Us*, vol. 2, 130.

176. Brown, "Adams and the Press," 192–94.

177. Cooper, "To the Electors of Northumberland County," *Aurora*, Sept. 11, 1799.

178. *Gaz. U.S.*, Feb. 11, 21, 1799; *Porc's Gaz.*, Feb. 11, 12, 1799. Remarkably, Duane failed to mention either the "riot" or the trial in the *Aurora*. The other Republican newspapers were equally silent.

179. Callender, *Prospect Before Us*, vol. 1, 3.

180. Much of what Callender wrote for the *Examiner* he presented to the public again in the two volumes of *The Prospect Before Us* in 1800.

181. *Aurora*, April 6, Dec. 9, 1797; *Porc's Gaz.*, April 6, 1797; Scharf and Westcott, *Philadelphia*, vol. 1, 490.

182. *Exam.*, Feb. 11, 1800; *Aurora*, Aug. 10, 1798.

183. *CUSR*, March 3, May 8, 10, 1798.

184. *Aurora*, Aug. 9, 1798; *Gaẓ. U.S.*, Dec. 21, 1798. In New Jersey, Aaron Pennington, editor of the Republican *Centinel of Freedom*, was beaten up in August 1798. Carl E. Prince, *New Jersey's Jeffersonian Republicans: The Genesis of an Early Party Machine, 1789–1817* (Chapel Hill, N.C., 1967), 38.

185. Scharf and Westcott, *Philadelphia*, 497; *Aurora*, Jan. 18, 19, 1799.

186. Malone, *Cooper*, 137–38; Richard J. Twomey, *Jacobins and Jeffersonians: Anglo-American Radicalism in the United States, 1790–1820* (New York, 1989), 72.

187. Briggs, "Gales," 119; Durey, *Callender*, 118–19, 126; Smith, *Freedom's Fetters*, 338.

188. Phillips, "Duane," 70–75.

189. Miller, *Crisis in Freedom;* Smith, *Freedom's Fetters;* Frank M. Anderson, "The Enforcement of the Alien and Sedition Laws," *Annual Report of the American Historical Association for 1912* (Washington, 1914), 115–26; Stewart, *Opposition Press*, 466–86; Levy, *Emergence of a Free Press*, 282–308; Banning, *Jeffersonian Persuasion*, 255–66; Durey, *Callender*, 127–35.

190. James Monroe was one leading Republican who saw the value of organizing sedition cases before the courts as "show-trials" on behalf of the party. See, e.g, Smith, *Freedom's Fetters*, 298–99n, 345–46; Monroe to Jefferson, May 25, 1800, Jeff. Papers.

191. When Duane was cited for contempt of the Senate in 1800 a petition of remonstrance that circulated in Philadelphia gained more than 3,000 signatures, a very large number. Phillips, "Duane," 89.

192. [New York] *Time-Piece*, July 25, 1798.

193. *Am. Pat.*, March 3, 1803.

194. Quoted in Brown, "Adams and the Press," 272, 258.

195. Reprinted in *Gaẓ. U.S.*, Aug. 18, 1802.

196. John C. Miller, *The Federalist Era, 1789–1801* (New York, 1963), 276; John Ferling, *John Adams: A Life* (Knoxville, 1992), 404; Elkins and McKitrick, *Age of Federalism*, 739–40; Brown, "Adams and the Press," iv.

197. Prince, *New Jersey Republicans*, 56–57; Banning, *Jeffersonian Persuasion*, 267–68.

198. I am talking here about a question of emphasis. I do not mean that Federalist emphasis on the role of the journalists has been ignored by other historians.

199. Appleby, *Capitalism*, 78, 104 (my italics).

200. *Aurora*, March 2, 1795.

201. *Aurora*, Dec. 2, 1795.

CHAPTER SEVEN. REFORMING THE REPUBLIC

1. John Daly Burk, *An Oration, Delivered on the 4 of March 1803, at the Court-House in Petersburg* (Petersburg, 1803), 15. See also Priestley to Jefferson, June 17, 1802, Jeff. Papers.

2. *Gaẓ. U.S.*, March 9, 11, 12, 1801.

3. Inaugural Address, in Paul Leicester Ford, ed., *The Works of Thomas Jefferson* (New York, 1904–5), vol. 10, 195.

4. See, for example, Duane's comments in *Aurora*, Sept. 5, 1806, and John Binns's in *Rep. Argus*, Jan. 7, 1803.

5. Forrest McDonald, "The Presidency of Thomas Jefferson: The Triumph and the Perils of Republican Ideals," in Lance Banning, ed., *After the Constitution: Party Conflict in the New Republic* (Belmont, Calif., 1989), 371; Richard E. Ellis, "Jeffersonian Divisions," in Banning, ed., *After the Constitution*, 391.

6. John Robert Nelson, Jr., "Hamilton and Gallatin: Political Economy and Policy-Making in the New Nation, 1789–1812" (Ph.D. diss., Northern Illinois University, 1979), 241. See also Richard E. Ellis, *The Jeffersonian Crisis: Courts and Politics in the Young Republic* (New York, 1974), 274–75. Lance Banning, *The Jeffersonian Persuasion: Evolution of a Party Ideology* (New York, 1978), 274, writes: "There were no radicals among the great triumvirate [Jefferson, Madison, and Gallatin] who guided the Republicans in power."

7. Roland M. Baumann, "The Democratic-Republicans of Philadelphia: The Origins, 1776–1797" (Ph.D. diss., Pennsylvania State University, 1970), 585.

8. Jefferson to Joseph Scott, March 9, 1804, Jeff. Papers.

9. *Exam.*, Sept. 23, 1800, April 17, 1801; Kim T. Phillips, "William Duane, Philadelphia's Democratic Republicans, and the Origins of Modern Politics," *PMHB* 101 (1977): 371.

10. Jefferson to Wilson Cary Nicholas, March 26, 1805, Jeff. Papers; Frederick B. Tolles, *George Logan of Philadelphia* (New York, 1953), 245.

11. Russell L. Hanson, " 'Commons' and 'Commonwealth' at the American Founding: Democratic Republicanism as the New American Hybrid," in Terence Ball and J. G. A. Pocock, eds., *Conceptual Change and the Constitution* (Lawrence, Kans., 1988), 165.

12. Jacob E. Cooke, *Tench Coxe and the Early Republic* (Chapel Hill, N.C., 1978), 438. Quiddism, from "tertium quid" (a third force), was not a coherent, fixed political position, but was used to denote any faction that was accused of departing from the "true" Republican line (usually from "the spirit of '76"). Coxe, before converting to Quiddism himself, called it "a hermaphrodite thing partaking of two characters, and yet having neither." Tolles, *Logan*, 246. Thus, Quiddism in Pennsylvania referred to the Constitutional Republicans, moderates who in state politics tried to ally with moderate Federalists to defeat Duane's Democrats. At the national level, John Randolph's Quiddism was the dissidence of Old Republicanism, more similar to Duane's politics than to the Pennsylvania Quids. In the New York factional wars of 1809, Cheetham called his opponents Quids, yet accused them of being under orders from Duane. Noble E. Cunningham, Jr., *The Jeffersonian Republicans in Power: Party Operations, 1801–1809* (Chapel Hill, N.C., 1963), 222–24; David A. Carson, "That Ground Called Quiddism: John Randolph's War with the Jefferson Administration," *Journal of American Studies* 20 (1986): 71–92; *Am. Cit.*, March 14, 1809.

13. *Aurora*, March 2, 1804.

14. There are some similarities between the divisions among the exiles after 1800 and those shown among Anti-Federalists after 1787. Moderate exiles and "elite" Anti-Federalists accepted the idea of rule by a natural aristocracy of talents, education, and experience. Radical exiles and populist Anti-Federalists desired a much closer connection between rulers and ruled, and wanted participatory democracy. For the divisions among Anti-Federalists, see Saul Cornell, "Aristocracy Assailed: The Ideology of Backcountry Anti-Federalism," *Journal of American History* 89 (1990): 1148–72.

15. Edward C. Carter, "The Political Activities of Mathew Carey, Nationalist, 1760–1814" (Ph.D. diss., Bryn Mawr College, 1962), 268.

16. [Thomas Cooper], *Consolidation: An Account of Parties in the United States, from the Convention of 1787, to the Present Period* (Columbia, S.C., 1824), 5.

17. *Aurora*, Feb. 22, Sept. 3, 4, 5, 30, 1806; *Am. Cit.*, March 15, 1800; *Rep. Argus*, Jan. 7, 1803; *Aug. Chron.*, Jan. 28, 1804.

18. *Aurora*, Sept. 6, 1806; [William Duane], *Experience the Test of Government: In Eighteen Essays, Written during the Years 1805 and 1806* (Philadelphia, 1807), 43.

19. Alexander Wilson, *Oration on the Power and Value of National Liberty* (Philadelphia, 1801), quoted in Robert Cantwell, *Alexander Wilson: Naturalist and Pioneer* (Philadelphia, 1961), 103.

20. *Rep. Argus*, Jan. 7, 1803.

21. Cooper to Jefferson, Oct. 25, 1802, Jeff. Papers. See also Duane, *Experience the Test of Government*, preface.

22. *Aug. Chron.*, Feb. 18, 1804.

23. *Aurora*, Sept. 30, 1806.

24. Jefferson to William B. Giles, March 23, to William Findley, March 24, 1801, in Ford, ed., *Works of Jefferson*, vol. 10, 222–25.

25. Carl E. Prince, "The Passing of the Aristocracy: Jefferson's Removal of the Federalists, 1801–1805," *Journal of American History* 62 (1970): 575. See also, Cunningham, *Jeffersonian Republicans in Power*, 69–70.

26. Michael Durey, *"With the Hammer of Truth": James Thomson Callender and America's Early National Heroes* (Charlottesville, Va., 1990), 143.

27. *Am. Cit.*, June 5, 1801.

28. David Denniston and James Cheetham to Jefferson, June 1, 1801, in Worthington C. Ford, ed., "Letters of James Cheetham," *Proceedings of the Massachusetts Historical Society* 3rd Ser., 1 (1907): 42–43.

29. *Temple of Reason*, May 20, 1801; *Am. Pat.*, Sept. 25, 1802.

30. *Temple of Reason*, May 13, 1801; Denniston and Cheetham to Jefferson, June 1, 1801.

31. Burk to Jefferson, June 1801, Jefferson to Burk, June 20, 1801, Jeff. Papers.

32. Thomas Leiper to Jefferson, March 8, 1801, Jeff. Papers.

33. Jefferson to Monroe, Dec. 13, 1801, Jeff. Papers. By August 1802 Granger had appointed 379 new postmasters, 250 of them replacements for unsatisfactory incumbents. Granger to Jefferson, Aug. 23, 1802, Jeff. Papers.

34. Callender to Madison, April 27, 1801, in Worthington C. Ford, ed., "Thomas

Jefferson and James Thomson Callender," *New England Historical and Genealogical Register* 51 (1896): 153–55.

35. Lyon to Jefferson, July 20, 1801, Jeff. Papers. Nor did Lyon refrain from complaining about the distribution of patronage. Lyon to Jefferson, Oct. 5, 1802, Jeff. Papers.

36. Jefferson to Monroe, [March] 7, Jefferson to Horatio Gates, March 8, 1801, in Ford, ed., *Works of Jefferson,* vol. 10, 202–6.

37. Henry Adams, *The Life of Albert Gallatin* (1879; reprinted New York, 1943), 281. Significantly, the one prominent Virginian who called for a clean sweep of offices was James Monroe, who had been closely associated with the penmen in Philadelphia in 1796–97. Daniel Sisson, *The Revolution of 1800* (New York, 1974), 44.

38. Frank van der Linden, *The Turning Point: Jefferson's Battle for the Presidency* (Washington, D.C., 1962), 12, 181; Cunningham, *Jeffersonian Republicans in Power,* 258–61. Callender's caustic reference to an editor wearing muslin gowns and petticoats was aimed at Smith. Smith's father had also been master of the Philadelphia Freemasons.

39. Phillips, "Duane," 133–37; Treasury Department to Gallatin, Feb. 8, Gallatin to Jefferson, Feb. 9, 1802, Jeff. Papers.

40. Clement Eaton, "Winifred and Joseph Gales, Liberals of the Old South," *Journal of Southern History* 10 (1944): 463.

41. Carter, "Mathew Carey," 266–68; Jefferson to Theodore Foster, May 9, 1801, in Ford, ed., *Works of Jefferson,* vol. 10, 251.

42. Cooper to Jefferson, March 17, 1801, Jefferson to Cooper, Nov. 29, 1802, Jeff. Papers; Dumas Malone, *The Public Life of Thomas Cooper, 1783–1839* (New Haven, 1926), 174–75, 154.

43. Phillips, "Duane," 206.

44. *Aurora,* Dec. 23, 1806.

45. *Rep. Argus,* May 20, 1803.

46. Sanford W. Higginbotham, *The Keystone in the Democratic Arch: Pennsylvania Politics 1800–1816* (Harrisburg, 1952), 64.

47. Andrew Ellicott to Jefferson, Dec. 1, 1803, Jeff. Papers. McKean in his 1805 inaugural message criticized recently arrived "political incendiaries," who sought "to acquire, for sinister purposes, the mastery of the passions and prejudices of the people." James Hedley Peeling, "Governor McKean and the Pennsylvania Jacobins (1799–1808)," *PMHB* 54 (1930): 344.

48. David Bailie Warden was the victim of similar sentiments, privately offered to President Madison by Gen. John Armstrong, when he was American consul in Paris, a position, it was argued, for which he was unfit because he was not native born. See Armstrong to Madison, March 3, 1811, in Francis C. Haber, *David Bailie Warden: A Bibliographical Sketch of America's Cultural Ambassador in France, 1804–45* (Washington, D.C., 1954), 14–15.

49. Stanley Elkins and Eric McKitrick, *The Age of Federalism: The Early American Republic, 1788–1800* (New York, 1993), 694.

50. *Am. Pat.*, Feb. 17, 26, March 8, 1803.

51. Phillips, "Duane," 204–9; Craig Hanyan, *De Witt Clinton: Years of Molding 1769–1807* (New York, 1988), 238–39, 249; [New York] *Morning Chronicle*, quoted in *Am. Cit.*, Jan. 17, 1806.

52. Phillips, "Duane," 195–202; Higginbotham, *Keystone*, 22.

53. Carter, "Mathew Carey," 271–72. Carey was also probably jealous of Duane's influence over the Irish, which supplanted his own.

54. Duane always argued that he was an American citizen by birth, but as he had been taken back to Ireland when he was twelve and was not in America when independence was declared, he was legally a British subject.

55. Phillips, "Duane," 231.

56. *Aurora*, Oct. 15, 1807: Higginbotham, *Keystone*, 144.

57. *Aurora*, Oct. 20, 1807.

58. Richard J. Twomey, *Jacobins and Jeffersonians: Anglo-American Radicalism in the United States, 1790–1820* (New York, 1989), 88.

59. See above, 153–55.

60. Cheetham to Jefferson, Dec. 10, 1801, in Ford, ed., "Letters of Cheetham," 46–48.

61. "A Citizen of New York" [James Cheetham], *A Narrative of the Suppression by Col. Burr, of the History of the Administration of John Adams, Late President of the United States, Written by John Wood* (New York, 1802); Cheetham, *Nine Letters on the Subject of Aaron Burr's Political Defection* (New York, 1803); James Cheetham, *A Reply to Aristedes* (New York, 1804).

62. Hanyan, *Clinton*, 357–69.

63. *Am. Cit.*, Feb. 24, 1806.

64. Ibid., Feb. 26, 1806.

65. *New-York Evening Press*, March 17, 1809.

66. *Am. Cit.*, July 27, 1808.

67. James Cheetham, *The Life of Thomas Paine* (New York, 1809), iv.

68. Jabez D. Hammond, *The History of Political Parties in the State of New-York* (Albany, N.Y., 1842), vol. 1, 260.

69. *Am. Cit.*, Dec. 31, 1807, April 4, 1809; Cheetham, *Paine*, 153; Louis Martin Sears, *Jefferson and the Embargo* (1927; New York, 1966), 200; Hammond, *Political Parties*, vol. 1, 263.

70. *Am. Cit.*, March 1, 1809.

71. Ibid., April 4, 1809.

72. Ibid., April 21, 24, 1809.

73. Ibid., April 15, 1809.

74. Ibid., April 22, 1809.

75. Ibid., May 1, 1809.

76. Cheetham, *Paine*, 122–23, 127.

77. Twomey, *Jacobins and Jeffersonians*, 59; George Cuming to Robert Simms, Jan. 18, 1816, Jan. 22, 1817, PRONI D1759/3B/6/33.

78. *Spirit of '76,* quoted in *New-York Evening Post,* March 25, 1809; *Am. Cit.,* March 21, 1809.

79. John W. Francis, *Old New York: or, Reminiscences of the Past Sixty Years* (New York, 1865), 335–38.

80. Francis, quoted in Twomey, *Jacobins and Jeffersonians,* 56–57.

81. *Am. Cit.,* Jan. 27, July 18, 1808.

82. Ellis, *Jeffersonian Crisis,* 20.

83. *Aurora,* March 15, April 28, 1796, March 21, 1798 (Callender); Margaret Evelyn Leslie, "The Social and Political Thought of Joseph Priestley" (Ph.D. diss., Cambridge University, 1966), 295–97; Durey, *Callender,* 87–90. The exiles were not alone in thinking the Constitution required revision. See, e.g., *Am. Cit.,* March 25, 29, 1800; Robert E. Shalhope, *John Taylor of Caroline: Pastoral Republican* (Columbia, S.C., 1980), 117–18; Banning, *Jeffersonian Persuasion,* 281–82; Ellis, *Jeffersonian Crisis,* 21. For the Anti-Federalist antecedents of these views, see Christopher L. Tomlins, *Law, Labor, and Ideology in the Early American Republic* (New York, 1993), 66.

84. For Cheetham's major role in the reform of New York City's municipal charter, see James Cheetham, *A Dissertation Concerning Political Equality and the Corporation of New York* (New York, 1800); Twomey, *Jacobins and Jeffersonians,* 125–30.

85. See, e.g., Duane's comments to Jefferson in 1806, explaining his attacks on Jefferson's cabinet colleagues but proclaiming personal loyalty. Dumas Malone, *Jefferson the President: Second Term, 1805–1809* (Boston, 1974), 147.

86. *Aurora,* Aug. 28, 1806.

87. *Aurora,* Aug. 28, 29, Sept. 30, 1806.

88. Phillips, "Duane," 247–48; Dumas Malone, *Jefferson the President: First Term, 1801–1805* (Boston, 1970), 448–57; Adams, *Gallatin,* 177–78.

89. Phillips, "Duane," 139.

90. There are, however, clear signs of compatibility. Jefferson's ideas on ward-republics were not incompatible with Duane's views on participatory democracy, but unlike Duane's they remained speculative. Richard K. Matthews, *The Radical Politics of Thomas Jefferson: A Revisionist View* (Lawrence, Kans., 1984), 81–87.

91. Birch was on the committee of superintendence assisting in Duane's senatorial candidacy. Reynolds was frequently named on Republican ward committees. One of the impeachment charges against McKean was for having unlawfully removed Reynolds from the Philadelphia Board of Health. McKean claimed Reynolds was violent and intemperate. See *Aurora,* Sept. 23, 1807, and passim; Peeling, "McKean and Pennsylvania Jacobins," 348, 351; Twomey, *Jacobins and Jeffersonians,* 67.

92. Peeling, "McKean and Pennsylvania Jacobins," 328; Ellis, *Jeffersonian Crisis,* 160. Higginbotham, *Keystone,* 18, suggests that Duane "sublimated personal grievances into questions of principle." Carter, "Mathew Carey," 270, makes essentially the same point.

93. Elizabeth K. Henderson, "The Attack on the Judiciary in Pennsylvania, 1800–1810," *PMHB* 61 (1937): 115.

94. Frank E. Manuel and Fritzie Manuel, *Utopian Thought in the Western World* (Cambridge, 1979), 337.

95. *Temple of Reason*, Feb. 13, 1802; Higginbotham, *Keystone*, 79–80.

96. Driscol in *Cork Gaz.*, Jan. 25, 1794.

97. Thomas Paine, "To the Citizens of Pennsylvania on the Proposal for Calling a Convention," in Philip S. Foner, ed., *The Complete Writings of Thomas Paine* (New York, 1945), vol. 2, 1004.

98. Morton J. Horwitz, *The Transformation of American Law 1780–1860* (Cambridge, Mass., 1977), 17–18; Raymond Walters, Jr., *Alexander James Dallas, Lawyer-Politician-Financier* (Philadelphia, 1943), 6; Tomlins, *Law, Labor, and Ideology*, 32–33.

99. Paine, "To the Citizens of Pennsylvania," 1003; Tolles, *Logan*, 251.

100. *Aurora*, Jan. 15, 1805, Aug. 21, 1806.

101. Ibid., Aug. 12, 1806.

102. Paine, "To the Citizens of Pennsylvania," 1003.

103. *Am. Cit.*, Dec. 9, 1805.

104. Duane, *Experience the Test of Government*, 6–7.

105. *Aurora*, Jan. 28, 1805.

106. Ibid., Jan. 15, 28, 1805.

107. Duane, *Experience the Test of Government*, 14, 56.

108. *Temple of Reason*, Feb. 27, 1802.

109. Higginbotham, *Keystone*, 53, 55; Ellis, *Jeffersonian Crisis*, 162–63. Duane's Philadelphia democrats played only a marginal role in this early agitation. Pressure mainly came from country democrats led by Simon Snyder and Binns's *Rep. Argus*.

110. *Rep. Argus*, July 15, 1803.

111. Ibid., June 14, 1805.

112. Ibid., Nov. 18, 1803.

113. Ibid., Feb. 24, March 2, 1804, June 14, 1805.

114. Twomey, *Jacobins and Jeffersonians*, 136–37. Twenty years later Cooper was again taking up radical positions, accusing the Republican party of having rejected its original principles, especially strict construction. Cooper, *Consolidation*, 5–6.

115. David Freeman Hawke, *Paine* (New York, 1974), 353–73; Jack Fruchtman, Jr., *Thomas Paine: Apostle of Freedom* (New York, 1994), 393–418; Jerry W. Knudson, "The Rage Around Tom Paine: Newspaper Reaction to His Homecoming in 1802," *New-York Historical Society Quarterly* 53 (1969): 34–63.

116. Eric Foner, *Tom Paine and Revolutionary America* (New York, 1976), 131–34.

117. Paine, "To the Citizens of Pennsylvania," 993, 1001–2. Most critics of the 1776 constitution objected to the unrestrained, populist legislation passed by the unicameral legislature. Paine obviously did not see the "equalizing" laws that favored the people rather than the minority propertied classes as a problem. The problem was the failure of the system to give enough time to the legislators to think through the possible consequences of their laws.

118. Paine, "To the Citizens of Pennsylvania," 995–1005.

119. Duane, *Experience the Test of Government*, 53, 43, 9–10, 52, 7, 55–56.

120. Henderson, "Attack on the Judiciary," 135–36.

121. Peeling, "McKean and Pennsylvania Jacobins," 343–49.

122. Higginbotham, *Keystone*, 215–16.

123. [John Binns], *Recollections of the Life of John Binns: Twenty-Nine Years in Europe and Fifty-Three in the United States* (Philadelphia, 1854), 245, 250–52.

124. My comments on émigré political economy can be found in Michael Durey, "Thomas Paine's Apostles," 678–81; Michael Durey, "John Lithgow's Lithconia: The Making and Meaning of America's First 'Utopian Socialist' Tract," *WMQ* 3rd Ser., 46 (1992): 679–84; Durey, *Callender*, 79–86.

125. Exile opinions can be found in James Thomson Callender, *Sketches of the History of America* (Philadelphia, 1798), 184–90; Mathew Carey, *The Olive Branch: or, Faults on Both Sides, Federal and Democratic* (Freeport, N.Y., 1969), 58–59; William Duane, *Observations on the Principles and Operation of Banking* (Philadelphia, 1804); Binns, *Recollections*, 232–34; *Am. Pat.*, Feb. 22, 1803; *Aug. Chron.*, March 31, 1810. See also, Willis G. Briggs, "Joseph Gales, Editor of Raleigh's First Newspaper," *North Carolina Booklet* 7 (1907): 120; R. R. Madden, *The United Irishmen: Their Lives and Times* (Dublin, 1858), vol. 3, 233; Higginbotham, *Keystone*, 225; Malone, *Cooper*, 222; Carter, "Mathew Carey," 290–98; David N. Doyle, *Ireland, Irishmen and Revolutionary America, 1760–1820* (Dublin, 1981), 226; Ronald Schultz, *The Republic of Labor: Philadelphia Artisans and the Politics of Class* (New York, 1993), 184–86.

126. "Justice and Humanity" [Paine], *Pennsylvania Journal*, March 8, 1775, in Foner, ed., *Writings of Paine*, vol. 2, 16–19.

127. Fruchtman, *Paine*, 418.

128. See above, 23–25. For the United Irishmen, *N. Star*, Dec. 12, 1792.

129. For a discussion of some of the exiles and slavery, see Twomey, *Jacobins and Jeffersonians*, 102–6.

130. For this approach applied to Thomas Cooper's career, see Stephen L. Newman, "Thomas Cooper, 1759–1839: The Political Odyssey of a Bourgeois Ideologue," *Southern Studies* 24 (1985): 295–305.

131. William H. Stafford, ed., *The Blennerhassett Papers* (Cincinnati, 1864), 45; John Bernard, *Retrospections of America, 1797–1811* (New York, 1887), 188–89.

132. *RSCIHC* (1798), 16; Madden, *United Irishmen*, vol. 3, 183–84; James J. Hoecker, *Joseph Priestly and the Idea of Progress* (New York, 1987), 242–43. I have been unable to confirm Sweetman's or Driscol's ownership of slaves.

133. Rollo G. Silver, *Typefounding in America, 1787–1825* (Charlottesville, Va., 1965), 29.

134. Clement Eaton, "Winifred and Joseph Gales, Liberals of the Old South," *Journal of Southern History* 10 (1944): 461; Briggs, "Gales," 121.

135. Quoted in Eaton, "Winifred and Joseph Gales," 464–65.

136. Larry E. Tise, *Proslavery: A History of the Defense of Slavery in America, 1701–1840* (Athens, Ga., 1987), 51; Lawrence J. Friedman, "Purifying the White Man's Country: The American Colonization Society Reconsidered, 1816–40," *Societas* 6 (1976): 5–6.

137. Eaton, "Winifred and Joseph Gales," 465.

138. Friedman, "American Colonisation Society," 5, 15–16.

139. Winthrop D. Jordan, *White over Black: American Attitudes Toward the Negro, 1550–1812* (Chapel Hill, N.C., 1968), 429, pithily sums up Jefferson's dilemma: "He hated slavery but thought Negroes inferior to white men." Jefferson had suggested recolonization in Africa in 1776. Gary B. Nash, *Race and Revolution* (Madison, Wis., 1990), 42–43.

140. *Aurora*, Dec. 29, 1795.

141. *CUSR*, March 17, 1798.

142. Binns, *Recollections*, 264, 74.

143. *Aurora*, Jan. 19, Feb. 6, 1805, Dec. 23, 1806.

144. *Cork Gaz.*, Jan. 8, 1794.

145. *Am. Pat.*, Oct. 2, 1802.

146. Ibid., Nov. 13, 1802. See also Callender's view that "The condition of the slave is very often much more comfortable than that of his master." *Rec.*, Aug. 25, 1802. Cooper thought they were better off than English laborers. Malone, *Cooper*, 288.

147. Michael Durey, "Irish Deism and Jefferson's Republic: Denis Driscol in Ireland and America, 1793–1810," *Éire-Ireland: A Journal of Irish Studies* 25 (1990): 74–75.

148. Gordon S. Wood, *The Radicalism of the American Revolution* (New York, 1993), 186.

149. Twomey, *Jacobins and Jeffersonians*, 105. For Jefferson's views on black inferiority, see Jordan, *White over Black*, 435–40.

150. M. Tait, "James Ronaldson, Baker, Typefounder, Philanthropist, and His Connexions in and around Edinburgh," *Book of the Old Edinburgh Club* 28 (1953): 48.

151. *Rec.*, June 3, 1803.

152. Although one might be tempted to exculpate Cooper if one historian's highly inaccurate pen portrait of him as the South Carolina "upcountry's . . . treasured cripple," a "fanatical . . . hunched-over old man," is accepted. William W. Freehling, *The Road to Disunion: Secessionists at Bay, 1776–1854* (New York, 1990), 256–57. It is instructive to learn that Cooper grew up in France and "spent a stormy career in and out of jails on both sides of the Atlantic."

153. Malone, *Cooper*, 289.

154. Daniel T. Rodgers, *Contested Truths: Keywords in American Politics Since Independence* (New York, 1987), 31.

155. S. H. Jeyes, *The Russells of Birmingham in the French Revolution and in America, 1791–1814* (London, 1911), 263–64, 273.

156. John Daly Burk may probably be added to this list. His *History of Virginia* totally ignored the role played by blacks in the revolution. Friedman, "American Colonization Society," 2.

157. Haber, *Warden*, 20–22.

158. For the influence of utilitarianism on antislavery sentiment in Britain, see David Brion Davis, *The Problem of Slavery in the Age of Revolution, 1770–1823* (Ithaca, N.Y., 1975), 354–55.

159. Gwyn A. Williams, *The Search for Beulah Land* (London, 1980), 77; Twomey, *Jacobins and Jeffersonians*, 102–4.

160. *American Universal Magazine*, June 13, 1797.

161. Lewis Leary, "Thomas Branagan: Republican Rhetoric and Romanticism in America," *PMHB* 77 (1953): 332–52.

162. Thomas Branagan to Jefferson, May 7, 1805, Jefferson to George Logan, May 11, 1805, Logan to Jefferson, June 10, 1805, Jeff. Papers.

163. W. Melancthon Glasgow, *History of the Reformed Presbyterian Church in America* (Baltimore, 1888), 79–80; John Neil McLeod, *Preparation for Death the Business of Life: A discourse on the death of the Rev. Samuel Brown Wylie* (New York, 1852), 18.

CHAPTER EIGHT. CONCLUSION

1. Gordon S. Wood, *The Radicalism of the American Revolution* (New York, 1993), 232. See also, written from a Marxist perspective, Charles Sellers, *The Market Revolution: Jacksonian America, 1815–1846* (New York, 1991).

2. Wood, *Radicalism*, 230.

3. This is the thrust of the arguments in Gwyn A. Williams, *Artisans and Sans-Culottes: Popular Movements in France and Britain during the French Revolution* (London, 1989); E. P. Thompson, *The Making of the English Working Class* (London, 1968); Colin Bonwick, *English Radicals and the American Revolution* (Chapel Hill, N.C., 1977).

4. Ronald Schultz, *The Republic of Labor: Philadelphia Artisans and the Politics of Class* (New York, 1993), 3–35; Alfred F. Young, "English Plebeian Culture and Eighteenth-Century American Radicalism," in Margaret Jacob and James Jacob, eds., *Origins of Anglo-American Radicalism* (London, 1984), 185–212.

5. Edward Pessen, *Most Uncommon Jacksonians: The Radical Leaders of the Early Labor Movement* (Albany, N.Y., 1970); Bruce Laurie, *The Working People of Philadelphia, 1800–1850 (Philadelphia, 1980);* Sean Wilentz, *Chants Democratic: New York City and the Rise of the American Working Class, 1788–1850* (New York, 1984), chaps. 4 and 5.

6. Schultz, *Republic of Labor*, chap. 7; Michael Durey, "John Lithgow's Lithconia: The Making and Meaning of America's First 'Utopian Socialist' Tract," *WMQ* 3rd Ser., 46 (1992): 675–94.

Bibliography

MANUSCRIPT COLLECTIONS

England

Public Record Office, London
HO42	Home Office, domestic
HO100	Home Office, Ireland
HO102	Home Office, Scotland
HO105	Home Office, out-letters
TS11	treasury solicitors' papers
WO1	War Office, in-letters

British Library, London
Add.MSS, 16919–25	Association for Preserving Liberty and Property papers
Add.MSS, 27809–12	Francis Place papers
Add.MSS, 33105–6	Pelham papers

Kent County Record Office, Maidstone
U840	Pratt papers

National Army Museum, London
6807/174	Nugent papers

Hampshire County Record Office, Winchester
38M49	Wickham papers

Northern Ireland

Public Record Office of Northern Ireland, Belfast
D272	McCance MSS
D1759	Irish letters from America
T1053/1	Minutes and records of the Presbytery of Antrim
T3541/5/3	John Caldwell, "Particulars of History of North County Irish Family" (typescript of original)
T1375	Robb papers

Scotland

Scottish Record Office, Edinburgh
NG1/1	Minutes of the trustees of the board of manufacturers
CH2/121	Records of the Presbytery of Edinburgh

University of Edinburgh, Special Collections
Ms.La.11.451/2   Forbes correspondence
National Library of Scotland, Edinburgh
MS 3825   Thomas Muir correspondence

Republic of Ireland
National Archives, Dublin
620 Series   Rebellion papers
MS 2300   McKenna correspondence
Library of Trinity College, Dublin
Ms 873   Madden papers
Ms 868–9   Sirr papers

France
Archives des Affaires Étrangères, Paris
Corr. Pol. Ang. 588

United States
Library of Congress
    Thomas Jefferson papers
    William Sampson letters
Historical Society of Pennsylvania
    Lea and Febiger collection
    Edward Carey Gardiner collection
American Philosophical Society
    Castle Collection, Bache papers
Maryland Historical Society
    David Bailie Warden papers
Philadelphia City Hall Archives
    Letters of Administration

PRINTED COLLECTIONS OF PRIMARY MATERIALS

Boyd, Julian P., et al., eds. *The Papers of Thomas Jefferson.* 26 vols. to date. Princeton: Princeton University Press, 1950–.

Campbell, Charles, ed. *Some Materials to Serve for a Brief Memoir of John Daly Burk.* Albany, N.Y.: 1868.

Chart, D. A., ed. *The Drennan Letters.* Belfast: HMSO, 1931.

Cobbett, William. *Porcupine's Works.* 12 vols. London, 1803.

Conway, Moncure D., ed. *The Writings of Thomas Paine.* 4 vols. New York: AMS Press, 1967.

Davis, Thomas W., ed. *Committees for Repeal of the Test and Corporation Acts: Minutes 1786–90 and 1827–8*. London: London Record Society, 1978.

Fitch, Raymond E., ed. *Breaking with Burr: Harman Blennerhassett's Journal 1807*. Athens, Ohio University Press, 1988.

Foner, Philip S., ed. *The Complete Writings of Thomas Paine*. 2 vols. New York: Citadel Press, 1945.

Ford, Paul Leicester, ed. *The Works of Thomas Jefferson*. 10 vols. New York: Knickerbocker Press, 1904–5.

Ford, Worthington C., ed. "Letters of James Cheetham." *Proceedings of the Massachusetts Historical Society* 3rd Ser. 1 (1907): 41–64.

———. "Thomas Jefferson and James Thomson Callender." *New England Historical and Genealogical Register* 51 (1896): 321–33, 445–58; 52 (1897): 19–25, 153–58, 323–38.

Grosart, A. B., ed. *The Poems and Literary Prose of Alexander Wilson, the American Ornithologist*. 2 vols. Paisley: A. Gardner, 1876.

Howell, T. B., and T. J. Howell, eds. *A Complete Collection of State Trials*. 34 vols. London, 1809–28.

[———.] *Parliamentary History of England, from the Earliest Period to 1803*. 36 vols. London, 1816–18.

King, Charles R., ed. *The Life and Correspondence of Rufus King*. 6 vols. New York, 1894–1900.

McDowell, R. B. "Proceedings of the Dublin Society of United Irishmen." *Analecta Hibernica* 17 (1949): 3–143.

McHugh, Roger J., ed. *Carlow in '98: The Autobiography of William Farrell of Carlow*. Dublin: Richview Press, n.d.

Mitchell, Stewart, ed. *New Letters of Abigail Adams, 1788–1801*. 2nd ed. New York: Greenwood Press, 1973.

Perkins, Bradford. "A Diplomat's Wife in Philadelphia: Letters of Henrietta Liston, 1796–1800." *William and Mary Quarterly* 3rd Ser. 9 (1954): 592–632.

Ross, Charles, ed. *Correspondence of Charles, First Marquis Cornwallis*. 3 vols. London: John Murray, 1859.

Rutt, John T., ed. *The Theological and Miscellaneous Works of Joseph Priestley*. 25 vols. London, 1823–32; reprint, New York: Kraus Reprint, 1972.

Stafford, William H., ed. *The Blennerhassett Papers*. Cincinnati, 1864.

Stephenson, Jean. "Records Furnished to the D. A. R. Library; . . . U.S. District Court, Charleston, S.C., 1792–1800." *National Genealogical Society Quarterly* 30 (1942): 125–27.

Syrett, Harold C., and Jacob E. Cooke, eds. *The Papers of Alexander Hamilton*. 26 vols. New York: Columbia University Press, 1960–79.

Thale, Mary, ed. *Selections from the Papers of the London Corresponding Society, 1792–1799*. Cambridge: Cambridge University Press, 1983.

Vane, Charles (Marquess of Londonderry), ed. *Memoirs and Correspondence of Viscount Castlereagh, Second Marquess of Londonderry*. 10 vols. London, 1848–49.

GOVERNMENT PUBLICATIONS

Report of the Secret Committee of the Irish House of Commons. Dublin, 1798.
Report of the Secret Committee of the Irish House of Lords. Dublin, 1793.
Report of the Secret Committee of the Irish House of Lords. Dublin, 1798.

CONTEMPORARY PUBLICATIONS

A. C. P., ed. *Equality: A History of Lithconia.* 1837; reprint, Philadelphia: Prime Press, 1947.

Anderson, Robert. *Life of Samuel Johnson LLD.* 3rd ed. Edinburgh, 1815.

[Anon.] *Look Before You Leap; or, a Few Hints to Such Artizans, Mechanics, Labourers, Farmers and Husbandmen as Are Desirous of Emigrating to America.* 2nd ed. London, 1796.

[Anon.] *A Narrative of Recent Occurrences within the Bounds of the Eastern Subordinate Synod of the Reformed Presbyterian Church.* New York, 1834.

[Anon.] *Poetical Works of Alexander Wilson.* Belfast, 1845.

[Anon.] *The Soldier's Friend: or, Considerations on the Late Pretended Augmentation of the Subsistence of Private Soldiers.* London, 1792.

Bernard, John. *Retrospections of America, 1797–1811.* Ed. Mrs. B. Bernard. New York, 1887.

[Binns, John.] *Recollections of the Life of John Binns: Twenty-Nine Years in Europe and Fifty-Three in the United States.* Philadelphia, 1854.

———. *The Trial of John Binns, Deputy of the London Corresponding Society, for Sedition.* Birmingham, 1797.

[Birch, Thomas Ledlie.] *A Letter from an Irish Emigrant to His Friend in the United States, Giving an Account of the Rise and Progress of the Commotions in Ireland.* Philadelphia, 1799.

———. *Seemingly Experimental Religion, Instructors Unexperienced—Converters Unconverted—Revivals Killing Religion.* Washington, Pa., 1806.

Burk, John [Daly]. *History of the Late War in Ireland, with an Account of the United Irish Association.* Philadelphia, 1799.

———. *An Oration, Delivered on the 4 of March 1803, at the Court House in Petersburg.* Petersburg, 1803.

———. *The Trial of John Burk, of Trinity College, for Heresy and Blasphemy.* Dublin, 1794.

Burke, Edmund. *Reflections on the Revolution in France.* London, 1790; reprint, London: Dent, 1964.

[Callender, James Thomson.] *A Critical Review of the Works of Dr. Samuel Johnson.* Edinburgh, 1783.

[———.] *Deformities of Dr. Samuel Johnson.* Edinburgh, 1782.

[———.] *An Impartial Account of the Conduct of the Excise towards the Breweries of Scotland*. Edinburgh, 1791.

———, ed. *Miscellanies in Prose and Verse*. 2nd ed. Edinburgh, 1792.

———. *The Political Progress of Britain*. Part 1, 2nd ed. Philadelphia, 1794.

———. *The Political Progress of Britain*. Part 2. Philadelphia, 1795.

———. *The Prospect Before Us*. 2 vols. Richmond, 1800.

———. *A Short History of the Nature and Consequences of Excise Laws*. Philadelphia, 1796.

———. *Sketches of the History of America*. Philadelphia, 1798.

[Carey, James?] "A Friend to Political Equality." *A Pill for Porcupine: Being a Specific for an Obstinate Itching which that Hireling Has Long Contracted for Lying and Calumny*. Philadelphia, 1796.

Carey, Mathew. "The Autobiography of Mathew Carey." *New England Magazine*, 1833–34.

———. *The Olive Branch: or, Faults on Both Sides, Federal and Democratic*. 10th ed. 1818; reprint, Freeport, N.Y.: Books for Libraries Press, 1969.

Carey, William Paulet. *An Appeal to the People of Ireland*. Dublin, 1794.

Cheetham, James. *A Dissertation Concerning Political Equality, and the Corporation of New York*. New York, 1800.

———. *The Life of Thomas Paine*. New York, 1809.

[———.] "A Citizen of New York." *A Narrative of the Suppression by Col. Burr, of the History of the Administration of John Adams, Late President of the United States, Written by John Wood*. New York, 1802.

———. *Nine Letters on the Subject of Aaron Burr's Political Defection*. New York, 1803.

———. *A Reply to Aristedes*. New York, 1804.

Cloney, Thomas. *A Personal Narrative of . . . 1798*. Dublin, 1832.

[Cobbett, William.] *A Bone to Gnaw for the Democrats: or, Observations on a Pamphlet, entitled, The Political Progress of Britain*. 3rd ed. Philadelphia, 1795.

[———.] *A Bone to Gnaw for the Democrats*. Part II. Philadelphia, 1795.

[———.] "Peter Porcupine." *The Democratic Judge: or, the Equal Liberty of the Press*. Philadelphia, 1798.

[———.] *A Kick for a Bite*. Philadelphia, 1795.

[———.] "Peter Porcupine." *A Little Plain English, Addressed to the People of the United States*. Philadelphia, 1795.

[———]. *Observations on the Emigration of Dr. Priestley, and on the Several Addresses Delivered to Him on His Arrival at New York*. Philadelphia, 1794.

[———.] "Peter Porcupine." *Political Censor, or, Monthly Review of the Most Interesting Political Occurrences Relative to the United States of America*. Philadelphia, 1796.

Cockburn, Henry. *Memorials of His Time*. Edinburgh, 1856; reprint, Edinburgh: Mercat Press, 1971.

[Cooper, Thomas.] *Consolidation: An Account of Parties in the United States, from the Convention of 1787, to the Present Period*. Columbia, S.C., 1824.

——. *A Reply to Mr. Burke's Invective against Mr. Cooper, and Mr. Watt, in the House of Commons, on the 30th. April, 1792*. Manchester, 1792.

——. *Some Information Respecting America*. London, 1794.

Creech, William. *Fugitive Pieces*. Edinburgh, 1815.

[Crichton, Thomas.] *Biographical Sketches of the Late Alexander Wilson, Communicated in a Series of Letters to a Young Friend*. Paisley, 1819.

Dickson, William Steel. *Scripture Politics*. Belfast, 1812; reprint (ed. Brendan Clifford), Belfast: Athol Books, 1991.

Dinmore, Richard, Jr. *A Brief Account of the Moral and Political Acts of the Kings and Queens of England, from William the Conqueror to the Revolution in the Year 1688*. London, 1793.

——. *An Exposition of the Principles of the English Jacobins; with strictures on the political conduct of Charles James Fox, William Pitt and Edmund Burke; including remarks on the resignation of George Washington*. 2nd ed. Norwich, 1797.

——. *A Long Talk Before the Tammany Society of Alexandria, District of Columbia*. Alexandria, 1804.

[Duane, William.] *Experience the Test of Government: In Eighteen Essays, Written during the Years 1805 and 1806*. Philadelphia, 1807.

[——.] "Jasper Dwight." *A Letter to George Washington, President of the United States*. Philadelphia, 1796.

——. *Observations on the Principles and Operation of Banking*. Philadelphia, 1804.

Dunn, Thomas. *A Discourse, Delivered in the New Dutch Church, Nassau Street*. New York, 1794.

Eddowes, Ralph. *Sermons Delivered Before the First Society of Unitarian Christians, in the City of Philadelphia; wherein the principal points, on which that denomination of believers differ from the majority of their brethren, are occasionally elucidated*. Philadelphia, 1817.

[——.] *State of Facts Relating to the Franchises of the City of Chester, and All Other Corporations in the Kingdom*. Chester, 1788.

——. *The Unity of God, and the Worship That Is Due to HIM alone: A Discourse delivered at the opening of the Church erected by the First Society of Unitarian Christians in the City of Philadelphia, on the 14th. February, 1813*. Philadelphia, 1813.

[——.] *The Whole Proceedings, in Several Informations in the Nature of a Quo Warranto, the King . . . against Mr. Thos. Amery . . . and Mr John Monk . . . of the City of Chester, on the Relation of Ralph Eddowes, . . . Merchant*. Vol. 1. Chester, 1791.

"English Barrister, An." *The Trials at Large of Robert Watt and David Downie, for High Treason . . . at Edinburgh, 1794*. London, 1794.

Finch, I. *Travels in the United States of America and Canada*. London, 1833.

[Fletcher, Mrs. Archibald.] *Autobiography of Mrs. Fletcher with Letters and Other Family Memorials*. Edinburgh, 1875.

Galt, John. *Annals of the Parish*. Edinburgh, 1821; Oxford: Oxford University Press, 1986.

Godwin, William. *Enquiry Concerning Political Justice.* 1793; Harmondsworth: Penguin, 1985.

Janson, Charles William. *The Stranger in America, 1793–1806.* London, 1806; reprint, New York: Lenox Hill, 1971.

Kennedy, James. *Treason!!! or Not Treason!!! alias The Weavers Budget.* London, [1795?].

Knox, John. *A View of the British Empire, More Especially Scotland.* London, 1784.

[Lawless, Valentine (Lord Cloncurry).] *Personal Recollections of the Life and Times, with extracts from the correspondence of Valentine Lord Cloncurry.* 2nd ed. Dublin, 1850.

Lee, "Citizen" [Richard.] *King Killing.* London, 1794.

[Lithgow, John.] "Timothy Telltruth." *The Collected Wisdom of Ages, the Most Stupendous Fabric of Human Invention, the English Constitution.* Philadelphia, 1799.

McLeod, John Neil. *Preparation for Death the Business of Life: A discourse on the death of the Rev. Samuel Brown Wylie.* New York, 1852.

McMaster, Gilbert. *The Upright Man in Life and at Death.* Philadelphia, 1852.

MacNeven, William J., ed. *Pieces of Irish History.* New York, 1807.

McSkimin [*sic*], Samuel. *Annals of Ulster.* New ed. Belfast, 1906.

Priestley, Joseph. *The Case of the Poor Emigrants Recommended, in a Discourse, delivered at the University Hall in Philadelphia, on Sunday, February 19, 1797.* Philadelphia, 1797.

[——.] *Memoirs of Dr. Joseph Priestley, to the year 1795, written by himself; with a continuation, to the time of his decease, by his son, Joseph Priestley: and observations on his writings, by Thomas Cooper . . . : and the Reverend William Christie.* 2 vols. Northumberland, Pa., 1806.

Reid, William Hamilton. *The Rise and Dissolution of the Infidel Societies in This Metropolis.* London, 1800; reprint (ed. Victor Neuberg), London: Woburn Books, 1971.

Rowan, Archibald Hamilton. *The Autobiography of Archibald Hamilton Rowan.* Ed. William H. Drummond. Dublin, 1840; reprint, Shannon: Irish University Press, 1972.

[Sampson, William.] *Memoirs of William Sampson.* 2nd ed. Leesburg, Va., 1817.

Sinclair, Sir John. *The Statistical Account of Scotland.* 20 vols. New ed. East Ardsley: EP Publishing, 1973–83.

Sweetman, John. *A Refutation of the Charges Attempted to Be Made Against the Secretary of the Sub-Committee of the Catholics of Ireland.* Dublin, 1793.

Teeling, Charles Hamilton. *History of the Irish Rebellion of 1798: A Personal Narrative.* Glasgow, 1828.

——. *Sequel to the History of the Irish Rebellion of 1798: A Personal Narrative.* Glasgow, [1828?].

"Touchstone, Geoffrey." *He Wou'd Be a Poet:, or, Nature Will Be Nature Still: An Heroic Poem.* Philadelphia, 1796.

[Tytler, James.] *Paine's Second Part of the Age of Reason Answered*. Salem, 1796.

———. *To the People and Their Friends*. Edinburgh, 1792.

[Vaughan, Benjamin.] *Two Papers by the Calm Observer, not printed in the Collection of his Letters Extracted from the Morning Chronicle*. N.p., 1795.

Wallace, Robert. *Various Prospects of Mankind, Nature, and Providence*. London, 1761.

Warden, David Bailie. *A Farewell Address to the Junto of the Presbytery of Bangor*. Glasgow, 1798.

Wilson, Alexander. *Oration on the Power and Value of National Liberty*. Philadelphia, 1801.

Wood, John. *A Full Exposition of the Clintonian Faction and the Society of the Columbian Illuminati*. Newark, N.J., [1802].

———. *A General View of the History of Switzerland, with a particular account of the origin and accomplishment of the late Swiss revolution*. Edinburgh, 1799.

Wylie, Samuel B. *The Obligation of Covenants*. Philadelphia, 1804.

———. *Sentiments of the Rev. Samuel B. Wylie, A. M. in 1803, Respecting Civil Magistracy and the Government of the United States: contrasted with sentiments of the Rev. Samuel B. Wylie, D. D. in 1832, on the same subjects*. Philadelphia, 1832.

———. *Two Sons of Oil*. Philadelphia, 1803.

CONTEMPORARY NEWSPAPERS

England

Berrow's Worcester Journal
Cobbett's Weekly Political Register (London)
Manchester Herald
Times (London)

Scotland

Edinburgh Evening Courant

Ireland

Cork Gazette
Dublin Evening Post
Freeman's Journal (Dublin)
Northern Star (Belfast)
Press (Dublin)
Rights of Irishmen, or, National Evening Star (Dublin)

United States

American Citizen (New York)
American Patriot (Baltimore)
Augusta Chronicle (Georgia)

Aurora and General Advertiser (Philadelphia)
Carey's United States Recorder (Philadelphia)
Charleston Daily Evening Gazette (Charleston, S.C.)
Constitutional Diary and Philadelphia Evening Advertiser (Philadelphia)
Daily Advertiser (Philadelphia)
Examiner (Richmond, Va.)
Exile (New York)
Gazette of the United States (Philadelphia)
New-York Evening Post (New York)
Pennsylvania Packet (Philadelphia)
Polar Star (Boston)
Porcupine's Gazette (Philadelphia)
Raleigh Register (Raleigh, N.C.)
Recorder (Richmond, Va.)
Republican Argus (Northumberland, Pa.)
Shamrock (New York)
Temple of Reason (Philadelphia)
Time-Piece (New York)
Virginia Gazette and Richmond Daily Advertiser (Richmond, Va.)
Wilmington Chronicle: and North-Carolina Weekly Advertiser (Wilmington, N.C.)

CONTEMPORARY MAGAZINES

American Universal Magazine (Philadelphia)
Annual Biography and Obituary for the Year 1818 (London)
Bee (Edinburgh)
Edinburgh Clerical Review
Gentleman's Magazine (London)
Irish Magazine, or, Monthly Asylum for Neglected Biography (Dublin)
Mirror (Edinburgh)
Monthly Repository (London)
National Magazine, or, Cabinet of the United States (Washington, D.C.)
Scots Magazine (Edinburgh)

SECONDARY SOURCES

Dictionaries, Finding Aids, Etcetera

Baylen, Joseph O., and Norbert J. Gossman, eds. *Biographical Dictionary of Modern British Radicals, 1770–1830.* Hassocks: Harvester Press, 1979.

Brigham, Clarence S. *History and Bibliography of American Newspapers 1690–1820.* 2 vols. Worcester, Mass.: American Antiquarian Society, 1947.

Evans, Charles. *American Bibliography*. 14 vols. Worcester, Mass.: American Antiquarian Society, 1925–55.

Filby, P. William, and Mary K. Meyer, eds. *Passenger and Immigration Lists Index: A Guide to Published Arrivals*. 3 vols. Detroit: Gale Research Company, 1981.

Gaines, Pierce W. *Political Works of Concealed Authorship*. 3rd ed. Hamden, Conn.: Shoe String Press, 1972.

———. *William Cobbett and the United States, 1792–1835: A Bibliography*. Worcester, Mass.: American Antiquarian Society, 1971.

Greaves, Richard L., and Robert Zaller, eds. *Biographical Dictionary of British Radicals in the Seventeenth Century*. 3 vols. Brighton: Harvester Press, 1982.

Johnson, Allen, and Dumas Malone, eds. *Dictionary of American Biography*. 12 vols. New York: Scribner's, 1927–58.

McConnell, J., and S. G. McConnell, eds. *Fasti of the Irish Presbyterian Church*. Belfast, 1951.

Stephen, Sir Leslie, and Sir Sidney Lee, eds. *Dictionary of National Biography*. 22 vols. Oxford: Oxford University Press, 1967–68.

Books

Adams, Henry. *The Life of Albert Gallatin*. 1879; reprint, New York: Chelsea House, 1943.

Allen, H. C., and Roger Thompson, eds. *Contrast and Connection: Bicentennial Essays in Anglo-American History*. Athens: Ohio University Press, 1976.

[Anon., ed.] *Thomas Jefferson: The Man, His World, His Influence*. London: Weidenfeld and Nicolson, 1973.

Appleby, Joyce. *Capitalism and a New Social Order: The Republican Vision of the 1790s*. New York: New York University Press, 1984.

Arendt, Hannah. *On Revolution*. Harmondsworth: Penguin, 1973.

Aspinall, Arthur. *Politics and the Press, 1780–1850*. Hassocks: Harvester Press, 1973.

Axelrad, Jacob. *Philip Freneau: Champion of Democracy*. Austin: University of Texas Press, 1967.

Bailie, W. Desmond, et al., eds. *A History of Congregations in the Presbyterian Church in Ireland, 1610–1982*. Belfast: Presbyterian Historical Society of Ireland, 1982.

Baker-Short, L. *Pioneers of Scottish Unitarianism*. Narberth, 1965.

Ball, Terence, and J. G. A. Pocock, eds. *Conceptual Change and the Constitution*. Lawrence: University Press of Kansas, 1988.

Banning, Lance, ed. *After the Constitution: Party Conflict in the New Republic*. Belmont, Calif.: Wadsworth, 1989.

———. *The Jeffersonian Persuasion: Evolution of a Party Ideology*. New York: Cornell University Press, 1978.

Barry, Jonathan, and Christopher Brooks, eds. *The Middling Sort of People: Culture, Society and Politics in England, 1550–1800*. London: Macmillan, 1994.

Bartlett, Thomas. *The Fall and Rise of the Irish Nation: The Catholic Question, 1690–1830*. Dublin: Gill and Macmillan, 1992.

Beeman, Richard, ed. *Beyond Confederation: Origins of the Constitution and American National Identity.* Chapel Hill: University of North Carolina Press, 1987.

Belz, H., et al., eds. *To Form a More Perfect Union: The Critical Ideas of the Constitution.* Charlottesville: University of Virginia Press, 1992.

Berkeley, Edmund, and Dorothy Smith Berkeley. *John Beckley: Zealous Partisan in a Nation Divided.* Philadelphia: American Philosophical Society, 1973.

Berthoff, Rowland Tappan. *British Immigrants in Industrial America, 1790–1850.* Cambridge, Mass.: Harvard University Press, 1953.

Bewley, Christina. *Muir of Huntershill.* Oxford: Oxford University Press, 1981.

Black, Jeremy, ed. *British Politics and Society from Walpole to Pitt, 1742–1789.* London: Macmillan, 1990.

Bloch, Ruth. *Visionary Republic: Millennial Themes in American Thought, 1756–1800.* Cambridge: Cambridge University Press, 1988.

Bolt, Christine, and Seymour Drescher, eds. *Anti-Slavery, Religion and Reform: Essays in Memory of Roger Anstey.* Folkstone: Dawson, 1980.

Bono, Paola. *Radicals and Reformers in Late Eighteenth-Century Scotland.* Frankfurt-am Main: Peter Lang, 1989.

Bonwick, Colin. *English Radicals and the American Revolution.* Chapel Hill: University of North Carolina Press, 1977.

Boorstin, Daniel J. *Hidden History: Exploring Our Secret Past.* New York: Vintage Press, 1989.

Bossy, John, and Peter Jupp, eds. *Essays Presented to Michael Roberts.* Belfast: Blackstaff Press, 1976.

Bradley, James E. *Religion, Revolution and English Radicalism: Nonconformity in Eighteenth-Century Politics and Society.* Cambridge: Cambridge University Press, 1990.

Bradsher, Earl L. *Mathew Carey, Editor, Author and Publisher: A Study in American Literary Development.* 1912; reprint, New York: AMS Press, 1966.

Brewer, John. *Party Ideology and Popular Politics at the Accession of George III.* Cambridge: Cambridge University Press, 1981.

Brock, W. R., and C. H. Brock. *Scotus Americanus.* Edinburgh: Edinburgh University Press, 1982.

Brown, Robert. *Paisley Poets, with Brief Memoirs of Them, and Selections from Their Poetry.* 2 vols. N.p., 1889.

Butler, Jon. *Awash in a Sea of Faith: Christianizing the American People.* Cambridge, Mass.: Harvard University Press, 1990.

Calder, Angus. *Revolutionary Empire: The Rise of the English-Speaking Empires from the Fifteenth Century to the 1780s.* New York: E. P. Dutton, 1981.

Cantwell, Robert. *Alexander Wilson: Naturalist and Pioneer.* Philadelphia: Lippincott, 1961.

Chandler, David Leon. *The Jefferson Conspiracies: A President's Role in the Assassination of Meriwether Lewis.* New York: William Morrow, 1994.

Chitnis, Anand C. *The Scottish Enlightenment and Early Victorian English Society.* London: Croom Helm, 1986.

———. *The Scottish Enlightenment: A Social History.* London: Croom Helm, 1976.

Christie, Ian R. *Stress and Stability in Late Eighteenth-Century Britain: Reflections on the British Avoidance of Revolution.* Oxford: Clarendon Press, 1984.

———. *Wilkes, Wyvill and Reform: The Parliamentary Reform Movement in British Politics, 1760–1785.* London: Macmillan, 1962.

Claeys, Gregory. *Thomas Paine: Social and Political Thought.* Boston: Unwin Hyman, 1989.

Clark, J. C. D. *English Society, 1688–1832: Ideology, Social Structure and Political Practice during the Ancien Regime.* Cambridge: Cambridge University Press, 1985.

———. *The Language of Liberty, 1660–1832: Political Discourse and Social Dynamics in the Anglo-American World.* Cambridge: Cambridge University Press, 1994.

Colley, Linda. *Britons: Forging the Nation, 1707–1837.* New Haven: Yale University Press, 1992.

Cook, Richard I. *Jonathan Swift as a Tory Pamphleteer.* Seattle: University of Washington Press, 1967.

Cooke, Jacob E. *Tench Coxe and the Early Republic.* Chapel Hill: University of North Carolina Press, 1978.

Cookson, J. E. *The Friends of Peace: Anti-War Liberalism in England, 1793–1815.* Cambridge: Cambridge University Press, 1982.

Coughlin, Rupert J. *Napper Tandy.* Dublin: Anvil Books, 1976.

Couper, W. J. *The Edinburgh Periodical Press.* 2 vols. Stirling, 1908.

Cowan, Ian B. *The Scottish Covenanters, 1660–1688.* London: Gollancz, 1976.

Cox, Joseph W. *Champion of Southern Federalism: Robert Goodloe Harper of South Carolina.* Port Washington, N.Y.: Kennikat Press, 1972.

Cunningham, Noble E., Jr. *The Jeffersonian Republicans in Power: Party Operations, 1801–1809.* Chapel Hill: University of North Carolina Press, 1963.

———. *The Jeffersonian Republicans: The Formation of Party Organisation, 1789–1801.* Chapel Hill: University of North Carolina Press, 1957.

Curtin, Nancy. *The United Irishmen: Popular Politics in Ulster and Dublin, 1791–1798.* Oxford: Clarendon Press, 1994.

Dabney, Virginius. *Richmond: The Story of a City.* New York: Doubleday, 1976.

Darnton, Robert. *The Literary Underground of the Old Régime.* Cambridge, Mass.: Harvard University Press, 1982.

Dauer, Manning J. *The Adams Federalists.* Baltimore: Johns Hopkins University Press, 1968.

Davis, David Brion. *The Problem of Slavery in the Age of Revolution, 1770–1823.* Ithaca, N.Y.: Cornell University Press, 1975.

———. *Revolutions: Reflections on American Equality and Foreign Liberations.* Cambridge, Mass.: Harvard University Press, 1990.

Devine, Thomas M., ed. *Conflict and Stability in Scottish Society, 1700–1850.* Edinburgh: John Donald, 1990.

———, and Rosalind Mitchison, eds. *People and Society in Scotland, Volume 1, 1760–1830.* Edinburgh: John Donald, 1988.

Dickinson, Harry T. *British Radicalism and the French Revolution, 1789–1815*. Oxford: Blackwell, 1985.

———. *Liberty and Property: Political Ideology in Eighteenth-Century Britain*. New York: Holmes and Meier, 1977.

Dickson, Charles. *Revolt in the North: Antrim and Down in 1798*. Dublin: Clonmore and Reynolds, 1960.

Dickson, David. *New Foundations: Ireland 1660–1800*. Dublin: Helicon, 1987.

———, et al., eds. *The United Irishmen: Republicanism, Radicalism and Rebellion*. Dublin: Lilliput Press, 1993.

Doyle, David N. *Ireland, Irishmen and Revolutionary America, 1760–1820*. Dublin: Mercier Press, 1981.

Drudy, P. J., ed. *The Irish in America: Emigration, Assimilation, and Impact*. Cambridge: Cambridge University Press, 1985.

Durey, Michael. *"With the Hammer of Truth": James Thomson Callender and America's Early National Heroes*. Charlottesville, Va.: University of Virginia Press, 1990.

Dwyer, John, et al., eds. *New Perspectives in the Politics and Culture of Early Modern Scotland*. Edinburgh: John Donald, 1982.

Edwards, Owen D., and G. Shepperson, eds. *Scotland, Europe and the American Revolution*. Edinburgh: Edinburgh University Press, 1976.

Ehrman, John. *The Younger Pitt: The Reluctant Transition*. Stanford: Stanford University Press, 1983.

Elkins, Stanley, and Eric McKitrick. *The Age of Federalism: The Early American Republic, 1788–1800*. New York: Oxford University Press, 1993.

Elliott, Marianne. *Partners in Revolution: The United Irishmen and France*. New Haven: Yale University Press, 1982.

———. *Watchmen in Sion: The Protestant Idea of Liberty*. Derry: Field Day Theatre Company, 1985.

———. *Wolfe Tone: Prophet of Irish Independence*. New Haven: Yale University Press, 1989.

Ellis, Joseph J. *Passionate Sage: The Character and Legacy of John Adams*. New York: Norton, 1993.

Ellis, Richard E. *The Jeffersonian Crisis: Courts and Politics in the Young Republic*. New York: Oxford University Press, 1974.

Emsley, Clive, and James Walvin, eds. *Artisans, Peasants and Proletarians: Essays Presented to Gwyn A. Williams*. London: Croom Helm, 1985.

Erdman, David V. *Commerce des Lumières: John Oswald and the British in Paris, 1790–1793*. Columbia: University of Missouri Press, 1986.

Fergusson, Sir James. *Balloon Tytler*. London: Faber and Faber, 1972.

Ferling, John. *John Adams: A Life*. Knoxville: University of Tennessee Press, 1992.

Field, Henry Martyn. *The Irish Confederates, and the Rebellion of 1798*. New York, 1851.

Fitzpatrick, W. J. *Secret Service Under Pitt*. London: Longmans, Green, 1892.

———. *The Sham Squire, and Informers of 1798*. 3rd ed. Dublin: M. H. Gill and Son, 1895.

Foner, Eric. *Tom Paine and Revolutionary America*. New York: Oxford University Press, 1976.

Foner, Philip S. *The Democratic-Republican Societies, 1790–1800*. Westport, Conn.: Greenwood Press, 1976.

Forbes, M. *Beattie and His Friends*. London, 1904.

Foster, R. F. *Modern Ireland, 1690–1972*. London: Allen Lane, 1988.

Francis, John W. *Old New York: or, Reminiscences of the Past Sixty Years*. New York, 1865.

Fraser, W. Hamish. *Conflict and Class: Scottish Workers, 1700–1838*. Edinburgh: John Donald, 1988.

Freehling, William W. *The Road to Disunion: Secessionists at Bay, 1776–1854*. New York: Oxford University Press, 1990.

Fritz, Paul, and David Williams, eds. *City and Society in the Eighteenth Century*. Toronto: University of Toronto Press, 1973.

Fruchtman, Jack, Jr. *Thomas Paine: Apostle of Freedom*. New York: Four Walls Eight Windows, 1994.

Fry, Michael. *The Dundas Despotism*. Edinburgh: Edinburgh University Press, 1992.

Gaustad, Edwin S. *Neither King Nor Prelate: Religion and the New Nation, 1776–1826*. Grand Rapids: Eerdmans, 1993.

Geffen, Elizabeth M. *Philadelphia Unitarianism, 1796–1861*. Philadelphia: University of Pennsylvania Press, 1961.

Gilje, Paul A. *The Road to Mobocracy: Popular Disorder in New York City, 1763–1834*. Chapel Hill: University of North Carolina Press, 1987.

———, and William Pencak, eds. *New York in the Age of the Constitution, 1775–1800*. Cranbury, N.J.: Fairleigh Dickinson University Press, 1992.

Glasgow, W. Melancthon. *History of the Reformed Presbyterian Church in America*. Baltimore, 1888.

Goodwin, Albert. *The Friends of Liberty: The English Democratic Movement in the Age of the French Revolution*. London: Hutchinson, 1979.

Greaves, Richard L. *Deliver Us from Evil: The Radical Underground in Britain, 1660–1663*. Oxford: Oxford University Press, 1986.

Green, Daniel. *Great Cobbett: The Noblest Agitator*. Oxford: Oxford University Press, 1985.

Green, James N. *Mathew Carey: Publisher and Patriot*. Philadelphia: Library Company of Philadelphia, 1985.

Haber, Francis C. *David Bailie Warden: A Bibliographical Sketch of America's Cultural Ambassador in France, 1804–45*. Washington, D.C.: Institut Français de Washington, 1954.

Hamilton, Thomas. *History of the Irish Presbyterian Church*. Edinburgh, 1887.

Hammond, Jabez D. *The History of Political Parties in the State of New-York*. 2 vols. Albany, N.Y., 1842.

Hanyan, Craig. *De Witt Clinton: Years of Molding, 1769–1807*. New York: Garland, 1988.

Hatch, Nathan O. *The Democratization of American Christianity*. New Haven: Yale University Press, 1989.

Hawke, David Freeman. *Paine*. New York: Harper and Row, 1974.

Hayter, Althea, eds. *The Backbone: Diaries of a Military Family in the Napoleonic Wars*. Durham: Pentland Press, 1993.

Henriques, Ursula. *Religious Toleration in England, 1787–1833*. London: Routledge and Kegan Paul, 1961.

Higginbotham, Sanford W. *The Keystone in the Democratic Arch: Pennsylvania Politics, 1800–1816*. Harrisburg: Pennsylvania Historical and Museum Commission, 1952.

Hill, Christopher. *The Experience of Defeat: Milton and Some Contemporaries*. London: Faber and Faber, 1984.

Hinde, Wendy. *Castlereagh*. London: Collins, 1981.

Hoffman, Ronald, and Peter J. Albert, ed. *Religion in a Revolutionary Age*. Charlottesville: University of Virginia Press, 1994.

Holt, Istvan, and Michael Ignatieff, eds. *Wealth and Virtue*. Cambridge: Cambridge University Press, 1983.

Holt, Raymond V. *The Unitarian Contribution to Social Progress in England*. London: Allen and Unwin, 1938.

Hone, J. Ann. *For the Cause of Truth: Radicalism in London, 1796–1821*. Oxford: Oxford University Press, 1982.

Hook, Andrew. *Scotland and America: A Study of Cultural Relations, 1750–1835*. Glasgow: Blackie, 1975.

Horne, Colin J., ed. *Swift on His Age*. London: Harrap, 1953.

Horwitz, Morton J. *The Transformation of American Law, 1780–1860*. Cambridge, Mass.: Harvard University Press, 1977.

Houston, R. A. *Scottish Literacy and Scottish Identity: Illiteracy and Society in Scotland and Northern England, 1600–1800*. Cambridge: Cambridge University Press, 1985.

Hunter, Clark, ed. *The Life and Letters of Alexander Wilson*. Philadelphia: American Philosophical Society, 1983.

Inglis, Brian. *Freedom of the Press in Ireland*. London: Faber and Faber, 1954.

Jacob, Margaret, and James Jacob, eds. *The Origins of Anglo-American Radicalism*. London: Allen and Unwin, 1984.

James, Francis Godwin. *Ireland in the Empire, 1688–1770*. Cambridge, Mass.: Harvard University Press, 1973.

Jewson, C. B. *The Jacobin City: A Portrait of Norwich in Its Reaction to the French Revolution, 1788–1802*. Glasgow: Blackie, 1975.

Jeyes, S. H. *The Russells of Birmingham in the French Revolution and in America, 1791–1814*. London: George Allen and Co., 1911.

Jones, Clyve, ed. *Britain in the First Age of Party, 1680–1750: Essays Presented to Geoffrey Holmes*. London: Hambledon Press, 1987.

Jones, Whitney R. D. *David Williams: The Anvil and the Hammer*. Cardiff: University of Wales Press, 1986.

Jordan, Winthrop D. *White over Black: American Attitudes Toward the Negro, 1550–1812*. Chapel Hill: University of North Carolina Press, 1968.

Kates, Gary. *The Cercle Social, the Girondins, and the French Revolution*. Princeton: Princeton University Press, 1985.

Kay, John. *Original Portraits*. 2 vols. Edinburgh, 1877.

Kenrick, Mrs. W. Byng, ed. *Chronicles of a Non-Conformist Family: The Kenricks of Wynne Hall, Exeter and Birmingham*. Birmingham: Cornish Bros., 1932.

Keogh, Daire. *"The French Disease": The Catholic Church and Radicalism in Ireland, 1790–1800*. Dublin: Four Courts Press, 1993.

Knight, Frida. *The Strange Case of Thomas Walker: Ten Years in the Life of a Manchester Radical*. London: Lawrence and Wishart, 1957.

Knox, J. Wendell. *Conspiracy in American Politics, 1787–1815*. New York: Arno Press, 1972.

Koch, G. Adolf. *Republican Religion: The American Religion and the Cult of Reason*. New York: H. Holt, 1933.

Kramnick, Isaac. *Republicanism and Bourgeois Radicalism: Political Ideology in Late Eighteenth-Century England and America*. Ithaca, N.Y.: Cornell University Press, 1990.

Langford, Paul. *Public Life and the Propertied Englishman, 1689–1798*. Oxford: Oxford University Press, 1991.

Laurie, Bruce. *The Working People of Philadelphia, 1800–1850*. Philadelphia: Temple University Press, 1980.

Lecky, W. E. H. *A History of Ireland in the Eighteenth Century*. 5 vols. London, 1892.

Leder, Lawrence H. *America—1603–1789: Prelude to a Nation*. 2nd ed. Minneapolis: Burgess Publications, 1978.

Lenman, Bruce. *Integration, Enlightenment and Industrialisation: Scotland, 1746–1832*. London: Arnold, 1981.

Levy, Leonard W. *Emergence of a Free Press*. Oxford: Oxford University Press, 1985.

Link, Eugene Perry. *Democratic-Republican Societies*. New York: Octagon Press, 1973.

Lynd, Staughton. *Intellectual Origins of American Radicalism*. London: Faber and Faber, 1969.

MacDermott, Frank. *Tone and His Times*. Dublin, 1939; reprint, Dublin: Anvil Books, 1980.

MacDonagh, Giles. *Brillat-Savarin: The Judge and His Stomach*. London: John Murray, 1992.

McDowell, R. B. *Ireland in the Age of Imperialism and Revolution*. Oxford: Clarendon Press, 1979.

———. *Irish Public Opinion, 1750–1800*. London: Faber and Faber, 1944.

McElroy, Davis D. *Scotland's Age of Improvement: A Survey of Eighteenth-Century Literary Clubs and Societies*. Pullman: Washington State University Press, 1969.

McGee, D'Arcy. *A History of the Irish Settlers in North America*. Boston, 1851.

McKinney, William Wilson. *Early Pittsburgh Presbyterianism*. Pittsburgh, 1938.

McKnight, David A. *Historical Sketch of the Sabbath-Schools Connected with the 1st. Presbyterian Congregation of Pittsburgh from 1800 to 1867.* Pittsburgh, 1867.

McNeill, Mary. *The Life and Times of Mary Ann McCracken, 1770–1866.* Belfast: Blackstaff Press, 1988.

Madden, R. R. *Down and Antrim in '98.* Dublin, n.d.

——. *The United Irishmen: Their Lives and Times.* 2nd Ser. 4 vols. Dublin, 1858.

Malone, Dumas. *Jefferson and the Rights of Man.* Boston: Little, Brown, 1951.

——. *Jefferson the President: First Term, 1801–1805.* Boston: Little, Brown, 1970.

——. *The Public Life of Thomas Cooper, 1783–1839.* New Haven: Yale University Press, 1926; reprint, AMS Press, 1979.

Manuel, Frank E., and Fritzie Manuel. *Utopian Thought in the Western World.* Cambridge, Mass.: Belknap Press, 1979.

Mapp, Alf J., Jr. *Thomas Jefferson: A Strange Case of Mistaken Identity.* New York: Madison Books, 1987.

Marshall, Peter H. *William Godwin.* New Haven: Yale University Press, 1984.

Mason, Roger A., ed. *Scotland and England, 1286–1815.* Edinburgh: John Donald, 1987.

Matthews, Richard K. *The Radical Politics of Thomas Jefferson: A Revisionist View.* Lawrence: University Press of Kansas, 1984.

May, Henry F. *The Enlightenment in America.* New York: Oxford University Press, 1976.

Mee, John. *Dangerous Enthusiasm: William Blake and the Culture of Radicalism in the 1790s.* Oxford: Oxford University Press, 1992.

Meikle, Henry W. *Scotland and the French Revolution.* 2nd ed. London: Frank Cass, 1969.

Miller, John C. *Crisis in Freedom: The Alien and Sedition Laws.* Boston: Little, Brown, 1951.

——. *The Federalist Era, 1789–1801.* New York: Harper and Row, 1963.

Miller, Kerby A. *Emigrants and Exiles: Ireland and the Irish Exodus to North America.* New York: Oxford University Press, 1985.

Miller, Richard G. *Philadelphia—The Federalist City: A Study of Urban Politics, 1789–1801.* Port Washington, N.Y.: Kennikat Press, 1976.

Money, John. *Experience and Identity: Birmingham and the West Midlands, 1760–1800.* Manchester: Manchester University Press, 1977.

Moody, T. W., and W. E. Vaughan, eds. *A New History of Ireland.* Vol. 4. Oxford: Oxford University Press, 1986.

Morgan, Edmund S. *Inventing the People: The Rise of Popular Sovereignty in England and America.* New York: Norton, 1988.

Morris, Celia. *Fanny Wright: Rebel in America.* Urbana: University of Illinois Press, 1992.

Mott, Frank Luther. *American Journalism: A History of Newspapers in the United States Through 250 Years, 1690 to 1940.* New York: Macmillan, 1941.

Nash, Gary B. *Race and Revolution.* Madison: Madison House, 1990.

Neale, R. S. *Class in English History, 1680–1850.* Oxford: Blackwell, 1981.

Newman, Gerald. *The Rise of English Nationalism: A Cultural History, 1740–1830*. New York: St. Martin's Press, 1987.

O'Brien, Gerard. *Anglo-Irish Politics in the Age of Grattan and Pitt*. Blackrock: Irish Academic Press, 1987.

———, ed. *Parliament, Politics and People: Essays in Eighteenth-Century Irish History*. Blackrock: Irish Academic Press, 1989.

Onuf, Peter S., ed. *Jeffersonian Legacies*. Charlottesville: University of Virginia Press, 1993.

Pakenham, Thomas. *The Year of Liberty*. London: Panther Books, 1972.

Palmer, Robert R., ed. *The Impact of the American Revolution Abroad*. Washington, D.C.: Library of Congress, 1976.

Perkin, Harold. *The Origins of Modern English Society, 1780–1880*. London: Routledge Kegan Paul, 1969.

Pessen, Edward. *Most Uncommon Jacksonians: The Radical Leaders of the Early Labor Movement*. Albany: State University of New York Press, 1970.

Phelps, Glenn A. *George Washington and American Constitutionalism*. Lawrence: University Press of Kansas, 1993.

Philp, Mark, ed. *The French Revolution and British Popular Politics*. Cambridge: Cambridge University Press, 1991.

Philpin, C. H. E., ed. *Nationalism and Popular Protest in Ireland*. Cambridge: Cambridge University Press, 1987.

Pocock, John G. A., ed. *Three British Revolutions, 1641, 1688, 1776*. Princeton: Princeton University Press, 1980.

Porter, Roy, and Mikulas Teich, eds. *The Enlightenment in National Context*. Cambridge: Cambridge University Press, 1981.

Prince, Carl E. *New Jersey's Jeffersonian Republicans: The Genesis of an Early Party Machine, 1789–1817*. Chapel Hill: University of North Carolina Press, 1967.

Ramsay, J. *Scotland and Scotsmen in the Eighteenth Century*. 2 vols. Edinburgh, 1888.

Read, Donald. *Press and People, 1790–1850: Opinion in Three English Cities*. London: Arnold, 1961.

Reid, James Seaton, and W. D. Killen. *History of the Presbyterian Church in Ireland*. 2nd ed. 3 vols. London: Whittaker and Co., 1853.

Robbins, Caroline. *The Eighteenth-Century Commonwealthman*. New York: Atheneum, 1968.

Rock, Howard B. *Artisans of the New Republic: The Tradesmen of New York in the Age of Jefferson*. New York: New York University Press, 1979.

Rodgers, Daniel T. *Contested Truths: Keywords in American Politics Since Independence*. New York: Basic Books, 1987.

Rogers, Patrick. *The Irish Volunteers and Catholic Emancipation (1778–1793): A Neglected Phase of Ireland's History*. London: Burns Oates & Washbourne, 1934.

Royle, Edward, and James Walvin. *English Radicals and Reformers, 1760–1848*. Lexington: University Press of Kentucky, 1982.

Sainsbury, John. *Disaffected Patriots: London Supporters of Revolutionary America, 1769–1782*. Kingston, Ontario: McGill-Queen's University Press, 1987.

Scharf, J. Thomas, and Thompson Westcott. *History of Philadelphia*. 3 vols. Philadelphia: Everts and Co., 1884.

Schultz, Ronald. *The Republic of Labor: Philadelphia Artisans and the Politics of Class*. New York: Oxford University Press, 1993.

Sears, Louis Martin. *Jefferson and the Embargo*. 1927; reprint, New York: Octagon Books, 1966.

Sellers, Charles. *The Market Revolution: Jacksonian America, 1815–1846*. New York: Oxford University Press, 1991.

Shalhope, Robert E. *John Taylor of Caroline: Pastoral Republican*. Columbia: University of South Carolina Press, 1980.

Sharp, James Roger. *American Politics in the Early Republic: The New Nation in Crisis*. New Haven: Yale University Press, 1993.

Sheppard, John H. *Reminiscences of the Vaughan Family, and More Particularly of Benjamin Vaughan, LLD*. Boston, 1865.

Shepperson, Wilbur S. *Emigration and Disenchantment: Portraits of Englishmen Repatriated from the United States*. Norman: University of Oklahoma Press, 1965.

Silver, Rollo G. *Typefounding in America, 1787–1825*. Charlottesville: University of Virginia Press, 1965.

Sisson, Daniel. *The Revolution of 1800*. New York: Knopf, 1974.

Smith, James Morton. *Freedom's Fetters: The Alien and Sedition Laws and American Civil Liberties*. 1956; reprint, Ithaca, N.Y.: Cornell University Press, 1966.

Smith, Jeffery A. *Printers and Press Freedom: The Ideology of Early American Journalism*. New York: Oxford University Press, 1988.

Smith, Olivia. *The Politics of Language, 1791–1819*. Oxford: Clarendon Press, 1986.

Smout, T. C. *A History of the Scottish People, 1560–1830*. London: Fontana, 1985.

Smyth, Jim. *The Men of No Property: Irish Radicals and Popular Politics in the Late Eighteenth Century*. London: Macmillan, 1992.

Soboul, Albert. *The Parisian Sans-Culottes and the French Revolution, 1793–4*. Oxford: Oxford University Press, 1964.

Spater, George. *William Cobbett: The Poor Man's Friend*. 2 vols. Cambridge: Cambridge University Press, 1982.

Spurlin, Paul M. *The French Enlightenment in America*. Athens, Ga.: University of Georgia Press, 1984.

Stauffer, Vernon. *New England and the Bavarian Illuminati*. New York: Columbia University Press, 1918.

Steinberg, S. H. *Five Hundred Years of Printing*. 2nd ed. London: Faber and Faber, 1959.

Stevenson, David. *The Covenanters: The National Covenant and Scotland*. Edinburgh: Saltire Society, 1988.

Stewart, A. T. Q. *A Deeper Silence: The Hidden Origins of the United Irishmen*. London: Faber and Faber, 1993.

———. *The Narrow Ground: Aspects of Ulster, 1609–1969*. London: Faber and Faber, 1977.

Stewart, David. *The Seceders in Ireland, with Annals of Their Congregations.* Belfast: Presbyterian Historical Society, 1950.

Stewart, Donald H. *The Opposition Press of the Federalist Period.* Albany: State University of New York Press, 1969.

Sunter, Ronald M. *Patronage and Politics in Scotland, 1707–1832.* Edinburgh: John Donald, 1986.

Tagg, James. *Benjamin Franklin Bache and the Philadelphia Aurora.* Philadelphia: University of Pennsylvania Press, 1991.

Thomas, William E. S. *The Philosophic Radicals: Nine Studies in Theory and Practice, 1817–1841.* Oxford: Oxford University Press, 1979.

Thompson, E. P. *The Making of the English Working Class.* London: Penguin, 1968.

Thorne, R. G. *The History of Parliament: The House of Commons, 1790–1820.* 5 vols. London: Secker and Warburg, 1986.

Tillyard, Stella. *Aristocrats: Caroline, Emily, Louisa and Sarah Lennox, 1740–1832.* London: Chatto and Windus, 1994.

Tise, Larry E. *Proslavery: A History of the Defense of Slavery in America, 1701–1840.* Athens: University of Georgia Press, 1987.

Tolles, Frederick B. *George Logan of Philadelphia.* New York: Oxford University Press, 1953.

Tomalin, Claire. *The Life and Death of Mary Wollstonecraft.* London: Weidenfeld and Nicolson, 1974.

Tomlins, Christopher L. *Law, Labor, and Ideology in the Early American Republic.* New York: Cambridge University Press, 1993.

Toth, Charles W., ed. *Liberté, Egalité, Fraternité: The American Revolution and the European Response.* Troy, N.Y.: Whitston Publishing Co., 1989.

Tucker, Bernard. *Jonathan Swift.* Dublin: Gill and Macmillan, 1983.

Turner, James. *Without God, Without Creed: The Origins of Unbelief in America.* Baltimore: Johns Hopkins University Press, 1985.

Twomey, Richard J. *Jacobins and Jeffersonians: Anglo-American Radicalism in the United States, 1790–1820.* New York: Garland, 1989.

van der Linden, Frank. *The Turning Point: Jefferson's Battle for the Presidency.* Washington, D.C.: R. B. Luce, 1962.

Wahlke, John C. *The Causes of the American Revolution.* 3rd ed. Lexington, Mass.: Heath, 1973.

Walker, R. S. *James Beattie's London Diary, 1773.* Aberdeen: Aberdeen University Press, 1946.

Wall, Maureen. *Catholic Ireland in the Eighteenth Century: Collected Essays of Maureen Wall.* Ed. Gerard O'Brien. Dublin: Geography Publications, 1989.

Walters, Kerry S. *The American Deists: Voices of Reason and Dissent in the Early Republic.* Lawrence: University Press of Kansas, 1992.

Walters, Raymond, Jr. *Alexander James Dallas: Lawyer-Politician-Financier.* Philadelphia: University of Pittsburgh Press, 1943.

Watson, John F. *Annals of Philadelphia.* Philadelphia, 1830.

Watts, Michael. *The Dissenters: From the Reformation to the French Revolution*. Oxford: Clarendon Press, 1978.

Wells, Roger. *Insurrection: The British Experience, 1795–1803*. Gloucester: Alan Sutton, 1983.

Werkmeister, Lucyle. *A Newspaper History of England, 1792–1793*. Lincoln: University of Nebraska Press, 1967.

Wharam, Alan. *The Treason Trials, 1794*. Leicester: Leicester University Press, 1992.

Wilentz, Sean. *Chants Democratic: New York City and the Rise of the American Working Class, 1788–1850*. New York: Oxford University Press, 1984.

Williams, Gwyn A. *Artisans and Sans-Culottes: Popular Movements in France and Britain during the French Revolution*. 2nd ed. London: Libris, 1989.

———. *Madoc: the Making of a Myth*. London: Eyre Methuen, 1980.

———. *The Search for Beulah Land*. London: Croom Helm, 1980.

Williamson, Audrey. *Wilkes, "A Friend to Liberty."* London: Allen and Unwin, 1974.

Wilson, David A. *Paine and Cobbett: The Transatlantic Connection*. Kingston and Montreal: McGill-Queen's University Press, 1988.

Witherow, Thomas. *Historical and Literary Memorials of Presbyterianism in Ireland (1731–1800)*. 2nd Ser. London, 1880.

Wood, Gordon S. *The Radicalism of the American Revolution*. New York: Vintage Books, 1993.

Young, Alfred F., ed. *Beyond the American Revolution: Explorations in the History of American Radicalism*. DeKalb: Northern Illinois University Press, 1993.

Young, Robert M. *Ulster in '98. Episodes and Anecdotes*. 3rd ed. Belfast, 1893.

Youngson, A. J. *After the Forty-Five: The Economic Impact on the Scottish Highlands*. Edinburgh: Edinburgh University Press, 1973.

Articles And Essays

Anderson, Frank M. "The Enforcement of the Alien and Sedition Laws." *Annual Report of the American Historical Association for 1912*. Washington, D.C., 1914, 115–26.

Anderson, Robert. "In Search of the 'Lad of Parts': the Mythical History of Scottish Education." *History Workshop Journal* 19 (1985): 82–104.

Ashworth, John. "The Jeffersonians: Classical Republicans or Liberal Capitalists?" *Journal of American Studies* 18 (1984): 425–35.

Aspinall, Arthur. "The Social Status of Journalists at the Beginning of the Nineteenth Century." *Review of English Studies* 21 (1945): 216–32.

Bartlett, Thomas. "An End to Moral Economy: The Irish Militia Disturbances of 1793." *Past and Present* 99 (1983): 41–64.

———. "Defenders and Defenderism in 1795." *Irish Historical Studies* 24 (1984–85): 373–94.

———. "The Burden of the Present: Theobold Wolfe Tone, Republican and Separatist." In *The United Irishmen*, ed. David Dickson et al., pp. 1–15.

Baumann, Roland M. "John Swanwick: Spokesman for 'Merchant-Republicanism' in

Philadelphia, 1790–1798." *Pennsylvania Magazine of History and Biography* 97 (1973): 131–82.

————. "Philadelphia's Manufacturers and the Excise Taxes of 1794: The Forging of the Jeffersonian Coalition." *Pennsylvania Magazine of History and Biography* 106 (1982): 3–39.

Ben-Atar, Doren. "Alexander Hamilton's Alternative: Technology Piracy and the Report on Manufactures." *William and Mary Quarterly* 3rd Ser. 52 (1995): 389–414.

Black, Jeremy. "Introduction." In *British Politics and Society from Walpole to Pitt, 1742–1789*, ed. Jeremy Black, pp. 1–28.

Bonwick, Colin. "English Dissenters and the American Revolution." In *Contrast and Connection: Bicentennial Essays in Anglo-American History*, ed. H. C. Allen and Roger Thompson, pp. 88–112.

————. "Joseph Priestley: Emigrant and Jeffersonian." *Enlightenment and Dissent* 2 (1983): 3–22.

Boston, Ray. "The Impact of 'Foreign Liars' on the American Press, (1790–1800)." *Journalism Quarterly* 50 (1973): 722–30.

Brewer, John. "English Radicalism in the Age of George III." In *Three British Revolutions: 1641, 1688, 1776*, ed. J. G. A. Pocock, pp. 323–67.

Bric, Maurice. "The Irish and the Evolution of the 'New Politics' in America." In *The Irish in America*, ed. P. J. Drudy, pp. 143–67.

————. "Priests, Parsons and Politics: The Rightboy Protest in County Cork, 1785–1788." In *Nationalism and Popular Protest in Ireland*, ed. C. H. E. Philpin, pp. 163–90.

Briceland, Alan V. "The Philadelphia *Aurora*, the New England Illuminati, and the Election of 1800." *Pennsylvania Magazine of History and Biography* 100 (1976): 3–36.

Briggs, Willis G. "Joseph Gales, Editor of Raleigh's First Newspaper." *North Carolina Booklet* 7 (1907): 105–30.

Brims, John. "From Reformers to 'Jacobins': The Scottish Association of the Friends of the People." In *Conflict and Stability in Scottish Society, 1700–1850*, ed. T. M. Devine, 31–50.

————. "The Scottish 'Jacobins', Scottish Nationalism and the British Union." In *Scotland and England, 1286–1815*, ed. Roger A. Mason, pp. 247–65.

Butler, Jon. "Coercion, Miracle, Reason: Rethinking the American Religious Experience in the Revolutionary Age." In *Religion in a Revolutionary Age*, ed. Ronald Hoffman and Peter J. Albert, pp. 1–30.

Carson, David A. "That Ground Called Quiddism: John Randolph's War with the Jefferson Administration." *Journal of American Studies* 20 (1986): 71–92.

Carter, Edward C. II. "A 'Wild Irishman' Under Every Federalist's Bed: Naturalisation in Philadelphia, 1789–1806." *Pennsylvania Magazine of History and Biography* 94 (1970): 331–46.

Clifford, James L. "Robert Merry—A Pre-Byronic Hero." *Bulletin of the John Rylands Library* 27 (1942): 74–96.

Colley, Linda. "Eighteenth-Century English Radicalism before Wilkes." *Transactions of the Royal Historical Society*, 5th Ser., 31 (1981): 1–19.

Corfield, Penelope. "John Thelwall in Wales: New Documentary Evidence." *Bulletin of the Institute of Historical Research* 59 (1986): 231–39.

Cornell, Sean. "Aristocracy Assailed: The Ideology of Backcountry Anti-Federalism." *Journal of American History* 89 (1990): 1148–72.

Crane, Verner W. "The Club of Honest Whigs: Friends of Science and Liberty." *William and Mary Quarterly* 3rd Ser. 23 (1966): 210–33.

Curtin, Nancy. "The Transformation of the Society of United Irishmen into a Mass-based Revolutionary Organisation, 1794–6." *Irish Historical Studies* 24 (1985): 463–92.

Davis, H. M. " 'Very Different Springs of Uneasiness': Emigration from Wales to the United States of America during the 1790s." *Welsh Historical Review* 15 (1990–91): 368–98.

D'Cruze, Shani. "The Middling Sort in Eighteenth-Century Colchester: Independence, Social Relations and the Community Broker." In *The Middling Sort of People: Culture, Society and Politics in England, 1550–1800*, ed. Jonathan Barry and Christopher Brooks, pp. 181–207.

Devine, T. M. "The Failure of Radical Reform in Scotland in the Late Eighteenth Century: The Social and Economic Context." In *Conflict and Stability in Scottish Society*, ed. Devine, pp. 51–64.

Dickerson, Oliver M. "Were the Navigation Acts Oppressive?" In *The Causes of the American Revolution*, ed. John C. Wahlke, pp. 26–48.

Dickinson, H. T. "The Precursors of Political Radicalism in Augustan Britain." In *Britain in the First Age of Party, 1680–1750: Essays Presented to Geoffrey Holmes*, ed. Clyve Jones, pp. 63–84.

———. "Radicals and Reformers in the Age of Wilkes and Wyvill." In *British Politics and Society from Walpole to Pitt, 1742–1789*, ed. Jeremy Black, pp. 123–46.

Dinwiddy, John. "Interpretations of Anti-Jacobinism." In *The French Revolution and British Popular Politics*, ed. Mark Philp, pp. 38–49.

Ditchfield, G. M. "Anti-Trinitarianism and Toleration in Late Eighteenth-Century British Politics: The Unitarian Petition of 1792." *Journal of Ecclesiastical History* 42 (1991): 39–67.

———. "The Campaign in Lancashire and Cheshire for the Repeal of the Test and Corporation Acts, 1787–1790." *Transactions of the Historical Society of Lancashire and Cheshire* 126 (1977): 109–138.

———. "The Subscription Issue in British Parliamentary Politics, 1772–79." *Parliamentary History* 7 (1988): 45–80.

Donnelly, F. K., and J. L. Baxter. "Sheffield and the English Revolutionary Tradition, 1791–1820." *International Review of Social History* 20 (1975): 398–423.

Durey, Michael. "The Dublin Society of United Irishmen and the Politics of the Carey-Drennan Dispute, 1792–1794." *Historical Journal* 37 (1994): 89–111.

———. "Irish Deism and Jefferson's Republic: Denis Driscol in Ireland and America, 1793–1810." *Éire-Ireland: A Journal of Irish Studies* 25 (1990): 56–76.

———. "John Hughes, Reluctant *Agent Provocateur* and Millenarian: A Note and New Documents." *Eighteenth-Century Ireland* 7 (1992): 141–46.

———. "The Radical Critique of 'Old Corruption' and the Beginnings of Public Service Reform in Late Eighteenth-Century Scotland: The Edinburgh Sasine Office as a Case Study." *Scottish Tradition* 16 (1991): 33–55.

———. "Transatlantic Patriotism: Political Exiles and America in the Age of Revolution." In *Artisans, Peasants and Proletarians: Essays Presented to Gwyn A. Williams,* ed. Clive Emsley and James Walvin, pp. 7–31.

———. "William Cobbett, Military Corruption and London Radicalism in the Early 1790s." *Proceedings of the American Philosophical Society* 131 (1987): 348–66.

———. "William Winterbotham's Trumpet of Sedition: Religious Dissent and Political Radicalism in the 1790s." *Journal of Religious History* 19 (1995): 141–57.

Dwyer, John, and Alexander Murdoch. "Paradigms and Politics: Manners, Morals and the Rise of Henry Dundas, 1770–1784." In *New Perspectives,* ed. John Dwyer et al., pp. 210–48.

Dyck, Ian. "Local Attachments, National Identities and World Citizenship in the Thought of Thomas Paine." *History Workshop Journal* 25 (1993): 117–35.

Edwards, Owen Dudley. "The Impact of the American Revolution on Ireland." In *The Impact of the American Revolution Abroad,* ed. R. R. Palmer, pp. 127–58.

Eastwood, David. "Patriotism and the English State in the 1790s." In *The French Revolution and British Popular Politics,* ed. Mark Philp, pp. 146–68.

Eaton, Clement. "Winifred and Joseph Gales, Liberals of the Old South." *Journal of Southern History* 10 (1944): 461–74.

Elliott, Marianne. "Irish Republicanism in England: The First Phase, 1797–9." In *Penal Era and Golden Age: Essays in Irish History, 1690–1800* (Belfast: Ulster Historical Foundation, 1979), pp. 204–21.

———. "The Defenders in Ulster." In *The United Irishmen,* ed. David Dickson et al., pp. 222–33.

Ellis, Richard E. "Jeffersonian Divisions." In *After the Constitution,* ed. Lance Banning, pp. 383–96.

Emsley, Clive. "Revolution, War and the Nation State: The British and French Experiences, 1789–1801." In *The French Revolution and British Popular Politics,* ed. Mark Philp, pp. 99–117.

Fairley, John A. "The Pantheon: An Old Edinburgh Debating Society." *The Book of the Old Edinburgh Club* 1 (1908): 47–75.

French, Roderick S. "Elihu Palmer, Radical Deist, Radical Republican: A Reconsideration of American Free Thought." *Studies in Eighteenth-Century Culture* 8 (1979): 87–108.

Friedman, Lawrence J. "Purifying the White Man's Country: The American Colonization Society Reconsidered, 1816–40." *Societas* 6 (1976): 1–24.

Fruchtman, Jack, Jr. "Politics and the Apocalypse: The Republic and the Millennium in Late Eighteenth-Century English Political Thought." *Studies in Eighteenth Century Culture* 20 (1981): 153–64.

Garvin, Tom. "Defenders, Ribbonmen and Others: Underground Political Networks in Pre-Famine Ireland." In *Nationalism and Popular Protest in Ireland*, ed. C. H. E. Philpin, pp. 219–44.

Gilpatrick, D. H. "The English Background of John Miller." *The Furman Bulletin* 20 (1938):14–20.

Grabbe, Hans-Jurgen. "European Immigration to the United States in the Early National Period, 1783–1820." *Proceedings of the American Philosophical Society* 133 (1989): 190–214.

Graham, Thomas. " 'An Union of Power'? The United Irish Organisation: 1795–1798." In *The United Irishmen*, ed. David Dickson et al., pp. 244–55.

Gronowicz, Anthony. "Political 'Radicalism' in New York City's Revolutionary and Constitutional Eras." In *New York in the Age of the Constitution*, ed. Paul A. Gilje and William Pencak, pp. 98–111.

Handforth, Pauline. "Manchester Radical Politics, 1789–1794." *Transactions of the Lancashire and Cheshire Antiquarian Society* 66 (1956): 87–106.

Hanson, Russell L. " 'Commons' and 'Commonwealth' at the American Founding: Democratic Republicanism as the New American Hybrid." In *Conceptual Change and the Constitution*, ed. Terence Ball and J. G. A. Pocock, pp. 165–93.

Heaton, Herbert. "The Industrial Immigrant in the United States, 1783–1812." *Proceedings of the American Philosophical Society* 95 (1951): 519–27.

Hempton, David. "Religion in British Society, 1740–1790." In *British Politics and Society from Walpole to Pitt, 1742–1789*, ed. Jeremy Black, pp. 201–21.

Henderson, Elizabeth K. "The Attack on the Judiciary in Pennsylvania, 1800–1810." *Pennsylvania Magazine of History and Biography* 61 (1937): 113–36.

Hole, Robert. "English Sermons and Tracts as Media of Debate on the French Revolution, 1789–99." In *The French Revolution and British Popular Politics*, ed. Mark Philp, pp. 18–37.

Houston, R. A. "The Demographic Regime." In *People and Society in Scotland*, ed. T. M. Devine and Rosalind Mitchison, pp. 9–26.

Howe, John, Jr. "Republican Thought and the Political Violence of the 1790s." *American Quarterly* 19 (1967): 147–65.

Hyslop, Beatrice F. "American Press Reports of the French Revolution, 1789–1794." *New-York Historical Society Quarterly* 42 (1958): 329–48.

Kiernan, V. G. "The Emergence of a Nation." In *Nationalism and Popular Protest in Ireland*, ed. C. H. E. Philpin, pp. 16–49.

Knudson, Jerry W. "The Rage Around Tom Paine: Newspaper Reaction to His Homecoming in 1802." *New York Historical Society Quarterly* 53 (1969): 34–63.

Kramnick, Isaac. "Eighteenth-Century Science and Radical Social Theory: The Case of Joseph Priestley's Scientific Liberalism." *Journal of British Studies* 25 (1986): 1–30.

———. "Liberalism, the Middle Class, and Republican Revisionism." In *Republicanism and Bourgeois Radicalism*, ed. Isaac Kramnick, pp. 1–40.

———. "Religion and Radicalism: English Political Thought in the Age of Revolution." *Political Theory* 5 (1977): 505–34.

———. "Republican Revisionism Revisited." *American Historical Review* 87 (1982): 629–64.

Latimer, W. T. "David Bailie Warden, Patriot 1798." *Ulster Journal of Archeology* 23 (1907): 29–38.

Leary, Lewis. "Thomas Branagan: Republican Rhetoric and Romanticism in America." *Pennsylvania Magazine of History and Biography* 77 (1953): 332–52.

Lottes, Gunther. "Radicalism, Revolution and Political Culture: An Anglo-French Comparison." In *The French Revolution and British Popular Politics*, ed. M. Philp, pp. 78–98.

Lovejoy, David S. "Two American Revolutions, 1689 and 1776." In *Three British Revolutions*, ed. J. G. A. Pocock, pp. 244–62.

McClelland, Aiken. "Thomas Ledlie Birch, United Irishman." *Proceedings of the Belfast Natural History and Philosophical Society* 7 (1963): 24–35.

McDonald, Forrest. "The Presidency of Thomas Jefferson: The Triumph and the Perils of Republican Ideals." In *After the Constitution*, ed. Lance Banning, pp. 366–82.

McDowell, R. B. "The Age of the United Irishmen: Reform and Reaction, 1789–94." In *A New History of Ireland*, ed. T. W. Moody and W. E. Vaughan, pp. 289–338.

———. "The Age of the United Irishmen: Revolution and the Union, 1794–1800." In *A New History of Ireland*, ed. T. W. Moody and W. E. Vaughan, pp. 339–73.

———. "Colonial Nationalism and the Winning of Parliamentary Independence." In *A New History of Ireland*, ed. T. W. Moody and W. E. Vaughan, pp. 196–216.

———. "Parliamentary Independence, 1782–9." In *A New History of Ireland*, ed. T. W. Moody and W. E. Vaughan, pp. 265–88.

———. "The Personnel of the Dublin Society of United Irishmen." *Irish Historical Studies* 2 (1940–41): 12–53.

Malcolmson, Robert W. "Workers' Combinations in Eighteenth-Century England." In *The Origins of Anglo-American Radicalism*, ed. Margaret Jacob and James Jacob, pp. 149–61.

Martin, Robert W. T. "From the 'Free and Open' Press to the 'Press of Freedom': Republicanism and Early American Press Liberty." *History of Political Thought* 15 (1994): 505–34.

Meacham, Standish. "Priestley in America." *History Today* 12 (1962): 568–73.

Miller, David W. "Presbyterianism and 'Modernisation' in Ulster." *Past and Present* 80 (1978): 66–90.

Moore, John Hammond. "Theophilus Harris's Thoughts on Emigrating to America in 1793." *William and Mary Quarterly* 3rd Ser. 36 (1979): 620–14.

Morrell, J. B. "Professors Robison and Playfair, and the *Theophobia Gallica*: Natural Philosophy, Religion, and Politics in Edinburgh, 1789–1815." *Notes and Records of the Royal Society* 26 (1971): 43–63.

Murdoch, Alexander, and Richard B. Sher. "Literary and Learned Culture." In *People and Society in Scotland*, ed. T. M. Devine and Rosalind Mitchison, pp. 127–42.

Murrin, John M. "Fundamental Values, the Founding Fathers, and the Constitution." In *To Form a More Perfect Union*, ed. H. Belz et al., pp. 1–37.

Nash, Gary B. "Artisans and Politics in Eighteenth-Century Philadelphia." In *The Origins of Anglo-American Radicalism*, ed. Margaret Jacob and James Jacob, pp. 162–82.

Newman, Simon P. "Principles or Men? George Washington and the Political Culture of National Leadership, 1776–1801." *Journal of the Early Republic* 12 (1992): 477–98.

Newman, Stephen L. "Thomas Cooper, 1759–1839: The Political Odyssey of a Bourgeois Ideologue." *Southern Studies* 24 (1985): 295–305.

O'Casaide, Seamus. "John Chambers: Printer and United Irishman." *Irish Book Lover*, July 1940.

Onuf, Peter S. "The Scholar's Jefferson." *William and Mary Quarterly* 3rd Ser. 50 (1993): 671–99.

———. "Watty Cox and His Publications." *Irish Book Lover*, 1933, 18–25.

O'Raghallaigh, Deasmumhan. "William James MacNeven." *Studies: An Irish Quarterly Review* 30 (1944): 247–59.

Peeling, James Hedley. "Governor Thomas McKean and the Pennsylvania Jacobins (1799–1808)." *Pennsylvania Magazine of History and Biography* 54 (1930): 320–54.

Pernick, Martin S. "Politics, Parties, and Pestilence: Epidemic Yellow Fever and the Rise of the First Party System." *William and Mary Quarterly* 3rd Ser. 29 (1972): 559–86.

Phillips, Kim T. "William Duane, Philadelphia's Democratic Republicans, and the Origins of Modern Politics." *Pennsylvania Magazine of History and Biography* 101 (1977): 365–87.

Phillipson, N. T. "Adam Smith as Civic Moralist." In *Wealth and Virtue*, ed. Istvan Holt and Michael Ignatieff, pp. 179–202.

———. "Lawyers, Landowners, and the Civic Leadership of Post-Union Scotland." *Juridical Review* 21 (1976): 97–120.

———. "The Scottish Enlightenment." In *The Enlightenment in National Context*, ed. Roy Porter and Mikulas Teich, pp. 19–40.

———. "Towards a Definition of the Scottish Enlightenment." In *City and Society in the Eighteenth Century*, ed. Paul Fritz and David Williams, pp. 125–47.

Philp, Mark. "The Fragmented Ideology of Reform." In *The French Revolution and British Popular Politics*, ed. Mark Philp, pp. 50–77.

———. "Rational Religion and Political Radicalism in the 1790s." *Enlightenment and Dissent* 4 (1985): 35–46.

———. "The Role of America in the 'Debate on France' 1791–5: Thomas Paine's Insertion." *Utilitas* 5 (1993): 221–37.

Plumb, J. H. "Merchant, Gentry and Intellectual: British Opinion and the American Revolution." In *Liberté, Egalité, Fraternité: The American Revolution and the European Response*, ed. Charles W. Toth, pp. 65–78.

Pocock, J. G. A. "Radical Criticism of the Whig Order in the Age between Revolutions." In *The Origins of Anglo-American Radicalism*, ed. Margaret Jacob and James Jacob, pp. 33–57.

Prince, Carl E. "The Passing of the Aristocracy: Jefferson's Removal of the Federalists, 1801–1805." *Journal of American History* 57 (1970): 563–75.

Rice, C. Duncan. "Scottish Enlightenment, American Revolution and Atlantic Reform." In *Scotland, Europe and the American Revolution*, ed. Owen D. Edwards and G. Shepperson, pp. 75–82.

Richey, Russell E. "The Origins of British Radicalism: The Changing Rationale for Dissent." *Eighteenth-Century Studies* 7 (1973–74): 179–92.

Risch, Erna. "Immigrant Aid Societies before 1820." *Pennsylvania Magazine of History and Biography* 60 (1936): 15–33.

Robbins, Caroline. "Honest Heretic: Joseph Priestley in America, 1794–1804." *Proceedings of the American Philosophical Society* 106 (1962): 60–76.

Rogers, Nicholas. "The Urban Opposition to Whig Oligarchy, 1720–60." In *The Origins of Anglo-American Radicalism*, ed. Margaret Jacob and James Jacob, pp. 132–48.

Rose, R. Barrie. "The Priestley Riots of 1791." *Past and Present* 18 (1960): 68–88.

Rowell, George S. "Benjamin Vaughan—Patriot, Scholar, Diplomat." *Magazine of History* 22, no. 3 (1916): 43–57.

Schultz, Ronald. "God and Workingmen: Popular Religion and the Formation of Philadelphia's Working Class, 1790–1830." In *Religion in a Revolutionary Age*, ed. Ronald Hoffman and Peter J. Albert, pp. 125–55.

Schwoerer, Lois G. "The Contribution of the Declaration of Rights to Anglo-American Radicalism." In *The Origins of Anglo-American Radicalism*, ed. Margaret Jacob and James Jacob, pp. 105–24.

Seed, John. "Gentleman Dissenters: The Social and Political Meanings of Rational Dissent in the 1770s and 1780s." *Historical Journal* 28 (1985): 299–325.

Sellers, Ian. "Unitarianism and Social Change." *Hibbert Journal* 61 (1962): 16–22.

———. "William Roscoe, The Roscoe Circle and Radical Politics in Liverpool, 1787–1807." *Transactions of the Lancashire and Cheshire Historical Society* 120 (1968): 45–62.

Shelton, Cynthia. "Labor and Capital in the Early Period of Manufacturing: The Failure of John Nicholson's Manufacturing Complex, 1793–1797." *Pennsylvania Magazine of History and Biography* 106 (1982): 341–64.

Sheps, Arthur. "The Edinburgh Reform Convention of 1793 and the American Revolution." *Scottish Tradition* 5 (1975): 23–37.

———. "Ideological Immigrants in Revolutionary America." In *City and Society in the Eighteenth Century*, ed. Paul Fritz and David Williams, pp. 231–46.

Sher, Richard B. "Moderates, Managers, and Popular Politics in Mid-Eighteenth Century Edinburgh: The 'Drysdale Bustle' of the 1760s." In *New Perspectives*, ed. John Dwyer et al., pp. 179–209.

Shulim, Joseph I. "John Daly Burk, Irish Revolutionist and American Patriot." *Transactions of the American Philosophical Society*, New Ser. 54 (1964): 3–60.

Smyth, James. "Dublin's Political Underground in the 1790s." In *Parliament, Politics and People*, ed. Gerard O'Brien, pp. 129–48.

Spater, George. "The Quest for William Cobbett: A Revisionist View of an English Radical." *Times Higher Education Supplement*, Sept. 18, 1981: 12–13.

Stewart, A. T. Q. " 'A Stable Unseen Power': Dr. William Drennan and the Origins of the United Irishmen." In *Essays Presented to Michael Roberts*, ed. John Bossy and Peter Jupp, pp. 80–92.

Tait, M. "James Ronaldson, Baker, Typefounder, Philanthropist, and His Connexions in and around Edinburgh." *Book of the Old Edinburgh Club* 28 (1953): 44–50.

Tinling, Marion. "Thomas Lloyd's Reports of the First Federal Congress." *William and Mary Quarterly* 3rd Ser. 18 (1961): 519–45.

Twomey, Richard J. "Jacobins and Jeffersonians: Anglo-American Radical Ideology, 1790–1810." In *Origins of Anglo-American Radicalism*, ed. Margaret Jacob and James Jacob, pp. 284–99.

Underdown, David. "Commentary." In *The Origins of Anglo-American Radicalism*, ed. Margaret Jacob and James Jacob, pp. 125–30.

Walvin, James. "The Rise of British Popular Sentiment for Abolition, 1787–1832." In *Anti-Slavery, Religion and Reform: Essays in Memory of Roger Anstey*, ed. Christine Bolt and Seymour Drescher, pp. 149–62.

Weinglass, D. H. "Ralph Eddowes." In *Biographical Dictionary of Modern British Radicals, 1770–1830*, ed. Joseph O. Baylen and Norbert J. Gossman, 144–50.

Wiggins, James R. "Jefferson and the Press." In *Thomas Jefferson: The Man, His World, His Influence*, pp. 141–49.

Williams, Gwyn A. "Morgan John Rhees and His Beula." *Welsh History Review* 3 (1967): 441–72.

——. "Tom Paine." *New Society* 6 (August 1970): 236–38.

Wood, Gordon S. "Interests and Disinterestedness in the Making of the Constitution." In *Beyond Confederation: Origins of the Constitution and American National Identity*, ed. Richard Beeman et al., pp. 69–109.

——. "The Trials and Tribulations of Thomas Jefferson." In *Jeffersonian Legacies*, ed. Peter S. Onuf, pp. 395–417.

Wright, Esmond. "Robert Liston, Second British Minister to the United States." *History Today* 11 (1961): 118–27.

Yarbrough, Jean. "Republicanism Reconsidered: Some Thoughts on the Foundation and Preservation of the American Republic." *Review of Politics* 41 (1979): 61–95.

Young, Alfred F. "English Plebeian Culture and Eighteenth-Century American Radicalism." In *The Origins of Anglo-American Radicalism*, ed. Margaret Jacob and James Jacob, pp. 185–212.

Dissertations

Baumann, Roland M. "The Democratic-Republicans of Philadelphia: The Origins, 1776–1797." Ph.D. diss., Pennsylvania State University, 1970.

Brims, John D. "The Scottish Democratic Movement in the Age of the French Revolution." Ph.D. diss., Edinburgh University, 1983.

Brooke, Peter. "Controversies in Ulster Presbyterianism, 1790–1836." Ph.D. diss., Cambridge University, 1980.

Brotherson, Gregory. "The Social and Political Thought of John Horne Tooke." M. Phil. diss., Murdoch University, 1993.

Brown, Walter Francis, Jr. "John Adams and the American Press, 1797–1801: The First Full Scale Confrontation between the Executive and the Media." Ph.D. diss., University of Notre Dame, 1974.

Carter, Edward C., II. "The Political Activities of Mathew Carey, Nationalist, 1760–1814." Ph.D. diss., Bryn Mawr College, 1962.

Gallin, Richard G. "Scottish Radicalism, 1792–1794." Ph.D. diss., Columbia University, 1979.

Gallop, Geoffrey I. "Politics, Property and Progress: British Radical Thought, 1760–1815." D. Phil. diss., Oxford University, 1983.

Gavre, William M. "Republicanism in the American Revolution: The Collapse of the Classical Ideal." Ph.D. diss., University of California, Los Angeles, 1978.

Hebert, Anne Catherine. "The Pennsylvania French in the 1790's: The Story of Their Survival." Ph.D. diss., University of Texas at Austin, 1981.

Hogan, Patrick. "Civil Unrest in the Province of Connaught, 1793–1798: The Role of the Landed Gentry in Maintaining Order." M.Ed. diss., University College, Galway, 1976.

Knudson, Jerry Wayne. "The Jefferson Years: Response by the Press, 1801–1809." Ph.D. diss., University of Virginia, 1962.

Leslie, Margaret Evelyn. "The Social and Political Thought of Joseph Priestley." Ph.D. diss., Cambridge University, 1966.

McCue, Daniel L., Jr. "Daniel Isaac Eaton and 'Politics for the People'." 2 vols. Ph.D. diss., Columbia University, 1974.

Nelson, John Robert. "Hamilton and Gallatin: Political Economy and Policy-Making in the New Nation, 1789–1812." Ph.D. diss., Northern Illinois University Press, 1979.

Nelson, John Wallace. "The Belfast Presbyterians, 1670–1830: An Analysis of Their Political and Social Interests." Ph.D. diss., Queen's University, Belfast, 1985.

Pendleton, Gayle T. "English Conservative Propaganda during the French Revolution, 1789–1802." Ph.D. diss., Emory University, 1976.

Phillips, Kim T. "William Duane, Revolutionary Editor." Ph.D. diss., University of California, Berkeley, 1968.

Robinson, Thomas P. "The Life of Thomas Addis Emmet." Ph.D. diss., New York University, 1955.

Sloan, William David. "The Party Press: The Newspaper Role in National Politics, 1789–1816." Ph.D. diss., University of Texas at Austin, 1981.

Stewart, A. T. Q. "The Transformation of Presbyterian Radicalism in the North of Ireland, 1792–1815." M. A. diss., Queen's University, Belfast, 1956.

St. Mark, Joseph J. "The Red Shamrock: United Irishmen and Revolution, 1795–1803." Ph.D. diss., Georgetown University, 1974.

Waldstreicher, David L. "The Making of American Nationalism: Celebrations and Political Culture, 1776–1820." Ph.D. diss., Yale University, 1994.

Wall, Brian. "The Social and Political Thought of John 'Walking' Stewart." B. A. Hons. diss., Murdoch University, 1994.

Walvin, James. "English Democratic Societies and Popular Radicalism, 1791–1800." D. Phil. diss., University of York, 1969.

Wheeler, William Bruce. "Urban Politics in Nature's Republic: The Development of Political Parties in the Seaport Cities in the Federalist Era." Ph.D. diss., University of Virginia, 1967.

Index